CONTENTS

To my loving wife of so many years, Margaret,
and to my children and grandchildren.

May the Lord bless and keep them!

EXPLANATORY NOTES

In Albanian, unlike in English, the article "the" is attached to the respective noun or name. When speaking of a specific person, the name "Hilë" (generic) becomes "Hila" (the Hilë, a specific person). To avoid confusion, I have used "Hila" instead of "Hilë" even when the latter form was called for in Albanian. My apologies to readers who know Albanian. I have tried to keep Albanian names constant but once in a while an inconsistency has crept in and the text may show Ndoja, Ndue, Ndojë or some other proper Albanian variation; my apologies. In Albanian, you may call a man "Mister" combined with his first name, his last name, or with a title. It may sound odd in English, but it is acceptable in Albanian. In English, we say "Mr. Mayor," or "Mr. President," but we don't say "Mr. General," "Mr. Doctor," or "Mr. Senator." Peculiar, isn't it? You may find instances of, say, Mr. Genc, in a dialogue. Now you know why.

The Albanian alphabet has some letters and diphthongs that are pronounced differently from the way we pronounce them in English. Here is a list with the corresponding English pronunciation:

ALBANIAN LETTER	ENGLISH PRONUNCIATION	ALBANIAN LETTER	ENGLISH PRONUNCIATION
a	as in "father"	t	= t
m	= m	g	as in "get"
b	= b	th	as in "thumb"
n	= n	gj	as in "ar**gue**"
nj	= as in "knew"	u	as in "boot"
c	as in "oa**ts**"	h	as in "heaven"
o	= o	v	= v
ç	as in "child"	i	as in "important"
p	= p	x	as in "**Z**imbabwe"
d	= d	j	as in "yolk"
q	as in "cute"	xh	as in "John"
dh	as in "this"	k	= k
r	rolled 'r'	y	as in French "une"
e	as in "pest"	l	as in "elite"
s	as in "soup"	z	as in "resemble"
ë	as in "berm"	ll	as in "ball"
sh	as in "shine"	zh	as in "azure"
f	= f		

INTRODUCTION

I began jotting down the first lines of these memoirs in 1985. As I write these introductory lines, it is the year of Our Lord 2004. Over the years, there were times when I wrote furiously, unable to stop putting on paper memories that crowded my mind. Such periods were often followed by long interruptions where other activities took precedence. Hence the long time span from inception to completion. If you consider, however, that it took me almost half my life to live these events, twenty-odd years of putting them on paper do not seem excessive.

Over the years, I heard many young and not-so-young people complain they knew little about their roots, about the "old country" whence their parents or grandparents had sailed from for these shores. Just as often they added that they regretted not having asked more questions of their elders while they were still alive. I wrote my memoirs, and have insisted that my wife write hers, to give our children and grandchildren the opportunity to know more about their roots if they so desire. I rather doubt that, while I am still alive, they will take out time from their many activities to sit down and read about people and times long past. Should they do so, I will be happy to try to answer their questions.

I said "try to answer" because there are some answers I do not know. An unexpected benefit of writing these memoirs has been the psychological relief as I wrote chapter after chapter. I no longer feel compelled to tell others about these events. Unfortunately, I have done so in the past well beyond the listeners' initial interest.

Over the years, my wife Margaret caught many mistakes in my original draft. She drew my attention to typos, awkward phrases, and needless repetitions.

My children and grandchildren come from families they can be proud of. They withstood the difficulties of two world wars. They knew hunger and persecution; they often paid a heavy price but preserved their ideals. Opa Walther rebuilt a life for his family and himself starting anew in his forties when he and three million Germans were forced out of Czechoslovakia. Opa Kortsha spent 15 years in communist prisons and forced labor camps. He was mistreated and tortured. He contracted tuberculosis but was refused treatment and hospitalization. We sent medication we received from Italy but the authorities forbade their use. In protest, he went on a hunger strike and died a difficult death. Both grandmothers were worthy of their husbands. My family can be proud of them.

Many strangers who helped my wife and me over the years were men and women of courage and integrity. I will always be grateful and pray for them in this life and beyond. I hope that our descendants will also honor their memories.

The reader may wonder how I could have kept a diary in the mountains when such records could have caused death and destruction if they had fallen into the wrong hands. Actually, I did not. The memories of those long three months burned themselves into my mind. I put them on paper within days after I crossed into Yugoslavia and took the notes with me wherever I went. Therefore, I could attach actual dates to specific events. That applied only to events in the Albanian mountains and the early days in Yugoslavia. Thereafter, you will notice that I speak of events and do not report them by date.

To my family (and all readers!): The important things in life are neither power nor wealth. Integrity, honesty, loyalty, love, and good will toward others will carry you far. Faith in the Lord will be your strength and your comfort in good times and in bad. Be good to each other. Love and respect each other and pass onto your children and their children our family values and our honored name.

CHAPTER SUMMARIES

1: On October 9, 1952, I fail my attempted escape with Ignace Kujxhija. I evade military service but brother Mergim is drafted. Hysni Kapo orders that I be reinstated; the governor's secretary denies the order exists.

2: October 9, 1952: Peter Kola arranges my meeting Kola Murreci, my liaison with the infiltrators from Yugoslavia. I say goodbye to Mom. With Kola we cross the River Kiri and reach Kola's house in the mountains.

3: Brief history of Albania from Skanderbeg until after WWI and early family history.

4: November 1936: Descriptions of early childhood and more world history. Background of Italy's occupation of Albania.

5: We leave Fiume and move to Albania in the summer of 1939. Hitler invades Poland on September 1, 1939. I return to Fiume to attend high school. The year 1940 marks the surrender of France and a partial occupation of French territory by Germany.

6: Italy floods Albania with goods and capital. Dad is appointed State Counselor. Our relatives leave Korça to stay at our house. Germany invades Yugoslavia and Greece in the spring, the Soviet Union in the summer of 1941. In Fiume, high school students patrolled the streets. My choir travels to Rome for a national choral contest.

7: Dad invites the German ambassador to our home. I sit in and learn that foreign friends have their own agendas. We Albanians must love and defend our country no matter what. Dad becomes secretary of education in Mustafa Kruja's cabinet.

8: I graduate and return to Albania. Dad's relations with Montanelli, his Italian advisor. Beso Gega asks for his daughter's release. Professor Safet Butka comes to dinner. Petrit Merlika gets married in Bari.

9: I start medical school in Padua. Italian authorities engineer Qazim Koculi's death. The Kruja government resigns. I join Balli Kombëtar. I pass exams in chemistry and physics and return to Albania for the summer.

10: The war turns against the Axis. In Albania, the Allies support the communists over their nationalist counterparts. The COMINTERN orders communist parties in the Balkans to attack the nationalist forces of resistance. Civil war ensues in Yugoslavia, Albania, and Greece. Italy surrenders to the Allies and German forces fill the void from Italy to the remote steppes of Russia.

11: The communists fail in their attempt to assassinate Mustafa Kruja. American bombers hit Tirana. I start volunteer work at the Tirana hospital. Police and gendarmerie in Tirana massacre hundreds of communists and communist sympathizers. I join a group of nationalist youth and go to Fier to make propaganda on behalf of the nationalist cause. We fail.

12: Balli Kombëtar sends the Battalion Besnik Çano to Kosova. I am transferred from the front back to Peja. The communists assassinate Iliaz Agushi in his apartment. Dad rejects my suggestion that we leave Albania.

13: The last German column leaves Tirana. Communist forces arrest Dad and me. We wind up at Burgu i Ri, Tirana's New Prison. There are early signs of friction among the Allies. Tirana demands the return of Albanian political refugees from Italy. I reproach Dad for having misrepresented Albania.

14: There were optimists and pessimists in jail; all hopes depend on the Allies. A 'Special Tribunal' judged the most important prisoners. Dad is sentenced to death but the sentence is commuted to lifelong imprisonment.

15: I study English "with" Ernie Pyl and begin a friendship with Hans Lüning. Dad and I spend six weeks in solitary confinement. Dad and I share a room with Fr. Anton Harapi, who is tried and executed

16: Former enemies of communism appear in court. Several are executed. In jail, I am interrogated and respond that Kosova should not be under Yugoslav rule. Eventually I am released. I seek employment, flunk an English test but am appointed a physician's assistant without pay at the Tirana Military Hospital.

17: I start working at the Military Hospital with Dr. Augi. Dad's life in a hard labor camp.

18: Descriptions of Nako Spiru's death and Dr. Augi's treatment of torture victims. Dr. Augi is given a suspended 5-year sentence for 'negligence while on duty.'

19: I am appointed a physician's assistant in Dukagjin. The Mbrojtje (Security Service) had torched the hospital to infiltrate the resistance and had failed. The inhabitants are very poor, traditionally neglected by government employees, and grateful for any help I can offer.

20: Description of my work in Dukagjin, one of the poorest and most primitive areas of Albania.

21: Back in Shkodra, I am appointed city health inspector. Ndue Vata and friends escape across Lake Shkodra. Greek refugees bring typhus to Shkodra.

22: Description of working conditions at my new job at provincial headquarters. Colonel Hilmi Seiti recruits informants. There is growing persecution against the Catholic Church. Qazim Ramadani offers to help Mergim and me escape from Albania. The attempt fails. Sejfullah Merlika makes a similar offer. Another failure. I am fired from my job for 'improper political behavior.'

23: An informant team, mother and son, sets traps for us; we avoid them through no merit of ours. Mergim and I wind up breaking stones in a quarry. I beat the draft, Mergim joins the Army's Labor Battalion.

24: Mom hates communism with a passion. I work at several construction sites. October 6th is a turning point in my life.

25: October 12–18, 1952: I attempt escape. I meet Kola Murreci's family and hide for several days in a 'tomb' underneath the oven. Finally, I meet the three infiltrators. Peter gives me his revolver and a hand grenade. We leave Kola Murreci's for a creek.

26: October 19–21, 1952: We travel to different bases. Hila fails to recruit Lazër Pali. Peter and Deda tell me that Yugoslavia views the Anglo-American Allies as enemies.

27: October 22–26, 1952: We meet the brothers Shuk and Luka, who ferry us across the Drini River. We touch base with Gjoka Lazri, leave his home, and spend the night in the open.

28: October 26–November 2, 1952: Marka Deda Alija brings food and helps us across a creek. The group from Yugoslavia that will get us across the Drini fails to arrive, and Deda refuses to enter the Drini without them.

29: November 2–10, 1952: At Gjoka's we meet Zef Toma. Gjoka reports that Skura has no news from Yugoslavia. Shuk refuses to take us back across the Drini. Zef Toma leaves us to seek help and decides to stay in Albania. Marash Bardheci promises to contact network. We move to a cave.

30: November 11–13, 1952: Marash needs to get us out of the cave and on our way ASAP. I prepare mental letters to Edward, Mustafa Kruja, and Valnea. We seem stuck, tempers rise.

31: November 15–December 2, 1952: I feel the call to become Catholic. Marash Bardheci tells Marash Ndoja about us. Marash decides to stay with us and forgo carrying food to his nephew in the concentration camp in Tepelena.

32: December 3–13, 1952: Marash returns; a group from Yugoslavia is looking for us. We meet three men who have come for us and leave for Fierzë and Porav. Warm weather melts the snow and forces us to cross the Drini River in daylight. Four men cross, Mark Zogu, Peter Toma, and I are left behind.

33: December 14–31, 1952: We leave the house near the Drini and seek refuge in a mountain hut. We make it to Gjokë Deda's home. Brief overview of events in 1944 before the communist takeover. Peter Toma and Mark Zogu leave for Porav. The rescue team from Yugoslavia arrives.

CHAPTER ONE

FAILED ESCAPE ATTEMPT—1951

Shkodra, October 9, 1952

It is the second Thursday in October. The tinge of fall is on the leaves and there should be a chill in the air. Instead, it is a hot, sunny day. The air is dry and dusty, as it has not rained in weeks. Man and beast move at the slow, deliberate pace typical of hot climates. Each has just so much energy and each must last through the day.

At 1:30 p.m., I leave home for the Cultural Center, the former Italian consulate. I duck into the shadows, trying to be unobtrusive. To be noticed can mean trouble, as there is always some informant who is short of his or her Judas quota for the month. For one like me, it is best to be neither seen nor heard. Things could be worse. Instead of removing old garbage piles to make room for a park, I could be reassigned to hard manual labor. Work resumes at 2:00 p.m., after the lunch break, and I'd better be there. As I approach work, thoughts surge through my mind—short-range thoughts. For quite some time now I have given up thinking beyond the immediate. Long-range planning makes me feel hollow for laying claim on a future, even if only in thought. Could today be different?

I project my thoughts as far as two o'clock. Will Peter Kola be there? Peter the faithful, Peter the loyal? Will he be at the gate of the Cultural Center to tell me whether the men of the underground will pick me up, will spirit me out of Albania? So far, I have failed nine times trying to escape from my native country. Will this be my tenth failure?

As I hasten toward the back entrance, my spirit sinks: Peter is nowhere in sight; one more glimmer of hope down the drain. I am so used to failure that I pull myself together with little effort. Clearly, there is no future for me beyond Albania's borders.

I pick up my shovel and go to the half-moon I have carved out of the pile of old garbage. About ten minutes go by, slow as molasses. Then lightning strikes. Could Peter be at the main gate? I am there almost before completing my thought. There he is, freckle-faced, sturdy, with big, rough hands, slightly stooped and bow-legged. His red hair and walrus mustache, his ready smile and wrinkled face usually give him a friendly look. Not today. He looks furious.

"I thought you stood me up again," he growls, red in the face.

"I came in through the back entrance. What's the word?"

He calms down. "Be at the pastry shop near the People's Park at four o'clock. A mountaineer named Kola Murreci will approach you and will ask you whether you are the doctor from Dukagjin. Answer 'yes' and enter the shop with him. Whatever the two of you do thereafter is your business."

Having delivered his message, Peter turns around and walks away, stooped but strong. I follow him with my eyes, with bells ringing in my heart. For now, it is back to my shovel. For the first time I allow my thoughts to stray. Could this be a beginning? Dare I hope?

Why did Peter say he had feared that I had stood him up for the second time? When Peter had come to see us a year earlier, in the fall of 1951, Mergim, Mom, and I were home. As usual, the conversation had quickly shifted to the political realities that consumed our lives. Dad was in prison. He had been there since the end of 1944. My brother and I were fired simultaneously from our jobs for "bad political behavior," victims of the purge of the spring of 1950. Until then, Mergim had worked as an elementary school teacher in Kallarat, in southern Albania, and I as public health inspector for the province of Shkodra. Henceforth, we could work only as manual laborers. Our first assignment was to break stones with hammers in a quarry at Mount Tarabosh. Our daily norm and pay were based on the eight-hour output of a nonexistent mechanical stone crusher. Fairness toward the worker was obviously of no concern. At least we earned enough to buy bread with our ration cards. We also had ration cards for eggs, meat, and clothing but these items were never available. Mom did not work and had no cards, not even food cards.

As "enemies of the people," as members of a prominent "reactionary" family, we were oppressed and, possibly, marked for extinction. Mergim and I could try to escape. But that raised other problems. Dad was in prison, out of the picture. Mom lacked the strength to flee. Besides, she would never leave Dad who needed food and help. Yet Mom was willing to have us escape so that we, her sons, could enjoy a better life. She must have considered that our escape would leave her and Dad under most difficult conditions. On the other hand, if Mergim and I were arrested, which was likely, her life would be even more difficult as she would have to provide food and other necessities for the three of us. This was our dilemma. Mergim and I did talk, among ourselves and with trusted friends, about a possible escape from Albania, as remote as it seemed under the circumstances. We read tea leaves and listened to foreign broadcasts, always hoping for a foreign intervention or an internal uprising that would rid Albania of communism.

During his visit on the Muslim feast of Bajram the year before, Peter had mentioned that a group of infiltrators was in the area and was willing to take persecuted people to Yugoslavia. Besides Mergim and me, a number of "enemies of the regime" were breaking rocks at Mount Tarabosh near Shkodra. All told, nine of us wanted to flee from Albania. We agreed with Peter that it was worth a try. I would be responsible for our group and Peter would be our link with the infiltrators.

Then things started going wrong. One day as Mergim and I returned from work, we saw a policeman at our gate. Our hearts sank. We were about to be arrested and had no place to hide. We had no choice but to enter the house. Fortunately, our guess was wrong. We were not about to be arrested. We found out that a youngster in the landlord's family had typhus and all of us would be under quarantine for several weeks. Furthermore, the police or public health inspectors would drop in unannounced several times a day to check whether everyone was present and accounted for. Unfortunately, Mergim and I would be locked in just as we needed to be free to organize our escape. My stomach was in knots. Perhaps there was still hope. Someone else may take over our liaison with Peter. Mergim and I, however, could only sit and wait.

Luckily, Victor Kujxhija was a member of our work detail at the quarry. In high school, he was arrested for plotting against the communists. He spent several years in prison, was tortured at length, and was beaten and tied to a pole at a forced labor site but never betrayed his friends. In fact, his prisonmates greatly admired him for his steadfastness and strength of character. At the quarry, he was tough and self-confident. I decided he would be the new liaison man for our group. Fortunately, Peter and the infiltrators accepted Victor and things began to move again. Every evening, right after work, Victor or his younger brother would bring us the latest news. They would call us from outside the eight-foot stone wall that surrounded our house. We, on the inside, would converse with our visitors from atop a ladder.

Finally, everything was set. Sunday morning, Victor would let us know where and when we would meet with the four infiltrators—and we would be on our way. Saturday evening, we began to sense that something was wrong when the younger brother came to the wall. He tried hard to sound confident.

"Victor has been summoned to Sigurimi [state security police] headquarters for 10 a.m. tomorrow morning. He will listen to what they have to say, and then we will pick you up. The original plan will be carried out as intended, except for the brief visit to Sigurimi."

To me this did not make sense and I attempted to convince the younger brother to talk Victor out of it.

"Listen, Victor must not go to Sigurimi headquarters. I am sure they don't know of our plans. Otherwise, they would arrest us right now or simply set a trap and catch us red-handed. If we leave before dawn Sunday morning, by the time the security organs notice that Victor did not show up, we will be gone. Once we reach the foothills we are in good shape. To go to Sigurimi at this point is like putting our heads in the noose."

Sunday morning came. It was a bright, sunny day. My brother and I made no special preparations as all we needed was for Victor to show up and tell us when and where to meet the infiltrators. We knew what to do. The morning hours dragged on. Mergim and I moved about our one-room apartment aimlessly. We were tense, on constant alert. We took in even the slightest outside noise and every movement along the outside wall. The morning went by uneventfully, and so did the afternoon. In the evening we resigned ourselves to the inescapable reality. Maybe that was what the "visit to Sigurimi" had been all about. Due to our quarantine, the group had decided to leave without us. We could not deny that we were an added complication. Mergim and I reached this conclusion at the same time, without rancor. Have a safe trip, friends. As for us, better luck next time.

But it was not over yet. The next morning, the younger brother came to see us. Sigurimi had told Victor they knew all about our plan. They warned him not to do anything foolish or else. According to his brother, Victor felt he had no choice but to abort the escape attempt. Having delivered his message, the young man left like a dog with his tail between his legs.

To me, the Sigurimi story was a fabrication. Sigurimi was not in the habit of giving avuncular advice. More likely, Victor got cold feet at the last moment and aborted the mission.

His decision turned out to be a true turning point in our lives. After our release from quarantine, I expected to be drafted. In the past, I had avoided the draft as I was seen as someone indispensable at work. Now I was available for military service. Trying to help me avoid the draft, Dr. Dhimitër Lito, a pulmonary specialist, had issued a report claiming that I had spit up blood but that the chest X-rays were negative. In view of that alleged episode, Dr. Lito requested that I return to the TB clinic in six months for another checkup.

The bogus report might have gotten me off the hook but presenting it entailed a considerable risk for me as well as Dr. Lito. A simple investigation would reveal that my name did not appear anywhere on the dispensary's patient register nor was there any chest X-ray of mine supporting Dr. Lito's report. Under the circumstances, I decided to take a chance and present the report to the draft board.

The day came for me to appear before the board with my hair cropped down to the scalp. This was supposed to show discipline and readiness to serve the fatherland, even though some who received draft notices were rejected or deferred for various reasons. Nonetheless, the visit to the barber was a must. Draftees shed all their clothes before appearing before the draft board to enable the noble members to assess the draftee's physical condition. Fortunately, on the day of my appearance there were no women board members present.

The members were strung out along one side of the table like disciples around the central figure of the communist party representative, a venomous version of da Vinci's *Last Supper*. In addition, there was the representative of the government, one man from the city block where I lived, two others sitting in for the Labor Union and the National Front, and the personnel representative of the road construction enterprise in charge of the quarry where I worked. A physician sat at the end of the table and a male nurse stood by a scale along the wall.

All were seated according to rank. According to communist practice, a person's arrogance reflected his or her true ranking more accurately than the title or the official position. Arrogance showed one's standing within the party, the secret police, and the powers of darkness. It was an index of services performed and the number of victims delivered. While communists were degradingly submissive toward their superiors, the fear they evoked among the lower party echelons and the hapless masses was a rewarding, inebriating part of their recompense. It was headier than their lowly privileges or their meager pay.

I entered the room, hands modestly folded in front of me. As I stood before the board, its members looked at each other with a barely concealed grin. They need not wonder about my political status or what military unit I should join. The forced Labor Battalion was about to put its loving, caring arms around another reactionary draftee.

The physician, a recent transferee to Shkodra, spoke up with unexpected harshness. He read Dr. Lito's letter and the recommendation that I return to the pulmonary clinic after six months. He called the letter a blatant attempt on my part to evade military service. Dr. Lito was a former political prisoner and an unrepentant enemy of the regime. What could one expect from a class enemy? Fortunately, the physician did not ask me when I had visited the clinic or whether I had my chest X-rays with me.

The doctor asked the nurse for my weight. I was surprised by the nurse's reply. As I stepped on the scale it registered 158 lbs. The nurse, however, reported my weight as 136 lbs., over 20 pounds less than the scale showed. The doctor shook his head. "He looks heavier than that," he said, but the nurse stood by his previous readout.

I was asked to leave the room. When they called me back, I was told that I should return to work and that the draft was postponed for one year. I was getting dressed in the anteroom when the nurse stepped out and whispered to me that the personnel man from the enterprise where I worked had told the board not to worry, he would see to it that I spit out my lungs on the rocks in the quarry, and everyone had laughed.

"What was the deal with my weight—why did you underreport it?" I asked the nurse.

"To lend credibility to Dr. Lito's report," he replied as he hurried back into the boardroom.

At one time, the nurse had worked for me, but I had never thought of him as a friend. That was not the only time I had misread people.

Thanks to Dr. Lito, I beat the draft. But we still had a surprise coming. In my stead, they drafted Mergim and sent him to the Labor Battalion.

A few months later, on a cold, damp day, I ran into Victor Kujxhija on a side street not far from our home. We were both bundled up. He tried to sound hearty and convincing. Just because we had failed once was no reason for us not to try again. And try we would, wouldn't we? There was much I could have said in return. Instead, I replied coldly that I was glad we had not escaped. I would have had no one to entrust Mom and Dad to. I had changed my mind. I was no longer interested in escaping. Should he try again, I wished him luck but he was not to contact me. That was the last time I saw him. I walked away saddened. I had just witnessed the end of a friendship born in the trenches.

That failed escape attempt took place in 1951; now fast-forward to October 1952. This newest chapter of my escape saga started on Monday, October 6, when Peter Kola came to our one-room apartment for Bajram, a Muslim holy day. On such occasions, Catholics would visit their Muslim friends while the latter returned the courtesy at Christmas and Easter.

"Blessed be this day of note." He spoke the traditional greeting with simple dignity, raised his demitasse, and took a sip of the black liquid that passed for coffee. I took this opportunity to tell Peter what had happened the year before.

"Peter, I hope you agree that whatever happened was not my fault. Mergim and I were under quarantine and had no way of predicting that things would go the way they did. Victor Kujxhija..."

Peter visibly stiffened in his chair. He cut me short.

"Listen," he said, "there was more to last year's story than you know. Four infiltrators from Yugoslavia came all the way to Bardhaj expecting you that Sunday morning. They carried four extra rifles and ammunition for you and your comrades. If only one of you had shown up, they—and I—would have had a body, a living human being, to show for the risks they took. If that was not bad enough, at that same time my father lay on his deathbed and sent for me. I was so concerned that something might happen to you and your group that I failed to heed my father's last request. In fact, he died without me seeing him for the last time. I should have known better than to trust city folks. There is no question in my mind that you are to blame."

I was stunned. I did not know that Peter's father had died, let alone that Peter had stayed in town because of us. Furthermore, Bardhaj was just beyond the city limit of Shkodra, on the other side of the river Kiri. Four men had left the relative safety of the mountains and had ventured as far as Bardhaj to pick us up. What a missed opportunity!

"Peter, you must believe me. I am truly sorry about your father and about the infiltrators. But Mergim and I could not move without Victor. And you know what he claimed happened to him. I am dead serious about escaping. In fact, right now I am in deep trouble. You know Xhevdet Bajrami, the city sanitary inspector?"

Peter nodded.

I proceeded to tell him about the following encounter:

A few days ago Xhevdet stopped me, right in the middle of Main Street, to give me good news. I never cared for that communist weasel. I had traveled with him on more than one occasion and had concluded that he was untrustworthy and full of hot air. Well, this time, it was worth listening to him. A few days before, he had been in the office of the governor's secretary. There he had seen a letter signed by Hysni Kapo, the communist vice-premier, and the number-three man of the regime, ordering that I be reinstated as public health inspector for the province of Shkodra. It was hard to believe. According to Xhevdet, this was not a request, this was a flat order.

After being fired from the Public Health Service, I wrote the customary letters to government and party officials professing my innocence. I asked that I be told if I had erred in some way to keep me from repeating any unintentional mistakes. In the absence of such mistakes, I hoped to be reinstated. Of course, I received no replies nor had I expected any.

And now, according to Xhevdet, there was an answer. "Are you sure you saw this letter on the secretary's desk?" I asked him.

"Of course I am. I saw it with my own eyes."

What happened next is hard to believe. When I looked up there was Teufik, the governor's secretary, hurrying by, his eyes to the ground, as was his habit. That way he looked important, always in a hurry, with little or no chance for anyone to stop him with inopportune questions or requests.

Teufik was about 40 years old, 5 feet 10 inches, with wavy dark brown hair. Some locks tended to fall on his forehead, giving him a boyish appearance. He had dark, piercing eyes and an athletic build. If you got to know him, he was quite likeable. He was one of a handful of party members who were graduates of an Italian military academy. During the civil war, he had fought in the ranks of the People's Liberation Army. After the war, he came under suspicion for alleged counter-revolutionary activities and spent some time in jail. It took Teufik much effort to be "rehabilitated." Back in the good graces of the communist party, he had risen to the position of secretary to the head of the province. Yet, he still felt vulnerable and wanted little chance contact with people. I knew him well because our offices had been across the hall from each other's. Furthermore, in a moment of weakness, he had confessed to me why he was arrested.

One day, he was with a friend at a café in Durrës. During the conversation, he had drawn some dog heads on a napkin. Shortly thereafter, he was arrested and asked to explain what had happened during the meeting with his friend. The drawing of dog heads, which they found in his pocket, had complicated matters. Sigurimi wanted to know the meaning of those drawings. Were they a code, some means of conspirator identification? If not, what were they? Why had Teufik pocketed the drawing if it had no meaning? Their questioning had been intense, their methods brutal. The last thing Teufik needed was to be arrested and tortured again; hence, his aversion to meeting people outside the defense perimeter of his office. For me, however, Xhevdet's statement was most important, so I stepped right in front of him.

"Comrade Teufik, I understand you have received a letter from comrade Hysni Kapo ordering my reinstatement?"

"What are you talking about? I do not know what you are talking about!" He said this while trying at the same time to walk away from me.

"Comrade Teufik, wait a minute. Comrade Xhevdet here tells me he saw the letter on your desk just the other day."

Teufik sank his eyes into those of Xhevdet. "You saw no such thing."

I asked Xhevdet to repeat what he had told me and Xhevdet repeated the story in just about the same words. Teufik looked at Xhevdet long and hard, and hissed.

"Let me tell you again, there is no such letter."

"I must have been mistaken," Xhevdet caved in, visibly shaken. With the impasse resolved rather abruptly, both communists took off in opposite directions and I was left there, in turmoil.

At this point in the story, Peter shifted in his seat as if to interrupt me.

"Hear me out Peter," I continued. "Chances are Xhevdet is telling the truth. Furthermore, for the secretary to deny even the existence of the letter, it is likely that the governor has already decided to reject Hysni Kapo's order. The communists have no substantiated charges against me or I would be under arrest right now. They need hard evidence to reject the vice-premier's order and the easiest way to gather such evidence is to arrest me and make me 'confess.' If arrested, instead of supporting my parents, I become a burden and one more reason for Mom to worry. Also, it is October. If I am not arrested, this time I will be drafted for sure. Being drafted is the lesser of two evils. Right now, however, I stand a better chance of going to jail for the second time."

Peter looked at me and said the unexpected.

"Another group from Yugoslavia is nearby in the mountains. They accept only people who are in dire danger and of some importance. I will try to contact them Friday. With luck, I should have an answer for you Friday evening."

I was speechless. I rose and hugged Peter. Faithful Peter had understood and was willing to give me another chance.

That happened the evening of Monday, October 6. I immediately sprang into action. Tuesday I stuffed cotton into my right ear and went to the Polyclinic right after work. The institute was across the street from the House of Culture, the former Italian consulate, where I was removing old garbage piles. I knew all the professional people who worked there. After all, the Polyclinic was one of the institutions under my jurisdiction as a public health inspector.

As usual, the place was jam-packed with patients. In the course of a normal business day, each physician saw about 200 patients. You can imagine the quality of service provided by this and other institutions like it. I quickly scanned the lines of patients waiting to be seen by a physician. The lines seemed equally long. So I picked one of my favorite physicians and approached the nurse.

"Can you please get me in ahead of the rest? I will take up only one minute of the doctor's time."

I did not want to be seen lingering around. You never knew who could see me or what could happen. A smile of recognition flickered across her face even though I was dressed in shorts and a mended shirt. She disappeared briefly into the doctor's office, came out and motioned for me to enter. The physician looked up, too tired to ask why I was there.

"Doctor, I have had an earache for a while and it is getting worse. I plan to go to Tirana to see a specialist. Without a physician's report, I must wait about two weeks to see the doctor. With such a statement from you, I can see a specialist immediately."

The doctor lowered his head and began writing. He filled out a form, put my name on it, handed it to me and turned to the nurse. "Next."

He never asked me for my name. That was the only sign of recognition he gave me. I pocketed the report and hurried out. Whether my plan would succeed or fail, one thing was for sure. The cotton would stay in my ear, at least for the next few days.

As I was leaving the Polyclinic, I felt good. I did not know whether it was a good omen, but my step was bouncy and the world seemed to smile. As I got close to home, a thought struck me. Peter would have an answer for me by Friday but Friday could be too late. Even if they did not arrest me, October was the month when recruits appeared before the draft board. Last year I had beaten the draft with Dr. Lito's help. This year I was helpless and would be drafted for sure. I ran up the steps two at a time. Mom was setting the table. She saw me and smiled; good, sweet, strong Mom. I looked for mail but none had arrived that day. There was no draft notice— yet. If the notice were delivered tomorrow, I may have to appear before the draft board in a matter of days, possibly as early as Friday.

We sat down to eat. We spoke little that evening, even less than usual. I knew what was on Mom's mind. What if I were drafted or arrested? How would she cope? She had no ration cards. What little she ate came off mine. She felt so guilty about it! Some time before, she had decided she needed a job, any job, to get her own ration cards. Mom could do many things. She spoke German and Italian and had a working knowledge of Turkish and Serbian. She was a good cook. She could take care of babies, children, or patients. She could be a clerk in a store or work in a factory. In fact, she had more ability and experience than most government employees. Yet, when she applied for a job, she was told the only job available to her was to clean public toilets. Instead of commodes, public toilets had platforms a few inches high with footholds and a hole in the middle. Customers crouched down and did their business. Some waste piled up on the rim, the rest dropped into the pit below. As toilet paper was unavailable, people cleaned themselves with water from aluminum cans that had once contained food. Mom was supposed to scrub these toilets and keep the cans clean and filled with water. Obviously, this was an insult, not a job offer. At my insistence, she did not take the job.

All I could think about was that by the time Peter contacted the underground, I might be in jail or on my way to the Labor Battalion in Tirana. Mom and I sat down to have dinner. When we were done eating, it had gotten dark outside and a rainstorm was pelting the city. Around nine o'clock the rain stopped. I told Mom I had to see Peter. I had been at his place once or twice before when Peter and his team sprayed the marshes with DDT. This activity came under the public health department.

I jumped on my bike and pedaled to his home. Fortunately, he was there.

"Peter, there is a good chance that I might be drafted or arrested before the week is over. Can you contact the infiltrators sooner?"

Peter nodded. "I will see you at the House of Culture Thursday at two o'clock."

When I returned home, Mom looked at me quizzically.

"Peter said he would hurry," I said softly.

I could not tell how she felt as she faced the dilemma. In the clutches of the government, I was in trouble. If I escaped, she was left alone at home. Mergim was with the Labor Battalion and had another year to go. Dad was in prison since November 1944. Her face remained expressionless the rest of the evening.

Wednesday felt like dead space, like a wedge between Tuesday and Thursday, between last night's visit to Peter and the meeting on Thursday, except, of course, if I were arrested or drafted on Wednesday. What a pity that would be, now that escape was a possibility, albeit not yet a reality. Wednesday passed and Thursday came.

CHAPTER TWO

GOODBYE SHKODRA

About 15 minutes have passed since Peter and I parted at the main gate. I am back to digging into piles of old, dry refuse. Minutes ago, I had felt imaginary walls closing in on me relentlessly, as they had done since 1943. At that point, our war against the foreign invaders had shifted to a fratricidal war to fend off communist attacks against us. Albanian nationalists could not fight on two fronts. Thus, during those years, we had drifted from fatigue to exhaustion, from exhaustion to despair, and from despair to defeat. Much had happened around me and to me during those nine years. Almost all of it had been bad as I went from a 19-year-old youngster in medical school to digging in a pile of long-abandoned Italian garbage. That's how it was until today, until a few minutes ago.

All of a sudden, I feel young, 28 years young. I hum as I dig. Somehow, a feeling of well-being, undefined but exhilarating, has replaced my helplessness. I feel as if I had taken a dizzying drink made of nine measures of feeling alive and one measure, one full measure, of hope. All my senses are alert, tingling, noticing everything and taking it in. In the yard surrounding the House of Culture, to one side, there is a well, frequently used by neighbors who come to fetch water. Unexpectedly, Zana, one of the cutest girls in town, enters through a side entrance and comes to the well with an empty pail in hand. She is about 16 years old and wearing a sailor dress. I know her well as she lives in my neighborhood.

"Zana, no girl is permitted to lift a heavy pail out of the well when I am around!" She blushes, smiles, and offers no resistance as I reach for the pail. I am just about done cranking the pail out of the well when I look at her with mischief.

"You know that service in the navy is set at four years?"

She nods.

"Well," I continue, "I would not mind serving four years under you." A flash of understanding sweeps across her face. Then she brushes it off. No, it can't be. Mr. Genc would never harbor such thoughts. She has known me as an anatomy instructor in high school, as a public health inspector, as a grown-up. As with most people in town, she probably has much respect for political prisoners and those in obligatory labor. She must have misunderstood. With her suspicion gone, I wish I felt guilty after my silly remark, but I don't.

"I understand that you are about to announce your engagement," she replies with a bright, innocent smile. Could she be such a skillful fencer, parrying my thrust, just in case?

"Zana, let me assure you that I have absolutely no such intentions. No young lady in Shkodra deserves such a dark fate."

"I know better—and you know better, Mr. Genc." She looks sincere and unaffected.

"Well, if you are so sure, then pray tell, who is the young lady?"

"You don't know?" she asks.

"Not unless you tell me." She hesitates a moment, takes a deep breath, and then mentions the name of a young woman, a student, from a much-persecuted family.

This time I answer in all seriousness. "I know that young lady from sight. I have never spoken to her nor have I gotten in touch with her family, directly or indirectly. Under more favorable circumstances, I would be honored if what you say were true."

I can tell that Zana doesn't believe me. "In fact, Zana, soon you will hear something that will prove to you beyond any doubt that I am telling the truth."

Zana leaves, and with her any fondness I ever felt for the Albanian navy. I keep digging and hauling my loads of refuse as I keep track of time. I must not be seen lingering around the candy store near the park. I must be neither early nor late for my meeting. But first I must see my foreman to let him know that I need to see an ear specialist in Tirana. After all, I must have room to disappear for a few weeks without arousing suspicion.

I approach him and feed him my story exactly at a quarter to four.

"You cannot go on medical leave without a doctor's report."

I show him my medical report.

"OK, go to Tirana. When you are well again, come back to work."

I had counted on his answering me by the book. I thank him and leave through the main gate. My hopes dim for a moment. After all, I may be back in a few days, if my bad luck holds true.

I move with my usual gait. Head down, shoulders sagging, I start walking toward home but turn right into the little street where the pastry shop is located. The church bell strikes four and from the opposite direction comes a tall, dark, mustachioed farmer wearing a black jacket and pants made of homespun woolen cloth. His once-white skullcap is pushed back. He walks like a mountaineer, lifting his feet high as if stepping over invisible rocks.

"Are you the doctor of Dukagjin?" he asks with a deep, pleasant voice.

"Yes, I am," I reply.

"I wonder whether you can help me."

"Let's enter the pastry shop and tell me about your problem."

We sit across from each other at a small table and place our order. He looks at me with a searching glance. He seems satisfied with what he sees.

"My wife is ill, too ill to come into town and doctors here do not want to climb our mountains to see patients. People say you care and you are a good doctor. Can you come with me?"

"Yes, I have a few days off. Perhaps I can help you. When and where do we meet?"

"Be at the Catholic cemetery at five thirty. We'll leave from there."

I am in a daze. We finish our modest pastries, shake hands, and leave separately. As I exit the small building, a thought strikes me. Twenty-eight years ago I was born on the second floor of that very same two-story house. Could this mark another beginning, a second birth for me?

I proceed to the corner and stop. There is joy in my heart. Never in my nine escape attempts have I gotten this far. I almost bump into Xhelal Dani, Qemal Dani's youngest brother, our cousins by marriage. During the civil war, the Dani family had sided with the Front of National Liberation and Uncle Riza was appointed a member of parliament after the communist takeover. Shortly thereafter, he had clashed with his former allies and was shot. At that point, our two families had buried the hatchet and had gotten close again.

Xhelal smiles as he greets me. "How are you and how is the family?"

I smile back. "As well as can be expected." He knows what I mean.

"Have you heard any good news lately?" He asks the question we all ask, hoping against hope. The good news could be something heard on the radio, from a leaflet dropped by U.S. airplanes invading the Albanian airspace, or distributed by the underground. No matter what the source, an entire people anxiously await good news—anything to indicate the end of the communist regime. I decide not to take any chances.

"I am afraid I have heard nothing special."

"I know," he replies, "I guess that's the way it's going to be for a while."

We nod to each other in parting. I am about two minutes from home. Now I must concentrate on my last preparations. I pass by Zana's house, past a small, denuded cemetery. What the regime has done to the cemetery is but one of the many acts of disrespect, of psychological violence perpetrated against the helpless. This little Muslim cemetery is quite old with no more than 30 graves. First, the communists started driving a herd of swine daily through the graveyard. Later, they removed the marble head stones and used them as steps in the stadium under construction a few blocks from here. They did the same to many other cemeteries in town and in surrounding villages.

The Qukej house looms a block ahead. I rush up the steps and into our room without running into any of the Qukej women. There is fear in Mom's eyes as she asks me "Have you been fired again?" She knows that there is worse than my being forced to work as a laborer.

"No, Mother. All is well. I am home early because I am leaving Shkodra for the border today."

"How much time do we have?"

"I will be leaving shortly after five o'clock."

"What do you need to take with you?"

I ask her for a blanket, some socks, some bread, and cheese. She moves about with a shuffle I had not noticed until now. Mom has always been strong; thin but strong. Today she looks drained. Suddenly I remember. I have to get her out of the room.

"Mom, could you please get me my briefcase so I can hide my knapsack in it?" As she leaves the room, I steal her big kitchen knife and slip it under my belt, in the back under my jacket. In preparation for my trip through town I don a brown striped suit that Sadije had sent me from Detroit after Uncle Faik's death. If I am to give the impression that I am seeking transportation for Tirana, I must dress up a bit. In rags, I could arouse suspicion.

Mom returns with my briefcase. It bulges a bit as I stuff the knapsack in but that's no problem. We still have a few minutes.

"Is Xhevat Quku home?" I ask. He is the oldest son of the landlord. He was sixteen when they arrested him in school. He survived torture and five years in prison and came out a man. I would like to entrust Mom to him.

Mom returns shaking her head. "He is out," she says laconically. "Have you thought everything through?"

"Yes, Mom."

"When can I expect to hear from you?" she asks.

Peter had said that I should be in Yugoslavia in one week. I give myself a little more time. "I should be in Yugoslavia in two weeks. At that point you can expect a telegram from Valnea saying that her brother is well." Valnea is a former schoolmate of mine in Italy.

The last few moments are awkward. Neither of us knows what to say. Finally, I break the silence. "Mom, it's time for me to leave." We are near the door that leads to the hallway.

"Son, be strong," are her parting words. What she means is, "Don't let them take you alive. Die like a man." We shake hands; no hugs, no kisses. If she hugged me, she would hang on to me and would not let me go. She closes the door behind me. I go down a few steps, cross the front yard, step through the gate and out of her life—forever.

I have a few minutes if I want to make it to the Catholic graveyard by five thirty. I stop at a small bar and have a shot of raki (Albanian whiskey). I never liked the stuff. Today I don't even notice as it burns its way into the stomach. I take small side streets until I come to the north end of the People's Park.

The pedestrian traffic gets heavier as I approach the Old Market. Somebody calls me by name. I turn and look straight at Hënza, Shpresa Dervishi's younger sister. I had dated her on and off in 1943 and 1944. If I had to describe her, I would say she was cute, short, and very kind. While I was in jail, she married an Albanian-American. This young man was a captain in the U.S. Army and was stationed in southern Italy toward the end of the war. In Bari, he had the misfortune of running into Bedri Spahiu, whom he had known before migrating to America. Bedri was now a communist general, one of the pillars of the regime. In fact, Bedri Spahiu was the prosecutor of the special tribunal in Tirana right after the war. He was a former teacher and had known my father well. In court, he had requested the death sentence for Dad.

In Bari, Bedri had asked the young captain to return to Albania where the people needed him. America had, after all, thousands of young men of his caliber but Albania needed every capable young man and woman to help rebuild the country and secure a better future. Unfortunately, for him, the young captain resigned his commission, and returned to his native Albania. In Tirana, he and Hënza met and fell in love with each other. When I visited Hënza after my release from jail, she told all this to me while her pretty face shone with love for her husband. I congratulated her and gave her a big hug.

Shortly thereafter, her husband was arrested as an American spy. He was placed in solitary confinement while Hënza was called to police headquarters. She was told bluntly that she had to divorce her husband who was a spy and a traitor. Hënza refused and was arrested on the spot.

A few years later, while still in prison, the warden called Hënza into his office.

"Your father is dying," he told her. "If you want to see him once more, you'd better divorce your husband now and get out while there is still time."

This time, Hënza accepted. She and her husband met in divorce court after years of separation. The proceedings were brief. Her husband never looked her in the face. Eventually, after seven years in isolation, her ex-husband was released from prison. She got in touch with him because she still loved him deeply. His reply was terse and to the point.

"When I needed you most, you divorced me." And that was the end of that.

I have just passed beyond the People's Park, on my way to the Catholic cemetery when Hënza calls out.

"Genc, where have you been hiding these last three days?" she says with a big smile. She radiates friendliness and her dimples are as pretty as ever. "I have been looking for you all over Shkodra."

"Hënza, my dear, it's so good to see you." We hug. "I am about to look for transportation to Tirana. If I find a truck today then I won't see you tomorrow. Otherwise, I'll be home tomorrow and we can get together. Go and see my mother tomorrow morning. I might be home."

I hardly stop as I say these words to her. We wave at each other, and I am on my way again when someone grabs my arm. It is Qazim Ramadani, a friend of my parents. In fact, all members of his family were friends of ours as long as I could remember. Qazim himself had been a sort of *bon vivant*. He had never had anything to do with politics, even though his uncle, as minister of the interior under King Zogu, had been a very powerful man. The communists had first employed Qazim as an accountant in a local enterprise. During those years, many reactionaries worked as accountants. Accountants had to have some schooling and many communists lacked training. The communists knew that reactionaries worked harder than anyone, as they needed their jobs to feed their families and to stay out of jail. Reactionaries were helpless, at the mercy of the party and the secret police. Guilty or not, reactionaries could be readily blamed for all shortcomings or irregularities at their enterprises. The communists knew it and so did their victims.

Qazim had worked a few years as an accountant. One day they accused him of theft and arrested him. He was tortured for two years, and tried to commit suicide twice—once by jumping into a dry well in the prison courtyard. While he was still in prison, the communists discovered that his boss was responsible for the missing funds. Nonetheless, the jailers continued their pressure on Qazim to the point where they finally informed him that he had been found guilty by the court and would be executed. Early one morning, they dragged him out of his cell and stood him up against the wall. The firing squad took up positions and pointed their rifles at him. The officer raised his arm, and then lowered it slowly, with a big, ugly smile on his face.

"This time we did it in jest. The next time will be for real."

When Qazim was released from prison, he was a changed man. Gone was his gentleness, his trusting smile. He hated the communists with an all-consuming passion. One day I mentioned to him that my communist boss had come to realize the error of her political ways. Qazim stared at me.

"Don't you ever defend your boss or any other communist. After the liberation, you and other students will come to Tirana asking for scholarships to complete your studies abroad. Let me tell you. Not one of you will go back to school until you have earned that privilege by helping us purge the country of the communist scourge. Only then will you be allowed to go to college. Those among you who have no stomach for the job will not go back to school. It's as simple as that."

My heart ached when I saw what they had done to that gentle man.

Now in the Old Market, he grabs me by my arm with his feet firmly planted on the pavement. "What's the hurry?" he asks with a smile. I looked him in the eye.

"Qazim, I am on my way to Yugoslavia. Please, go home and stay with Mom. Right now she is all alone."

He shakes my hand.

"Good luck. I am on my way." I know I can count on him. In fact, he had attempted to get me across the border at one point but things had gone awry at the last minute. That had been the story of my life. Was it about to change?

I am on my own again. I pace myself as I move toward the cemetery. I get there shortly before five thirty. There is a public restroom nearby. I promptly slip inside behind the wall but not before I notice a couple walking hand in hand in my general direction. I almost burst out laughing. He is a Yugoslav refugee who sought asylum in Albania when Tito broke relations with the Soviet Union. Rumor has it that he is working for the Albanian secret police and sneaks back into Yugoslavia from time to time. I feel like asking him whether he has anything for his parents. I must admit, though, it is a fleeting thought and I have no problem controlling my impulse as well as my laughter.

I walk out from behind the wall as the clock from a nearby church strikes five thirty, and there, right on the dot, is my guide—unruffled, tall, and full of self-confidence. Who could ask for more?

"All set?" he asks with a smile. "At the Kiri River we'll take off our shoes and socks and wade to the opposite shore. Don't worry, the water is not deep."

We walk a short way and sit down to bare our feet when a platoon of security guards comes marching toward us. A young officer heads the column. I freeze.

"Getting ready to ford the river?" he asks. "It's a nice evening and the water level is low. You should have no problem."

Kola Murreci mumbles something in reply. The officer nods and is on his way again. Only then do I notice that his men are carrying small barrels on their backs. It is the water detail.

I go back to removing my footwear when I noticed someone with a handkerchief tied low over his forehead walking straight toward us. I have a sinking feeling; first the security platoon and now this pirate-like character! Will we ever get to enter the river? At that moment, I recognize the man. It is Peter Kola.

"Genc, you are about to leave the city. From that moment on you are out of my hands and are no longer my responsibility. Give me something to show your mother that you made it out of Shkodra." I am touched. I give him my briefcase that I need no longer.

"Take this to Mom and she will understand. Besides, she also has a gift for you."

We embrace. The time has come to bid farewell to Shkodra. Because of circumstance, Peter failed to get me out of town the first time. This time I might get lucky.

A few days before, Peter had told me, not without hesitation, that while the infiltrators had agreed to take me across the border, they had asked for 10,000 lek to pay the bases (the homes that would hide us along the way) for my food and other expenses. I don't remember how we scraped together the money. In addition, Mom had set aside one of my shirts as a gift for Peter.

Peter turns back as Kola Murreci and I walk toward the river. The last traces of daylight are disappearing rapidly. We step into the water. It is not cold. At least I feel nothing. A few moments later, we step ashore near the agricultural cooperative of Bardhaj, near the place where the four infiltrators had awaited our group the year before.

Kola and I start toward the foothills, Kola walking ahead with that deceptively slow pace of mountaineers I knew from my year in Dukagjin. Mountaineers keep that pace whether they are climbing a steep footpath, going down a mountain slope, or walking along the bottom of a valley. Between stops, they cover much ground. If there is need, they can move fast.

Darkness envelops us rapidly. In fact, soon it is so dark that I find myself totally blind. Fortunately, I can hear Kola's steps and the footpath is flat and clear. Suddenly, Kola speaks. "Two men are coming toward us. Stay calm and let me do the talking." We stop.

"Good evening, men," Kola starts the conversation. "How are you? Are you tired?"

The conventional Albanian phrases sound reassuring even though I cannot see the men who are no more than three feet from us. It is a strange sensation. Against any logic, it feels as if they could not see me either. Just in case, I cross my hands in the back and feel for my knife. It is there, but the conversation is relaxed and nonthreatening.

"We are from up the river," they said, mentioning a nearby village. "We will stay overnight in Shkodra where we have some early business. Where are you going?"

Kola mentions a village about three hours to the north.

"Have a safe trip." I hear soft steps as the two men go their way.

Our path begins to climb. Kola keeps his pace and I am right behind him. Maybe he is walking slowly for my sake or maybe my training in Dukagjin and my harsh stint as a laborer have prepared me for the occasion. I am neither euphoric nor depressed. In fact, I am not thinking beyond my next few steps, the next few minutes. The fear and helplessness that had paralyzed me for so many years seems to have stayed behind at the Kiri River. I no longer feel hemmed in and powerless in the hands of the regime. A feeling of relief, of having cast off heavy chains pervades me through and through. It feels good. For the time being, at least, I have wings on my feet.

As we move up the foothills, we go from darkness through semi-darkness and, finally, we step once more into the rays of the setting sun. The mountaintops above Shiroka beyond Lake Shkodra are painted dark against a red sky. Like fireflies, electric lights are glimmering in growing numbers in faraway Shkodra. We stop for a moment to take in the view. I can't make out any features of the city except for the lights. I know, though, that one of those lights shines in Mom's window and that it is both a light and a prayer.

Kola pushes on until we are deep in the woods. Before I can see it, I smell the water of a nearby spring. Perhaps I smell the wet leaves and the rotting wood on the ground. Someone had pushed a piece of iron pipe into the hillside and a steady stream of clear, cold water gushes out in a silver arc and into a wooden trough that is running over. On the ground, the water forms a rivulet that gurgles peacefully downhill. Kola stops, drops his backpack, and kneels down to drink. Then he moves over, sits down cross-legged, and smiles.

"Time to eat, don't you think?"

We have not stopped since we met the two men in Bardhaj. That was hours ago. Up to now, I have felt neither hunger nor fatigue. I had told myself that I was going to keep pace with Kola and not be a burden to him. Now that he suggests we make a break, I accept with pleasure. Sitting down near a spring to break bread with the man who is shielding me from danger adds to my sense of freedom. The moon has risen, the air is crisp, and the wind rustles high up in the trees. It feels good to be alive. In silence, we eat some bread and feta cheese. Then Kola rises for another drink of water. I do the same and am ready to go when Kola says that we will stay and sleep for a while. We see large, lush meadows, the high flats of Mount Cukal that in the moonlight shimmer through the trees. Here, in the past, government security forces ambushed parachutists coming from Italy. It may be safer to cross the meadow in the early morning hours when sentries, if any, might be napping. Kola, of course, knows best. We lie down with our knapsacks as pillows. I have a blanket but as Kola has none, I leave mine in the knapsack. I say my prayers: "Our Father who art in heaven... Hail Mary full of grace..." Before I know it, I am fast asleep.

OCTOBER 10

Kola awakes me at about two o'clock in the morning. The night feels chilly; the moon and the stars are high in the sky. It feels good to be moving again. We reach the edge of an enormous meadow that glistens like liquid silver bathed in moonlight. Eons ago, glaciers had inched their way toward the plains, churning up the ground before them. When they finally stopped, a lake formed, fed by the crystal-clear waters of the glaciers. Over the following millennia, the lake had disappeared, replaced by this luscious meadow known to the people as Lake Cukali. There it is, shimmering in all its glory. I take it all in without stopping. Kola is moving through the knee-high grass at a good clip. It takes us less than ten minutes to traverse a corner of the brightly lit meadow. The view is so unreal, so charmed that I feel safe from harm. I shouldn't. Later that day we learn that the police had surrounded the lake in force as they expected infiltrators to come by parachute that night. Why nobody stopped us, I will never know.

We walk until early afternoon. We stop at another spring and drink and eat again. This time Kola picks a spot where the trees are less dense. Some bushes protect us and, beyond them, I see a farmhouse. When we are done eating, he looks at me half smiling.

"I need to see someone in that farmhouse. You stay here where you will be safe. I'll be back in about half an hour."

I would like to tell him either to take me with him or to forget the visit to the farmhouse. I have no choice; I nod in agreement. When three-quarters of an hour have passed without Kola showing up, I begin to worry. A shepherd comes my way. First, I hear him call his sheep and then I see him. He and his sheep are coming directly at me. I have to move. The bushes further up the hill are thicker. I hide there, even though it means moving away from the spot where Kola left me. I move cautiously, ducking behind the foliage, the noise of my steps mercifully covered by bleating sheep, rustling leaves, and creaking twigs as the sheep graze up and down the hill. Fortunately, the shepherd has no dog but I don't realize it until after he passes me by.

By now, I am furious. First, Kola is late by about an hour. Next, the shepherd could have discovered me without my having the ghost of a chance of talking my way out of my predicament. Finally, I am not where Kola had left me. Then I see him. He is climbing uphill, slowly scanning the bushes with his dark eyes. When he sees me, he smiles warmly, like a cat enjoying the prospect of a succulent meal, if cats could smile. A widow lives all by herself on that farm, he says. She is always hospitable and obliging toward him. Afterwards he had fallen asleep. The rascal!

It is time, though, that we get going if we want to make it to his house before midnight, but first we have to cross a bare hilltop. Without waiting for an answer, he turns around and sets out in long steps toward the other side of the hill. I follow without a word. By the time I reach safety, my anger has evaporated. Kola is a scoundrel; there is little doubt about that. He has a way with words, with gestures, and with timing. He sure knows how to manipulate people. He plays me like a fiddle. What choice do I have?

We start to climb again. Before I realize it, we are next to a stone wall about three feet high that surrounds a farmhouse, larger and more impressive than the one belonging to the lovelorn widow.

"I have to speak with the village elder. Sit here near the gate at the foot of the wall and keep your head down. I'll be back in a few minutes."

He crosses the front yard and disappears inside the house before I know what hits me. I swear under my breath. Kola is the closest thing to a magician I have ever seen. He knows how to disappear faster than anyone I have ever known. What is worse, he can do it whenever he so chooses without ever giving me a chance to clear my throat, let alone speak.

This time I hear them coming. The village elder is a man in his sixties, also powerfully built but somewhat shorter than Kola. They are joking with each other. Almost on my belly, I scurry away from the gate and around the corner. The two mountaineers laugh heartily as they shake hands. Heaven knows what they are up to. Kola takes off and the host returns inside. I wait a minute and then I half run and half slither after Kola. He has stopped out of sight and is waiting for me. He must have more confidence in me than I do.

By now, it is late afternoon. Our path first seems to hug a densely wooded mountainside and then moves away and downhill. The day had been cloudy but, as night falls, the clouds begin to disappear and the moon once more reaches with long delicate fingers between the tree branches and down to our footpath. Kola is bobbing up and down in front of me, broad shouldered and self-confident. I have his strong face before my eyes, his mischievous smile and his easy manners. It is hard to stay mad at him for long. Besides, I am at his mercy. Yet, I do not feel in danger—quite the contrary. At one point he stops. "Are you hungry? We will be home by about nine o'clock. Then we can eat."

We keep going and shortly after nine Kola stops and whispers, "We have arrived. There is my house. We will enter the stable and you will stay there. I will see if we have guests. Either way, I'll let you know."

Both the house and the stable are of stone and look rather impressive in the moonlight. We enter the stable. It is occupied by a number of healthy-looking, tranquil cows. Kola disappears. When he returns about fifteen minutes later, he explains that a cousin has come over and is with Kola's wife and children.

"Tonight you stay in the stable. Tomorrow we prepare your hiding place. I brought food. Eat while I prepare a place for you to rest."

I reach for the food, but instead of eating, I watch Kola. He rolls together some wooden barrels, places boards on top and covers them with corn stalks. "Sit down and eat. Don't worry about the cows. They mind their own business. Will you be all right?"

"Don't worry about me. I'll be just fine."

"Good night, then. Sleep well and I'll see you tomorrow."

Kola disappears. I eat and when I am done, I jump on my temporary bed. The stalks feel hard but I am tired and I know that I will fall asleep without trouble. I unfold my blanket, cover myself, roll the knapsack up like a pillow, and lie down. My thoughts go to God and to Mom. Before I know it, I am asleep, but not for long. Somebody tugs at the cornstalks. I wake up and there is a cow pulling and munching at the same time. The beast is breathing noisily, or so it seems to me. I am furious. I push the animal away and lie down again. Within a split second, another cow tugs and pulls, and my head is dragged along with the cornstalks. I have taken just about all I can. I sit up, grab a stalk and start whacking the animal over the head. Then the thought strikes me. What if I am hitting the bull? From where I sit, I cannot tell. Above all, I know I should not make noise. So, I decide to compromise. I remove the cornstalks and throw them on the ground. The cows, and bull, can have the stalks if they let me get some sleep.

OCTOBER 11

Before I know it, Kola is shaking me awake. It is early dawn and the cows will be let out. I have to stay inside and keep quiet, as the cousin will be in the house until after breakfast. When I tell Kola about my problem with the cows, he chuckles. I wonder whose side he is on.

When he walks out of the barn, he leaves me sitting on my "bed." In daylight, it becomes obvious that I should have been more grateful. Had I not been atop that improvised structure, I would have been much closer to the cows and the end product of their active digestion. I spend most of the morning perched on my platform.

For the first time in days, I have time to think. Over the next few months, I will have plenty of chances to do so as we hide or rest during the day and travel at night. Presently, though, it is a novel experience. I felt better when I was putting distance between Shkodra and me. I knew the perils and pressures of the city and felt safer in the woods. The threat was the same, but the level had gone down as I was not under constant surveillance. The thought of possible betrayal, of course, is scary. I reach for my knife in the small of my back but cannot find it. I search high and low but my knife is gone. It is not the end of the world but helplessness is an old companion that just does not want to leave me. Kola returns.

"Soon we will have you in a safe place. Today you will stay here in the stable but tonight, once my cousin is gone, you will meet the family and join us for supper."

"Thanks. As long as I am safe, I am fine."

Kola continues. "Today I am meeting a man who can tell us where the group is. Then we will know when they will pick you up."

Having said those few words, Kola leaves the stable. This is the first time he mentions the group. Officially, such infiltrators from across the border are known under different terms of endearment such as mountain criminals, foreign stooges, or infiltrators. In the eyes of the oppressed majority, however, they represent hope.

CHAPTER THREE

ESCAPE FROM ALBANIA – 1924

L et me begin with a brief summary of Albanian history starting with the time of its national hero, George Kastriota Skanderbeg. In the fifteenth century, Europe came under attack by the hordes of the Ottoman Empire. The Turkish armies occupied Egypt and part of North Africa, much of the Arab peninsula, Israel and Syria, Byzantium, Greece, Romania, Albania, and part of Yugoslavia.

When they reached Albania, they saw a chance to settle the score with Skanderbeg whom they had held as a hostage through his childhood and youth. He had received military training under the Turks and had excelled in battle. At the Battle of Niš against John Hunyadi, Skanderbeg broke ranks and with his Albanian warriors deserted from the Turkish camp, went to Albania, reclaimed his possessions and, at the head of a coalition of Albanian princes, over a period of 25 years repulsed 13 Turkish invasions of the Albanian territory. He became known for his incredible physical prowess. The Ottoman sultan asked once that Skanderbeg send him his sword as he was known to cut a bull in two with one stroke of his sword. Some time later, the sultan returned the sword with a message that the fame of the sword was greatly exaggerated as the strongest man in the sultan's army had been unable to cut a bull in half with one blow. "The next time," Skanderbeg replied, "I'll also send you my right arm." Skanderbeg also excelled because of the strength of his character. His nephew, his sister's son, showed an invading Turkish army a path that would permit them to outflank Skanderbeg and hit him from the rear. Skanderbeg defeated the Turks and captured his nephew. It blew my mind when I read that Skanderbeg had forgiven the nephew. Even today such great Christian behavior would be out of the norm.

The successful resistance to the Turkish onslaught earned him the title "Defender of the Holy See." Pope Callixtus III named him commander of the upcoming Crusade and Europe's kings accepted to fight under Skanderbeg's command. Normally, the ruler who contributed the most troops would become supreme commander. Skanderbeg was offered the post because of his paramount military achievements. The death of the pope put an end to the military plans to free the Holy Land from the Turks. With the death of Skanderbeg in 1468, Albania lost its freedom, and Christianity its champion.

Albania and most of the Balkans came under the Turks for almost 500 years. In Albania in particular, the foreign invaders did much harm as they forbade the use of a written Albanian language. There were no schools or books in Albanian. There was no Albanian printing press anywhere throughout the Ottoman Empire. Anyone who went to school learned Turkish, how to read and write in Turkish, how to think in Turkish, thus absorbing Turkish culture and mores. Furthermore, the Turkish masters bestowed honors and material goods on those who served the Sultan.

Albania's ancestors, the Illyrians, had embraced the Christian faith since St. Paul's early travels to the Balkans. Following the Turkish occupation, most Albanians living in the plains were forced to become Muslim. Over the centuries, part of the Albanian population in the south kept its religious affiliation with the Orthodox Church. Likewise, part of the city dwellers of Shkodra and the inhabitants of the mountains to the north remained faithful to the pope and the Church of Rome. The Turks, who saw nothing worth fighting and dying for in these mountains, displayed a religious tolerance toward their inhabitants they had denied to the inhabitants of the plains. In Albania, this state of affairs continued until the beginning of the twentieth century. The majority of the population endured the foreign yoke with patience rooted in hopelessness. After all, Europe was eager to trade with Turkey even if it meant the loss of the Christian faith and of freedom in the Balkans.

On the eve of World War I, Albanians revolted against the Turks. Muslims and Christians, young and old, took to the mountains and faced the Turkish Imperial troops that had once thrust terror into the hearts of Europeans as far north as Vienna. My father, among hundreds of other patriotic youths, fought valiantly until the Turkish troops had to withdraw. During these turbulent years, Dad was jailed five times and sentenced to death twice, both times by foreign powers he had fought against. The Albanian revolutionaries hung up their victorious arms when their leaders gathered in Vlora and signed the Declaration of Independence on November 28, 1912. Among the signatories was Mustafa Merlika-Kruja, Uncle Bashkim's father.

Albania declared its independence on November 28, 1912. The Turkish Empire would hang on and survive for a few more years, until 1922 when the Turkish Republic replaced it.

Shortly thereafter, Albania was declared a principality under the rule of Prince Wied, a German prince. His throne toppled almost immediately, under the onslaught of Balkan wars and World War I that exploded following the assassination of Archduke Ferdinand of Austria in Sarajevo. World War I ravaged Europe for four years. Austrian, Italian, and French troops invaded Albania. At the end of various conflicts, including World War I, Albania's neighbors again displayed their lust for Albanian territory. European diplomats created Yugoslavia and enlarged Greece at the expense of half of Albania's lands and population, in blatant disregard of history and the rights of the indigenous populations. Had it not been for President Wilson and his firm belief in self-determination for all peoples, there may not have been an Albania at the end of World War I. Albania still suffers under the injustices perpetrated by European diplomats almost a century ago. Unfortunately, the country's military and economic impotence greatly contributed to the neighbors' appetites in the past and continues to do so to this day.

During World War I, Italian troops had occupied the port and hinterland of Vlora, a port across from Italy, on the east shores of the Straits of Otranto. At the end of the war, Italy refused to withdraw her troops as, with Italian troops on both sides of the Otranto channel, the Adriatic became an Italian lake. The Albanians had no choice but to take up arms one more time. Under the command of Qazim Koculi, a graduate of a naval academy, three years after the end of World War I, their determined assault pushed the Italian troops into the Adriatic. Mussolini, at that time a Socialist member of the Italian parliament, wrote in his diary that he cried more because of this territorial loss than when Austro-Hungarian troops defeated the Italian forces at Caporetto in World War I. At Caporetto 600,000 Italian troops had either deserted or surrendered to the enemy. Eighteen years later, in 1939, Mussolini would invade Albania and thus "redeem" the honor of Italy. He carried his revenge even further. At the end of 1942 and under the murkiest of circumstances, he had General Rivolta, commander of the Italian forces in Vlora, kill Qazim Koculi, the hero of Vlora.

Let us go back to the years following World War I. During those years of imminent danger, Fan Noli, an Albanian Greek Orthodox priest who had immigrated to the United States, returned to Europe to serve his country. Friend and foe alike recognized his brilliant defense of the Albanian cause at the League of Nations in Geneva. The generous help in men and material given by the Albanian diaspora in the United States, and President Wilson's firm determination to secure the right of self-determination for all peoples, laid the foundation for an independent, albeit mangled, Albania. Albanian territories, from Tivar to the Mountain Region in the north, from Kosova to Metohija and Ohër in the east, to Çameria in the south, went to Albania's neighbors and with them half the population of Albania.

The following biographical details are few and sketchy based on what little I heard and remembered from my parents and other relatives. Unfortunately, the Turkish administration in Albania kept no written records of births, deaths, and the like. Thus, genealogical research would be of little help.

My paternal grandfather, Zeqir Llëngu, died at age 27 while working as secretary to the governor of the province. My paternal grandmother's name was Ziqe. After her husband's death, she remarried and had two daughters, Nigjar (who married Hysni Mborja, Bessie's uncle), and Gjylka (who became the wife of Zyhdi Tapija). Upon Ziqe's death, her husband married again and had several children, among them Uncle Edward (Liço). While we considered him an uncle, he and Dad had two half sisters in common but no actual blood links. Unfortunately, I never met my paternal grandparents and this is all I know about them. I can tell you, I missed them because the old love the young, but the young also need and seek their grandparents.

Dad was born on January 10, 1893. I don't know his place of birth but our family stemmed from the village Vinçan near Korça. As a youngster, he served as a guide to Albanian rebel bands fighting the Turks in the Korça area. Having gone to an elementary school in Albania (where all subjects were taught in Turkish), he attended a Turkish high school in what is now northern Greece. When he came of age, he joined anti-Turkish guerilla forces led by Spiro Bellkameni and Mihal Grameno. During World War I, Dad taught grade school in Mollagjesh, a village near Elbasan in central Albania. One day he came into town and saw some of his friends sitting in a railroad car—part of a train operated by Austrian troops. His friends were leaving to attend the university in Vienna, Austria. Dad ran to his school, grabbed a kerchief with his meager belongings, and got on the train. An Austrian sergeant made the roll call but when he counted noses, there was one more body than names on his list. He challenged Dad, who seemed older and had a mustache that went from ear to ear. Dad pointed at a name on the sergeant's list. The sergeant shrugged his shoulders and off they went. Once in Vienna, some students interceded on Dad's behalf and the Albanian consul granted him a full scholarship. He registered to become an engineer. The flu epidemic toward the end of World War I threatened his very life and left him with impaired eyesight. Unable to do the drawings required by his engineering courses, he switched to history and philosophy and earned his doctoral degree *summa cum laude* in eight semesters.

One day, I asked Dad why he had been in such a hurry to return to Albania. After all, he should have given himself at least a year to learn German, a language with complex grammar.

Dad looked at me sternly. "That would have meant depriving some other student of the chance to study in Vienna," he replied, "at the expense of the Albanian people." In Dad's eyes, that would have been a veritable crime.

My maternal grandfather was Rauf Angoni from Gjirokastra. His family was among the prominent families in town and was related to other such families such as the Selfo family, the Çabej family, and even Enver Hoxha's family (Mozi, my sister-in-law, is a Selfo; Toni, her son-in-law, is a Çabej; Enver Hoxha, the butcher of Albania). Grandpa studied medicine in Turkey and left the military service with the rank of major. In civilian life, he served as medical officer for the city of Shkodra and practiced medicine in his private office until his death in the summer of 1932. Being Muslim, he was the physician of choice of the Catholic half of the city while Dr. Saraçi, a Catholic, was the family physician of the Muslims. There were also a few other physicians in town but Grandpa and Dr. Saraçi had the largest practices. Mom told me Dr. Saraçi assisted at my birth. When she was in labor and screaming, my Dad, pacing the floor downstairs, urged Dr. Saraçi to cut up the baby and save the mother's life. Dr. Saraçi replied that everything was going well and that Dad should not worry. Thank goodness Dr. Saraçi did not listen to Dad!

Grandfather Angoni was known as an excellent diagnostician even beyond the borders of Albania. When medical clinics in Vienna acquired X-ray units, many a radiologist was impressed that Grandpa had identified complex pulmonary illnesses by just listening to the patient's chest.

Grandpa was a true healer. When patients needed a prescription but had no money, he did not charge for the visit and paid to have the prescription filled. He never owned a home but lived in a flat in a very simple two-story house in Shkodra. I was born in that house and, 29 years later, I met a man in a candy store on the first floor of that very building. That man then led me out of Shkodra, on the first leg of my flight to Yugoslavia.

My maternal grandmother, Myhbire, was born in Shkup (Skopje), capital of present-day Macedonia. She was 13 years old when she married Grandpa, who was already a physician! That is how things went in those days. When I met her in the summer of 1938, she was very short, bent over, and a chain smoker. Years later, I discovered that she looked very much like Mother Teresa. They were both offspring of the Albanian population in Macedonia. Judging by their looks, they could have been sisters. I saw my grandmother frequently, particularly after 1948 when Mom, Mergim, and I moved to Shkodra. Except as a baby, I never met Grandpa and remember him only from one photo where he wore a Turkish military uniform.

My grandparents had four daughters and a son. Makbule, the oldest, was a very fine lady, kind and soft-spoken. She married Riza Dani, of the Danis of Shkodra. They had one daughter, cousin Agim. Naxhije was the second daughter. She married a veterinarian, Sejfi Vllamasi, who received a high professional award from the Pasteur Institute in Paris. They had no children. You will read more about these two families later on. My mom, Seadet, was born on January 11, 1906 in Prishtina, Kosova. She grew up in Shkodra and, like many young girls from prominent Muslim families, attended a school run by Catholic nuns. From what I have gathered, she was a tomboy. Later on, I will write more extensively about Mom and Dad and the years that followed. The youngest sister was Shqipe. She was very bright but had a difficult life and died young, after an unsuccessful gall bladder operation. Memduh, the fifth child, was the only son in the family. I remember him vaguely from when I was 4–5 years old in Vienna. He was dark, tall and handsome, had a beautiful singing voice, and was lots of fun. In Vienna, he was registered at the Faculty of Medicine but, as I heard from my parents, he cared more for girls than books or exams.

Fan Noli, an Orthodox priest living in Boston, returned to Albania in 1923 and headed the government of the new state. In those years, my maternal grandfather was the medical officer of the city of Shkodra and his modest home became a hotbed of Albanian nationalism. Riza Dani became a member of the newly formed parliament. Sejfi Vllamasi became a member of Fan Noli's cabinet. Dad held no government post but, being of the same political persuasion, became a member of the political circle of Noli supporters that met in my grandfather's home.

Mom was engaged to a physician before she met Dad. This was an arranged engagement and pleased my grandmother very much. Then, one day, Mom told her parents that under no circumstances was she going to marry the man they had chosen for her. Grandma hit the ceiling. It was unheard of that a young girl would buck the will of her parents. To dissolve the engagement would bring shame to both families, to ours and to the physician's as well. But Seadet was adamant. Finally, Grandpa intervened. He was not going to force his daughter to marry a man against her will.

"If you like the physician so much," he said to his wife, "you marry him." Shortly thereafter, Mom met Dad, and henceforth Nekija Lame carried love letters from one to the other.

As part of the engagement, my grandparents organized a picnic to which they invited some close friends, all from Shkodra. The men of Shkodra were renowned for their courage and their prowess with firearms. Korça, on the other hand, was considered the intellectual capital of Albania. At the picnic, a friend of the family, not knowing Dad's past, posed a challenge.

"Here in Shkodra," he said, "we do not give our daughters to men unless the latter know how to handle a gun. Now you are from Korça and have your doctorate from Vienna. That's all well and good, but can you shoot?"

"I do not have a gun with me," Dad replied.

"Fine," said the speaker. "I am going to put my silver tobacco box on this tree branch and give you my handgun. If you want to marry the young lady, first you will have to hit the box at thirty paces."

He stepped off the distance and gave the gun to Dad. Dad took aim and fired sending a bullet right smack through the middle of the box.

"Sheer luck," the man said as he picked up the ruined silver box. "I will set it up again and you shoot once more. If you hit it again, I'll believe that you know how to shoot."

"We also have a tradition in Korça," Dad replied. "We do not shoot twice at the same target. Put another silver box on the branch, and I will fire again." The man was not going to risk another silver box and Dad passed the test.

My parents were married on May 3, 1923, and I was born in Shkodra on February 16, 1924. By December of that same year, Ahmet Zogu, who had been minister of the interior in Fan Noli's cabinet, overthrew the government and proclaimed himself president. The circle of friends and political allies who met in Grandpa's home scattered. All three sons-in-law escaped, taking their families with them. Dad, Mom, and I escaped across Lake Shkodra into Yugoslavia where we spent the next couple of years.

Dad taught at the University of Belgrade and things simmered down for a while. I began to learn Serbo-Croatian and my parents used to tell me that—with some difficulty—I would climb the steps to the university building where Dad worked. I would present myself at the receptionist's desk and would ask her whether there was any mail for Dr. Djevat Kortsha. My parents would laugh as they told me this story and I never found out whether I had ever received any of Dad's mail.

Another story dealt with something that happened with a chicken. One day I tied a string to the leg of a chicken in our backyard. I held a twig in my hand and, as I straddled the chicken, I urged it to take me to Albania. Rev. Lazër Shantoja, a Jesuit priest and friend of the family, witnessed the scene and wrote a little poem on this subject. As far as I know, a copy of the poem is somewhere among my wife Margaret's papers.

At about this time, Ahmet Zogu (Zog), who had promoted himself to lifelong president and later to king, sent two men to Belgrade to ax my Father to death. Fortunately, the attempt failed. Shortly thereafter, Zogu reached an accord with the government of Belgrade, which stipulated, among other things, that all Albanian political refugees be returned to Tirana. This took place during the winter of 1927. Dad wasted no time, boarded a train with Mom and me, and as the sun came up we were safely in Austria where we spent the next ten years or so until November 1936.

My parents did not know it then, but the years in Austria, hard as they were, would turn out to be the best years of their lives. The Great Depression was wreaking havoc on both sides of the Atlantic. Dad could have taught at a university had he been willing to relinquish his Albanian citizenship. This he would not do. For the next 10 years, we lived on what little Dad earned with his writings and with money uncle Faik sent from Detroit. First, we lived in Vienna where I attended a Montessori kindergarten. Here I distinguished myself during the great winter freeze when the pipes inside the kindergarten froze solid. I organized a gang of children who took turns wrapping our hands around the pipe. To our delight, after a while, one or two drops of water would come off the faucet. This was no small success, was it?

Later we moved to Graz where life was cheaper. Few Albanians lived in Graz at that time. There was Uncle Riza with Aunt Makbule, Bule for short, and my cousin Agim. There was Qazim Koculi, the victor of Valona. The few other Albanians included a handful of college students and some transients who came for medical or other reasons. Agim and I got along famously, much better than when I was born. Let me explain. Until my arrival, she was the pride and joy of her parents and the entire clan as she was the only child in the family. Then I appeared, a boy, any Albanian parent's and grandparent's delight. One day, Grandma, Mom, and other members of the family were sitting together in one room while I slept in my crib near the fireplace in another. Agim had disappeared. Grandma got suspicious and entered the room where I lay, just in time to see Agim shoving a red-hot poker between the bars of my crib. Grandma immediately grabbed the poker away from her.

"What were you trying to do?" she yelled at Agim.

"This time, I was only going to poke his eyes out," Agim said. "If he continues to misbehave, the next time I will kill him!"

Life in Graz was pleasant and tranquil. I started kindergarten and two of my early memories are linked to that period. There was a cute little blonde in my group. One day, she was standing nearby, holding a big ball under her arm. I hit the ball and when the young beauty bent over to pick it up, I kissed her on the nape. Ever since I have liked brunettes; the two great loves of my life would turn out to be brunettes.

The other incident dealt with our fate as exiles. Dad came home one night and Mom told him to ask why I was sad and sitting in a corner. When Dad asked me, I told him I was crying because we would die and they would bury us in foreign soil, far away from Albania.

I was too young and too well shielded to realize that we were strapped economically. Obviously, I was also left out of any important things that were going on around me. For instance, King Zogu, who according to some

Albanian wags had installed himself firmly on the throne of Nasredin Hodja, was planning to come to Vienna with his sisters and a full entourage. This was the opportunity the political exiles had been waiting for. A committee was formed and two former army majors, Azis Çami and Ndokë Gjeloshi, volunteered to assassinate the king. Dad, Qazim Koculi, and Uncle Riza were in on the plot. The two officers attacked the king as he was leaving the Vienna Opera. The king entered the limousine first, followed by Lesh Topallaj, his aide-de-camp. The officers fired and mortally wounded the aide-de-camp, hoping that he would fall backwards, outside the car, giving them a clear shot at the king. Instead, he fell forward, providing the king an excellent cover. Çami then circled the car and came up near the driver. He pointed the gun at the driver, who promptly ducked, thus giving Çami a clear field. He pointed the gun at the king from a distance of no more than five feet. He pulled the trigger but his pistol jammed. By now, the Austrian police had recovered and had grabbed both would-be assassins. The aide-de-camp died on the spot while the king himself survived without a scratch.

While the Austrian prosecution could not prove that there was a link between the Albanian émigrés in Vienna and the two plotters, the government nonetheless forced all Albanian exiles residing in Vienna to leave the country. Those in Graz were deemed innocent and were allowed to stay.

Dad became involved after the shooting. He demanded that the trial of the defendants be moved from Vienna to a smaller, industrial city in Austria. The defense lawyer objected and even called Dad an "agent provocateur." Dad felt offended and challenged the lawyer to a duel. At this point, the lawyer enquired about the reasons that had prompted Dad to request a change of venue. Dad's rationale was simple. Vienna was the capital of the former Austro-Hungarian Empire and part of the population would be pro-monarchic. Hence, jurors could be for King Zogu and against the defendants. In an industrial city, chances of a jury disposed in favor of the defendants were much better. The lawyer understood, intervened with the court, and was able to change the location of the trial. The two defendants were sentenced to a number of years in prison and were eventually released.

The plot also had an impact on me personally. One day I overheard Dad and Qazim Koculi discussing the plot in great detail, after the fact, including their personal involvement. I was sitting at a desk in the next room, doing homework. My eyes fell on a photograph of Aziz Çami with Mom,

Dad, and me. I was so worried that the police might find the photograph and suspect Dad's involvement that I scratched Major Çami's face off the picture. Dad had entered the room and stood behind without my noticing him. He hit me so hard that I flew off my chair and unto the floor.

"Why did you do this?" he kept asking as he held me tightly in his grip.

"Don't you understand?" said Qazim Koculi. "The boy was just trying to protect you. Let him be."

I was frightened beyond speech. I had always liked Mr. Koculi. He was rather short, rotund, and very kind. Dad had told me that he and Aziz Çami were the heroes of Vlora and I looked at Mr. Koculi with admiration. I often imagined him in a naval uniform because Dad had told me he had been an officer in the Turkish navy. Just like us, Mr. Koculi had fled Albania when Zogu had come to power, leaving his wife and two children behind. Over the years, he had sort of adopted me. He brought me little gifts from time to time. When I had scarlet fever, Dad took me to Mr. Koculi's apartment to bathe, since we had no bathtub in our apartment. In the past, Mr. Koculi had made my life more comfortable. This time, I was convinced, he had saved it.

My maternal grandfather died early in 1932. We were in Judendorf when Mom left for Albania. In all fairness to Zogu, Mom had no trouble getting a passport even though Dad was an enemy of the king. Comparatively speaking, Zogu was a gentleman whose rule was much more civilized and respectable than that of the communists a few years later. While Mom was gone, Dad and I ate our main meal at a restaurant; breakfast and supper we ate at home. Dad always ordered only one main course at the restaurant, divided the food into two unequal halves, and always gave me, the eight-year-old, the bigger half. Years later, he told me that he had done so to save some money in case Mom returned ill from Albania. That's exactly what happened. When Mom came back, she was suffering from malaria.

As I said, I was too young to understand much of what was going on. Mom told us that there were many mourners at Grandpa's funeral. Also, that Grandpa was buried at public expense because the family was too poor to cover the funeral expenses, but also in recognition of the services he had rendered to the poor whom he had served with dedication for so many years. Mom's words would come back to me a few years later when I visited Shkodra. Their full impact, though, would not hit me until much later, as I grew in age, wisdom, and understanding.

Mom returned from her visit to Albania in the summer of 1932. I did not know it then, but she had traveled to Albania heavy with child. That December Mergim was born and I was no longer an only child. The name Mergim meant *exile*, as he was born in Graz. The fact that my parents chose an Albanian nondenominational name was in line with my Dad's political beliefs that first names should have no religious affiliation. He, and those who believed as he did, wanted to select such names and do away with labels that divided Albanians into the three prevailing religious groups. Hence, I was named Genc after an Illyrian king. My cousin's name was Agim meaning *dawn*, Mustafa Kruja's four sons were named Petrit (*falcon*), Fatos (*hero*), Bashkim (*unity, union*), and Besim (*faith*). As it turned out, only a few Muslims adopted this practice.

Before Mergim was born, for a little while I had a younger brother named Ylli (*star*). My first memories of him go back to when I was about four—he was pudgy and robust. Then, one day, he fell ill and was taken to a hospital. Whenever I asked about him, I was told that he was in the hospital and that he would come back when he was well again. Time went by and I asked less and less about my baby brother. I don't recall a funeral but years later I was shown his grave and the headstone. The headstone was about six feet tall, a simple obelisk with a crying angel on top. We would visit the grave occasionally and by then I had only vague memories of my brother Ylli.

Many years later while on vacation in Graz, I went to St. Peter's cemetery but could not locate his grave. The cemetery had been bombed during the war and besides, I was told, all graves were routinely dug up after a number of years to make room for others. And yet years earlier, after we had moved to Fiume, I distinctly recall Dad telling Mom and me that he had bought Ylli's gravesite in perpetuity.

Some childhood memories stand out in my mind. One of them was the feast of St. Nicholas, on December 6 in Graz. It always began with a dreaded knock at the door. When Mother opened the door, there was the devil, covered with soot and rattling his chains.

"Where is that boy of yours, that little boy who does not study, obey, or even eat as he should? Where is he so I can teach him a lesson?" More rattling of chains!

In a sense, I was grateful. With all that noise, nobody could hear my chattering teeth or my knees knocking together as I hid behind Mom's skirt. While the devil made those charges, I examined my conscience. I did well in school even though I could do better. I was obedient compared to some schoolmates and friends. But that charge about eating poorly. Did he know that I stuffed my breakfast croissants into the big stove in our living room? Neither Mom nor Dad had ever mentioned it to me! Then I heard Mom defend me against such wanton charges with the loyalty that only mothers can muster.

Suddenly, there was St. Nicholas. He pushed the devil aside. St. Nicholas said I was a good boy. He knew that for sure and had brought me some gifts. The old gent would reach into his bag and give me a handful of nuts and maybe an apple or two. Sometimes I might even get an orange. To my relief, at this point St. Nicholas would step back and wave. Mom would close the door and I would be safe for another year. I could hear St. Nicholas and his companion shuffle upstairs to the next apartment for their next performance. Well, perhaps those children deserved the devil's rebuke. They were not nearly as good as I was.

As I recall, at the beginning of each school year, our teachers took us to church. My most vivid memories go back to the Church of the Sacred Heart of Jesus in Graz. I think the entire school went to this large and beautiful church even though many of my schoolmates were Protestant. Did the latter actually go to a Catholic church? I don't remember. I do remember the huge church, or so it seemed to me, the beautiful stained-glass windows, and the massive portals. The statues of saints spoke of heaven. The heavy columns supporting the central nave and the lateral aisles reached skyward. Shafts of light scanned the building like angels' fingers; clouds of incense wafted upwards. Their penetrating fragrance and the mighty sounds of the organ all combined to make me feel like nowhere else. I united my prayers with those of the others. I don't know what the teachers prayed for. We little ones prayed for good grades. At home, neither Mom nor Dad taught me any religion. We never went to any churches, mosques, or temples. It was in this church, at age 7, that I first felt the call to become Catholic. That desire never left me. Even before I was baptized, Catholic churches in Italy, Yugoslavia, Greece, and the United States were home to me and offered me refuge. Prayer stayed with me, particularly in difficult times. Years later, it gave me reassurance that while times were bleak, while communism could persecute, hurt, and kill me, it could never destroy my soul unless I willed it. Hence my constant prayer that God would let me draw strength from

His love and justice to resist and oppose the ever-present surrounding evil.

As I started school in Graz, good grades meant a lot. I wanted to please Dad, who expected much of me. Dad was a graduate of the University of Vienna. Because he refused to become an Austrian citizen, he could not apply for a job. He was home practically all the time. He spent almost ten years translating documents dealing with Albania that had appeared in *Acta et Diplomata Austro-Hungariae* (the printed collection of Austrio-Hungarian diplomatic documents). He considered such documents as being essential for the formation of future Albanian diplomats, of history professors, and the like. But since he was always home, he also wanted to know what I did in school, how well I did, how much homework I had, and so on. He checked the latter and was always ready to help—his way. Often, especially in math, he would explain things differently from how the teacher had explained them in class. For me that meant nothing but trouble. When Dad sensed that he had lost me, he would put more pressure on me. The more he pressured me, the more I got scared and the more he lost me. Mom would intervene on my behalf. That made matters worse. It was a vicious circle where the mere thought of it paralyzed my brain. In retrospect, there is no doubt that Dad helped me very much, not so much because of the specific knowledge I gained but because he taught me how to study. Were it not for Dad, I would have never gotten the grades I got through school, including college and graduate school. On the other hand, his refusal to share with me the pleasure my scholastic progress gave him contributed to a feeling of inadequacy that haunted me well into my forties.

Mergim was born in Graz on December 30, 1932. At the insistence of my father, Mergim did not receive Austrian citizenship. I do not recall what steps my father took to bring this about, but he was proud to be Albanian and demanded his Austrian-born son be Albanian. Years later, after the communist takeover, Uncle Edward suggested that we approach the Austrian embassy and explore the possibility that Mergim leave Albania, since he was born in Austria. Heinrich v. Wimmersperg, Margaret's sponsor who was active among Austrian-Americans, contacted the Austrian authorities in the United States without success. According to them, Mergim was born to foreign residents and was not entitled to Austrian citizenship.

Shortly after Mergim was born, Uncle Faik visited us in Graz on his way to Albania. He was older than Dad and was very kind and loving. I was nine years old and I remember how he described in vivid terms the gifts he would send me upon his return to Detroit. Two stood out in my mind. He was going to send me a real car, albeit a small one, so I could drive to school and around town. He would also send me a small airplane that I could fly if and when I felt like it. I no longer believed in Santa Claus but I did believe Uncle Faik. For a while, those two announced presents enhanced my status among the boys at Grabenstrasse 46. It was clear to everyone that only those in my good graces would be asked to join me in my travels by car or by air, depending on my whim and the prevailing weather. Somehow, those gifts never arrived. Pity!

On his return from Albania, Uncle Faik arrived with his bride, Sadije. When Mom was in Albania the summer before, she had visited Dad's family in Korça. She was received with the honors due to the wife of the head of the family and had dutifully visited his numerous relatives in and near Korça. Visiting so many homes had been a mixed blessing. I recall Mom telling me how fed up she was with being served a spoonful of jelly and a glass of water on each such occasion. One day, her hosts had taken her to a sidewalk cafe in Korça. To her surprise, the waiter had offered, among other things, bananas. Mom welcomed the change and ordered a banana. To her eye-popping surprise, instead of a banana she was served a candy banana and the usual glass of cold water!

Mom had visited Dad's two half sisters, Nigjar and Gjylka. They had received her with much love, as they both adored their oldest brother. There was no question, though, that while Gjylka was a very loving person, Nigjar, the older sister, was difficult, particularly toward her sister-in-law Sadije. Mom was very impressed with Sadije and the kindness she showed Nigjar. One night, she asked Sadije how she could stand Nigjar who was so mean to her; Sadije tried her best but could never do enough to please Nigjar. Sadije just shook her head and replied that Nigjar suffered from a crippling form of tuberculosis of the spine (Pott's disease) and her physical suffering had affected her disposition. Mom made a mental note. According to Albanian tradition, Sadije was almost beyond marrying age as she was still single at the ripe old age of 24. Upon her return to Graz, Mom wrote to Uncle Faik, a bachelor, saying that Sadije was neither the youngest nor the prettiest but she would make someone an excellent wife. When Uncle Faik went to Albania, he made a beeline for Sadije's house and asked her brother Hysni for her hand. He may have already done so in writing before ever seeing the young woman. According to Faik, Mom's word was good enough for him. That's how Faik gave up his freedom and returned to Graz with a brand-new wife.

Unfortunately for me, Sadije's arrival was not all sweetness and light. A few months before Mergim's arrival, and upon the advice and with the financial help of Uncle Faik, we had moved to a larger apartment. It had a large kitchen, a maid's bedroom, a family room, a living room, a dining room, and two bedrooms. It also had a bath with a bathtub and a gas-fired water heater, a rarity in those days. It had a washbowl, a mini-washbowl with a nozzle with a vertical water jet to rinse the mouth after brushing one's teeth, and a bidet. It had a bathroom antechamber that Dad used as a darkroom. This was the best-equipped apartment we had ever rented. Then, one month or two before the baby's birth, Herr Nowak, the landlord, declared bankruptcy. He owed Dad some money and now he paid us back in furniture and copies of two paintings with Albanian motifs by a Serbian artist. One showed several Slavic women being guarded by their Albanian captors, and the other showed two fighting roosters surrounded by an Albanian crowd. I do not know why he had bought those pictures in the first place. They were impressive, though, and we owned them until a few years later when the communists confiscated the pictures as well as most of our household belongings.

Anyhow, because of Mergim's imminent arrival, the impending harsh winter, and Uncle Faik's help, we had a nice place to stay. It was at this apartment that Faik and Sadije found us. Unfortunately for me, Sadije brought her wedding pictures, some magazines with bridal gowns, as well as travel literature of various maritime companies featuring passenger ships that plied the Atlantic. Mom, who always liked to spin romantic tales, got ahold of a 10-year-old girl, known as *"Fette Gerta"* (Fat Gerta) among us boys, and encouraged her to make plans which linked Gerta and me in a romantic (read "sick") union. The girls in our apartment building were delighted with the whole situation, the boys made fun of me, and I hated every moment.

Our apartment was in a five-story building that housed many boys and girls roughly my age. There was Walter Kühnel who, at 13, was the oldest. Günther Zankl was next in line. He had two sisters. There was Günther Kuschl with his sister Lotte. This second Günther, also known as Bobby, was my best friend for as long as we lived there. When I spent a vacation in the Italian Alps in 1972, on my way back to Nuremberg, I visited his parents in Kindberg.

When we moved into this building, it was the first time that I found a number of playmates under one roof. It also happened that I was the least acquainted with the rough-and-tumble world of middle-class pre-teens. I don't recall ever meeting Mr. Kühnel. Mr. Zankl was a paint manufacturer and Mr. Kuschl owned two pharmacies. Their offspring were well brought up but the boys had adopted manners toward the opposite sex that made me the natural victim of girls starved for polite behavior. When I walked into this environment, I was invited to be part of all girlish games that always revolved around "family situations." They liked to play father and mother, prince and princess, or king and queen. Gerta, being then 10 and thus the oldest among the girls, was always the queen, the princess, or the mother. You can imagine who was expected to be the king, the prince, the father, or some other male figure. Furthermore, I was linked by the machinations of a romantic (cruel) mother to this rotund beauty who wanted nothing better than to walk hand in hand with me before the envious eyes of the other girls, making me a helpless target for the cutting comments of my boyfriends.

One day the dam finally broke. I was not going to let Gerta get away with it any longer, particularly because there was nothing I could do to my mother. One day and in front of everyone, I insulted Gerta with that cruelty that only children are capable of.

"I am sick and tired of playing king, prince, father or any of those games with you. Stay away from me. You are so fat that if you were put on the stove you would melt and only a few bacon rinds would be left of you."

Gerta ran away crying while I struggled with my guilty conscience amid the boisterous approval of my boyfriends. Shortly thereafter, Mrs. Zankl called me and chided me gently, pointing out that Gerta's weight problem was due to sickness and that I should not make matters worse. I was glad that Mrs. Zankl went no further. I was even gladder that Dad did not hear about the incident, which saved me from a well-deserved spanking. As far as Gerta was concerned, she was no longer my problem. And that was all I was interested in. For the record, according to Bobby's mother, Gerta married an Englishman after the war and moved to England.

Anyhow, if Mom had not pushed so hard to play "romantic" games with Gerta and me the whole thing would have never happened. Maybe Mom got married too young. I recall her telling me that, even after she was married at 17, when Dad left for the office she played with dolls. Can you imagine? For the first two years of my life, she dressed me like a girl; me, a boy, the heir to the family name if not to the throne. She always wanted a girl. Girls were so gentle, so graceful, and so much nicer to dress up! I was the next best thing to a girl. I don't know how Dad put up with it. All I can say is that it was by sheer luck that Freud never heard of me and that I had not read his books before age two. The consequences could have been disastrous.

Because of the presence of three boys of roughly my age, Grabenstrasse 46 also had an ambience different from my past experiences, particularly at Christmas. According to Austrian tradition, several days before Christmas, a room in our apartment became off limits as far as I was concerned. On Christmas Eve, at the stroke of midnight, a bell rang and I could enter "the room." And there, in all its glory, stood the Christmas tree with slim wax candles burning brightly on its branches. Glittering ornaments, candy wrapped in paper, and apples and oranges hanging from the branches lent it such a festive air. There were always presents for me under the tree. They were not expensive but they were fun presents: a model train, some lead soldiers.

One year, at Grabenstrasse 46, Santa Claus seemed to have considered us four boys as a group. I got a castle (maybe two feet square and two feet high measured at the tip of the tower). My three friends also got castles and toy soldiers. I remember us four boys placing our four castles to form a square while painted lead soldiers stood on the parade ground. What a splendid spectacle that was. That was the Christmas of 1932. Mergim was born a week later. Within 10 years, my three Austrian friends would wear the German uniform. One, Walter, would die in Russia. Günther and Bobby survived the war but Bobby would die of tuberculosis a few years later. In another twenty years or so, I would be hiding in the Albanian mountains, helpless, were it not for kind and brave strangers.

Not long after Mergim's birth, we moved to a much more modest apartment at Schillerstrasse 20. This was around 1934 and the Depression was ravaging Europe as well as the United States. Uncle Faik was still helping us but life had become so expensive, and his help so irregular, that by the end of 1936 Dad decided to move to Fiume, Italy. Fiume was a "porto franco," a port city where goods paid no import duty. Financially, it would be much easier for my parents to make ends meet. As it turned out, the move had a major impact on my future.

CHAPTER FOUR

FIUME 1936

When we arrived in Fiume in November 1936, we first rented a room in a modest hotel. It was near the waterfront and from our terrace we could see the busy piers. Through the open windows we could smell the sea, that typical smell of salt and iodine that I remembered from my first trip to Italy. We could hear the crowded pedestrian traffic, bits and pieces of loud, mostly friendly conversation. People normally spoke louder than in Austria. They stood closer together and touched each other while speaking. They dressed more elegantly and perhaps in somewhat stronger colors whenever they went out. They usually sought refuge indoors during the noon hours and in the early afternoon and stayed up longer, walking along the seashore and the boulevards well beyond what was considered bedtime in Austria. All in all, the climate was warmer, the spring came earlier, and winter was not as severe as in Graz. For me the move represented a major change even before I started school and merged into the flow of Italian life.

Fiume was smaller than Graz. It had flourished under Hungary as it was its only seaport. It had, however, a charm all its own with wide streets, parks, and the Molo Lungo, the long breakwater that offered a rocky side to swimmers toward the Adriatic and mooring facilities on the inside toward the city. Every so often, we could hear the roaring engines of a twin-engine seaplane landing or taking off near the Molo (pier) San Marco. Few businesspeople usually climbed in or out, but it gave a touch of class to Fiume, which had lost importance and prestige once it joined Italy at the end of World War I.

From our hotel room, we could see the masts of larger ships mooring beyond depots and buildings. Sometimes we would walk over and see these ships. Occasionally, there would be an Italian destroyer, a submarine, or even foreign navy vessels, particularly cadet training ships. Life in Fiume was very different from what I was used to in Graz.

On December 1, mere days after our arrival, Dad took me to the Regio Ginnasio-Liceo Dante Alighieri, the Royal Jr. High School named after the Italian writer-poet Dante. Dad had already met with the principal and told me that I would attend the seventh grade, and that after the upcoming Christmas vacation I was expected to be able to follow the lessons in class and take oral and written exams, all in Italian. My classmates had had three years of French. To make things easier for me, I would be permitted to have German as a foreign language. Also, at the end of the seventh grade I and the rest of the class would take oral and written exams in every subject taught in the fifth, sixth, and seventh grades—all, of course, in Italian.

Dad dropped me off at school early and someone, a janitor I assume, took me to an empty classroom. The room was smaller and darker than what I was used to, perhaps because the school building was older than the Lichtenfels Realgymnasium I had attended in Graz. For the moment, the classroom was quiet, almost eerie. Then, all of a sudden, the door flung open and a horde of boys my age stormed into the classroom. They were yelling, laughing, and pushing each other hard. When they saw me, they stopped. Everybody fell silent, even if only for a moment. Then they surrounded me and fired words at me, in Italian of course. I didn't know what they were saying and answered the best I could: I repeated "Albania" again and again, unfortunately with the accent on the wrong syllable. They quickly lost interest in me. They turned toward each other, resumed talking in a loud tone of voice—their normal level of conversation I guess—and forgot all about me.

Sometime later, a boy approached me. "Sprichst Du deutsch?" he asked.

Finally, someone who could speak German! I was no longer alone in my new world. He told me his last name was Kraal and that he would be glad to help me. Moments later, the teacher arrived. She was pushing 40, of medium height in a blue flowery dress and a bit on the plump side. When she spoke to the students, I noticed she lisped. I suspected she was introducing me to the class. Then she turned toward me and spoke to me in halting German. Kraal's German was much better but I could understand her. She told me that she would help me when necessary but that I was expected to make every effort to learn Italian as quickly as I could. I assumed the principal had briefed her in my regard.

Those first few weeks passed quickly. The boys no longer looked at me as if I were a creature from outer space, someone who could not speak Italian, obviously someone not too bright. Before I knew it, the Christmas vacation was upon us.

From day one, my life as a student changed drastically. School lasted usually from 8 a.m. to 1 p.m. six days a week. There was a short break around ten o'clock. At school's end, I would come home for lunch, rest a bit, and then I would start studying the day's lessons using a dictionary and entering the Italian words I did not know into a notebook. In addition, Dad made me study from Book I of the Mertner Method for German-speaking individuals who wanted to learn Italian. Its intent was the same as that of Berlitz; its method much different. Mertner had fought on the Italian front in World War I. As the Austrians and the Italians frequently overran each other's trenches (with heavy casualties on both sides), Mertner found pages of Italian newspapers left behind. He tried to understand what they were saying and found out that pretty soon, with the help of a dictionary, he was able to understand short news items. He attributed his interest in reading these Italian newspapers to the fact that the news items were much more interesting than the traditional texts used to teach a foreign language. "My aunt's pen is black," or, "My brother's dog is under the table," or similar gems were boring. The fact that an airplane had been shot down over Mount Grappa or a hailstorm had destroyed the crops in Ferrara was current and much more interesting.

For the first few weeks in our new apartment, by sheer willpower, I kept up with the daily school lessons and my Mertner assignments. A lesser spirit might have groaned. I knew better than to groan with Dad around. Aside from hours spent in the classroom Monday through Saturday, I was cooped up all day and had few contacts with the outside world. The Christmas vacation was looming large on the horizon and I expected the daily rhythm to change significantly. How significantly, I was about to find out.

Once the vacation started, reveille—minus the bugle—was at 0700 hours. Wash-up and breakfast were over by 0800. Dad and I would sit down and tackle our daily workload consisting of a quiz covering words I had studied so far (I was learning about 100 new words a day). At this pace, my vocabulary was growing rapidly. It came from my daily school lessons and from lessons covered by my classmates in the fifth, sixth, and seventh grade. Latin and math covered about the same ground I had studied in Austria, except that I had to learn words and expressions in Italian. German as a foreign language was, of course, no problem. I attended no German lessons and had no reason to study German grammar.

By 10 a.m. we made a break and I had 15 minutes to entertain myself. I usually played ping-pong against the wall. Then the lesson restarted until noon when Mom served lunch. By 1300 hours, Dad and I resumed our work until about mid-afternoon, at which point we went for a walk and covered orally, in Italian of course, the lessons of the day and whatever lesson Dad chose as the topic for that afternoon. Back home, we resumed the formal lesson until dinnertime. By eight o'clock, we were back at work. Bedtime was around 9:30 and now I had time to study the 100 new words or so I had encountered that day.

This went on for a few days until Mom protested very vigorously with Dad. "If you have decided to kill the boy, can't you find a more merciful way?" or words to that effect.

Dad stared at her for a moment or two and then said, in a tone of voice that admitted no contradictions, "Pack a suitcase with Mergim's and your things, enough for two weeks. Tomorrow you leave for Nervi where you and Mergim will spend the rest of the vacation with Mustafa Kruja (Mergim's godfather). I will call him tomorrow to let him know that you are coming." That was that.

The next day Mom and my brother, who was all of four years old, left for Nervi and Dad and I went back to our routine. The rhythm was intense but I could see the progress I was making and that was a great boost for me. A few days later, we got a letter from Mustafa saying that he was glad that Dad was studying with me. He also stated that he thought that the best we could hope for was that I would flunk Italian and Latin in June and would pass the make-up exams in September. He wished us good work and told us not to worry about Mom and Mergim. My sense was that worrying about the two of them was the farthest thing from Dad's mind—or from mine, for that matter.

Mom and Mergim returned at the end of the Christmas vacation and I faced my first day back in school. I had been told that on the first day of school I would be required to take an oral exam in Italian. It turned out that the teacher had chosen the Austrian siege of Milan as the subject for my first exam. I described how the Austrian troops under the command of General Radetzky had reached Milan but I stopped because I did not know how to say "surrounded" in Italian. I formed a circle with my fingers and said "*umzingelten*" in German. The teacher said "*circondarono*" and I went on with my narrative that the Austrians had surrounded and conquered Milan. My first exam went quite well and the teacher seemed satisfied.

I was pleased with my performance but when I told Dad about it, I also added one question that had bothered me all day. The way the Italian history book described the Austrian campaign depicted Radetzky as a brutal and hated conqueror who had persecuted the Italian nationalists. In Austria, our textbook had spoken of Radetzky as the brilliant general and the gallant fighter who had entered Milan at the head of his brave troops. Which description was true? I was confused. He replied that both were true. For the Italians, he was an invader, for the Austrians he was the brilliant conqueror. This was my first inkling that history was not an exact, "hard" science. The facts were the same, but the interpretation varied.

For me the worst was over. I studied more intensely than ever before but I could also see the rewards. My Italian was improving daily and so was my performance in school. More important, I was starting to communicate with my schoolmates and was making friends. One day, perchance, I stepped out on our kitchen balcony at home. A voice yelled from above.

"Genc, what are you doing on that balcony?"

I looked up and there was Lucio Mandarà, a classmate of mine, on a balcony one floor above ours in the apartment house next to ours.

"This is where I live," I replied. "What about you?"

"I have been living here for years," he answered laughing.

"Now what we have to do is to either agree on a time when we meet on the balcony or find a way of calling each other to come to the balcony."

"I know how to call you," I replied. "I will make this sound," and I made a sound like a whistle. It started out like a "prrrrrrrrr..." but at a very high pitch. Lucio tried it and could also make that ear-piercing sound. Now we had a way to call each other out onto the balcony, and since the neighbors did not protest it served us well for several years.

While we lived in Graz, Dad had asked me to make that sound in front of Prof. Schmerz, a distinguished surgeon and friend of his. Prof. Schmerz had listened carefully, had touched my Adam's apple while I made that sound and had told us that the sound resembled that made by howling monkeys and that I would no longer be able to make it once my voice changed. Actually, Lucio and I called each other in that manner well beyond puberty.

In World War I, Prof. Schmerz happened to be walking past the Imperial Palace in Vienna early in the morning. Several drunken young officers were coming out of the Palace and started to feed apples to their horses. Prof. Schmerz protested that horses at the Imperial palace in Vienna were fed apples while he could not get fresh fruit for the wounded at the Military Hospital. As a result, he was sent to a concentration camp. This was the first time I had heard about concentration camps in World War I. Soon after the German occupation of Austria in 1938, Prof. Schmerz, who was Jewish, sent Dad a postcard to Fiume where he told him that students had been assigned to watch him in surgery lest he intentionally hurt his Aryan patients. In his postcard he added that he was ashamed to be German and that, by the time we received the postcard, he would no longer be among the living. He had signed the postcard *"Dolor"* ("dolor" in Latin means pain, the same as "schmerz" in German). Shortly thereafter we heard from a friend that Prof. Schmerz had committed suicide.

Before I knew it, winter was over and we were well into spring. I must admit that the spring of 1937 worried me, because the exams covering the last three years were approaching rapidly. Taking exams was never my idea of fun and the upcoming exams, by their sheer scope, loomed larger than anything I had experienced up to that point. June was finally upon us. We had both oral and written exams in each subject and here I made another discovery. Each day I woke up with a knot in my stomach and each day I felt better as soon as I tackled and passed the exam of the day. This feeling of well-being, however, did not last. Obviously, that day's exams had not been as bad as I had imagined but those still staring me in the face—those were the truly tough ones!

This went on until I finished all my exams except for the German language exam. I did not know what to expect. I had found out where the exam would take place. I had understood from my snickering classmates that our parallel class was a girls' class and they had studied German as a foreign language. We were all beyond the age that disliked girls but to be the only boy in an all-girl class could be tough. When I entered the classroom, everyone was already seated. Without looking left or right, I saw a sea of girls, all staring at me. I did notice a few boys, however, and that bothered me because I felt they were trespassing as I was supposed to be the only boy at this exam. Well, these feelings disappeared as soon as Professor Spiegel handed out the exam. It was a translation from Italian into German. The entire text was less than half a page long and straightforward. We got the text at 9:00 a.m. and I was done by 9:10, a scant ten minutes later. I double-checked my translation and found no errors. I stood up and handed my paper in. The professor asked me whether I had double-checked my work and I nodded. When I had entered the classroom, I had felt all these eyes following me, probably filled with curiosity. Once again, I felt all eyes on me as I was leaving, this time probably with wonderment or envy.

Now I had all my exams behind me. A few days later and full of dread, I walked to school where all final grades were posted along the entrance stairwell. I could not believe my eyes. I had passed every exam, including Italian, for grades five, six, and seven, and I could not wait to tell my parents. I ran back all the way to our apartment building, rushed up the stairs, and gave them the good news. Mom hugged me. Dad did not say much but I did overhear him say to Mom that when Mustafa Kruja had predicted that I would flunk Italian and Latin he had shown that he did not know the Kortsha boys.

I remember I did not touch a schoolbook all summer long but by now, I was reading Italian fluently and read various books for fun, both in Italian and in German. I remember reading the autobiography of the Red Baron and *The Three Musketeers* in German, and some of Jules Verne's books in Italian. In retrospect, I remember in much more detail the difficulties of the school year than the carefree summer months that followed.

Finally, it was fall. I was leaving my classmates who continued to study French and was switching over to the parallel class that would study German. I had been eagerly looking forward to going to school with girls even though it meant letting go of some of my boyfriends. That first day in school was something else. I found out where the boys had come from, the ones that had taken the German exam the preceding spring. They came from little towns near Fiume where they had German as a foreign language. They came from Laurana, Abbazia, Mattuglie, and other such places, well known for their attractive location along the seashore or a bit further inland. They were boisterous teenage boys, easy to make friends with. In fact, one of them, Giancarlo Tiribilli, would be one of my best friends until our graduation from high school. Giancarlo was about 6 feet tall, with dark, wavy hair. He had broad shoulders but was not the athletic type. At a moment's notice, he could turn on his Florentine dialect and sound very affected. Normally, he spoke in Italian rather than in the dialect of Fiume. After the war, he studied law and became a successful prosecutor but, unfortunately, died young.

Then there was Piero Nutrizio. Also dark with wavy hair, about 5 feet 10 inches, with large shoulders and a very slim waist. He was a boxer and good at shotput. When we met many years later, in 1990 in Padua, his left leg was shorter by about 10 inches. He never told me, and I did not ask him, what had happened to his leg. He walked with difficulty, and told me that he had been on the side of the Yugoslav partisans during the war after witnessing the crimes of the Italian forces against the Slavic populations of the area. It is funny but, even though I had fought against the communists, we felt a bond between us, the bond of those willing to sacrifice for something they believed in.

There was also Edi Buda, about my height with wavy dark hair (many had wavy dark hair) and not much of a student. It was not for lack of ability. Simply put, Edi had other priorities such as billiards and, a couple of years later, girls. When we met after so many years, he told me he had a good business manufacturing light fixtures. Unfortunately, a number of his customers never paid their bills, and eventually he was pushed into bankruptcy.

Gianni Pisano was a modest piano player, short, with dark straight hair held in place with gobs of brilliantine, a gooey hair cream. Eventually, he would become a physician. He and I shared our birthday. In class, we were seven boys. Most of them had little impact on my life and I will skip their names and other details.

Then, of course, there were the girls. There were 14 girls in our class. Many of them were better students than the boys. There was Gemma Murrighili, the daughter of a railroad worker. She was petite and pretty, an excellent student particularly in Italian and the soft sciences. I will mention her again as we would run around with the same crowd in high school. There was Jole Pescatori, the daughter of a career army officer, very friendly and helpful. There was Clementina Niccolì, also known as Nucci. She was the prettiest girl in our class and she knew it. I had noticed her even before we became classmates. One day, Lucio and I on our bikes made it a point to circle the apartment building where *"La bella Nucci"* lived. For reasons I no longer remember I had to brake hard, flew over the handlebar and skinned the palms of my hands. I still have a small scar at the base of my right thumb as a reminder of that day. When I saw her years later, she told me she had taught high school and had never married. Then there was Valnea Curatolo. She was quite tall, with soft brown hair and a light complexion. She was an excellent student and well liked in class. I liked her at first sight. She and Rosaria DeGaetano sat in the first row, Giancarlo Tiribilli and I right behind them. I held back from talking to Valnea as I was afraid she might discover that I liked her. That would have been a disaster, right? You will hear more about her from time to time.

The school year went by in a hurry. I was doing well in class, and I made new friends without cutting off the old ones. I got involved in sports, particularly fencing. Fiume had an excellent fencing coach by the name of Callegari. He was nationally known but so was his dislike for the fascists. Hence, he was transferred to Fiume, a small port near the Yugoslav border, little more than a spot on the map.

Fencing as a sport had evolved over the millennia. Presently, three types of weapons were used at sporting events. There was the saber, sometimes seen in film fencing scenes, which allowed the fencer to slash or stab the opponent from the head down to the waistline. Next was the foil, a weapon limited to stabbing the opponent in the chest. Finally, there was the epée, a weapon meant to stab the enemy from head to toe.

I took my training seriously. For six months, we did nothing but exercises, going through fencing positions without holding a weapon in our hands. Mr. Callegari wanted to develop our leg and arm muscles and have us attain the necessary coordination for attacking and pulling back safely. In addition, I suspect he also wanted to get rid of those who were not serious about fencing and who eventually did drop out. The day came when we, the survivors, saw daylight. Mr. Callegari told us to acquire padded fencing attire and a foil. The attire consisted of a white top with buttons along the side of the neck and chest. It had a standing collar, a padded right arm and padding from below the neck all the way down to the groin. A flap went from the front, below the crotch, and to the back where it was buttoned in place. We also bought white knee pants, white socks, and flat white leather shoes.

Our fencing master collected money for individual fencing masks and foils. He had us purchase foils even though our first training would involve sabers, of which there were plenty in the gym. Eventually, we would train with epées, foils, and sabers. The blades of all three weapons were about 3 feet long. Foils and sabers weighed about 17.5 oz. while the epée was heaviest at 27.16 oz.

Now the real fun began. We dressed up, with our weapon in hand, and learned to advance and move backward on a runner of rubbery material about 3 feet wide. From a distance, we probably looked like ducks in a row. Soon we were paired off and, eventually, held regular fencing match-es. I did well and enjoyed it very much. Part of the fun was that my friend Lucio also stuck it out and so we went together to fencing lessons. The fact that I was the better fencer did not seem to bother him.

During these years, home was in Via Parini 10, next door to Lucio. I lived four houses away from the apartment building where Milena lived, and about 150 yards from Valnea's home and the bakery her mother owned. Furthermore, there were several girls in our class that lived in our general neighborhood that took Via Parini to walk to school. Thus, I often walked with one or the other and that made the walk less boring.

During the eighth grade, Fatos, Mustafa Kruja's second-oldest son, came to live with us. He had attended a boarding school in Turin and had not done well. Hence, Mustafa sent him to stay with us and benefit from Dad's tutoring. Fatos was the kindest person one could imagine. In school, he got along with everybody. At home, he was willing to work hard and Dad was certainly not an easy taskmaster. Fatos began to do better in school. He had no problem passing eighth and ninth grades, even though at the end of the ninth grade we had to pass exams covering all subject matters of the last two years. He went to Zara at the end of the ninth grade and graduated from high school in 1942.

Unfortunately, he spent 45 years under communist rule in Albania, most of them in concentration camps. Years later in Tirana, Margaret and I met him and his wife, a courageous and strong person he had married while in one of the camps. They had a daughter who had gotten married, had left

Albania, and now lived with her husband and two children in Germany. Margaret and I will never forget the complete lunch Fatos' wife Klora put together for us with the aid of a small electric hotplate in their one-room apartment. They both belonged to that small group of people who had emerged from years of suffering unscathed by hatred. God love them!

During my summer vacation of 1938, Dad sent Mom and me to Albania for a month or so. I was curious about the country and its people. I spoke fluent, accent-free Albanian, knew quite a bit about the country as seen through the eyes of my parents and particularly Dad. I imagined Albania to be mountainous, the people brave and generous. I pictured a rotten government as it was headed by King Zogu, who had tried to kill Dad more than once. On the day of our departure, Dad brought us to a gleaming white Italian passenger ship docked at one of the piers in Fiume. I was eager to visit Albania, my native country. In Austria and Italy, I was always the foreigner. Now, I would belong, even if for only a few weeks.

The food aboard ship was excellent and sleeping accommodations adequate. We stopped in Zara for a few hours. At our next stop, our ship dropped anchor in deep waters a few miles offshore from Split. We were told we could take a dip in the Adriatic. It was a wonderful, sunny day and I had never seen waters of such a deep blue, ink-like color. I donned my swimming trunks and jumped into the water. It was pleasantly cool. I swam for a little while and then climbed aboard ship, back to the sunny deck and the wonderful food. Later, I found out that sharks were occasionally sighted in these waters.

Our last stop was Dubrovnik and after that: Durrës, Albania. The port of Durrës lay before our eyes; crowded, noisy, and full of people moving in all directions. There were people with handcarts, small carts drawn by donkeys, horse-drawn carriages, and cars. I spotted some American passenger cars. Compared to their Italian counterparts, they looked massive and radiated strength. *If we could only ride in one of those*, I said to myself. Mom pointed out a gentleman at the end of the gangplank.

"That's Qazim Ramadani, your godfather's younger brother. He has come to pick us up."

Mom was right. Qazim had spotted us at about the same time. He waved and we waved back. It felt good to know we were not alone.

We descended the gangplank with our luggage, hugged Qazim, and off we went toward one of those magnificent American cars I had admired from the deck just a few minutes ago. The trunk of the car was so large that our luggage practically got lost in it. The best part was still to come. When I climbed into the passenger compartment, I noticed a very pleasant smell, the smell of a new car. The driver started the engine. All I heard was this subdued rumbling, something akin to being inside a Bengal Tiger but without the fear. When the car moved, it seemed to defy potholes. When it came to a stop, it could not have been gentler, barely swaying, like a ship gently rocking with the waves. I fell in love with that vehicle. I wished I could drive an American car when I grew up!

We had not gotten very far when the driver stopped the car. Qazim invited us to enjoy some pastries at the Café Bella Venezia. I really did not feel like leaving the car but it was not up to me. When it was my turn, I ordered some fine-looking pastry and lemonade. When I sank my teeth into the pastry, I wished I could have spit it out but I knew better than that. As I struggled to swallow this first mouthful, I noticed Mom had been watching me.

"This is very good pastry," she said to me, looking deeply into my eyes, "once you get used to the taste of the butter and the eggs."

"Why do they taste different?" I asked.

"Each country makes butter in slightly different ways. And the taste of eggs depends on what they feed the chickens."

"I noticed no difference when we moved from Austria to Italy," I replied, unwilling to accept Mom's explanation.

"You'll see, everything will be all right once we have been here for a few weeks," Mom continued with a smile.

I must admit that having to eat that kind of food did not appeal to me at all. I did not care what the farmers fed their chickens! Well, all was not lost. There was still that beautiful American car awaiting us outside the café.

Finally, we left the pastry shop and were on our way. We had traveled about an hour or so and I began to feel sick to my stomach. It had to be the pastry I had forced down my throat at the Café Bella Venezia. The name means "beautiful Venice" and I had nothing but the best memories of the real Venice, of Venetian ice cream and Italian soft drinks. There was no comparison with what I had to ingest in Durrës at the Café Bella Venezia! Obviously, one could not judge a book by its cover, or a pastry shop by its name.

Well, I felt worse and worse. Soon I asked to be let out of the car. The driver stopped and I barely got out before I puked into the ditch along the roadside, filling it to the rim, or so at least it seemed to me.

"He got carsick," said Qazim. I appreciated the diagnosis but I resented the fact that he had said so smiling, and without a word of commiseration for the way I felt. I was beginning to hate Albania.

Eventually, we made it to Shkodra. The car stopped in front of a small two-story building. Mom pointed out that it was my birthplace. Her words were lost on me as I worried about what was coming. I did not have to wait long. We climbed the rickety stairs and here were my aunt Shqipe and my grandmother. They hugged and kissed me, and hugged and kissed me until I freed myself to come up for air.

"Boys don't like to be kissed," they said, as they smiled at each other. Their eyes, on the other hand, said very clearly that they were not going to resist the urge just because I did not care for it. The fact that I was 14 years old, a head or so taller than my aunt (Grandma was minuscule) and strong enough to break their backs did not seem to faze them.

They showed me to my room. It was very small with a big bed covered with a patterned wool blanket.

"Lie down," they said to me. "The trip must have tired you out. Rest a little and you will feel better."

I lay down and they covered me with the blanket. I was most uncomfortable. The blanket was heavy, hot, and scratchy. I never could stand wool next to my skin! I wanted to get up, wash my face after all that kissing, and find a cool corner somewhere. I wanted neither drink nor food. I didn't want to see Mom either if my aunt or Grandma accompanied her. All I wanted to do was sulk in silence and dream of the day when we would go back to Italy. Unfortunately, we had just arrived but I could dream, couldn't I? Eventually, I got up, washed my face and appeared in the tiny living room.

"Are you feeling any better?" my Grandma asked.

"Yes," I replied, "much better." In truth, I felt a little better than just before puking. Well, they had waited for me and now we ate. They had prepared stuffed peppers and tomatoes with a rather spicy sauce. It tasted almost as good as when Mom prepared such dishes in Fiume. I attributed this to the spicy sauce that probably killed any peculiar taste the food might have had otherwise.

That evening Mom and I had a rather long and meaningful conversation.

She explained to me that my Grandma and aunt were doing the best they could. They were poor because my grandfather, a distinguished and much-beloved physician, had died poor. He had treated needy patients for free and had often paid for the prescriptions they could not have afforded otherwise. We were just going to stay here a few weeks and then it would be over for us while they would continue the same life they had endured since Grandfather's death in 1932. I was to pull myself together. I was her older son and she was very proud of me. She would always be available to listen to me in private—out of earshot of our relatives. I understood and promised to do the best I could to overlook the difficulties and problems that would arise during our visit. I also said that I would do the best I could to be polite but that I would not lie. Mom nodded in agreement.

Well, things did not get any better as time went by. On the first floor was a little grocery store. A wood floor with plenty of cracks between the boards separated our bedroom upstairs from the grocery store. Fruit flies, lots of little fruit flies, visited my bedroom, particularly at night. Mom slept on the bed and I on a mattress on the floor. I covered myself only with a sheet and often covered my head to keep fruit flies away from my face. Under the sheet it got hot, of course, but that was better than having the little buggers crawling into my nose and ears.

I managed somehow as long as I did not have to be with my aunt. I liked Grandma. She was loving and kind and asked questions and then listened to my answers. My aunt was a pain. She had stacks and stacks of movie magazines in her room. She read them—no, she devoured them—when she was alone. Then she would seek me out, throw her arms around me, and try to wrestle me to the ground. Well, I had promised Mom I would be good but I never promised I would be that good. When attacked, I busted my aunt's embrace and then twisted her wrists, her hand, her arm—anything I could get ahold of without getting too personal—until she cried out in pain. I was old enough to know what was going through her mind but I was not going to be a part of it, not even for play.

Qazim would drop in quite often and together we would visit friends of the family. Many had known Dad from way back when he was the principal of the local high school and they loved and respected him. I answered their questions about Dad truthfully and as well as I could. One question came up frequently that bothered me a lot.

"How do you like Albania?"

Everyone got the same answer. "I like it a lot but I don't think I would want to come again without Dad." My answer was truthful, at least the second part. That was the most Mom could expect of me. I knew that Dad would not come back as long as King Zogu ruled the country. As far as I knew, Zogu was going to be in charge for years to come. From where I stood, that was not so bad, now was it?

One day, Qazim announced that he and I were going to Ulqin, a seaport in Yugoslavia, just a few miles from Shkodra. There I could go swimming and enjoy myself. To me any change in the status quo was a change for the better. A few days later, he pulled up in a ritzy American car and off we went. What he had not told me was that a few of his friends would join us on this trip. Not that I minded his friends or grown-ups in general but for weeks—for years it seemed to me—I had not been with youngsters my age and grown-ups were interested in things I was not. That turned out to be the fly in the ointment on this trip.

We arrived in Ulqin, got rid of what little luggage we had in hotel rooms we had reserved, and went to a café on the beach. One of Qazim's friends looked at me and then said to Qazim in broken Italian, "What are we going to do with him when we go out to have fun?"

That's when I spoke up, also in Italian. "Whatever you want to keep from me, don't do it in Italian." That took care of that. I did not want to waste my time speculating on the kind of fun they were seeking; all I can say is that Qazim did things in a way that never caused me embarrassment or trouble.

Eventually the day came when we said goodbye to Grandma and my aunt. I endured their hugs and kisses. After all, an American car was standing outside with the engine running, ready to take me away from Shkodra. It was not going to take me directly to Durrës but to Kruja, which was quite close to Durrës, closer than Shkodra. It was a move in the right direction.

Mom and I were going to Kruja to attend the wedding of Mustafa Kruja's sister. Not that I was particularly interested in weddings, Albanian or otherwise, but I was getting out of Shkodra. Besides, I had nothing to say in this regard.

We made it to Kruja and this time without my getting carsick. Kruja was atop some foothills with higher mountains right behind it. The villa where we stayed overlooked the plains to the very shores of the Adriatic Sea. Quite a few guests had arrived before us. They were a boisterous group, mostly men. The women disappeared in the kitchen or blended in with the landscape. Children, and there were some, were even less important than the women. This pecking order became obvious at mealtime. The men started out drinking and eating appetizers from morning until evening. I must say, the appetizers were quite substantial: roast lamb, cheese, hard-boiled eggs, scallions, fried liver, kidneys, and lots of *kukurec*. This last item was new to me. It consisted of braided small intestine (scrupulously cleaned, of course) holding in place spicy morsels of liver, heart, kidneys, and the like. It was cooked on a skewer and looked succulent while fresh. With time, it tended to dry out. The men had a good time.

We children got nothing between a skimpy breakfast and dinner around midnight. This was not my idea of fun. I complained to Mom but she told me that there was nothing she could do because other mothers would have protested if I had been treated differently from their children. By the time midnight came around, the food was cold, the fat on the lamb's meat had congealed, and I for one barely ate lamb when it was at its best. Furthermore, what food survived until midnight came in a pot that was planted in the middle of the table. Famished women and children thrust their hands into the pot, trying to grab whatever they could. I refused to sink so low as to reach into the pot to compete for chunks of congealed lamb.

After a couple of days of sulking, I asked Mom to do something if she did not want to see me waste away. Mom promised that at midnight I would get my favorite: *Palatschinken*, an Austrian version of crepe Suzette. Well, midnight came and I sat ready with fork and knife in my hands. An old woman was sitting next to me. Mom pushed a plate of *Palatschinken* toward me.

"What is that you are about to eat?" the old hag asked.

"It's something they prepare in Austria for sick people," I replied.

"Let me try it." As she said so, she reached and ripped off a chunk of *Palatschinken* from my plate. The orange-brown polish on her fingernails was half gone near the tips and her fingers looked crooked and disgusting. Besides, she had put her hand on my food and that was enough to get me mad. While pensively chewing, she smiled, smacked her lips, and voiced her approval of this Austrian food for those under the weather. I was furious. I pushed my plate in front of her, told her she could have it, and stormed out of the kitchen. I did not care what anybody thought of my behavior, including Mom.

Well, all good things come to an end—and, thank God, so do the other kind. The next day the guests started leaving. Qazim Ramadani picked us up and Mom and I left that afternoon for Durrës. That same evening we would be homebound for Fiume. The ride to Durrës took maybe an hour and before I knew it, we were in the home of Hysen Mushqeta, an old friend of Dad's.

Hysen Mushqeta was prosperous but also very generous. According to Albanian tradition, a girl needed an ample dowry before she could become a bride. Most girls, by the time they became teenagers, would start sewing and embroidering, embroidering and sewing, lest they be found wanting when a good "catch" appeared on the horizon. Each year, Hysen Mushqeta provided complete dowries for two girls from poor families. During his conversation with me, he stressed that Albanian farmers needed to learn modern agricultural techniques.

He looked me in the eyes and said, "If you earn a degree in agronomy, I will buy adequate land for you—if you are willing to settle in a village and teach our farmers how to till the soil and care for their animals properly. Remember to tell your Dad about our conversation."

Of course, I did. Dad agreed with pleasure and for some years, I thought I would study agronomy when the time came. Events followed their own path, however, and the three of us, Hysen Mushqeta, Dad, and I, became pawns of destiny. Hysen Mushqeta was shot and mortally wounded by the communists before they came into power, Dad died after 15 years in jail, and I—well, you will find out what happened to me as you continue reading.

Hysen Mushqeta and his family lived in a two-story house built to European standards. The rooms were large and well furnished. The bathrooms had modern fixtures and were spotless. On top of the house was a beautiful terrace from where it seemed you could touch the ships in port. Ours had not arrived yet but I made it a point to say that I wanted to be on the terrace shortly before 10 p.m. so I could witness the arrival of the ship.

The rest of the day went by in a hurry. We enjoyed the food and the warm hospitality of Hysen Mushqeta and his family. A cool evening followed a hot day and the sea breeze was most pleasant. That evening Hysen Mushqeta's teenage niece and I climbed the steps to the terrace. It was a marvelous night. The stars were bright, the night air cool, and the girl quite pretty. Had it not been for the incoming ship that was going to take me out of Albania, I might have written a short poem and dedicated it to the young lady next to me. Under the circumstances, all I could think of was the white ship that would take me back to Fiume.

The clock struck 10 p.m.; it was time to say goodbye. We took leave from our hosts and Qazim Ramadani, our faithful friend, took us to the port of Durrës. The ship that would take us back to Fiume was there, brightly lit and in full splendor. I could hardly wait to climb aboard. Qazim showed our passports to the guard at the entrance to the port. The guard looked at our passports and disappeared. He returned with an officer who informed us that our passports were no longer valid as they were within six months of their expiration date. I panicked as I realized that our return trip was in jeopardy. Qazim made a couple of phone calls trying to find the mayor at 10 p.m. He saw that I was all shook up.

"Don't worry, one way or another I will get you aboard this ship," he told me.

He called City Hall and was told that the mayor was out of town. He insisted that he needed to speak with whoever was second in command and was given the phone number of the vice-mayor who could be reached at his villa on the seashore. Qazim reached the vice-mayor and talked to him for a while. To me all this was wasted effort. The validity of passports was regulated by law and ours were no longer valid. Qazim asked the officer to take the phone. The officer took the phone and nodded a couple of times. When he put the phone down, he turned toward the guard and ordered him to let us board the ship.

I was speechless. True, Qazim was the nephew of the minister of the interior, who was a very powerful man. Our passports, however, were no longer valid. How could anyone overrule the law? As the years went by, I learned much more about laws and the authority of people in power. Anyhow, we got aboard that beautiful white ship that very evening and, by midnight, we were underway, northbound for Fiume.

The return trip was uneventful. The weather was splendid, the food excellent, but I could not wait to see Dad. Finally, we pulled alongside the pier in Fiume. There was Dad, reliable, strong, and solid as a rock. It was great to hug him again. Later I wondered whether perhaps the fact that he was my guarantee that I would not go back to Albania added to the warmth of that first embrace.

Dad, of course, wanted to know every detail of our trip to Albania. In describing one of our visits to a friend's home, my narrative went along these lines:

"There we stood before the large locked gate of our friend's house. We used a heavy knocker but were not sure they would hear us inside the house, as it was quite a distance from the gate. Then, before we knew it, the large gate swung open, silently, without anyone in sight. I did not know what to think. How did the heavy gate open all by itself? Now what? Were we supposed to approach the house? Was anyone home or was this gate mechanism somehow automated? What would happen if we proceeded inside the courtyard?

"By this time, Mom grabbed me by the arm and together we ventured toward the house. Moments later a lady appeared atop the stairs bidding us welcome. At this point I solved the riddle of the magic gate. There was a long rope that ran from inside the house to the handle that opened and closed the gate. When we knocked, someone inside had pulled the rope and the gate had swung open. Ingenious, wasn't it?"

Well, Dad was delighted with my story. "I want you to put some of your adventures in writing, will you? You have such a nice way of describing things that I know I will enjoy reading about them as if I had been on this trip with you."

"Dad, I really would rather tell you about such things than put them on paper."

Dad looked displeased. Lines formed around his mouth and I could see his eyes harden. "Genc, I expect you to write about the trip in detail. I know you can do it. And now let's go swimming."

Dad knew I liked to swim but I also knew that if I was going to object to putting my adventures in writing, I'd better do it now.

"Dad, I really don't want to write about the trip to Albania."

"Listen, son, the rest of the family and I are going swimming. You stay home and start writing."

My parents and Mergim left for the seashore and I stayed home. Dad could leave me behind but my mind was made up. I was not going to write about that darned trip to Albania. I sat at my desk and started looking out the window. Ever so slowly, the sun disappeared behind some dark clouds. It did not take long and the first raindrops, huge drops, started pounding against our windows. I cannot say I was sorry. In fact, it seemed to me that

Mother Nature was taking sides, and this time she was on my side. I felt vindicated and happy.

Within the hour the rest of the family returned, wet as poodles. I knew better than to gloat. I was a little scared, however, because I did not know how Dad would react to my writer's strike. He came into the room, glanced at my desk, saw that I had not written a single line, and moved away without saying a word to me either then or later. Somehow, the threatened storm had blown over. Not the one outside the house. That was coming down with rare fury. The storm that had been brewing between Dad and me was over. What a relief!

What was left of summer went by in a hurry and, before I knew it, I started school.

The ninth grade for me was more of the same. I did well in school, had a good time with my classmates, did well in sports, and enjoyed myself very much, taking everything for granted.

However, in the spring of 1939, unbeknownst to me, dark clouds had been gathering on the horizon. Back in 1924, the Yugoslavs had helped Ahmet Zogu assume power in Tirana after taking the presidency away from Bishop Noli. Upon taking power, Ahmet Zogu had declared himself president and, in 1928, king of Albania. Over the years, he had come to view Italy as the least dangerous of Albania's neighbors and had begun to depend heavily on Italian economic and organizational support. Albania had become deeply indebted but Italy seemed satisfied with the way things were going. In fact, in April 1938, Count Galeazzo Ciano, Italy's foreign secretary and also Mussolini's son-in-law, was King Zogu's best man when the king married the Hungarian Countess Geraldina Apponyi. She was a very pretty young woman who had been working as a librarian in Budapest. She belonged to the Hungarian aristocracy, even though her family had fallen on hard times. Rumor had it that King Zogu had sought to marry a princess from a reigning house in Europe but had been rebuffed.

King Zogu may have wanted to gain greater acceptance for himself and for Albania, but he eventually decided to marry a young Hungarian noblewoman. Unfortunately for the royal couple and the nation, less than a year later, on April 7, 1939, Italian troops invaded Albania. During those days, Dad stayed glued to the radio, hoping that at least France, England, and the United States would raise their voices and perhaps take some diplomatic action on behalf of Italy's most recent victim. Actually, the Soviet Union was the only country that protested. Neither the crowned heads of Europe nor any government throughout the world uttered one word of condemnation against the aggression as Albania disappeared from the ranks of independent nations. When Italy attacked and conquered Ethiopia in 1935 and 1936, respectively, the League of Nations imposed sanctions on the aggressor. But this time nobody said or did anything on behalf of Albania, the hapless victim. Instead, the major countries declared in so many words that Italy's takeover of Albania did not alter the balance of power in the Mediterranean and little Albania was left to her own devices.

Closer to home, despite the fact that Dad and King Zogu had been bitter enemies throughout their political lives, on April 6 Dad crossed the bridge from Fiume to Sušak, Yugoslavia, and sent King Zogu a telegram asking him to admit political refugees into Albania so they could fight side by side against the Italian invader. Zogu did not reply. His wife had given birth to a son just a few days before. On April 7, King Zogu gathered some of his faithful and traveled to the Greek border. There he sent most of them home and continued with a small group into Greece. Subsequently, he proceeded to the Middle East and later to Egypt.

Meanwhile in Albania, Italian troops were pouring ashore en masse—division after division, Alpini and Bersaglieri, fascist militia units and armored troops—while the Italian navy, if not the first then certainly the second most powerful fleet in the Mediterranean, protected the troops and their supply lines. The Italian air force had absolute dominance over the Albanian skies and covered the entire country with propaganda leaflets, delivering at the same time the unwritten message that bombs could take the place of the leaflets at the will and whim of the occupying forces.

One small unit, under the command of Major Abaz Kupi, one of the king's most trusted officers, had opened fire on the Italian troops as they landed in Durrës. On the Albanian side, Mujo Ulqinaku lost his life. The Italians did not say if there were any casualties on their part.

Originally, Italy had offered Mustafa Kruja and his group financial support and weapons to remove King Zogu from power with the understanding that Albanians would organize and carry out the uprising. At the last minute, Italy notified the conspirators that Italy had decided to take direct action against Tirana. At this point, Albania's tragedy proceeded as scripted in Rome. Italy was going to declare Victor Emanuel king of Italy and emperor of Albania and Ethiopia.

Mustafa Kruja had left Italy for Grenoble some time before in protest over the fact that the Italian authorities had been reading his mail. After the invasion, he and several Albanian political opponents of King Zogu sent a telegram to Rome requesting that the Albanian crown be given to a prince of the House of Savoy. The international situation was tense and the signs of an imminent conflict were on the horizon. Their thinking was that if Italy entered World War II and lost the war, an Italian prince would be more interested in saving his throne and Albania's future than in remaining faithful to his links with a defeated Italy. Mustafa Kruja and the other signatories of the telegram had a historical precedent in mind. Napoleon had rewarded some of his marshals, such as Bernadotte and Murat, by appointing them kings of Sweden and of Naples, respectively. As the Napoleonic wars progressed, both kings had disassociated themselves from Napoleon even before his final defeat at Waterloo.

At first, Mustafa Kruja's telegram remained unanswered. Dad refused to sign what became known as the Grenoble telegram. Eventually, the Italian government replied that by giving the crown of Skanderbeg to the king of Italy, his majesty was bestowing an even greater honor on the Albanian nation than if the crown had gone to a prince of the House of Savoy. A change of sorts did come about, though. For reasons I don't know, the Italians did change their mind about the king's title. On April 12, Victor Emmanuel assumed the titles of king of Italy and of Albania, and emperor of Ethiopia. Years later, the communists branded the Grenoble telegram another example of treason against the fatherland.

While our apartment in Fiume was mourning that 7th of April, 1939, my little world had its own problems linked to the international events. Weeks in advance, my friends and I had planned an outing for Saturday, April 8. Would Dad allow me to go? It was not that I was insensitive to what was happening in Albania, but our little picnic would in no way affect these unfortunate events one way or another. I asked Mom whether there was hope that Dad would let me join my friends that Saturday. She thought he would and offered to talk with him. She was back a few moments later with a favorable answer.

The next day, Mom packed me some sandwiches. I mounted my beautiful—and heavy—Austrian Puch bike, and off I went with Lucio, Valnea, Nucci, and a few other classmates. I must admit I feared that one of them might mention Italy's action in Albania as I would have probably answered in spades and perhaps broken out in tears. Fortunately, no one spoke a word about what was going on in my native country and we all had a good time. We boys used the opportunity to show off before the girls. I was good at soccer and to have Valnea watch me was just great. Well, at one point, somebody kicked the ball into the sea. I stepped on a boulder trying to retrieve the ball, lost my balance and had to jump into the water over the top of another boulder in front of me to avoid being hurt. Once in the water, retrieving the ball was no problem. Actually, when the ball fell again into the water, I jumped in displaying the nonchalance one could expect of someone who was already wet. I did pay a price, though. I had a beautiful watch. It had a metal plate that covered the face and had three windows allowing rotating discs to mark the hours, minutes, and seconds. Unfortunately, the watch was not waterproof and this was Saturday. I could not get the watch to a repair shop until Monday and, by that time, the inner works had rusted. They were able to get it to tick again but shortly thereafter, the watch gave up its ghost for good.

Another event comes to mind as I reach back into the far-away past. The German ambassador to Italy at that time was von Mackensen. He was coming to speak to German expatriates and Germans from all over Italy were flocking to Trieste. Our German maid was going to that meeting and Dad gave me permission to join her. It was quite an evening for a non-German. The language, of course, was no problem. I could understand the enthusiasm, the patriotism, and the sense of belonging of the audience. The fact that Germany had risen to the level of a world power gave those present a great sense of pride. Hitler had retaken the Saargebiet, had rebuilt the economy, and had strengthened the armed forces. In addition, he had brought about the union with Austria and had annexed the Sudetenland. These successes were even more impressive compared to the impotence and misery in which Germany had wallowed at the end of World War I. The bringing together of Germans, be they in Austria or Czechoslovakia, appealed to us Albanians as we had about half our brethren living beyond our borders in Montenegro, Kosova, Macedonia, and Greece. It should also be stressed that Austria and the Sudentenland would have voted overwhelmingly for a union with Germany if a free election had been held. Subsequently, our sympathies for Hitler's successes dropped to the freezing point when he occupied the rest of Czechoslovakia by force of arms. But that was still months away. Hitler's criminal persecution and extermination of Jews, gypsies, and political opponents would remain a secret for me and many Europeans until the end of World War II. By the time we heard about them, we and half of Europe had lost our freedom. The world as we had known it had crashed and the outlines of a new world order, of a new balance of power, were emerging slowly and dimly, at least for the time being.

By the time our maid and I returned from Trieste, it was 3:00 a.m. When the alarm rang at 7:00 a.m. and I had to get up for school, I was absolutely bushed. In fact, that morning we had a written final exam in Latin and I was not looking forward to it. Once in class, though, something electrifying happened. Our professor paired us students off according to our proficiency, and guess what? He put Valnea and me together! My tiredness was gone instantly. During the test, I noticed that Valnea had made an error in translating from Italian into Latin. I bumped her with my elbow and pointed out her error. To be of help to her made me feel on cloud nine! Let me add as a matter of clarification that cheating in Italian schools carried no stigma. School was war, with the professors on one side and students on the other. A popular saying goes: "Everything is fair in love and war." Well, this was war!

Within days, the semester was over. We took exams covering all subjects taught in grades eight and nine. The morning came when our grades would be posted in the lobby. I walked there with hesitation. I knew I had done well; the question was how well. I looked at my grades and they looked great. Then I looked at the grades of my classmates and that's when my eyes popped! I ran all the way home. Dad was in the bathroom, shaving.

"Dad, Dad," I yelled. "I am first in my class overall and first in Italian." Dad never missed a stroke.

"You have done your duty." That was all he said. Crestfallen, I went to Mom and told her about my grades and Dad's reaction—or lack of reaction.

"Don't be fooled," she said. At this very moment he is very proud of you."

Mom may have been right but Dad never came back to the subject nor did he in any way show his pleasure.

CHAPTER FIVE

ITALY INVADES ALBANIA – 1939

At the end of the school year, we started packing. Dad hired a mover to ship our furniture and most of our belongings to Albania. My parents, Mergim, and I would carry some clothes and a few belongings with us in our suitcases. Moving from Austria to Italy had required no particular effort on my part. This move to Albania was just as easy, except for a problem I had not anticipated when Italy invaded Albania on April 7. Would I have to stay in Albania and change schools once more? Would I say goodbye to Fiume and adapt to a new social and political environment? I would have wanted to stay in Fiume but knew we lacked the means to pay for room and board. I knew that Dad would not be impressed by the friendships I had formed in Fiume. Was this perhaps a case where Mom could be of help? I felt in a daze.

The day of our move to Albania finally came. It was a hot summer day when we boarded one of those beautiful white ships that plied the Adriatic. We got aboard some time after mid-morning and soon thereafter a bell summoned us to the dining room. We were barely seated when the waiters came carrying trays heaped with sliced sausages and cheeses of all kinds. Breads and hard rolls were already on our table. I figured that since this was our first meal aboard, it was unlikely that they would serve anything else. Armed with fork and knife—and a healthy teenager's appetite—I dug deep into the vittles and got myself seconds and thirds with unbounded enthusiasm. Eventually, the waiters removed the trays and begun serving soup. Then came meat dishes, fish, salads, desserts, fruit and—once more—various cheeses. I was what the Italians call *"una buona forchetta,"* i.e., I could eat a lot. Drunkards drown their sorrows in alcohol. That day I buried mine under heaps and heaps of food. Just for the record: I did partake of every dish they offered, not with the initial enthusiasm but with enough dedication to please every chef and helper who had contributed to that sumptuous first meal aboard ship. I learned my lesson, though, and I enjoyed every meal until we reached Durrës but not with the abandon I had mustered for that first meal.

Shortly before we reached Albania, Mom went into her cabin to change clothes. A few months before, her only brother Memduh who lived as a refugee in Paris, France, had died of tuberculosis and Mom had worn black ever since. She and her sisters had agreed that they would not tell Grandma that she had lost her only son. Thus, Mom shed her mourning clothes and wore regular summer garb when we left the ship. Within minutes, before we even left the harbor, Mergim caught his foot, fell, and broke his left arm. I remember how much Mom blamed herself for Mergim's accident. She felt that the accident was punishment for her having violated Albania's mourning traditions that required women to wear black for a whole year after the death of a close relative.

That, of course, changed our plans. We left for Tirana where Professor Lozzi set Mergim's arm by applying a large, heavy cast. It was so heavy that he had trouble standing straight. Then things happened in a hurry. Dad returned from a visit with Mustafa Kruja who had urged Dad to take Mergim to Bologna to the famous Istituto Ortopedico Rizzoli. Mustafa Kruja's youngest son, Besim, had broken his arm as a youngster. Serious complications had impaired his full recovery and had limited his use of the arm. If Dad lacked the money to take Mergim to Bologna, Mustafa would take care of the expenses. Thus, Dad and Mergim left for Bologna while Mom and I took the bus to Korça to meet Dad's clan. In Dad's absence I, the older son, would represent the family. Despite my young age, I was not flattered.

We left Tirana and about six hours later, after much bouncing and swerving, made it to Pogradec, a small town along the shores of gorgeous Lake Ohrida. Up to that point, the scenery had been interesting but not spectacular. As our bus descended the twisting highway, the view widened and we began to see the marvelous blue of the lake and its luscious shores. The scenery was enchanting. Somehow, I felt I had seen this scenery before although this was my first visit to Pogradec. Was this a case of déjà vu?

It took another twenty minutes or so before we stopped in front of a small hotel. We got off to stretch our legs when a man and a dozen or so younger people began staring at Mom and me. They stood before a small bus. The man was rather short, well dressed, and distinguished looking. He walked toward Mom, his right hand outstretched.

"Seadet, welcome. It gives me great pleasure to see you again after so many years. Where are Djevat and Mergim? Are they coming later?"

"Muamer, I am very happy to see you. Yes, Djevat and Mergim will come later. It's a rather long story. I'll tell you when we get home."

"Fine. Please get on this smaller bus that will take us directly home. I'll take care of your luggage."

So, that was Uncle Muamer. He had rented a bus to pick us up. He must have been quite disappointed that Dad was not with us. Anyhow, I had a chance to look at the others who had come with Uncle Muamer. There was one young man named Edward, probably three or four years older than me. Then there were a few more young people but no one bothered to introduce them to us, and so they remained anonymous for the time being.

With our luggage piled on the bus, we left for Korça and stopped at Dad's house. It was a two-story building surrounded by a rather large yard and walled in to a height of about 8 feet. There was the usual heavy front door and a small building near the entrance, some sort of a stable, I guessed. A path with cobblestones led to the house and ended at an open space under the large porch of the floor above. To the left, a few steps led to the basement and a longer flight of stairs went up to the second floor. We climbed those steps and entered a rather large room with a sofa along three walls. Women all dressed in black sat cross-legged all along three walls, giving the room a mournful appearance. They sat there perched like vultures, with tilted heads and wrinkled necks, smiling, staring at me like at a long-anticipated meal. I am sure they meant well but that's the way I saw them.

The first one was an old woman I had never met before. She rose half-way, stated that she had raised Dad, took me into her arms and kissed me with abandon—and lots of saliva—on both cheeks. Next came Aunt Nurije whom I knew from Austria. It was she who told me that Mom was at the hospital having a baby when Mergim was born. She too rose, embraced me, and plastered me with smackers, one on each cheek. She had also raised Dad. And that's the way it went all around the room. After the first three or four women had assaulted me with their unwanted kisses, I gave up looking at the individual salivating on my cheeks. They all dressed the same and looked the same to me. They had all raised Dad, who must have been overwhelmed by the attention and love they had lavished upon him as he grew up. After all the kissing and drooling, I was disgusted and furious.

"If you don't mind, I want to wash my face."

Mom knew how I hated being kissed. She took me downstairs and then descended the steps that led into the basement. I followed her, boiling inside. I had to get rid of the rivers of saliva that had to be running down my cheeks (at least, that's the way I felt). As I stomped down those three steps, I forgot to duck and banged my forehead against the transom. That did not help at all. Now beside the saliva that I could wash off I also had a bump on my forehead that would stay with me for a few days. What a beginning!

Well, things did improve, at least for a while. Edward came to pick me up. It was the time of the obligatory evening stroll and all the young men of Korça walked up and down along the U-shaped main drag at the center of town. They greeted each other every time their paths crossed while craning their necks hoping to see those few girls, mostly high school students, who took their evening stroll pretending to be unaware of the hungry looks they got from the boys.

At one point Edward hissed, "Ignore them."

The ones I was supposed to ignore were two girls that looked familiar. When they passed they smiled, pleased that I had acknowledged their greeting despite Edward's imperious order.

"Edward, who are these girls? They look vaguely familiar."

"They were with us on the bus from Pogradec to Korça. One is my sister Dashka and the other Muamer's oldest daughter, Lumka."

So that's who they were. They were not introduced to Mom and me on the bus and, if Edward had his way, I should continue to ignore them ever after.

"Can we join them and walk with them a while?" I asked.

"They would laugh us out of town," Edward replied. "They" were probably the ones that counted, i.e., Edward's friends. That loss of face had to be avoided at any cost, of course. Well, I did not share his views about separation of the sexes but decided to conform to his wishes, at least for the time being.

It got dark and Edward accompanied me home. Most of the old ladies had flown the coop and were probably nesting at their usual places, away from our house. That was a blessing. We had dinner and Mom and I, having had a long day, withdrew for the night. It had been hot in Korça and Mom had set up the two beds on the porch. I sank to the bottom of the soft mattress and fell immediately asleep—but not for long. I woke up feeling hot and itching all over.

"Mom, Mom, I'm sick."

Mom woke up, lit a kerosene lamp she had placed near her bed, and walked over to where I lay. In the darkness I could see legions of bugs crawling all over my bed. I had never seen such bugs before nor was I pleased to make their acquaintance.

"Get up," Mom said to me. She picked up the mattress, shook it over the railing of the veranda and laid it on the floor, away from the bed.

"There is not much I can do to get rid of these bedbugs tonight. Tomorrow I will take care of them. Tonight do the best you can."

It took me a while to fall asleep again but I was grateful that Mom was going to take care of the problem. I didn't know how, but I knew that when she promised something, she kept her word. In fact, the next morning she got kerosene, matches, a handful of newspapers, and went to work. She bunched up newspapers, dipped them in kerosene and burned the bottoms of the legs of the iron bed frames. Then she burned the springs and the supporting fixtures, and finally, inspected the mattresses to make sure that no bed bugs were hiding in the folds. She procured some empty aluminum cans, filled them with water, and placed the legs of the bed frames inside the cans.

I was impressed. Having burned out the hiding places of the bedbugs, Mom now made it impossible for them to reach the bedposts without falling into the water. Clearly, the human intellect had triumphed once again. Years later, in jail, I saw famished bedbugs climbing up the walls, crossing the ceiling to points above their victims' bed, and dropping down on the beds and the hapless victims. The bedbugs in Korça were either less hungry or less smart because, for the rest of our stay there, we had no more problems with bedbugs. I must add though that Mom had asked the two old ladies with whom we shared the house to do the same rigorous cleanup with their beds. I am sure they conformed in part because Mom said so but mostly because they were mortified when they heard about my battle with the bedbugs the night before.

Some time went by and Dad and Mergim finally returned from Bologna. Mergim's cast was small and very light. He could raise his left arm in every direction but could not open the elbow. Eventually the cast was taken off. Unfortunately, despite exercises, hot soaks, and the like, to this day Mergim is unable to straighten out the elbow completely.

Shortly after his arrival, Dad decided to take us to Dardha, a beautiful mountain village not far from Korça. It was most picturesque, surrounded by dense woods and rolling mountains. Upon arrival, I noticed that a creek that ran through the village had a funny smell, like rotten eggs. In fact, the village was known for its sulfur springs. Tourists from surrounding areas flocked to Dardha because of the healing properties attributed to the water. I was more impressed with the ability of the water to give a golden sheen to silver coins immersed in the creek. This patina was temporary but it was fun to watch while it lasted.

One day Dad showed up with a stranger, an Albanian of Nordic appearance. He was tall, muscular, and blond with blue eyes. He was personable and very friendly. His name was Lazër Fundo. Even more surprising than his looks was the fact that he was a communist and a friend of Dad's. When the civil war exploded in Albania, he joined the communist guerillas in the mountains. Because he was an idealist who disapproved of the aims and methods of the Slav-dominated communist movement in Albania, he was bludgeoned to death by his companions while asleep. The orders for his execution had come from the very top.

The closer we got to September, to the beginning of the school year, the more nervous I got. I was desperately clinging to the hope that Dad would send me to Fiume to continue high school. Dad had told me he would look into it but that's all I knew. It meant that he would let me know whatever there was to know—in due time. Meanwhile, I had to be patient and that was hard for me. I had changed school systems once when we moved from Austria to Italy. I liked Fiume, and I liked my schoolmates very much. I did not want to have to change again.

Meanwhile, a number of major events had taken place in the international arena. In March of 1939, Neville Chamberlain, prime minister of Great Britain, had guaranteed Poland's independence. The Poles, aware of the danger that threatened them from both east and west, had turned that guarantee into a full alliance. Next, France and Great Britain sent emissaries to Moscow trying to forge a coalition with Stalin against Germany. These emissaries spent weeks and weeks in Moscow seemingly without progress. Then, during the last week in August, right under their noses, Germany's Foreign Secretary von Ribbentrop arrived in Moscow. He and Molotov, his Soviet counterpart, proceeded to sign the German-Soviet Non-Aggression Pact, a clear indication that the Soviets had been dealing with Hitler in secret while officially discussing a possible alliance with the West. Von Ribbentrop returned to Berlin with the pact in his pocket; the Western emissaries returned home empty-handed.

On September 1, Dad and I returned to Korça. As we passed by a candy shop, we heard Hitler's unmistakable voice on the radio saying, "As of this morning, German troops have penetrated 18 kilometers into Polish territory." According to German officialdom, Germany had exhibited incredible patience in the face of continued Polish provocations. The military response of September 1 was well justified and the rest of the nations could not help but agree with the German decision to strike back. Germany had finally reacted to border incidents provoked by the Polish military.

To prove its point, Berlin showed newsreels that provided documentary evidence of Polish attacks on German border positions. What turned up after the war shed a different light on these "facts." The documentary Berlin had offered to justify the invasion of Poland had been prepared ahead of time. A group of common criminals in German prisons was offered a chance to be part of a movie. They received Polish military uniforms and were to simulate an attack on certain German frontier posts. They were issued weapons and blank ammunition, as befits a movie. They started the "attack," firing at the German military that were manning the watchtowers. The German guards returned fire, not with blanks but with regular ammunition. The "attacking Poles" were killed. Subsequently, so was the German border unit that had fired back at them. The German plans had required that no witnesses survive the filming of this "documentary." In 1939, Europe and the world at large were unaware of this, of course. Within a few weeks, Germany defeated Poland, and German and Soviet troops partitioned the country between the two of them.

World War II had started and no one could know how and when it would end. I distinctly remember Dad saying that he hoped that the powers involved would fight to exhaustion on both sides lest Albania's rights once more be trampled underfoot. I did not quite understand what he meant, nor did I ask. Personally, I felt as if I had received a sharp blow to my head as my hopes to return to Fiume rapidly vanished into thin air.

I was wrong. Soon after Hitler's speech, Dad told me that because of my scholastic record I was being granted a scholarship to continue my schooling in Italy; furthermore, I would stay with the Mandarà family, with my best friend Lucio. Yippee! Things now really started to move. Mom packed my belongings, we embraced, and off I went with Dad to the bus station in Korça. We were already on the bus when some acquaintance spoke up to Dad.

"Have a good trip, Djevat Bey."

Dad replied, "If I knew I had even one drop of *bey* blood in me, I would cut my wrists!"

As the bus left the station, I questioned Dad. "Why did you give the man such a sharp answer? He was just trying to be polite honoring you with a title."

"To be a *bey* means that I or someone in my family had been a favorite of the Turks that kept us enslaved for 500 years. I fought against the Turks and you think I should feel honored if someone called me a *bey*?" I dropped the subject. I was returning to Fiume and that's what counted.

The next few days disappeared in a blur and before I knew it, Dad and I were in Durrës in a small rowboat that was carrying us to a beautiful white ship that would take me to Bari. Dad came aboard to check out my cabin. After a quick hug, Dad went down the ladder and the little boat started carrying him away. My eyes filled with tears. I could barely make out his outline as he waved. Soon he was lost against the background of the shore and I moved away and went to my cabin. For the first time in my life I was truly alone, responsible for what I would do and say.

I repeated the guidelines Dad had given me: "Remember that our family's good name goes with you. Never do anything to be ashamed of, and above all, never, never lie." He had also given me cash and had asked me to use it prudently. Finally, I was to give him a monthly account of how I spent the money. In Fiume, I would live with the Mandarà family. I had no idea how long it had taken Dad to make the arrangements. One thing was obvious: When Dad said that he would see what he could do to get me to continue my schooling in Fiume, he had meant it. Dear, dear, Dad.

It felt great to be on my own. My cabin was well lit. I had a bed and all the amenities I needed. Even though the war had started in Europe, Italy was neutral, the ship was brightly lit, and the next day I would be in Bari. Then a train ride of about 24 hours to Trieste. Finally, I would make a decision: I could take the train or the bus to Fiume. These busses were called *Freccia del Carnaro*, the "Arrow of Carnaro"—Carnaro is in that part of northern Italy. The busses of this line were sleek, painted deep red, and were at least as fast as the train.

When I reached Trieste and got on the bus, reality grabbed me. I was actually going to Fiume. I would see my friends again, go to the same high school building I had entered since the seventh grade, and live with Lucio, my dear friend. School had already started a few days earlier but that should be no problem. During the trip to Fiume, it started to rain. But to me it did not matter. I knew that winding highway quite well. I pushed my face against the window. Each turn of the highway took me closer and closer to Fiume. My prayers were being answered in full!

This was my first time away from home. Life at Lucio's was strange at first. His father was a stern, unsmiling individual. During the summer he had suffered from some intestinal infection that had bothered him a lot. One day, as he sat at the sandy beach near Santa Croce, Sicily, he felt the urge to enter the tepid seawater. He knew that it would burn like the dickens but he could not resist the temptation. He waded knee-deep into the water, and sat down. According to his own words, the burning was almost more than he could endure. Gradually, the pain began to subside. He sat a while longer, got out, and from that moment on, he began to heal. When I got to Fiume, he was still anemic and had to eat horsemeat every day. His wife prepared these horse steaks in the frying pan. They looked delicious, succulent and tender. Well, one day, he gave me a bite of horse steak. It was tougher than the dickens! Anyhow, I was glad he let me try it because now I no longer envied him as he thoughtfully chewed his way through his daily steak.

Mrs. Mandarà was a dear person. She was a good cook, always kind, always ready to help. She spoke accent-free German, a rarity in Fiume although the city had been under the Hapsburgs for a long time. She was frugal and modest in her attire. I liked to hear her play the piano, even though she did so rarely.

Lucio was the same good old Lucio I had known now for three years, for one fifth of my entire life. When you consider that I had never attended the same school for more than two years, this was a record. Continuous change had been one of my life's characteristics. I was born in Albania, spent two years in Yugoslavia as a toddler, and then 10 years in Austria, first in Vienna and the rest in Graz. Once I started school, we moved—and I changed schools—practically every two years. At home we spoke Albanian. Outside the home, I had to speak German in Austria and now Italian. I needed to find a base to which I could cling, hold on to, with which to identify myself. The obvious answer was my family that, for the time being, was in Albania.

The school year started with a screech. I had no trouble catching up, even though my schoolmates were a few days ahead of me. Nonetheless, something had changed drastically. I did not know it, but in the ninth grade I had been the students' favorite. Now, there were little incidents here and there where my classmates showed ill will toward me. I had no idea what I had done—or failed to do—to earn their disfavor. So, I retreated into my internal fortress and decided to weather the storm as long as it took. After all, I had been the outsider all my life and if it had to be that way, that was OK with me.

To this day, I don't know what happened in the tenth grade. At the end of the ninth grade, I had dated a classmate for a few days and before leaving for Albania had written her a very bashful note that she had made public. Everyone who had read it had had a good laugh at my expense. She was now dating an upperclassman and, eventually, would marry him.

During the school year, we had soccer matches among students of our high school. The makeup of the teams changed according to circumstances. We wore uniforms and soccer shoes with cleats consisting of corks screwed to the sole of the shoes. After some use, the corks wore off and the bare screws tended to stick out.

The upcoming match was between "single" players and the team of the "married," meaning those with steady girlfriends. I was left halfback of the singles team. The boy who was going steady with my former date played for the married team. During the match he and I ran to recover the ball that was coming down from on high. Intentionally, I jumped early. I was coming down while my opponent was on his way up. I stuck my foot out and my shoe scraped against my opponent's thigh. He started to bleed profusely. I don't remember whether I apologized but, even if I did, it would have done little good. A strong reaction of the girls against me made me think that my former date was behind this whole thing. Well, I had struck a nerve and that was what I had been after. I must admit that, afterwards, I felt less proud of myself than when I had first hatched and executed my revenge.

The winter of 1939–1940, the first winter of World War II, resembled shadow boxing more than a real war on the western front. Nothing was happening along the Maginot Line, the French defensive line along the border with Germany. Northern Europe, however, saw a new conflict. The Soviets demanded that the Finns give up East Karelia. Rebuffed, the USSR attacked Finland and got a bloody nose at first. Eventually, size prevailed. Despite the valor of the Finnish troops, its brilliant military leaders, and the merits of its cause, Finland eventually capitulated. It was a tragic defeat.

At this point, Western European governments had bigger problems than to worry about Finland. The winter had gone by in eerie silence with few shots being fired between Germany and France. The pundits speculated about what was to follow on the western front, spinning theories that went from one extreme, namely peace coming to Europe and preserving the status quo, to the other of Germany conquering the entire continent.

There was much speculation about whether, when, and how Hitler's armies might start rolling again. We did not have to wait very long. In the spring, the German attack began with the usual fury. Holland, Denmark, and Belgium were overrun in nothing flat. The Maginot Line was out-flanked, the British Expeditionary Force was reeling back toward Dunkirk, and the German troops were threatening Paris, the glittering, fascinating French capital. Paris fell early in June, after hearing the rumble of German guns for the second time in 25 years. The day before, I had been teaching Italian to Suzanne, the French wife of my cousin Xhevdet Asllani. That day she stated flatly that Paris would never, never fall into the hands of the *Boches*, a disparaging name the French reserved for the Germans. Hitler forced France to sign the surrender at Compiégne, in the same railroad car where defeated German generals had surrendered at the end of World War I.

After the fall of the French capital, the Germans seemed to get ready to invade Great Britain, as they began bombing British cities and attempted to destroy the Royal Air Force. What would later be known as "Operation Sea Lion" had begun but would never go beyond those initial moves.

I suffered a serious health problem in early spring of 1940. I fell ill suffering from a recurrent high fever. Every other day it started out with shivers and then a high fever would start. The physician took blood and ran tests. It was neither malaria nor the Mediterranean fever. I don't know what other tests he ran but the fever kept returning. I was getting weaker and weaker and was out of school for about six weeks. Mrs. Mandarà was very dear and tender toward me. Finally the fever ran its course. The physician sent me to a cancer institute and asked for X-rays of my abdomen. The diagnosis was peritonitis specifica, i.e., tuberculosis of the peritoneum. I got a very gooey black ointment and was told to apply it to my belly and cover the area with gauze. Over the years, this diagnosis turned out to be in error; thank God!

When I returned to school, I had forgotten all about my classmates' hostility. My big problem was catching up with all I had missed. I began studying furiously and was making good progress—except in Art History. We had a teacher, a mutilated veteran of World War I, who had been an architect and was now hammering into our heads the works of Italian artists of centuries past. Lucio stayed up with me, sometimes until 3:00 a.m. to help me memorize long lists of works by many—too many—artists. There was so much to memorize that I just could not cope with it. I would get tired, a mental block would set, in and that was the end of my studies for that night.

Every Wednesday I had nightmares. Art History class was on Thursdays. I had asked for extensions in order to memorize those horrible lists and eventually got to the end of the semester with no place to hide. On the day of my final oral exam, the teacher called my name and I faced Calvary. He asked only one question: "Paintings, sculptures, and mosaics in the Cathedral of Milan." I was sure that it would take several books to adequately answer the question before me. I had neither the time nor the knowledge to start composing such books. On the other hand, if I could give a halfway decent answer, I could probably overcome this last hurdle, as I had received passing grades in all other subjects. I don't remember what I said, but eventually the teacher nodded and I returned to my seat. As far as grades were concerned, that year would not mark another triumph. I passed without having to repeat any exams in the fall. That was the best I could hope for and that was what I got.

CHAPTER SIX

WWII 1939-1941

As usual, I spent the summer vacation in Albania. It wasn't much fun because I had no personal friends, no schoolmates, no roots. I spent the summer with Dad and the family, mostly in Korça, and with relatives about my age. Resistance against the Italians was stiffening. The Italians reacted by bringing in abundant supplies of food, clothing, and other goods. Materially, people lived better in Albania than in Fiume where most food items had to be imported. For example, Mom wanted to hire a maid. For her monthly pay, Mom offered two napoleons—Dad was making 16 as state counselor. The gypsy woman patted her belly, said, "Long live il Duce who has filled us with pasta!" and stalked out of our rented house.

Dad had asked to be appointed principal of the middle and high school in Shkodra, the school he had founded in 1923. He had two reasons for doing so. Italy had invaded Albania in April 1939. We returned to Albania in July. He chose to return months after the invasion to make the point that he did not return with the invading forces. By seeking to be appointed principal of the school, he wanted to stress that he had not benefited from the occupation. Well, the Italians did not appoint him school principal, probably for those very same reasons. Furthermore, they knew Dad and his nationalist views and did not want him to mold the Albanian youth against Italy. So they sidelined him by making him a member of the state council, a job with a modest income and of little consequence. Either way, as a school principal or as counselor of state, Dad would have been unable to send me to attend classes in Fiume. Fortunately, I had the scholarship granted me the year before and did not have to worry in this regard.

Italy entered the war on the side of Germany against France and England in June of 1940. Mussolini had done so rather precipitously, just as France was about to surrender to Hitler. People believed that Italy was ill prepared for the war. Mussolini felt he had to enter the war if he wanted to carry any weight next to a victorious führer. History would prove him wrong. The Tri-partite—Rome, Berlin, and Tokyo—lost the war. Mussolini did end his life on Germany's side. Disguised as a German soldier, he was captured and shot by Italian partisans and preceded Hitler in death by several months.

In one respect, I was better off than the year before. In Tirana I had made a few friends, including two younger sisters of Shpresa's, the future Shpresa Dervishi, named Hënza and Yllka. We went together on picnics, bicycled a lot, and had fun. We were young, healthy, and full of dreams and hopes. There was, of course, also a dark side. The Italians had occupied our country and we were very much against them. The war was going on and the anti-Italian resistance developed and grew.

Late summer came and I got ready to return to Fiume. This time, I took a boat from Durrës to Bari and from there I traveled to Fiume by train. From the railroad station to Lucio's it was just a hop, skip, and a jump. He and I would share the same bedroom; he on the sofa and I on the bed. This was the second year I would spend with them. There was much less to get used to and our friendship took off from where it stood at the end of the school year two months earlier. In fact, our friendship would last a lifetime.

This school year, I decided to make a change as far as Art History was concerned. All summer I had nightmares on Wednesday nights, on the eve of the Art History class. I decided then and there that—if I could help it—I would never again fall into last year's predicament. I kept a black book where I entered the subjects, the date a student took an oral exam, and the grade he or she received. From the second bench where I sat I could easily see the teachers entering the grades in their registers. Thus, I knew exactly who had taken what exam and on what date. The Art History teacher always liked to examine two students during each class session. I would volunteer to take my exam at the beginning of the semester when the list of artists and their works was short. As most students tried to defer the Art History exam as long as possible, I gambled that the teacher would run out of time and never call me back for a second oral exam. There was, of course, a risk inherent in this strategy. I took my chances for the next two years and got As with little effort, albeit with little added knowledge in Art History.

Having gotten rid of the mysterious illness that had plagued me in the tenth grade, I was doing quite well. I was class president and one of the top students. I was asked to join the varsity soccer team of our high school and was among the best young fencers in town.

In the 11ᵗʰ grade, we had a woman teacher for Latin and Greek. She had a funny way of teaching. The first semester, not one student got a passing grade. The purpose was to get us to study as hard as we could. Well, the good students were stung by the low grade and hit the books hard. The majority did not react. They knew that she could not flunk the entire class. They plodded along at their usual pace, confident that eventually they would get a passing grade. The poor students could not be bothered as they were used to failing grades. Well, miracles do happen. The teacher got pregnant—got out of the class and out of our hair. A young male teacher by the name of Uglietti (pronounced "Oolieti") took her place. He was relatively short but powerfully built. He always had a plugged nose but his lessons were so interesting that soon we stopped noticing his handicap. His grading system was also very different. He was not reluctant to give high marks. In Italy it was said that only God deserved a 10, teachers could get a 9, and an 8 was reserved for the best students. Well, I got a 9 in Latin and you can imagine how I studied so I would not slip back. There are various ways to make students hit the books: giving them unfair low marks or making them work hard to keep up their high scores. I need not explain which I preferred.

Scholastically, this year was also much easier for me than the previous year when I had suffered from ill health. I was a "bachelor," but not by choice. Since the eighth grade I had this secret love for Valnea Curatolo. As I grew up, my feelings for her also matured. She was an excellent student, friendly toward all, a good skier, and fun to be with. I could not help it, but there was more distance between the two of us than I would have liked.

In the 11ᵗʰ grade, things started getting more interesting. A new student by the name of Sandro Bolchi (pronounced Bowlkey) entered the tenth grade. He was tall, dark, with a five o'clock beard even though he shaved regularly. He looked like an athlete but did not participate in any sports. He was very friendly, sociable, and one day he invited us to the apartment where he lived with his parents. Surprise No. 1: It was the same apartment that our family had previously occupied. Surprise No. 2: Sandro claimed that his father had a baritone voice of operatic caliber. Well, we did not believe him. His father was a major in the Italian army and anyone with an operatic voice would be on stage, not in the army.

On the day when Sandro invited us to his home, we shuffled in, resigned that we would have to listen to his father sing who knows what. The father was also tall, quite heavy around the middle, and wearing his uniform. Sandro had told the truth, at least as far as his father's rank was concerned. Yes, he was a major. His wife sat down at the piano while the major announced that he would sing the aria *"Sì vendetta, tremenda vendetta..."* from Verdi's *Rigoletto*. It was a difficult aria, even for professional baritones. We shuffled uncomfortably in our seats and prepared ourselves for what was to come. Our group of friends used to go to the opera when the Carro di Tespi Lirico (Mussolini's gift to the opera-loving masses) brought Italy's best opera singers to Fiume. In other words, we knew a good singer when we heard one. Mrs. Bolchi played the opening notes. Surprise No. 2 struck us like lightning: Major Bolchi had a most beautiful baritone voice, comparable to the best we had ever heard on the operatic stage! His voice was powerful, resonant, modulated, and most expressive as he told of the hatred of Rigoletto for the Duke of Mantua and sang with a father's tender love about his daughter Gilda.

We were stunned. We couldn't quite applaud. How does one applaud a friend's father? You don't congratulate parents. Of course parents are good at what they do. That's why they are parents. We just sat there mesmerized. We could not understand why he was not singing on stage with Italy's best. He must have read our minds.

"I was a young lieutenant when I had a chance to meet Tito Schipa [a world-famous tenor of the mid-1930s]. He offered to get me an audition at La Scala, Milan's great theater. He did not rush me. 'Think it over and let me know by the end of the week.' Those were the years of the Great Depression. I didn't know whether I would make it as a singer. Besides, would people still pay hard-earned money to go to the opera? I thought long and hard. Somehow, the army seemed to offer a safer career. I made up my mind and that's what I told Tito Schipa.

"His reply was terse: 'I hope you won't regret it.'"

We all thought with regret that Major Bolchi would have had a splendid career as an opera singer but, by now, he was too old to undo that unfortunate decision.

The Bolchis were also good hosts and loved being surrounded by youth. They invited us to come again and Sandro offered to teach us ballroom dancing, at which he was very good. The following Saturday Lucio, three or four others, and I showed up, all very embarrassed and sure that we would trip over our own feet. Fortunately, there were no girls present.

Sandro was an excellent teacher. We sought our partners and Lucio and I, started dancing together fairly well, if not with abandonment. We were progressing better than any of us had anticipated. After about three sessions, Sandro announced that his parents and he thought that the time had come to invite some girls. We had dreaded (or dreamed about?) this moment. Out went the invitations. The girls were all from our class. We invited Milena, Valnea, Nucci, and Gemma; to our surprise and delight, they all accepted.

That first Saturday came and none too soon. Lucio and I were so excited that, on one hand, we feared we might not live long enough to see that Saturday and, on the other, that we would faint or worse, once we put our right arm around a girl. Two years before, in the ninth grade, I had been at an afternoon dance and Lidia Desimoni had asked me to dance with her. I had protested forcefully saying that I did not know how to dance. Lidia had insisted, saying that there was nothing to it and that she would teach me. She took my left hand with her right hand, put her left hand on my shoulder, and dragged me to the dance floor. Then disaster struck. Lidia was a very good-looking blonde. She wore a light blue dress with a semi-transparent bodice. When I put my right hand around her back, I thought I felt her soft, silky skin. I let go and bolted off the dance floor. She followed but did not utter a word; her whole physical expression—from head to toe—was one big question mark. I mumbled something that was supposed to explain why I was leaving, took the next streetcar, and did not recover my composure until I was safely inside my room. Here, I buried my head in homework but could not get rid of the memory of how unsettlingly soft her back had been.

Now, two years later, my classmates Milena, Nucci, Gemma, and Valnea would actually come to dance with us beginners. How deliciously disconcerting. What if I panicked like the last time? I told myself that now I was two years older and certainly more mature, less likely to panic. I did not anticipate any problems with three of the girls, but what about Valnea? She had been my "flame" since the eighth grade. OK, what were the possible alternatives? What if I did not dance with her? That was not an alternative. Courtesy required that each boy dance with each girl at least once. What if I danced with her just once and then ignored her the rest of the evening? Now, why would I want to do that? She was the only one who really mattered to me. Besides, if I survived that first dance, why would I want stay away from her? Of course, if I fainted during that first dance...

Finally, the girls arrived. They had dressed up but not too much. However, as they entered the room, we boys noticed that they were wearing perfume. The Bolchi parents were very gracious and there was no awkwardness at all and that helped us boys overcome our shyness. The record player started and, somehow, Milena and Sandro drifted together. I moved toward somebody, I don't remember who it was because my mind was on Valnea but I didn't want to appear too eager to dance with her. The first record was a slow fox, just right for our dancing ability. Wonder of wonders, the girls thought we boys danced well enough to make it fun for them also. The mood warmed up considerably as our fears began to recede.

Eventually, I danced with Valnea; since I had also danced with everyone else, she became my steady dancing partner. I couldn't believe that we were dancing well together, that I was holding her in my arms, smelling her perfume, feeling her movements follow mine. Me, fainting? Who spoke of fainting? This was more fun than I had anticipated, and it continued until about suppertime when the group broke up and everyone went home for dinner.

At the dinner table, Lucio's father asked rather sternly where we had spent the afternoon. We told him we were at Major Bolchi's. What were we doing there? he wanted to know.

"We danced with some girls from school."

"You danced while our soldiers are dying, fighting for our country?"

I could have told him that in Germany people danced, including their soldiers, who had been fighting longer than their Italian allies, but prudence told me to keep my mouth shut. It was a wise decision. Captain Mandarà never returned to the subject although he would comment from time to time that jazz was a Negro distortion of music. We in Italy were blessed. We could spend our time listening to Monteverdi, Rossini, Puccini, Verdi, and even to Mozart, Bach, Brahms, Wagner, and other European greats! Anyhow, he would grumble from time to time about frivolous entertainment while we kept dancing at the Bolchis practically every Saturday while school was in session. Captain Mandarà's thoughts were his own. Major Bolchi outranked him. That helped. Besides, it took more than one man's opinion to stop youngsters who were just coming into their own.

Actually, we did more than dance. One afternoon, we boys painted our faces black (inspired by Mr. Mandarà's comments about jazz being Negro music?), fake musical instruments in hand, and mimicked a black band playing *Tiger Rag* while Sandro Bolchi and Milena Lekovich gave a torrid rendition of the dance. I was behind the drums and had a field day. Everybody laughed, including Sandro's parents. Our dance was off to a great start.

After a while, we began tackling more ambitious projects. We decided to stage a play, *Addio Giovinezza*, (Goodbye Youth). Sandro and Milena, of course, played the lead roles; Valnea was the mother; Nucci, Lucio, and the rest took up the slack. I refused to act, so I became the official prompter.

The play became an important part of our after-school lives. Sandro and Milena fell madly in love. There were other minor crushes within the group. The play was well received when we gave it before a group of friends at the Bolchi apartment. The friends suggested we rent a theater and open the play to the public at large. Well, you can imagine the excitement in our ranks.

Now everybody was stage struck. The girls and boys could see their names on large posters and I had a real prompter's box, halfway below stage level, from where I could rescue some unfortunate actor or actress who happened to fumble a line or two. Rehearsals at the theater assumed a new dimension and the cast's mood swung from despair to delight and back—several times a day! I felt secure and protected in my cubicle. Besides, not being under pressure, I knew every line of every part. Nothing touched me, nothing upset me. My Olympian mood rendered me downright unflappable. Eventually, it dawned on me that my mood was not due to any merit of mine. It was simply the result of cowardice, of wanting to feel safe when those who stepped on stage faced the public.

Well, the dreaded, much-awaited night came and went—just like that. The actors, the makeup lady who was also in charge of costumes (namely Mrs. Bolchi), and, of course, the prompter were all at the theater quite early. Some members of the cast were clearing their throats, others were tugging and pulling their sleeves, jackets, skirts, and whatever else happened to get between their fingers. Everybody was eager to peek between the curtains, hoping, expecting to see the public streaming into the theater. Well, maybe it was too early, we told each other at the beginning. When things did not improve with time, we were baffled at first, then discouraged, and finally floored when only a handful of people showed up. We could have handled those few at the Bolchi apartment without having to rent a theater!

Eventually, it dawned on us. The theater owners had been willing to accommodate us on a holiday when few people would come to the theater. We went through with the performance. It was indeed a sad event. We left the theater crestfallen, in silence. No one had anticipated what had happened. We had expected a big success. We could have even put up with a failure, but this? To be totally ignored and left out in the cold, twisting in the wind? Our spirits did not pick up until the Saturday after when we returned to the Bolchi apartment for one of our regular dances. Blessed youth! Not even a week had gone by and here we were, dancing, laughing, and having a good time. Things, however, were about to change in a hurry. Again, unanticipated events would affect our lives drastically.

War activities had been surrounding our little island of Fiume without a direct impact on our lives, at least for the time being. On October 28^t, 1940, Mussolini sent seven Italian divisions (155,000 men) across the Greek border. Why did the attack take place on October 28^t? Because Mussolini loved historical dates and October 28^t marked the 18th anniversary of Mussolini's takeover of the Italian government in 1922. This time, however, things went wrong from the very beginning. Within 10 days, the Greek forces stopped the attack, entered Albania, and occupied the southern third of the country.

This affected my family in Albania. When Greek troops entered Korça, many of our relatives came to Tirana and moved in with our family. The ladies, all much younger than Mom, saw themselves as guests. They would get up in the morning, enjoy their breakfast, doll up, and go out to visit friends and relatives. They would return for the noon meal and take off again. In the evening, they were back for supper and stayed home until the next day when they started all over again. Even though Mom had a maid, the very unfairness of this setup was getting to her. If one adds the British air raids and Mom's feeling of helplessness and panic under bombardment, it is not surprising that she demanded that Dad find an appropriate solution. So, one day Dad called a family council and announced that Mom, Mergim, and he were leaving for Fiume. Our relatives could stay in the house and run it any way they chose. Mom needed medical treatment and, as soon as her health permitted, the three of them would return to Tirana. And that's what they did.

In Fiume, they rented an apartment near the Opera. Mergim attended school in Fiume, Dad took care of Mom's frayed nerves, and I, of course, was delighted to have them nearby instead of in faraway Tirana. I saw them often and benefited in more ways than one from their presence because, despite wartime rationing, Mom always had something good for me to munch when I went to see them.

The previous November, British planes had penetrated Italian air defenses at the port of Taranto and had torpedoed and sunk three Italian battleships. In March of 1941, Germany invaded Greece through Romania and Bulgaria soon after British forces, 58,000 strong, had landed in Greece to help thwart the impending German attack. The Italian navy had left port to intercept British convoys bringing troops and supplies to Greece and their naval escort. The two naval forces met near Cape Mataplan and it ended with the Italian battleship *Vittorio Veneto* severely damaged, with three Italian cruisers and two destroyers sent to the bottom of the Mediterranean Sea. Mataplan was the last naval battle between British and Italian forces in World War II.

On April 6, 1941, German troops invaded Yugoslavia and Greece. Italy joined the attack and on April 17, Yugoslavia surrendered. Greece surrendered to the Axis forces less than a week later. Thus, after a Balkan campaign lasting about two months, German forces captured 340,000 Yugoslav, 220,000 Greek, and 20,000 British and Commonwealth troops. German losses amounted to 2,500 dead, 6,000 wounded, and 3,000 missing in action. Now, Germany took a breather.

The Greek surrender followed a hasty retreat from occupied Albanian territories. Our relatives returned to Korça, and my parents and Mergim returned to Albania. Their stay in Fiume had been good for Mom and when they got home, life went back to normal.

World War II went on. On June 22, Hitler invaded the Soviet Union with 150 divisions and a total of three million troops. When World War II began, communist parties in Europe had applauded Poland's occupation by German and Soviet troops. Only when Hitler invaded the Soviet Union did communist forces in occupied countries begin their armed attacks against the Axis.

Yugoslav and Greek nationalist underground forces had continued their resistance after their regular armies had been defeated by German and Italian troops. Now the communists joined the nationalist forces. Civil war in the Balkans was still a ways down the road.

In the spring of 1941, Yugoslav underground units were mounting sporadic hit-and-run attacks in areas around Fiume and beyond. We high school students, as members of paramilitary organizations, were called to patrol the streets of Fiume. When it was my turn, I donned my navy paramilitary uniform and reported for duty. Four of us were issued long Carcano rifles, similar to the one allegedly used by Lee Harvey Oswald to kill President Kennedy in Dallas. We received white ammunition belts but no ammunition. I questioned this procedure but was told that our officer, also a civilian in military disguise, was armed. He had a miniscule pistol that he showed us with great pleasure and pride.

We were scheduled to be on patrol for several hours. To our chagrin, we discovered that we were assigned to the outer edge of our city where none of the girls were likely to see us. We began our rounds and stopped a few pedestrians who dutifully showed us their ID cards. Then, our five-man patrol challenged a man in his 20s who looked a bit disheveled. For the occasion, we assumed a firmer, sterner attitude to better project the authority that went with our mission. He reached for his ID card but, instead, pulled out a large handgun, ran around the next corner and opened fire. The five of us ran for cover as fast as we could. The assailant's gun barked like a large mastiff. When our leader returned fire, his mini pistol sounded like the petulant cough of a Chihuahua. Here we were, four men with long rifles, cowering behind a wall and hoping that our assailant would run for safety rather than relieve us of our impressive-looking, useless weapons.

When we returned to the barracks, I told the man in charge not to bother calling me again because I would not come unless we were issued live ammunition. I heard later that they stopped those useless night patrols. In my mind, I blamed the usual Italian way of doing things half-heartedly, such as arming people but withholding the ammunition. It turned out they were not the only ones. Many years later, some Arabs drove a truck loaded with explosives near a major U.S. military installation in Beirut, Lebanon. The sentries challenged the driver. When the truck failed to stop the sentries could not open fire as they had not been issued ammunition for their rifles "in order not to offend the local population." Rifles yes, ammo no. The local population could see rifles but had no way of knowing that the guards had no ammunition. Hundreds of Marines were killed in the blast. I will never understand these finer points where diplomacy and the military intersect.

In the spring of 1941, the city of Fiume and its surrounding areas were running out of food as the Yugoslav underground was tightening its stranglehold. Eventually, the order was given to evacuate the city, so Dad took us to Bologna where we spent the next few weeks. In Bologna, there was no school, no choir, no sports, no Saturday dances, no nothing. How boring! Finally, we returned to Fiume. There were no signs that there had been any fighting within the city. All seemed normal. It was probably an instance where the authorities preferred to overreact than to be caught flatfooted.

School started at an accelerated pace. Now teachers had to cover the same subject matter but had less time to do so because of the weeks everybody had been out of town. Thus, they began to cover more and more material, loading us with more homework. We protested, the principal intervened, and the pace slowed down—for a little while.

We choir members had bigger worries. We were all good students and our city choir had been preparing to go to Rome for a national choral contest. Because we had lost weeks of practice, we almost didn't make it. Mercifully, the judges granted us an extension. When they returned, they gave us a passing grade. So, the trip to Rome was on! Our choir, all one hundred of us, got ready. We had our uniforms washed and pressed. Each choir member had a small suitcase whose contents should last us for the duration. The actual contest in Rome involved two steps: A total of 72 choirs from all over Italy would compete. The top 50 percent would stay in Rome for the great spectacle while the bottom half would return home before the event.

When we got to Rome, we were housed in very impressive old palaces near the Vatican. On the day of the contest, we were wound up as tightly as violin strings. We marched to the building where the contest would take place. I remember, as we marched through the streets of magnificent Rome, that we felt like soldiers about to go into combat. We loved each member of the choir as never before, the boys as well as the girls. After all, we had to depend on each other because we would either win or go under together. We had to await our turn and time was oozing away like molasses. Finally, someone came out and called, "Fiume!" Our choir director looked at us. No commands were given as we fell in line, marched into the auditorium, and climbed up the steps. First came the girls: the sopranos, followed by the altos, and then the boys: the tenors and then the baritones. Last came us basses, who formed the foundation, the background, and lent harmony, support, and emphasis to what the rest of the choir was singing.

We went through our repertoire in a daze. Before we knew it, it was over. We had our chance and now we had to await the verdict. Our choir director seemed confident.

"You certainly did a fine job. Usually, at the end of a piece of music, you would come down a note or two. Today, you actually ended up higher than the key you started in. You did well. Indeed, you did very well."

As I recall, we placed second, after Trento. We had every reason to be proud. When we first arrived in Rome, we had rehearsed at the Terme di Caracalla. You may recall the first concert in Rome by the Three Tenors, Domingo, Carreras, and Pavarotti—that's where they sang. Now, having survived the contest, we started rehearsals at the Foro Mussolini, a modern stadium built in the style of Greek or Roman stadiums rather than their modern equivalents. It was large, full of statues at the top, with tiers of marble steps. We marched twice daily from our dorms to the stadium and back. We were so thirsty and the water pitchers in the dining room so small that the boys would steal each other's glasses and drink the water before the victim could do anything about it. I was not going to steal anybody's water but I was not going to let anyone drink my water either. So, as soon as we sat down at the table I would spit into my glass, making sure that everyone saw me do it.

Two unusual events happened during our stay in Rome. One day, as I walked into our dorm, one of the boys was reading aloud from a newspaper. An assassination attempt had been made against King Victor Emmanuel III during his visit to Albania. One of the boys yelled, "Let's get the Albanian!" Several others turned toward me, ready to jump me. I pulled back into a corner of the room and pulled my dagger. Daggers were part of our uniform.

While those nearest me hesitated, another boy yelled, "Let's not be stupid. The newspaper says that the assailant was a Bulgarian, not an Albanian."

Phew, that was a close one. Shortly thereafter, when I returned to Albania, it turned out that the assailant had indeed been an Albanian but that the press had called him a Bulgarian so as not to give the impression that the Albanians did not love their king!

The other event took place on a Sunday. Of the 3,600 choir members that had survived the contest, about 3,300 went into town while the remaining 300, all boys as I remember, went to Mass at St. Peter's Basilica. I was the only one from Fiume.

As Mass started, a priest walked by. One of our clowns approached him and asked with a grave demeanor, "Would it be possible for us to see the Holy Father?" We could have killed the b.....d! He had chosen to attend Mass. Could he not be serious for once? Well, to our great surprise, at the end of Mass the priest returned.

"The Holy Father is expecting you."

We could have fainted. Dazed, we followed the priest. He walked us across St. Peter's Square and into a side entrance. A Swiss Guard in uniform, with helmet and halberd, stopped us while an officer, in a black uniform with a ruffled white collar and a sword at his side, opened a hidden cabinet, pulled out a telephone, and announced our arrival. I felt let down when I saw him use the telephone. I would have expected him to send a messenger on horseback, in keeping with the surroundings.

The officer took one look at us and asked us to leave our daggers with the guard. Then he changed his mind and had a guard lead our group up some marvelous flights of steps. We were agog. Many frescoes we had been studying in our Art History class were right here before our eyes.

Eventually, we reached the second floor and—to our surprise—stepped out into some beautifully kept gardens full of luxuriant trees, bushes, and flowers. The guard then handed us over to a major-domo who led us into a corridor. He stopped in front of a roly-poly man who could not have been over 5 feet 4 inches tall. He looked unimpressive, even though he wore a purple cassock with a gold cross on his chest. In a squeaky voice, he directed the major-domo to lead us into the small reception hall.

I looked down at him from atop my 6 feet 2 inches and commented, "There are three hundred of us."

In his squeaky voice he replied that the large hall was for 2,000 couples. I later learned he was Cardinal Maglione, the Vatican's secretary of state!

As we entered the small reception hall, the décor overwhelmed us. The carpet was crimson red. So were the silk walls. The chandeliers were all of crystal, the papal canopy purple silk and gold. We youngsters, including our officers, took up about one third of the reception hall.

Then the pope entered. Pope Pius XII, born Eugenio Pacelli, was tall and ascetic looking, dressed in white from head to toe. He seemed to glide rather than walk. He looked at us and acknowledged our presence with a slight nod. Then he walked toward our officers and started to talk with them. I was bursting with envy that they had a chance to speak with the pope. Then, Pius XII started walking along the rows of choir members and exchanged a few words with each and every boy. Finally, he was approaching where I stood. I was the last of the basses and next to me was the first tenor, a little squirt who was not yet shaving. The pope stopped in front of me, gave me his hand, I knelt down and kissed the papal ring.

"When are you leaving?" he asked.

"Tuesday, Holy Father."

He moved on and asked the tenor, "How old are you, my son?"

"Fifteen, Holy Father."

The pope shook his head murmuring to himself. "Too young, much too young."

I heard his comment but it did not make sense. We were not too young to sing in a choir! The more I thought about it, the more the pieces of the puzzle started falling into place. The priest whom our clown had approached at Mass had probably mistaken our attire for military uniforms. Here were hundreds of soldiers who on Sunday, instead of following more worldly instincts, had come to Mass. Furthermore, they were hoping (praying?) to have a chance to see the pope. When word reached the Holy Father, the latter decided to make room in his busy schedule for such unusual visitors. This would explain why he considered us "too young"; not too young to sing in a choir but too young to go to the front to face the brutality of war.

That afternoon, when the rest of the choir members returned from their visit to Rome, those of us who had gone to Mass had something to tell them!

Finally, the day came for the great performance. At the Foro, we were across from the tribune meant for the authorities, too far away to recognize Mussolini when he entered the stadium. We could tell, though, because the trumpets blared and all heck broke loose. We performed, all 3,600 of us. Eventually the performance drew to a close, and we returned to our dorms tired and with a certain sense of letdown now that it was over.

The next day, I said farewell at the railroad station. They were returning to Fiume while I was going to Albania. Just as I was hugging the girls goodbye, word reached us that the choir from Trento had been disqualified and we were declared the winners of the 1941 national choral contest. This was the perfect occasion for a tired "Yippee!"

CHAPTER SEVEN

IN FOREIGN POLICY:
NO FRIENDSHIP, ONLY COMMON INTERESTS

The summer vacation of 1941 was not bad at all. In Tirana, I had now a group of friends, including some girls, who were fun to be with. We went on picnics, took bicycle rides, and had a good time. I had finished the 11ᵗʰ grade with high marks and did not have to worry about studying during the summer. So I enjoyed myself as I looked forward to my senior year. After that I knew I was college bound, but what would I study? The answer to that question still lay immersed in fog. At that point, however, I felt there was no need for me to worry too soon.

That summer, Dad decided to teach me an important lesson. Many Albanians were pro-German. I, in particular, shared such feelings as I grew up in Austria. This pro-German stance went back to the fact that Germany and Austro-Hungary were historically interested in Albania, in its language and traditions, and had stood up for Albanian rights. Russia, since the days of the tsars, had seen herself as a defender of the Slavs in the Balkans. The French had a strong foothold among the Slavs as well as in Greece. The only non-Slavic and non-Greek population in the area was the Albanians. Hence, a pro-Albanian stance coincided with German and Austro-Hungarian interests.

The Italian government had declared von Panwitz, the German ambassador to Albania, a *persona non grata* because of his ill-concealed lack of esteem for Italy and for the fascist regime. In response to the Italian request, during the summer of 1941 the Germans replaced him with a young career diplomat acceptable to their Italian allies. Upon his arrival, the new German ambassador hosted a gathering of Albanians who were graduates of German or Austrian universities and thus Dad was included. Dad in turn invited the new ambassador to our home and asked me to be present during the conversation—stressing, however, that I should keep my ears open and my mouth shut.

The German ambassador arrived at four o'clock sharp. During the conversation, Dad brought up some serious charges against the Italians. They had imposed the fascist emblems, the *Fasci Littori*, on the Albanian flag while Italy's flag did not display them. They had introduced Italian into Albanian grade schools beginning with the first grade when the young pupils should learn to read and write Albanian. They had arrested teachers of the Albanian language, Albanian literature, Albanian history and geography, and had sent them to a concentration camp on the island of Ventotene off Italy's west coast. According to Dad, if Rome did not repeal these and other similar measures, he could foresee an armed insurrection by the Albanians and perhaps a repetition of the events of 1920 when Italian troops were forced out of Vlora and had to leave Albania for good. I was holding my breath as Dad spoke so bluntly to the German ambassador whose job it was to maintain a good rapport with Rome, considering his predecessor's fate.

Dad and I did not have to wait long for the German ambassador's reply. In his view, there was a big difference between 1920 and 1941. Presently, Italy had several fully armed divisions on Albanian soil. There was a world war in progress and Albanian irregulars would hardly stand a chance against the vastly superior Italian forces. Keep in mind, the ambassador added, that the king of Greece was from the ranks of German nobility and that Germany always had strong feelings of friendship for Greece and its ancient and glorious culture. Despite these strong bonds, Germany had bailed out the Italian war machine when Greek forces repulsed the Italian attack and German units had smashed the Greek resistance in nothing flat. Germany, according to the ambassador, also had strong traditional feelings of friendship toward Albania. If, however, we Albanians unexpectedly endangered Italy's position on this side of the Adriatic Sea, Germany would have no choice but to forget its traditional pro-Albanian feelings and come to the aid of its ally. Dad then changed the topic and the ambassador left shortly thereafter.

"Well," Dad said to me, "did you hear how Germany truly feels toward Albania? You must never forget that it is Germany's duty to defend its interests under any and all circumstances. Friendships are fine between individuals. Between nations there are no friendships, only common interests. It is our duty as Albanians to stand up and fight for Albania. It is also our duty to seek allies to further our cause. But remember this: No one other than us Albanians are duty-bound to love and protect our country's interests. Not the Germans, nor anyone else!"

As I write these words, I am in my mid-80s. Obviously, Dad's words have stuck in my mind ever since.

In September 1941, just before the start of classes, I returned to Fiume and took up residence at Lucio's. School started, my friends were all there, and God was in heaven! The trouble started when our professors began loading us with homework to make up for the time lost the previous year when we had evacuated Fiume. The students in our class protested, particularly the ones with weak scholastic records. Professors promised less homework but soon returned to their old ways of overloading us. Eventually the class decided that a delegation had to speak to our high school principal. They chose three students and asked me to head the group.

Our principal was a very learned and soft-spoken gentleman by the name of Silvino (Little Silvio) Gigante (Giant). The name fit. He was short and thin. As to his last name, the only big thing about him was his nose. It was downright formidable. He was also considered the premier Italian translator of Hungarian authors, like Lajos Szilahy, who were much in vogue at that time. Our principal also happened to be the brother of the governor.

He received us in his office, listened to us impatiently, and stated flatly that ours was a class of asses and that we had to work harder if we wanted to graduate. I rose to my full 6 feet 2 inches, cleared my throat, and expressed surprise that asses had made it to the 12th grade while he was the principal. Furthermore, that we, the class representatives, were good students and had no particular problems coping with our homework, but that we had been charged by our classmates to speak on their behalf. The principal shook his head impatiently, promised he would speak to our professors, and waved us out. Our professors slowed down for a while but by the beginning of December, three months after school had reopened, it was clear that they were going again at full blast.

Our class got together to discuss this most serious matter. After a long discussion, we concluded we had to take drastic steps if we wanted to get the professors' attention. We decided we would go on strike. Under the fascist regime strikes were frowned upon but we felt we had no choice. Once the resolution was taken, we saw ourselves as crusaders fighting for a sacred cause. We picked the day and swore to each other that all of us, the academically strong as well as the weak, would hold hands and stay out together. This was a detail the poorer students insisted on, as they feared that some of us would go to school and leave the others in the lurch. Well, the designated day came. As per our agreement, we gathered in front of our school and then marched off.

That day there was excitement in the air all around us, beyond what we could rightfully expect. We paid no attention to what was stirring and walked as a group to the nearby sea and the piers that lined the seashore. Once we crossed the Rubicon and cast our die, we didn't know what to do with ourselves. That's when our less scholastically inclined schoolmates came to the rescue. They had more experience then the rest as to what one could do if one skipped school.

"Let's go to a bar," they suggested, and to a bar we went.

Nobody challenged us or asked to see our ID cards. We pooled our money and bought a couple of bottles of liqueur. One thing was for sure, we were not a drinking crowd. It took us a while to finish the two bottles but—eventually—we succeeded. By then we were in a pretty good mood. So what should we do now? Someone suggested that we write our names on a strip of paper, put the paper in one of the bottles, and throw it into the sea, the way Robinson Crusoe and other stranded people had done. After all, when we thought of our predicament, a group of students persecuted by bloodthirsty professors led by a micro giant, we were about as stranded as anyone had ever been!

Fortunately, by the time the alcohol fumes and our self-righteousness dissipated, it was time to go home—as if we were returning from school. There I got together with Lucio, eager to tell him how things had gone. He, of course, had known about our plans but not about their execution. I told him all about our adventures. He lay back, listening quietly, drumming the fingers of one hand against those of the other, as he did when he was thinking.

"Do you know that Japan attacked Hawaii yesterday and that both Japan and America have entered the war? Japan, of course, is on our side."

I hadn't heard. We had picked that Monday because it had suited our plans. How were we to know that Japan had chosen the Sunday before to enter the war? "Well, tell me, what happened at school?" I asked. "Did they hold a meeting?"

"Not at all. They took us out and organized a massive rally where the authorities gave the usual speeches but with one difference. They stressed time and again that Japan had never lost a war and that victory was a foregone conclusion."

"Did anyone say anything about our class skipping school?"

"I haven't heard anything, but we will find out tomorrow, in school."

That was not a very consoling fact. One thing was for sure. Our daring gesture had been overshadowed by the Japanese attack. How could the Japanese do this to us?

The next day, school did not go very smoothly. Our Italian literature teacher spoke sternly to us. According to her, we had done something very foolish and the principal and the professors had decreed that we would be suspended for three school days—one third of the class at a time. So, we would all lose three days of instruction and would have to study that much harder. That applied to all students except for one who had come to school when the rest of us had committed that abominable gesture.

So, there had been one traitor among us after all. To make things worse, the teacher told us that he, Gianni Pisano, had taken some oral exams in our absence and had done rather well, better than in the past. That, of course, was hard to believe. More likely than not they had paid 30 pieces of silver to the one Judas among us in the form of easy exams and—what was downright despicable—had done so in our absence. Heaven knows, Gianni needed good grades. As far as we, his classmates, were concerned, he would be an outcast, a pariah, for the rest of the year, which was equivalent to permanent ostracism since we were in the 12th grade and by next summer we would disperse for good.

Soon thereafter, our teacher of Italian literature talked to me before the entire class. She assured me that the "traitor" had strong reasons for coming to school that Monday, December 8, and that he had explained his reasons to her satisfaction. Then she asked me to accede to her wishes and to speak to him again. I knew I could not refuse her. So I told her that I accepted her judgment and would speak to him if there was need to do so but that I could not tell the class what to do. That was a personal decision each student had to make on his or her own. Having made those two points, I felt I had made my stand perfectly clear. The class agreed with me that I had no choice but to do as I had said. As I recall, eventually the ostracism faded away and no harm resulted in the long run.

School was going well, the end was in sight, and a new phase, going to college, lay ahead of me. For the time being, however, I still did not know what I was going to study. I had to make up my mind soon because—whatever I decided—university courses started with a bang. Each school, from agriculture to zoology, and everything in between, started with college courses related to the specialty. General courses, such as language, math, and so on had been covered in high school and were given only if one pursued a degree in languages, math, etc. Dad's friend, Hysen Mushqeta, had offered several acres of land in some Albanian town or village if I studied agronomy and was willing to teach the farmers how to farm scientifically. I had had botany and biology in the sixth grade but did not care for either. I had never had zoology. At this point, I could not see myself studying agronomy. Dad had started out studying engineering but had to quit when the flu epidemic affected his eyes and he was unable to do technical drawings. Thus, he was obliged to switch and chose to study history and philosophy. I was not interested in engineering; history and philosophy also failed to attract me. My maternal grandfather had been a physician. His only son had registered in medical school but had never taken any exams. I did not like the idea of dealing with sickness or death. In fact, while staying at Lucio's, a young man living in our building had hanged himself. Many in our building had rushed to see the poor man's body. Not me! I wanted no part of the gruesome picture. I knew that eventually I would have to make a choice as far as college was concerned, but was not ready to take that step. Soon enough, however, things would take care of themselves.

In school, things were going my way. My grades were high, I was class president, and I was doing well in sports. I was asked to join the high school soccer team. In fencing, I was city champion for my age group in foil and saber. One day our teacher of Italian literature assigned students to work in tandem and present a detailed report on some writer of note. When it was my turn, I was paired off with Valnea. I was to give a biographical sketch of Machiavelli while she would discuss his writings.

Personally, I would have preferred to report on Machiavelli's works. Even after so many centuries, he was colorful and controversial. Well, I would do the best I could with what was asked of me. On the positive side, Valnea and I would work together at the library. She meant a lot to me. We met, of course, in school and we danced together for hours on Saturday afternoons at the "Via Parini Club" but here was a wonderful opportunity to be with her by ourselves.

Well, the sessions at the library were less satisfying than I had hoped. She spoke with warmth of an older classmate who was now attending medical school in Bologna. Well, if that was the way she felt, that was OK with me.

When the day of our presentation came, I was tense and ready to go. Everything went well until my closing sentence. I was prepared to say, "And with him died one of the great men of Italy." Instead, I said "And with him died one of the great men of the great Italy." I could have kicked myself. Italy had occupied my country and here I was lauding "the great Italy"! I can still feel myself blush even after so many years.

In January 1942, Dad came to Fiume to see me. He told me that his best friend, Mustafa Kruja, had become premier of Albania the preceding November and had asked Dad to become secretary of education. So far, Dad had refused. What did I think? Should Dad accept the office?

The Italians had occupied Albania and were striving to assimilate the country as quickly as possible. Years of economic deprivation and the many problems afflicting the Albanian nation of one million inhabitants made the Italian conquest seem benign. Albania's neighbors, Yugoslavia and Greece, had been drooling for years at the prospect of splitting Albania into two halves with the north becoming part of Yugoslavia and the south going to Greece. Italy was having some tough economic times because of the war but, for political reasons, Albania had only a *pro forma* rationing system, no military draft, nor any of the wartime restrictions Italy was enduring. Albania was like a little island bathed in sunshine, except that the favorable living conditions were strictly artificial because they were intended to make it easier for Italy to rule at that point and to assimilate little Albania when the time was right.

Under these circumstances Dad was being asked to join the cabinet. I spoke strongly against such acceptance. Dad had earned a high reputation as a man of intellect and a patriot. He had been jailed five times during the insurrection against the Turks and the war against Albania's neighbors. He had been sentenced to death twice. He had been a political refugee for 15 long and hard years during the rule of King Zogu. To accept now the post of secretary of education would negate his past and turn him into a collaborationist with Italy. Having delivered my response in no uncertain terms, I felt good also because Dad fully agreed with me.

A few weeks after his return to Albania, he wrote telling me that he had accepted the post of secretary of education. In his letter he said that we would discuss this development in detail when I returned home for the summer vacation.

When Dad returned from Fiume to Tirana, his friend Mustafa Kruja said that when he had accepted the premiership he had insisted that Dad should be secretary of education. The Italians had balked but now had given in. King Victor Emanuel III had already signed Dad's appointment as secretary of education. Dad's refusal at this point was not only an open challenge to the Italians but would also put Mustafa Kruja in a most difficult position.

Now, the ball was in Dad's court. Before accepting the appointment, he insisted on three conditions:

1) The Italian language that was being taught from the first grade on would be removed from the curriculum. In grade school students had to learn Albanian. Italian would be taught starting in junior high.

2) All Albanian high school professors who had been sent to a concentration camp on the island of Ventotene would be released and appointed at the pleasure of the secretary of education.

3) Mr. Sestilio Montanelli was the Italian advisor at the ministry of education. Under the previous administration, no document could leave the ministry without Mr. Montanelli's approval and signature. Henceforth, he would act as an advisor and would offer opinions only if requested by the secretary of education.

The Italians accepted and so Dad accepted the appointment. What we did not know at that time was that Jacomoni, viceroy of Albania, had informed Ciano during the previous fall that the cabinet of Shefqet Verlaci had lost its effectiveness and needed replacing. There was a group of patriotic Albanians, meaning Mustafa Kruja and the other refugees during the Zogu regime, who were held in high esteem by the people. The only way to compromise them and ruin their reputation was to entrust the government to them. This information came out only after World War II. At first glance, it might seem as no more than an evil Italian maneuver meant to discredit Albanian patriots. There was more to it. The Italians were trying to discredit a group of potential leaders who otherwise might be able to direct passive and active resistance against the Italian invader. The willingness of Dad and his friends to take over the government was based on their belief that Italy needed stopping from within. To do so, they had to assume the reins of government and risk their personal and family honor and reputation.

After 45 years of communist rule and propaganda, to this day Mustafa Kruja, Dad, and their companions have been branded quislings. Thus, the Italians gained little and Dad and his friends lost a lot. It will be up to Albanian history writers to put them historically in the place they deserve. I am not too optimistic. Marshall Petain in France played a similar role in France. To my knowledge, there has been no major effort to rehabilitate that hero of World War I and the man who tried to do his best for France in World War II.

Meanwhile, our group of classmates continued to dance and have fun at the Bolchi residence on Saturday afternoons. We went together to the opera during the winter season and enjoyed ourselves immensely, listening to great operas sung by Italy's best. It gave us the opportunity to be together, it was musically exciting, and cost very little. Some love affairs within our group flourished, grew cold, and ended. But the friendships even between former young lovers continued unabated. I had been secretly in love with Valnea for years. We had our ups and downs, but neither phase had ever reached blinding heights or depths of despair. Now, somehow, things began to fall into place. Eventually, I asked her for a date and she accepted. As I was going toward our meeting place, I saw Milena who greeted me with a friendly smile, as always. Minutes later Valnea arrived. She had a puzzled look.

"Milena saw me," she said. "She waved and exclaimed, 'Finally!'" Valnea looked me in the eye. "Did you tell her that we had a date?"

"Absolutely not," I replied. "I did see her before I came here and all she did was wave and smile. I haven't told anyone about our date."

Well, that was the beginning. We dated almost every afternoon and competed fiercely with each other in school. To my satisfaction, at the end of the year I beat her by several points. In Italian high schools grades ranged from 10 on down; a passing grade had to be equal to or better than 6. Anything below 6 was a failing grade. As I have mentioned before, according to scholastic tradition, 10 was for God, 9 was for the professors, and 8 was the maximum students could aspire to. Anyone earning an average of 8 received a full university scholarship, all expenses paid. By the end of the school year, it was my good fortune to have earned this grade point average and the scholarship that went with it.

CHAPTER EIGHT

HIGH SCHOOL GRADUATION

Because of the war, at the end of the 12th grade we did not have to take the so-called "maturity exams." Hurray! We students of the two parallel classes celebrated the event with an all-nighter at the house of one of the girls from the parallel class, the class that Lucio attended. The house was on a hill. It was quite large and tastefully furnished. The girl's father was in the military, a superior officer as far as I knew. That evening, we boys wore suits. There was nothing special about that. In school, we all wore shirts, ties, and jackets. I always wore one or the other of my two suits. The girls all wore black smocks in class, some with white collars of various kinds. Tonight they wore dresses, smelled of perfume, and wore nice shoes. As I recall, none of the girls wore jewelry. The evening was a modest event by any standards. We had something to eat and drink, reminisced, spoke little about the future. Reality was finally knocking at our door. My Italian boyfriends were likely to be drafted. And then what? Who would win the war, the Axis or the Allies? The magic of the high school years had come to an end. The bubble was about to burst. We had no choice but to face what was at best an uncertain future.

From my point of view, this was another transition, certainly a major one. But I was young and looked forward to what lay ahead. I was getting ready to leave Fiume once more to spend my vacation in Albania, except that this time I would not return to Fiume but start medical school in Padua. Valnea would study pharmacy also in Padua and as far as I was concerned, that was all that counted.

I had finally decided I wanted to study medicine. My grandfather had been a physician. I had been good in sciences. I liked taking care of people and felt that medical school was right for me. Valnea's father was not a physician. He had attended medical school for several years but never finished. He developed a treatment for tuberculosis and the state had authorized him to have two private clinics, one in Merano and one in Sanremo, where he treated TB patients under the supervision of licensed physicians. I cannot exclude that subconsciously I may have felt that studying medicine would get me into his good graces. Following my decision to attend medical school, when Dad went to the health spa in Abano that summer, he stopped in Padua and met the dean of the medical school. During the conversation, he informed the dean that I would be one of his students that fall. As far as I was concerned, the die was cast.

The time had come, of course, to say good-bye to the Mandarà family. I had spent three years at their home sharing their meals and the bedroom with Lucio. They had been happy ones. Even during my prolonged illness in the 10th grade, Lucio and his Mom had been very good to me and letting go of them was not easy. On the other hand, Mr. Mandarà and I had never been close. We always behaved correctly toward each other but no more than that. When the day came, I packed my modest belongings, hugged Lucio as well as his Mom, shook hands with Major Mandarà (who had been recently promoted to that rank), grabbed my suitcase, and left for the railroad station.

I was returning to Albania with mixed emotions. Scholastically, I had done well, with a grade point average of 8 and hence with a full scholarship in my pocket as long as I maintained a decent GPA. In college, except for the thesis, the highest grade was 30. Eighteen was the lowest passing grade; to keep the scholarship, I had to maintain a grade point average of 24. I knew that Dad would be pleased with my high school GPA even though I would never hear a word of praise from him. On the other hand, Albania was under Italian occupation. Anti-Italian demonstrations had already taken place, some by students, and Dad was secretary of education. I knew his deep enmity toward the occupying power. After all, he had fought all his life against Turks and other enemies of Albania. He had opposed Zogu and had spent 15 years in political exile. Presently, I was deeply troubled. Did his friends and the population at large realize that his being a member of the cabinet was dedicated to fighting the invader from within?

My return trip to Albania was uneventful. That summer we moved to a nice apartment in "New Tirana" (south of the center of town). I helped move clothing and other smaller items to the new location. To do so I had to learn how to drive but that was another plus in my life. Dad's chauffeur took care of that and everything would have been fine except that Mergim, who at that time was all of ten years old, could also drive.

One day Mergim was driving on Tirana's main boulevard when a traffic cop noticed this "midget" behind the wheel of a Lancia car. He made a note of the license plate and showed up at the door of our apartment. Fortunately, it was Mom and not Dad who answered the bell. There stood the policeman with papers in his hands.

"Madame, your young son has been driving your car on public streets. He is much too young to have a valid license. Here is the ticket for the traffic violation. I need to see the head of the family to inform him of this violation and of possible consequences should this happen again."

I am not sure how Mom handled this incident. She never told me the gory details. Somehow, she was able to prevent Mergim from receiving a deep imprint of Dad's right hand where it would have hurt. The incident also marked the end of the young man's driving excursions, including in our apartment's immediate neighborhood.

The second car-related incident makes me blush even today. My brother and I had to drive somewhere. I sat down behind the steering wheel and Mergim sat demurely next to me. I put my driving gloves on, turned the ignition, depressed the clutch, put the car in gear and expected the car to start rolling smoothly. Instead, the car jumped forward and came to a full stop as the motor coughed and died. It had to be another one of those instances when I had released the clutch too soon and the engine had died for lack of fuel. I tried again, but this time I gunned the engine as I released the clutch. Well, the same thing happened again. I sat embarrassed and at the end of my wits. Mergim timidly offered to try his hand. We changed places. To my great satisfaction, the car lurched forward, and the engine died—just as it had done with me.

Mergim looked down, hesitated a moment, and then exclaimed, "No wonder the car won't move! You have not released the emergency brake!"

Sheepishly, I returned to the driver's seat, released the hand brake, and we took off. I felt awful. Here I was, on the threshold of college with all the accoutrements of that lofty state in life, but when it came to driving, I still needed the help of a fourth grader!

As secretary of education, Dad was able to stem to some extent some dangerous Italian initiatives. He reduced the function of his Italian "adviser" to a true advising function. Previously, Signor Montanelli had claimed that to function properly in his capacity, he had to see all documents. Dad changed that. Montanelli would see the documents Dad wanted him to see and would give advice when Dad asked for it.

One day, two of Dad's acquaintances were in his office when Montanelli asked for permission to go to the viceroy's office as the latter had asked for him. Dad agreed and Montanelli left. Dad's friends expressed surprise that Dad held Montanelli on such a short leash. Two years later, Fuad Asllani, one of the two visitors, testified at Dad's trial to give evidence as to Dad's firm behavior *vis-à-vis* Montanelli, who was intended to be the Gray Eminence, the true power at the ministry of education.

Among Dad's visitors, there was also Beso Gega. The Italian Carabinieri had arrested his daughter, who worked as a teacher. Mr. Gega, a pharmacist and a friend of Dad's since the days of the struggle against the Turks, came to ask Dad to release his daughter Liri from prison. Dad started to pull out her dossier when his friend interrupted him.

"Whom do you believe, me or the Italian Carabinieri? Of course, they claim that my daughter is a communist. Lies! She is not a communist, she is anti-Italian, pure and simple."

Dad asked him in return, "Do I have your word of honor as to the truth of what you just told me?"

"Yes," Beso answered, extending his right hand. The two old friends shook hands and Dad ordered that Liri Gega be released from prison. Subsequent events would prove that Liri Gega was among the top communist leaders of that time.

Coincidentally, at about the same time Dad was able to lay his hands on a document issued by the Italian Carabinieri that identified Dad as a communist and asked that he be kept under surveillance on his travels.

During this period, the Albanian professors who were sent to a concentration camp on the island of Ventotene, in Italy, were released and returned home. Before their internment, they had taught Albanian, Albanian literature, Albanian history, and geography and were removed to weaken subjects that could counteract the Italian influence in Albania's school system. One of the conditions Dad had set before he agreed to become secretary of education was the return of these professors. Dad now invited Safet Butka, one of these professors, to dinner. Dad and several of the men in the professor's family had been friends since the days of the war against the Ottoman Empire.

At dinner, our guest accused Dad of collaborating with fascist Italy, Albania's archenemy. I blushed and was ready to react but Dad motioned to me to hold my peace and turned to our guest.

"Safet, I have appointed you to teach at one of the newly opened Albanian schools in Kosova. You are now back in Albania. You can accept the appointment in Kosova or you can join the nationalist resistance. We will both fight the Italians, you from without and I from within."

Teaching in Kosova was a plum as Kosovars welcomed Albanian teachers as heroes. Kosova had suffered for many years under Serb persecution. The unification with Albania had been a dream of all Albanian nationalists on both sides of the border. On the other hand, the resistance against the Italian occupation was solidifying and the desire to join Balli Kombëtar was strong among Albanians favoring the establishment of a republic. As Dad said, the choice was up to professor Butka. Within a year, he would face a crisis that would cost him his life.

The summer of 1942 held a pleasant surprise for me. Dad rewarded me for my success in school with a two-week vacation in Italy. My response was immediate. I chose Abbazia as the vacation spot but Mom objected.

"Abbazia is a place we know well. Abbazia is near Fiume and we spent three years in Fiume. Let's go to Merano or someplace we don't know."

Mom had hit the nail on the head. I wanted to spend the two weeks in Abbazia exactly because it was near Fiume, i.e., near Valnea.

To cut the discussion short, I replied, "Mom, Dad said this is my vacation and I choose Abbazia." I am sure that Mom guessed why I wanted to go there. Having made her objection known, generous Mom consented. Had she known what would follow, she might have continued her efforts for a change of venue.

Another detail of our vacation was the marriage in Bari, Italy, of Petrit to Elena, a young Italo-Albanian woman. Petrit was Mustafa Kruja's oldest son. He had graduated from the University of Grenoble with a degree in engineering and his bride-to-be held a literature degree from an Italian university. Mom, Mergim, and I would travel together with Mustafa Kruja and the wedding party from Bari to Bologna where our ways would part. My parents had not been invited to the wedding, celebrated by the Rev. Lazër Shantoja, a good friend of Mustafa Kruja's and of our family. Mom and Dad thought that perhaps they were not invited because Mustafa Kruja suspected that Dad might object that the wedding be celebrated in a Catholic Church and that Petrit had perhaps converted to the Catholic faith.

Be it as it may, I had other reasons for remembering this railroad trip. When traveling by train, one could pick up simple fast food from vendors while the train stopped for 2–3 minutes at some railroad station. In our case, roasted rabbit and other delights were brought to our first-class compartments and we dined in style. Why not? After all, Mustafa Kruja was prime minister of Albania. In Bologna we spent a night at the Hotel Papagallo that, at that time, was first rate. That afternoon Mustafa gave money to his second-born son Fatos, who had been with us in Fiume in the ninth and tenth grades. Fatos was to buy a watch for me and one for himself, since he had graduated from high school in Zara. I felt somewhat inhibited and bought a Juvenia, an excellent medium-priced watch. Fatos, who felt no such inhibitions, bought a top-of-the-line Movado.

The next morning our ways parted and we three Kortshas left for Abbazia. It was Sunday noon when we arrived. On Sundays no buses ran between Abbazia and Fiume. Instead of spending the rest of the day with Mom and Mergim, that afternoon I rented a bike and scooted to Fiume as fast as I could. That was my first get-together with Valnea on that vacation. She would come to Abbazia Monday through Saturday, often with Lucio. That second—and last—Sunday of my vacation, I rented a bike and pedaled impatiently to Fiume. It was a wonderful vacation for me but not for Mom, who spent most of her time alone with Mergim. Of course, she could always come to the beach to see my friends and me, and did so from time to time. In the evenings Mom, Mergim, and I dined together.

Well, good things cannot last forever. At the end of our vacation, we left Abbazia and returned to Albania where I would spend the rest of the summer. Before the beginning of the academic year I would return to Italy and start medical school in Padua.

As it turned out, I had one more hurdle to overcome. Dad notified me one day that Mustafa Kruja's son Bashkim, his third son, had been suffering for years from stomach pain. Thus far, all medical help had failed to give him relief. Dad had proposed that Bashkim go to Görlitz an der Neisse to see an internist Dad had known in Graz and whom he held in high esteem. Mustafa had agreed and Dad had offered that I accompany Bashkim, who spoke no German. Dad sweetened the pill by telling me that I could take all winter clothing with me and instead of returning to Albania I might want to spend the few remaining days of vacation in Fiume before going to Padua. That clinched it.

Bashkim and I did not get along too well. He was two or three years older than I and at that age that made quite a difference. Furthermore, he was a teaser and I did not like being teased. Before joining him in Ortisei, a mountain village in northern Italy, I had to obtain German visas for the two of us in Rome. I flew from Tirana to Rome and the next day went to the Italian Foreign Office to ask for assistance in obtaining the visas. I was to meet an Italian functionary who would introduce me over the phone to his German counterpart. From then on I would be on my own.

The Italian official did so, and as I was leaving his office he said to me, "Good luck, it will take several weeks before you can get your visa."

This sounded ominous. Where was I to spend those weeks—in Rome, Ortisei, or back in Tirana? I took a cab to the German consulate. The building was impressive. I entered, asked for the visa section, and was shown to the proper office. The secretary announced me to the official in charge. When I entered his office, I found him standing behind his desk. We shook hands and I greeted him in German. If he was surprised, he did not show it. We conversed for a while as I explained the purpose of our trip to Germany. He asked for our passports. Bashkim and I both had diplomatic passports as family members of high government officials.

"Mr. Kortsha, please return this afternoon at 4:00 p.m. for your visas." I tried to hide my surprise in view of what the Italian functionary had told me, and sailed out of the office as fast as I could before the German official changed his mind.

When I returned at 4:00 p.m., only a janitor was around, dusting and mopping. I asked to see the visa officer and the janitor replied that the ambassador had called the entire staff to a meeting and the offices would remain closed until the next day. I insisted on the strength of the German official's assurance that morning, as well as because of my desire to reach

Fiume as soon as possible. Finally, I persuaded the janitor to at least go to the functionary's office and see whether he had left a note for me. The poor man complied and when he came back, he held an envelope in his hand. Inside were our two passports with the German visas and a note in which the official apologized for being unable to hand me the passports in person. He wished us a good trip and a pleasant stay in Germany. The next day, at the Italian Foreign Office, the functionary who had told me it would take weeks to get the visas could not believe his eyes when he saw our passports. I believe this quick turnaround came about because of our diplomatic passports but perhaps, in small part, also because of my flawless German.

Now that I had overcome this big hurdle, all I had to do was to reach Ortisei, get Bashkim, and take the train to Germany. The train ride up to Ortisei was fascinating. The little village was nestled on a mountainside, surrounded by luxuriant bushes, trees, and gorgeous mountain peaks that cradled the village among meadows full of flowers. The very air seemed different, lighter and sparkling. In a sense, it was too bad that I would be there just overnight but I was in a hurry.

I informed Bashkim of my plans, and asked him to pack his bag so we could take the first train to Görlitz. Bashkim replied tersely that he did not intend to travel that far by train without sleeping car accommodations. I was thunderstruck. This did not make any sense. He had never traveled in such luxury before, not even recently, when his older brother had gotten married. Furthermore, I was there to do him a favor—and I wanted to leave promptly. Did that not matter at all?

Obviously, Bashkim was in no hurry to go to Germany. The next morning I contacted a travel agency in Bolzano and learned that there were no beds available on trains bound for Germany for at least a week. Had it not been for my Dad, I would have told Bashkim to go fly a kite. Now I had no choice but to settle down and spend a few days in Ortisei. It did not take too long to discover why Bashkim was in no hurry. The daughter of the innkeeper where we stayed was young, healthy, and full of good will toward Bashkim who did not seem to mind. Besides admiring the scenery that was magnificent, there was little else for me to do. I climbed a few paths, read a little, and one day decided to go to Bolzano to talk to the travel agency and to get a haircut.

At the travel agency, I learned there would be no sleeping car accommodations in the foreseeable future. However, since we traveled in first class, securing seats shouldn't be a problem. As far as I was concerned, that did not sound too bad and might get Bashkim off dead center.

When I entered the barbershop, the barber was engaged in animated conversation with another man. There were no other customers in the shop. The barber motioned that I take the chair near him. I sat and waited... and waited, and waited. I had spoken in Italian but noticed that he was speaking to his friend in German. I got the general idea. After all, this was what the Germans called the South Tyrol. I turned and spoke in German, indicating that I was in a hurry. The barber's eyes lit up. He immediately gave me his full attention and did a fine job. I had to suppress a smile. Speaking German had done wonders for me at the consulate in Rome and now it served me well at the barbershop in Bolzano.

I returned to Ortisei and when I notified Bashkim that there would be no sleeping car in our future, he agreed to leave promptly for Germany. I did not know whether this was a good or a bad omen as far as the innkeeper's daughter was concerned. Frankly, I did not care. A day or two later we went to Bolzano and boarded the train that—via Vienna—would get us to Halle where we would board another train for Görlitz. I was carrying a very heavy suitcase full of summer and winter clothes because I would proceed first to Fiume and then to Padua without returning to Albania in between. I was young and vigorous and a heavy suitcase was just a reminder that, after Görlitz, I would again be a free man. The suitcase was not that heavy, after all.

Our first-class accommodations were very comfortable. Third-class compartments had wooden bench seats for eight passengers. Second-class passengers sat on upholstered seats, also eight to a compartment. In first class, the upholstered seats were of deep red velvet, very comfortable, and intended for only six passengers per compartment.

When the train stopped in Vienna, a beautiful young woman boarded the train. As fate willed it, she entered our compartment and her chauffeur placed her suitcases overhead. She sat herself across from us going to great length to ensure that we realized that she was not even aware of our presence. That did not last long. Bashkim, who spoke no German, tried Italian and French, and did his very best to engage her in conversation. I must say he got her attention and, eventually, she even gave him a luminous, beautiful smile.

I turned the other way and tried to catch a few winks. I woke up when Bashkim was struggling to get her heavy leather luggage off the overhead rack. Too bad, the beautiful siren had reached her destination and our compartment would plunge into deepest darkness once she left. As far as I was concerned, the darker, the better. All I had on my agenda was sleep. Bashkim settled down with a content smile that might have indicated that he had reached whatever goal he had set for himself.

I woke up the next morning having slept in relative comfort. I wondered how we would be able to buy food in Germany during our stay. Usually, when I traveled from Albania to Italy, it would take several days until I got my ration cards. In the interim, I was a welcome guest of the black market, i.e., I ate at restaurants and paid the waiter something extra under the table. Early that morning, a railroad conductor asked for our names. He confirmed that we were going to Görlitz, and handed me two sets of ration cards, each for three days, to bridge us over until we could get the regular visitor's ration cards in Görlitz. No doubt, the Germans were well organized.

In daylight, I could see that our railroad car was near the end of the train. When the train stopped, we were too far away to read the name of the railroad station. By the time we got rolling, we were going too fast to catch the name of the station. I decided to go in search of the conductor to ask when and after how many stops we would reach Halle. It took me a while to get the information I needed. Halle was our third stop. According to schedule, we would get there by 10:30 a.m. By the time I returned to our railroad car the train had stopped in the middle of nowhere. Bashkim was dragging his suitcase to the exit.

"Why do you want to get your suitcase off the train?"

"We are in Halle," he replied.

"No, we are not. Halle is three stops from here. Don't get your suitcase off the train." While we were carrying on this conversation, the train started to move. I asked, "Where is my suitcase?" Through the window, I could see my beautiful blue-striped, cloth-covered suitcase getting smaller and smaller as the train gained speed.

I was incensed. "What gave you the idea we were in Halle?"

Bashkim had seen some men working along the railroad track and had asked "Halle?" and they had nodded. He had lowered my suitcase first and was about to do the same with his. I had also noticed the men working alongside the train. They wore striped black and white tops and trousers and had the big letters KG on their uniforms. KG stood for *Kriegsgefangener*, which means "prisoner of war."

Now I might never see my suitcase again. I had to speak with the station chief in Halle and did so as soon as we arrived. He was recognizable by his red cap. I explained my predicament. We went to his office from where he called his colleague at the station where Bashkim had unloaded my suitcase. "*Ja, ja*...They are just delivering your suitcase to my colleague," he explained to me. I whispered to him that we would wait for the suitcase in Halle. He shook his head and spoke into the phone.

"Please, forward the suitcase to Görlitz. The traveler will pick it up at the railroad station there." Then he turned to me and said, "You proceed to Görlitz as planned. The suitcase will reach you in a couple of days." He marched out of his office and that was that.

Bashkim and I did as we were told. We took the next train to Görlitz. We arrived on time and took up two rooms at a hotel not far from the station. Now all we had to do was keep the appointment at the hospital, meet with the police official in charge of foreign visitors, and get our ration cards. Of course, we also had to retrieve my suitcase, assuming that it ever got there.

I started our activities with a visit to police headquarters. A police lieutenant received me and we talked politely about the purpose of our visit, our intention of staying in Görlitz until my travel companion had completed his medical tests, and our return to Italy once the medical evaluation was completed. Before the end of the conversation, the lieutenant gave me ration cards for nine days and asked that Bashkim come to his office the next day. I agreed but added that I'd better come with him as he did not speak German.

Unexpectedly, the lieutenant snapped, "But he must speak German."

I snapped right back. "*Herr Leutnant*, he must speak Albanian. He may speak German, Italian, English, or whatever, but only Albanian is a 'must' for him." I saw myself out of his office and never again crossed the threshold of police headquarters, and neither did Bashkim. For the record, we did not receive a summons to go to this office.

After a couple of days, we went to the railroad station to see whether my suitcase had arrived. My name did not appear on the list of people waiting for their luggage. I explained to the clerk that I had not sent the suitcase through regular channels but hoped to receive it here in Görlitz as the station chief had assured me in Halle. The clerk took me to the luggage deposit and there, big as life, was my suitcase. The clerk remarked that it was against regulations for an unlocked suitcase to be sent via the Reichsbahn. I reminded him that the suitcase was dropped off by mistake and that I had kept it unlocked on the train to have access to the contents. That made sense to him. Next, he asked me to describe the top layer inside the suitcase. Once he was satisfied that I was the legitimate owner, he closed the suitcase and took it to his office. Here he began lengthy calculations and informed me that there was a surcharge as the suitcase had not been mailed according to regulations. I cast a long and meaningful glance at Bashkim when I saw the clerk work with three-digit figures.

When the clerk was done, he looked up and said, "That will be two thirty-four."

"You mean, two marks and thirty-four pfennige?" I asked.

"Yes," he replied, "that's correct." I could not believe my ears.

"In Italy," I said, "I might have gotten a thank-you note from the person that had absconded with my suitcase. Had I known this was the way you handled luggage in Germany, I would have dropped mine off at the Brenner Pass and mailed it to Görlitz."

"Why didn't you?" he replied. I gladly paid the paltry charge and took my suitcase back to our hotel.

Things at the hospital went according to plan. Bashkim and I presented ourselves at the appointed times and everything—all tests and medical exams—went as scheduled. We were done three days earlier than we had allowed for and took the train back to Italy, having stuffed ourselves with the goodies for the extra days our ration cards had entitled us to. The trip was uneventful and we made it to the Brenner on time. We crossed without difficulty and separated on the Italian side of the border. Bashkim returned to Ortisei and I was on my way to Fiume. I regret to say that the medical visit in Germany did not help Bashkim's stomach problems. On the positive side, Bashkim and I separated without a serious clash.

I had done what Dad had asked of me and now I was a free man, in charge of my destiny, on my way to Fiume and then to Padua where I would start medical school. I expected that college life would be very different from what I was used to but I felt confident that I could handle just about anything that lay ahead.

CHAPTER NINE

MEDICAL SCHOOL IN PADUA

The days in Fiume passed as quickly as a dream, a happy dream turned into reality, a reality that would continue in Padua but on a higher plane. Leaving the Mandarà family was not easy. I would miss Lucio, who was not coming to Padua. He promised that he would show up from time to time and that made parting less difficult.

I left for Padua before Valnea did, and checked in at the Casa dello Studente. This was a neat four-story building, with its own cafeteria and a basketball court. The first impression was good. My room number was 234, easy to remember. The first meals were not bad. Within days, the food got worse and worse and I finally stopped eating there, even breakfast. There were also some strict house rules. No outside male students could visit "inmates" after 10:00 p.m. Girls were not allowed in the dorms, not even during the day. No hot plates were permitted in the rooms, and there were a few more don'ts that escape me now.

My room was on the second floor and was comfortable and relatively big. It had a large window from where I could see the basketball court and the main street in front of the building. I had a sofa that turned into a bed, a desk with several drawers and a lamp, an office chair, a couple of other chairs, and a bookshelf. The washbasin with hot and cold running water and a toilet were recessed in a closet behind a door. There was also another closet where I stored my clothes and the rest of my belongings. Hired help cleaned our rooms.

I obeyed most rules except the one about hot plates. The food at the Casa dello Studente was plain miserable and I needed to prepare breakfast. I also wanted a hot cup of soup for dinner and some food I smuggled in from the outside, which needed reheating. Beside, Mom sent me packages that included sausages, coffee and tea—things that were practically unobtainable with ration cards. My hot plate became a true necessity.

My main meal was at noon and always at a restaurant, though not always at the same restaurant. The reason for this was simple. New customers were treated better. After a while, the helpings declined in both size and quality. Changing restaurants was, therefore, my response to this common practice. It resembled the moves and countermoves of German and Allied forces such as the German submarine "wolf pack" attacks that sank hundreds of Allied supply ships a month and the Allied response by sea and by air that eventually blunted and destroyed this formidable German weapon. Maybe my moves and countermoves had less impact than naval warfare, but in my case it too was a question of survival.

Coffee at that time was a rare commodity. I gave coffee to waiters under the table. They, in turn, brought me bigger and better helpings by hiding a second slice of meat under the noodles or the vegetables on my plate. Once I brought my favorite waiter a pair of bicycle tires from Albania and he repaid me with bigger and better helpings for months. Bicycle tires were practically unavailable on the open market.

I was told to make two visits upon my arrival in Padua. The first was to a government office. I looked up someone whose name had been given to me and when we met, he bid me welcome and gave me an envelope with some ration cards that would bridge me over until I got my regular coupons. Delicately, he had placed the cards inside an envelope. When I returned to my room, I looked at the contents of the envelope and was flabbergasted. In addition to food coupons that I needed right away, there were coupons for clothing articles such as shoes, leather gloves, shirts, and the like—well beyond those covered by regular ration cards. I could have sold the coupons or exchanged them for personal favors. Instead, I simply put the envelope in my desk drawer, used some coupons for personal needs, and forgot the rest.

Dad had also stressed that I meet with Professor Bucciante, our professor of anatomy. I called for an appointment and went to see the professor, who was in his office wearing a white hospital coat. He rose and greeted my very courteously, showed me around the lab, and then asked me a question.

"What do you call the liquid portion of the blood?"

I had no idea.

Next: "Do you know the difference between plasma and serum?"

Again, I drew a blank. I wonder what conclusions he drew from my lack of knowledge. Blushing, I shook his hand and left, feeling less assured of myself then when I had first entered his office.

Valnea soon joined me in Padua and things began to fall into place. To go from one lesson to the next I had to walk to the various buildings. Those of chemistry, physics, histology, and biology were close to the Casa dello Studente, while anatomy and related matters were taught at a building complex quite a distance from where I lived. At noon, Valnea and I had lunch together and spent afternoons studying together or separately until fairly late at night.

I decided to take the colloquium of osteology (oral exam on the skeleton) as soon as possible and get ready to take the exams of chemistry and physics in June. Over the summer, I would study histology and biology and take the exams in September. That would bring me up to date with my class schedule and scholarship requirements.

We Albanian students spent little time together except in class at the end of lectures. One day, as we were exiting from an anatomy class chatting with one another, an Italian student approached and told me to stop speaking in my native tongue and to use Italian. The Italian authorities had forbidden the use of Slavic languages on campus but certainly not Albanian, since we shared a king with Italy. I pointed that out to him but it seemed to make no difference. He gave his books to another student and I did the same. At the same time I told my friends in Albanian that, one on one, I could take him. If other Italians joined in, I expected my friends to come to my help. Then some Italian students intervened, restrained and pushed my opponent away, and I thought that was the end of that.

Well, it was not. Valnea and I were at lunch at a restaurant when he showed up with three or four other students. I rose as I could better defend myself standing up and placed myself so I could easily grab our long-necked water bottle—just in case. Well, the Italian students approached us, pushed him forward, and he stammered a lame apology. This was not what I had expected. I tried to keep a poker face, and after a few moments of silence, I accepted his apology and the group left. Why they insisted on his apologizing and who was behind the whole thing I never found out. I was relieved because I had not cherished facing four or five attackers in front of Valnea.

I had another restaurant adventure soon thereafter. Valnea and I were having lunch at another restaurant that was practically empty when a young second lieutenant made a grand entrance, looked around, and then came to our table.

"As there are no other free tables, I will sit here with you," he said. I didn't quite know how to react or what was on his mind. I soon found out.

"I just returned from the front," he volunteered. "I have seen quite a bit of combat and am glad to be back in Italy."

Now I understood. Here was a war hero who was seeking well-deserved admiration from Valnea. He held the stage for several minutes. He spoke of military preparations, of actual attacks against the enemy, dropped a few names of generals, and wound up mentioning a few of the glorious deeds his troops had accomplished under his command.

Both Valnea and I sat in silence during his soliloquy. I didn't know how she felt. I for one was at a loss for words, at least for the moment. Then something struck me. I recognized his divisional insignia on his lapels— and now it was my turn.

"Wasn't your division one of the first, if not the first, to cross the border into Greek territory?"

He nodded with pride.

"But wasn't it also your division that was forced back by the Greeks? In fact, didn't soldiers of your division, once you reached Lake Ohrida, jump into the water seeking to hide from your pursuers?"

The lieutenant began to squirm.

"And isn't it true that it turned into some kind of turkey shoot as the Greeks picked off the poor Italian soldiers when they came up for air?"

None of this had appeared in the Italian, or for that matter, Albanian press. I had heard these details from our relatives who had fled Korça. Now I had the chance to use the information to my advantage. The lieutenant did not know what to answer. He blushed, rose to his feet, turned around, and left without a word. I enjoyed the scene immensely.

Valnea looked at me and said, "Military uniforms have never impressed me." And that was the end of that.

Dad had asked for a monthly expense account when I was in high school. He still wanted it now that I was in college, with the exception of 100 lire that I did not have to account for. I guess he was making allowance for the fact that now I would be dating. Actually, 100 lire a month was quite a bit of money if one considers that lunch in a good restaurant was around seven lire, tickets to the movies cost about the same, and even opera tickets were only slightly more, at least for the seats that we students tended to go for. Other Albanian students, who spent more than I did on girls and fun in general, had complained to me more than once that the scholarship was inadequate and that I should talk with Dad about giving me more money. Actually, I had no money problems. I received the same stipend as everyone else. By the end of the school year, I had saved 11,000 lire and bought myself a microscope with three objectives and two oculars and took it with me to Albania.

Just before Christmas, I made arrangements to spend my vacation in Albania. It turned out to be quite a trip. My train was scheduled to leave Padua at "00:00 hours" and I interpreted that to mean 1 a.m. Luckily, I was already at the station when the train pulled in just before midnight, jam-packed with passengers. All I could see from below were people crammed together like sardines, including at the entrance and exit platforms.

Somebody yelled from above, "Reach up the suitcase; we'll stack it with the rest in the toilet."

I lifted up one suitcase and somebody grabbed it. When I pushed up my second bag with the gifts for my family and friends, an arm shot out of the crowd and pushed it down. On the sleeve was a full colonel's insignia. I pushed the arm aside, somebody took my bag, and I climbed aboard. The man who had tried to push my bag down was staring at me. He was short, rotund, and in his fifties.

"Do you know who I am?" he asked me.

"Yes," I replied, "You are a colonel."

After a moment's hesitation, he asked again, "Do you know who I am?" He seemed taken aback by my reply but said nothing. Had he asked, I would have told him I was a medical student.

The train took off on schedule at midnight, at 00:00 hours! As the train rattled along, we passengers swayed to and fro but eventually found enough room for our feet. I kept half listening to my friend the colonel, who was telling us what military academy he had graduated from, what war colleges he had attended, and the like. It was not very exciting stuff but at least it made standing less boring. No lights were permitted for fear of Allied air attacks. As my eyes got used to the dark, I noticed a German soldier who lay stretched out in the corridor just beyond our cluster, his knapsack under his head and his rifle between his legs. He was soundly asleep. I realized that if he stood up like the rest of us, we would be less squeezed together.

"Colonel," I asked, "did you study foreign languages while at the academy?"

"Of course," he replied. "French and German."

"Would you please tell this soldier to stand up and make some room for the rest of us?"

"But...but, he is German," the colonel stammered.

I stretched one foot toward the German soldier and poked him in the shoulder.

"*Steh auf,*" I barked. Without a word, the German soldier stood up, straightened his cap, pushed his knapsack toward the wall, and held on to his rifle. The colonel was dumbfounded. Who was I that the German soldier had obeyed me so promptly? A German officer? I looked awfully young, but then one never knew. The colonel had stopped talking and there was silence for a while. All one heard was the rattling of the train. Now we had a bit more room, which made standing a little easier. What if the German soldier had ignored my words? I really had nothing to lose. After all, I was just a freshman in medical school.

I wish the incident had ended at this point but it didn't. Eventually, a passenger stepped out of the first compartment and got off the train. The colonel turned toward me and with a polite gesture offered me the empty seat. To my shame, instead of asking the older man to sit down, I took the seat and promptly fell asleep. When I woke up, the colonel was gone.

I made it to Tirana without further incidents. My parents and Mergim were in good health and food was aplenty. Our apartment was nice and comfortable. Dad had the same driver and bodyguard as before, and Mom had the same mother and daughter who cooked and cleaned for us. Nothing seemed to have changed. Yet, there was a restlessness in the air that I had not noticed in years past.

The hostility toward Italy and the Italians had become palpable, and so had an incipient resistance that involved many, particularly the young. Armed guerillas, both nationalist and communist-directed, were beginning to strike here and there. While such actions were at a relatively low level, they represented a major change in the Albanian political climate. There was also considerable confusion in Albanian public opinion. Often it was hard to tell whether these actions were done by nationalists motivated by patriotic feelings or by communists, as the latter skillfully used their so-called National Front of Liberation to recruit new members, communists as well as nationalists, ranging from the unknown to well-known personalities.

Two years after exploding in Europe, the world war was still going relatively well for the Axis powers. Yugoslavia had been occupied without much effort and Albanians had seen their lifelong dream of a union with Kosova come true. After the Italian debacle, Greece collapsed, thanks to German intervention. The Italian authorities in Albania had become less sure of themselves, less focused on how to deal with the Albanian problem, probably because of the utter failure of the Italian military—from North Africa and the Mediterranean to Greece and the Soviet Union. It was painfully evident to all, including the Italian people, that Italy could not live up to Mussolini's bombastic claims of being an equal partner of the Tripartite Pact of Rome-Berlin-Tokyo.

By now, the overall balance of the war had begun to shift. The German armies were still deep in Soviet territory, at the gates of Leningrad, Moscow, and Stalingrad. Yet, something was remiss. The Germans seemed to have lost their ability to act with lightning swiftness. Their submarines were no longer sinking Allied vessels at a rate exceeding the ability of the latter to build replacements. British and American bombers were striking day and night at cities and factories anywhere in Europe, despite Field Marshal Göring's early boast that no Allied bomber would ever reach the skies of Berlin.

After World War I, all foreign troops had left Albanian territory except those of Italy that hung on to Vlora and the hinterland. This gave them a strong military footing across the straits of Otranto and provided Italy a stranglehold on the Adriatic. Under pressure by Albanian volunteers under the command of Qazim Koculi, and lacking the support of the Italian parliament, these Italian troops were forced to withdraw. At that point, Mussolini, a Socialist member of parliament, wrote in his diary that he had cried more for the defeat of Vlora than for Caporetto where Austrian troops had inflicted heavy casualties on Italy's armies.

Back to December 1942. The Italian authorities had reneged once too often on promises made to Prime Minister Mustafa Kruja and he and his government resigned. This prompted the viceroy of Albania, Francesco Jacomoni, to fly to Rome to seek a solution that would make the Albanian government reconsider its decision.

As this political crisis was taking place, Qazim Koculi, the hero of Vlora, had gone south to study ways to counteract communist anti-government activities. Here, in a trap set by the Italians with Albanian mercenaries, Qazim Koculi lost his life. Twenty-two years after the debacle of Vlora, Mussolini finally had his revenge. As soon as the news reached Mustafa Kruja, he informed Jacomoni that the resignation of his government was final. Kruja then sent a telegram to the widow of Qazim Koculi saying that she was mourning her husband of so many years, that, he, Mustafa Kruja was mourning his friend of some 40 years, and that the Albanian nation was mourning its hero. Still in power, Mustafa Kruja had the telegram published in the Albanian press. The telegram stressed three points: The Koculi family had suffered a grievous loss, he had lost a personal friend, and Albania had lost the hero who had chased the Italians into the Adriatic. Undoubtedly, the Italians took note of it. As was customary, each cabinet member was awarded a medal and could pick his next job—every member, that is, except Dad who received no medal and returned to his previous job as member of the state council.

In January 1943, I met Luan Gashi who was studying engineering at the University of Padua and had just returned from Albania. He started to tell me that the National Front (*Balli Kombëtar*) was striving to better organize the nationalist resistance against the Italians. The organization was led by eminent Albanians under the leadership of Mid'hat Frasheri, the son of a famous nationalist family. I liked what I heard. It was in line with what Dad had taught me all my life and so with pride and joy in my heart I joined the ranks of the nationalist resistance movement. Luan promised he would keep me abreast of further developments and would ask me to become active if there was a need. I was very pleased because other students whom I held in high esteem, such as Karl Harapi, Rustem Buzo, and others, were also part of this group.

It was now the spring of 1943. Almost the whole school year had passed in a hurry and I was just weeks away from the upcoming exams. My routine between studies and what little fun I allowed myself was pretty much established. Studying took up most of my time and in between, Valnea and I spent time together. During the week, we had lunch together. On Sundays, we attended Mass at Saint Anthony, Padua's beautiful cathedral. Twice we went to the opera and enjoyed the marvelous music and the beautiful God-given operatic voices of the performers.

Then I got a message that Dad would stop in Padua on his way to the thermal spa of Abano. That was an unexpected development. I told Valnea it was likely we would not see each other for a few days. Meanwhile, I preferred that she stay home as I thought it was best that his path and Valnea's not cross. I did not recognize how silly this was of me. Valnea did, and promptly defied my request by spending the evening with our high school companions Milena and Nuccy, I soon found out.

That afternoon, I went to the railroad station to pick up Dad. We chatted easily as he and I always got along well. I had the greatest respect and love for him. He was my dad, the man I wanted to pattern myself after! At some point during our conversation and out of a blue sky, Dad asked, "Are you still dating that girl from Fiume?"

"Yes," I stuttered in reply.

"Good, I would like to meet her. Why don't you invite her to join us tomorrow for breakfast?" Stunned, I nodded.

We had reached Dad's hotel. I helped him with the luggage, bid him good night, and zipped over to Valnea's. I whistled our whistle and she appeared at her window. I told her the news, and we had breakfast and spent the next day with Dad. It was an uneventful day and there really was no reason why it should have been otherwise.

As it turned out, there would be a parallel event. When Valnea's father came to Padua, he in turn wanted to meet me. He was pleasant, intelligent—and cagey. We were sitting at an outdoor café when he winked at me to keep me quiet. He started to tell us that during World War I his ship had anchored in Durres and he had noticed that Albanians were very dark skinned.

Valnea burst out, "But Dad, those were not Albanians, those were gypsies." He smiled in reply. All he had wanted to know was how strongly she felt about me. He was also interested in how I felt about his daughter. That evening we had dinner in Venice. On the vaporetto going back to the train station, it got rather cool. Instinctively, I took off my jacket and put it around her shoulders. He looked at me but said nothing. He had just gotten his answer.

My studies were going well. I studied hard all year and with good results. I got the highest grade on my oral exam on the skeleton and was on schedule with my preparation for my exams in chemistry and physics. By the time the exams came around, I had studied the physics text of 1,000 pages about seven times and the chemistry book three times from A to Z. Anatomy would present a problem the coming year. Anatomy was a two-year course and I had started with the second-year program, thus lacking the foundation that had been laid during the first year. That would be a problem but there was no need to worry about it now.

In Italy, we had no quizzes, midterms or other exams. The final grade depended on one oral exam taken in public before two or more professors. That morning I registered to take the physics exam. I was third or fourth in line, but military personnel had preference and usually got easier questions. That day, Professor Drigo had flunked every student beginning at 8:30 a.m. until 2:00 p.m., including all the military.

Just ahead of me was a girl with whom I had taken the colloquium of osteology and we had both aced it. Finally, I would see how a good student would fare with Professor Drigo. He tormented her for a while and she finally—and barely—made it. Now it was my turn. I descended the steps of the amphitheater and sat facing two professors with a table between us. A blackboard rested on the table. I was still confident but had lost some of the bounce with which I had entered the amphitheater that morning. The questions started and I made it a point to illustrate my answers with the proper formulas.

Drigo seemed pleased. He asked for an additional formula. I wrote it on the blackboard and Drigo asked me to explain what the symbols stood for. It turned out that I had misunderstood the function of the symbol ε, which I thought was the dielectric constant. Drigo asked for another formula, and again I misinterpreted what ε stood for. Drigo consulted briefly with his colleague, turned around, and informed me that I had earned 28 out of a maximum of 30. In Italy, a student could refuse a passing grade he or she deemed inadequate. I said I would refuse the grade and retake the exam in September.

The professor stared at me and said, "In September I will flunk you."

As the grade for the whole semester depended on that oral exam and satisfied the requirements of my scholarship, I accepted it reluctantly.

The main hospital in Rome had lost a radioactive source and Professor Drigo had built a detector with which he was able to locate the missing source, succeeding where his predecessors had failed. He was sure that now he would be promoted to full professor. When that promotion was denied, he took it out on the students.

In chemistry I knew my stuff but fell short when I was asked how I would remove calcium from water. I said that I would boil the water but the professor asked how I would remove the last traces of calcium. When I could not come up with the answer, he also gave me 28 out of 30. Let me add that a score of 18 was sufficient to pass an exam but I had studied hard and wanted my 30. It was not meant to be. After the exam, I found the answer in a footnote of the chemistry text. I should have added oxalic acid to the water to form calcium oxalate, which is very insoluble.

Having completed the two major examinations I had prepared for, I got ready to return to Albania. With the 11,000 lire I had saved, I bought myself a beautiful microscope so I could better study histology during the summer. In September, in addition to histology, I also expected to take my biology exam to be ready for my second year in medical school in Padua.

Just before leaving, Luan Gashi asked me to buy several reams of paper Balli Kombëtar needed to print anti-Italian leaflets that we would distribute at night throughout Tirana and beyond. It was not a very exciting assignment but I could see that such paper would come in very handy.

One more incident happened at that time. A fellow student approached me to ask a favor. The communist party had ordered him to return to Albania ASAP. Would I take the exams of chemistry and physics for him? After all, he was going to fight for our country. Helping him maintain his university standing in Padua was the least I could do for him. It did not take me long to say "No" to his cheeky request. The gall of it. I was supposed to cheat, lie, and endanger my university standing because he was going to fight for the communists!

After the German invasion of Yugoslavia in 1941, two Yugoslav communist agents, Dushan Mugosha and Miladin Popovic, accomplished what the Albanian communists had been unable to do by themselves. They brought together the three communist factions of Shkodra, Tirana, and Korça that had existed since before World War II, and thus created the Albanian communist party. Later, both agents spent most of the war in the Albanian mountains organizing the Front of National Liberation (FNL) along the lines the Soviets had developed and used so successfully in country after country.

The idea was very simple. The FNL was an organization "of the masses" with room for anyone who was willing to fight side by side with the communists. The communist party and its members formed the backbone of the FNL. They pretended to "share the power" with non-communists of stature and distinction. Such individuals were carefully chosen from among those who were satisfied with the semblance of power, with minor participation in the decision making process, and who did not mind collaborating with the communists. The presence of such individuals at the top gave the communists a semblance of respectability among the "silent majority." The communists, however, were the true movers within the fighting units. They were disciplined and were among the bravest, ready to risk and sacrifice "for the cause." Thus, the communist leadership stood at the helm while the communist troops formed the military backbone, earned the respect of, and led the simple masses into battle initially against the invader, and later increasingly against the nationalists.

Initially, the leadership of the FNL included Major Abaz Kupi, known for battling the Italian troops in Durrës when they first stepped on Albanian soil on Friday, April 7, 1939. He was a staunch supporter of King Zogu who had left him in charge of the royalist forces before fleeing the country with his queen and his newborn son. Initially, the ranks of the FNL had included royalists and other nationalists who opposed the

Italian and German invaders, who believed in an Allied victory, and did not mind working side by side with the communists. Actually, Albanian nationalists were the first to oppose the Italian occupation. They realized that if the Allies were to lose the war, Albania would suffer under Italian rule—who knew for how long. Hitler's Blitzkrieg had stunned and paralyzed Europe at first, but by the time the German troops invaded Albania in the fall of 1943 following Italy's surrender, the fortunes of war had shifted and an Allied victory was only a matter of time.

Events began to take place in rapid sequence. British and American planes kept dropping military supplies and liaison officers to the communists. Abaz Kupi quit the FNL and continued a modest resistance against the Germans while his forces came under communist attack. The nationalist front Balli Kombëtar became the No. 1 target of the communists in line with orders from Moscow. As the German units began their withdrawal from Greece through Albania, Enver Hoxha and his brigades followed in their footsteps. After the communist takeover, many nationalists who had belonged to the FNL, among whom were my uncle Riza Dani and Mozi's father, were executed under one pretext or another. What was left of the FNL became a tool of the communist party.

Albania officially became a satellite of Jozip Broz Tito, who in turn began to orbit around the Soviet sun. Dushan Mugosha and Miladin Popovic returned to Yugoslavia and a newly appointed Yugoslav ambassador replaced them at Enver Hoxha's court. Dushan became a general and Miladin got the top political job in Kosovo.

At this point, the communist troops killed Albanians by the thousands in both Albania and Kosova. Enver of course had a free hand in Albania. The massacres in Kosova did not take place until the Fifth Albanian Attack Brigade "freed" Kosova and disarmed the Albanian population. Then the commander of the Brigade, Shefqet Peçi and his political commissar Ramiz Alia, handed the province and the population over to the Yugoslav communists that decimated the male population. An Albanian teacher in Kosova decided to take revenge and shot Miladin Popovic. The assassination attempt succeeded and both Miladin and the Albanian teacher died in a blaze of gunfire.

In Padua, I said goodbye to Valnea and left for Brindisi, from where I would fly back to Albania for my summer vacation. In Brindisi some Italian officers bumped me and several other civilians off the plane. It turned out that they were anything but eager to reach their assigned posts in Albania while I, reluctantly, had to spend one more night in Brindisi.

Eventually, it was my turn to fly to Tirana. Mom and Dad were awaiting me at the airport. Nobody questioned me about the reams of paper in my luggage. Everything went well and on schedule. Everything, that is, except my plans about studying that summer and returning to Padua in September. In fact, down the road, within 16 months to be exact, my life and that of our family would change beyond recognition.

CHAPTER TEN

COMINTERN AND THE BALKANS

The summer of 1943 went by in spurts, propelled by cataclysmic events. The fortunes of war were turning against the Axis and my hopes of returning to Padua in the fall began to recede inch by inch. United States shipyards were launching more ships than the German U-boats were able to sink and more U-boats were being sent to the bottom of the seas than Germany was able to build and man. This gave the Allies greater freedom of the seas compared to the beginning of the war.

For the first few years, the German Supreme Headquarters had filled the airwaves with triumphant military music and special bulletins announcing victory after victory from Poland to France, from the Balkans to the Soviet Union, from 1939 until 1942. Now the military music and the victory bulletins were gone and German bulletins spoke more and more of "maneuvers intended to shorten the front," a euphemism for "retreats." Since their defeat at Stalingrad and Kursk, the Germans were pulling back all along the Soviet front. Rommel, the brilliant commander of the German 7th Tank Army in France, the Desert Fox who had rescued Mussolini's armies in North Africa, was finally beaten by Field Marshal Montgomery. He was recalled to Germany in the spring of 1943 as American and British troops mopped up what was left of Axis forces along the North African shores. In a speech mourning the loss of Africa, Mussolini said that all Italy was suffering from "the African Malaise." Italian wags immediately responded by saying that the African Malaise could be treated with "English salt," i.e., with magnesium sulfate, a common laxative.

On July 10, 1943, the Allies landed in Sicily. Two weeks later, on July 24, Mussolini convoked the Fascist Grand Council—the highest authority of the Fascist regime—which had not met since the beginning of the war. By a majority vote, the Grand Council decided to remove Mussolini from office. Even Galeazzo Ciano, Mussolini's son-in-law, voted against the dictator. The next day, King Victor Emmanuel III discharged Mussolini from his post of prime minister and had him arrested on the spot.

To keep him out of the hands of the Germans, Italy's new prime minister, Marshal Badoglio, first sent Mussolini to the island of Ponza and later had him sequestered atop the seemingly impregnable Mount Gran Sasso. On September 12, 18 days after Mussolini's arrest, German gliders crash-landed on the Gran Sasso, overwhelmed the Italian garrison, and put Mussolini on a small single-engine plane, nestled between the pilot's feet. There was danger that the plane was too heavy and would not reach takeoff velocity at the end of the makeshift runway. The pilot pointed the plane toward the eastern slope of the Gran Sasso that dropped off sharply, hoping there would be enough space for the plane to drop at first without hitting anything and eventually gain sufficient speed to reach altitude and return to base. The gamble worked. That evening Mussolini and Hitler embraced in Munich.

In Tirana, I was still studying for my fall exams. My hopes of returning to Padua, to my life as a student, were running out like dry sand between my fingers. I felt helpless. One day, I sat staring at my biology book while an Italian radio station broadcast Soviet military music underscoring the narrative of a Russian mother mourning her dead soldier-son. I sat there wondering: How could an Italian radio station glorify the Red Army? Then it hit me. Of course it could—if the radio station was in Allied hands! For someone like me who was strongly committed to the cause of a nationalist Albania, this Allied endorsement of communism was ominous. As part of their strategy, the Allies continued to airdrop liaison officers and significant amounts of weapons, ammunition, and uniforms to the communist-led forces of the Front of National Liberation.

Meanwhile, Western aid to our nationalist forces was doled out with an eyedropper. Didn't the Western Allies see what the communists were up to? Didn't they realize that the communist allegiance to democracy was no more than lip service? Didn't they ask themselves why Mehmet Shehu, the communist butcher, had executed Allied pilots who had sought refuge with the communists because Allied airplanes had mistakenly dropped a batch of left boots without the corresponding right boots? What about Allied pilots and their crews who were shot down and were rescued by our nationalist forces? They were escorted to the Adriatic coast safely where British submarines picked them up. Couldn't the Allies recognize who was on their side and who was not?

There was an obvious answer to such questions. It was clear that the fortunes of war were favoring the Allies and that was precisely what we Albanian nationalists hoped for, since we shared the democratic ideals of the West. Unfortunately, at this stage of the war, the Allies, and particularly the United States, suffered from tunnel vision. They demanded total commitment to the war against Germany, no matter what the cost to Albania. As nationalists, we had to weigh Albanian lives lost and villages destroyed against the potential damage to the German forces. An Albania in ruins and replete with cemeteries was unacceptable to us.

Mehmet Shehu, on the other hand, proclaimed that Albania needed no more than 100 young men and women to survive the war and secure the nation's future. Allied support decisively helped the communist side. As time went by, however, British officers with the communists in the mountains became increasingly aware that the Red attacks were directed mostly against us nationalists, not against the German war machine. Unfortunately, while the war was still on, Allied headquarters in the Mediterranean paid little heed to these officers' warnings from Albania.

In the fall of 1943, our National Front and the communist-led Front of National Liberation reached an agreement at Mukaj. The agreement assigned Albanian villages into nationalist and communist zones and stipulated that Kosova would freely decide its destiny at the end of the war. Two years earlier, in the spring of 1941, Kosova had rejoined Albania after the German invasion of Yugoslavia. Tito, trying to win support from the Kosovars, was promising the Albanian majority that, if they joined his cause, they would be free to vote for independence at the end of the conflict. We, of course, put no faith in Tito's promise, since the Yugoslav emissaries Mugosha and Popovic had received orders to scuttle the Mukaj agreement by any means because of the clause concerning free elections in Kosova.

Nor did we put much hope in the Allied Atlantic Charter. The charter, made public on August 14, 1941, proclaimed that the will of the peoples would be heard and respected after the Allied victory. We remembered only too well Lloyd George's promise to the Armenians during World War I that if they joined the war against Turkey, at the end of the war Britain would favor the establishment of a free Armenia. The Armenians fought bravely against the Turks but were eventually overwhelmed and massacred. The mass killing triggered no Allied action nor was a defeated Turkey held accountable for killing more than one million Armenians. After the war, Lloyd George, British prime minister from 1916 to 1922, repudiated his earlier promise to the Armenians, stating that British naval units could not scale the mountain peaks of Armenia. Such lessons of history were hard to forget.

On September 3, Marshal Badoglio, Italy's new premier, signed Italy's surrender in Sicily in great secrecy. General Eisenhower, Allied supreme commander, officially announced Italy's surrender five days later. Within hours, German forces sprung into action from Sicily, throughout Italy and the Balkans, to the far steppes of the Soviet Union—wherever Italian forces were stationed. German troops occupied Albania with lightning speed. A few days later, we found out that they had entered Albania in such a hurry that their artillery units had little or no ammunition. The bluff worked. The commanding German general gave the Italian troops in Albania three choices. They could join the German armed forces, keeping their rank and pay. They could surrender and be treated as prisoners of war. If they did neither within 24 hours, they would be shot on sight.

Most Italian troops surrendered, and it was quite a spectacle. At the center of Tirana, I saw three German soldiers, two on foot and one behind a motorcycle-mounted machine gun, disarming hundreds of Italian troops waiting in line. The officers were taking off their belts and pistols, and dropping them on the sidewalk. The enlisted men were handing their rifles to the two German soldiers who smashed them against the sidewalk. This did not go on for very long. The soldiers got sore hands and had the prisoners pile the weapons up on the sidewalk.

In Korça, in southern Albania, a day or two later, two German military trucks pulled up in front of the hospital. The commanding officer, a surgeon with the rank of major, notified Dr. Selahudin Mborja, the director of the hospital, that the Germans were taking over one wing of the building. While they were conversing in French, a young lieutenant reported that some soldiers had shot and wounded a pheasant that had limped into a nearby cave. Inside the cave, they stumbled upon two Italian officers. What was the lieutenant supposed to do under the circumstances?

His superior asked tersely, "Lieutenant, can you read?"

"*Jawohl, Herr Major.*" Thus, the major reminded his subordinate that more than 24 hours had passed since the publication of the German edict giving Italian military personnel three choices. The Italian officers had neither joined the Wehrmacht nor had they surrendered. That left only the third alternative. A few bursts of machine gun fire broke the silence and the situation was back on track.

Mussolini, in the meantime, under German protection, founded the Republic of Salò on the shores of Lake Garda in northern Italy. This republic included all Italian territories from south of Rome to the German border. In a sense, this was an ironic turn of fate. In far-away 1922, Mussolini, on his way to Rome at the head of victorious fascist forces, intended to abolish the Italian monarchy. He changed his mind at the last minute and, with his bombastic style the world would soon get to know, he declared to King Victor Emmanuel III, "Your Majesty, I bring you the Italy of Vittorio Veneto," as if Italy's triumph over the Austrian forces at Vittorio Veneto had been his to bring.

Now, 21 years later, Mussolini, deposed by the king, founded the Republic of Salò, willed into existence by the Germans whom Mussolini had dreaded ever since Hitler's rise to power. This republic kept shrinking as the German troops continued their withdrawal toward Germany's borders. Mussolini attempted to flee with the retreating troops wearing a German uniform and accompanied by his mistress Clara Petacci. The Germans and the partisans had agreed that the partisans would let the convoy pass unhindered but reserved the right to inspect the trucks beforehand. The communist guerillas recognized Mussolini and took him off the truck. His mistress asked for permission to stand by his side and both were shot on the spot. It was April 8, 1945. The führer took his own life in his bunker in Berlin three weeks later, on April 30. World War II in Europe ended with Germany's unconditional surrender on May 8, 1945.

The nationalist forces in Yugoslavia, Albania, and Greece had opposed

Italian and German forces from the very first days of the attack by the Axis forces against their respective countries while the communists had sat on their hands for two years and had even favored the Axis for fighting the "plutocracies," i.e., France and Great Britain. The communists joined the battle only after Hitler attacked the Soviet Union in 1941. After the Italian surrender in the fall of 1943, one more factor had a major impact on the Albanian political scene. Following the German defeat at Stalingrad and Kursk, the Soviet General Staff became convinced that the German defeat was only a matter of time. Hence, the communist International (Comintern) ordered communist parties in the Balkans to unleash attacks against the nationalist forces while continuing to fight the Germans, at least nominally.

Their strategy was as simple as it was brilliant. As long as the Soviet Union was one of the Allies, the communists could count on Anglo-American help. On the other hand, the nationalist forces, under attack by the communists, would have to fight simultaneously on two fronts, against the Germans and against the communists. The nationalists would have to scale down their war against the German armies and perhaps even be forced into a *de facto* armistice with them. Should the nationalist forces emerge victorious at the end of the war, they would be tried as collaborationists with the Germans. If they lost against the communists during the civil war, so much the better. For the communists this was a win-win situation. For us it meant certain defeat.

These events played out on the international stage, some of them in secrecy, and would not see the light until decades after the end of World War II. Their impact on the Albanian microcosm will become clear in the following chapters. For the time being, the best we could hope for was to survive and wait for the day when the Allies landed in Albania in hot pursuit of German forces. Then, we had a chance to explain and defend our cause. Until then, we had to defend Albania's interests as best we could, try to swing public opinion over to our side, and fight, fight, fight.

Only Churchill saw beyond the approaching end of the war and tried to persuade the United States and the Soviet Union to land in the Balkans rather than in Italy. Stalin wanted to keep Allied troops out of the Balkans as he was planning to draw the entire region into the Soviet orbit. He handily convinced Roosevelt that the Allied superiority in aviation and armored forces would be much more effective in Italy than in the mountainous Balkans. Roosevelt, in turn, sought to reassure the Soviet Union that the Western Allies did not intend to mount or allow anyone else to mount another surprise attack against the USSR. As proof of good Allied intentions, he was willing to hand the Soviet Union the landmass of central Europe that any aggressor from the west would have to cross before reaching Soviet soil. The Balkans were part of the deal. The Big Three decided that British and American forces would land en masse in Sicily and Italy but not in the Balkans.

Winston Churchill had major misgivings as he recognized the important role of the Balkans in keeping the balance of power in Europe. Some British contingents eventually landed in Greece and fought the communists. By the time American troops took over the anti-communist campaign in Greece, Albania and the rest of the Balkans were securely in Stalin's hands and the Iron Curtain had split Europe in two.

The Balkan communists had their own clear goals. They expanded the civil war by assassinating prominent nationalist personalities throughout Yugoslavia, Albania, and Greece. These daily killings were well planned and effective. Since these hit-and-run execution squads were rarely caught, their actions increasingly paralyzed the government and terrorized the public. In Albania, intellectuals, and particularly the military, refused to take sides, hoping to avoid antagonizing the communists and to emerge unscathed after an Allied takeover at the end of the conflict.

The day came when German forces withdrew from Greece and Albania. The communists, in cautious pursuit, took over most of Greece and all of Albania. When Allied forces asked to land in Albania, Enver Hoxha replied there was no need for such a landing as the country "had been liberated." This was at the end of November 1944. The war in Europe had less than six months to go. Germany surrendered in May of 1945 and Japan capitulated in August.

It was only after the end of World War II that Allied priorities shifted significantly. Now the Allies directed their attention to Soviet communism and its satellites.

Lord Cadogan, a British political personality and Churchill's close collaborator, was the highest-ranking Allied representative to visit Albania. At the Hotel Dajti in Tirana, Lord Cadogan encouraged Albanians to rise against their communist oppressors, promising that as soon as Albanian revolutionaries freed one city from communist rule, Great Britain would intervene militarily. I heard this from my mother, who with other wives of persecuted Albanian nationalists had met with Lord Cadogan in Tirana. Albanian resistance forces rose up against the communists and freed Koplik, a city north of Shkodra. For several days, the communists disappeared from circulation throughout the north. When Allies forces failed to intervene, the communists resurfaced, asserted themselves ever more cruelly, and drowned the revolution in blood. The uprising hardly caused a ripple on the international scene. Anthony Eden, at a meeting in San Francisco, stated that because of lack of political clarity in Albania, Great Britain was not in favor of recognizing Enver Hoxha's government at that juncture. That was all.

In central Europe and the Balkans, a heroic resistance continued for a number of years but was doomed to fail. Allied efforts to topple Enver Hoxha's regime failed, thanks mostly to Kim Philby and associates and half-hearted Allied commitment to the struggle. By the time the Soviet Empire imploded in the late 1980s and early 1990s, Soviet satellites had paid a staggering price in suffering and death. To this day, some of these countries are still dominated by their erstwhile communist rulers.

Chapter Eleven

Civil War

In Albania in the fall of 1943, before the ink had dried on the Mukaj agreement, the Albanian communists scuttled it, on orders of the Comintern and of their Yugoslav masters. Enver Hoxha and Co. made sure they kept their nationalist counterparts in the dark about this turnabout and about the cataclysm they were about to unleash on Albania. Following the agreement the National Front had just signed, it dispatched Besnik Çano and Qeramudin Sulo to southern Albania to notify those villages that would provide food and assistance to the nationalist forces and those that would support the Front of National Liberation and the communists. On their way south, the two young men were waylaid and executed by communist units. Next, these units proceeded to attack National Front forces in the south, claiming the latter had tried to collect tithes from villages assigned to them, i.e., to the communists, a ludicrous claim now that Enver Hoxha had torn up the agreement.

The nationalist commander was Safet Butka, the professor who at dinner at our table in Tirana had accused Dad of having betrayed the nationalist cause. That evening Dad had told him that he, Safet, was free to choose. He could accept his appointment as a teacher in Kosova or he could join the nationalist resistance and fight the Italians his way. Dad had chosen to fight the Italians from within. Now, a few months after the dinner at our home, Safet Butka found himself surrounded and attacked by Albanian communists. Rather than fire on Albanians, he chose to take his own life, an early victim of the civil war that over the next two years would spill blood in cities and mountains of Albania. These were the opening salvoes of the civil war. They marked the prelude to almost half a century of communist rule that

139

cost the country its best sons and daughters and left behind deep physical and moral wounds that to this day refuse to heal.

Early on in their campaign, the communist killer squads shot Hysen Mushqeta in Durrës. As I have mentioned before, Hysen Mushqeta was a patriot who had fought for Albania and against the Turks from the early days of the revolution. At one point, he had been mayor of Durrës. It was he who had offered to donate property to me if I graduated with a degree in agriculture and accepted to teach farmers modern farming methods. Hysen Mushqeta had also established the yearly tradition of providing a dowry to two young women from poor families so they could get married. Being a generous and patriotic individual put him high on the communist death list. He was shot in Durrës but survived the attack and was brought to The General Civilian Hospital in Tirana for intensive medical care. He died at the hospital after drinking poisoned milk given him by communist nurses.

On October 12, our phone rang. It was a call from a dentist cousin of ours. He had just finished taking care of Mustafa Kruja. When the latter got into his car, another car blocked the street and its occupants opened fire. Mustafa and his two bodyguards were wounded. The dentist had provided first aid but more medical assistance was needed. I told Dad to stay home and practically ran all the way to the dentist's. The guards recognized me and let me go upstairs to see Mustafa. He was seated in the dentist chair, his forearm bandaged. He had good color and seemed undaunted. Blood-stained pieces of gauze and bandages lay strewn all over the floor. After greeting Mustafa and assuring myself that he was not in imminent danger, I checked the other two wounded men. One was an army captain, the other a gendarme. Both were blood relatives of Mustafa. The captain was very pale with a wound under the orbit of one eye and another at the top of his head. It looked as if a projectile had entered through the orbit and had exited at the top of the skull. The pulse was regular and fairly strong. That was not uncommon in people with head wounds. His skin was white and clammy. I feared the worst. The gendarme had a superficial wound and was in no danger. The dentist had already called for a German military ambulance that was due to arrive any moment.

I was downstairs waiting for the ambulance when a young man, sloppily dressed with long hair and a cap pulled low over his eyes, entered the house. No one seemed to recognize him but the guards did not prevent him from climbing the stairs. I pulled my gun and followed him silently. I watched his every move when we entered the room where Mustafa was. The young man did not reach into his pockets or under the jacket. If he had, I would have beaten him to it. After a few long moments of silence, Mustafa recognized him and greeted him by name. It turned out he was a relative and harmless. Unnoticed, I took a deep breath and holstered my revolver.

The German ambulance finally arrived. Mustafa Kruja and his wounded bodyguards climbed in the back. I sat up front with the driver, pulled my revolver, and held it between my knees. A friend of Dad's, Koço Kotte, poked fun at my "heroics" and told me to holster the revolver. I neither replied nor did as he told me. We were going to drop off Mustafa and the gendarme and then we would go to a German air force hospital where they would take care of the captain. The driver took off but took a route other than the direct one. I did not speak up, thinking that the driver had received instructions how to get to the Kruja villa. We reached a point where continuing would have caused us to overshoot. I spoke to the driver and it turned out that he had no instructions whatsoever as to where we were going. We reached the villa, Mustafa and the gendarme got off, and the ambulance left for the German hospital. The captain seemed to have stabilized. After a quick examination by the surgeon on duty, it turned out that the captain had suffered two wounds, one under the orbit of the eye and the other on top of his head. Both wounds were superficial and not connected. He received first aid treatment, and then the ambulance took him home. I returned to our apartment, which was not far from the hospital.

A day or so later, we heard that on the day of the assassination attempt against Mustafa Kruja, the communists had set up a second ambush about 300 feet from the dentist's office. The fact that the German driver did not take the shortest route to the Kruja villa had saved our lives.

Another victim of the communist death squads was Aziz Çami, an early freedom fighter against the Turks. He had also participated under Qazim Koculi in the campaign that had forced the Italian troops to abandon Vlora at the end of World War I. Mussolini had Qazim Koculi killed around Christmas 1942. The communists shot from behind and killed Aziz Çami in the fall of 1943. In the early 1930s, Aziz Çami had fired on King

Zogu as the latter was leaving the opera in Vienna, and had done time in an Austrian prison after the failed attempt. When we went to pay our respects to Aziz Çami's remains at the morgue at The General Civilian Hospital in Tirana, the communist nurses had put a cigarette between his lips.

Aziz Çami's death was a direct attack on the Central Committee of the National Front (Balli Kombëtar), whose member he had been from early on. His funeral was a major event attended by many well-known Albanians and by a large group of nationalist youth. On the way to the funeral, not far from me, a gun fired. When I turned around, I saw a group of people standing behind a pickup truck. They looked worriedly at a body lying on the ground. I rushed toward them and saw one of our members on the ground, covered with blood but still alive. A car was passing by. I stopped the car and asked the Italian driver to get out as we needed the car to get the wounded to the hospital. The man objected, claiming that the car was practically out of gas. I waved him off, got the wounded man into the car and started toward the hospital. We ran out of gas within a few hundred yards. I got out, stopped a horse-drawn carriage, ignored the protests of a number of semi-veiled women in the carriage, put the wounded man in the back seat, and took off toward the hospital. By the time we reached the hospital he had died.

He was the younger brother of Dr. Dibra, a neurologist who lived near the hospital. I looked around the morgue. No one there was eager to notify the physician of his brother's death. I had no choice but to do it myself. As I walked toward Dr. Dibra's house, I thought of how to break the news to him. I decided to do it in stages.

The doctor was at home. I told him that his brother had been shot but was alive. As we hurried toward the hospital, I told him that the wound was quite serious and eventually, just before we entered the building, I told him of his brother's demise. I need not try to describe the older brother's grief for his younger sibling. I left as soon as I could because I still had time to make it to the funeral.

By now, the crowd was all around the gravesite. The band had stopped playing Chopin's Funeral March, a piece of music we were hearing more and more often. It is interesting to note that the military bandleader was an NCO who continued to direct the band after the communist takeover, except that now he had been promoted to lieutenant. It is safe to assume that he, as a member of the communist movement, had truly enjoyed bringing many good nationalists to their graves.

At the funeral, there were few speeches. Everyone was in a hurry to get away, very much aware that crowds made good targets for the roaming communist death squads, and attendees at Aziz Çami's funeral made for particularly attractive targets. As I was half listening to the speeches, I kept looking around as I fingered my 9 mm Beretta and the spare clip in my pocket. About a year later, in prison, I met a former partisan who told me that he and his men had surrounded the cemetery during Aziz Çami's funeral with heavy machine guns, with orders to open fire on the crowd. At the last moment they were told that the operation had been cancelled. At that point, he didn't know why. I couldn't help but wonder how much my friends and I could have done with our sidearms against heavy machine guns.

As time went by, I learned how to differentiate between Italian and German aircraft by the sound of their engines. Early one afternoon, I heard the deep, throaty sound of numerous heavy aircraft engines that were neither Italian nor German. I stopped in my tracks. Suddenly, I heard the whistling sound of falling bombs as German anti-aircraft batteries opened fire. I ran into my parents' bedroom yelling, "We are being bombed!" We rushed down the staircase toward the basement where we found families who occupied the lower floors and had preceded us. Among them was the family of Lt. Colonel Lamponi whose 16-year-old daughter Luciana had just been rejected by a young man who lived in the same apartment building. She vented her feelings with these hate-filled words: "We should push all Albanians out of the building while the bombs are falling." I knew what had happened and kept my mouth shut. Within a few weeks, she and her family climbed aboard a German truck convoy and left Tirana bound for Italy. In Montenegro, communist forces attacked the convoy and the Lamponi family reportedly died in the ambush.

I climbed the stairs out of the basement and stepped out into the open. A German soldier was just rounding the corner.

"Did you ever see anything like this?" I asked, all shook up.

"I was at Stalingrad," he replied dryly and walked on without missing a step.

The American bombers had dropped a veritable carpet of bombs as they had made one pass over Tirana. Soon we heard reports of casualties. About a hundred yards from our apartment building, a grandmother had stepped out of her home holding a baby in her arms. The grandmother was killed instantly, but the baby was unhurt. A number of small dogs were struck by shrapnel and killed. The bomb craters were very shallow, indicating the use of anti-personnel bombs. All told, about 300 people were killed and about 700 wounded.

This was by far the worst bombardment Tirana had ever suffered. For days we heard tales of children who had been maimed by what looked like fountain pens or other such gadgets. We could never establish whether such incidents were true, and if so, whether the Americans had dropped such innocent-looking explosive devices or whether they had been planted by the Germans to create anti-American feelings.

At this point, our hospitals were overrun by hundreds of wounded civilians. The most serious cases had priority and were treated by surgeons. The rest had to await their turn. Physicians, religious sisters from Italy, and Albanian nurses took care of them, cleansed their wounds, removed dead tissue, and provided follow-up care. A friend of mine, also a medical student, and I volunteered at the hospital and began working there regularly—without pay, of course.

As time went on, we were also getting more and more wounded communists who, I am sorry to say, were intentionally neglected by the Italian sisters. Even though I was an active anti-communist, I did not tolerate that these wounded be neglected. We were enemies and fought each other in the field. In the hospital, they were entitled to the same treatment and care as anyone else. To achieve this, I had all communists put in one room. With Albanian nurses we provided needed care and soon things were under control.

One day, ideology raised its head unexpectedly. One of the wounded communists was running a high fever and was on a meatless diet. One morning, as I was making the rounds, I heard him tell the rest of his comrades, "Once we are in power, there will be no discrimination whatsoever. All patients will get meat."

A little more than a year later, some friends and I found ourselves in jail. After a few months, wanting to get out of prison even for a few hours, we asked to be sent to the hospital, claiming all kinds of imaginary ailments. I had rubbed my eyes until they were red and claimed that I was suffering from conjunctivitis. With the help of the prison doctor, my fellow prisoners and I were on our way to the hospital—on foot for lack of transportation. This was a break for us as we would see more of Tirana and might run into friends. When we reached the hospital, two young nurses who had assisted me in the surgical ward the year before came to me and expressed great surprise that I was in prison, I who had obviously been a communist and had helped the wounded partisans with such determination. "Well," I said, "it's one of those things." The nurses looked bewildered but dared ask no more questions—nor did the take any action on my behalf.

Late in 1943 and extending into January 1944, German troops had begun an offensive against the communist forces, cornering and nearly destroying them. I say "nearly" because when the communists found themselves without an escape route, the German offensive came to a halt and the troops withdrew. After the war, we learned from German sources that they had refrained from destroying the communists so that the civil war in Albania could continue unabated, thus reducing attacks from either side against German garrisons and convoys.

During and after the German offensive, mass defections weakened the communist ranks. In our apartment building in Tirana, several communist defectors arrived dreading the communist death squads more than us, their nationalist opponents. Knowing what would happen to them in case of a communist victory, some defectors joined the ranks of the police and fought actively against their erstwhile comrades. This strange alliance between former enemies unleashed the strongest attack against communist cells and guerilla forces in Tirana. On the night between February 3 and 4, hundreds of communists were arrested and few among them lived to see the dawn.

It was a blood bath that deeply affected friend and foe alike. The communists had sowed wind and had reaped whirlwind. But not even we, their opponents who had been at the losing end of the civil war from the beginning, could rejoice at an illegal operation of such proportions. As time went by, it became obvious that the communists regrouped and their ranks continued to swell with steady Allied backing while our nationalist forces melted away gradually, unable to stem the Red tide.

Being idealistic, we young members of the National Front continued to fight. A group of volunteers, about six of us, left on a mission to drum up support for the nationalist cause in Fier and its surroundings. In Tirana, we jumped on a truck loaded with oranges and left southbound, in high spirits. As we traveled, we started tasting, actually devouring the cargo. It was sweet and juicy.

After a few hours, we knocked on the cab to get the driver's attention. He stopped near a bridge, understanding our need. At the head of the bridge was a German sentry. We ran down the embankment and relieved ourselves with youthful exuberance. Once we felt better and quieted down, we heard someone sobbing. Under the bridge, cowering in the deepest shadows was an Italian soldier. He told us that he had surrendered to the Germans in Vlora. He was suffering from a severe case of dysentery and the Germans had put him on a convoy and were taking him to the Military Hospital in Tirana. The column had stopped at the bridge and he had gone under the bridge, suffering from severe abdominal cramps. When the column was ready to leave, he had lacked the strength to climb up the embankment while the truck with his few belongings and the all-important documents had taken off with the rest. He was sure that the German sentry did not know all this and would shoot him for lack of ID papers. We told him that he need not worry. We would carry him up the embankment. If the German soldier made any hostile moves, we would protect him, claiming that he was our prisoner. Then we would put him on the truck and get him out of this predicament. Later, we would make arrangements to ensure his safety and survival. He seemed reassured. We carried him up the embankment. I explained to the sentry what had happened.

The German shrugged his shoulder and answered very simply, "Leave him here with me. I'll put him on the next German convoy that comes this way and we will get him to the hospital. No problem." The Italian prisoner agreed, we wished him well, and left. That was the last we heard of him. I hope he made it.

In the morning we were in Fier. We went to the command post of the National Front, washed up, and grabbed some breakfast. Here we met with other members of our organization. I was glad so see Luan Gashi, the man who had recruited me for the National Front in Padua the year before. He told us that not much was going on at the time. There was only one man in prison. He was a local farmer. Our forces had searched his place and had found the body of one of our soldiers buried in his dung heap. The man denied knowing anything about the dead soldier. He was kept in prison while the investigation continued. I felt torn.

I remembered Dad telling me the following story. At the time, Dad was a teacher in a little village when they had caught a man who was trying to rape a neighbor's wife. Dad had conducted the interrogation and once he was satisfied he knew the facts, he had sentenced the man to receive ten lashes on the soles of his feet. The man had challenged Dad's authority to pass sentence, but Dad had replied that he was the judge of Askundi (Nowhere) and the man had submitted to his lashes.

Did it behoove me to take action—in other words, to force the prisoner to confess? The man had been in prison for a while and no one seemed to be doing anything to get to the bottom of this matter. After all, one of our soldiers was dead and no one seemed to care.

I tried to sound self-assured. "Leave me alone with the prisoner and I'll make him talk." I felt someone had to stand up for the dead man.

Luan shook his head. "No, this is a matter for the local police. We are neither in charge nor responsible for keeping the public order. The deceased was our soldier and we will do all we can to have the police pursue this matter until we know who committed the crime."

I was glad I was off the hook. After all, I could not find it in my heart to beat the man or use some other type of violence against him. I was trying to live up to what I thought Dad expected of me. But when push came to shove, I could not do what I knew was wrong.

About 30 years later in Detroit, a friend of mine came to see me. Our conversation drifted to the war years and he mentioned that he had defected from the communist ranks only toward the end of the civil war. Early in 1944, he was in Fier where his communist guerilla unit had killed one of our soldiers and had hidden the corpse in the dung heap of an unsuspecting farmer. The farmer was arrested and the communists were able to get away without being discovered. I can imagine how I would have felt if I had done violence to an innocent man!

There was little for us to do in Fier. So we decided to visit some outlying villages and tell the people what we stood and fought for. We climbed some foothills and met people who belonged to our National Front. One of them fed us and then had us meet an Italian soldier whom he was hiding from the Germans. The Italian was an expert machine gunner. He had taken his weapon with him when he had sought refuge with our friend. Now he demonstrated the use of the heavy water-cooled machine gun and we all took turns firing the weapon. Often, we do not think of Italy as an industrial power. In reality Italy had—and has—an excellent heavy industry, including an arms industry of repute. In fact, a few years ago, NATO selected the Italian Beretta pistol as the sidearm of choice.

The next day we marched uphill for a while, and chose a modest farmhouse to make the case for our nationalist struggle. The owner received us with typical Albanian hospitality. He offered us bread, cheese, and home-brewed whiskey. As the conversation proceeded, he asked us to spend the night at his place but apologized that he could not offer us the kind of elaborate meal and bedding we nationalists had come to expect. He would have been less concerned if we had been communist partisans, because they shunned frills and were satisfied with simple food and modest accommodations. And this after we had tried to explain to him that we were fighting for our country, that we wanted to protect our land from foreign invasions, and that we wanted to bring freedom and well-being to Albanians throughout Albania!

Obviously, he was unwilling to believe in our cause. We rose, said goodbye to the man, and left his house. We marched back to our base where we did not have to fear a communist night attack. The next morning, as we were descending toward Fier, we saw American bombers overhead, probably returning from a bombing mission over the Rumanian oil fields. We waved and waved in sign of friendship when, all of a sudden, we heard the unmistakable whistling of bombs hurtling toward earth. We hit the ground when the bombs began exploding all around us.

The bombing ended as suddenly as it had begun. The pilots probably had to get rid of leftover bombs before they could land at their airbase and we, a handful of armed individuals, may have made an interesting target among those barren mountains. Dirt and stones hit some of us. One of our friends sheepishly admitted that he had wet his pants. Luckily, by the time we reached town, his pants were dry again.

We had begun our trip south in high spirits, hopeful that we would be able to change minds and bring communist sympathizers over to our side. Unfortunately, we failed, and what was worse, we failed to realize that the communists had outmaneuvered us among the population at large.

Chapter Twelve

The Battalion Besnik Çano

Our return from Fier to Tirana was uneventful. The trip had left us with a deep feeling of failure. We knew how much we loved our country. We were also fully aware that the communists would be a veritable scourge if they emerged victorious. Yet many Albanians obviously favored the communists. Either they did not understand the danger of a communist victory or we were unduly worried. From my point of view, the signs of the gathering storm were unmistakable.

The political assassinations by the communists continued. Communist ranks kept swelling and their support by the Allies remained unabated. We could do little about it and felt helpless as the noose around our necks was getting tighter. The one ray of hope continued to be the solidarity with our Kosovar brothers. During the difficult years of conflict, Kosova was our breadbasket. Equally important, if not more important, was the fact that they had sent volunteers to help us in our struggle against the communists. Meanwhile, Albania's officer corps stood idly by, in self-serving neutrality. The Albanian police seemed increasingly impotent and the armed units of various notables, mainly from northern Albania, had proven to be of little value and had crumbled soon after their deployment in the field.

That summer of 1944, leaders of the National Front Balli Kombëtar decided to form a volunteer unit to fight side by side with our Kosovar brothers against Tito's forces in Kosova. About one hundred young volunteers signed up. I was among them.

One day, at Balli Youth headquarters, a young man was enthusiastically singing as he led the rest of us in a blood-stirring rendition of patriotic songs.

"Did you register as a volunteer?" I asked.

"No," he replied. "I just want to get some of these fools to sign up. I am not going." After the communist takeover, he became part of a radio comedy team that made fun of the nationalist movement and particularly of its leader, Mid'hat Frashëri.

Our battalion took the name "Besnik Çano" after one of the two Balli members the communists had killed as they unleashed the civil war in our country. We volunteers wore whatever appropriate clothing we could muster and had to bring our own weapons. I picked a tan military jacket and a pair of black riding pants of Dad's. I wore knee socks and heavy boots. I had my trusted 9 mm Beretta pistol, a spare clip, and an Italian military carbine plus ammunition.

The day set for our departure was warm and sunny. The air was clear and the heat of the day was fading when we gathered in late afternoon at our youth headquarters. At the head of our column were our commander, a young lawyer, Seit Kazazi, and his next-in-command, Halim Begeja, who was a well-known athlete, soccer player, and teacher. The flag bearer was Rizvan Banka, a friend of mine from Tirana. I was in charge of first aid and health matters. We climbed aboard our trucks and waved goodbye to those left behind. Mom stood there on the sidewalk, looking lonely, sad, and forlorn as we set out on the first leg of our journey.

We left at dusk as plans called for traveling at night to avoid strafing by Allied fighters. Our morale and our hopes were sky high. We would show our gratitude and solidarity to our Kosovar brothers. We had links of blood, a common language, and millennia of shared history. Now we would fight against the same enemy, the Yugoslav oppressors, and for the same cause, for a Kosova united with Albania.

Before our departure, Dad had warned me, "The Kosovars will be delighted to see you and will seek to keep you out of combat. Instead, they will parade you up and down Kosova, they will show you the most beautiful sights of their land, and they will wine and dine you to show you their gratitude. Make sure you go into combat. Otherwise, when you return, the communists will say you went to Kosova to buy cheese!" Those words had stuck with me. Besides, I still felt the sense of failure with which we young volunteers had returned from our trip to Fier. This time would be different if I could help it.

We reached Shkodra late at night. Together with two young men, I slept at the home of a family that had offered to take us in. The next day in mid-morning, we met in the central square, basking in the glow of admiration we thought we detected in the eyes of local beauties who made it a point to walk by nonchalantly attracted—we thought—by our manly appearance, our weapons, and our attire.

The day went by in a hurry. That evening we mounted our trucks again and took off in a northeasterly direction. The evening was warm and the sunset spectacular. During the night, it got very cold as the trucks kept climbing up tortuous mountain roads. I was glad I had a blanket with me. I put my rifle between my legs and wrapped the blanket around me so I could throw it off in a hurry and use my rifle if I had to.

When dawn broke, a very cold dawn as I remember, we found ourselves way up in the mountains. The mountains seemed to reach all the way to the sky. As the highway emerged from darkness, we could see it was being repaired by Italian prisoners of war. They were in rags, without top coats, shivering, and stretching out their hands begging for food. We began tossing them loaves of bread. One could not help but wonder. Until a few months ago, they were the enemy, the rulers of Albania. Now they were begging for bread and we were feeding them out of our limited supplies. *Sic transit gloria mundi*! It also bore testimony to the fact that Italian troops in Albania had behaved generally well to the extent that many found refuge with Albanian farmers until the end of the war when they returned to Italy.

One of our companions, an ex-communist, chided us for throwing bread to the "fascists." He obviously still felt the hatred the communists tried to instill in all their members. We told him to shut up and did so in no uncertain terms. We nationalists fought the enemy; we did not fight helpless prisoners.

By the time we reached Prishtina, the sun was high on the horizon, the sky was blue, and our hearts throbbed with pride. We were in Kosova! We were among our brothers and sisters who, over the years, had been severed from Albania by foreign diplomats who gave Kosova to Serbia against all evidence and historic realities. Thus, these diplomats had brought upon Kosova and the Kosovars grief, death, and destruction. By a stroke of the diplomatic pen, Slovenes and Croats, the people of Montenegro, the Bosnians, the Macedonians, and some Hungarians had also been squeezed together to form Yugoslavia. This was of no consolation to us. We wanted a Kosova freely joined to Albania as an integral part of our nation. Well, now we were here, ready to delve into all the emotions and joys of the moment.

At this point, I got two assignments. First, I had to take our commander to the hospital. The diagnosis was clear. He had a severe sinus infection. At the hospital they stuck a needle through his palate, drained the sinus, gave him sulfa drugs, and we were on our way. Next, I was appointed flag bearer of our battalion as Rizvan Banka was accidentally wounded in the arm. The wound was not serious but he had to keep his arm in a sling. Henceforth, I would march at the head of our battalion, proudly carrying the Albanian flag.

Our next stop was Peja. From here we would go to Morina to take up a sector along the front against Tito's forces. Things were getting interesting. That's what we had come for and now it was about to become reality.

In Peja we got off the trucks and were told to line up in formation, as the commander of the garrison, Major Neshat Hasho, would inspect our ranks. When we fell in line, I had a chance to look at our group. Seen through my eyes, we had looked pretty good until then. Sure, we all wore different clothes, some were tall and some were short, and practically no one had been in the service. But we had known each other for years; we shared the same ideals and fought the same enemy. We shared the brotherhood of the trenches. We were like schoolmates who may have looked funny the first few days of school, but once we got used to each other, we looked normal while those of all other classes looked odd, if not worse. I did not know it then, but I would meet Major Hasho two more times—once in prison in 1944–1945 and again a couple of years later in the Military Hospital, when he was brought in as a prisoner.

Now, however, I was looking at our group through the eyes of an experienced garrison commander, starting with our leaders and down to the last man. Major Hasho stepped out of the building and took one long look at us. He turned to our commander and said in a fairly loud voice words to this effect, "Your men have all kinds of different weapons, from Italian rifles to German Mausers, to Greek Manlichers. There is no way I can supply you with ammunition for these different types of rifles. I recommend that we issue long Carcano rifles to your battalion."

The major was obviously right. All who needed to handed in their weapons and ammunition and received long Italian rifles. I had the impression that Major Hasho had in mind a few salty comments but kept them to himself. I must admit that the impression we gave was not that of a well-honed fighting force. How could we be something we were not? Anyhow, we got our weapons and ammunition and spent that night in Peja.

The next day we climbed aboard our trucks, the engines started to roar, the exhaust pipes belched smelly, dark diesel fumes, and we were on our way to the front in full daylight. Allied airplanes were apparently no threat in this part of the country.

Wherever we drove through, people would come out of their houses and wave, throw us flowers, and greet us as if we were the prodigal son returning home. Our trucks began climbing up some winding mountain roads. We were told we had to cross a high pass and from there we would descend to the plains of Morina. The trip would take several hours. The area was picturesque. We chatted, sang, and felt good all over. We were finally on the way to the front.

The sky was clouding over and the temperature was falling as we proceeded up the mountains. When we reached the Çakor Pass, our column stopped. Several trucks loaded with Kosovar fighters were coming up the mountain from the opposite direction. They stopped and some of our men went to touch base with them. When they returned, they told us they had seen a man who had been struck across the abdomen by a burst of machine gun fire. His bowels were protruding between his fingers as he tried to contain his intestines. He had asked them who we were.

When they told him, his eyes had smiled and he had whispered, "I know I am dying and no one can do anything for me. But now that I see you young Albanians here, willing to fight side by side with us, I don't mind dying."

Our column started the descent into the Morina Valley. The encounter with the dying man had cast a shadow on our youthful enthusiasm, but not for long. At our age, we were sure of ourselves, of our immortality. Come what may, we could handle it.

That evening we reached Morina and pitched our tents, 10–12 men per tent. Then we sat down to a meal. We felt rough and manly as we pulled our knives and cut off slices of bread, bits of cheese, and chunks of tomatoes. We lay on the ground and covered ourselves with blankets we had brought from home. We wished each other good night and fell into a deep sleep.

The next morning we woke up early. It was quite cold. The mist in the valley was breaking up. We could see foothills and mountains covered with pine and deciduous trees. Everything was green and luscious. In the valley all around us there were few buildings and even fewer fields. One small building, more the size of a hut, could be a little store. As I looked around, I had the impression that we were the only ones occupying part of the valley. From a practical point of view, we had yet to find out where there was a spring, a well, a water fountain, or a creek. Someone knew where to go for water. We gave him our canteens and when he returned, we washed our hands and faces. I don't think anybody shaved; that would have been sissy stuff and sissies we were not. Our bones and joints ached from sleeping on the ground but we would not show it nor did we complain. After all, we were volunteers, we had come to fight, and discomforts such as these were part of the deal.

Now we had a chance to get ourselves acquainted with our rifles. For me it was easy because I was familiar with the Carcano rifle. I knew how to take it apart. I cleaned it as best I could and got mentally ready for lunch. After all, this was Kosova, the breadbasket of Albania. Meat, eggs, cheese, and the like were abundant here and one thing we did not have to worry about was food.

Our cooks started fires under two big copper kettles. Soon the water was boiling. They added chunks of meat, vegetables, and whatever other goodies they had found. Soon lunch would be ready and we would sit under God's blue sky and enjoy a hot meal. "Hunger is the best cook," a German saying goes, and our mouths were watering in anticipation.

To make things official, I stepped forth to inspect the food, and to my horror, discovered that our volunteer cooks had forgotten to clean the copper kettles thoroughly before adding water and the ingredients. What I saw were two bubbling, boiling cauldrons covered by a thick bluish-green layer of what looked like copper sulfate. If we ate the food from those cauldrons, we could get very sick—if not worse. Hence, I saw no alternative but to order the cooks to dump the contents of the two cauldrons and to bury the contents in the ground. So much for our first meal. I regret to say that over the next few days, all we had was bread, cheese, and tomatoes to keep body and soul together, a far cry from Mama's cooking or from the abundance of food all around us in Kosova.

One day our commandant called me and two other men from our squad into his office. We were to go on patrol with a German and help him locate partisan machine-gun nests. Soon thereafter, we met our German NCO and started climbing a nearby mountain. We climbed for about three hours without ever resting or taking a breather. When we were near the top, the German stopped and told us we could now rest for a while. Petrit Toto, one of my comrades, was so tired that he did not bend down to retrieve an ammunition clip that had fallen from his belt. Hamit Troplini and I sat down, trying not to show how bushed we were.

As we were reclining on the ground, the German turned to me and said, "How would you break that branch?" pointing at a nearby tree.

I replied that I could try, and aimed my rifle at the branch.

"No, no," the German said. "How could you do it without shooting?"

I translated his words to my comrades-in-arms and we collectively shrugged our shoulders. The German got up, climbed the tree nearest to the one in question and jumped, landing with both feet on the branch he wanted to break off. The branch gave way under his weight and he grabbed the tree trunk to keep from falling. He climbed off the tree.

"That's how you can do it." I was less impressed by the originality of his approach than by his physical strength after chasing up that mountain. Then he turned to me. "I need one of you to help explore enemy lines. Who will it be?"

I explained to my friends what was going on and we decided to draw lots. Hamit Troplini won, or lost, depending on one's point of view. He and the German NCO got ready to take off. Petrit and I decided to take a snooze since we had enough food for one meal and that we would eat at day's end, just in case there was some nocturnal fighting.

When we woke up, the German NCO and Hamit Troplini were seated and may have been back for some time. The German was all steamed up. Hamit Troplini, in his opinion, lacked discipline and was no longer acceptable to the German. When I asked why, he would not tell me. So I asked Hamit. It turns out that while the German was marking communist machine-gun nests on his map, Hamit had crawled out as far as he could on an overhang, had grabbed a hand grenade, ready to drop it on the enemy position. The German had shaken his head violently to indicate that all he wanted to do was identify the locations of these machine guns and was against dropping any hand grenades or to start any kind of military action. Hamit had still motioned that he wanted to drop the hand grenade but had eventually accepted what the German NCO was telling him. I assume what the German needed was to mark these locations on his map for the German artillery in the valley. When I asked Hamit why he had persisted, he replied that he wanted the German to know that we Albanians perhaps did not know how to break branches off trees without shooting but we neither shunned nor feared military action. For better or worse, that's what had happened.

We spent that night in the woods, completed our mission the next morning, and returned to base around noon. The German NCO invited me to break bread with him, knowing well that there would be little food in my tent. I politely declined his offer stating that I first had to report to my commander and then I would go to my tent and eat with my comrades. And that's what I did.

When I reached the commander's quarters in a stone building nearby, I found him and his staff seated, ready to partake of a fragrant small roasted lamb. When Seit Kazazi saw me, he broke out in a big smile.

"We have been looking for you all over the camp but could not find you. Sit down and get some of this succulent lamb." Embarrassed, he explained, "The Kosovar unit next to ours sent us this lamb. It was too little to feed the battalion and returning it would have offended the donors. So we decided to consume it here at headquarters."

I did not make his job any easier. I simply made my report, told him that I was returning to my tent to eat with my comrades, and left. I grabbed some dry bread inside our tent and decided to sleep off some of the tiredness that was still in my bones. I had barely fallen asleep when my friends woke me up. A German soldier stood there and told me that the NCO had sent us some German Kommissbrot, some margarine, cheese, and artificial honey so we would have an idea what the German soldier's ration consisted of. By the way, the amount of food sent by him sufficed for all the occupants of our tent. I asked the soldier to thank his NCO on our behalf and made sure no one touched any food until after the soldier's departure. Once he left, the twelve of us divided everything very carefully and ate it with relish and appreciation.

That night we were awakened by automatic gunfire and by exploding hand grenades as communist forces attacked us. We took up positions but the attackers disappeared as quickly as they had struck. Our sentries had failed to detect them in time. The next day we checked the likely infiltration routes, set up new sentry positions, and got ready for what the next night or nights would bring.

Our daily routine was rather monotonous. We got up, cleaned our weapons, and went to the one and only store that offered cheese, jellies, fruit, and some baked goods. We could also buy needles, thread, and other such items to repair whatever damage our clothes might have suffered. I for one was in need of such repairs. One day I had been on patrol on horseback with a German NCO and in dismounting, I somehow caught one pant leg in the packsaddle and ripped open the inside seam. I did fix it, of course, but it looked awful—as if some toddler had grabbed a needle and black thread and had unleashed his fury and lack of skill on my pants.

Anyhow, in Morina nobody paid any attention to how we looked, and since I had only one pair of pants, my choice was limited. And so was our menu. We tried to have one hot meal a day and as long as food was abundant, taste was secondary. Fortunately, it was summer and fruits and other food items were available for a price.

We washed neither often nor thoroughly. Nobody noticed as we probably all smelled the same. Besides, washing with ice-cold water from a nearby creek was not tempting and we opted for relative cleanliness only when we had no choice. It was bad enough that when we wanted a change of underwear, sooner or later we had to go to the creek and wash our things in cold water. There was no one to do our laundry nor was there a barber in Morina. After a while, we got to look and smell rather raunchy. This was war and we looked like warriors, unkempt and rough.

One day we had an incident that could have gotten out of hand. One of our patrols had searched a house in a Slavic village some distance from our positions. They had found small-arms ammunition and were interrogating the women. There were no men in the house because they had all joined Tito's forces in the mountains. While our volunteers were trying to get the women to provide information we might use, they heard a young girl scream. They rushed to the barn and found a member of the patrol trying to rape her. The patrol arrested the man and brought him to our commander. We all gathered, heard the case, and began proposing what to do with the culprit. It was obvious that the accused could no longer remain in our ranks. We had come here to fight the men, not to attack their women. Sooner or later, someone from the battalion would seriously harm or even kill the attacker who had brought dishonor to our outfit. We had no jail we could keep the man in and so the one solution that came to mind was to make an example of the would-be rapist and execute him. This would have certainly vindicated our honor in our eyes, in those of the Albanian population, as well as before the Slavic villages in the area. I tended to agree with those who held this opinion.

Our commander, after listening to the debate, spoke up. The man had attempted to commit a vile act but had been stopped in time and had been arrested by the squad. This intervention alone had restored the honor of the battalion. We had no jail where we could keep the culprit. Furthermore, we had no legal standing to pass and carry out a death sentence. The thing to do, therefore, was to return him to Albania as a prisoner and put him before a regular court that could mete out the appropriate sentence. The arguments presented by our commander carried the day and the man was returned to Albania. By the time we got back to Tirana, it never occurred to me to inquire what had happened to him. It was a good thing that our commander was a lawyer, both for the culprit as well as for the rest of us.

At night, several times a week, the partisans would attack with rifle fire and mortars. We would scramble into position, return fire if we saw the enemy, and return to our tents after it was all over. One night, a young volunteer near me started screaming all of a sudden.

"We are surrounded, we are surrounded!"

I turned around and yelled at him, "If you don't shut up, I'll stuff my fist down your throat!" It worked.

About a year later, while I was in prison in Tirana, I saw him approach our iron gates, wearing the uniform of an NCO of the State Security Service. When I caught his eye, I whispered, "Good for you that they did not discover that you were a member of the Nationalist Youth."

He looked at me and said coldly, "It was the communist party that sent me to Kosova with the battalion."

One day, our commander called me to his office and told me that I was to accompany two sick men to the hospital in Peja. I was to make sure they received proper medical care. Furthermore, I was to stay there even after they were able to return to the battalion because other patients may have to be hospitalized. In addition, I was to buy provisions for our unit and ship them properly and on time to Morina. I objected as strenuously as I could. I had come to Kosova to fight, not to buy cheese.

He looked me in the eye and replied, "This is an order." I had no choice. I saluted and left his office.

That night the communists attacked us again. The first out of our tent was Bardhyl Borshi, our machine gunner. I followed him with the ammunition box. We fell flat on the ground because the communists had come close to our tent. I saw one of them, aimed, and was about to pull the trigger when Bardhyl rose to his full height in front of me. He had seen one of the infiltrators and was going to open fire with his pistol. I released the trigger just in time. Bardhyl never realized how close he had come to being shot from behind. Phew!

The attack had come shortly after midnight. At 3:00 a.m., I was awakened as the truck that would carry the two patients and me to Peja had arrived. Inside the cab, seated next to the driver, were two men. I squeezed in beside them and kept my eyes and ears peeled. The night was dark and threatening. The mountain road was barely lit by the headlights of the truck. The three men spoke little; in Serbian, I thought. I lifted my pistol out of the holster and kept the weapon out of sight, between my knees. We bounced along on the highway for a few hours when I saw the first brush strokes of dawn. The men had loomed threatening in the dark. Actually, all three, including the driver, were Albanian. If there had been any danger, it would have been from an ambush along the mountain road, not from them.

The truck dropped us off at the hospital. The two patients were properly registered. They took a shower, changed into hospital garments, and looked quite civilized when I saw them in their beds. The physicians were Albanian and so were the nurses. I knew that my friends were in good hands. I left them for the time being and walked to the home of Rifat Begolli, a colleague of Dad's. His family had already asked me the first time we were in Peja to stay with them. I really could not think of a good reason to refuse their hospitality even though I would have preferred to rent a room and be on my own. As soon as I showed up, they received me with all the respect and honor they would have extended to Dad. I took a shower, put on fresh underwear and socks, excused myself, and made a beeline for the tailor at the center of town. Finally I could have my riding breeches professionally fixed and pressed. This time they came out looking like new.

I spent several weeks at the Begolli home. I got used to their food, which was so salty that by the end of the meal I had a solid crust of salt around my lips. I slept comfortably, showered regularly, and had no worries about any ambushes. One brother was the mayor of Peja and the other the commander of the gendarmerie. After the communist takeover, the Yugoslav communists executed both brothers and paraded the head of the gendarmerie officer on a platter for all to see. But those events still lay ahead of us.

After a while, I became impatient and started to ask our battalion commander for permission to return to the battalion. Finally, he gave me the true reason why he wanted me in Peja, away from the front. The German unit must have informed their superiors of my knowledge of German and had presented an official request to our battalion commander that I be assigned as liaison between the German and the Albanian forces. Our commander felt that this was not in our best interest, and had replied that I was stationed in Peja where I was assigned several responsibilities on behalf of our battalion and was not available.

After I left Morina, Hamit Troplini took my place and carried the ammunition for the machine gunner of our squad. The battalion had almost ended the assigned stay at the front when the Slavs attacked one night. The machine gunner and his helper were running to take up their positions when they hit the dirt because of incoming mortar fire. The mortar shells exploded nearby. Hamit Troplini fell on top of the ammunition case and a shell fragment hit him above the forehead, shearing off the top of his skull. He died instantly. When the battalion brought back his remains, we buried our fallen comrade with simple military honors in the Peja cemetery. The participation of the local population was most touching. Personally, I could not help but think that it could have been me had I not left Morina.

The battalion spent a couple of days in Peja. We returned the rifles provided by the garrison. The volunteers finally had a chance to get cleaned up, have their hair cut, get their laundry done, polish their shoes, and eat good, wholesome, and abundant food. Because I had developed a number of local contacts as a liaison for our battalion, I spent much of my time with Commander Seit Kazazi. One late morning he and several of us volunteers were passing through the city's main square when we noticed to our right and across the square a kind of cage mounted on a pedestal. Inside the cage there were two or three men. Next, I noticed that Seit Kazazi had turned his head away to the left where there was nothing special to see. He noticed that we were looking at him.

"Those are Albanian communists captured in a clash between Kosovars and Yugoslav partisan bands. Because of their collaboration with the enemy, they are being paraded through several cities before being executed."

Somebody said to him, "That still does not explain why you are averting your eyes and refuse to look at them."

"I recognized their leader. We were schoolmates in high school. Our eyes met when we entered the square and he looked at me, silently begging from a distance that I intervene in his favor. I cannot and I won't do it. But I do find it hard to look at him because at one time we were close."

The three men were shot in public a few days later. Following the communist takeover in Albania, Seit Kazazi took to the mountains to continue the armed resistance. At one point, he entered Shkodra illegally and went to his home. A maidservant betrayed him to the police that laid siege to the house. A gun battle ensued and Seit Kazazi, hopelessly surrounded, committed suicide in the basement.

After Peja, the battalion spent another week or so traveling through Kosova to show the flag. The people could not do enough for us and the reception we got everywhere was overwhelming.

One instance stands out in my mind. We were in Ferizaj, a city inhabited by Muslims. The banquet lasted into the wee hours of the morning. We were dead tired and eager to go to bed. As usual, we were assigned to different homes, two to three men per house. My two companions and I were brought to a home surrounded by high walls. Awaiting us at the large gate was our host, a man in his fifties with gray hair and a gray moustache. He showed us the way to the living room on the second floor. This looked like a typical Muslim home with tapestry on the walls, low divans along three walls of the guest room, and ornate copper plates hanging from the walls. He welcomed us officially into his home and told us what an honor we had done him by accepting his invitation. I responded with a few polite words expressing thanks for all the assistance that Kosova was giving Albania and that it was our privilege to fight the common enemy side by side with the brave sons of Kosova.

Because of the late hour and the fact that Muslims kept their women out of sight, what happened next caught us by surprise. Two young girls entered the room. One carried a washbasin and soap. The other had a large and ornate copper pitcher and towels in her hands. She put the washbasin on the floor while the other got ready to pour warm water over our feet. The father asked us to take off our shoes. In a Muslim home, this was unheard of. We were young men and yet had a chance to see these girls of marrying age. We were being treated like most honored guests. What added to our embarrassment was the fact that we had been wearing those socks for days and our feet smelled to high heaven. We looked at each other but there was no way out. I, as the flag bearer and speaker for the group, was first in line. Reluctantly, I removed boots and socks and instinctively curled my toes trying, as it were, to keep the foot odor from pervading the room. The girl with the copper pitcher bent over and wet my feet while the other washed them with soap and warm water. In so doing, she was also massaging my feet. It felt so good that it did not take long for me to uncurl my toes. Then her sister handed her a towel and she wiped my feet. I was all set. Then she repeated the same procedure with the other two young men. Before we knew it, the young women had brought thick mattresses, sheets, and blankets and then disappeared. Their father asked us whether we needed anything else and then bid us good night.

The next morning we joined the battalion, mounted our trucks and left for the next city. Eventually, our round trip through Kosova came to an end as we left for Prishtina. Here, our battalion commander was to meet with some German officers before leaving for Tirana. He chose a few of us to accompany him to the German command. Before entering, we had to resolve a problem. The assassination attempt against Hitler at Rastenburg in East Prussia had failed and the German armed forces had replaced the military salute with the Nazi salute. We of course did not intend to salute the Germans in this fashion. After a brief discussion, we agreed that we would use the Albanian Royalist salute by placing our right hand on the chest at the height of the heart with the edge of the hand pointing outward. As we entered the room, we were greeted with a clicking of heels and a sonorous *"Heil Hitler."* We responded as we had previously agreed. I don't recall anything memorable being discussed at that meeting. We left after a short while and joined the battalion, eager to return to Albania.

We left Kosova and didn't even stop in Shkodra as we pushed on to Tirana. We arrived there during the wee hours of the morning, jumped off our trucks, and dispersed after agreeing that we would meet that afternoon at 4:00 p.m. in front of the building that housed the Central Committee of Balli Kombëtar.

I reached our apartment building and realized I had no keys for the main entrance door. I hit the lock with my rifle butt, the door swung open, and I ran to the third floor two steps at the time. By the time I unlocked the door to our apartment, Mom was there, flinging her arms around my neck, and right behind her was Dad. We talked briefly and then we all went to bed. Mine was made and ready. It was good to be home again.

The next afternoon we men of the Battalion Besnik Çano put on our uniforms and armed ourselves for the last time as a unit. Several representatives of the Central Committee came to greet us and one of them, Ali Klissura, spoke eloquently, putting our trip in perspective and honoring once more Hamit Troplini, our comrade who had sacrificed his young life in the Morina Valley. I handed over the battalion flag signifying that the battalion was officially dissolved. Sadness hung over us all and sorrowful days would soon follow.

I shook hands and said farewell to Seit Kazazi and to Halim Begeja, our second in command. This was the last time I saw Seit. I would briefly meet Halim in 1955 in New York, a few hours after my arrival in the United States. Years later, I saw two battalion members in Toronto a couple of times. One of them was Bardhyl Borshi, our squad's machine gunner, the other Rizvan Banka, the first flag bearer of the battalion.

Sometime after my release from jail, Mom and I were chitchatting about various things and I asked her about her and Dad's decision to let me join the Battalion Besnik Çano. By the summer of 1944, it must have been obvious to my parents that the war against the communists was lost both in Yugoslavia and in Albania; furthermore, that the battalion's efforts could have no impact on whether Kosova would remain a part of Albania or would return under Yugoslav rule. What had prompted them to let me risk my life for a lost cause?

Mom replied that she and Dad had discussed the matter at length. If they had prevented me from going, I might have obeyed grudgingly but would have concluded that they were hypocrites, that all their preaching of loving Albania and being willing to fight for it had been mere lip service. It would have destroyed what they had tried to teach me all my life. If, on the other hand, I disobeyed and joined the battalion against their will, it would have caused a serious rift within the family. She and Dad had concluded that they had to take a chance—they had to let me go to war, in order to keep intact what they had taught me and believed in.

After the return from Kosova, things kept going from bad to worse. The communists were continuing their war on every front against Balli and nationalism in general. Our volunteer units were attacked systematically; nationalist personalities were killed in the streets and in their homes while the communists made only token efforts against the Germans. The Allied kept supporting the communists despite clear evidence that the communists throughout the Balkans were in hot pursuit not of Germans but of their own political goals. Enver Hoxha was using war and terror to bring Albania under communist rule. Tito was doing the same in Yugoslavia, and so were communists in Greece. Romania and Bulgaria were a different chapter. They fell into Stalin's hands when Soviet troops overran both countries.

During the summer of 1942, we had moved into a new apartment, one of 16 apartments in Building #1. There were four such parallel buildings that ran north and south. Now, two years later, someone fired at a passing German patrol from the flat roof of Building #4. The German patrol turned around and moved into the building. I happened to be there and neighbors asked me to make myself available as an interpreter to avoid misunderstandings and possible reprisals. While the Germans had suffered no casualties, they took such incidents seriously. When I approached them offering to serve as an interpreter, they gladly accepted. They searched the rooftop of #4, found no one there, saw that families living in those apartments were anything but troublemakers, and left without wasting time or taking hostages. We were greatly relieved because in times of war no one could anticipate the consequences of such incidents. This event would surface again a few months later when Dad and I were in prison.

That summer of 1944, there was another incident that unfortunately ended in the death of the prominent head of a Kosovar family from Prishtina. Ilias Agushi and Dad were members of the Mustafa Kruja cabinet. Mr. Agushi also had an apartment in the same complex with us. One day his male secretary climbed the stairs to the apartment and asked whether Mr. Agushi was home. The housekeeper said yes and asked him to enter. The man responded that all he wanted to know was whether his boss was home. Then he went downstairs, nodded to the assassins who were awaiting his signal and left the building. The terrorists climbed the steps, rang the doorbell, burst into the apartment and shot Ilias Agushi dead. One can imagine how that alarmed all of us who had been living under tension for quite some time. It was another example of the "class struggle," the ideological cover name communism gave to terror as a weapon, which it had successfully used elsewhere in the past and was now applying to Albania to destroy the strong and bend the weak.

One day Dad was at a friend's home a couple of miles from our apartment. The phone rang and someone alerted us that a terrorist on a bike had been circling the block where Dad and his friends had gathered that afternoon. I immediately called Dad and passed on the news. A little later, I was waiting at the window when I saw Dad's car pulling into the courtyard. As Dad stopped the car, a young man on a bike came out of nowhere and hit the brakes next to Dad's car. Dad pointed his revolver at the young man before the latter could lift his hands off the handlebars. When Dad pointed the revolver at the young man's chest, the latter almost fell off his bike. They talked briefly, but I could not hear what they said to each other nor could I make out whom the young man was. The man left and Dad entered our building.

Here is what had happened. Dad had received my warning and was on the lookout. When the young man on the bike stopped near the car, Dad had him covered. It turned out that the young man was a physician, the brother of Elena, Mustafa Kruja's daughter-in-law.

I asked, "Dad, how come you did not pull the trigger when you had been warned about a young assassin on a bike circling the block where you and your friends were meeting?"

"You never fire unless you are sure of your target," was his terse reply.

Dad was a man of convictions. Mom and I worried that he often went out on foot to his office at the Council of State and never wanted any bodyguards as did most other people whom the communists might want to assassinate. One day we suggested that he reconsider his decision but his answer came along these lines. First, it was nearly impossible to find someone so devoted that he would sacrifice his life for the person he was supposed to protect. Most people did it for money and the only way to enjoy this money was by staying alive. Next, Dad was a very fast walker. Anyone wanting to follow and catch up with him would betray himself by the noise of his footsteps. As far as hiding behind a corner and stepping out when Dad approached, Dad never walked along walls but always in the middle of the street. That would deny an assailant the advantage of surprise and would give Dad time to draw. One could have come up with some objections but Dad had more experience in such matters and who was I to offer advice?

One day we talked about leaving Albania before the communist takeover that seemed to be coming ever so quickly. Dad's rationale went something like this: He had been in exile for 15 years during Zogu's regime.

Those had been hard years. Presently, we had no financial reserves and any escape from Albania would present insurmountable economic problems. He had done nothing to deserve punishment. Come what may, he was not going to go once more into exile.

I knew better than to argue with him. On the other hand, I was part of the Nationalist Youth Organization and exposed to the realities of the daily anti-communist struggle. I was convinced that the communist take-over would start with a bloodbath and that Dad would be among its early victims. Before he had accepted the post of secretary of education in the Kruja cabinet, the communists had offered to pay him a cabinet member's salary on condition that he refuse the job. Dad had replied that if he accepted the position, it was not for the money. As secretary of education, he had opposed the communists wherever and however he could. As a cabinet member, he had decided on the strongest anti-communist measures ever taken by an Albanian government of those times. I decided I had no choice. If I could not get through to him, I would stay in Albania and do my best to protect him and our family.

CHAPTER THIRTEEN

COMMUNIST TAKEOVER

The communists were on a roll. As the Germans withdrew from Greece and southern Albania, communist forces moved in behind them, crowed "victory," and imposed their political and administrative apparatus on the "liberated territories." On November 1, they entered half of Tirana but marked time because the Germans were not ready to withdraw. Our part of Tirana was still "free," so to say, as the communists stood by, avoiding locking horns with the German troops that were firmly entrenched in their positions.

One evening, from our terrace windows I could see tracers crisscrossing the sky. The communists usually fired from rooftops and the Germans responded from the ground. Suddenly, I saw tracers fired from the top of the minaret of the mosque on Skanderbeg Square aimed at the German bunker that controlled access to and from four major streets. The base of the minaret was about 150 feet from the bunker. It was foolish to attack the bunker with small-arms fire and downright preposterous to open fire from the unprotected minaret. The German bunker fired back. The first shell missed by a hair. The second struck the slender tower midway. The upper part of the minaret shook, broke, slid off sideways, and crashed to the ground. All this seemed to be happening in slow motion. It was unlikely that the partisan who had fired from the minaret could have survived. It was one more futile death in a senseless struggle. The Germans were going to withdraw according to their timetable, ignoring the halfhearted pressure the communists were exerting on them.

Most of the noise that surrounded us day and night came from propaganda, not from communist guns. After the war, the Albanian partisans would claim that they had dislodged the German troops from Albania and that 28,000

167

Albanians had lost their lives in this struggle. Communist figures were always inflated and only communist figures have been available since the end of the war. To this day, to my knowledge no one has tried to verify such claims. After the war it became evident that Italian and Czech partisans, and perhaps many more, had struck similar deals with German troops in retreat.

During those last few months before the communist takeover, the nationalist authorities had become ever less effective in those parts of the country still under their nominal rule. In early November, some representative of the communist Youth asked me to come with friends to a certain address near Radio Tirana. I invited Astrit Permeti and Faslli Nepravishta to join me. When we got there, they ushered us into a room where three communist Youths awaited us. The gist of their statement was that the Albanian people would soon be free. The Front of National Liberation would take power temporarily until nationwide elections could take place. For the first time in its history, Albania would have a freely elected government. We, the youth of Balli Kombëtar, had a chance to join the victors and contribute to the reconstruction of Albania.

As I was the one the communists had contacted, both sides looked at me for an answer. My reply was simple: What we heard sounded promising. We would stand on the sidelines until we saw the victors in action. If their deeds matched their words, we would gladly join forces to rebuild our country. We shook hands and left. Within days, I would be arrested and meet the fathers of my two friends in prison. General Aqif Permeti, Astrit's father, would be shot, Faslli's father, Abidin, would draw a lengthy prison sentence.

November 16, 1944 was the last day of the German presence in Tirana. Some distant relatives had moved in with us to escape the dangers of living in no-man's land. We still had enough food but were prey to conflicting feelings. On one hand, there was the fear of the imminent partisan occupation, on the other a certain curiosity as to how the Reds would run things. Two events marked that afternoon as the last grains of sand of our way of life were trickling away.

That afternoon, we saw German soldiers moving swiftly inside the "Lana" ditch that ran along our apartment building in a northerly direction. We could see only their heads bobbing up and down. Suddenly, our phone rang. The call was for Dad. It was from Tahir Kolgjini, a former head of the Albanian police.

"I am in front of the Hotel Dajti with one foot on the ground and the other ready to climb aboard the last German column of trucks about to leave Tirana. Do you want me to send a car to pick you up?"

Dad smiled, shook his head, and replied, "Thank you for the offer, but no. Have a safe journey." Thus vanished the last opportunity our family had to escape the imminent communist takeover. A few hours later, the communist forces knocked at our door.

That happened around midnight. The atmosphere was confusing. The inhabitants of the various apartments opened their doors and congregated on landings and steps between floors. Formerly hidden sympathizers wore badges with pride for the first time in public. Others hid their hostility toward the partisans at this moment of surrender, looked at the victorious enemy with curiosity, and rolled with the punches—up to a certain point. The partisans wore rumpled makeshift uniforms. Their officers were better dressed, in contrast with what I would have expected. One officer drew a list out of his leather satchel and began to rattle off names. Among others, he mentioned Dad and Bahri Omari, a former member of the Balli Kombëtar Central Committee. The officer asked these men to get ready. They were to go to the nearest military command post for interrogation—a mere formality, he added. Bahri Omari's wife demanded to accompany her husband.

The officer turned holier than thou. "This is the People's Army. The men whose names are on the list will be safe in the hands of their brothers, unlike the past when Balli Kombëtar arrested people at night and shot them a few hundred yards from their homes."

Dad intervened, saying that Bahri Omari's wife had the right to accompany her husband since she was Enver Hoxha's sister. Enver Hoxha was head of the provisional government and the communist top dog. The officer hesitated. He consulted with his fellow officers in whispers. Then he delivered their decision. There was no need for Bahri Omari's wife to accompany the group. The interrogation would be postponed until daylight. The men could return to their families. The next morning, the bodies of those arrested the previous night were found in ditches near their homes, riddled with bullets.

November 17 started out as a gray, dull morning. Partisans marched in and out of our apartment building and we could find neither rhyme nor reason to their coming and going. A young servant girl, who had babysat for a family on the first floor, turned up in a British military uniform with a red star on her cap. She looked good, much better than her comrades-in-arms of either gender. As we did the night before, we fed the partisans assigned to us. They kept mostly to themselves and avoided direct contact with us.

In the afternoon, some urchins ran across our courtyard. One of them was wearing a military cap with "scrambled eggs" on the visor. Judging by the insignia, it had to belong either to General Permeti or General von Mirdascz. As General Permeti lived in our neighborhood, it was likely that he was under arrest and that his home had been ransacked. At dusk, another officer read names off a list, and this time I was among those being arrested. Not knowing what would happen to us, I handed Mom my wallet and my wristwatch, just in case. Our little group marched off at dusk. The clouds had vanished and a marvelous sunset painted the horizon in brilliant red. We walked for a few minutes and then were told to stop next to a ditch. I looked at the partisans escorting us. They made no sudden moves nor did they remove their rifles from their shoulders. Then we started walking again, this time toward apartment buildings at the bottom of the foothills at the southern edge of Tirana. A few months before, our Battalion Besnik Çano had gathered in the courtyard at a farewell-to-arms ceremony attended by members of the Central Committee of Balli Kombëtar. Times had changed.

By now, it was dark. We heard the crackle of German machine guns and small-arms fire at a distance. No one seemed to know what was happening. The next day we heard that a handful of Germans had been surrounded at the Burgu i Ri, the large prison at the outskirts of town. Meanwhile, the last German column had reached Vorra, halfway between Tirana and Durrës. When the Germans heard the shots, they detached a platoon that turned back, broke the communist encirclement, and freed their comrades.

We reached the building that had formerly housed the Balli Central Committee. Our guards led us down a flight of steps and herded us into a room in the basement. Several men were already there, among them General Aqif Përmeti and Fejzi Alizoti, a high functionary and member of several governments under the Turks as well as under King Zogu. Young communist officers entered, stared at the prisoners, and asked for their names. When they heard some well-known names, they gaped at them, like visitors at the zoo staring at exotic animals.

At one point, a partisan came in and asked one of the officers for instructions because German and Italian prisoners were asking to go out to relieve themselves.

"Request denied," the officer snapped in return. The partisan turned around and disappeared.

Fejzi Alizoti remarked, "You can shut people's mouths but not their..." He and the rest of us would soon find out what the "liberators" were capable of.

The door opened and Colonel Nexhip Vinçani walked into our room. He embraced first Dad and then me as we exchanged the traditional greetings. His family was from Vinçani, the village of my ancestors. Nexhip was bright and a good student. Dad had helped him get a scholarship to study in Italy. During the civil war, he had joined the partisan forces. He spoke to us in a friendly manner and then left. I would not see him until 1994, two years after the so-called fall of communism in Albania.

In 1994, I looked for him because he was the highest-ranking communist I had known since before the war. I wanted to ask him about the inner workings of the Red regime, for he had been high enough to be in the know. He was living in Tirana, in a brand-new home. Inside, the rooms had a bare minimum of furniture. His daughter led us to his bedroom where there was a metal bed frame with a thin mattress. Against the opposite wall were a small table and a chair. She asked us to sit down, pointing at the bed. When his daughter helped him into the bedroom, I would not have recognized him except for a scar at the corner of his mouth. He wore a dark suit and a white shirt that hung on him like on a scarecrow. I rose, embraced him for old times' sake, and could not hold back.

"Nexhip, what have they done to you?"

"They kept me 50 weeks in a mental institution," was his reply. I was shook up. It was common knowledge what "treatment" inmates received in such institutions. Nexhip had been of athletic build. After the communist takeover, he had graduated with highest honors from the Frunze Academy in Moscow. Upon returning to Albania, he supposedly had compared the Soviet and the Albanian communist regime in ways unfavorable to the latter. If that was not bad enough, he had competed for the number-two spot on the political ladder and had lost. He was removed from his high army post and demoted. Years later, when the regime had wanted to fortify Albania's shores against a possible American landing, he was reinstated and given the assignment. Once he completed the necessary fortifications, he was sent packing again. I hesitated to ask what prompted his hospitalization in a mental institution. Fifty years had passed between that meeting on the first night of our arrest and our encounter in Tirana in 1994. Over that half-century, many families had suffered and many lives had been destroyed, including Nexhip's, despite his war record and former rank of general.

But back to the events of November 1944. The next day, the guards marched us toward the center of town until we came to a low building surrounded by an eight-foot wall. Despite its sturdy doors and iron bars on the windows, it did not look like a prison. It was the former branch of a bank and never intended as a prison. I did not mind. We had survived that first night when prisoners were shot on their way "to being interrogated at the command post." Now it was important that our families find us to keep them from worrying. Tirana had grown considerably when people from southern Albania had come to seek refuge from the horrors of war. As it turned out, this influx had increased the effectiveness of the grapevine. Late that morning, Mom arrived and brought us some food. Thank God for Mom! She could see us from the gate through the windows and was able to let other families know of the whereabouts of their relatives.

During the day, we had no big problems even though the room was too small for the number of prisoners that were squeezed in. Not so at night; the only way all of us could catch a few hours sleep was for half the prisoners to remain standing while the other half slept on their side. There was not enough room for us to sleep on our backs. After a few hours, those standing up lay down while the rest got on their feet. Nobody got a full night's rest but some sleep was better than none.

Having survived that first night of my arrest, I asked Mom to bring me my wallet and wristwatch. The next day I saw her hand both items to the partisan at the gate. When he came to me, he gave me my wallet but no watch. When I asked him about my watch, he denied receiving it from Mom. Later, I saw my watch on his left wrist. The watch had gone to the victor!

We stayed in this prison for a few days and then were moved to the Burgu i Ri. That prison consisted of two two-story buildings a few yards apart from each other. Each had four large rooms on the first floor, front and back, separated by hallways and by an entrance hall and a staircase in the middle. On the second floor, there were two large rooms, equivalent to the four on the first floor. In the middle, on top of the staircase, there was a small room in Prison 1. The restrooms were at the far end on both floors. In front of these two buildings was an area about 50 feet wide that extended along the entire façade of the two buildings. It was separated from the rest of the large front yard by a barbed-wire fence and a gate about 15 feet high. Beyond the barbed wire was the very large front yard that was out of bounds for prisoners. The prison offices were at the far end.

The day we arrived, we were assigned to Prison No. 1, to one of the large rooms on the top floor. Several women occupied the small room on top of the staircase, among them three young German women.

When we entered our room, we were pleasantly surprised. Obviously, this had been built as a prison with barred windows and sturdy doors with hefty steel bolts. Compared to our previous prison, however, here we had enough room not just to sleep on our backs but also to hold foot races if we so desired. We had neither beds nor blankets. Furthermore, we had no electric power; neither did the rest of Tirana. We did have running water, however, and restrooms on our side of the bolted doors. That was important, particularly for the older men among us. That night, we lay down on the floor, glad to be alive and to have room to stretch out.

That first night we found out the cells were full of bloodthirsty bed-bugs. When our families brought us field beds, we tried to rid ourselves of these bloodsuckers by putting tin cans filled with water under the feet of our beds. That did not help, since the insects crawled up the wall and across the ceiling. Once above a prisoner's bed, they dropped down and began gorging themselves with the prisoner's blood. The next morning, we used newspapers as torches and burned the suckers into oblivion. That turned out to be the right approach.

Those first few days, the two cells at the north end of the first floor were packed with German and Italian prisoners of war. There was a striking difference between the two groups. Most of the Italian soldiers had no uniforms. More likely than not, their communist captors had also "liberated" these uniforms, removing their insignia and adapting them for their own use. Yet the Italians were cheerful, singing often at the tops of their voices, and sometimes singing a refrain stating that for them the war was over. They did this while washing up with cold water (no warm water was available), scrubbing themselves, and gushing with joy. Some of them ran around happy as larks, with only a couple of rags the size of handkerchiefs covering their nakedness. True, for them the war was over, but Italy was still torn asunder by the war. The front was moving steadily from south to north with incredible destruction and loss of Italian lives. For the prisoners in Albania, however, the war was over.

The German prisoners presented a different picture. They seemed crushed and gloomy, even though they still had their uniforms and seemed in fair shape. They gave the impression that, once their military organization had crumbled, they had gone to pieces. They were sullen and filthy. They sat in their room in darkness, too dispirited even to roam around the prison behind bolted doors.

One day some fellow prisoners in our cell asked me to act as interpreter because they wanted to buy valuables from the German prisoners of war. When we entered their room, I told the Germans the purpose of our visit. A murmur rose from all four corners. At first, I could not make out what they were saying. Then I heard some voices.

"Quiet, the captain wants to speak."

Now that our eyes had gotten used to the darkness, we saw a man rise.

"I protest most vigorously against the treatment we are receiving from the Albanian authorities. Such treatment violates all rules of the Geneva Convention dealing with prisoners of war. I demand that all applicable articles of the Convention be strictly enforced and that my men and I be treated accordingly." At the end of his speech he remained standing. I had expected anything but such a speech. I was furious.

"Captain, first of all remember that we have been arrested and receive the same treatment you are. If you want to protest, talk to the guards, not to us. Furthermore, where was your great respect for the Geneva Convention when you and your troops were executing Albanian hostages? What about the villages your troops destroyed and burned to the ground in reprisal for Albanian attacks against you? Where were you and your articles of the Geneva Convention?"

Neither he nor his companions said a word in reply. It took me a moment or two to regain my composure.

"The men with me are here to buy any valuables you may want to sell. If anyone is interested, please speak up."

Some soldiers started to dig into their pockets while the Albanians sharpened their eyes trying to see what was for sale. Once the bargaining started, there was no need for me. The Germans held out their merchandise and indicated a price. The Albanians made clicking sounds with their tongues to indicate that the "valuables" were not worth that much. The Albanians would offer some money and the Germans would shake their heads asking for more. The Albanians would reluctantly offer more money and the game went on until the German grabbed the money and let go of whatever he had in his hand.

While I stood there feeling like a bump on a log, a German soldier touched my hand and offered me his wedding band. I had no need for it but he looked so lost. I offered him a good price for it and he accepted without haggling. While the others were still very busy, I walked out of the room holding the ring in my fist. First, I showed it to Dad and then pocketed it. A few years later, when I needed money, I tried to sell it. The buyer said the ring was not made of gold. Perhaps I had overpaid when I bought it or the buyer was trying to cheat me out of my money. Either way, I hope the German prisoner had made good use of what I had paid for the ring. He had needed it more than I did.

Soon our room got crowded as more prisoners arrived day and night from all parts of the city and beyond. Conditions, however, remained bearable. Our families had found us right away. They had brought us mattresses and/or field beds, and of course, food as the prison administration was not providing any.

Within days, the prison population had grown to the point where all rooms were full and space was at a premium. We guessed that the total population had reached—and probably exceeded—the one-thousand mark. Each day partisans would enter our rooms and read this never-ending list of about a thousand names in each room. The procedure took hours and hours and never gave them a clear picture of whether every prisoner was accounted for. It was a bother also because we had to stand while they were reading off the entire list of names. Eventually, they realized they needed a new system. To make sure that every prisoner was listed, they decided that everyone had to see the director in person and be registered anew. They paired us off by twos and when it was my turn, a former colonel and I entered the director's temporary office in our building. My companion raised a clenched fist to his forehead in the communist salute. I saluted the director, Janaq Karabataqi, with a nod. We answered the director's simple questions, saluted once more, the same way as we had when we had entered, and left his office. Outside, the ex-colonel smiled at me and said, "This is how you fool these idiots," referring to his salute with the clenched fist. A few months later, he and a number of other prisoners faced the firing squad.

Those first months under communist rule were a period of pressing questions and elusive, ever-changing answers. The Allies had special missions in Tirana. There were British and American representatives. That was comforting. Then there were also the French and the Soviets and their role was unclear. Also unclear was the role of the Yugoslav representatives who had founded the Albanian communist party and had shaped its policies during the war. When the Allies requested landing rights in Albania, Enver Hoxha replied that the Germans were already gone and that British and American troops were not needed. The Allies had not insisted.

On the diplomatic front, the British brought experts to Albania whose official mission was an obvious cover. Among them was Colonel Oakley-Hill, who had served as an organizer of the gendarmerie under Zogu. He had also entered Albania secretly during the war and had met the leadership of the Albanian resistance. He spoke Albanian fluently and was well acquainted with Albania's past and present political leaders.

Another distinguished British visitor was Lord Cadogan, a collaborator and friend of Prime Minister Winston Churchill. When a group of ladies, including my mother, met with him, Lord Cadogan stated that if a counterrevolution freed but one Albanian city, His Majesty's government would intervene militarily to set things straight. Unfortunately, this was not to be. The revolution of Postriba erupted and freed a portion of northern Albania, including the city of Koplik. Communists in Shkodra and environs disappeared from streets and public places for a few days. When nothing happened, they resurfaced, government forces counterattacked, and the revolution drowned in blood.

This climate of confusion also prevailed in jail. No one knew for sure how the communists would run the country. There were some ominous signs. One afternoon a truck stopped in the prison yard. Two guards dragged a hapless human figure through the courtyard gate into Prison No. 1 and then dumped him in our cell. I recognized Fr. Lazër Shantoja, a Jesuit priest and friend of our family. I approached him and saw his bare feet. They were grotesquely swollen. The small toe of his left foot was dangling by a strip of skin. I had a few bandages, some iodine, sulfa powder, and small scissors among my personal belongings. I cut off the toe and proceeded to bandage his foot. While I was ministering to him, he told me his story.

"I was arrested in Shkodra and put in a small room. After a while, an important-looking man in uniform but without rank insignia entered. I rose in sign of respect. 'Do you know who I am?' he asked. 'No,' I replied. 'I am Mehmet Shehu.' I knew that he was the commander of the First Assault Brigade, and the prime butcher of the war. 'I am pleased to know you,' I replied. 'We'll see if you will be pleased,' was his reply as he stalked out of the room. Shortly thereafter they took me to another room and the tortures started."

I was barely done cutting off the toe when two soldiers came into the room. Without a word, they picked Fr. Lazër up, dragged him out of the room, put him back on the truck, and left. A short while later we heard that Fr. Lazër Shantoja was executed by a firing squad. This was the first time we had tangible proof of communists torturing a prisoner.

During those first months, torture was not routine. Several months passed before they tortured Osman Kazazi, a fellow prisoner and a former leader of the National Front (Balli Kombëtar) Youth Organization. This was an isolated case. What they wanted from him was material they could use against National Front leaders Bahri Omari and Kolë Tromara.

The communist regime was also trying to extend its reach beyond Albania's borders. The press published lists of political refugees, Balli members, royalists, and others who were in Allied hands. Some had escaped from Albania into Greece. Some had followed the German troops on their retreat from the Balkans and had reached Italy via Vienna. Some important nationalist leaders had escaped by boat from Ulqin to Italy. It was first whispered, and later confirmed, that a German motor boat had led them through German minefields near the eastern Adriatic coast. The communists wanted "the traitors" back.

Eternal optimists in our prison saw this extradition request as a positive sign. These men the communists were asking for were leaders of the resistance, compared to many of those presently in prison who were small potatoes, at least in their own eyes. In fact, self-perception played tricks with the majority, if not all, prisoners.

The jail population ranged from decision makers to low-ranking employees, from generals to soldiers and policemen. We had exponents of the two major nationalist organizations, Balli Kombëtar and *Legaliteti* (Royalist Movement) down to simple members such as me. The one thing we all had in common was that the communists considered us political opponents.

I decided to make the most of my time in prison. Here I had the chance to meet people who had directed the Albanian government for decades before the communist takeover. Furthermore, now I could observe them without the accoutrements of power, 24 hours a day, from the moment they opened their eyes in the morning to when they bid good night to their cellmates at night. I could see "cause and effect"; how they reacted to news and events, how they faced reality. Under no circumstances but in jail could I have observed them from such a close distance. I made it a point to devote a couple of days to a VIP—and even some non-VIPs— about whom I wanted to know more.

One day I was walking with one such person who, among other important positions, had headed the Albanian parliament. He was quite short and I was among the tallest prisoners. People watched us walking together in the front yard and dubbed us "Victor Emanuel and Umberto." Victor Emanuel was the king of Italy and the offspring of first cousins. He was very short. To bring fresh blood into the royal dynasty, Victor Emanuel married the daughter of the king of Montenegro, a miniscule Balkan kingdom with a bloodline that had never married into any other royal house. Their offspring, Prince Umberto, grew to be very tall for the times; hence, the comparison involving our short VIP and me.

"You know," my VIP of the day said to me, "in jail we have a strange mélange of people. Some were recognized leaders and some, shall we say, anonymous followers." He was obviously including among the important people the two prime ministers, both of them assigned to our cell; also two generals, two former the heads of parliament, and umpteen ministers, members of various governments, colonels of the various services, and other superior officers, not to mention military of lesser rank.

Then he turned to me and said, "You for instance."

I felt great because I knew he would rank me with the "nobodies."

"You fought against the communists, weapons in hand. You were a member of Balli, of the strongest anti-communist organization in our land. You belong here. But what about me? I conspired with General Ezio Garibaldi to overthrow Mussolini. Events overtook us and we were unable to carry out our plans. Clearly, I should not be in prison with the rest."

I was dumbfounded. The old gentleman, instead of absolving me, had ranked me with those who belonged in prison. Did he not realize that I was the only one among my friends to be in prison? Did he fail to see that in realistic terms I was only a follower and by far not a Pied Piper? His words wreaked havoc with my self-perception. I tried not to show how I felt.

"If you conspired with General Ezio Garibaldi against Mussolini, why don't you ask the general to come to Albania and testify in your behalf?" I stuttered, trying to hide my disappointment.

"Under the present circumstances, until he can get a passport, get transportation, and come to Albania, that would take at least three months. Why should I spend another three months in prison?"

One day I was walking with Fejzi Alizoti, who had held important positions from the time Albania was still under the Ottoman Empire (before 1912) until a few years before, under King Zogu. He may have been a lawyer and was of keen intellect. He explained to me that a basic juridical tenet stipulated that no law could be made retroactive. In view of that definition, none of the prisoners could be held responsible for past actions as long as they had been within existing laws. From a juridical point of view, in his opinion, none of the prisoners presently in jail could be sentenced to more than two or three years of imprisonment. Unfortunately, within a few months, Fejzi Alizoti and 16 others would be executed by court order. In fact, when the firing squad had fired its volley, Fejzi Alizoti had fallen to the ground with the others. He had suffered no lethal wound and asked the prosecutor that, according to international law, his life be spared. The prosecutor, Bedri Spahiu, replied that the Special Tribunal did not recognize international law, and then fired his sidearm, killing him instantly.

Osman Gazepi, an ardent supporter of the former king, was a fellow prisoner. He had reached the rank of major under King Zogu, and was considered a buffoon and one of the king's most faithful followers. Communist officers who visited our prison from time to time had often tried to tease Osman about his former loyalties. One day they asked him, "Would you like for King Zogu to return to power in Albania?" This was a trick question. If Osman said yes, it could cost him some additional years in prison. If he said no, he would deny his old leader and friend. Instead, Osman Gazepi replied, "Of course, I want him to come back. But I want him to be the phonograph record and you the stylus." The young officers did not know what to make of the answer and left visibly confused.

The gray interim period continued for a while. Before the Special Tribunal convened, this was how some of the best minds in jail foresaw the future. One day, the usual group of VIPs in our room had gathered at one end of the medium-sized cell when Osman Gazepi entered he room. He and I sat apart but near the VIP circle.

Osman raised the following question: "Gentlemen, what do you think the communists will do with us?" It was the question of the day, uppermost in everybody's mind.

The learned VIPs spoke out, one at a time. "Well, there is no question that they won the war. We are in prison and they can do as they please."

Others spoke up. "They fought and won. That is true. On the other hand, they are also bright and will understand—sooner rather than later—that it is easier to win a war than the peace."

"Right, they will also recognize that while they had the strength and courage of youth, we have the experience needed to run a government."

"Of course, the hullabaloo against us on the radio and in the press is so much propaganda and they know it."

"They know that, while we opposed communism, we always served our country with integrity and often against our self-interests."

Several had spoken up and it sounded as if we could expect the director of our prison to enter our room with a smile to tell them that they were free to leave any time it was convenient. Now it was Osman Gazepi's turn.

"Gentlemen. The communists went to great trouble to gather us one by one—like olives in harvest season—you think they will let us go scot-free?"

Osman Gazepi had injected reality into some wishful thinking by individuals who should have known better. At first, there was silence. No one stirred. Then the group broke up and the men busied themselves with insignificant details such as fetching water or straightening out their beds (or what passed for beds) in prison.

From time to time during this period, the prison administration gave us cornbread. Much of the time, it was thick, wet, and barely edible. Sometimes it was full of mold. Whenever guards brought the bread into prison, they dropped the canvas sacks between the two rows of iron bars that separated us from the courtyard. We prisoners then picked up the bread and brought it into the prison. One day I was watching this procedure when one of the bags broke and moldy bread fell on the floor.

The prison secretary who was supervising the delivery told one of the guards that the leftovers should not be fed to the pigs in the pens behind the administration building.

I spoke up. "What about us?"

The secretary looked at me surprised. "If anything happens to the pigs, I am responsible!" he said as he shook his head and walked out.

One day I said something to Dad I will regret as long as I live. Dad despised lying above everything else. He always told me that no matter what I did, I always must tell the truth and take the consequences. Only cowards lied and cowards were neither respected nor could they respect themselves. Dad had also told me about the struggle against Turkish domination in Albania. The country had been under the Ottoman Empire for five centuries. It had been exploited. Albanians were forbidden to develop a written language or have Albanian schools. The country had suffered in every respect. When the revolution started, Dad, as a young boy, had first helped the insurgents as a guide and later fought in the ranks of two guerilla bands, one headed by Mihal Grameno and the other by Spiro Bellkameni. When Albania finally declared its independence, Dad was 19 years old. During our years in exile, Dad had told me about Albanian hospitality, Albanian bravery, Albanian loyalty, and the Albanian code of honor. In my mind, no other country or nation could come close to Albania and the Albanians.

The years went by. The Italian invasion of 1939 was overwhelming. Then came the civil war. The communists attacked the nationalists filled with hatred, like furies out of hell. As I looked around in prison, some older inmates matched the ideals that Dad had described as characteristic of Albanians. Many more fell short of those ideals and some were unpaid spies trying to gain favor with the authorities.

"Dad," I said to him one day, "why did you lie to me? What happened to the Albanians you had talked to me about for so many years? Look around you and tell me what you see. A few patriots and the rest informants, crooks, and wheeler-dealers. Are these the Albanians I am supposed to be proud of?"

Dad looked at me while tears started rolling down his cheeks. "My son, what I told you was the truth as I lived it during the revolution for our independence. We entered a village, whether we knew anyone in that village or not. As soon as the people saw the double-headed eagle on our shirts, they invited us in, they fed and protected us until we left again. That was the Albania I was talking about. The years under Zogu have been truly catastrophic."

I had never seen Dad cry. I did not regret making my comments to him. What I regretted was that I had accused him of lying. That I will never forget, nor can I forgive myself for using that word.

Initially, no families were allowed to visit prisoners. One evening, the guards called Beso Gega to the iron bars at the entrance to Prison No. 1. I was curious and followed him. He walked to the bars and I sat, inconspicuously, on the steps behind him. A young woman and a boy in his teens had come to see him. I had no idea who they were. The woman spoke first.

"Dad, why did you transfer from the prison in Gjirokastra to Tirana?" No conventional greeting or anything of the sort.

"Liri, is that all you can say to your father?"

So this was Liri Gega, the best-known communist woman leader, at least among us anti-communist militants, better known than the wives of Enver Hoxha and Mehmet Shehu. When we were still a fighting force, she was high on our list of candidates for arrest or worse. So that's what Liri Gega looked like. Liri did not bother to answer. A painful silence followed. Then her father spoke up.

"I demanded to be transferred, first because the prison walls in Gjirokastra dripped water day and night and my rheumatism was killing me, and second, because there was nobody in town who would feed me."

"And who is going to feed you here?" she retorted.

"Well, you, your brother..." And here the old man's voice trailed off.

"You are wrong," was her curt reply. She turned on her heels and left, followed by her brother who trotted behind her.

Instead of returning to his cell, Beso Gega walked toward ours, with me closely behind him. He walked to where Dad was.

"Do you remember when I came to your office when you were secretary of education? Liri was a teacher and had been arrested as a committed communist and I interceded for her. You asked me whether she was a communist or whether she opposed Italy's occupation of Albania and I said that she was fighting the Italians, that Beso Gega's daughter could never be a communist; and I gave you my word of honor. Right then and there, you ordered that she be released from jail."

"I remember," Dad replied.

"Well, that day you broke your oath of office twice. First, when you freed her from jail; and, second, when you did not have me arrested." Then, Beso Gega got up and left our cell.

Dad looked puzzled. I told him what had just happened. Dad and Beso Gega had fought against the Turkish occupation. Thirty years later, they both opposed the Italian invaders with many Albanians, some nationalists and some on the side of the communists. The civil war had not started yet and in 1942, it was most difficult to separate the nationalists from the communists, and also because the Trojan horse, the communist-led Front of National Liberation, added to the confusion. After the war, the true nature of the various so-called "Fronts of National Liberation" became quite evident on whatever continent the communists started their quest for power.

Liri Gega hovered near the top of the communist hierarchy for a few years until she was accused of deviationism, sentenced to death by a communist court, and executed while pregnant.

Shuk Gurakuqi was the offspring of a patriotic Catholic family from Shkodra. He had spent 15 years in political exile during the years Ahmet Zogu was in power. He was secretary of finance in Mustafa Kruja's cabinet, and was known and respected for his honesty. He was a dear friend of our family.

One day as we walked together, being in a playful mood and knowing that he was a confirmed bachelor, I asked him, "Is it better to remain single or to get married?"

"If you want to live like a king and die like a dog, stay single. If you want to live like a dog and die like a king, get married."

His answer was intentionally cryptic. After a pause, while I was trying to make sense of what he had just told me, he spoke up again.

"As a bachelor you live like a king and are responsible only to yourself and for yourself. You come and go where and when you want. You spend your money and your vacations as you please. That's living like a king. In your old age, however, if you need help there is no one there to care for you and when you die, chances are you are alone in a hotel room while the help waits in the hallway for you to die so they can rent it to someone else.

"When you are married, your wife and children run your life and your first and most important task is to take care of them. If you are old and sick, however, they are at your side. When death knocks at your door, your loved ones will care for you and be all around you until you draw your last breath. Now that I have explained these things to you, the choice is yours."

I had asked the question in jest and had received an answer that was half flippant but also had a serious side to it, particularly under the communists where family members were potential hostages. Since I had no intention of considering marriage seriously, either then or within the foreseeable future, I did not worry about the alternatives his answer presented. Nonetheless, his answer has stayed with me since early 1945.

There were clusters among fellow prisoners. There were those who had been supporters of King Zogu and there were those who had opposed the king and had been in exile 15 long years. There were those who had fought against the communists as well as a few who had been party members and who now shared the prison with the rest of us. We had former officers who had opposed the communists as well as those who had defected from the ranks of the partisans. Yet in jail there was no significant division or hostility among these groups as we all shared the same fate..

We had a sergeant of the prison guards who may have been pushing 50 and was considerably older than the rest of his unit. He was tall, thin, always wore a black raincoat, and was rather reserved. He was not obnoxious toward us prisoners. One day, after the siren blew and our morning walk was over, we re-entered the prison. To our surprise, the sergeant remained in the main hallway. We thought there was an official reason for his presence among us—that perhaps a search for forbidden items was about to start.

He saw our questioning looks and said words to this effect: "You are asking yourselves what I am doing here among you instead of on the outside looking in. Many of you fought against the communist forces and hope in an Allied landing or some cataclysmic event that will overturn the communist regime. That will be your day.

"I fought with the partisan forces and this was to be my day. Instead, I am being accused of being a member of a communist splinter group and find myself in jail pending a detailed investigation. Your day may yet come. I for one will have lost in either case."

Sometime in 1945, I believe, the regime came up with a monetary reform with an exchange rate of 10:1 (ten old lek for one new lek, I seem to recall). The reform allowed each citizen to have no more than 10,000 new lek. Those who had more than 100,000 old lek were to loan that money to the state and would be repaid "in due time." The rich did not want to admit they had more than 100,000 old lek. Holding on to the old currency was not an option. Hence, many went to friends who had little money and gave them old lek that they were to exchange for new ones. The monetary reform was to be completed promptly.

The very day after the monetary reform, the government imposed war profit taxes that could amount to hundreds of thousands of new lek. All rich merchants were arrested. Those who could not pay were jailed for non-payment; those that did pay were arrested as they could not have legally had more than 10,000 lek. Those arrested were tortured to the very edge of death. Some gave up hundreds of thousands of gold coins. One supposedly chose death by torture rather than give the communists the fruits of his labor. This was another page from the manual of proletarian justice and equality.

One day Mom informed us that she and Mergim were being evicted and the furniture confiscated. She had spoken with the president of the republic, Omer Nishani, and had protested that even Mergim's bed was being taken away. The president had answered that it was time Mergim learned to stand on his own two feet. Anyhow, the day she and Mergim were to leave the apartment, she would be unable to bring us food.

I tried to save some food for that particular day but somehow failed. On the designated day, I skipped breakfast and no one noticed. At lunch, one of my friends asked me why I was not eating and I replied that I was not hungry. He and my other friends seemed satisfied with my answer and each turned to the food in front of him.

We had an ex-policeman among us who had found a way to earn enough money in jail to support his family on the outside. Every morning he got up early and started a fire, with permission of the prison authorities, I am sure.

His wife brought him some condensed milk that he diluted with water and then sold for ten cents a cup. Many prisoners liked to have some warm milk in the morning (in Europe we never drank cold milk from the ice-box. It was supposedly bad for the stomach). The man thus made enough money to make it worth his while.

He was short, thin, with dark hair and skin, bow-legged, and anything but handsome. In fact, he looked almost diabolical. He did not buy my answer that I was not hungry. He watched me for a short while. Then he literally jumped to his feet and came to me.

"Look," he said, "if I am not good enough for you to break bread with, I understand. Otherwise, get up and join me. I have enough bread and bean soup for two. I insist. Please join me but bring your spoon. I have only one."

The way he worded his invitation made it impossible for me to refuse without offending him. Besides, my youthful appetite was strongly in favor of accepting his invitation. I thanked him and we enjoyed a bowl of hearty bean soup together. The food hit the spot. I don't know how my friends reacted to his thoughtfulness and generosity. Personally, thereafter I never saw him in any other fashion than that of a kind soul who was willing to share his food with a needy person. He was also probably one of the few in our cell who had known true hunger. Over the coming years, we would all learn what true hunger felt like.

I remember the day when the newspapers reported the death of Alqi Kondi, the head of the Albanian communist youth organization. According to the grapevine, he had crashed his motorcycle into a tree and had died of severe head injuries. I was standing in the corridor when some Balli Youth members came zipping down the corridor. They stopped and spoke to a prisoner next to me whom I did not know.

"Did you hear that Alqi Kondi died in a motorbike accident?"

"Yes."

"Is it true it was your motorbike he killed himself with?"

"Yes, that's true."

"Might you have a city bus in storage somewhere the communists could confiscate?"

Without waiting for a reply, they took off laughing.

CHAPTER FOURTEEN

EARLY MONTHS IN PRISON

For months, we had been asking ourselves what fate had in store for us. The optimists kept daydreaming, while the pessimists were depressing and shunned by the rest of the prisoners. I could not make up my mind which I wanted to be. When I woke up in the morning, I felt great. I was 20 years old, healthy, and strong as an ox. As soon as reality set in and I realized that I was behind bars with about a thousand other individuals, it hit me that Dad's life was in grave danger. That's when the pendulum swung in the other direction and the prison walls closed in on me. The eternal optimists were sure that the Allies would soon land and rid Albania of its communist rulers. They held this belief even though the Germans kept withdrawing and the front kept moving steadily north, away from Albania. These optimists would smile; if challenged, they would whisper, "See what's happening in Greece? The same will happen in Albania. You'll see."

In Greece, there had been clashes between British troops and Greek partisans. Rumors claimed that while Churchill was leaving Athens for the port of Piraeus, communist forces had hit the convoy. Churchill had ordered British forces to return fire and take up positions in Athens. Later, the British forces had extended their perimeter and held part of Greece under their control. Eventually the British would withdraw and U.S. forces would take over. However, this would not take place until some years later. Where Albania was concerned, Enver Hoxha had firmly rejected the Allied offer to land in Albania, claiming the situation was well in hand. Unfortunately, these hands were not those of liberators but of a communist regime that would bring the country death and destruction.

Dad also was unruffled and strong in his optimism. "You'll see, nothing bad will happen to us," he would say to me.

One day I challenged him. "If you are so sure that everything will turn out well, please tell me so I can share your confidence and relax."

Dad smiled. "Of course I don't know what will happen. I do know, however, that if and when things go wrong we will have enough time to worry. Why ruin the present needlessly?"

Then came the day when reality came crashing in. This came about during the early months of 1945. A "special tribunal" was set up to judge the first batch of "war criminals" in the hands of the "people's justice." Some 60 prisoners were informed they would appear before this court and received written charges. There was an obvious pattern to these charges. The most serious were leveled against one member of each cabinet while his former colleagues received lesser charges. Similar charges were also made against superiors and flag officers of the various periods since 1924 to the recent present. The number of hostile witnesses for each accused was set at five. I remember the words of Bahri Omari, brother-in-law of Enver Hoxha, when he received the names of his five accusers.

"This first one I remember because..." Then he proceeded to mention favors he had done for four of the five witnesses. "I don't recall having done any favor for this fifth one. I don't quite understand why he wants to testify against me."

The prosecution witnesses that were going to testify against Dad were also individuals for whom he had done favors. One of them was a former teacher who had asked Dad to transfer him to Vlora because the Italian authorities were persecuting him as anti-Italian at his present post. Dad agreed but found out later that the communist party needed the man in Vlora and had used Dad as an unwitting accomplice. Another witness had received a license to open a store, again through Dad. And so on.

Besides a general charge that Dad had been secretary of education, he was also accused of having engaged in pro-Italian propaganda and, what was most serious, that during his tenure he had stolen the sum of 500,000 francs. Dad did not remember anything remotely connected with this charge. He decided to enlist the help of Ali Hashorva, his former secretary at the Department of Education.

At the last moment, some prisoners were added to the list of the accused. They did not fit the profile of the majority. One, Luigj Filaj, had been my brother's music teacher. The man had never engaged in any political activities. Yet he, with the rest of the accused, would travel every day to the Movie Theater Kosova where the trials were to take place.

Every morning trucks rolled into the prison yard. The rumbling of their engines conveyed a sense of inevitability and doom. The prisoners were handcuffed in pairs and had to climb on the trucks. They spent the rest of the day on hard benches in the movie house and returned in chains each afternoon. Prisoners who had already appeared before the judges had to keep going to court until the last prisoner had been heard.

I stayed in the same cell with Dad until the prosecutor demanded the death sentence for him. That day I had to move upstairs and remained there until after the court handed out the verdicts.

Before the trial, Mom went to see Hysni Kapo, one of the judges and a top leader of the new regime. She asked him whether it was appropriate to hire a lawyer. The question was fully justified since this was the first political trial staged by the Red regime. Hysni Kapo's answer was ominous.

"If you have money to burn, go ahead and hire a lawyer."

Despite his chilling answer, Mom hired the best lawyer she could.

The trial was a farce. The presiding judge was Koçi Xoxe, a tinsmith from Korça. He was the number-two man in Albania. He had been imprisoned by the Italians, had gotten out of jail, and rejoined his partisan brethren in the mountains. He came to see us in jail and surprised us with a question.

"Are you trying to escape? Have you started digging your way out beyond the walls of your prison? Don't be afraid. It is your duty to try to escape. It is the director's duty to prevent such attempts. We dug such tunnels when I was in prison."

No one had the courage to point out the difference between the way prisoners were treated in the past and what would happen under the communist regime. No one dared to contrast the present group of prisoners who had directed the country when Koçi Xoxe was in jail with the present communist leaders who were neither gentlemen nor qualified for the posts they held.

At the special tribunal, Koçi Xoxe headed the panel of judges that included Mehmet Shehu. Mehmet Shehu would remain near the top of the communist pyramid for many years. Bedri Spahiu was the prosecutor of the special tribunal. He, like Enver Hoxha, was a native of Gjirokastra. He joined the communist party early on, fought in the civil war against the nationalist forces, and reached the rank of lieutenant general. He made it his mission to destroy distinguished Albanian personalities that had opposed the communist movement both in Albania as well as those who had fled abroad toward the end of the war. A few years later, he assumed the office of secretary of education. By 1955, he had run out of favor with Enver Hoxha. He spent years in prison and in concentration camps, a victim of the Red regime he had helped create. He remained an unrepentant communist to the end.

When it was Dad's turn in court, Bedri Spahiu leveled several charges against him. Dad had been secretary of education in Mustafa Kruja's cabinet and a close friend of Mustafa. Dad readily agreed with these charges. Next, that he had made propaganda in favor of fascism. Dad responded vigorously. Propaganda, he said, could be done orally and in writing. He challenged the prosecution to present a single speech or even one article in support of this charge. He told the court that after the Italian occupation, at a conference held at the viceroy's palace, Lorusso Attoma, the viceroy's secretary, had approached a group of counselors of state. He had invited them to write articles on behalf of Albania's union with Italy and promised that authors would receive an honorarium of five napoleons, about one third of their monthly salary. Dad had refused, saying that he was not a writer. Lorusso Attoma replied by listing some of Dad's writings. At that point, Dad had stated that he had broken his pen on April 7, the day in 1939 when Italian forces had landed in Albania. In court, Dad added that Omer Nishani, president of communist Albania, had been present during that conversation and could testify that Dad was telling the truth. What Dad did not say was that Omer Nishani had indeed written on behalf of the union of Italy with Albania. Since the communists kept dossiers on everyone, it was likely that Bedri Spahiu and his cohorts were well aware of this detail.

The major charge was that Dad had stolen 500,000 francs during his tenure as secretary of education. Dad rejected the charge. It soon became apparent that the prosecutor had not done his homework. Dad's former secretary had obtained a copy of the documents that supported the statement Dad made before the court. That sum was a surplus from the FAPI agricultural fund and each ministry had received comparable payments. At the Ministry of Education, the sum of 500,000 francs went to pay teachers an extra salary. The prosecutor interrupted saying that only certain teachers, those with fascist tendencies, had received an additional salary. Dad replied that each and every teacher had received a 13th salary from that fund and that their signatures were on record. The prosecutor rebutted, saying that Dad was trying to corrupt Albania's teachers and turn them into pro-Italian puppets.

To this Dad replied, "If you believe that Albania's teachers would sell themselves for one monthly salary, then I plead guilty to this charge." That was the end of that.

When Dad returned to prison, I asked him how he could have admitted being a friend of Mustafa Kruja, the *bête noir* of communism. Dad's answer was straightforward and to the point.

"First of all, it is true that I am a friend of Mustafa's. Furthermore, if I had denied it, the prosecutor could have presented argument after argument in support of that charge. The best way to lay it to rest was to admit the friendship and go on to the next point."

Gjergj Bubani was a journalist, a fellow prisoner, and one who appeared in court daily with the rest of the prisoners. He had been listening to our conversation. He turned to me, saying that Dad had presented the strongest possible defense under the circumstances. That was quite a statement, coming from a professional wordsmith and strong debater.

The trials continued until the day when the prosecutor asked the court to impose sentences ranging from death by firing squad to verdicts of innocence for some prisoners. These were the few that had been added to the group just before the trial.

Dad was among those for whom the prosecutor had asked the death sentence. That morning the guards made me move to the cell block upstairs. The move itself was easy; it involved a collapsible field bed, a mattress, and a handful of personal belongings. The concrete walls, the heavy doors, and the steel bolts behind the doors, however, set me worlds apart from Dad. I was now upstairs and all I could do was try to catch a glimpse of Dad, handcuffed to another prisoner, when he got on or off a truck.

The day came when Koçi Xoxe passed sentence on each of the men standing before him. Some, including Dad, had fought for Albania's independence against the Turks. Others had contributed in one way or another to strengthening the political and social fabric of the country and had turned Albania into a viable member of the European community. Those sitting in judgment and about to pass sentence had fought for communism jointly with their comrades abroad. When the bell tolled for communism five decades later, half of Europe would lie in ruins socially, economically, and morally. Communism had fought hard to create the new man and when it succeeded, the world was the worse off for it.

Before noon the morning of sentencing, an officer came to visit a prisoner in our cell block. He started rattling off the sentences he remembered. He mentioned Dad's name as among those the court had condemned to death.

I was stunned and sat there alone. No one wanted to come near me as there was little they could say. Some time went by. It seemed an eternity. Then I heard the trucks in the courtyard and rushed to the window, but could not see too well. I left the upper cell block, ran downstairs, and hid in a cubbyhole across from the entrance. That room was occupied by a prisoner with pulmonary TB. I whispered to him that the prisoners were returning from the last session of the special tribunal. He understood and made room for me. Armed guards unlocked the two sets of iron bars and took up positions. Then came the prisoners, still handcuffed in pairs. Finally, I saw Dad. He was chained to another prisoner, but not to the one to whom he had been handcuffed throughout the trial.

I burst out of the cubbyhole. "Dad, what's the verdict?"

"I am safe," he replied, his face etched with sorrow.

The guards rushed me and pushed me back. My knees gave and I collapsed backward, against the wall. Dad was safe. Thank God!

When the prisoners were secured in the lower cell block, I returned upstairs with wings on my feet. As I was entering the cell block, Ramazan Jerani was coming in from the cell block across the hall, with his mattress on his shoulders. He was in his fifties, slightly bent, a fine man, and a teacher for whom I had a lot of respect.

Euphoric, I asked, "Are you coming or going?"

"I am returning to our cell block. I moved out this morning because I did not want to be here if they had sentenced your dad to death. There was another father-and-son couple involved in this trial, but they are not as close as you and your dad." He smiled and went back to his old bedding place.

Once I saw my way clear, I went downstairs to see whether I could speak with Dad. The heavy doors separating his cell block were still bolted shut. Through a window, I asked someone inside to call Dad. When Dad came, he looked at me, tears streaking down his cheeks. "They commuted my death sentence to lifelong imprisonment. Don't congratulate me. They are going to shoot my friends." At this point his voice trailed off.

Shortly thereafter, I was permitted to return to Dad's cell block. Now we were together again. Sadly, 17 men from the group were to be executed once the appeal process had run its course. Yet, selfishly, I could not help but feel greatly relieved. Now, with the death sentence no longer hanging over Dad's head, I was as eager as anyone to listen to the eternal optimists and hope and pray that something would happen to remove the scourge of communism from Albania and wherever else it was possible.

During the trial, on April 12, President Roosevelt passed away. To honor his memory, one of the lawyers asked that the court show clemency to the prisoners. The prosecutor replied that showing clemency would make Roosevelt turn in his grave.

Once the trial was over, it was clear that Hysni Kapo had been right when he told Mom that hiring a lawyer was a waste of money. In our case, Dad was to be the sacrificial lamb for the Kruja cabinet. The charges against Dad turned out to be weaker than the communists had anticipated. They also found that Koço Kotte, besides his official duties as member of the cabinet, had also directed a newspaper. On page one, the paper had followed the official line of the times—exalting fascism and Albania's union with Italy. Inside, it had presented a much more realistic picture of events in Albania, often at odds with the official version. The court held page one against Kotte and thus the latter took Dad's place and was executed for the Kruja government.

Throughout the proceedings, the lawyers were severely restricted in how strong a defense they could mount on behalf of their clients. Eventually, they could only ask the court for clemency instead of producing evidence contradicting the official charges. A handful of lawyers who tried to do more were branded enemies of the communist party and eventually paid the price.

We did not have to wait long for the last act of the special tribunal. The appeals for clemency were duly filed and rejected. The 17 prisoners sentenced to death were executed within days by a firing squad.

Some rumors surfaced but were difficult to verify. It was said that a former colonel had lain on the floor of his cell and had refused to get up when soldiers had come to escort him to the place of execution. A fellow prisoner, a former general, had rebuked him, "Do you recall when you and I sent men to their death in combat? Act like a man now that it is our turn!"

From his limo, with drawn curtains, Enver Hoxha had supposedly watched the execution of his brother-in-law—Bahri Omari.

Life in prison changed a lot and yet remained the same. As far as I was concerned, it changed much for the better. When I woke up in the morning, I no longer had that sense of oppression, that heavy burden that had weighed me down for so many months. After all, Dad would live and one never knew what surprises life held in reserve. Doubtless, I mourned for the men who had been shot, victims of contrived political charges. On the other hand, Dad, my beloved Dad, was no longer in danger.

Now Dad told me that he had given his last will and testament to another prisoner who had appeared with him before the special tribunal but was not in danger of being sentenced to death. The man was Ali Kuçi, a former merchant and a good friend of Dad's.

Mr. Kuçi had been a merchant before the communist victory. He was about 5 feet 8 inches tall, portly, with a fleshy, wrinkled face and gray, wavy hair. When I asked him about the testament, tears started rolling down his cheeks. He apologized and asked for my forgiveness; he had opened the little envelope and read Dad's last words to me. Grave as the infraction would have been if Dad had been shot, now that he was safe, it mattered little to me. I assured him that I carried no resentment toward him, took the little envelope, and found a place where I could read the contents without being disturbed. Dad had written just a few lines addressed to me:

My dear son,

This is the sixth time I am a political prisoner and the third time that I am sentenced to death. The first two, foreign powers were going to execute me for fighting against them on behalf of Albania. Those charges were true and they had every right to do so. This time, Albanians are sentencing me to death as a traitor to my country. *Treppenwitze der Geschichte.* [translated as, "An ironic twist of history!"]

I leave you little else beyond an honored name. To your mother I leave my silver cigarette case, to you my gold cufflinks, and to Mergim my fountain pen. The war will soon be over and travel will be possible again. Take your mother and your brother and join Uncle Faik [Bessie's dad] in Detroit.

Signed,
Xhevat

I scanned the letter and pocketed it. Thereafter, I reread it from time to time. Those few lines were imbued with tragedy. They spoke of a man who had fought for Albania since early youth. In exile, he had refused to renounce his Albanian citizenship, preferring hardships and privations for him and his wife. After the Italian occupation, he continued his lifelong fight, this time from the inside. He had risked his good name and now he would die as a traitor. He could see no future for his widow and two sons except to tell them to leave his beloved Albania, which had no room for him or his family.

Now other details gained an importance they had lacked before. We had access to hot water and could bathe, for a fee of course. Our families brought us food once a day and we made it last for at least two meals. It was a burden for the families, not only financially, but also physically. Mom, for instance, had to carry the stacked food containers a good three quarters of an hour and then walk another three quarters of an hour back to the apartment she was now renting.

Once inside the prison yard, the families handed the food to guards that stood between the two sets of bars that separated us from the outside. The guards stirred the food and broke the homemade bread to make sure they contained no messages before handing them to the intended recipients.

The guards used the same spoon to stir soup, meat, vegetables, or whatever else the families brought in. One day a prisoner offered his own wooden spoon to the guard to stir the food. It was his birthday and his wife had prepared his favorite dishes. The guard seemed not to have heard. He removed the covers off the food containers, bent down, picked up some dirt with his spoon, dipped the spoon into the food, stirred it, and handed the containers to the prisoner without looking at him or missing a beat.

It was not uncommon for guards to kick prisoners as they entered or left a prison building. NCOs encouraged such behavior as it led to bad relations between the guardians and the guarded. One morning we heard that some prisoners had tried to escape. The attempt was unsuccessful. It turned out that several prisoners had made a run for it with the help of a guard who had intentionally looked the other way. We never saw that guard again. More likely than not, the guard was shot.

From time to time the guards carried out unannounced searches of our cells while we were walking in the front yard, and frisked us as we came back in. I had nothing to hide except a medium-sized pocket knife. In prison, I had my military boots and a pair of wooden clogs. I wore the boots in bad weather and the clogs the rest of the time. When I wore the clogs, I hid my pocket knife in one of the boots and stuffed some paper into the tip to keep the knife from sliding out if they picked up the boots. If I wore the boots, I kept my pocket knife under my French beret and when they searched me, I would raise my arms in mock surrender smiling at the guard. The system may have been naïve but it worked.

The prison authorities also tried hard to prevent unauthorized news from entering the prison. Their efforts were fruitless as long as there was direct or indirect contact with the outside world. One fellow prisoner had a little dog that came when his wife brought food. The dog would scoot between the bars, put his paws on his master's legs, and lick his hands when the man petted and stroked the cute little critter. In so doing, the man also retrieved a message from under the dog's collar. Later that day, the man would share with us whatever news the dog had smuggled into the prison.

Mom used several different methods. She baked bread and hid a vial with news in the heel of the bread. The guards usually broke the bread in two somewhere near the middle. The heel was hard and difficult to break and therefore the safest part of the loaf. Other times, she brought us books. On the cover page, she marked a fictitious date supposedly when the book was bought. The month indicated the page where the message started. Beginning with the top line, she put a pencil dot over the first time a given letter appeared on that page and continued marking one letter per line. It took us some time to put together the entire message but it worked. As this was our method of choice, we never shared it with any prisoners, including our friends.

A third method came into play when we met with her face to face with two sets of bars and a complement of guards between us. Once, she wanted to let us know news concerning Bishop Fan Noli, an Orthodox prelate and former prime minister of Albania overthrown by Zogu in 1924. Bishop Noli now lived in the United States. As she started talking to us, she began with four words from a poem of his ("*syrgjyn gjallë, syrgjyn vdekur...*") and completed the sentence by saying that he was not coming. We had regretted it when government sources had announced his visit. The communists had made a much ado about this event, interpreting his visit as an endorsement of the regime by the bishop. Now our sorrow had turned into joy. Mom was the first who brought the news to us. Brave Mom, smart Mom!

CHAPTER FIFTEEN

FATHER ANTON HARAPI

In prison, early on, we did get rid of bedbugs. We had other parasites, however, that were more dangerous that we could not get rid of. These were the so-called stool pigeons, the informants, a dangerous breed of "bird" that perched on a prisoner's bed or fluttered nearby inside the prison or outdoors, and chirped anti-communist words into the prisoner's ear and then reported the prisoner's response, correctly or in distorted fashion, to the prison director. Whatever these "birds" reported was always detrimental to the prisoner. If the prisoner agreed with the anti-communist whisperings of the "bird," his response was duly reported. If the prisoner disagreed, he was accused of agreeing simply because he obviously knew that the "bird" was an informant. As Dad put it, these informants were eternal. Within their lifetimes, they had served Zogu, then the Italians, the Germans, and now they worked for their communist masters. Informing was like a profession—once an informer, always an informer. The communists turned out to be the most interested in what these "birds" had to offer, but paid the least for such services.

To avoid becoming a target, one had either to be asleep or to study. Otherwise, before you knew it, a bird of this kind would perch near you and the conversation would go something like this.

Bird: "Wasn't the cornbread awful today? It was moldy, downright inedible!"

If the prisoner agreed, that was the wrong answer; if he disagreed, that too was wrong. Initially, I trained myself to sleep most of the day and all night long. This waste of time I could ill afford. Instead, I decided to study

French. I found the language fairly easy because of my Italian and my eight years of Latin.

Then one day that spring of 1945, the V-E Day issue of *Life* magazine fell into my hands. On the cover was a sailor kissing a pretty girl in Times Square. I had read somewhere that 60 percent of English words were either of Latin or German origin. As I knew both languages, I thought that would not be a problem. Boy was I wrong. I could not understand the text, no matter what page I turned to. On the spot, I decided to switch from French to English. I could cheat my way through in French. Now I decided to learn English.

When Mom brought us some food that day, I asked her to bring me whatever I needed to study English. Within days, Mom brought me two books by Ernie Pyle, a German-English/English-German dictionary, some notebooks, paper and pencils, and, thoughtfully, an eraser.

Now I was in business. I had studied Italian in 1936 by the Mertner method. This method stayed away from the traditional boring approach of using phrases such as "My aunt's cat is under the table. The carafe is on the credenza." Mertner had served in the Austro-Hungarian army in World War I. The Austrian and Italian troops had moved back and forth as they occupied and gave up their mountain trenches in a war of attrition. Mertner had often found Italian newspapers in the enemy trenches that offered short news items about various events. With a dictionary, he could understand the simple, straightforward newspaper text. After the war, he adopted this approach to learning foreign languages. He presented a news item, say in Italian, followed by a word-by-word translation, in parallel with a correct German version. That method had served me well when we moved to Fiume and I had to learn Italian in a hurry. Now, nine years later, I would adapt it to studying English.

I began by translating Chapter 1, word for word. It did not take me long to understand what Ernie Pyle was saying. I remember it covered the American landing in North Africa. I memorized about 100 words a day and repeated the words of previous days until I had them down pat. In less than a month, I knew about 3,000 words and did not have to go to the dictionary as frequently as in the beginning. Before I knew it, I was enjoying what I was reading and, on top of that, I reaped some unexpected benefits. First, English was beginning to make sense to me, a step forward compared to my blank stare just a few weeks before when I had looked at

Time magazine. Next, Ernie Pyle took me to North Africa, to the Far East, and all over the world, well beyond the prison walls in Tirana. One day he put me next to a GI who was fishing along a river. Suddenly Eisenhower showed up behind the soldier.

"Hi, soldier."

"Hi, General." And, according to Pyle, the soldier continued fishing.

Never in my life had I run into an army where a soldier would reply in such a manner to a general. In those I was familiar with, the soldier would have jumped up and snapped to attention. He would have clicked his heels, and saluted; not so in the American army, at least not according to Ernie Pyle.

But there was more to my learning English. As I grew up, I had been taught that a brave man was never scared. To hide the fact that I was scared and therefore a coward, I had gotten into many a fight in and out of school. I could not let people in on my secret, now could I? As I grew up, I did not know how I would behave in combat—if and when the time came. It turned out I was scared, particularly before we started firing back at the enemy. Then the adrenaline took over and things got better. Pyle, on the other hand, was saying that everyone was scared, the brave and the not-so-brave. Except that the brave would do what was expected of him—despite his fear. Now that was something I could live with, something that would restore my self-respect. That felt great!

One shortcoming of my approach to learning English was the obvious lack of hearing spoken English. I had no one to teach me the correct pronunciation. Furthermore, if I wanted to write something in English, there was nobody to correct it. With us in prison was Akile Tasi who had spent years in the United States and had edited the Albanian-American newspaper *Dielli*. He was so much under siege by would-be students of English, however, that I decided not to approach him. Meanwhile, my vocabulary and knowledge of English idiomatic expressions kept growing day by day.

The German and Italian prisoners of war we had first met when we reached Burgu i Ri left early on, destination unknown. We still had with us the three German women prisoners and now we had another five to ten German male prisoners who kept more or less to themselves. One day I met one of them. He was tall, slim, and self-assured in a pleasant sort of way. I engaged him in conversation and we seemed to hit it off from the very beginning. We started walking together in the morning and afternoon and, after a few days, I knew a few details of his previous life. His name was Hans Lüning. He was a graduate of a police academy, was drafted, and had served on the Russian front in an infantry unit with the rank of captain.

He told me about an event from his Russian campaign. At one point, a young major had joined his unit. He was younger than Hans, who was born in 1921. The major was the son of a general and had received the Iron Cross with oak leaves, swords, and diamonds, comparable to the Congressional Medal of Honor. These details had made Hans's unit suspect that the newcomer had received special treatment as the son of a general. Soon Hans had a chance to get to know his young superior better. One day the two of them went out to reconnoiter the terrain, just the two of them. Suddenly they found themselves in a trap. Two Soviet troopers jumped them, took away their weapons, tied their hands behind their backs, and started marching them toward the Soviet lines. Apparently, the Soviets had been on patrol and were lucky enough to capture the two German officers. Having walked for a while, the foursome stopped for a brief rest. The Germans were put in a barn, still with their hands tied behind their backs. The Soviet soldiers stayed outside. Inside the barn, Hans felt depressed. It was likely that they were near the Russian lines and soon both German officers would experience the horrors of being in the hands of Soviet interrogators. At this point, Hans heard the young major whispering in his ear.

"Now is our chance. I have a small handgun hidden in my boot. I don't intend to use it unless it is absolutely necessary. How good is your jiu-jitsu?"

"Pretty good," replied Hans.

"I figured that. Now we will ask our captors to take us out to relieve ourselves. They will probably agree and take us out one at a time. Can you see that tree through the window? You go first. At the tree, ask your guard to untie your hands. He will probably do so but keep you covered with his gun. You busy yourself for a minute. I will scream and call my guard in. Your guard will turn. Jump him, grab his gun, and run back to the barn. I will jump my guard. If necessary, help me. OK?"

Hans nodded. They called the guards and things went as the young major had predicted. When Hans returned to the barn he saw that the major had jumped his guard who lay unconscious on the floor. Hans cut the ropes, freeing the major's hands. Hidden behind the door, the major had called the second guard. When the guard entered and was seeking to adjust his eyes to the dark, the major had jumped and hit him with both feet in the back.

"What shall we do with the two soldiers?" Hans had asked.

"They did not hurt us, we'll let them live. Let's tie their hands and feet, put them inside, and leave their weapons outside the barn. We don't want to take their weapons with us or else their unit will shoot them. Once back, with their weapons in their possession, they can concoct any story they want. Let's retrieve our automatic pistols and get going. We should be able to make it back to our lines shortly after dark."

Hans concluded his narrative. "The young major was the son of a general. This may have helped him in some way. There is no doubt in my mind, however, that he had earned his high medal on his own merit."

Hans told me one day that during the war, when the German army attacked, it would send up to three waves against enemy positions. If they were unable to break through, the attack was called off, at least for the time being. In Stalingrad, Hans had counted up to 11 Soviet waves attacking the German positions, one after the other. There were times when the German troops had to come out to remove the piles of corpses so they could see the next Soviet wave. The Red soldiers kept coming with Soviet machine guns pointed at their backs in case they wanted to retreat. In fact, the last waves of Soviet troops had to grab the weapons of their fallen comrades, as they, their replacements, had none.

Hans had suffered a severe head wound at Stalingrad and was evacuated by air. The majority of wounded were left behind as their wounds were less severe and the Soviets would treat them in captivity. This turned out to be a disaster waiting to happen. The Soviets treated their prisoners, including the wounded, in a most barbaric way, as the world found out after the war.

Hans was sent to Berlin and, after recovery, he was assigned to military intelligence in Greece. Here, he received a fictitious name, rank, and uniform. Officially, he was a sergeant assigned to an artillery unit. In reality, he served in German intelligence as a liaison with the nationalist resistance movement of General Zervas. In this capacity, he traveled between German and Greek headquarters, and to various Greek units in the field.

One morning, Hans happened to arrive at a village that had been taken over by the Greek partisans during the night. He was taken prisoner and was brought before three British officers, a colonel and two majors. According to international rules of war, Hans gave his name, rank, and serial number, in this case all of them fictitious.

The British officers began by asking questions about the strength of Hans's artillery unit, the number of rations delivered each day, the names and numbers of officers commanding the unit, and the like. Hans refused to provide information beyond name, rank, and serial number. Finally, the colonel tired of this game.

"You are Captain Hans Lüning, you work for German intelligence under commander so-and-so, and you liaise with General Zervas. You are a graduate of the police academy, joined the service in such-and-such a year, were wounded in Stalingrad, and flown to Berlin." The colonel gave him additional accurate information about his biography and career.

Now it was Hans's turn. "You, sir, are colonel so-and-so," and Hans rattled off the colonel's career highlights. He continued by giving detailed biographies of the two majors standing next to the colonel. The colonel rose from his chair and, followed by his two officers, left the room. One of them turned toward Hans, winked with a smile, and closed the door behind him.

"How did you know all those details about the three British officers?' I asked Hans.

"Shortly after the three of them came to Greece, we received their dossiers from Berlin," Hans replied. "Besides, we also dealt with them directly after their arrival. We provided them with lists of names of Greek communists in various cities while they provided us with the names of their partisan comrades in the mountains."

I was flabbergasted. How could enemies, such as the Germans and the British, engaged in a deadly struggle with each other, maintain such links, particularly the British officers whose lives after all depended on the protection offered them by the partisans in the mountains?

Hans answered my unspoken question. "Remember, no matter who wins the war, the victor will have to deal with the communists. The struggle between international communism and the West will be the continuation of World War II."

"How high up must one be to have this broader vision of the present and future conflict?"

"Lower than you think," Hans replied. "I was in Greece, on a ship traveling from Crete to continental Greece. Suddenly someone yelled from the bridge, 'Periscope in sight!' The German crew rushed to battle stations. All guns turned toward the submarine that rose to the surface. We soldiers thought it might be one of ours. It turned out to be British. Several uniformed men appeared on the bridge and one of them ran some flags up the mast with the message, 'Happy hunting against the communists.' The Brits waved in our direction and we waved back. The sub began to dive again and was gone before we had recovered."

I had just learned a major lesson on international relations in times of war.

Hans and I became good friends. One day, at the start of our morning walk, I looked for Hans in the courtyard as we took our daily walks together. He was nowhere in sight. Finally, I located him lying on straw in his cell.

"Hans, come on out, it is time for our walk."

"I can't. I have no pants."

"What do you mean, you have no pants?"

"Last night I washed the colonel's pants and, since they were still wet, I loaned him mine."

Hans's behavior touched me. To hide my feelings, I pretended to be mad.

"Hans, the war is over. Germany has surrendered and the *Wehrmacht* no longer exists. You are no longer a captain and he is no longer a colonel. Why would you want to wash his pants?"

Hans replied sharply. "They made him a colonel because of his ability and it's his ability I respect, not his rank."

The colonel was a man in his fifties. Of medium height, he had light eyes, a ruddy complexion, and reddish-blond hair. He was slim and muscular. One would not call him handsome but he had quiet strength that inspired confidence. Initially, he was kept in a high-security prison in Tirana. One night he had managed to unlock the door of his cell with his wooden spoon. Dressed in a German summer uniform, wounded in the chest and heel, he had walked from Tirana as far south as Vlora, where he had collapsed in a ditch. He was captured and brought to our prison. That was all I knew about him at that time.

Years later, Hans and I met again, this time in Germany in 1969. Walter Wolf, my brother-in-law, located him through the German Red Cross. Thereafter, Hans and I have met every two to three years or so. One year he told me that the colonel was actually a general. He had been governor of Corfu during the war. His conduct there had been such that he was sure that, once he got there, he would be well received by the Greeks. That is why he had walked to Vlora, from where he intended to swim to Corfu. Without food, he had collapsed in a ditch where the communists had recaptured him.

During one of our conversations, Hans returned to the evening in prison when he had washed his superior's pants. He told me that the general suffered from hemorrhoids and that day his pants had gotten bloody. Hans did not want the general to be seen in that condition and had washed the pants. As the pants had not dried in time for the morning walk, Hans had given the general his pants and had remained indoors where I had found him lying on the floor. As Hans told me the full story, it made a lot of sense and said much about my friend Hans.

During one of our morning walks, a guard started reading some names off a list. Dad's and my name were among them. All those whose names were read had to return to their rooms, pack, and await further instructions. We did not have to wait long. As the other prisoners returned to their cells, we gathered in the front yard. By now, we were about forty prisoners. Without leaving the premises, we were herded into the lower-floor cells of Burgu No. 2. The room was quite dark compared to the glaring sunshine outdoors. As we entered and our eyes adapted to the dark, we saw a man sitting on a field bed with his head turned toward us. It took a moment or two before some in our party recognized the man on the cot. Then the man on the cot, Dad, and Shuk Gurakuqi, former secretary of finance in the Kruja government, nodded to each other without words, like friends who had fought the good fight for many years. The rest of our group, who knew the man less well, gathered around him and made loud noises, as if to fill the gap that separated them with words. I recognized the man from photographs but had never met him before. Our fellow prisoner—and now roommate—was Father Anton Harapi, a Franciscan of renown. He was a distinguished man of letters, known for his integrity and love of people. He was loved by the poor and humble while the rich and mighty had respected and included him in their power calculations. Personally, I was delighted to see this legendary patriot but waited for Dad to introduce me. I did not know then we would spend 42 days together in that cell.

Fr. Anton wore his Franciscan habit. He seemed rather short, with a thin, deeply lined face, a large bulbous nose, and big ears. The dominant features, however, were his deep-sunk, light eyes that seemed to radiate with an inner light. In the days that followed, I would see those eyes question intently, brim with forgiveness, and flash with contempt. Most of the time they shone with friendliness. As we entered the room, he looked at us with his head tilted to one side, bird-like, calm, curious, and at peace—the peace of one who had seen and suffered much.

When Germany invaded Albania after the Italian surrender on September 8, 1943, the German authorities made a series of proposals. Albania could declare itself independent and neutral. It could determine its form of government without German interference. The German military would buy food and other locally available goods at market prices and would sell to Albania medicines and industrial products, also at market prices. All Germany expected was free access to Greece that was under German occupation. If Albanians interfered in any way with the movement of German troops and supplies, the well-known rules of German warfare would apply.

Albania proceeded to adopt a form of government headed by a council of four regents representing the major geographic areas and religious groups. Fr. Anton was asked to join the regency as a representative of the Catholic population. He replied that he would accept the burden of office on condition that he received permission from the Holy See and that he would never sign a death sentence. Having received permission from the Vatican and given the exemption he had asked for, he accepted. There was no guarantee, however, that the communists would spare him at the end of the war. In fact, several other Albanian personalities were asked to serve on the Council of Regents but refused as they wanted no part of a political office that would put them at risk with the communists.

For them, maintaining peace and order in Albania was a worthy cause—but not at that price! Many non-communist personalities played it safe at that point by refusing to side either with the nationalists or the communists. In fact, one such person, when asked to assume a major office, had replied that he was "for tomorrow, not for today," i.e., that he would be available when the Allies liberated Albania, not while the civil war was raging on.

I noticed that Fr. Anton struggled three times a day trying to put drops into his ears. The drops probably did not do much good because he failed to pull the outer ear upward to straighten the auditory canal. I offered help, which he readily accepted. One day, as I was pulling his rather large ears before releasing the medication, I asked him whether he had ever suspected the day would come when I would pull him by his ears three times a day.

He looked up. "Why don't you ask instead why I need these eardrops?"

I had often wondered but had lacked the courage to ask. "OK, please tell me why do you need these eardrops?"

The story goes like this. When the communists came into power and extended their control to the Albanian mountains, Fr. Harapi and Lef Nosi, another former member of the Council of Regents, sought refuge in the mountains of Dukagjin. At one point, the pastor hid them in his rectory in Pult. Not long thereafter, a battalion of soldiers combed the area for enemies of the regime and pitched their tents in the churchyard, having searched the church and rectory from top to bottom—except for the corner room on the second floor of the rectory, occupied by the fugitives. Following the search, several officers took up quarters in the rectory on both sides of this corner room, unaware of their clandestine neighbors.

Soon things got quite complicated. Communist troops tromped in and out of the rectory at all hours of the day and night. The food for the stowaways, however, could be prepared only at regular mealtimes lest anyone get suspicious. Since it was dangerous to serve the food at unusual times during the day or night, the housekeeper, who was in on the secret, loaded trays with food, carried them to the corner room, and entered in view of anyone who happened to be in the hallway. Doing it quite openly and without apparent fear may have provided the best cover. This went on for as number of days.

Finally it was decided that for their own safety, the two ex-regents had to leave—the sooner the better. A farmer was brought into the plot. On the appointed day, the old farmer came in full daylight, tied his mule to a tree amid the encamped soldiers, and entered the rectory. After a while, the farmer came out acting as a guide. Lef Nosi, on the mule, wore a Franciscan habit, and Fr. Anton led the mule by the reins, dressed as a poor farmer. The strange procession left the courtyard undisturbed. Soldiers and officers alike made way for them and never asked any questions. The two ex-regents, the mule, and their guide were on their way.

(Fr. Anton Harapi told me this part while we were in isolation together. I don't know how far they went or how many other hiding places the two fugitives visited after Pult.)

The day came when both Lef Nosi and Fr. Anton were somewhere in the mountains on a farm alone with a small boy. The rest of the family had left to tend to their chores. The little boy knew that the two elderly guests had to be protected from communists. When he saw a communist patrol walking along the edge of their property, he unleashed the dog. These guard dogs are very fierce. They are kept on a chain during the day and unleashed at night to protect the house and stable from wolves. The dog attacked and the soldiers shot the dog. Having become suspicious, they searched the premises. Except for the little boy, the house was empty. In one room, however, they found dentures soaking in a glass of water. Dentures in a farm house in the mountains? They also found linen towels with the initials A.H. Did the initials stand for Anton Harapi?

Having found no one else in the house, the soldiers ran outdoors, fanned out, and started combing the surroundings. A wooded area extended from the back of the house toward the mountains. If Fr. Anton had been hiding in the house, he could not have gone far. He would not have had time, and besides, he was an old man. The soldiers split into two groups and formed a large circle. Once they secured the perimeter, they began closing in toward the center. Fr. Anton could hear them coming. Now they were within sight. When they were only about 100 feet away, he stood up, a hand grenade in each hand, and threatened the soldiers. The latter promptly jumped him and arrested him.

"Did you hurl the grenades at the soldiers?" I asked.

"How could I? I could not kill."

"Then why did you threaten them if you had no intention of following through?" I asked rather testily.

"Because I hoped that they would shoot me on the spot and spare me what I knew would follow." He stopped briefly. "Unfortunately, they jumped me and handcuffed me.

"Lef Nosi and I were arrested but were separated immediately. I was brought to Shkodra and questioned. At one point, they brought a generator into the interrogation room. They wrapped one lead around my genitalia and stuck the other against one of my eardrums. They turned on the electrical current. It hurt. Eventually, they perforated first one and then the other eardrum."

That day he said no more. The rest of his tale came in bits and pieces over the next few days.

"I was questioned for quite a while," Fr. Anton continued one day. "They wanted to know every detail of my stay in hiding. They wanted to know who had offered us refuge, who had taken us from one hiding place to another, who had fed us, and who had offered transportation or other support. Somehow, they forgot to ask about one man who had helped us and who is still alive and free. I fear that at my trial they will correct this oversight and ask me about him."

"There is no need to tell them," I blurted out. "Could you give them the name of someone who has died in the meantime?"

"Are you saying that I should lie?" he challenged me.

I shut my mouth but felt like saying, "What is such a lie compared to saving a human life?"

"There is no question that I will be killed," Fr. Anton continued. "My plan is to play dumb, offer myself as an easy target, and make them forget about the farmer."

In truth, I could not understand his reasoning. Not telling the truth under these circumstances did not appear sinful to me. Fr. Anton, however, had absolutely no doubt that this was the only way to save the life of a poor mountaineer without lying.

One advantage of being in isolation was that we had fewer spies among us. In our room we had only two, both former noncoms of the gendarmerie, and both Catholics from Shkodra. One day something interesting happened. Fr. Anton celebrated daily Mass regularly. Every day the nuns brought him simple food, bread, and boiled fruit that came in wine instead of water or syrup. That's how Fr. Anton got the bread and wine for his Masses.

When Fr. Anton celebrated Mass, the Catholics in the room attended except Shuk Gurakuqi. One day Fr. Anton asked him why he would not attend Mass. Shuk replied that he would not attend as long as the two informers participated and received Holy Communion. Fr. Anton called the two informers and read them the riot act! They could no longer attend Mass until they repented, confessed, and stopped being informers. All this took place before Fr. Anton went to trial. It took courage for the helpless Franciscan to challenge the cruel and godless communist system, but Fr. Anton had plenty of courage.

[After 42 days we were released from isolation and joined the rest of the prisoners. I was released from jail on December 17, 1945, after 13 months of incarceration.]

In early 1946, Fr. Harapi was brought to public trial. Like the special tribunal that had judged Dad and the first group of defendants, the court sessions were held at the Movie Theater Kosova. Admission was by special tickets available only to "true believers." Depending on one's viewpoint, those present were either the cream of the crop or the scum that had risen to the top of the revolutionary cauldron. Over the next few weeks, the audience would applaud or boo on cue, under the baton of the special prosecutor Bedri Spahiu.

While only a select few could attend the trial in person, everybody could hear the proceedings on the radio, or anywhere on the streets of Tirana, where loudspeakers at full blast made it impossible to avoid the trial proceedings.

According to precedent, the trial would open according to a detailed script. The judges and the prosecutor would march on stage in military uniforms of subdued splendor, their splendor signifying the "glorious victory of the people" and the sartorial modesty to stress that these were no foreign conquerors, but rather the worthy sons risen from the ranks of the people's army, who single-handedly had defeated the forces of Fascism and Nazism. At least that was the communist version of what happened during the war. That was not quite true, but that is another topic.

Now they, the representatives of the people, were ready to mete out justice to the nation's worst criminal: Fr. Anton Harapi, representative of the treacherous Vatican, chief villain and architect of nefarious plots that had robbed the poor and had given to the rich. Never mind that the Franciscans took a vow of poverty, but they used religion, the opiate of the people, to deceive the masses. All one had to do was look at the accused and hear the tale of his crimes. Anyone with any sense of justice would rise to his feet demanding that the accused be sentenced to death. At least, that was what the communist script hoped to achieve.

There were a few flaws in this scenario. When the judges and the prosecutor marched in, their uniforms were not exactly modest. After all, they were modeled after their Yugoslav counterparts who were no shrinking violets, beginning with Tito himself.

When the members of the court climbed on stage, Chief Justice Koçi Xoxe was clearly identifiable by his golden rank insignia and his uniform that was bulging at the seams because of his corpulence. Not so Bedri Spahiu, the prosecutor, who looked thin and bilious. Perhaps his hate-filled appearance came with the job.

More important than its appearances was the court's hidden political agenda, its motivation, its quest for how best to serve its masters in Belgrade who wanted Albanian patriots out of the way. It was the court's job to achieve this "in the name of the Albanian people."

Then they brought in the prisoner, ascetic in his simple Franciscan garb, with clear, luminous eyes. There was no sign of arrogance or false humility in him. Fr. Anton looked as he had lived, at peace with himself, with the serenity of one whose convictions and faith had coincided with his chosen life. Those in the theater could not help but notice the contrast between the accused and his judges. Besides, there was one major detail that did not fit the official scenario. They had not anticipated Fr. Anton's demeanor. It became obvious as soon as the prosecutor started to weave his web and set his traps.

"Fr. Anton, did Francesco Jacomoni ever visit your parish in Mirdita?"

"I am not sure."

The prosecutor decided to change his approach. "Have you seen this picture before? Isn't this the viceroy with his sycophants? Aren't you standing next to him, surrounded by the notables of Mirdita?"

"Boy, you're right!"

The presiding judge started to laugh so hard that he hid his face behind the notebook in front of him, shaking silently, lest he appear undignified. The audience took the cue and erupted in loud laughter.

The prosecutor turned toward the public with a smirk on his face, as if he had slyly engineered the whole scene.

"So then, the viceroy did visit you, after all."

Fr. Anton, on his part, was following his script to the letter. It was painful to watch—or rather, for us on the street, to listen to—a dialog that portrayed the priest as a bumbling old man. He had told me before my discharge from prison that he would do anything to save the life of the one farmer who had sheltered him and whose name had escaped the communist investigators thus far. He, Fr. Harapi, knew that he would be executed but had decided to fight to the last on behalf of his farmer friend, even at the risk of incurring undeserved ridicule. All this because he could not lie, even to save a life.

The enemies of the communist regime, the silent majority, felt let down and greatly disappointed. They had expected a courageous, brilliant defense of the nationalist position. Instead, they heard a "feeble-minded" old priest make a fool of himself. It hurt me that I could not speak up and tell the truth. What was worse, even Mom, who knew the truth, felt Fr. Anton had disappointed everyone. I tried in vain to point out Fr. Anton's self-sacrifice. Here was a man whose sole treasure on earth was his reputation as a man of high integrity and intellect, who now was sacrificing his reputation to save a humble farmer's life. No man has greater love than to give his life for his friends. Now Fr. Anton was walking in the footsteps of his Master. That's not what Mom wanted. What she had wanted and expected was a splendid defense of our traditional values and beliefs and a sharp attack, yes attack, against the communist pack of lies by a man of strong mind and unbending will, by someone willing to die standing up.

The trial ran its course. Fr. Anton and the other defendants, Lef Nosi and Maliq Bushati, were found guilty and were sentenced to death by firing squad. There was the usual appeal for clemency and the anticipated denial. A few days later, the sentence was carried out and the three defendants were executed on the outskirts of Tirana.

Thirty-two years later, in 1998, Fr. Primus Ndrevashay told me what he had heard from Peter Freeman (Sinishtaj), commander of the firing squad that had executed these three prisoners. "Peter Freeman" was the name the man had assumed when he had started a new life in Canada. Freeman had told him that when they shot the three prisoners, two had fallen to the ground while Fr. Anton had vanished from sight, surrounded by a cloud. He, the commanding officer, had walked over to where the bodies lay and had drawn his gun to administer the *coup de grace*. The bodies of Lef Nosi and Maliq Bushati lay crumpled on the ground while Fr. Anton Harapi's remained out of sight, surrounded by the cloud. It took several minutes for the cloud to dissipate. Then, and only then, did the soldiers see the body of the poor one of St. Francis lying in the majesty of death.

In 2004, Viktor Dosti was visiting with us. When I told him Fr. Anton Harapi's story, he added an interesting detail. Years ago in Albania, a soldier who had been part of the firing squad had told him the same detail about the cloud that had obscured Fr. Anton's body for a time following his execution.

CHAPTER SIXTEEN

TIRANA MILITARY HOSPITAL

With the fear of the death sentence for Dad gone, life in prison became routine. Mom brought us food regularly, I studied English, informers bothered us much less, and the signs of a conflict between the Western Allies and the Soviet Union were becoming increasingly obvious. The question was how long we would have to live under communism. Unfortunately, time was running out for some fellow prisoners. With the first big trial out of the way, the communists were setting up new trials for military personnel that had opposed them during the civil war. A number of officers began their road to Calvary. We saw a repetition of the phases characteristic of the special tribunal sessions. There were the trumped-up charges and the false witnesses. The prosecution became ever more strident and the lawyers' defense increasingly diluted until it turned into a mere plea for clemency. The appeals procedure turned into no more than a formality and executions by firing squads into a numbing routine.

This last stage, the execution of the prisoners, became semi-public. I remember a particular morning when we had seen a squad of partisans, shovels on their shoulders, leaving early that morning for a field behind our prison. It had rained during the night. The clouds had cleared away and the morning was drenched in sun. The puddles the rain had left behind shone like polished mirrors. Then we saw an imam accompanied by a guard disappear behind the prison. Around 10:00 a.m., we heard the ominous clanging of iron gates swinging wide open. The prisoners who had been condemned to death fell into formation in the front yard of the prison.

Their uniforms seemed freshly pressed and their boots were polished to a shine. As they marched across the yard, they instinctively avoided the puddles. They marched proudly, their heads held high, singing a modified version of the Albanian national anthem. Instead of saying, "but Albania will live because we are fighting for her..." they sang, "but Albania will live because we are dying for her..."

Hans and I watched the marchers. I had a knot in my throat. Then I heard Hans speak up.

"I have been present when people faced the firing squad. I have never seen anyone marching to his execution singing."

That noon, the wife of Major Alo Kuçi and the sister of a man who was executed that morning, stood outside the iron bars with food for two people. A prisoner looked at her, embarrassed. He wondered whether she knew that her brother no longer needed food.

She looked the prisoner straight in the eye and said, "Why are you embarrassed? I know they shot my brother this morning. I was there behind some bushes. There is no need to be embarrassed. Just before the soldiers opened fire, my brother and his comrades yelled, 'Long live Albania!' They were true men and died like men."

One of the guards spoke up. "Why, are we not true men?"

The question lingered a moment or two, suspended in air. No one bothered to answer. Then it dissipated without a trace, like water vapor in the sun.

Two years later, I met Mrs. Kuçi at the Military Hospital. We recognized each other but gave no outward sign. We had a job because of the work we could do, she as a cleaning woman and I as a physician's assistant. To hold on to our jobs, we also had to make ourselves useful in other ways. In our case, we held classes teaching soldiers how to read and write —without pay of course.

Had it not been for the changing seasons, the days, weeks, and months in prison would have gone by almost unnoticed, one day flowing into the next. Shortly after my release from solitary confinement, I was called across the courtyard to the administration building. The guard took me to a room and told me to sit down and wait because someone wanted to see me. After a few minutes, a man about my age entered the room. He was there to ask me a few questions, he said. He did not introduce himself as there was no need to. He was Mynir Tirana, first cousin of Agim Dani. I was also a cousin of Agim's.

His questions were neither difficult nor tricky.

"Were you a Balli member?"

"Yes."

"When did you join?"

"During the winter of 1943."

"Where?"

"In Padua, at the university."

"Why did you join?"

"To fight the Italian invader."

While he was asking these questions, covering information they already possessed, I kept wondering what his ultimate goal was.

"Did you go to Kosova as a member of the Balli Youth Battalion?"

"Yes."

"Would you have gone had you known then what you know now about the fraternal links between the Albanian people and those of the Yugoslav Federation?"

So that was what he was after. He was offering me a chance to say that I had changed my mind, and in retrospect would not have gone to fight against the Yugoslav communists in Kosova. While he was not promising anything explicitly, I had a chance to recant with the hope that this might trigger my release from jail. Several thoughts crossed my mind. Only a handful of Balli Youth members with activities comparable to mine were in jail. I suspected that my imprisonment was some sort of private vendetta. As to the broader picture, during the war, Tito had promised the Kosovars free elections at conflict's end to determine whether they wanted to stay with the Yugoslav Federation or join Albania. After the war, no such elections ever took place. Yugoslav communist brigades tried to disarm the Kosovars but were unable to do so. Albanian communist brigades entered Kosova and proceeded to disarm the Kosovars who willingly surrendered their arms to their brothers. Now that the Kosovars were helpless, Tito proceeded to slaughter Albanian men by the thousands near Ulqin.

As I looked at Mynir, I had two choices. I could "repent" and perhaps go free or I could express my true feelings and run the risk of staying in jail. Besides, a no was also the truth. I looked straight at Mynir and replied, "No, it would have made no difference."

He rose, slammed his notebook shut, and left the room. His abrupt departure confirmed that he had wanted to give me a chance and I had let him down. Sometime in August, there was an amnesty and a few prisoners were released from jail. My name was not among them. We heard later that someone had taken my name off that list at the last moment. Who had done so? Mynir, perhaps?

The next chance for an amnesty came on November 28, on the occasion of Albanian Flag Day. Rumor had it that this would be a big one. All kinds of reasons were given. One was that the communists wanted to regain some of the popular support they had lost after nationwide mass arrests and executions. Others thought that by letting smaller fish out, the families of the latter might be more willing to cooperate with the regime. Also, these individuals could be gainfully employed and would be more likely to tow the party line because they had more to lose than if they had stayed in jail.

I held my tongue, but there was no question that I hoped to be released, the sooner the better. I understood that an amnesty, an act of forgiving political offenses, probably applied only to people who had been found guilty and sentenced by a court while I was never tried. I was willing, however, to forget some of these legal technicalities. If my name was on the list, I decided I would not challenge the decision on legal grounds nor would I refuse to leave the jail. To say the least, it would have been impolite on my part and I did not intend to hurt anyone's feelings.

The 28th of November came and the list of prisoners to be freed appeared in the press. In our cell, I was asked to read the names of the lucky ones. The list included the names of several hundred prisoners from all over Albania. Considering the total prison population, several hundred was not very many. Anyhow, I began reading and pronouncing each name carefully to let it sink in. There was always someone in our cell who knew an individual or who asked me to repeat the name and the prison the person was being released from. To complicate matters, neither individual names nor those of their prisons were in alphabetic order. I read, and read, pronouncing all kinds of names while my mind was seeking just one name, namely my own. As I kept reading and nearing the end of the list, my heart sank lower and lower as I did not see my name. I was almost at the end when there it was, clear as daylight: Genc Korça (that was how the communists forced us to spell our last name). I read the name with no show of emotion, or at least I tried to.

Several of my cellmates yelled, "Congratulations!"

"Let me finish," I replied while my heart was thumping in my chest.

Dad looked at me with a big smile on his face.

"Now," he said, "you will go home and take care of your mother and Mergim."

From that day on, no matter what I did or where I found myself, I always kept my ears open, waiting for the roll call that would set me free. Days passed and finally weeks and nothing happened. Now that the news of the amnesty was out, the communists seemed in no particular hurry to release the prisoners. Since my name had appeared in the newspaper, various prisoners had wished me well, everyone telling me to forget my time in jail as soon as possible. Only Ramazan Jerani told me the opposite. It was he who had switched to another cell the day that Dad was being sentenced to death. Now he told me that I should never forget the 13 months I had spent in prison. When I asked why, he replied that people always remembered the worst times in their lives and he hoped that I would never suffer more than I had suffered in jail.

On December 17, Dad and I were having lunch together. Nineteen days had gone by since November 28, and on December 17 I completed 13 months in prison, to the day. As we were dipping our wooden spoons into the food that Mom had brought us, my spoon broke. Dad looked at me with a big smile.

"Today you will be a free man. That's what your spoon is telling you."

I liked what Dad was saying even though nothing had moved yet. Then it happened. That afternoon the guards came in, read the names of prisoners to be released, including my own, and gave us a few minutes to get ready while they stood by. I gathered my few belongings like a whirlwind, hugged Dad, waved to the rest, and scooted out of the cell like greased lightning.

With a handful of others, we crossed the front yard and entered the administration building. The director, Janaq Karabataqi, and a group of security officers were expecting us. We lined up in single file, ready for the next step that would lead us to freedom.

The director had the rank of captain of *Sigurimi* (security service). He was in his mid-thirties, of medium height, and on the heavy side. Outwardly, his behavior toward us prisoners had been more or less correct. He had never insulted or kicked us as the guards did from time to time. We had no way of knowing what he really was like. Overall, he did not seem to be a bad person.

He started out with a brief speech. He greeted us with a few friendly words and stressed the generosity of the people's regime and its kindness in forgiving our past and accepting us among the ranks of the free with equal rights and privileges as the rest of the population. He paused, possibly to leave room for applause. The silence with which his words were received was awkward—downright embarrassing. He decided to fill the void by closing with a few slogans, sure to evoke applause in our ranks.

"Long live Comrade Enver, long live the people's regime, long live our party!"

There came some applause from our ranks. I did not applaud. I could not help it. I had to blow my nose at that very moment. I averted my head, blew my nose noiselessly, wiped it, and pocketed my handkerchief just as the applause ended. Then I smiled an embarrassed smile, hoping that I had not interfered with the solemnity of the moment.

Now that we had listened to the obligatory comments and had responded as was expected of us, we ex-prisoners thought we would be free to go; not so. With guards all around us, we were told to step outside and follow the guards. By now it was after 6:00 p.m. The guards led us out of the prison compound, south on Tirana's main boulevard, beyond the city square with Stalin's bust, past the ministries, and west to a building that had housed the general staff before the communist takeover. Now it belonged to the security service.

We climbed to the second floor and walked through a door marked "Captain Stefo Grabocka." We found the captain standing behind his desk. He was of medium height, with dark, piercing eyes. He was the brother of the NCO at the Burgu i Ri, who was mentally dull and physically repulsive. The captain was the older and more gifted of the two.

"You are being released from jail because of the generosity of the Party and the people. You have a chance to prove yourselves worthy of this magnanimous act. Don't forget. We will be watching you and at the first false step, you will find yourselves back in jail, and this time there will be no mercy for you."

He looked us over once more, one by one, and then dismissed us with a nod. When we turned around, the guards were gone. We hesitated a moment, and then left, each for his own destination.

I knew where Mom and Mergim were staying. It was a villa owned by Engineer Hivzi Korça. As I walked toward the villa, I had a chance to ponder the words of Capt. Grabocka. He did not welcome us or mention our rights as citizens. He told us we bore the sign of Cain on our foreheads and reminded us what we could expect if arrested a second time. I could not help but wonder if he disapproved of Karabataqi or of the words with which the latter had addressed us. Perhaps someone from Karabataqi's office had called Grabocka and informed him of our lame response to Karabataqi's kind words and Grabocka had wanted to give us a more realistic picture of where we stood *vis-à-vis* the people's regime. Whatever the case, I was hurrying home and that was what counted.

The hours and days ahead of me would be busy and important. There was so much to tell Mom and Mergim about Dad's and my months in jail, and besides, there were so many things to do and decisions to be made.

I reached the villa, climbed the few steps, and rang the doorbell. The door opened and there was Mom; tough, tender Mom. She flung her arms around my neck and would not let go. Eventually, we both had to let go in order to breathe. Mom had carried a heavy burden with Dad and me in prison. It was not just our absence but the sequence of events, the need for Mom to face so many difficulties by herself, to make tough decisions, to keep everything going and take care of Dad and me in jail.

Then came the flood of words. Question followed question in rapid succession, often without leaving time for an answer. The important alternated with the trivial. A veritable dam had broken. Words gushed, swirled, and sometimes went against the current in an effort to squeeze the most information into the least amount of time. Actually, it was less the quest for information and more the need to release tensions, new and old, that had been dammed up for too long. Slowly our conversation became more structured, it began to make sense, and we proceeded as one topic after another was completed and laid aside.

We went to bed late and got up early the following day, Tuesday, December 18, 1945. This was the first day in 13 months that I woken up in a room without bars on the windows. Mergim had to go to school and Mom had to start preparing the food for Dad. She insisted that she take the lunch to prison, as she had done for over a year. She said that it was part of her daily routine. Furthermore, I had to rest, soak in freedom, such as it was, and meet with the owner and a family that lived in the basement, the latter a former army major and friend of our family. I suspected she wanted to keep me away from the jail, the guards, and any informants who may have harbored some grudge or itched to display their power for evil.

Mom had made one thing very clear shortly after I had come home the evening before. She expected me to take over the family responsibilities. What were we to do for a living? We had some savings in gold coins, unfortunately very few. Where should we cash them? Having gold was illegal and anyone caught trading gold could be arrested and tortured. The torture was necessary to "convince" the prisoner to give up all the gold in his possession and to reveal the names of others who may have cashed the gold, or who had been connected with such transactions in any way. It was a fishing expedition on the part of the government with inflicting unceasing, excruciating pain an integral part of the process.

I needed to find a job. Even if we could sell some gold coins for the time being, we needed a visible source of income. What were we to do with Dad's extensive private correspondence? Did it contain information that could lead to further prosecution? What should we do with our car that was hidden in the *Teqe* (monastery) of the Halveti sect? Such decisions could not wait. I had to make them and I was not yet 22 years old.

Much happened over the next few days. Visitors came and went. I went out to see my friends and take evening strolls, ogling the pretty girls. I spent most of my time with old friends, all of them previous Balli members, all of them from persecuted families. In a society where guilt by association was part of the legal system, this was not a good idea. On the other hand, whom else could I trust and be comfortable with?

One of my friends was Fasli Nepravishta, son of Abedin Nepravishta, a former mayor of Tirana, the other, Astrit Permeti, son of former General Permeti. I had been in prison with both their fathers. Mr. Nepravishta had been sentenced to 20 years and General Permeti had been shot. In fact, the day of his execution, we had seen one of the guards wearing the boots and uniform, without insignia, that the general had worn in prison.

One evening, Astrit and I were walking along the main drag of Tirana when we ran into two sisters. Both were young, pretty, kind, and very understanding. The younger one was in her early twenties, tall, slim, with dark hair, and very shapely. Her sister was probably around 30 years old. She may have been widowed. At their insistence, after dinner we took them to the basement ballroom at the Hotel Dajti, the best hotel in Tirana, built by the Italians in the early 1940s. As we sat at our table, I felt conspicuous and uncomfortable. It was a long way from Burgu No. 1 to the Dajti Ballroom in the company of two pretty women! I did not need this kind of exposure.

We had just completed our first or second dance when Gjovalin Luka and another communist sat at our table while asking whether they could join us. Gjovalin was from Shkodra, the son of a former rich merchant. The other's name escapes me. Both were former partisans, both members of the communist constitutional assembly. We all shook hands and introduced ourselves. The two intruders could not keep their eyes off our dates. Soon they asked them to dance. The two young ladies played it coy. "Please ask our escorts," they replied. As we had little choice, we smiled and made virtue of necessity. Before long, other eager would-be dancers were besieging our table asking to take our dates for a spin. Most were either well-known communists or in army uniforms. What they lacked in dancing ability, they made up for in enthusiasm. I made a big show of keeping a list with a flourish, pairing names with the kind of dance they were asking for. When the right dance came up, I would turn toward the lucky man on my list and would invite him to dance with my date. The man would jump to his feet, eager to show that he had graduated from fighter in the mountains to skilled ballroom dancer. Needless to say, the evening was not without its hilarious moments.

As the evening progressed, things got a bit more complicated. Terpsichore, the muse of dance, must have decided that the time had come to push the Commies off the dance floor. The band started playing Viennese waltzes and big band music that presented more of a challenge than those on the dance floor could handle. The number of eager dancers began to melt away. At last the four of us—Astrit and the older sister, and the younger sister and I—were the only ones left gyrating to the rhythms of the band. The rest had sat down and were watching us with mixed emotions: one part admiration, two parts envy, and a dash of pure hatred.

We did not remain the sole owners of the dance floor for long. Two foreign couples had come in earlier and joined us now. They were Australian and British, as I recall, and were in Tirana on official business. When the tune finished, the four couples stopped, turned toward the band, and clapped. One foreign couple came up to us. The lady greeted us with a friendly smile. Her partner looked at the young woman next to me and grinned with condescension born of past intimacies.

"Do you speak English?" the man asked me, his eyes fixed on my date.

"A little."

"Is she your wife?" he continued, always staring at her.

"No," I said.

"Your sister?"

"No."

"Then how do you know her?"

"The same way you do, except long before you."

My date stood tall and pretty, smiling innocently, while we men traded insults. I thanked God she did not understand English. I should have felt guilty because my last reply was not true. His insult, however, was more than I could take and deserved such a reply. At least that's the way I felt at that moment.

A few years after the chance encounter on the Dajti Hotel dance floor, the younger sister was arrested as a Western spy. She was kept in jail for a while and then released. We never found out what they had done to her or asked of her in prison. Whatever it was, it was too much for her. Some time after her release, she took her own life.

Uncle Riza, the husband of Mom's oldest sister Makbule, had sided with the communists during the civil war. Early in 1946, he came to Tirana to take part in a session of parliament as a representative of Shkodra. He had an apartment at the Hotel Dajti and Mom and I paid him and his family a visit. He looked subdued. At one point, he asked me to follow him into the next room.

"I am about to deliver a speech in parliament and I wanted you to hear it first. As you know, your mother and I don't get along and I did not want her to tell me 'I told you so!'"

He began reading. He accused the government and the Party of having misled the people, of having lied when they had promised that a victory of the National Front of Liberation would bring the nation freedom and democracy. He said that the truth had turned out to be the exact opposite of what they had promised.

"Uncle Riza, I am too young and inexperienced to give you advice. It seems to me, however, that while what you are saying is absolutely true, you may be arrested and executed if you give this speech in parliament."

"I know what they will do to me but I don't want to be remembered as one who helped the communists stay in power. As you know, while you were in jail, my only daughter Agim passed away of typhoid. Life has no more meaning for me. This is one way to end my life with dignity."

Uncle Riza did give the speech. Nako Spiru accused him of lying and said, "If there were no freedom of speech in Albania could you have delivered such a speech in parliament?"

At the end of that day's session, Uncle Riza was arrested. He was transferred to Shkodra where his mustache was plucked until his upper lip swelled to monstrous proportions. He was tortured, sentenced to death, and executed.

At this point, the communists had killed Uncle Muamer, Dad's brother (they had two half-sisters in common), and Zyhdi Tapija, Dad's brother-in-law. One other brother-in-law was in prison, soon to be followed by Uncle Sejfi Vllamasi, husband of Mom's second sister Naxhije. Uncle Riza was the third in our family to be shot by the communists.

My need to find a job had become urgent. I would have been unable to answer any question, no matter how simple, if the authorities inquired how I was able to support my family. Under the circumstances, this was a serious matter. Within days there was an item in a newspaper. It said that Radio Tirana was looking for an English translator. The only qualification was, as I remember, that the individual be versed in English and Albanian. I decided to apply. Even if I did not get the job, showing need/goodwill was a plus on my behalf.

I registered and found myself in the company of five or six other well-intentioned individuals, all about my age. From chatting with one another, it became apparent that none of us had lived in an English-speaking country. Only one of the group seemed to have some affiliation with the communist party. We were ushered into a room where we received a printed, rather short news item in English. The text was straightforward with one minor exception, a short phrase that was somewhat unclear. It did not take me long to translate the text into Albanian. Within a short while, our group gathered again outside the office building and compared notes. All of us had translated the news item the same way except the one with the possible party affiliation who had translated the tricky phrase differently. A few days later, we found out that he had been hired for the job. Was his the only correct translation? Was he somebody's protégé? Did he have the right party connections? One thing was sure: I had to continue job hunting.

Among the many visitors, my cousin Mirie and her husband Stefan Prifti also came to see us. Mirie was the adopted daughter of Gjylka, Dad's half-sister. The husband, Zyhdi Tapija, had been taken to prison with the early waves of arrests in Korça. He was a telegrapher by profession, known for his skillful handling of the Morse code in receiving and sending messages. To us his arrest did not make any sense as he was never involved in politics. What may have militated against him was the fact that both his brothers-in-law were strong anti-communists. One was Dad, the other Muamer Liço, executed by the communists as an active member of Balli Kombëtar.

Mirie brought her father food in prison and had caught the eye of Captain Stefan Prifti, then director of the jail. One day he called the young girl into his office and made her an offer. If she married him, he would save her father's life. Mirie may have discussed the matter with her mother and accepted the offer. The two were married. Her father was executed in due course.

During their visit to our apartment, Captain Prifti, now commander of the Tirana Garrison, told us that he had served for a time in the Albanian contingent of the Royal Guard in Rome. During his stay in Rome, he told us, he had met with Pope Pius XII and during a political debate had "nailed the pope to the wall due to his superior knowledge of Marxist dialectics." Mom was ready to explode and give the liar a piece of her mind. I gave Mom the evil eye, so she bit her lip and kept quiet.

As it turned out, that was for the better. Having told us about his "intellectual triumphs" in Rome, he turned to me and asked me why I was not gainfully employed. Everybody of good will was expected to help rebuild the country following the communist victory over fascism. This latter point was highly debatable, of course, but I chose to resist the temptation. Instead, I told him that I had tried once, unsuccessfully.

"Try again. You are a medical student. Come and see me some day and I'll see what I can do."

Mirie spoke up, "Why should he come and see you some day? Why don't you ask him to come and see you tomorrow?"

"Fine," Stefan said, "come and see me tomorrow at 4:00 p.m."

I thanked him and nodded appreciatively at Mirie.

The next afternoon at 4:00 p.m., I entered his office. He received me courteously and offered to write a note to Major Ibrahim Dervishi, head of the military medical service. In his note, he wrote that comrade Korça had studied medicine in Italy and had worked at The General Civilian Hospital in Tirana. Could our military make use of his services?

I thanked him and walked without delay to Major Dervishi's office at the southern end of the main boulevard. As luck had it, Major Dervishi was in his office and could see me. The major was quite tall, heavy set, with a fleshy face and a heavy black mustache.

"Are you related to Djevat Kortsha?"

"Yes, I am his son."

"Were you with the partisans during the civil war?"

"No, I was a Balli member. I was released from jail a few months ago and am looking for work."

"How do you know Stefan Prifti?"

"He married my cousin."

The major thought for a while in silence. "Major Sinan Imami needs competent people at the Military Hospital. I am sending you there as a volunteer. You can work as a physician's assistant. The job is without pay. You can hand him my note tomorrow."

"Thank you, I understand."

He wrote the note to Major Imami and I was on my way.

CHAPTER SEVENTEEN

DAD AT HARD LABOR

Major Sinan Imami was the medical director of the Military Hospital, the intended recipient of the note I was carrying. He had received his medical degree in France, had served as a medical officer in Albania for years and had worn various military uniforms reflecting his long career and the various regimes that had ruled Albania since the time of King Zogu. He was tall, dignified, with a relatively long face, heavy eyebrows, and a brown mustache that covered the ample space between nose and upper lip. Despite the fact that he had been a member of Balli Kombëtar, the communists had appointed him director of the Military Hospital. Rumor had it that his intimate knowledge of the hospital, of its facilities and services, his administrative ability, and his nimbleness in avoiding political quicksands had led to his appointment and subsequent longevity at this post. Besides, throughout his tenure as director, the political commissars were at his side—by virtue of their party standing—and had always had the last word on any individual, problem, or subject. No doubt, Major Imami knew his limits and was prudent enough not to test them.

When I presented Dr. Dervishi's note to Major Imami, one eyebrow shot up and he wrinkled his forehead. Over time, I would see this expression on his face time and again. His unspoken question was how could a son of Djevat Kortsha have access to Major Dervishi? Might there be an unsuspected political side to my life? If so, why was I being appointed a physician's assistant *without pay?* That, again, spoke to my not being a communist or an informant. In Dr. Imami's mind, the reason for my appointment was unclear but he was a patient man. Time would tell. Besides, whatever the mystery, it was not likely to affect him personally.

Major Imami asked how many years of medical school I had completed and any hospital experience I had, but asked no personal questions. He stressed I was being hired without pay and informed me that I would start work as an aide to Dr. Augi, head of surgery. As far as he, Dr. Imami, was concerned, I could start work immediately. As I was more than willing, Major Imami took me upstairs to introduce me to Dr. Augi.

We walked along some highly polished hallways to Dr. Augi's office. Coming from the outside, the office seemed rather dark. It was small and painted in dark green, like the rest of the rooms. There was one desk under the only window, and a metallic chest of drawers. There was one chair behind the desk, a few more against the wall, and an examining table in the middle.

Dr. Augi stood up with a friendly smile on his face. Dr. Imami told him the contents of the note, stressed again that I would serve without pay, and sailed out of the office, carrying one shoulder higher than the other.

Dr. Augi asked me whether I spoke Italian, was happy to hear that I did, and asked me to sit down. He was pushing fifty, a bit rotund, and no more than 5 feet 7 inches or so. He was almost bald, with gentle blue eyes, soft, tender hands, and the speech and manners of a gentleman. What a relief at a time when ignorance, rudeness, and aggressiveness carried the day. Instead of asking personal questions, he showed me a bound register in which he had entered all the names of patients he had operated on, the diagnosis, and a description of the surgical technique for each case.

"Would you find it difficult to translate and transcribe these entries into another register in Albanian?"

"No problem, sir; the terminology is clear and I will be happy to do what you ask of me."

Dr. Augi had registered and described in detail all operations he had performed. Such documentation was essential for his career once he returned to Italy. Over the next few weeks, I set up the Albanian equivalent to Dr. Augi's register. Almost all operations were either appendectomies or hernias, likely problems in young, healthy men. Occasionally, there was something more complicated such as a kidney stone, a gallstone, a stomach ulcer, or gunshot wounds. Sometimes there had been amputations, but these were rare. Translating these procedures was no problem. I would have liked to have more contact with patients, but for the time being transcribing past surgical cases in the register took precedence. Each morning

Dr. Augi took me on his rounds through the two wards and gave me instructions that I either carried out myself or passed on to the nurses. Then for me it was back to the register entries.

As time went by, I told Dr. Augi my family background and vicissitudes and he told me some of his. His family was from Sicily. He had served in the Italian army as a surgeon with the rank of major. He had surrendered to the Germans on September 8, 1943, had served at the Military Hospital, and that is where he was when the communist takeover occurred. Albania's new rulers informed him that Italy had agreed to allow some specialists to remain in Albania until their services were no longer needed. Italy, a defeated Axis power, may have had little choice in this matter. Dr. Augi's future and that of several other Italian physicians was in the hands of their communist masters.

Dr. Augi served as a civilian. His colleagues had joined the partisans in the mountains and were now part of the Albanian military. They wore the Albanian military uniform and the rank they had held in the Italian army. Some were more guarded than others in discussing political matters. None seemed to wear the uniform with ideological pride.

Those first few weeks at work went well. Dr. Augi was a good teacher and I was eager to learn everything I could in the field of medicine so dear to my heart. The nurses—a few Italian nuns and some Albanian partisans—had graduated from courses lasting from a few weeks to a few months, and were pleasant and cooperative. There was one older male nurse, a man in his fifties, who was an informant and wore the bilious looks of his profession. Leonardo da Vinci could have used him as a model for Judas Iscariot. As a true professional, I am sure he had exercised "the profession" for years under several regimes. He was readily identifiable, thus easy to avoid or neutralize.

In the beginning, the Italian nurses staffed the operating room. They wore white habits, but the mother superior was in black. They were long on experience, had worked with Dr. Augi for years, and made the operating room run smoothly and efficiently. They were particularly nice to me and eager to teach me, sensing that I was at the receiving end of the communist whip. They were caring, friendly, and kind to everybody. Patients and personnel liked them very much but no one dared display affection toward them, as that would have been unhealthy in the prevailing anti-religious and particularly anti-Catholic climate. In fact, the only one who got away with telling the truth was a mental patient in the neurology department. One day, he climbed half-naked on the window sill in his padded cell. He held on to the iron bars and, as the mother superior walked by, he belted his approval, yelling, "Long live the sisters, black and white, long live the sisters, black and white..." Who said there was no freedom of speech in Albania? Maybe not for everyone, but some could yell the truth and get away with it.

Behind the hospital buildings was a rather large church that probably dated back to the years of the Italian presence in Albania. Now it was no longer used as a church. In fact, within a few months of my being hired the administration changed it into a club where banquets and dinner dances took place. Anyone who objected to this changeover would have been "politically incorrect" and in danger.

I worked without pay for about four weeks. That meant I had to walk close to an hour to get to the hospital in the morning; I worked my eight to ten hours a day and returned home on foot at night. Those were long days but they also were good days. I worked with Dr. Augi, a surgeon and a gentleman. I was working in my favorite field and was gaining knowledge and skills. As an unpaid worker, I could not eat in the mess hall. So I brought my lunch to work. My situation was not ideal but it was far better than it had been just weeks before.

Then one day Major Imami notified me that I had received a permanent appointment and would be on the payroll as a physician's assistant. Here he mentioned a paltry sum but I was delighted. The money, no matter how little, was welcome. It would pay for at least part of our family expenses. More important, now I could say that I held a job and could feed the family, even though the money fell short of our needs.

It turned out that it was neither my ability nor my dedication to the job that got me hired. Sometimes we played volleyball at the hospital because I was trying to organize a team. Major Dervishi, an avid sportsman, had witnessed my efforts and had ordered Major Imami to give me a paying job. That was how it happened. Not very flattering, huh?

Soon, I earned the confidence of Dr. Augi and began to prepare papers and patients for surgery, dress wounds, and remove sutures. He taught me how to check the patients' pulses, examine throats, palpate abdomens, and check for hernias. Next, he had me use a stethoscope to listen to normal lungs and hearts. After a while, he also had me listen to chests of patients with pneumonia or irregular heartbeats. I learned how to interpret X-rays of fractures and I helped apply casts. In other words, I was in seventh heaven, professionally at least.

Once Dr. Augi felt confident that I had thoroughly assimilated the concept of sterile tools, operating fields, and surgical procedures, I learned how to put the patient under with ether. It involved applying a gauze mask to the patient's nose and mouth and dripping the anesthetic slowly, while continuously checking his eye reflexes.

One day my blind devotion to sterility could have had catastrophic consequences. The operation was almost complete. I had stopped administering ether, but out of habit I checked the patient's eye reflexes. To my horror, they were gone. I alerted Dr. Augi. He tore off the sheets covering the patient's throat and chest. The patient was trying to breathe as indicated by a rhythmic lowering of the portion between the trachea and the top of the breastbone. Because of an obstruction, no air was getting through. Dr. Augi asked for a scalpel and told me to bring a tracheotomy tube. I ran out, found one, and started sterilizing it. Then I heard Dr. Augi's voice:

"Bring the tube here immediately."

Bewildered, I grabbed the tube with sterile gauze, rushed into the operating room, and handed it to Dr. Augi. He had already slit the patient's trachea. He inserted the tube and the patient started breathing freely. Later, in the office, he explained to me that the soft palate of the patient had swelled up, blocking the trachea and making it impossible for the patient to breathe. Then he added, "How long does it take to sterilize an instrument by boiling it?"

"Ten minutes," I replied.

"And how long can the brain live without oxygen?"

"Four minutes."

As soon as he started questioning me, I understood my error. Dr. Augi then changed the subject. He had just taught me a lesson. Rubbing it in was neither useful nor his intent. On that occasion, I learned another important lesson. People of lesser training, such as I, learned and applied the rules. It took someone more knowledgeable to know when to bend them. Life taught me later that that was true in other fields, not just in medicine.

Two more surgeons were on staff. One was Dr. Jul Koliqi. He came from a well-known Catholic family from Shkodra. He had studied medicine in

Italy and had specialized in surgery. He held the rank of lieutenant. He was tall, clean-shaven, and probably had a "poor biography," meaning that he had neither fought in the communist ranks during the civil war nor had he joined the party after its victory. He had dark eyes, brown hair parted on the side, and a quick wit. He and Dr. Augi got along well even though there was no obvious friendship between the two. This was perhaps a defensive stance, as friendship with an Italian "fascist" prisoner of war would have probably hurt Dr. Koliqi's standing in the eyes of the authorities. Technically he was competent and played a supporting role to Dr. Augi.

Then there was Dr. Petro Cani. He was presented as a physician and surgeon even though rumor had it that he had attended medical school in Athens but had not graduated. No one had publicly said so. When I met him at the Military Hospital, he was a first captain.

He was tall, heavy set, with broad, hefty shoulders. Even though he was probably in his late twenties, he had lost most of his light brown hair. He had a fleshy face, protruding eyes, a strong voice, and an assertive presence.

He had broad shoulders not only physically but also politically. He had fought on the side of the partisans during the civil war and had barely survived the German winter offensive of 1943–1944. Relatively soon he was sent to attend medical school in Zagreb from where he returned after one year with his medical diploma.

Dr. Cani also permitted himself a certain latitude that others would not presume for themselves. We had a patient with an echinococcus cyst of the liver. Dr. Augi, who would be on vacation for a couple of weeks, instructed me to prepare the patient for surgery after his return. The next morning, Dr. Cani asked me to prepare the patient for surgery.

"But Dr. Augi told me to hold the patient until his return from vacation."

"How is a young surgeon to learn if all the interesting cases are reserved for the head surgeon? Go ahead, prepare the patient for tomorrow. When Augi returns, I'll explain everything to him."

Reluctantly, I did as I was told. Gaining experience had been uppermost on Dr. Cani's mind. He did not mention the patient's survival chances. For the record, Dr. Cani removed the cyst and the patient healed promptly. Had the cyst broken or leaked during surgery, the patient could have died of anaphylactic shock.

Many years later, Dr. Cani's courage served him well and boosted his career. Mehmet Shehu, then prime minister, had an attack of acute appendicitis. None of the available surgeons volunteered, since recovery was anything but sure. On the other hand, delaying the operation could have been fatal. Dr. Cani operated and the patient healed fully.

One day all technical personnel had to attend a conference. Our political commissar, a young man with strong political credentials and little else, stepped on the podium and gave us the news of the day. Yugoslav scientists had been able to get penicillin from the blood of bulls' ears. The commissar underscored the great scientific breakthrough achieved by "Albania's great friends and protectors in Belgrade."

It bothered me to just stand there and listen to such nonsense. I turned to Dr. Cani and asked innocently, "Comrade Doctor, is the blood in a bull's ear different from that in the rest of the body?"

I had barely finished my question, when Petro Cani interrupted the commissar.

"Why did they take the blood from the bull's ear and not from his legs, or tail, or from anywhere else?" His question was dripping with irony.

As soon as Dr. Cani asked the question, I was panic-stricken. The commissar lacked knowledge in technical matters and would be unable to answer Dr. Cani's caustic remark. In this particular case, it not only embarrassed the commissar but it also made fun of the Yugoslavs, the likely source of the news item. That was dangerous ground to tread on. What would have happened if the commissar had asked Petro Cani whether this was his question or whether someone had whispered it into his ear? What if Cani had pointed the finger at me? As it turned out, no one challenged Cani and I was able to get away with it. I learned my lesson, however, and became much more careful when dealing with Dr. Cani.

We had another incident involving penicillin. Some of the antibiotics at the hospital bore U.S. labels and some came from the Soviet Union. At another conference, they told us that all the penicillin we received came from Soviet sources—but that the bottles bearing American labels had first been exported from the Soviet Union to the United States. There they were relabeled and reached us as if produced by U.S. pharmaceutical companies. In disregard of this communication, shortly thereafter all technical personnel were secretly instructed that only U.S. penicillin should be used on exponents of the ruling class. Truth is a many-splendored thing!

One day, one of our young patients was dying from pneumonia. As in other cases, treating him with Soviet penicillin seemed to push his temperature sky high, possibly due to impurities in the antibiotic. One morning his mother came to the front yard of the hospital. The poor woman had somehow been able to purchase American penicillin. She saw me wearing a white lab coat, ran over to me, pressed several bottles of penicillin into my hands and begged me—as a mother—that the penicillin be administered to her son. Then she turned around and left without waiting for an answer.

I took the bottles to Dr. Imami and told him the story.

"How is her son?" he asked.

"He is near death, Comrade Major."

"OK, administer the penicillin."

That's what I wanted to hear. I ran to his pavilion, gave the patient his first shot of aqueous penicillin, and instructed the nurses to keep injecting the antibiotic every three hours. The fever started receding, and within days the patient recovered.

Shortly thereafter, we had another technical conference during which our commissar explained that the young patient had recovered due to the cumulative effect of the Soviet penicillin. The weakness of the argument was that penicillin had to be injected every three hours because it did not have a cumulative effect. That may have been the reason why it was the commissar and not a physician who held the conference. Any physician, even a communist one, would have hesitated to spout such absurdities.

By now I was a regular member of our operating team. I scrubbed with the surgeons. I learned the sequential use of instruments during the various surgical procedures so as to be ready with the right instrument at the right time. I will never forget the first time I actually assisted at a surgical intervention. Several members of a security unit had suffered wounds in clashes with the underground resistance. I scrubbed side by side with Dr. Augi. The nurses helped me dress, fastening the surgical gown and mask securely in place and helping me put on the sterile gloves. Now I was ready.

Dr. Augi's first patient was the one who had been wounded most severely. Unfortunately, the operation ended abruptly as the patient expired on the operating table. It was a difficult lesson but one that everyone in the medical field has to learn eventually.

One day I did not scrub and was the only staff person available on the floor. A woman came holding a baby in her arms. She was dressed as a nanny. That was highly unusual as nannies had been a symbol of the past. She said she was from Czechoslovakia and that the baby was Mehmet Shehu's son. She pointed at the baby's left arm. The upper arm had popped out of the shoulder joint. Putting it back in place was a simple maneuver, particularly in a baby. The problem was that the baby was Mehmet Shehu's son. Mehmet Shehu was the butcher of Albania and had been part of the special tribunal that had sentenced Dad to death.

I asked her to wait and walked into the operating room. Dr. Augi listened to me and then replied, "Mehmet Shehu's son is no different from any other baby. You know what to do."

That did not help me very much. All I could think of was, "What if something goes wrong? What if the baby starts screaming at home? What if Mehmet Shehu finds out I was the culprit and makes a political example of me?"

By the time I reached my office where the nanny was waiting, there was no longer time for delaying tactics. I had her seat the baby on the examining table, wrapped my left fist with cotton, and lifted the baby's arm gently to about shoulder height. Then I placed my wrapped fist in the baby's armpit and lowered the baby's arm. Before it knew what was happening, the head of the humerus had popped into place. The baby did not utter a sound. Phew, thank God! The nanny thanked me with a smile, took the baby into her arms, and wafted out of the office.

I could not help wondering if Mehmet Shehu would know or even bother to ask who had taken care of his son. The years went by. The young man studied electrical engineering, and died at an early age. Rumor had it he electrocuted himself.

Professionally, things were going well. I alternated between aseptic and septic surgery, and learned as much as I could. The lack of a well-prepared technical staff with the right political credentials also made it easier for me to keep my job.

Occasionally Dr. Imami would take time out to give me an unwelcome lecture. One day he asked me to take a walk with him in the courtyard of the hospital. On that occasion, he pontificated that Dad had made a serious mistake sending me to school. I would have been better off had I become a cobbler. I suspected I knew why he was saying such things to me. I resented his considering me a cat he could kick with impunity while he cowered before the political wildcats that surrounded him all day long. I responded with a question.

"Is that what you would have done if God had given you a son?"

The silence that followed showed I had hit the mark.

Another time he gave me a little speech when he notified me that I had received a miniscule raise.

"I was glad I could get you money for your work in the hospital. I hope you duly appreciate it."

Again, I didn't hold back. "Comrade Doctor, I appreciate the fact that my superiors consider my work satisfactory. As to the monetary value of the raise, it is the equivalent of a couple of shots I give privately to patients after work."

During my stint at the hospital, I had one more run-in with Dr. Imami. As usual, when patients came to our department, we put their military boots under the bed. For a week after the operation, the patients stayed in bed. When they got up, they put on their boots for the first time

One day a patient got up and looked for his boots but they had disappeared. There was an inquest. I was told that I was in charge of all material goods in the department, and therefore was responsible for the missing pair of boots. I replied that if I was responsible, we should keep the patients' boots under lock and key until the owners were ready to use them. I was told that presently this was not possible.

On payday, I went to our finance office and got paid, but was also informed that the price of the boots had been deducted from my pay. It so happened that Dr. Imami was receiving his pay at the same time. He came over to me.

"I regret the affair of the missing boots. The hospital administration was about to penalize Dr. Augi as head of the department. After discussion, we decided to charge you with the loss. Here, let me give you some money to defray part of the deduction."

I should have been grateful. Instead, I turned toward him and said loudly and distinctly, "Comrade Director, if the deduction was imposed unjustly, I am sure you would not have signed the order. If it was imposed justly, then I deserve it and will pay for it in full."

He turned away without saying a word.

Things on the job were going better for me in other respects also. I got a pair of tires and inner tubes for my bike, so I no longer had to walk to work and back. I now covered the distance in a fraction of the time. The bike also permitted me to give shots to civilian patients upon recommendation of various physicians. I am mentioning the tires also for another reason. I knew from experience that under the new regime rank and arrogance went hand in hand. The lower a person's position, the humbler the person's approach when dealing with party or government personnel.

I had received an authorization for a pair of bicycle tires and had a full 30 days to redeem it. In truth, I was so busy that I could not see my way clear to go to City Hall and complete the transaction. On the very last day, I could no longer procrastinate. When I pulled up at the municipal building, there was the usual armed guard and a line of people a block long. I knew I would never make it during office hours if I had to await my turn. I whipped my bike around, drove straight to the main entrance, and snapped at the guard, "Watch my bike."

Then I dismounted, removed my briefcase from the bike, and entered the building as if I owned it. At the door to the office, I pushed my way through the people who were standing in line. Inside they took care of me promptly. After all, I worked at the Military Hospital—I had to be someone with strong party affiliations! When I came out, the bike was where I left it. I made sure I did not thank the guard—that would have been out of character—and pedaled back to the hospital. Communists always brag about their classless society. What a farce!

Our life as a family was getting more normal in some respects. We had a regular income, albeit one insufficient to cover our living expenses. We found a reliable individual who sold what few gold coins we had. That kept us going for a while.

We had another problem. The *baba* in charge of a Muslim monastery of the Halveti sect had agreed to hide our family car in a shed on his property. He was a friend of Dad's and was trying to help us at considerable risk to himself. Even during the time when both Dad and I were in prison, he had been good to Mom and had always welcomed her.

Shortly before the feast of Ashura, Mom had been at the monastery and had told Baba about a dream she had. In her dream, he had asked her to give the monastery some sugar for the upcoming feast and Mom had answered that she was sorry, but she had only one small jar with sugar in the house and that was all. Baba listened to her dream. Then, as she was leaving, he said to her, "Don't forget to come with your sons and see me on the occasion of Ashura."

Mom had replied, "You mean 'with my son,' because my older son is in jail."

"Don't think of who said the words, just come."

That year, the feast of Ashura was a few days before I was released from prison and Mom made it in time to visit the monastery and Baba with both her sons. Thus, the three of us had a chance to partake of the Ashura dessert, the sweet named after the feast. Baba's use of the plural "sons" had turned out to be prophetic.

We had dreaded for quite a while what would happen once the communists discovered our car in Baba's barn. It did not take long for someone to blow the whistle. The police came, searched the premises, and confiscated the car without taking any further steps against Baba or against us. What a relief—and how indicative of the times—that we were glad the government confiscated the car without any ill consequences for us!

At the hospital, I worked hard and did my best. After all, I had a family to support. I got along with people and greatly appreciated my warm friendship with Dr. and Mrs. Augi. Mrs. Augi must have been in her fifties. A bit on the heavy side, she had brown, wavy hair and a warm, friendly smile. She was most considerate, quite circumspect, and glad when she could let her guard down with me.

They had been married for a number of years but had no children. They lived in a modest bungalow on the hospital grounds. In Dad's absence, Dr. Augi was the only person to whom I could go for advice. I was struggling with a problem. My income was not nearly enough to pay for our living expenses, modest as they were. We discussed this in our family. Two alternatives came to mind. One, we could take Mergim out of school as soon as he was old enough to become an apprentice in some trade and thus increase our income. Or we had to take a chance, sell the few gold coins we had, and hope that the authorities would not put our income and expenses under a magnifying glass. Mom insisted that I make that decision and I felt that it was best that Mergim leave school. When I mentioned the decision to Dr. Augi, he spoke strongly against it, mainly because it meant taking chances with Mergim's future.

Dr. Augi returned to the subject a few days later with a third alternative. He and his wife had discussed the matter and were offering to adopt Mergim. This was an unexpected turn. We discussed the matter with Mom. This time she spoke up. She was unwilling to give up her son, and that was that. Mergim was a strapping young teenager; bright, healthy, with great personal charm. She could understand that both Dr. and Mrs. Augi would have liked to have him as a son. They too, however, could understand that Mom was unwilling to give him up.

While life for the three of us was as normal as could be under the circumstances, Dad's life had gone from bad to worse. That summer of 1947, Dad had been in prison for almost three years, deprived of his dignity as a man. He and the rest of the prisoners were treated worse than cattle. The prisoners spent spring, summer, and fall at work camps. These three seasons were also times of nightmares for their families. Every spring the story was the same. When Dad asked for medicine to induce constipation we knew he would soon go to a work camp. The prisoners were herded on trucks and chained together. The trip took several days, during which no prisoner could get off the trucks for any reason. As long as they were constipated, they were OK. They could always urinate in place. At their destination, they were assigned to barracks. Here they would wash up and clean their sores as best they could. Each shipment of prisoners was kept together and away from the hundreds and thousands of other prisoners assigned to the same project. Their daily work lasted from dawn to dark, without breaks. They ate before and after work. The food was almost inedible and not enough to sustain a man at hard labor.

Most projects involved draining swamps. The only tools were picks, spades, saws, and mallets. The prisoners worked in water up to their midriffs, shoveling mud while trying to keep their footing. As on the trucks, they could not leave their assigned spots for any reason. So they stood and shoveled, stood and shoveled, amid the heat, the leeches, and the mosquitoes.

All along the canals, on both sides, were the guards. They too suffered under the heat and mosquitoes. When the guards got bored, they sought ways to break up the monotony. One day an old man was not shoveling fast enough to please the guard. He kept slipping in the mud and by the time his shovel came out of the water, there was hardly any mud left on it. The nearest guard decided to teach him a lesson. He struck the old man with his rifle butt on the back of his head. The prisoner fell forward, disappeared under water, and failed to come up for air.

After a minute or so, the guard grinned. "The swine is trying to trick me."

The other prisoners stopped working. A few more minutes went by. Not a ripple broke the surface of the swamp.

"Get the swine out of there!" the guard barked. Two prisoners bent down, grabbed the body, and dragged it out. They laid the corpse next to the ditch. The two prisoners who dragged the old man's body out slipped back into the muddy water and everybody started shoveling again.

Another dead prisoner. The guard did not have to worry about killing the old man. Nobody would ask any questions. If the prisoner had any family, his family would miss him, even mourn him. He would never go back home, would never see the day of freedom. The old man had stopped suffering. Perhaps it was better this way. The surviving slaves were worn out, dead tired, trying to survive one day at the time. Would any of them ever make it home? Some would. The rest would disappear in unmarked graves all over the country. Human feelings had no room among communists, only class hatred.

Only prisoners who ran a fever were considered too sick to work. If you had no fever, you were not sick. Those were the rules. One day Dad had a high fever. When the prisoners lined up for work, Dad was still lying on his bunk atop his matted straw. The prison officer came and had the doctor, also a prisoner, check Dad's temperature. Then the officer personally checked the thermometer. Clearly the prisoner was ill. That day, the rest of the prisoners marched beyond the barbed wire enclosures to their places of work. Dad was marched only as far as the barbed wire. There they tied him down, atop some barbed wire loops. He stayed there as long as the prisoners were at work. Then the guards untied him and he returned to the barracks.

When Mom and I first heard this story, we did not believe it. Even the communists would not sink that low. When Dad returned his clothes to be laundered, we saw bloodstains and holes in the material in a pattern characteristic of barbed wire. Then we believed.

CHAPTER EIGHTEEN

TORTURE VICTIMS

As time went by, life at the hospital got more difficult the more it became integrated into the communist system. There were the ridiculous aspects of hospital life, such as the Yugoslavs' penicillin from bulls' ears, the Soviets as the only source of penicillin in the world, etc. In the Soviet version of history, Sir Alexander Fleming was not even a footnote in the discovery of penicillin. Officially, the Albanian communist party cheered and applauded with all its might this bold lie while at the same time reserving American penicillin for their VIPs.

One day, the psychiatric department sent a nurse with a patient for evaluation. The young recruit claimed to be deaf and dumb. How much was a put-on and how much was true? Dr. Cani took charge. He asked the young soldier some questions but could get no response. Off we went to the operating room. I put the patient under with ether. As he began to regain consciousness, Dr. Cani started asking questions.

"What's your name?"

The patient gave his name.

"Where are you from?"

"From Kavaja."

"Who told you to pretend you were deaf-mute?"

"My uncle."

"What's his name?"

The patient gave the uncle's name.

"Does your uncle hold office?"

"Yes, he is head of our village."

The patient was allowed to recover and was then sent back to his department under escort, after Dr. Cani wrote up the results of the examination.

I found myself in a bind. The male nurse from our department present at the 'interrogation' was our distinguished stool pigeon. If I did not report the incident to the commissar, I would be found wanting. Obviously I did not want to do so as my sympathies were with the patient. I had to decide quickly what course I would take. I returned to surgery and filled out the registry with the operations of the day. While making the various entries, I could not help but think what would happen to the young recruit and—even worse—what was about to happen to his uncle. I spent almost an hour in the office to give our stoolpigeon time to act. Then I told him to watch the station while I went to see the commissar.

"Do you want to inform him about the deaf-mute?" he asked me.

"Yes," I replied with a grave face.

"There is no need for you to go, I have already informed him."

"Then that's taken care of." I changed direction and walked toward the mess hall. It was time for lunch.

One morning when I approached the hospital's main gate, instead of responding to my salute, the sentry blocked the entrance and motioned that I should go to the side entrance. There I entered the hospital without difficulty. As I climbed the stairs to surgery on the second floor, Zihni Hazbiu, a male nurse, approached me and whispered into my ear.

"A 'big one' bit the dust last night."

"Don't even joke about such things," I replied reproachfully.

In the office, Dr. Augi looked at me and motioned that I sit down near him.

"Last night, around 8:00 p.m., they brought in a man who had either shot himself or had been shot in the chest. They told us that it was Nako Spiru. Allegedly, he had dropped his pistol accidentally, and the gun had fired. The man seemed to have lost a lot of blood. The version that the gun had fired accidentally was a hoax. When a gun falls on the desk or a floor and fires accidentally, the bullet entry is lower than the exit wound. Here the opposite was true. Obviously, the shot had been fired with the gun pointed downward. Because the outer clothing had been removed before Nako Spiru was brought into surgery, I did not see any powder marks on his clothes that would have been there if the gun had been pressed against his chest. This could be a case of suicide or, more likely, the man had been shot by someone standing above him. This was no accidental death."

The director immediately sent word that Soviet surgeons from the civilian hospital next door be brought in. Meanwhile, Mehmet Shehu and his security forces surrounded the hospital, controlling who was entering or exiting the premises.

"We started a blood transfusion. Obviously, there was serious internal bleeding because the transfusion did not help at all. After the second transfusion, I suggested that we stop giving the patient any more blood. As the patient was too weak for thoracic surgery, there was not much else we could do."

"What did the Soviet surgeons say?"

"They insisted that we continue the transfusions. We did so and after having used seven donors [at that time we used direct transfusions from donor to patient], the patient died on the operating table at 10:00 p.m."

"Did he say anything while he was still alive?" I asked.

"Yes, during those two hours he kept moaning, 'O Lord save me, O God save me, O Lord save me, O God save me."

I was thunderstruck. Nako Spiru had studied at Turin University for two years. In Albania, he had moved rapidly up the ranks of the communist party. After they assumed power, he was in charge of the campaign against religious beliefs. Most recently, he had headed the Five-Year Plan. He had married Liri Belishova, also a communist and a member of the Central Committee.

I shared what little I knew with Dr. Augi. Time had come to circulate and find out what the grapevine was saying.

Some time before, some minor luminary in the communist party had died and Dr. Imami had been severely reprimanded because the Military Hospital had distinguished itself by its absence at the funeral. This time, Dr. Imami was going to make sure that we participated in full force.

We formed ranks and we marched to the cemetery. We listened to speeches and mourned the loss of this great man who had given his life at his desk, serving the people and the party until the very last. Eventually the speeches ended, the crowds dispersed, and we returned to the hospital. Here something strange was going on. Members of the communist Youth were dancing in the front yard of the hospital and one of the master sergeants was laughing and swaying as the dancers circled in front of him.

"Comrade, we just buried Comrade Nako. Do you think it is right to dance at this point?"

He looked at me with a strange expression. "Comrade Nako died accidentally, he did not die in battle."

I could not quite make sense of what was going on. Shortly, however, things became clearer. Rumor had it that the evening before, Koçi Xoxe had chaired an important meeting. Koçi Xoxe was the second most powerful man in the communist hierarchy. At the meeting, Nako Spiru had reported that Albania had sent large quantities of leather and wool to Yugoslavia, yet the military boots and uniforms received in return were of cardboard and cotton, respectively.

"Are you telling us that the Yugoslavs are cheating us?" Koçi Xoxe had asked.

"Comrade Koçi, as head of the Five-Year Plan it behooves me to present the facts to you. Furthermore, the toothpaste we are getting is such that users wind up with bleeding gums."

"Comrade Nako, you have 24 hours to present all necessary export and import documents supporting the charges you just made against our Yugoslav allies."

The meeting had broken up, Nako Spiru had returned to his office, and the rest is history.

A few days later, a representative of the communist party held a meeting with all party members on the hospital staff and notified them that Comrade Liri Belishova, Nako Spiru's widow, had been expelled from the Central Committee and was appointed a teacher at an elementary school in a nearby village. Wow, what a plunge—from member of the Central Committee to village teacher! Under this system no one was safe, not even major exponents of the regime.

Among his other duties as a surgeon, Major Augi took care of prisoners requiring surgical attention. Through him, I gained access to that ill-famed room that served as a prison in the officer's ward. One day we were alerted that an ambulance was bringing a prisoner to the hospital. I immediately thought of Dad. When they wheeled the prisoner into the operating room, it was not Dad but Dr. Ahmed Saddedin, our family physician. He lay there ashen-faced.

Dr. Augi began to unwrap the prisoner's wrists while he mumbled to me, "Get rid of that officer who has entered our operating room."

I looked toward the door. There stood a lieutenant, probably the one who had accompanied the prisoner. I walked toward him.

"Comrade Lieutenant, it would be better if you left the operating room," I whispered.

"Why?" he asked defiantly.

"Because the sight of blood and the odor of medicines may bother you."

"I am head of the torturing squad," he replied with an ugly grin. "Don't worry about me."

"At least sit down," I mumbled, unable to come up with more compelling reasons. I pushed a chair in his direction and returned to the operating table. I looked at Dr. Augi with a helpless shrug.

Meanwhile, Dr. Augi had unwrapped the patient's wrists. They displayed deep, irregular cuts as if someone had tried to saw them open with a blunt instrument. Dr. Augi injected an anesthetic along the cuts. Suddenly there was a thud behind us. The lieutenant had slipped off the chair and lay sprawled on the floor. We looked at each other. As I had not scrubbed, I grabbed the lieutenant by the shoulders and dragged him out of the operating room. I did not know what had made him faint. Perhaps it was the fact that we were trying to help and not hurt his victim, a thought so farfetched it had never crossed the lieutenant's mind. Anyhow, I was glad to get the bastard out of our sight. I handed him over to his "colleagues" and returned to the operating table just in time to hear Dr. Augi ask for sulfa powder.

"Doctor, why are you trying to save me? They'll torture me again and I don't have the strength to take it anymore."

Dr. Saddedin looked at me while addressing Augi. Dr. Saddedini had recognized me but knew better than to let on. After all, he didn't know who else was in the operating room with us. Augi gave no indication that he had heard the prisoner. He sprinkled the powder into the wounds and stitched them up. I bandaged them and left the operating room just as the guards were entering to claim their charge. One of them had told a nurse that the prisoner had tried to cut his wrists with a small spoon pipe smokers use to scrape the bowl of their pipe. Obviously, the prisoner was guilty and had a bad conscience, the guard said. It never entered his mind that there was a more plausible explanation of why the old physician had tried to take his own life.

One day someone from main registration at the hospital asked us to prepare the operating room for a prisoner. When they wheeled him in, he was poorly dressed, skinny, and forlorn under the blanket on the gurney. He had been severely beaten and had bled profusely. The nurses started to clean him up while I took the patient's history. He was a pilot working for the Ministry of Health. He had taken off from Tirana airport to spray DDT on marshes around Tirana. The weather had suddenly turned bad. Fog had made it impossible for him to land in Tirana or at some nearby airport and he had flown to Korça where he was able to land. He was immediately arrested, accused of trying to fly to Greece, and severely tortured. While he was telling us these things, he reached into his pocket and pulled out a photograph.

"These are my two little daughters. They are my angels. Why would I want to escape and leave them behind?"

He looked at me with eyes filled with tears.

The surgeon applied some stitches and the little pilot was taken out of the operating room and out of our lives, another wreck strewn along the path of the glorious communist victory.

Other memories come to mind when thinking of tortures and prisoners linked with the Military Hospital in Tirana. One day I was called to the infamous prison room. I took a male nurse and a cart with me as I entered the room. An NCO of the security forces with two armed soldiers stood guard inside the room. On the low bed was a prisoner. Despite the darkness, I recognized Major Neshat Hasho, a career artillery officer. I had met him twice before; the first time in Peja in 1944 when our volunteer battalion was getting ready to leave for the front. Major Hasho was commanding the garrison. He had disliked our use of different rifles, and demanded that we all use a common type.

The second time I met Major Hasho was in prison in Tirana when we did time together. When the communists decided they needed to train their own artillery cadres, they freed him, gave him his old rank back, and pressed him into service. At that point, I lost track of him.

This third time, we met in the prison room in the Military Hospital in Tirana. He lay in bed, pale with eyes that spoke of intense suffering. When I removed the blanket, I saw that he had two broken legs. Splintered bones stuck through multiple wounds. Whitish worms crawled over both legs. I could feel the security people watching us with diffidence. The male nurse and I spoke the southern dialect. The south of Albania was the cradle of Albanian communism. The nurse was an NCO, and I was in civilian clothes, possibly an officer. We must have passed muster, at least for the time being. First, we cleaned the wounds of both legs thoroughly. I turned to the nurse.

"Prepare two leg splints."

He lined two splints with layers of cotton. I grabbed one leg with one hand just below the knee and the other above the ankle. I pulled the knee and the ankle apart to avoid pinching any nerves or blood vessels as I placed the leg in the splint. The prisoner was scared and obviously in pain.

"Genc, please be careful. Don't hurt me."

He was trembling from head to toe.

"How come you know his name?" the head guard snarled.

"I heard the nurse call him by name."

I was grateful the prisoner had a ready answer. I started to bandage the prisoner's legs in their splints.

"Wrap them tight," the guard hissed, "he always tries to unwrap them at night."

I was not going to take anymore from the head guard. "Comrade, mind your own business. I know what I am doing and you are interfering."

At this point Neshat Hasho erupted. "Comrade Sergeant, don't be a *Tartar*!"

"Whom do you call a traitor?" the sergeant shot back as he raised his left hobnailed boot over the low surgical bed and close to the prisoner's face, but without touching it.

"Step on my face! Go ahead, step on my face!"

Neshat Hasho no longer cared about anything, not for his safety, not for his life. For a moment, it seemed as if this scene would never end. The tension broke when the head guard answered icily, "I would, but I have no orders to do so."

Then he turned toward his two apprentices. "Chain his hands to the sides of the bed so he won't unwrap his legs."

The nurse and I were done for the time being. We packed and left the room. The door had barely closed behind us when the beating started, one dull thud after another, while the prisoner screamed to high heaven. We had left him lying on his bed with both legs in splints and his hands chained to the sides of the bed. Where were they hitting him? We left in a hurry as there was nothing we could do. The beatings stopped after the officers in the adjacent ward complained about the noise. What human tenderness, what heartwarming compassion on their part!

That afternoon, Dr. Augi and I were in the office. A security officer entered. "How long will it take for the prisoner to heal?" he asked Dr. Augi.

"Barring complications, it will take six months, perhaps longer."

The officer thanked Dr. Augi and left the office. We looked at each other, feeling helpless. The reality we were experiencing mocked the Hippocratic Oath. The next morning the nurse and I went back to dress the prisoner's wounds. The prison room was empty, but the head guard was lolling around.

"Where is the prisoner?" I asked.

The sergeant beamed an ugly smile. "It would have taken the pig a long time to heal and even that was not sure. We took him out last evening, here behind the hospital. The prisoner was not man enough to stand on his own two feet so we propped him up in his bed. I stepped behind him and let him have it with my automatic rifle. Remember? He wore a white woolen sweater. You should have seen the tufts of wool squirting like jets from a water hose."

The guard had really enjoyed himself. Just thinking about it gave him pleasure.

I learned later that Major Neshat Hasho had been arrested a second time. Somehow, he was able to reach the roof of the prison. When he jumped off, he broke both legs. I did not know how he was treated in prison before and after his failed escape attempt. I could imagine what the guards did to him after the nurse and I left the room. There was no question; he had suffered much. I am sure he had done his best to endure whatever they had done to him both before and after he broke his legs. But to say that he was not man enough to stand on his own two feet when he was about to be shot was scurrilous. This is how Neshat Hasho's life ended. I wondered where his killer was, how he felt about his role in this sordid execution, and how he would try to hide it if the day ever came when human values would again prevail in Albania.

Of the prisoners who passed through that infamous room, another unfortunate individual stood out in my mind. When Dr. Augi was notified there was a prisoner in need of attention, he motioned that I follow him. I always dreaded such moments. When we entered the room, the prisoner was lying on his side. He was a man in his fifties. His eyes were lifeless, his body sagging. There was a bandage around his upper chest. A stench emanated from the prisoner, the worst I had ever experienced.

While I began to undo the bandages, Dr. Augi lit a cigarette. High between the prisoner's shoulders was a wound the likes of which I had never seen. It was perfectly round, about five inches in diameter and about one inch deep. It was clean, without a trace of pus or scabs. The flesh underneath seemed healthy. The stench was such that I had to use all my strength to keep from vomiting. Dr. Augi told me to dress the wound and left the room while I bandaged the prisoner as best I could.

"I will be back to dress the wound again this evening," I told the guard. He nodded.

"How did they inflict such a wound? A wound so regular, so clean, and yet so terrible?" I asked Dr. Augi back in our office.

"They must have pressed a round, blunt object between his shoulder blades; maybe a piece of pipe. Maybe they tied the prisoner to a tree, with a branch stump pressing between his shoulders. Whatever they did caused a deep necrosis and the dead tissue had sloughed off." That was the technical answer; it also bore witness to the tragedy the prisoner and all of Albania was enduring.

Dr. Augi continued. "I apologize for walking out on you. I just could not take it anymore."

That evening, before going home, I re-entered the prison, trying to make the prisoner's life as comfortable as I could. They had given him a bowl of beans for lunch. He had slumped forward and had died with his face in the bowl. I called the guard.

"The prisoner is dead."

I left the building, picked up my bike, and left for home. That evening I had no desire to eat or speak to anyone, not even to Mom.

Over the years, I watched Dr. Augi work long hours for little pay. The communists treated him with respect and suspicion; with respect for his undeniable surgical skills, yet with suspicion because he was a gentleman and in no way inclined to pay even lip service to communism.

The following happened at Christmas. Dr. Koliqi was Catholic. The other doctor, Dr. Petro Cani, was Orthodox by birth and a communist, i.e., an atheist, by persuasion. Dr. Augi offered to be on call for Dr. Koliqi to allow the latter to be with his family. As fate willed it, an officer with acute symptoms was rushed in on Christmas Eve. He died before his history could be taken. This happened on Dr. Augi's watch. Was this a case of negligence or even of clear-cut sabotage, the communists asked? After all, Augi was Italian and a bourgeois! The case went to court and dragged on for a while. Augi was under great stress. If he were condemned to prison, who would take care of his wife?

The days passed slowly. He walked from his bungalow to the hospital in the morning, and walked the same 100 yards back in the evening, day in and day out. Rarely did he and his wife venture into town, communist xenophobia being what it was. One morning he shed his white coat and went to court to be sentenced for negligence unbecoming a physician. He returned later that morning. The judge had sentenced him to five years in prison. Upon request of Dr. Ibrahim Dervishi, who vouched for the professional integrity of Dr. Augi, the judge suspended the sentence. What this meant was that Dr. Augi was not found innocent but that, because of mitigating circumstances, he would not have to go to prison unless he broke the law again. When he returned to the hospital, Dr. Augi felt crushed. His professional integrity had been found wanting. How painful for a physician of his character.

"Would you do me a favor?" he asked me that day. "Albanian friends of mine have asked me to perform an appendectomy on their 10-year-old son. Can you assist me this evening after hours?"

"Of course," I replied. "Just tell me when and where you want me."

He said he would tell me later that day.

That afternoon I did not scrub, but administered ether to patients undergoing surgery. Dr. Koliqi assisted Dr. Augi. About 6:00 p.m., the nurses brought in the last patient of the day. It was a transfer from another department. The man had a cavity in one lung and the surgeons would cut the corresponding branch of the phrenic nerve. I recall it was a sunny late afternoon.

Everybody was bushed. Dr. Augi looked out the window. He was pensive and even more reserved than normal. When he turned around he was at the left side of the patient. Dr. Koliqi proceeded to paint the left side of the chest with iodine. Then he put the surgical sheets in position, leaving open the area around the left collarbone. Dr. Augi injected local anesthetic all around the area, asked for the scalpel, and made an incision above the clavicle. He isolated the nerve and cut it. The left half of the diaphragm would be immobilized for months until the nerve healed, thus giving the cavity time to calcify and the patient time to heal. At this point, Dr. Augi spoke to the patient.

"How are you feeling?" he asked in broken Albanian.

The patient said he was fine.

"On what side are you sick?" Augi continued.

"On the right side," the patient answered.

"Where are his X-rays?" Augi asked.

I rushed into the prep room to retrieve them. They were not there. None of the operating room nurses had seen them. I ran to the pulmonary diseases department. When I got ahold of the X-rays, I felt crushed. The cavity was in the right lung, just as the patient had indicated. I ran back into surgery and propped the X-rays against the window lit by the evening sun. Augi was stone-faced. In the morning they had found him guilty and given him a suspended five-year sentence. What would they do to him now? He sutured the patient, removed his surgical gown and his gloves, and walked over to the department for pulmonary diseases. He explained to the lung specialist what had happened.

"Can I cut the right phrenic nerve at this time?"

The Albanian physician shook his head. "Not before six months."

This meant that the healthy lung would be immobilized for six months while the sick lung would have to work twice as hard. Dr. Augi walked back to the main building. I walked with him to the director's office, opened the door for Dr. Augi and remained outside. When he came out, I searched his face for an indication of what had happened. Augi had described the event to Dr. Sinan Imami, taking the entire responsibility upon himself. I asked him why he had done so.

"Dr. Koliqi was my assistant. I wielded the scalpel, mine was the responsibility," was his reply. "Go home," he added. "It's late."

When I returned the next morning, I was full of forebodings. Would Dr.

Augi have to go to prison? If so, would they add five years to the sentence because of yesterday's surgical mishap? What about Mrs. Augi? What would happen to her? When I entered the office I shared with Dr. Augi, he was already there. We chatted a few minutes, trying to avoid speaking about the events of the previous day.

"When are you going to operate on that youngster you mentioned yesterday?" I asked.

"I operated on him last night."

"Weren't you too tired?"

"A surgeon has no right to be tired. The boy and his parents had worried all day about the appendectomy. I had to operate and relieve their anxiety. By the way, everything went well."

Thank God!

I did not ask him whether he had heard from the authorities because of the incident of the previous evening. That day, we heard nothing, nor the day after, nor any day for that matter. I was glad that the authorities recognized that what had happened in the operating room that afternoon was a mistake, a sad mistake affected by circumstances. The surgeon felt guilty because of what had happened. The authorities must have concluded that was enough punishment. They simply chose to overlook the event. I suspect this was one more time that Dr. Dervishi had intervened on Dr. Augi's behalf.

CHAPTER NINETEEN

DUKAGJIN—BREAK WITH TITO

Things were going relatively well for us. I was doing well on the job. I got along with my superiors and coworkers, including Dr. Imami—as long as he did not make me a target of one of his ponderous tirades. We had moved to a simple but sufficiently large apartment for our needs. In fact, we sublet a room to an Italian physician who worked at the Military Hospital and the extra income was welcome. We had a circle of friends but missed Dad who was suffering physically and psychologically under an implacable regime that treated prisoners as slaves. In addition, there was always the threat of further punitive action on the part of the communist party and the government against us, the "class enemies."

According to a rumor that was making the rounds, families such as ours would have to leave Tirana to make room for the new elite, their storm troopers, and their families. It did not take long for this bit of news to take on substance. Long lists appeared on the walls of the municipal building with the names of families that were supposed to leave Tirana within a matter of weeks. Our name was on the very first such list. I tried to plead my case at the hospital but Dr. Imami told me that we were all necessary but no one was irreplaceable. We tried to appeal to the authorities but to no avail. Unfortunately, we had no friends among the powerful, so we packed our few things, found a truck that was leaving for Shkodra, and said farewell to Tirana, making sure we had left nothing behind, including our black angora cat, Lapushi.

For the first few days in Shkodra we stayed with Grandma and Aunt Shqipe. Then we moved across the street where the Quku family was kind enough to offer us a room with a toilet. There was no kitchen, but Mom decided to install a little electric hot plate in the anteroom to the toilet, with a curtain separating the two. It was far from ideal but it was the best we could get under the circumstances.

Under the same roof lived the head of the family, his brother, their two families, as well as the widow and children of the oldest brother who was deceased. The men were tall and gaunt. They wore suits with baggy pants since they liked to sit cross-legged. They wore shirts without the detachable collars, never wore neckties, and covered their head with a black fez, a sort of felt hat without a brim, characteristic of Muslims. This was an affirmation of their religious faith at a time when most others sought to avoid anything that might displease the Party stalwarts and their minions. Both brothers had been merchants. They were an upright family, hospitable and helpful. There were many kids around, lively but not mischievous. The two older boys were in prison. They were arrested in school for anti-party activities and were in prison or at forced labor, depending on the season of the year.

My next problem was to find a job. I volunteered for work at the local hospital and tried to make myself useful in surgery. A colleague of mine from Padua, Ismail Troshani, had been one year ahead of me in school and had worked now for quite a while with Dr. Mborja, the only surgeon at the hospital. The two of them and the complement of nurses formed a good team and there really was no need for me. I could always find work to keep myself busy but I realized it was unlikely that I would be hired.

Jakup Troshani was the hospital commissar, the man who had a finger in every pie. He was approaching 40, short, thin, and stooped for his age. He had dark hair, dark eyes, and a perennial five o'clock shadow. He looked at people with palpable malevolence that he wore like a badge of honor. He slinked around the offices with one shoulder carried lower than the other. A few weeks had gone by since my arrival when Comrade Troshani sent for me.

"Comrade Genc, you have been appointed a physician's assistant in Kodër Shëngjergj [Hill of St. George], in Dukagjin. You will have an office at the Regional Committee. You will have the right to write certain prescriptions and a pharmacy will fill them. This shows the confidence the Party has in you and in your technical ability.

"Right now, you can reach Theth by truck. There you will need to find someone with a mule to carry your things to the house of the pharmacist where you can live until you find a place to stay permanently. Have a safe trip."

He handed me an envelope confirming my appointment and shook hands with me. I turned around and left his office mumbling a few incoherent words of appreciation.

I had not expected this turn of events. Dukagjin was one of the poorest and most primitive areas of Albania. Most of the population was illiterate. It was known for its anti-communist resistance. I would live and work there under very poor conditions and find myself in an environment where I may have to tiptoe very carefully to avoid political traps along the way.

I wished I knew someone from that area so I could prepare myself for what lay ahead. I also had to put a positive spin on my appointment when I told Mom about my transfer. The positives were obvious. I had a job and an income. This was most important as we had run out of gold coins. The negatives were equally plain. Mom would be on her own while Mergim continued his high school education. I would be away from home living and working under most primitive conditions but probably able to send them part of my salary. This was not the worst that could have happened to us. Seen from that perspective, this was a positive development.

Now it was a matter of getting "the show on the road." I still had the field bed I had used in jail. This time I would add a few more personal belongings and some medical books. I must admit, the more I thought about it, the more I liked the idea of being gainfully employed. At the travel agency I found a truck bound for Theth, bought my ticket, and got ready to leave for a job that was new to me and would take me to a region I knew only by name and reputation.

The day I left Shkodra, the weather was warm but overcast. I hoisted everything aboard the truck, seated myself next to my meager belongings, and off we went. For the next hour or so we traveled along the shores of Lake Shkodra. The road was bumpy but bearable. At Koplik, we turned northeast and started climbing along a poorly maintained road. We bumped and ground our way between ever-higher foothills and mountains. I used to get carsick seated in comfort in a passenger car. This time I traveled in the back of the truck. The cool wind blew through my hair and refreshed my face. If I felt like puking, all I had to do was lean over the side of the truck and relieve myself. I must admit, though, that I enjoyed the ride, the scenery, and the challenges that lay ahead. I felt great. Not even the presence of a member of the Mbrojtje (security forces) on the truck dampened my spirit.

After about a three-hour ride, we made it to Theth. The air was cold and invigorating. It made my face and lungs tingle. The view was dazzling. A crown of snow-capped mountains rose majestically above a deep green valley, like diamonds surrounding a large emerald. Steep were the mountains and few the paths that hurtled down to the houses dotting the mountainsides. A river sprang from the mountains and foamed its way into the depth of Dukagjin. This was the northernmost tip of the land of Lek Dukagjini, the warrior and the legislator of the Code of Honor. The province was also one of the bastions of the anti-communist resistance. I looked around and felt welcome.

The driver awoke me from my reveries. He pointed out a solidly built larger building across the valley.

"That building belonged to the Franciscans. Priests and seminarians from Shkodra spent their summers in Theth." Clearly, the Franciscans knew where to build. Unfortunately, they would soon fall prey to one of the most radical and cruel persecutions the Catholic Church would suffer in modern times.

I had to force myself to let go of the view. I needed to find transportation to the house of the pharmacist Lel Vata. According to the driver, it would take me about five hours to get there on foot once I got going.

The village elder found me a muleteer who—for a reasonable fee—would get my belongings to what would be my abode for the next few weeks. We started going south. Soon we descended from the Theth plateau toward Ndërlysaj and from there we walked for about four hours to Bregu i Lumit. My guide told me that we had another half hour to walk to get to the house of Lel Vata. We ambled along the river at that seemingly leisurely pace of our mountaineers, whether they walked on flat ground or climbed up or down a mountainside. It would take me a few months to learn how to walk "properly."

As we reached a bend in the river, I could see the house of the pharmacist. It was a low building with stone walls and a slate roof. Two women came out and welcomed me. Obviously, they had expected me and were full of curiosity as they looked me over, taking in every detail from my looks and build to my clothing and footwear. I was not sure whether I measured up to their expectations. Regardless, the hospitality they extended me could not have been more prompt or gracious.

First, they gave me a chance to wash up. They already had prepared some hot water and soaking my feet felt great. Then they offered me food, which I declined as it was close to dinnertime. While they hustled about, they told me that their brother Lel was still at work but would be home soon. Only after they had taken care of me did they start asking questions about my family and so on. Now it was my turn to take a good look at them both as to their appearance and their personality. They were more sophisticated than I would have expected. It turned out that they had spent years in Shkodra, and it showed. The older sister was in her twenties, the younger in her late teens. Neither one was married. Their brother was also single. Neither they nor I touched on politics.

That changed rapidly as Lel came home. He was short and sickly thin. He had dark, unruly hair, wore dark clothes, was unshaven, and had a mustache— a must for a native male of Dukagjin. He greeted me effusively, plunged himself down, and let the sisters serve us dinner. Between bites, he let me know how much he despised the communists who had cut a bloody swath when they entered Dukagjin. Then he proceeded to tell me all about the people who worked at the provincial headquarters, beginning with the head of the executive committee. I tried to remember as much as I could for future use. Once I met the people, I would be able to put names and faces together. I would form my own impressions and reevaluate Lel's descriptions of them using his opinions of the various people, to take stock of Lel's powers of observation and his sincerity. As he spoke I kept a reserved attitude, which was quite easy as he was speaking of people and conditions I did not know.

It had been a long day for me, one rich in new impressions. The sisters prepared my bed that they had placed in a corner of the one big room the four of us shared with domestic animals kept behind a fence. The next day we had to get up early and Lel and I would climb the hill to the building where my office and his pharmacy were located.

Before going to bed, the sisters formed a little pile of embers in the fireplace and covered them with ashes. They made sure the door was locked and that we men were in bed. Then they blew out the kerosene lamps and lay down for the night.

The next morning when Lel and I were awakening, I noticed the sisters were up, had already started a fire, and by the time we men were ready for breakfast, they removed the freshly baked thin tortilla-type cornbreads from the fireplace. While we washed up, the sisters rolled the round, low table to the center of the room and served bread and feta cheese. We ate and soon were on our way. I carried a knapsack with my books on my back, eager to go to my office.

The regional offices occupied a two-story building that at one time had been the bishop's see. It consisted of a rather large stone building that had seen better days and presently housed the administrative offices of the province, a tribunal, and my "clinic." Another building nearby had been taken over by the police and the state security service.

My office consisted of a rather large room equipped with two desks, an examining table, and some chests of drawers for supplies and instruments. There was also a filing cabinet. Overall, I was satisfied with what I saw. I met a male nurse and several sanitary agents whose responsibility it was to inspect schools and what few stores there were to ensure that they complied with the basics of health and safety. These men reported to me even though some had the political credentials I lacked.

The night before, Lel had explained why Kodër Shëngjergj had a well-equipped pharmacy but no physician. Years before, there had been a hospital headed by a physician. Initially, the anti-communist resistance was quite active and ever present. To combat their elusive enemies, the state security people had hatched a plan. A man, posing as an anti-communist, had torched the hospital and had tried to join the guerillas in the mountains. When they heard what he had done, they tied him hand and foot and dropped him at night near the police station. When word spread that the guerillas had delivered him to the police, the regional Party committee had no choice but to have him tried for arson. He was sentenced to several years in prison where he fell ill and died of tuberculosis.

Once the hospital was gone, the authorities transferred the physician back into town. Because of the clumsiness of central planning, Dukagjin not only retained the pharmacy but kept receiving regular shipments of drugs, including penicillin, that were in critically short supply in the cities, not to speak of villages.

That morning I met my boss, a young man from Shkodra by the name of Mustafa. He was tall, slim, with wavy red hair and a red mustache. He had the right political credentials but never threw his weight around and never interfered with my technical or administrative responsibilities. In fact, during my one year in Dukagjin, I never could determine how he felt about me or my work.

Shortly after my appointment, a young nurse joined us. She had graduated from nursing school at a city hospital but had refused orders transferring her to some village. As punishment, she was assigned to Dukagjin. I welcomed her, indicating that her presence would make my life easier when dealing with female patients. At the same time I had to hide a smile, remembering the words of Jakup Troshani, the political commissar at the hospital in Shkodra, when he had explained to me why I was being transferred to Dukagjin: "This shows the confidence the Party has in you and in your technical ability." As it turned out, Dukagjin was for those the Party "respected" as well as those who had refused to obey orders; quite a quilt of people.

I was beginning to learn some things about the people of Dukagjin. On the surface, they had all the drawbacks of poverty and of a lack of formal education. Men, women, and children washed rarely. Taking a shower was not simply a matter of turning on faucets and lathering oneself with soap. To begin with, soap was seldom available. What passed for soap in the one and only co-op store in Theth would have failed muster in any civilized country. Besides, getting to the co-op took hours on foot one way. Assuming the soap was available, water had to be carried to the house in buckets from the nearest spring or river and had to be heated. That required wood that had to be gathered and carried home from the forest. Nothing was simple. Water and wood were mostly for cooking. For the time being, living with Lel and his sisters offered me better—and cleaner—living conditions. They had lived in Shkodra and the river and the woods were just a few feet from their home.

Many mountaineers were either illiterate or semi-literate. This of course was a handicap as far as acquiring formal knowledge was concerned. As I would soon find out, however, it did not affect either their common sense or their wisdom.

No regime as far back as anyone could remember had ever treated the population with justice and respect. Hence, the code of the mountains had come into being several hundred years before and was still used to resolve disputes, despite draconian measures by the communist authorities to impose their type of justice.

The code of the mountains, known as the Code of Lek Dukagjini, covered every possible subject from watering rights to murder. The code stressed the inviolability of a person's honor and was very harsh in this regard. An insult to a man's honor had to be paid for with blood—the offender's blood. If two men were involved in an altercation and one was unarmed, he had to get a weapon and return to face his opponent. Killing an unarmed person was dishonorable and treated as such. In case of death and before the blood feud became effective, the killer had to attend the funeral of the victim. A truce could be struck by decree of the council of elders or the intervention of the clergy. If a man involved in a blood feud had to leave his house for a serious reason and did so in the company of a woman, his enemies would let him pass, since no honorable man would hide behind a woman's skirt without a weighty reason. If the Ottoman police pursued a man involved in a feud, he could seek refuge in the house of his mortal enemy who would not only open the door but would also defend him to the last, as the Turks were the common enemy.

Special rules protected a "guest." Any stranger seeking food and shelter was welcomed and treated as an honored guest. The host would offer the guest the best food and accommodations available to him. Once the guest left, he remained under the protection of the host until he sought shelter at someone else's home.

Here was an important detail: If anyone harmed a stranger, his host would come to his defense or avenge him if he was killed. While feuding families could forgive each other for blood spilled or even deaths inflicted, no one could ever forgive the blood of a guest. This was important because forgiving a family member's death was never done lightly. On the other hand, it would have been easy forgiving a stranger's death. The Code made this impossible.

There were many other rules, all intended to uphold and regulate justice without government intervention. Unfortunately, this tendency continues among mountaineers in Albania and, to some extent, even among Albanian immigrants to the United States who find it difficult to leave their century-old traditions behind.

Faced with life in these beautiful mountains, I decided to make the best of it. Initially it was hard for me to ignore the heavy body odor that surrounded the people. After a few weeks I no longer noticed it. I was either becoming accustomed, as one does after spending time in a smelly room, or I had began to smell like them.

Next I began practicing a principle I had learned in jail from an Italian translation of Dale Carnegie's *How to Win Friends and Influence People*. Dad, by the way, was so impressed with the book that he translated it into Albanian. Carnegie stressed that a person's name was most important to that person. Thus, I made it a practice to remember the names of the villagers who came to my office. It made them feel respected and important. That was just what I wanted, because government employees and city folk had always treated them poorly.

To carry that principle further, I made it a point to receive them well and to go to their homes when I wanted to follow up on a patient. If it took me time and effort to get to their homes, they rewarded me with their friendship, which by far exceeded any of my efforts on their behalf. In addition, there was great joy and satisfaction in putting my modest medical knowledge to good use. No matter how I looked at it, my transfer to Dukagjin was a winner, irrespective of what the communists had intended.

Staying at Lel's was a gentle transition from living in Shkodra to the life in Dukagjin. He and his sisters made me feel welcome and tried to make my life as comfortable as possible. I was young, in good health, and willing to go the extra mile to understand and adapt to the mentality of the natives of our mountains. I came to realize that Lel did not always come home at the end of the workday. It was none of my business.

Then one night it was getting late when we heard him half hollering, half singing. We could not quite make out what he was saying except that the name of *Druzhe* (Comrade) Tito was part of the refrain. We got concerned because his hollering was not exactly respectful and speaking of Comrade Tito in any other way could be very unhealthy. He was obviously drunk. When he entered the house, he was grinning from ear to ear.

"Down with Comrade Tito and down with Yugoslavia."

We tried to muzzle him.

"You don't know what has happened. We have just broken relations with Comrade Tito. To hell with him and to hell with the Yugoslavs."

We could not believe our ears. While Lel's noisy behavior had scared us initially, at least he had not endangered himself or anyone else. It was late and Lel was drunk, or at least half-drunk. His sister put him to bed while I lay down on my field bed.

I said my nightly prayers with more feeling than usual. I could not fall asleep, however, as various thoughts swirled through my mind. Could this unexpected development be a step in the right direction? Might some of the political prisoners who had traditionally opposed a strong collaboration with Yugoslavia be released and even be asked to take the country on a new course? Would this development weaken the communist party's grip on the country, as Yugoslavia had been the Party's founder and main supporter? Eventually, mental and physical tiredness prevailed and I fell asleep.

The next day at the office, it was obvious that the local Party leaders had lost their bearings. They had forced the friendship with Yugoslavia down the throats of the people of Dukagjin, and had persecuted, pillaged, tortured and killed anyone who refused to follow the Party line despite centuries of enmity between our mountain people and our Slavic neighbors to the north. At this point uncertainty reigned among the communists. They were eagerly waiting for instructions from Tirana, instructions that were late in coming.

Meanwhile, the people rejoiced behind their poker faces. Unfortunately, it did not take long and the news from Tirana spelled out a new message, violently anti-Yugoslav and ever more groveling toward the Soviet Union. In fact, the change was trumpeted as a great victory. Yugoslavia had been full of duplicity toward Albania. It had exploited Albania politically and economically, causing untold damage. The Soviet Union under the brilliant leadership of Comrade Stalin had unmasked Tito, expelling him from the socialist camp, and Tito was crawling to the feet of his true masters, the capitalists, the enemies of the people. Stalin had stated that he could overthrow Tito by just wiggling his little finger. What Stalin did not reveal was that before the breakup, he had encouraged Tito to "swallow" Albania. This came out when Milovan Gjilas, the Yugoslav ex-communist leader, published *Conversations with Stalin*. There he describes Stalin encouraging the Yugoslav delegation to "swallow" Albania. When asked to explain what he meant by "swallowing," Stalin moved his hand to his mouth as if he were getting ready to swallow it.

It turned out later that Stalin had tried to purge the ranks of the Yugoslav communist leadership and bring a pro-Soviet faction to power. Try as he might, Stalin was unable to get rid of Tito while the latter succeeded in neutralizing Moscow's maneuvers within Yugoslavia. At this point, Tito quit the Soviet bloc and received economic and military aid from the West. Later, to assert himself as an international leader, he headed the so-called nonaligned bloc of nations with India and other countries as members.

Some past events surfaced now in Albania in a new light. At the time of Nako Spiru's death, Yugoslavia saw Koçi Xoxe as its Gauleiter in Albania. According to the Yugoslav blueprint, Nako Spiru, who had alerted the

Albanian leadership to economic irregularities in the relationship between the two countries, had to be silenced. Enver Hoxha and Mehmet Shehu were to be removed from office and eliminated. Stalin failed inasmuch as he could not remove Tito. The Yugoslavs in turn failed in Albania, where Mehmet Shehu arrested Koçi Xoxe. Xoxe, the former chief judge of the special tribunal, was brought before a court and wound up facing the firing squad. Enver Hoxha remained supreme head with the support of Mehmet Shehu. Liri Belishova, Nako Spiru's widow, was brought back to Tirana, returned to the Central Committee, and promoted to the Politbureau. That was a thumbnail sketch of the events of 1948—of the first crack to appear in the Iron Curtain. Others would follow over the years.

During the years of Yugoslav domination, a Lieutenant Baba had come to Dukagjin to uproot any local resistance. His goals were despicable and his methods hateful. In one case, a prisoner had broken out of jail and had disappeared without a trace. The guards had opened fire but may have missed and failed to capture the fugitive. A patrol had found blood on a bush halfway down a hill leading to a farmhouse. They asked the owner whether he had seen or had any dealings with the fugitive. The owner vigorously denied all such charges. Next, the investigators took the four-year-old daughter of the owner aside and asked her whether her father had dressed the wound of someone who had come to the house bleeding, and the child said yes, her father had indeed bandaged the hand of someone who had come to their home. At this point, they arrested the owner and Lieutenant Baba questioned him personally. But he was unable to get the man to admit any contact with the fugitive. The lieutenant ran out of patience. He brought in the prisoner's two children, the four-year-old girl and her little brother.

"Listen and listen well," he said to the prisoner. "If you refuse to cooperate, I will shoot your son." He knew how much a son meant to Albanians in general and to farmers in those mountains in particular.

"You don't believe me that I will shoot your son. Well, you'd better." He drew his pistol and killed the little girl. "Now do you believe me that I will shoot your son if you won't cooperate?"

The poor farmer swore that he knew nothing about the fugitive, that he had never seen him after his escape nor had he heard where he had found refuge. As he had threatened, the lieutenant aimed his pistol at the little boy and pulled the trigger. The little boy fell dead on the floor.

Enraged, the prisoner spit his words at the lieutenant, "Yes, I bandaged the fugitive's wounds and sent him on his way. I know where he is hiding. I further know where local resistance fighters are, where they have their cache of weapons, and where and when they intend to strike."

The lieutenant raised his pistol once more and shot the man dead.

When Albania broke off from Yugoslavia, Gjovalin Luka, a member of parliament, came to Dukagjin to investigate crimes committed by the security forces. There was a meeting at Kodër Shëngjergj, outside our office building, and the people spoke of such horrible events. Gjovalin Luka glibly attributed such crimes to Yugoslavia and the pro-Yugoslav faction within the Albanian communist party.

Rumor had it, probably planted by communist sources, that Enver Hoxha had personally ordered that the recently promoted Captain Baba be brought before a court and be made to pay for his crimes. The people of Dukagjin used this chance to vent their pain and emotions. I am sure that no one, beginning with Gjovalin Luka, had any illusions that the recent break with Yugoslavia would improve the political situation in Albania. Furthermore, it was one more instance where keeping people from talking openly could not keep them from thinking clearly and drawing their own conclusions.

I had the opportunity to feel the pulse of the population soon after the meeting. It was a Saturday afternoon. I was getting ready to close shop when Sabri, a noncommissioned officer of the security forces (Mbrojtje), entered my office. I had met him before. He was of average height, with red hair and a red mustache. He wore metal-rimmed glasses that made him look like a schoolteacher. What was unusual about him, besides his appearance, was that he had none of the aggressiveness and arrogance characteristic of Mbrojtje people. Instead, he had the reputation of being courteous and fair in his dealings with the population.

He entered my office smiling and began with the words, "Comrade Genc, what are you going to do..."

I interrupted him. "I am sorry; I cannot come to a meeting as I have to see a seriously ill patient." I had no intention of going to another of those terribly boring meetings we had to attend on weekends. I made it a point to spend weekends in various villages to avoid such political gatherings.

"Where are you going and who is your patient?" he asked.

I had to think fast. "It is a woman across the river I need to see. She lost her baby at birth and came down with a life-threatening infection. I gave her penicillin and my nurse continued the series of shots. Now I want to examine her once more to make sure she is out of danger."

"Where does she live?"

"She is the daughter-in-law of Pal Mirashi in the village of Vuksanaj."

Pal Mirashi was well known for his superior intelligence throughout Dukagjin. Anti-communists appreciated his wisdom; the communists had imprisoned him and continued to view him an enemy.

"Excellent," said the NCO. "I always wanted to meet the man. I'll come with you. You take care of your medical business, I'll use the chance to talk with Pal Mirashi. When are you leaving?" he asked me.

"In about half an hour."

"I'll be here."

This was an unwelcome development but there was nothing I could do. Around 5:00 p.m., the NCO showed up with a big smile on his face.

"I brought you a pistol to carry with you tonight. Vuksanaj is fairly dangerous territory, often frequented by the resistance."

My first thought was to reject the offer. Carrying a gun under the circumstances might give my friends the idea that I had switched sides. Besides, I could not be sure that the gun actually worked. The NCO could have altered the firing pin or the ammunition. I could ask him to let me fire the gun to get a feel for it. This, however, might show that I did not trust him. I pocketed the pistol, a German Luger, without a word. We had just gotten across the river when we ran into the head of the local communist Youth organization.

"Good evening, men."

We answered in kind.

"Where are you going?" he asked, and when he found out he called the NCO aside and whispered something in his ear. The NCO bid him farewell and then turned to me.

"He warned me that Pal Mirashi is a reactionary."

I did not quite know how to take these words.

"Look, I am here to serve the people. I do not ask what their political beliefs are. Otherwise, I could not do my job."

"Of course, of course," the NCO said smiling. "I told the young man that no Albanian harms a guest and there was no reason for him to worry."

We continued on our way and reached our destination shortly afterwards. At Pal Mirashi's they welcomed us even though I could not help noticing the funny way they looked at me. I examined the young woman who, thanks to the penicillin, had fully recovered. We ate dinner and when we lay down to sleep, Pal Mirashi came to make sure that we were comfortable. At this point, the NCO brought up politics.

"For years you, our elders and fathers, warned us against the Yugoslavs. You told us how they had invaded these regions, how they slaughtered people, how they tried everything to annex these regions to Yugoslavia. We did not listen or believe you. Instead we arrested you, we tortured you, and sometimes we killed you. I have come here to apologize to you tonight."

Pal Mirashi answered without hesitation. "If you had said these things to me anywhere else, I would not have answered you. You are in my house; you are our guest and I owe you an answer. It has been now four years since the communist party took over. For four years, you have fed us poison and have forced us to eat it saying that it was honey. What you have just said is like honey. I don't know whether your party has indeed honey, but if it does you will give us honey for another four years and we will refuse to eat it, convinced that it is poison. Now good night and sleep well."

With these words, he left the room and took the lamp with him.

The next morning we had breakfast, embraced our host and his family according to local custom, and wound our way back to where we had come from the day before. When we reached our village, I took out the Luger to return it to him.

"No, keep it," the NCO said. "I'll come by your office tomorrow and pick it up."

I nodded and walked toward the school building where I was staying at that time. It felt funny having a gun in my pocket. In fact, I had not had a gun in my hands since the communist takeover. Again, I was tempted to fire the gun to see whether it worked. Then I rejected the idea. Firing it would have attracted the attention of people, including the police and Mbrojtje. So I dropped the idea but could not help wondering whether the NCO had left the gun with me, or had brought it with him in the first place, because he trusted me or rather wanted to test me. Was he being naïve or duplicitous? Was he a dove or a snake? I guess I'll never know.

CHAPTER TWENTY

FROM DUKAGJIN BACK TO SHKODRA

I got to know the area and the people quite well as I traveled on foot from village to village. In time they understood that I truly cared for them. They in turn repaid me many times over. I was forming true friendships with people whose native intelligence and strength of character I came to admire greatly.

I also made a special friend. One day at a gathering, I met a stray dog. He was short, about the size of a beagle, with rather long red fur and an up-turned tail. He desperately sought friendship with the scared look of a stray that had been kicked around a lot. When he saw me he must have sensed that I was different from the other men present who despised dogs unless they were big and fierce, able to stand their own against roving wolves. The little stray came to me, rubbed against my leg, asking to be petted. I liked him and scratched his little head behind his ears, in a sense one stray making friends with another.

From then on, he never left my side. He blossomed, now that he belonged to someone. His personality changed. He looked self-assured with his furry tail flying like a proud banner as he made his way across Dukagjin, always about ten steps ahead of me. I called my new friend "Bubi." When we came to a crossroad, Bubi would stop, turn his head, and look at me quizzically. When he saw which way I was going, he would turn that way and proceed with obvious pleasure and assurance. When villagers saw Bubi, I could hear them shout, "The doctor is coming, the doctor is coming!" I was never quite sure whether they called Bubi "the doctor" or whether they meant me. Either way, the title was inappropriate.

During my stay at Kodër Shëngjergj, I changed homes several times. During the time of the event I am about to describe, I lived alone in a little tower next to the main office building. Inside, near the entrance to the tower, there was a primitive fireplace and a flight of steps that led to my bedroom upstairs. While this arrangement offered privacy, it also offered little comfort, as I had to fetch water for my own use and could count only on the daily ration of bread—which was daily in name only.

I had eaten nothing for a couple of days when a little old lady came to my first aid station with some complaint. I took care of her and she in turn gave me two fresh eggs. Boy! I rushed to my abode. Near the fireplace, I still had some dry wood. I grabbed what few scraps of paper I had and tried to build a fire. I never got beyond the trying stage.

I heard a timid voice calling. I turned my head, away from the clouds of smoke and dust I had stirred up as I was blowing into the fireplace, and looked out. There was a little girl, no more than five or six years old, with her few sheep.

"Comrade Doctor, would you like me to start a fire for you?"

I stared at her. Was she making fun of me? I didn't think so. She looked so innocent and full of good will.

"Go ahead," I replied. "Let me see how you do it."

I gave her some matches. She gathered a handful of dry grass and a few twigs, built a little mound in the fire place, and before I knew it, the grass started to burn and the twigs to glow. Then she added small branches, one at the time. In minutes, she had a lusty fire going. She got off her hands and knees, and smiled timidly, waiting for me to dismiss her.

"Thank you, little girl. It was nice of you to help me. I think I'll boil myself a couple of eggs."

She nodded, gathered her few sheep, and disappeared around the next bend. Big deal, I told myself. I too could have lit the fire with dry grass and twigs just as she had done. It just so happened I did not have any by my fireplace. So, there!

I filled a small pot with water, just enough to cover the two precious eggs, and climbed the steps to my bedroom. There I grabbed what medical books I had and threw them out the window. What good was my medical knowledge if I couldn't even light a fire to boil a couple of eggs? I was disgusted with myself.

On the feast of St. Michael, a farmer knocked at the door of my little tower. He had come from the village of Gimaj because a little boy was very sick. He had a fever and coughed a lot. When the boy coughed, he complained of a stabbing pain in his left chest. When he spit out some phlegm, the color was somewhere between rusty and red. The farmer's description fit pneumonia to a "T." I went to the pharmacy, grabbed some bottles of penicillin, distilled water, a couple of syringes, some aspirin, and cough syrup, and we were on our way. The village of Gimaj was on the same mountain slope as Kodër Shëngjergj. We did not have to cross the river, so we got there quickly. I examined the patient and when I listened to his left lung, I could hear the characteristic whistle of pneumonia that no medical student could ever forget. I started a series of penicillin shots and repeated the treatment every three hours. By evening, the young patient was beginning to feel better.

In the meantime, I had a chance to look around. St. Michael was the patron saint of the village. Outside the patient's room, the farmer had dug a pit and a few feet removed from the fiery pit was a lamb roasting as a child turned the crank ever so slowly. The fact that the lamb was not above the pit made it possible for the fat to drip into a wooden container without burning up in the flames. Obviously, it took hours before the roast was ready.

In preparation, the grandmother of the patient was preparing special candles for the occasion. She took a wick and rolled it in tallow to the thickness of her little finger. Then she gave it a spiral base and raised the tip of the candle straight up, similar to a cobra getting ready to strike. When it was time, she started praying and pronounced the words "Kyrie eleison, Christe eleison, Kyrie eleison," the only Greek words used in the Roman Catholic Latin Mass.

I asked her, "Mother, do you know what those words mean?"

"No," she replied.

"They mean 'Lord have mercy, Christ have mercy, Lord have mercy.'"

"Are you one of ours?" she asked, meaning, a Roman Catholic.

"No," I replied, "I am Muslim."

"Too bad," she said, "You would have made a good priest."

She continued with another question. "Do you know something about America?"

"I haven't been there, but I have read about America."

"Tell me, is America above or below ground?"

"Why are you asking?"

"This grandson of mine," she said while pointing at the patient, "came back from school one day and told me that some Italian had uncovered America."

In Albanian, the verb "uncover" also means "discover," hence the confusion. I told her about Christopher Columbus and the discovery of America. That satisfied her.

Late that evening they brought me some meat, bread, and cheese and I ate seated next to the patient. I must say, I had never had tastier lamb than the one they served that night.

The patient's fever had started to go down and he said he felt better. That of course added to the joy of his relatives and gave me much satisfaction. I was truly impressed how well the patients in the mountains reacted to any kind of medicine. In the case of penicillin, it was particularly satisfying to me that, thanks to the aberrations of central planning, the antibiotic was available in Dukagjin where there was no physician and was as rare as hen's teeth in major cities. I continued administering the penicillin every three hours throughout the night. The next morning I sent a farmer to bring the male nurse to Gimaj to continue the penicillin treatment and give me a chance to go home and catch up on sleep.

To keep my medical successes in perspective, I will mention one more episode. A farmer brought his little boy to my first aid station. The child had a skin eruption and no fever. I checked his eyes, nose, throat, lungs, and heart and everything seemed to be normal. I excused myself and went to my books. Let me hasten to add that after the boiled eggs episode, I had retrieved my precious books. I looked and looked and—by elimination—arrived at the one possible conclusion I could think of. I reentered my office and told the farmer in my best professional tone that his son had chicken pox.

"I know," replied the father. "I just wanted you to give me a note so my son would be excused from school."

If I had but asked the father, I could have saved myself some trouble. I had never seen a case of chicken pox before. Now I added it to the short list of illnesses I recognized.

It was around midnight one night in January or February of 1949 when I heard furious and persistent knocking at the door of the school building where I was staying at the time. I shared a room with two male teachers from Shkodra. We woke up and stared at each other. Bright moonlight through the window cut the room in two as it sliced a chunk of darkness off the floor and opposite wall.

"What shall we do? Shall we answer?"

"Well, we cannot put our heads under the pillows and pretend we are not here."

One of the teachers got up, threw something over his shoulders, and opened the door. There stood an employee of the provincial department of finance, a young and fairly friendly individual. His cheeks were red, his face perspired.

"Good evening," he said. "It looks nice and warm in your room. May I come in?"

We had no stove but it had not taken long for three young men sleeping in a small room to heat the room to a comfortable temperature, even in the winter.

"What brings you here in the middle of the night?" one of the teachers asked him, trying to keep his voice steady.

Our "guest" was nice enough during the day but he was also a member of the communist party. His visit that night could spell trouble. He looked at me and smiled.

"Please get dressed and come to the Mbrojtje command post; nothing to worry about, just a few routine questions."

My mind began to race. He could not have come to arrest me all by himself. I was bigger and stronger than he. True, he probably carried a weapon, but with the three of us in one small room, disarming him would be a cinch. The formula he had used about my having to answer a few routine questions was frequently used when someone was being arrested. If he had come to arrest me, more likely than not security forces had the school surrounded. Why would they send him in alone to bring me out when the pros could do it much better? The whole thing did not make sense. I decided to challenge him.

"Look, you are too nice a guy to do this to me. If anything, I would have expected you to warn me as soon as you found out that I was to be arrested."

While I was uttering these words, I rose and approached him, ready to jump him. He replied with a smile.

"Forget what I told you. We need you to take care of a man who was shot a few hours ago. Get dressed, grab whatever you need, and let's get going. I'll tell you more once we are on our way."

That made more sense. I dressed warmly, we shook hands with the teachers, and left the school house. My first aid station was about 10 minutes away.

"Tell me what happened so I know what to take with me."

"Here is what happened," he replied. "Yesterday toward evening, a patrol of the Mbrojtje led by Sabri, their sergeant major, entered a house in Ndërlysaj intending to spend the night there. The head of the family received them well, according to local custom. He hung up their weapons on the wall since they were now under his protection. They had a drink or two and then the women set the table before them. As they began to eat, the dog barked in the yard.

"'It must be my boy who is taking fodder to the barn,' the host said by way of explanation.

"The sergeant major rose, followed by his troops, and made for the door. They knew that no dog would bark at a member of the family. As they stepped out, they saw several men huddled together near the barn, talking with the eldest son of the house. When the strangers saw the uniforms atop the stairs, they opened fire. The soldiers ran back into the house to grab their weapons. The sergeant major who had been closest to the railing was last, and was hit in the right leg. The soldiers combed the area but the criminals got away, at least for the time being."

By this time, we had reached my first aid station and the attached pharmacy. I grabbed ample supplies of gauze and bandages, disinfectant, heart stimulants, sulfa powder, penicillin, a tetanus shot, syringes, and whatever else I could think of. Within minutes, we were on our way.

Now that I was relaxed, I took in the beauty of the winter night. It was extraordinarily beautiful. The air was crisp and clean. It had snowed on and off for days and the fresh snow reached halfway up the calf. It crunched underfoot and glistened as far as the eye could see. It covered the bare branches of chestnut trees, giving them a soft thickness. It dressed the pine trees in a glorious formal white encrusted with silver, their trunks showing through here and there like dark garments. The moon sparkled bright amid a galaxy of stars that punctuated the clear sky. What a beautiful, wonderful night!

Back to reality. I knew Sabri, the sergeant major. He was from Berat, a redhead with a little mustache. He was polite, friendly, and the opposite of the stereotype NCO of the Mbrojtje. He could make you want him for a friend. He had joined me when I had visited Pal Mirashi in Vuksanaj some time before and on that occasion I had gotten to know him better.

Anyhow, he had a reputation for being fair minded. Now he lay wounded a few miles away. How serious was his wound and what would the Mbrojtje do to the men of the house? The host had obviously expected the infiltrators that night. He had tried to deceive the sergeant and had failed. His oldest son was also involved. He had met with the infiltrators and had probably alerted them to the presence of the security forces. What would happen to the men of the house and the entire family? What kind of an example would the communists want to set? Would they confiscate the cattle? Would they burn the house, kill the men? In the past they had done this much and worse. One could never tell.

My companion and I kept walking at a swift pace for five hours without stopping to catch our breath. As we approached the house, I could see the brightly lit windows and men in uniform swarming all over the place. A lieutenant led me to the sergeant major. He was lying on his back on the floor. Two soldiers crouched next to him, one on either side, holding up a broom propped under his right knee. The sergeant major looked at me with a big smile.

"I knew you would come here as soon as you could. Please tell someone to bring me some water. I am dying of thirst."

"Do you have any other wound except the one in your thigh?" I asked.

"No," he replied. "Otherwise, I am fine."

I turned to a soldier who was crossing the room. "Please, bring the sergeant major some water."

The sergeant smiled again. "They have given me only whiskey and honey..." His voice trailed off. He didn't want to complain.

"It won't be long now, and you will have all the cold water you will want to drink."

"Thanks, Comrade Genc."

The wounded man looked well. His color was good, his pulse strong and rhythmic, his breathing regular. I removed the dressing from the wound. The shot had gone midway through his thigh without touching the femur or a major blood vessel. He could move his leg and toes without any problem. There was no nerve damage. Of course, he had lost blood, his lips were cracked, and his tongue dry. I asked the soldiers to remove the broomstick and lower the leg carefully. Just as I opened my bag to dress the wound, the wounded man spoke again.

"Comrade Genc, where is the water?"

I turned to look for the soldier when I noticed an officer looking over my shoulder.

"Comrade Lieutenant, I asked a soldier to bring the sergeant major some cold water. What's keeping him?"

"Look, Comrade Genc, we don't know as much about medicine as you do, but we do know that you don't give water to someone who has been shot." I was being accused of endangering the life of the man, obviously because I was an enemy of the regime. Before I could answer, the sergeant spoke up.

"Comrade Lieutenant, if Comrade Genc says that it's alright for me to drink water, I want water. I trust him completely."

The lieutenant hesitated for a moment. Then he nodded and a soldier brought a can full of cold water. We lifted the sergeant on his elbows and gave him his first drink of water since the previous afternoon.

It was getting light outside. I washed and disinfected the area where the bullet had entered and exited. Sulfa powder on the wound, a clean dressing, and then I was done as far as the wound proper was concerned. I gave the patient a tetanus shot and started the penicillin. He would get a penicillin shot every three hours; that's the way we did it then. I put a rolled-up blanket under the patient's leg and covered him lightly. He smiled, reached for my hand, and squeezed it. Had it not been for the atmosphere of crisis, the continuous coming and going, and the danger to the host and his family, the sergeant major would have been ready to fall asleep. Yet he did not permit himself the luxury.

The host and the other males of his family had been squeezed into a corner of the house, away from the women and children. The officers and other communists gathered in the main room with the sergeant major. They asked me to step out and for once I was glad to oblige. This was one case I really preferred not to be part of. I stepped out of the room and out of the house and filled my lungs with fresh air. Only now did I realize how stale the air had been indoors with so many unwashed bodies crammed inside, perspiring, some from revenge, the family out of fear.

As it turned out, I could hear some of what was being said inside. Some argued that the men of the house be shot immediately. They had been conspiring with the infiltrators. That was clear. That was reason enough to kill them. In addition, their execution would be a warning to others who fed and hid such criminals and were willing to serve as their eyes and ears. It was bad enough risking one's life daily against the enemies of the regime. It was time to hit the enemy and hit him hard. Depriving him of local support was one way to tilt the battle in favor of the forces of justice. As could be expected, escalation set in. I heard others argue that, in addition, the house should be burned to the ground, the cattle removed, and the trees cut down. That would serve the enemy and his helpers right.

I did not recognize the voices but one thing was obvious. No one had dared so far to oppose such incendiary words. No one, that is, until the sergeant major spoke up.

"Comrades, I disagree. We don't know whether the men of the family knew the infiltrators were coming. They heard the dog bark, the eldest son happened to be feeding the cattle, and when we stepped out we saw him with the criminals. It does not mean he was expecting them. In fact, he could not have timed it so accurately. Infiltrators travel at night. Yesterday it was barely dusk when we reached the house. Anyone expecting them would have expected them much later and would have had time to warn them of our presence. Second, if we had returned fire and the men of the house had been killed in the crossfire, that would have been one thing; shooting them today is another. We take pride in our system of justice. How can we bypass our courts and claim we are better than the oppressive regimes of the past if we execute the men without a trial? No, I firmly believe that our people's revolution demands we bring the men before a court that will judge them according to the best interests of the communist party and the people. Ours is not to exact revenge. It is our duty to protect the Albanian people, and in this case, to protect them from being victimized by the criminals who challenge our victory and oppose the people's regime. I urge all of us to think and act as communists. There is only one alternative before us: We must bring the men before a people's court and let the court decide. Any other approach is unworthy of the Party and of us."

There it was, the voice of reason. The words had been a bit bombastic, but according to the rhetoric of the time. Furthermore, it was unclear whether he truly cared about the party's reputation or was simply trying to save a family from total destruction and made use of the political jargon to further his cause. Either way, he deserved respect.

The silence that followed his words showed the impression his words had made. I heard shuffling of feet as the meeting broke up. The officers came out and started giving orders. Some soldiers put together a primitive stretcher. Others gathered their backpacks and shouldered their weapons. I went inside and filled my bag with what was left of my tools of the trade. As I peered into the depth of the house, I saw the head of the family and his eldest son in chains, surrounded by a cluster of soldiers. As we stepped out, the soldiers split into two single columns. One led the way toward Theth, toward the highway that led to Shkodra. Then came the stretcher carried by four men, followed by me and the rest of the soldiers.

We were on our way. The men of the house were in chains, but alive. The women and children, their house and property had not been harmed. Everyone was safe—for the moment. Thank God! Matters could have been much worse.

We started climbing toward Theth. The paths were narrow and the stretcher heavy. The soldiers took turns and even some local communists carried the stretcher for a while. At one point, a civilian communist wanted to help with the stretcher but did not know what to do with his rifle. I offered to carry it. As soon as he handed the weapon to me, he yelled, "Comrade Lieutenant, Genc has my rifle!"

The lieutenant fell back and relieved me of the weapon. Clearly, I was an enemy, not to be trusted with a rifle and five rounds even for a moment. I surrendered the weapon and fell in line.

The day was beautiful. In Theth the soldiers loaded the stretcher on a truck and some of them accompanied the wounded NCO to Shkodra. The rest of us backtracked, and a few hours later I was back at the school, ready to make up for the sleep I had lost.

One day I was in bed, weak and suffering from diarrhea. I had just crawled back to my field bed when there was a knock at the door of my little tower. I dragged myself down. There stood the police lieutenant, one of the least charming representatives of the communist power structure in Kodër Shëngjergj.

"My wife is ill. You know where we live; hurry!"

I put on my footgear, sandals with heavy truck tire soles, and trudged over to see the patient. The woman was in her twenties, lying in bed, surrounded by some old local women who were clucking words intended to comfort and encourage the patient. Once I shooed the women away, I could see what the problem was. The young woman was pregnant and the water bag had broken. The umbilical cord was protruding, without evidence of a heartbeat. Even from a distance, the old women were saying that they could push the cord back in and everything would be OK. The lieutenant looked at me.

"If she were my wife, I would take her to a hospital in Shkodra as soon as possible. Meanwhile, I would make sure that the umbilical cord didn't slide back into your wife's body."

The lieutenant did not reply. The old women protested. I turned on my heels and left to return to my humble home away from home.

About 20 minutes went by and there was another knock at the door.

"Doc, get up, we are going to Shkodra."

"I can't. I am sick myself."

"Get up and get ready. The communist party has sent you here to serve the people."

What choice did I have? I put on my topcoat—it was quite cold— grabbed a little bag with heart medication, a syringe, a pair of scissors, and some bandages, and off we went. In the meantime, the lieutenant had commandeered a stretcher, and drafted four strong men from nearby homes. We put the woman on the stretcher and off we went. We started climbing toward the pass leading to Shosh when, after a mere half hour or so, the woman asked that they lower the stretcher as she felt she was about to have a bowel movement. What she felt was the baby's head pressing against the rectum; the mother's womb was rejecting the dead preemie.

I asked the men to lower the stretcher and give me some privacy. They left except for the lieutenant who looked over my shoulder. As luck had it, the little body was in the right position. I had no problem forming a forceps with my fingers and removing the lifeless body. The placenta, however, would not come out. I pulled out the rubber band from the woman's underwear, tied the cord, severed it and told the woman to hold the band and make sure the protruding part of the cord stayed outside her body. Meanwhile, the lieutenant placed the tiny body in a grave along the side of the footpath. As I recall, he placed no marker on the site.

We started up again. The lieutenant would have the men carry the stretcher for a couple of hours. Then he would summon replacements from homes along the road as we continued toward Shkodra. I for one felt weak and miserable. Strangely enough, my tummy was not bothering me. Instead, my feet were hurting because my sandals fit poorly. On top of everything else, I knew that the lieutenant was a syphilitic. I did not know whether his wife had also been infected. In my mind, I could think of 101 complications that might interfere with her recovery and that—eventually—it may be held against me.

After 18 hours of steady walking, we finally made it to Shkodra. I went with them to the hospital, made sure the woman was taken care of, and dragged myself home. Mom was happy to see me unexpectedly but dismayed to see me in that condition. As I removed my heavy woolen socks, I pulled off some toenails. I washed up, collapsed in bed, and enjoyed sleeping on a real mattress. Under Mom's loving care, and thanks to the resilience of youth, I fully recovered after one week of TLC (tender loving care).

My first thought was for my patient. I went to the hospital, but to my consternation I could not find any trace of her in the hospital registry. Gravely concerned, I asked the registrar whether perhaps a patient by that name had passed away during the last week. That too proved futile. After some more searching, it turned out that the lieutenant's wife had recovered promptly and had left the hospital after three days. It had taken me a full week to get well...

It was spring in Dukagjin. Some high mountaintops still had snow but everything else was clad in luxurious green. The mountainsides were full of little lambs and nature rejoiced all around us. Each spring, alas, also brought a First of May and 1949 was no exception. This time there was a new first secretary of the communist party and he was going to celebrate the great feast day of the proletariat with a special ceremony of his own invention. He was articulate, quite tall, muscular, with regular features. He wore his suit well. He was from Mirdita, the other northern province that challenged Dukagjin for first place for its poverty and lack of formal education of its inhabitants as well as for their bravery.

The first secretary had decreed that all employees, one by one, were to pay him a visit on the First of May. Once in his office, each had to pronounce a toast and down a shot of whiskey. This presented me with two problems. First, I hated the taste of whiskey and never drank it if I could avoid it. I didn't think, however, that I could skip it this time. Second, what kind of toast would I offer in honor of the occasion? I waited in the anteroom for my turn. When I entered, I noticed that the office was bare except for a desk near the window. The first secretary stood behind the desk, two whiskey glasses in front of him. He handed me mine, picked up his, looked me in the eye and waited. I cleared my throat.

"I congratulate the communist party for the good it has done for the Albanian people."

I put the glass to my lips, closed my eyes, and swallowed the contents. When I opened my eyes again, I saw the secretary staring at me. His glass, of course, was still full.

"I understand," was all he said.

I turned around and left his office. I don't recall who was next and frankly, I did not care.

A few days later, I had a chance to go to Shkodra. I laid my hands on the May 1 issue of the communist daily newspaper and looked for the congratulatory telegrams published on page one. Half the page was taken up with excerpts from the telegram sent by the Muslim clergy to Comrade Enver Hoxha.

" May Allah and Baba Fetah favor and bless the communist party and its Great Leader..."

The other half of that page had excerpts of the telegram sent by the clergy of the Albanian Orthodox Church.

"May the Lord God, may Jesus Christ, and may the Holy Spirit bless and protect the communist party..."

In the middle of the page was the full text of the telegram sent by the hierarchy of the Catholic Church. It went something like this:

"Congratulating the communist party on the good it has done on behalf of the Albanian people; we pray that it may always use its power to strive on behalf of our country."

I was struck by the similarity of this last telegram with my toast in Dukagjin.

Shortly after the First of May, my boss called me into his office and notified me that I was being transferred to Shkodra where I was to assume the duties of sanitary inspector for the city. We shook hands and I was out of there. It took me a few days to say goodbye to my friends and find a man with a mule with whom I would travel, perhaps for the last time, from Dukagjin to Shkodra. I entrusted my dog Bubi to a farmer at whose home I had lived for a while. Then came the day of my departure. I still had my field bed, my books, and my personal belongings. All I needed now was a muleteer and his mule. I waited until about mid-morning but no mule showed up. Finally, I asked the man who was to procure the mule.

"Tell me, when will the mule be here? It's getting late and I would like to be on my way."

"Any time you are ready."

"What do you mean?"

He walked over to the bundle representing my earthly goods, tied it together with sturdy ropes, heaved the burden on his shoulders and said, "Let's go."

I could not believe my eyes. I had walked from Kodër Shëngjergj to Shkodra a number of times and knew that it would take somewhere between 10 and 18 hours to cover the distance. I could not believe that the brother of my former landlord was going to carry my belongings on his back, all the way to Shkodra. He saw my expression of disbelief.

"Don't worry. I'll carry your things. Lead the way and let's get going."

I was leaving Dukagjin with mixed emotions. Procuring food had sometimes been difficult, even as an employee with ration cards. Bread was not always available, not to speak of other food items, rationed or otherwise. Professionally, life had been tough at times because of my crisscrossing Dukagjin on foot, but most rewarding. The Lord and penicillin had saved two lives. A number of other patients had benefited from my interest in and caring for them, certainly beyond my modest medical capabilities. I had made a number of friends as I learned to look beyond their poverty and primitive living conditions. Twice the communists had tried to hurt me. When they first came into power, they had kept me in jail for 13 months. In jail I had the opportunity to get to know many Albanian leaders of years past. Where else could I have met them in such numbers and under such trying—and therefore revealing—conditions? A few years later, the communist regime had transferred me to Dukagjin as punishment befitting an enemy of the regime and gave me, the Albanian who had grown up abroad, the chance to meet and live with "*malësors*" (highlanders), the backbone of the anti-communist resistance. The communists had intended otherwise; the Lord had used them in mysterious ways to further my education.

I hugged the members of the family one by one, gave the children a bit of money, and waved a last goodbye as we started to climb the hill that would get us to the main path past my office. It was not quite three hours to Guri Kuq ("the Red Rock"). The Rock was the tough part of the trip, whether coming or going. It took about one and one-half hours to climb the Rock or descend from the top to the valley. The footpath snaked relentlessly back and forth, and resting halfway was not the answer. One had to clear the Rock and from then on things fell into place. During my stay in Dukagjin, I had learned how to walk uphill and downhill at the steady pace characteristic of our mountain people. They never seemed in a hurry but covered distances in remarkably good time. In addition to keeping a steady pace, they also rarely stopped to rest. That was part of the secret.

At the foot of the Rock, I breathed a sigh of relief. We had cleared the big hurdle. Even if my companion faltered along the way, I could pay him off, hire a muleteer, and proceed for Shkodra. My companion, however, walked steady at the normal pace.

While still in Dukagjin, I kept reviewing my memories of these last 12 months. I had met some good people and had been able to help them in modest measure. I had spent part of my time living in their homes as an intimate member of their families. I had laughed when their children had watched me in disgust as I brushed my teeth with toothpaste, with a mouthful of foam. I had wept inwardly when I heard their stories of suffering and persecution. I had attended weddings and shared their banquets that were second to none in their hospitality and generous friendship. And yes, incredible as it may seem, often I was able to send my entire salary home to Mom as I could live on what the families fed me in exchange for the wheat bread I received as an employee. The villagers were eager to secure this bread for their children. In exchange, they shared their cornbread and their meals with me. For me, this had been a good year. Raised abroad since I was a baby, I had the chance to meet the simple, humble, brave people of our mountains. Now I was returning to a city, with its advantages and its spies, with its comforts and its intrigues. Anyhow, it would be good to be with Mom and Mergim, to sleep in a regular bed, to have some of the comforts of living in a city. On the down side, I had to face once again the heavy-handed communist infrastructure that seemed more removed in the mountains but oppressively permeated city life 24 hours a day.

As we entered Shkodra, I asked my companion to stop at a weighing station. It turned out that the load he had carried on his back weighed close to 180 lbs. I could not believe my eyes. We made it home, I paid him what we had agreed on and then some.

Mom had prepared a meal. We ate and then my friend started his trek back home. I bathed, changed into clean clothes, and went into town to meet my friends, whom I had not seen for about one year.

CHAPTER TWENTY-ONE

TYPHUS

L ife in Shkodra moved at a more rapid pace than in Dukagjin. I presented myself to the head of the health section and asked him for instructions on when and how to start my new job. I would start immediately. I was to make sure that all applicable regulations were implemented. I also had to inspect and take care of the needs of seven institutes our section was responsible for. No, we had no secretary. There was only one secretary at City Hall and she worked for the mayor. If she had time, she might be willing to help. Helping me, however, was not part of her job. I asked for a typewriter, some paper and carbon paper, a list of the seven health institutes, and a copy of health regulations. My boss told me to do the best I could in this regard. He had a meeting he had to go to. He made a grandiose exit and practically never showed up at the office again.

My boss was about 5 feet 10 inches tall. He had a dull face and the lack-luster personality to match. He was a poster figure for laziness personified and was, of course, a member of the communist party. He suffered from syphilis, for which he was treated at the clinic for skin and sexually trans-mitted diseases. To my knowledge, that was the only contact he ever had with the health field. Apparently that satisfied the communist party's require-ments to head the city health section of Albania's second or third largest city.

I went to see the mayor's secretary. My office was on the third floor, hers on the second. I found her seated behind her desk. She was in her mid-twenties and friendly. I told her my needs and she provided me with an old typewriter, some paper, carbon paper, various office supplies, and a list of the seven health institutes. As far as health regulations were concerned, she suggested that I contact the provincial health section. As it turned out, they were able to answer my questions and provide copies of regulations I needed in my daily work.

My office at City Hall had two desks, one for me and one for my boss. I was able to scrounge a rickety typewriter table built for midgets. When I wanted to type, I had to bend low. Furthermore, the table was so narrow that I could barely squeeze my knees between the table legs. This got me into trouble. One day, the mayor cracked open the door to my office, stuck his head in, and asked me where the boss was. I replied he was out, while I struggled to stand up. As soon as he heard my answer, he shut the door and was gone. A few days later, at a staff meeting, he accused me of being disrespectful toward him and his office. He described what had happened and stressed that I did not get up when he stuck his head into my office, but he didn't mention that I had tried to get up but failed to do so because of my mini typewriter table and his rapid disappearance.

A brief description of the mayor may provide some insight into his character. Gjon Jaku was at the time mayor of Shkodra. He was of medium height, dark complected, and had black hair parted on the side. He had a habit of lowering his head and looking at you through his heavy eyebrows. His back was bent, his shoulder blades stuck out, and he walked with his toes pointed outward. He looked and acted like a hoodlum.

One time during the war, he was walking through some woods to join the partisans. When he came to a mountain spring, he saw an Italian officer taking a drink. He engaged the Italian in conversation and then said to him, "Those are nice boots you are wearing."

"Yes," answered the Italian, "and they better last me a while because I won't be able to get new ones until the war is over."

"Would you give them to me? I am joining the partisans to fight against the Germans."

"I can't. I refused to surrender to the Germans and now I want to join a partisan unit."

Gjon Jaku drew his sidearm, shot the Italian officer dead, and put on his boots, totally insensitive to the fact that he had just killed a human being for a pair of boots

Life at the office was anything but fun. I had to learn how to type, albeit with two fingers, but still within time constraints and deadlines. If I made a typo, I was in trouble. Almost everything I typed had to have an original and seven copies, seven for the institutes and one for our files. My office supplies and paper in particular were very skimpy. I learned from experience that by heating much-used carbon paper near a stove, the carbon layer would melt and I could prolong its useful life.

Often I had to pass on information to the seven institutes our department was responsible for. Sometimes I had to make decisions, always without the benefit of instructions from my boss, who continued to be conspicuous by his absence. Please keep in mind that under that regime, any error by someone like me, no matter how slight or innocent, was treated as sabotage.

Being responsible for health aspects of a city the size of Shkodra ranged from arranging vaccinations for schoolchildren to dealing with citizen complaints when the butter sold by government cooperatives was rancid, and this in a system where the government was always right. Case in point: If tomatoes at a co-op store had rotted and a customer wanted to buy potatoes, he or she had to buy the same amount of tomatoes by weight, since the state economy could not show losses.

One day, a city worker was sitting on the steps outside my office. As I walked by, I noticed the man was crying.

"What happened? Why are you crying?"

"My wife just had a baby daughter."

"This is a blessing. You must not cry."

"This is our fifth child. How can I feed my family with my income?"

Sadly, I had no reply for the man.

Another day, I greeted a group of workers on their way home from work who had emptied cesspools with buckets during their shift. They smelled to high heaven. I decided to do something about it. I called the director of public baths and asked whether these workers could take a daily bath free of charge after work. He agreed and I, with youthful enthusiasm, notified the sanitation crew. A few days later I ran into one of them.

"Tell me, how is it working out now that you can bathe before you go home?" I expected a very positive reply, perhaps even a word of thanks.

"We don't go to the public baths."

"Why not? Would that not make it much better for you and your families?"

"No it doesn't. After we bathe, we would still have to put on our filthy work clothes. Now, if you could get us an extra pair of coveralls, we could take a bath after work and go home clean."

The man was right, of course, but under the circumstances, getting them extra work clothes was out of the question.

While all this was stressful, there were a few instances where I could not help but smile, inwardly of course. Employees at City Hall had to be members of the government-sponsored union. There were 21 of us and 20 held various offices. These ranged from head of the union to secretary and treasurer, from individuals charged with entertainment to those responsible for food and drinks, from those cleaning and arranging the facilities to those preparing and hanging slogans and decorations, etc. In our case, the only person not holding an official position was the janitor. He was quite old. He was bent and shriveled by age. His big, bulging eyes seemed to look without seeing. He was practically bald and always had a white growth of hair on his cheeks, more than a stubble but never enough to be called a beard. At our meetings, while the 20 of us worked passionately for his pleasure and well-being, he sat in a corner, collapsed in his chair, with his tongue hanging out one side of his mouth, blissfully unaware of what was going on all around him. It was pathetic, a tragic-comic picture of a dictatorial regime, cruel and vindictive, going the extra mile to present an appearance of care and benevolence toward the people.

One morning, I noticed with concern that something was wrong. I had double vision. My hands were not shaking visibly but I had trouble writing. I asked a couple of physicians with whom I met at work and they both laughed it off.

By accident, I noticed that if soap got into my eyes, the double vision disappeared, at least for a while. After a few days, the double vision disappeared but the tremor persisted. I could write with great effort but controlling the tremor also strained my wrist. I took some vacation time and went to Tirana to see Dr. Augi. He listened carefully, summarized what I had told him to make sure he had understood me correctly, and then gave me his opinion. The double vision might return. The symptoms could be due to stress but they could also be the beginning of multiple sclerosis. There were no readily available tests for MS and there was no known therapy. I left Dr. Augi and Tirana quite discouraged. As the years went by, it turned out that I was not suffering from MS. To this day, however, writing by hand is hard for me.

At one point I learned that I was getting a new boss. I had no idea why my present boss was leaving. If they removed him for incompetence and dereliction of duty, for once they were right. My new boss would be Zina

Ashta. She was the wife of Kolë Ashta, who at that time was in charge of a manufacturing facility. Husband and wife were both Party members. I heard that when the Catholic bishop of Shkodra had passed away some years before, Zina had pelted the funeral with rotten tomatoes. I was glad I was losing my present boss but wondered whether the new one would be an improvement. I was politically vulnerable. The character and temperament of the boss would make a difference. All I could do was wait and see.

Monday came. Zina Ashta showed up right on time. She was about 40, of medium height, with black hair and a dark complexion. She moved well and seemed decisive.

"Good morning. I am Zina Ashta, and let me state right off the bat that I know nothing about public health. I intend to rely on you in technical matters. Don't let me down. I in turn will protect you politically."

She sure did not waste any time. I assured her that I would do my best and that I would never let her down knowingly.

"Good; keep me informed on important matters so I can answer questions I may get from the mayor or from the communist party secretary. You set the agenda but keep me informed."

That was that. Events confirmed that she meant every word she said that first morning.

Here is an example of her street smarts and decisiveness. A handful of men in Shkodra made a living grilling and selling meat patties on street corners. One day the mayor ordered that unless these vendors kept the raw and cooked meat patties inside glass enclosures, they could no longer sell their wares out in the open. They had ten days to comply. As neither such enclosures nor materials to build them were available, the public health agents were instructed to ensure that the vendors were off the streets after the deadline.

The deadline expired on a Wednesday. On Thursday, I passed the public market on the way to the office. There on the corner was a stand of the local food cooperative and there was a cook behind the grill offering meat patties for sale. Neither the raw nor the cooked meat patties were behind glass. It was obvious that our department had been used to chase private vendors off the streets for the benefit of the food cooperative. I was furious but helpless at the same time. My knees buckled and I puked into the ditch that ran alongside the street. Eventually I pulled myself up, crossed the street, and went to my office. Zina arrived a few minutes later.

"What happened to you? You look sick."

I described to her what had happened.

"Call our public health agents. Tell them to go to the private vendors and tell them that they are free to ply their trade. As for you, go home. You are in no condition to work today."

I had to admire her. She did not try to force the food co-op off the street to avoid butting heads with her superiors. Instead, she chose to permit the private vendors to ply their trade because she could make a case for such a move. The agents dispersed to notify the 11 private vendors and I took the rest of that day off.

During a morning session with the public health agents, one agent reported that the cooperative was selling carbonated drinks produced locally. This was a violation of health regulations as we had not been notified ahead of time and had not analyzed the water or the ingredients before the carbonated drink had reached the market. I remonstrated with the mayor who told me bluntly that the economy was more important than public health. The inhabitants of Shkodra drank well water because the city had no central water supply. It turned out that the water used to produce the carbonated drink was highly contaminated with E. coli. Lab results in hand, I went to the mayor's office to ask that the plant immediately stop production. When I gave the news to Gjon Jaku, he shook his head.

"As usual, public health lags behind the marketplace. The plant has already stopped producing pop for lack of popular demand."

The fact that some people might have been infected with E. coli did not bother him a bit. What is worse, there was not a chance that he might be called to answer for violating a health regulation or to pay for his transgression.

One day I was visiting the orphanage, one of the institutes our department was responsible for, when two nurses pulled me aside.

"As you know, the director of our orphanage is the sister of the first secretary of the communist party for Shkodra. This evening she is throwing a big party and has invited all the VIPs of our city for an evening of fun and good food. There will be baklava, halva, burek, and many goodies none of us has tasted in years."

"Where did she get the flour, sugar, and all the other ingredients from?"

The nurses giggled. The answer was obvious.

I returned to the office in a hurry.

"Comrade Zina, I assume you will spend the evening at the orphanage?"

"Why would I want to do that?"

"Have you not been invited? All the VIPs have been invited. You, of course, don't need an invitation to the orphanage. You are in charge of it. I understand that they will be serving all kinds of goodies, such as baklava, burek, and more."

"You must be dreaming. Where would they find the ingredients for such a spread?"

"Comrade Zina, I may be wrong. This rumor, however, has been making the rounds for days. Why don't you go there tonight and find out the truth?"

I changed the topic at this point for fear of appearing too heavy-handed.

The next morning, Zina came to work and sat down at her desk. She started to chat about this, that, and the other but said nothing about the evening at the orphanage. Finally, I could not stand it anymore.

"Comrade Zina, did you go yesterday evening to the orphanage?"

A dark shadow clouded her face.

" *##^&?!!!"

I prefer not to repeat the expletives she directed at the woman in charge and at the communist party. She ended by cursing those who had stolen the food from the children's mouths to entertain and amuse the communist elite. The information provided by the nurses had obviously been accurate.

"Comrade Zina, this is an instance where an individual may have abused her official responsibilities. In no way can you call the Party responsible for such an outrage."

I felt I had to protect myself. Zina might be truly incensed but that did not mean that she had changed her political allegiance and I, after all, had precipitated the incident by alerting her to what was going on. She never mentioned that evening again and I did not suffer any ill consequences. Thank God!

One morning, the cooperative in charge of food supplies notified our department that an employee had reported that some of the fruit jellies and marmalades were covered with mold. Our public health agents collected samples and took them to the Center for Hygiene for analysis. It turned out that if the moldy layer were removed, the remainder was edible. That was good news that gave us a chance to protect commercial interests and the pubic health at the same time.

One afternoon I went to the depot to see what the public health agents were doing. I found one, seated on the floor, with a spoon in hand. He was removing the moldy layer from the jars and resealing them. Next to him, I saw jars filled with a clear yellow jelly with mold on top.

"What kind of jelly is this?"

"It's quince jelly."

"Are you sure? Quince jelly is usually full of hard little seed-like particles."

"True, but these have been strained out. This quince marmalade is only for VIPs. It won't be sold to the public."

While he spoke, he removed the lid from one of these containers, carefully spooned out the moldy layer, and spit into the jar. Then he looked at me with a smile. I didn't know what to do. I could not condone what he did, at least not officially—not if I wanted to protect myself. On the other hand, I was not going to turn him in. I looked sternly at him.

"I am sure you will do what is right," and without giving him a chance to answer, I stalked out of the depot, mounted my bike, and got out of there as fast as I could.

I had met Ndue Vata in Dukagjin when his wife needed medical attention for a minor skin condition. In Shkodra we became friends. He was handsome, self-assured, with brown wavy hair. One day he came to our one-room apartment with an important proposal. During the war he had fought on the side of the partisans and had attained an officer's rank. Once he saw that the wartime propaganda of justice and freedom for all was replaced by a fierce class struggle intended to destroy the educated, the well-off, and the clergy, he quit the Party without attracting the ire of the ever faithful. Here is what he had to tell us that day.

"I am getting ready to escape to Yugoslavia with my wife and some friends. We are planning to do so in full daylight. We are going to take a boat to cross Lake Shkodra. We will have musical instruments aboard and sing, eat, and have fun as we aim toward Shiroka on the opposite shore. Once we are halfway across the lake, we will turn into Yugoslav waters. When the Yugoslav patrol boats approach, we will ask for political asylum.

By the way, we have already had a dress rehearsal, except that time we landed in Shiroka and returned to Shkodra. The next time we won't. What do you say, will you come with us?"

Mergim and I were stunned. The idea was simple and daring. Because it had never been tried before, it was likely to succeed.

"Of course we are interested," I replied.

"Fine, leave everything to me. I'll give you advance notice once we are ready."

Ndue Vata left and Mergim and I were absolutely delighted. Here was the opportunity we had been waiting for. Ndue was a serious individual, prudent and determined. If successful, everyone in Shkodra would know that same day the outcome of the flight and Mom would not have to worry about us. We really had to make no preparations. All we had to do was show up on time.

Some days went by. Infiltrators from Yugoslavia brought leaflets that carried an ominous message for Mergim and me. They praised Koçi Xoxe, who had presided over the special tribunal that had sentenced Dad to lifelong imprisonment in the spring of 1945. In 1949, Enver Hoxha and Mehmet Shehu had executed Koçi Xoxe as a Yugoslav stooge. At that point, Albania had become a satellite of the USSR. If Koçi Xoxe was a hero in Yugoslavia, Mergim and I could expect trouble once we got there. The authorities might return us to Albania, as they had done in some cases. We felt we had no choice but to let Ndue Vata know that we had changed our minds. He regretted it but informed us that his preparations had gone too far for him to back out at this point. We understood and Mergim and I both wished him luck.

On the feast of St. Roccus, the patron saint of Shiroka, Ndue Vata and friends crossed successfully into Yugoslavia. The venom the communists spewed out against the escapees made everyone's joy even greater.

Just as I was mastering the ropes of my job as city health inspector, a major crisis hit Shkodra. First I will offer some historical background. Churchill, in an effort to limit Soviet expansionism in the western Balkans, had reached an agreement with Stalin. Romania would be part of the Soviet zone of influence while Greece remained part of the British sphere.

British units under the command of General Scobie landed in Greece as part of the Allied effort to open several European fronts against Hitler. The ongoing struggle between Greek nationalist and communist forces had to be settled, and Churchill personally went to Athens to facilitate such an agreement. An accord was reached but failed almost immediately when Markos Vafiades, the communist leader, decided to attack General Zervas and his nationalist forces. While Churchill was still in the Piraeus harbor in Athens, communist artillery tried to shell the British navy ship that carried Winston Churchill. The British leader, in response to the communist concerted attacks against the British and the Greek nationalists, ordered General Scobie to strike back at the communists with all means at his disposal.

Some biographical notes of Markos Vafiades may serve as a stenographic account of the ups and downs of communists in the choppy seas of communism. Markos Vafiades started out as a laborer. He was a founding member of the Greek communist party and fought against the Germans in World War II. He became supreme commander of the communist forces and assumed the rank of general. In 1947, he formed a provisional Greek government that failed to gain international recognition. In the summer of 1948, Tito's Yugoslavia broke out of the Soviet camp. Within days Greek nationalist artillery was allowed on Yugoslav soil from where it began shelling communist forces in northern Greece; so much for political fair play and loyalty.

In 1949, General Markos had to leave Greece and seek asylum in the Soviet Union. Here Stalin purged him from communist ranks in 1950. After Stalin's death he was rehabilitated in 1956, only to be purged again in 1964 and returned once more to communist party membership in 1969. He returned to Greece after a general amnesty in 1983 and was elected to parliament in 1989 as a member of the Panhellenic Socialist Movement. He died in 1992 in Athens, remembered by many and mourned by few.

In the years following World War II, the United States replaced Great Britain on behalf of the nationalist Greek government against a communist takeover. With U.S. assistance, the Greek nationalist army was finally able to crush communist efforts to drag Greece behind the Iron Curtain. The year was 1949. The Iron Curtain separated the free world from the Soviet empire that extended from the Baltic to Eastern Europe and the Balkans, with Greece being the one exception. The Iron Curtain would remain standing until 1989 when it started coming apart with the fall of the Berlin Wall. Albania was among the last to rid its country of its former Red rulers. Or so it seemed—at least for the time being.

Now back to Albania and the year 1949. When the Greek communist forces withdrew from northern Greece, they entered Albania in disarray, forcing large numbers of civilians to accompany the fleeing units. Male and female partisans went to Kruja, a small town north of Tirana. The civilian population came to Shkodra. Under this arrangement, Albania offered them shelter; Poland and other communist countries fed and clothed them.

These refugees brought with them memories of war, of loved ones lost or killed in the changing fortunes of a prolonged civil struggle, and of tortures and persecutions by the communists. They also brought with them typhus, which would soon explode into a full epidemic among the population of Shkodra.

Typhus, not to be confused with typhoid, is caused by rickettsiae, bacteria named after Howard Ricketts, an American pathologist. These bacteria infect various parasites. In the case of human epidemics, they are carried by lice and find fertile ground where people live in crowded, unsanitary conditions such as concentration camps, prisons, and the like. In Shkodra, we had 63 cases scattered across the city. We began massive powdering of people with DDT in affected homes, schools, dormitories, prisons, hospitals, and—of course—among the Greek refugees. Homes of patients were put under quarantine with the entire family locked in until the patient regained his or her health.

According to law, each such home had to be under police guard around the clock. I wrote to the city police department requesting 24-hour police protection for each home under quarantine. At the height of the epidemic, this would have amounted to close to 200 police officers assigned to this task. Having received no answer from the police department, I wrote to the Ministry of the Interior, which was in charge of the country's security forces. Again I received no answer but at least I had covered myself. Instead of having 24-hour police coverage, we provided a handful of police officers with lists of all family members under quarantine at each site. The officers would drop in unannounced, check whether all family members were present, and then go on to some other home under quarantine. Such random visits were the best we could do under the circumstances.

One day a Soviet physician and her interpreter came from Tirana to inspect our campaign against the typhus epidemic. I explained to her our basic strategy and showed her our city map with about 60 flags marking the homes under quarantine. She nodded thoughtfully but said nothing of significance. I offered that we go to some of these homes and my guest agreed. She picked one home at random and off we went. She did not want to enter the home but only asked why there was no police officer at the gate. I explained the situation and the interpreter conveyed the information to the physician. The physician repeated the question.

"Where is the police officer?"

Even I understood that much Russian.

"Did you tell the doctor what I said?"

"Yes," the interpreter replied.

"Then please tell her again. We do not have enough police to have a 24-hour guard at every home."

The interpreter gave the doctor my answer. Our Russian guest looked me in the eye and said once more, "Where is the police officer?"

Now I understood. What she needed was to report some shortcoming, i.e., some "investigative result" of her visit.

"There is no police officer present at this point."

The physician nodded and said something to the interpreter who made a note. Now our Soviet visitor could return to Tirana and report that police coverage around the clock was not being implemented, in violation of applicable regulations. She had found a deficiency and had thus done her job. I had written to the police department and the Ministry of Interior of the need for such protection and had done my job. Nothing changed because of the physician's visit or my letters as far as the homes under quarantine or the safety and health of the affected family members were concerned, but we had all covered our *derrières* and that's how the regime functioned.

Another visitor of note during the typhus epidemic was Riza Butka, an inspector of the Ministry of Health. After looking at various administrative details of our work in the field, he asked to see a patient who was still under care at the local hospital. The woman in question suffered from a high fever and depression. A few days before, she had jumped from a third-story window, landing on ropes loaded with drying laundry. This setup had softened the fall and she had suffered only bruises. Her husband told us that his wife was Italian and that her brother had sent them two doses of tetracycline. He showed us a telegram confirming that the medication was on its way. Tetracycline had been developed recently and was effective against typhus. Unfortunately the antibiotic was unavailable to us. The husband asked the inspector whether the Ministry of Health had tetracycline and Riza Butka confirmed that the Ministry had indeed some doses of the antibiotic. The husband of the patient first asked for one dose and offered to replace it with one due to arrive from Italy. When the inspector refused, the husband offered both doses for one dose that he needed urgently to save his wife's life. Again the inspector refused and we left the patient's room embarrassed. Outside, I asked the inspector for an explanation.

"Here is what's happening. We have four doses at the Ministry that are reserved for the top brass in case of an emergency."

"I understand, but Italy is barely a half hour away by plane. The Ministry could replace the medication in nothing flat. Wouldn't it look good if the Ministry came to the aid of this poor woman?" She was the only one with complications among all the typhus patients.

"I regret it, but we can do nothing for this patient. Unfortunately this is not the only thing that's wrong with the way the Ministry of Health is being run, or for that matter with the way the regime is running the entire country."

This was quite a broadside against the government and the communist party. The Butka family was well known for its patriotism. Dad had fought with members of that family against the Turks. A professor and member of that family, Safet Butka, had returned from Ventotene and had insulted Dad at dinner in our home (See Chapter 8). A year later, Safet Butka had committed suicide rather than fire upon the communists at the beginning of the civil war (See Chapter 11).

Riza Butka was probably the black sheep in the family and must have joined the partisans when the rest of the family was strongly linked with Balli Kombëtar. How far could I trust Riza Butka? Were his words to be taken at face value or was he setting a trap?

Our subsequent conversation became ever more explicit in our criticism of the government and the communist party. We parted, trusting each other and promising to keep in touch.

By now the epidemic was under control and petering out. To my surprise, I was summoned to the office of the first secretary of the communist party because Comrade Tonin Jakova wanted to congratulate me in person for the way I had directed the campaign against typhus.

I had seen him before. He had a certain polish and good manners—for a communist. His office was quite elaborate by local standards. When I entered, he was seated behind his desk. Near the window was Lec Plani, a fellow student at the medical school in Padua, where he had been one year ahead of me.

Comrade Jakova stood up, reached across the desk and we shook hands. Smiling broadly, he proceeded to congratulate me on the skill and dedication with which I had conducted the campaign against typhus. Lec Plani tried to forge the iron while it was hot.

"Comrade Jakova, Genc has proven his ability by the way he directed the campaign against the typhus epidemic. Why not send him to a university where he can complete his medical education and become even more valuable to the people of Albania?"

This was a totally unexpected development, particularly since Lec was sticking his neck out for someone like me, an "enemy of the regime."

Tonin Jakova replied with a smirk.

"When we build a university in Trush, it will be his turn to go to medical school."

Trush was a godforsaken village half buried in mud during the rainy season. This was the communist party's answer; forget the smiles and the handshake. That was what I could expect from the communist regime in Albania, no matter what my performance.

One day at the office, Zina Ashta told me that I was being promoted to provincial health inspector. She hated to lose me and I was going to miss my working relationship with her. She had proven loyal and had lived up to what she had told me when she took charge of the city health department. She had said that she needed my technical support and that she in turn would protect me politically. Now she warned me that the environment at my new job was politically charged. With her warning still ringing in my ears, I went to see Aurel Ashiku, my new boss.

CHAPTER TWENTY-TWO

CATHOLIC PRIESTS MARTYRED

The provincial government offices were located in a massive building, three stories high, with large windows, and hallways and offices with wood floors and high ceilings. It was relatively cool in the summer thanks to its thick stone walls. Stoves kept employees warm during the winter. The office of the head of the province had a wide balcony facing the street that separated the building from the local high school across the street. Trees lined sidewalks on both sides of the street. Before the communist takeover, the building had housed the prefect's office and ancillary departments, comparable to its present communist administrative functions.

During one of his visits to Shkodra, Enver Hoxha, the dictator of Albania, addressed the people from the large balcony. For security reasons, treetops on both sides of the street were cut off, officially to provide the people with an unobstructed view of the beloved leader; more likely, to make sure no hostile snipers were hiding in the treetops. The people could come no closer than the front yard of the high school separated from the provincial headquarters by a low wall topped by an ornate iron fence, and by the street and the two sidewalks. As an added precaution, all people living in homes surrounding the government building had to leave until the "the beloved guest" had left town. That evening, the "guest" was to travel to Puka, a city several hours by car northeast of Shkodra. The military had posted soldiers along the road all the way from Shkodra to Puka, with machine-gun nests at strategic sites. That evening, Enver Hoxha left, traveled a while toward Puka, then turned around and spent the night in Shkodra. This is an example of VIP security as practiced behind the Iron Curtain.

The provincial health inspectorate consisted of two large offices on the second floor. I shared the office, a telephone, and a typewriter with two other health inspectors who had fought on the side of the partisans during the war. They had a middle school education or the equivalent gained in the service. Occasionally they showed their teeth. One day one of them decided to type a piece of correspondence, and in so doing pulled gobs of paper out of the typewriter each time he made a typo. Eventually I remonstrated with him, pointing out that the paper supply had to last us through the end of the month.

"If you truly cared for the people's property, you would have joined the partisans during the anti-fascist war," he spit out with politically correct logic. There was nothing I could say in return.

A door led to the director's office. At that the time our director was Aurel Ashiku, a man close to 50, a graduate of the school of pharmacy of Zagreb, Croatia. He was of average height, with black hair that was graying at the temples. He was intelligent, the scion of a respected Catholic family of Shkodra. He dressed well, had good manners, and was soft spoken. He had married some years before and had a son. One day, during the Italian occupation, his wife ran off with an Italian officer. Her husband caught up with the couple in Durrës, just before they boarded a ship that would have carried them to Italy. He brought his wife back to Shkodra and divorced her. This event embittered him deeply. After the war he remarried, this time with one of the leading communist women in town. Zenepe Golemi was very active in the local party committee, zipping from one meeting to the next, while her husband sought ways to profess his loyalty to the communist party, despite his social roots and upbringing.

The way he spoke, his manners—everything about him—was in strident contrast with his professed far-left political views that he bore on his sleeve. His conversion had opened a chasm between him and his brother Alfred who spent years in prison, a victim of communist persecution. Despite his upbringing, his family tradition and the split his political conversion had created within the family, Aurel never deviated from the official party line during the time I worked with him.

A counterweight to Aurel was Dr. Kel Naraçi. Also in his late forties, he was tall and slender. He was a graduate of a medical school in Italy and had married an attractive and bright Italian lady. He was a staunch anti-communist but resilient and able to avoid the dangers of hazardous political shoals and crosscurrents. He successfully headed the Center for Hygiene because of his medical and administrative skills. When depressed or in trouble, I could seek refuge in his office or at his home and get sufficient "oxygen" to weather the crisis.

The professional work environment at the provincial headquarters was a cut above the one at the city health department. From a professional point of view, Aurel Ashiku was competent, both technically and as an administrator. As a person, however, he had neither political strength nor the loyalty Zina Ashta had toward her staff. Dr. Naraçi was strong, both professionally and as a man. His staff adored him. His loyal support got me out of trouble more than once. The head of the province was Qamil Gavoçi, a communist who was resourceful and flexible compared to Gjon Jaku, the mayor, who lacked any redeeming qualities. While the work environment on my new job was more challenging and interesting, it was also more insidious and replete with hidden mines when compared to city hall.

While Zina Ashta had kept me informed at least to the point where I could do my job, my present boss asked me from time to time to bring the typewriter and some supplies to his office so he could prepare material he did not want me to see. I paid him back by giving him sheets of brand-new carbon paper. Afterwards I could read in a mirror what he had typed behind closed doors.

Many of his regular directives went to 20 or 30 recipients. They were generally short and of a standard format. When I needed a document for myself that I knew he would not sign, I typed it in a format similar to the rest and smuggled it in with a bunch of directives that he signed automatically after reading and approving the first copy.

I no longer worked with the health agents with whom and through whom I got the job done at the city level. Now I met once a month with about 30 male and female nurses and a midwife, all of whom worked in small cities or villages across the province. They were all graduates of short training courses. Some were motivated and sought to do a good job. Some were Party members; the rest clearly were not but had to keep up appearances to keep their jobs.

After a while I got things to run smoothly. We were dealing with health matters, after all, and I could identify with the job most of the time. If I ran into a problem, I tried to work my way around it without making waves. I made it a point, however, not to violate my principles.

At one point, I was asked to run a weekly radio program on health matters. Everything I was going to broadcast had to be approved first by the communist party committee. One evening I was going to speak on the subject of the smallpox vaccination. I wrote a brief history of the discovery of the vaccination and closed with advice to the parents that all children be vaccinated. The subject was straightforward and whoever approved my programs at the Party committee raised no objections.

Under normal circumstances, there was nothing wrong with the broadcast. Under communism, however, all inventions and discoveries were always credited to Russian, or even better, to Soviet scientists. Thus, Alexander Popov and not Guglielmo Marconi had invented the radio; the first person to have successfully undertaken powered flight was a Russian and not the Wright brothers; Soviet physicians, not Sir Alexander Fleming, had discovered penicillin, and so on. However, in the broadcast I gave credit to Edward Jenner, a British physician, for the vaccination that practically eliminated the deadly scourge of smallpox. I pronounced his name Jenner as it is pronounced in English, and I described the mass inoculations for children and gave credit for the initiative to the Ministry of Health and not to the communist party of Albania and to its all-knowing, all-caring leader Enver Hoxha. Somehow I got away with it.

We rarely had any inspection from Tirana. Our health section had two major responsibilities. One was to implement health programs. The other was administrative and seemingly more important. The People's Republic ran on the basis of statistics. We received request after request for statistical data regarding various types of inspections to food cooperatives, flour mills, restaurants, and public facilities. In addition, we had to provide statistical information on vaccinations, health visits, school inspections, and the like. These requests came from various government and party offices, mostly from Tirana but also from Party headquarters in Shkodra. Gathering the data was time consuming and risky because of the need to provide consistent answers to multiple requests concerning activities undertaken over long periods.

In self-defense, somewhere I scrounged a massive register, filled it with data reflecting every activity we engaged in, kept that register up to date, and had the perfect tool to provide consistent answers to repetitive questions at a moment's notice with a minimum of effort. This register saved us much time and avoided the risk of contradicting ourselves. That could have been serious. I was of course the one at risk. I was the "enemy of the people" responsible for keeping the office going. I was the weakest link, the one without protection, the one who would be blamed for everything.

In this People's Republic I had learned that appearances counted more than substance. That turned out to be the saving factor when Eleni Terezi, undersecretary of the Ministry of Health, stopped in one day to inspect our office. She was in her mid-thirties, short, with wavy blond hair. She appeared arrogant and decisive, a clear indication of her standing in the Party. Her husband was Josif Pashko, a man who had held various major assignments, a pillar of the regime. Eleni had the reputation of being the aggressive, strident half of this duo. At public trials, she was known to jump to her feet screaming, "Killing these criminals is not enough. Let's burn them with gasoline!" She also had a taste for things extravagant, indeed unheard of, for those times. At her little son's birthday party, she had not only offered abundant food and sweets but had also used a movie projector to entertain her young guests. Who had ever heard of such sybaritic luxury!

When we met in my office, she had obviously not done her homework. She asked me, "Are there instances when your boss does not implement the law?" She assumed that the boss, being a Catholic college graduate from Shkodra, was obviously the reactionary in charge because of his technical ability while I, from the predominantly communist south, was the second in command, the Party's man in this setup.

"Yes," I replied. "Health regulations require that a family member with a positive sputum and X-rays confirming the diagnosis of pulmonary tuberculosis be given a separate room. I have presented the file to Comrade Aurel twice, and twice he has refused to take action."

"Show me the file."

I did, and she glanced at the it.

"Aurel Ashiku was right. You are from the south and don't know the family in question. The Kazazis are reactionaries. We have killed two of their men, one a member of the anti-communist resistance, the other when he left the mountains and secretly entered his home in Shkodra. According to the file, the grandmother with her daughter and two small children share one room. The grandmother is the one suffering from tuberculosis. Eventually, when those children grow up, we will have to eliminate them. Why not let Grandma do it for us?"

I had known the Kazazi brothers well. One had been a member of the Kruja cabinet, the other was my commanding officer when our battalion went to Kosova. They were men of character and integrity. I had mourned them both. Here was a woman—a mother—speaking. I had a hard time hiding my distaste for her and the ideology she stood for.

One morning Aurel Ashiku called me into his office.

"Dukagjin will have a new hospital. It will again be built in Bregu i Lumit and the site for it has been chosen. Since you spent some time in Dukagjin and know the area, go to Bregu i Lumit and help the construction crew get started."

This was unexpected. I enjoyed the idea of revisiting some of my old friends in Dukagjin. There were, of course, some of the local authorities who would not be overjoyed to see me again, but as far as I knew, I had more friends than enemies there. Besides, a few days away from the office would do me good.

"When do you want me to leave for Dukagjin, Comrade Aurel?"

"As soon as you can."

I really needed no special preparations. I knew the way and hoped no one from Shkodra would accompany me. That turned out to be the case, and so early the next morning, wearing proper clothing and my trusted sandals, I started out on my trip. Until Prekal, the road was more or less flat and it took about five hours to cross the valley and reach the foothills. Then there was the 1½-hour climb up Guri i Kuq, the Red Rock, a couple of hours to Kodër Shën Gjergj, where my former office was, and another few minutes to the farmhouse where I was planning to spend the night. I had lived there for a few months. There I had come to admire the women of Dukagjin and their incredible efforts from dawn to late at night to keep the family going. I had with me small gifts for the children and some much-appreciated wheat bread.

The two brothers and their families were happy to see me again. We talked until late that evening. I carried news from the city and they brought me up to date on what had happened to various friends since my departure. The next morning, just before starting downhill to Bregu i Lumit, I asked about Bubi, my adopted canine friend. I had left him with the two brothers before I left for Shkodra.

"The wolves devoured him."

Bubi was a small dog that could not function as a guard dog. They had had no use for my little friend, had put him out at night, and thus sealed his fate. I felt let down. I could have told them a thing or two; I could have chastised them, I could have vented my anger. It would not have made a bit of difference. Dogs, unless they could hold their own against wolves, were of no use. No one in Dukagjin wasted food on a pet. Sadly enough, the fact that Bubi had been my friend had made no difference.

I shook hands with the brothers, hugged the children, said goodbye to the women, and left. In my heart, though, I mourned Bubi, who had brought friendship and warmth into my life in Dukagjin. In life and in death he had been unwanted. I was perhaps the only one who had made room for him and accepted him as he was—a small, unwanted dog, eager to give love and loyalty to anyone who made a little room for him near the fireplace and in his heart. Bubi was gone and I was left with warm memories mixed with sadness at the thought of the times Bubi and I had spent together.

My next stop was at Bregu i Lumit. I met with some of my friends and in particular with Zef Hajdari, on whose property the hospital would be built. Over dinner he explained to me that his property ran along the main footpath through Bregu i Lumit. If the hospital was built parallel to the path, he would lose his entire property; if the hospital was perpendicular to the path, he would still have some land he could cultivate for his family's needs.

I pondered the problem that night, and the next morning I instructed the construction crew that the hospital would be built perpendicular to the footpath. I took leave from my friends and started the return trip to Shkodra. A month or two later, Aurel Ashiku called me in his office.

With venom in his voice, he said to me, "I made a serious mistake when I sent you to Dukagjin to choose the hospital site. I should have known that you would side with the *kulak* rather than take the side of the people."

In the communist jargon, kulaks were rich farmers that had to be destroyed as class enemies.

I replied with vigor. "Comrade Aurel, if the hospital is built along the footpath, every passer-by will go in to demand free medicine, from aspirins to vitamins or some other pills. I had that experience when I worked there. Anything for free attracted the people, whether they needed the medicines or not. As the hospital will be now, travelers will have to get off the path. This might separate the needy from the rest. A second reason is that the hospital will face south and all rooms with a southern exposure will have sunshine from morning until evening. That prompted me to decide as I did."

Aurel Ashiku shook his head and repeated what he had said at the beginning of our conversation. It became clear to me that the communists' intention was to build a hospital and at the same time deprive Zef Hajdari, the class enemy, of his property—without appearing to do so. I had stood in their way and my boss had drawn his conclusion in line with what he had heard from his communist bosses.

I never knew whether they had countermanded my decision and built the hospital along the footpath. Years later a friend, Shpresa Dervishi, showed me an issue of an Albanian magazine. On the first page was the picture of the hospital in Bregu i Lumit. What do you know—the hospital was built the way I had laid it out.

During this period, the head of the dreaded security services in Shkodra was Colonel Hilmi Seiti. He was about 5 feet 7 inches tall, sturdy, with wavy, reddish-blond hair. Originally he was from Çamëria, that part of northern Greece from where the Greek government had forcibly removed the Albanian population at the end of World War II. He had a ready smile but could be trusted only as far as one could throw an elephant. One day Hilmi Seiti's office notified a man that he was to see the colonel on a certain day, three or four days hence. Anyone summoned to security headquarters experienced high psychological stress. All kinds of thoughts crossed the individual's mind, from examining his recent behavior to what informants might have told the colonel about him. Having the person wait a few days before meeting the colonel was intentional and was meant to prolong the agony and bring it to a feverish pitch.

Once the summoned man entered the office the colonel, according to a time-tested and well-rehearsed routine, welcomed the visitor, asked him sit down, and offered him a cigarette and a cup of coffee. Having gone through routine inquiries about the man's personal health and family well-being, the colonel became more specific.

"My friend, you know that we are surrounded by enemies, such as the traitor Tito to the north and revanchist Greece to the south. Italy is of course in the hands of Western imperialism and all are conspiring against our People's Republic. Do you share my concerns?"

"Yes, of course," was the unavoidable answer.

"How do you see our Party's and Comrade Enver's efforts to resist such nefarious plots? Do you think they are working in the best interests of our Albanian people?"

"Of course they are," was another answer made with dread, because by now it was obvious where the colonel was going with his questioning.

"Good, I am happy that we see eye to eye on such vitally important matters. Tell me, if you saw the fatherland in danger would you help our communist party and Comrade Enver defend our people against foreign aggression?"

Again, nothing but a positive answer was possible at this point even though the victim realized that the noose was about to tighten around his neck. "Of course," the man uttered.

"Very good. Let me tell you, my friend, that Albania is in grave danger, in greater danger than ever before. You know, of course, that the imperialist powers are sending armed infiltrators into Albania in an attempt to overthrow the People's Republic. No patriotic Albanian can allow these traitors and their masters to succeed and rob our nation of the legitimate fruits of its victory against the fascists. We need the help of every Albanian who feels like you and I do. We need to mobilize all our forces and cut off the head of this movement that is trying to sink roots within our country. Can we count on you to do your part?"

Here the monologue usually stopped to give the hapless victim time to formulate an answer and then continue the charade, depending on the answer.

"Of course, I want to defend Albania but I am old and no longer able to carry arms."

"We understand that. There is no need for you to carry arms. For that we have the young men and women who are eager to defend the communist party and the fatherland. For you we have something else in mind. There are many enemies within our borders; class enemies, cruel, selfish people who bled Albania's people until yesteryear and who desperately want to bring back those dark days of our history. Here, take this pen and write.

"Write your name, your parents' names, and your address. Then write 'I am a friend of the people's security organs. Should I reveal this secret to anyone, I accept to be judged by the special tribunal of the Ministry of the Interior. Now we will give you the names of five people, people you know well and with whom you have frequent contact. We want you to tell us what you talk about, how they think, particularly *vis-à-vis* our government, our communist party, and Comrade Enver. OK?"

For the man being questioned, this was the trap and the victim had two choices: either to accept and become an informant or to refuse at great risk to his person.

The man had known all along where this was going to end.

"I am sorry; this I cannot do."

"I am surprised," replied the colonel. "We were doing so well up to this point, weren't we? OK, then go home and forget the whole thing. I must say though that I am disappointed."

That, unfortunately, was not the end. A few days later two loose women presented themselves to the man, armed with an order that enabled them to occupy two rooms in his house. As part of Hilmi Seiti's plot, the women were to ply their "trade" full blast.

A few days went by. The man was furious and decided to see Colonel Seiti.

"Comrade Colonel, those two prostitutes you sent to my home must go. I have a 15-year-old daughter and no father in his right mind can allow such a situation to go on."

The colonel listened and then replied, cold as ice. "True, those women are corrupt in one sense but you, you are corrupt in every sense. You are a fascist who is willing to deprive the Albanian people of their liberty, their future, their just destiny. Write down the text we talked about the last time and sign it, and those women will leave your house immediately."

"No, that I won't do."

The man rose and left the colonel's office, wondering what would happen to him. Strangely enough, the two women left and nothing happened to him. The man could not believe his good fortune—and he should not have.

A few days then a few months went by. Meanwhile, a handsome young police officer started courting the man's 15-year-old daughter in secret. Such affairs were always in secret because Albania in general and Shkodra in particular took a very dim view of love affairs not formally approved by both sets of parents. Young people had to become engaged before they could begin to see each other. Marriage would follow quickly, uniting the two young people for good. In this case, however, the affair continued in secret, the young girl became pregnant, and, having completed his assignment with the young girl, the police officer was transferred, destination unknown. Next, Colonel Seiti had the girl brought to his office in secret.

"Young woman, we are security organs and we know everything. We know that you are pregnant. Albanian law will punish you most severely if you abort the baby. I realize also that your father is an old-fashioned ogre who will kill you as soon as he finds out that you are pregnant. For us, this is a matter of law. Go home and don't do anything stupid. We will be watching you."

One can imagine the young girl's predicament, her bewilderment, her anxiety, caught between the law and the Code of Honor. For her it was a lose-lose situation. After about a week, Colonel Hilmi Seiti called her once more to his office.

"All week I have been unable to rest or sleep, thinking of you. There is only one way out of this dilemma. I have to assume the responsibility of my decision. I cannot let your criminal father destroy your young life. You will have an abortion and I may have to face the consequences of my decision."

The young girl could not believe her ears. Here was a way out, here was salvation coming from a totally unexpected direction. The pregnancy was still in the initial stages and the abortion proceeded without a hitch.

The colonel was not yet done with the young girl who had just emerged from a situation that, up to that point, had seemed unavoidably deadly. One can imagine her relief and her elation under the circumstances.

"Now that criminal, your father, won't be able to hurt you. Tell me, who cares more for you and your future, your father or the communist party?"

She probably stammered words of thanks to the man who had engineered the whole plot.

"Now we will give you a chance to prove your gratitude to the Party. Here are paper and pen. Write your name, your parents' names, your address..." And he proceeded with the rest of the formula her father had refused to write. In addition, he gave her five names of people she was supposed to spy on as well as the monthly date and time she was to meet with a security officer in secret to present her report about her month's activities.

Originally the colonel had wanted to recruit her father because the people of Shkodra trusted and respected him. Having failed with the father, the colonel inducted the daughter into the ranks of informants. Furthermore, he recruited her in a manner that would assure her hatred for her father and would prompt her to report most faithfully on what went on in her family. The young girl, of course, never suspected how all this had come about.

How did people know what happened in this case? The story of Hilmi Seiti's despicable action started circulating throughout Shkodra. As to the dialogue aimed at forcing innocent citizens to break down and become informants, it was boilerplate.

One evening I was walking through the city park when a friend of the family greeted me hurriedly and disappeared in the shadows. That could be a bad sign if it meant that our friend had heard that I was about to be arrested and did not want to be seen with me. It so happened that on my way back I ran into the same friend half an hour later. Again he tried to avoid me, but this time I grabbed him by the arm.

"Tell me, am I about to be arrested?"

"Let me go. No, I have not heard anything about you. Come to dinner tomorrow evening and do not tell your mother you are coming to our home."

"OK, I will see you tomorrow evening."

I was baffled. I let him go but what he told me did not make sense. I decided to push the incident out of my mind until I could get a full explanation the next evening. Meanwhile, I did not mention the incident to Mom.

The next evening, I told Mom I was going out to dinner and she did not ask for an explanation.

Dad and the head of the house I was about to visit had been friends since the time we lived in Fiume. He was a merchant and Dad had helped him with export formalities. The younger brother had worked as a government employee and later as a teacher. The family was well known and highly respected in Shkodra. Neither brother had ever been involved in politics.

At the friend's home, the women greeted me with the usual warmth. The older brother welcomed me in the living room, and soon thereafter the younger brother, the man I had met the evening before, joined us. The conversation touched on the usual topics, our reciprocal health, the fact that life was getting increasingly difficult, etc. Then the older brother excused himself saying, "I know that you two have things to discuss. I'll see you later, before you go home.

This was highly irregular. Traditionally, the head of the family discussed important matters, not someone else, such as a younger brother. Anyhow, the ball was still in their court. The women set the table for two, brought us the food, and disappeared. We began to eat and my host started telling me the reason for this invitation.

"Several weeks ago, I received a summons from Colonel Hilmi Seiti. I was to see him at his office at the end of the week. I began to worry. Had someone spoken ill of me? Had someone spied and turned me in? Had I said anything that could be interpreted as anti-party or anti-government? I just did not know, no matter how often I asked myself these questions.

"On the day I was to see the colonel, to say that I was badly shaken would not tell you how I felt. I entered his office and Hilmi Seiti asked me to sit down. This is how he started the conversation: 'You have a relative who was an important member of King Zogu's entourage. We know that your relative met with Mussolini in Rome. We know what they discussed but want you to tell us what they talked about as proof of your sincerity.'

"I was totally confused. None of the things I had so painfully mulled over in my mind for almost a week was on the table. Instead, Colonel Seiti was talking about an event I knew absolutely nothing about.

"'Colonel, I have no idea whatsoever about this meeting with Mussolini. I was a child at that time. If the matter was ever discussed in our home, it was never in my presence. You must believe me.' Hilmi Seiti seemed unconvinced. 'Go home for now,' he told me. 'Come and see me in a week and we will discuss this matter in depth.' The colonel stood up and I left the office to return home, more confused than ever.

"One week later I was back at his office. This time I was wearing extra clothes so I could stay warm in case they arrested me. The colonel pierced me with his eyes but said nothing. I blurted out that no matter how hard I had pondered the matter he had brought up the last time, I had absolutely nothing to tell him.

"'Forget it,' the colonel said, brushing the whole affair aside. 'I want to know from you something that is related to a recent break-in at your school.' I felt greatly relieved.

"'Please make me a drawing of the layout of your school. Mark doors and windows, and show me where the thief forced his way into the building and what he stole.'

"I did as he told me but the more detail I was putting into the drawing, the more I began to wonder. The police had investigated the break-in and I was sure that the colonel knew much more about the incident than I could possibly know. While I was answering his questions, I began to feel more and more uncomfortable—I began to suspect that the colonel had something else in mind, something more important, something more sinister than a break-in that had netted the thief a few pencils, erasers, and notebooks. When I finished telling him what I knew of the incident, the colonel looked at me.

"'Tell me what you know about the disappearance of your colleague,' and here he mentioned a teacher who had disappeared without trace some time before.

"'I am sorry, Comrade Colonel, I know absolutely nothing about the man and what happened to him.'

"'You must know something,' he countered. 'You taught at the same school for years and must have talked about many subjects many a time.'

"I did not know what to say. Of course, I knew the teacher. Over the years, we had talked about a number of things but had never been particularly close. Maybe the teacher had been arrested and was accusing me of who knows what crimes. On the other hand, maybe he was a prisoner and they wanted me to provide information they could use against him.

"'Comrade Colonel, I have known the man you are talking about. However, we never had any conversations worth remembering. I am sorry but I am really telling you the truth.'

"The colonel kept staring at me. 'Are you trying to protect him, to defend him? Are you both enemies of the regime?'

"'Of course not, Comrade. But nothing comes to my mind worth talking about.'

"'All right, then tell me something less than memorable you two discussed over the years.'

"I did not know how to get off this subject. There was nothing I could tell the colonel and he seemed unwilling to change the subject. A painful silence followed. Finally, the colonel got up and motioned that I do the same.

"'Let's go into the basement. I want to show you something.'

"In the basement, he got me into a corner and pointed at some dark red splashes on the wall.

"'What do you think? Where did those stains on the wall come from?'

"'I don't know, Comrade Colonel.'

"'So you don't know? I will tell you what they are. Your friend, the teacher, was arrested. He refused to cooperate and here we beat him until his blood splashed in all directions. He remained unrepentant and this is the corner where we finished him off. Now that you know, let's go back to my office.'

"He asked me to sit down. Then he continued.

"'Are you going to persist in the same attitude as your friend? Will you continue to tell me that you don't know, no matter what I ask you about, or are you going to prove to me that you are a patriot who loves his country? Will you remain in the ranks of those who oppose the people and our hard-earned victory, or are you willing to join those that serve the country and the Party with loyalty and integrity?'

"I must admit, I broke down. I was afraid of what they could do to me in view of how they had killed my colleague. I thought of myself and my family.

"'Comrade Colonel,' I said, 'I have always loved Albania and I am not going to change now.'

"'Good,' Hilmi Seiti said and for the first time he smiled at me.

"'Take pen and paper and write: I—and now follow up with your name and the names of your parents—declare that I am a friend of the security organs. If I ever divulge this secret, I accept to be judged by the special tribunal of the Ministry of the Interior.'

"Then he gave me the names of five people I was to report on, covering the details of the encounter and what we had talked about. He also mentioned the place and the name of a security officer with whom I would meet every month. When I was done, we got up, shook hands, and the colonel saw me to the door. I cannot tell you how I made it home. I was not sure my legs would carry me that far.

"You are not among the five people who were assigned to me. That's why last evening I did not want to be seen with you in case they asked me what we had talked about. Listen, Genc, our families have been friends for years. I have entrusted you with this terrible secret, with this dishonor I have brought upon my family. In the past, you have mentioned that you intend to escape. In case you do, I ask you to give my name to a foreign secret service. Tell them that I am ready to do anything to cleanse my honor and that of my family, even if it costs me my life. What do you say?"

Here was a man, an honest man, whom the communists had broken, forcing him to become an informant. It was likely that at least one person on his list was also an informant, unbeknownst to my friend. This was par for the course. It was on this double coverage and the fear of each other that communist security thrived. What was I now supposed to do? How would he take it if I denied any intention of escaping to the West? If I told him I was trying my best to escape from Albania, would he have the strength to keep this secret under torture? No man could truly be expected to resist the prolonged and sophisticated methods of torture the communists had learned from the Yugoslavs and the Soviets and used with great abandon. I made up my mind.

"Yes, my friend, I am still trying to escape and one of these days I may make it to Yugoslavia and beyond. I regret that it has come to this, but I promise you that I will do as you wish if a serious and worthy opportunity should arise."

He smiled and thanked me. It had gotten late. We rose, shook hands, and I left for home without seeing either the older brother or the other family members. Mom and Mergim were ready to go to bed. That suited me fine as I had no intention of sharing with either one what I had just learned.

The persecution of the Catholic Church was getting ever more systematic. At one point, the communist party offered the Church that the clergy be paid by the government. The government would first approve promotions within the ranks of the Church before they reached the Vatican, and seminaries would be allowed to reopen on condition that Marxism-Leninism be taught one hour a week. The man representing the Party's proposal was Tuk Jakova, a Catholic and former carpenter from Shkodra. The discussions led nowhere as the Church authorities refused to include Marxism-Leninism in the curriculum. They stated that they could not teach materialism and religion at the same time. When asked how religion would survive without young priests filling the ranks as their elders passed away, the priests answered that God would provide.

The communist party could ill adapt to failure. They sacked Tuk Jakova, accusing him of fraternizing with the enemy, and unleashed ever more brutal attacks against priests. Many were arrested and tortured. Several prayed in court for their persecutors who did not know what they were doing. About 70 percent of priests, both Jesuits and Franciscans, joined Father Anton Harapi in suffering a martyr's death. I cannot do justice in describing the persecution endured by the Catholic Church. Anyone interested in the topic will have to draw on Albanian publications that appeared in print abroad over the years and in Albania after the fall of communism. I do want to mention two episodes typical of the Church's persecution by the communists.

One happened during my time, right after the rupture of "fraternal relations" between Tirana and Belgrade. One night a platoon of security forces secretly entered the Franciscan church in Shkodra and planted Italian and German rifles and other weapons under the altar of the Blessed Mother. They snuck out again and marched up to the main gate of the rectory. Their commanding officer was Lieutenant Pierin Kçira, a former student at the Franciscan high school. The lieutenant knocked at the gate. When the old pastor answered, the lieutenant told him that his men were there to search the church. Then the lieutenant pushed the priest aside and entered the church with his men. They went directly to the altar of the Blessed Mother. Lo and behold, what did they find under the altar? Italian and German weapons, indisputable proof that the Church had cooperated with both Axis powers, and even more important, that the Church was gathering arms to fight against the regime. By sheer coincidence, they had brought with them a photographer who recorded the presence of the weapons under the altar.

According to communist legal procedures, it was necessary that the old priest confess his part in the "crime" of storing weapons in church. No matter how hard they pressed him, no matter what tortures they used on him, the priest never changed his story that he knew nothing about the hidden weapons. The lieutenant, his former student, tried everything he had been taught to make the prisoner confess.

One day he had an idea. As they were crossing the yard, two police jeeps were parked in front of the building. After the war, the Western Allies had sent jeeps, trucks, food supplies, articles of clothing, and other goods to Albania. The government had appropriated whatever they needed, some for the armed services and some for their own needs. That is how the two jeeps got into the hands of the security organs. The rest of the goods they put up for sale at government stores. The lieutenant had the priest's arms tied—one to the front bumper and the other to the rear bumper of the two jeeps. Then one of the vehicles started moving away from the other, practically tearing the priest's arms out of their sockets. The priest still refused to confess. The priest was sentenced to death based on the photographic evidence presented in court. He was dragged into his cell to await the rejection of the automatic appeal for clemency. At this point the priest was no longer tortured and was fed as his sentence had been passed.

The man who broke down at this point was Lieutenant Kçira who knew that he and his men had planted the weapons under the altar. The lieutenant repented. He tried to contact the underground but they would not touch him with a flagpole. He went to his office, typed some anti-government leaflets and distributed them at night. It took the government but a few days to trace the leaflets to the lieutenant's typewriter. The young man was arrested and brought before a court. He confessed and was sentenced to a prison term. The sentence meant little because the authorities could pardon him whenever they wanted. The lieutenant had served them well during, as well as after, the war. True, he had published the leaflets, but he could be reeducated and still be useful to the Albanian communist party. Once the court passed the sentence, the former lieutenant felt safe. He asked the judge whether he had permission to add one more statement. Expecting an apology for publishing the leaflets, the judge gave his permission.

Then came the bombshell: "My men and I planted the weapons under the altar in church."

First there was a hush in court and then the Party faithful started screaming, demanding that the traitor receive the death sentence. The young man was handed over to his former colleagues who tortured him with a vengeance. They dragged the young prisoner, whom they had reduced to a pulp, to jail and dumped him in a cell next to the old priest, his former professor and recent victim. The priest had no knowledge of what had happened in court. Yet when they brought the priest some food, he dragged himself to the iron bars, pushed the food into the young man's cell and said, "Eat, you need it more than I do."

A friend told me another episode that took place some years after my escape from Albania. A Catholic priest was arrested and sentenced to lifelong imprisonment. Later, the government decreed that the longest prison term could not exceed 25 years, and the priest's sentence was reduced to that maximum. He served out his sentence and was released. A farmer approached him and asked Father to baptize the farmer's baby boy. Afterwards, word leaked out and the priest was arrested once more. This time he was sentenced to death and executed. My friend could not tell me whether the farmer had acted in good faith or had set a trap at the request of the government.

Mom returned home one day after running into Qazim Ramadani, a family friend (for biographical detail, see Chapter 2). During their conversation, he had mentioned that he had contacts with infiltrators from Yugoslavia and asked whether my brother and I might be interested in escaping. Such a move would put Mom in great difficulty. If we escaped, there would be no one left who could work and take care of her. Dad was in prison, condemned to lifelong imprisonment. Mom would have had to try to provide for both. Beginning in the spring and through fall, prisoners dried marshes, dug canals, and built hydroelectric power plants. They had to work without proper tools, were fed starvation diets, and suffered inhumane treatment by their guards. Mom knew all this. Yet, when she gave us the message, she accepted the possibility that we might leave her for good. Only a mother could willingly face such a sacrifice for the sake of her children.

The three of us had discussed the matter a number of times. Mergim and I were in danger of being arrested any time under whatever pretext or for no reason at all. That would have made matters even worse than if we escaped. Mom would be worried sick about what was happening to Mergim and me after our arrest. Furthermore, in addition to Dad, once we emerged from months of investigation and torture, she would want to take care of us even though we might be sent to different prisons or work camps, thus complicating her life even more.

When Mom gave us the news, it did not take long for Mergim and me to decide that this might be destiny knocking at our door. I got in touch with Qazim. He confirmed everything Mom had said, adding that he would take over at this point. He could give us no details, for obvious reasons. Mergim and I had to be ready to leave at a moment's notice. Once we were contacted, we were to follow instructions. That was all we needed to know. I thanked him and now it was simply a matter of waiting until things fell into place. This could have been a period of increased anxiety. Instead, Mergim and I relaxed because we could see light at the end of the tunnel. Several weeks later, Qazim came to see us. He was upset.

"What happened? Why did you fail to meet the infiltrators as we had agreed on?"

"Qazim, we don't know what you are talking about."

"The infiltrators entered Shkodra and you failed to show up. Did you change your mind?"

"Where and when were we supposed to show up? No one contacted us." Something had gone wrong at the last moment.

Qazim hesitated. "Are you telling me that nobody contacted you?"

"Yes, that's what we are saying."

Qazim shook his head. His anger had given way to disappointment, to sadness. Without uttering a word, he shook hands with us and left. We never heard from him or from any other source what had gone wrong. It was another failed attempt to leave the paradise called the People's Republic of Albania.

Mergim and I had one more chance to escape from Albania. In Chapter 11, I wrote of the communist assassination attempt against Mustafa Kruja. The gendarme wounded on that occasion was Sefullah Merlika, fondly known as Big Sefa. He was tall and sinewy, with light brown hair. He had easy manners, a ready smile, and inspired confidence at first sight. He moved with the grace and strength of a feline. Other than that, there was nothing catlike about him.

One day he had come to Shkodra and had run into Mom. He had mentioned to her that he was in contact with infiltrators from Italy and offered help in case we needed it. Mom had inquired whether he could help Mergim and me out of the country. In reply, Sefa had asked that I contact him to work out the details, and he gave Mom directions to his home.

I traveled to Tirana as soon as I could. There I asked a friend to accompany me to the village where Big Sefa lived. I did not tell my friend the purpose of the visit and told him that once we were near wherever I was going he would wait for me under some shady tree until I returned.

We rented two bikes and took off. As we approached Vorra, about half-way between Tirana and Durrës, we noticed a man on a bike who seemed to be following us. At Vorra, I had to turn right toward Shkodra to reach Big Sefa's house. I told my friend to proceed west toward Durrës while I turned north. The man who had been following us disappeared from my sight. I pedaled another half hour or so and reached Big Sefa's home. As luck had it, he was there.

We sat on chairs in his front yard under a big fig tree that gave us shade and privacy. Big Sefa got us something to drink. He started out by telling me that he had a clandestine radio with which he communicated with Italy. He had been in touch with every group before they parachuted into Albania. Another group was getting ready to come. This group was also bringing some medication for the daughter of Qazim Koculi, who was ill. He told me he would get in touch with Mergim and me and would give us sufficient time to come to wherever we would meet the infiltrators. I thanked Big Sefa from the bottom of my heart and left.

At Vorra, I picked up my fellow traveler and we returned to Tirana with saddle sores from riding inferior-quality bikes for hours and hours. Nonetheless, a sharp observer could have detected the bounce in my step and the smile on my face.

A couple of weeks went by without word from Big Sefa. Then we heard that he had been arrested. Next we heard that he had been executed but, brave as he was, he had not mentioned our encounter under torture. After my escape form Albania, I learned that an Italian air force captain at the airport of Foggia was at the service of the KGB and had betrayed every group of operatives before they had left for Albania. Just in case, there was also Kim Philby in London ready to inform on the upcoming drop of parachutists.

Shkodra had several marshy areas along its periphery. In the past, the Rockefeller Foundation had provided funds to fight mosquito breeding grounds. I don't know whether such funds were still available after World War II, but the campaign against malaria was still associated with the Rockefeller name. During the years of my work in Shkodra, we had crews that sprayed DDT along the edges of these marshes with very good results. The man in charge was Lush Radoja, a man close to 60. Lush did a good job and his men liked him. He also drank quite a bit. Not that he imbibed excessively, but quite regularly as his bulbous red nose indicated. One day he came into my office when I was alone.

"Is Comrade Aurel in?" he asked.

"No, he is at a meeting."

"Good. Comrade Genc, you are a good man and the communists don't like you."

"Have you heard anything concrete in this regard?"

"No I haven't, but clearly you are not one of them. You come from a good family, have gone to college, and have neither an important job nor have they sent you back to school. People are not blind, you know?"

I was relieved that Lush had not heard anything specific against me. "Lush, tell me. What's on your mind?"

"I'll be frank with you. A friend of mine and I are planning to escape with our motorboat. We were wondering whether you wanted to join us."

Lush was a good man and I liked him. I was not sure of his discretion and judgment. I decided to test him. "Tell me, who is the friend who wants to escape with you?"

"You know Lel Vata. We have discussed our plans in detail and are ready any time you are."

Lush obviously should not have told me Lel's name. Besides, Lush liked to drink and that was another reason why I decided to reject the offer.

"Lush, thank you for thinking of me. I have too many family obligations that tie me down. Regretfully I have to decline your offer." I felt I had to make a strong case against my escape. In case Lush blabbered to someone else about his escape attempt, at least it would show that I had no intention to undertake such an adventure.

A few days later, Lush and Lel were arrested in a bar, charged with try-ing to escape from Albania. I wonder who had blown the whistle.

I enjoyed the challenges of my work and had fun as a member of the city choir. I was also a member of the volleyball team representing Shko-dra, and enjoyed traveling with friends to national championships.

This was fine, except that it would all come to an abrupt end. When our choir traveled to Tirana, I led the choir as we marched in the stadium with other participating choirs. During rehearsals, some "well-wisher" behind a mike and amplifier was never satisfied with us. We were either too close or too far behind the unit ahead of us. Soon it became obvious that he was taking the opportunity to harass us as Shkodra was viewed as a reactionary city, i.e., a bastion of anti-communism. When his voice blared once more in our ears, I yelled back, "OK, OK we know what's on your mind!"

It shut him up, but I am sure it did not do me any good. The night our choir was to perform "The Shkodra Wedding," I was asked not to appear on stage—because I was too tall. That was fine with me. I had great fun with some personal friends and returned to our barracks at the end of the performance. When we returned to Shkodra, I held my breath for a while as I waited to hear from the authorities. Nothing happened and I resumed my regular routine.

In the meantime, I signed up to learn Russian. I spoke several lan-guages but I lacked a Slavic language. I was pleased to have this oppor-tunity but never made it beyond the third lesson. At the beginning of the fourth lesson, the teacher took me aside and informed me that I had to leave his class. He offered no explanation and I did not ask. Within days I was also notified that I had been expelled from the city choir and from the volleyball team.

Things were taking a turn for the worse. At the office, a courier from the Party committee showed up one day and asked for my boss. Since the boss was out of the office, I took the envelope the courier had brought. When my colleagues left that afternoon, I steamed open the envelope. There it was, in black and white. "Comrade Genc Korça will be removed from office for improper political behavior."

Family in Graz *circa* 1933

My dad and the family dog

Naval officer and his family

11th grade photo

**Medical student in Padua,
1943**

Father

My mother and father in costumed picture

High school class in Italy, *circa* **1941**

With fellow volunteers in Kosovo, 1944

Tirana central square, *circa* **1950**

Bled—last stop before freedom

**Free less shoes with Zef
Shllaku in Austria
(shoes removed due to
frostbitten toes)**

Gene and Margaret Kortsha

The Kortsha family

Chapter Twenty-Three

Another Failed Escape Attempt

I had found out sometime in March that I was to be fired but lightning did not strike until May when Aurel Ashiku called me into his office. He did not stand up as he spoke to me.

"Comrade Genc, I hereby notify you that you are removed from your job for improper political behavior. Collect your personal belongings and leave the office promptly."

As was frequently the case, he had a frozen smile on his face, more of a smirk than a smile. This time, however, a malicious glee shone through. He did not shake hands with me nor did he express any regrets—or thanks for the job I had done. That would have been out of character and could have given the wrong impression, and "Comrade Aurel" wanted none of that. Nor would I have wanted to shake hands with him or respond to any hypocritical comments on his part. I had looked long and hard for any positive character traits in him without success. I felt sorry for him because he had embraced a cause and a mentality that clashed with his family tradition, his upbringing, and his Catholic faith. I found it easier to forgive him than to respect him. Thus, we parted without tears. I could not help but wonder how much of my job would fall on his shoulders as neither of the other two health inspectors had made an effort to understudy my job.

Something happened, however, that shed new light on how my two colleagues had seen me and my work. While I was still employed, we received three speeches we had to collate. Each one was 10 or 15 pages long. One was a May First speech to be delivered by secretaries of the communist party throughout the province; another dealt with pre- and post-natal care, and the third with problems of the agricultural sector. All three speeches arrived in multiple copies. I suggested that we start with the first speech and put all pages 1 on the floor along the wall. Next, we would proceed with page 2, and so on until we were done with all three speeches. That was how we did it.

On May 1, something happened that could have landed me in jail, if not worse. Communist party secretaries throughout the province read the speech on the occasion of the feast of workers. To begin with, the way they delivered these speeches was funny. These speeches were in the Tosk, or southern dialect, while the Shkodra province had its own northern dialect. Northerners sounded funny when they tried to speak Tosk, akin to someone from New Jersey affecting a southern accent. To make matters worse, none of them had read the speech ahead of time. Otherwise they would have discovered the error and avoided embarrassment.

On May 1, as they were delivering this speech in public, when they got to a certain point, the subject switched from commemorating the feast of the proletariat to pre- and post-natal care. There was great confusion, embarrassment, and perhaps some laughter among the listeners. This was a classic case of sabotage and the search for the culprit began immediately. The investigation revealed that an enemy of the people, namely I, had a hand in collating the speeches and my neck was on the line. Fortunately one of my former colleagues, I don't know which one, assumed the responsibility for this dreadful mistake. Thanks to his proletarian roots, he was not punished. In truth, I could not be sure that I had not made the mistake but I could say in good conscience that I would have done my best to avoid such a slipup as it would have landed me in the fire. I am equally sure, though, that the logic of my defense would not have kept me out of jail.

Meanwhile, I was busy writing letters to the Shkodra party committee, the Ministry of Public Health, and to Hysni Kapo, the vice-prime minister in charge of public health. According to the custom of the times, I had to ask that if I had "sinned" I be told of my error so I could avoid it in the future. On the other hand, if I had not sinned, then I respectfully asked to be reinstated in my previous job. Such efforts were futile but were part of the ritual.

While I waited a week or two to give the authorities time to review my case and decide what to do with me, Mom came home one day and told me a surprising story. The year before, Mergim graduated from high school and was appointed to teach at a grade school in Kallarat, a small village not far from Vlora, in Albania's deep south. In a nearby village, a brother and sister from Shkodra were also teaching and the three young people met regularly as they knew each other from Shkodra. A woman had stopped Mom on the street and had introduced herself as the mother of the siblings. Now came the incredible part. The woman had added, in passing, that the area was regularly infiltrated by resistance fighters coming from Greece and that the three young teachers had met with them several times.

Neither Mom nor I knew the siblings or their mother. Yet she had mentioned the infiltrators without stressing this detail in any particular way. I could not understand why Mergim had never told us anything about this as this could be a safe route of escape for both of us. I decided to leave immediately for Kallarat and see how Mergim and I could exploit these lucky circumstances. I got on the bus and traveled from one end of Albania to the other. I had never been in Vlora before but that was no problem. Nor did I expect trouble getting to Kallarat. I might have to be extra cautious and perhaps avoid the beaten path. Having learned some fundamentals of traveling on foot in Dukagjin, I was confident I could make it with a minimum of help from others.

As I got off the bus in Vlora, an acquaintance approached me.

"What are you doing here? Mergim just left for Shkodra."

"Why would he do that?"

"He was fired from his job for improper political behavior."

That was unexpected. I had no choice but to take the next bus for Shkodra. Throughout the trip, I could not help but wonder. Why had we not heard that Mergim had been fired? Why had he not tried to reach me so we could have escaped together to Greece? After all, for us Greece was much better than communist Yugoslavia. I had to be patient until I reached Shkodra and had a chance to speak with my brother. When we met, I rattled off my questions.

"Instead of writing to you that I had been fired as a teacher, I thought it was better that I return to Shkodra and discuss the matter in detail, including what to do under the circumstances. As to the infiltrators from Greece, that is untrue. Why would the woman in question make up such a story?"

His answer to the first question made sense. The answer to the second question, unfortunately, was obvious. The woman had set a trap and hoped to benefit from it if the trap closed on us. She was undoubtedly an informant trying to chalk up another success.

Mergim added that he had gotten along with the siblings and that he had visited with them quite often, bringing with him food for himself and for the two of them, as Kallarat was better off than their village. In addition, he had lent the man some money, the equivalent of a month's salary.

"Has he paid you back?"

"Not so far."

"Why have you not demanded that he pay his debt?"

"I was too embarrassed."

I decided that I was going to demand that they pay back the money as soon as they returned to Shkodra. A few days later, someone pointed out the brother to me. He was of medium height, thin, and rather frail. He was average looking with no particular facial traits. He was no charmer but then I was probably prejudiced against him.

"I am Mergim's brother."

"Yes, I know."

"You owe Mergim money and we expect you to pay it back."

"You are wrong. We owe Mergim nothing. He was often at our home and ate our food."

"That is not true. In fact, the opposite is true. Mergim brought food from Kallarat for himself and for the two of you."

"Yes, but he also slept with my sister."

I was stunned. What kind of a man, what kind of brother would call his sister a slut and charge for her services? I could not help showing my disgust. He averted his face, his eyes darted right and left, like a rat with a bad conscience. He was the true son of his mother. He was also a worthy offspring of a system that thrived on informants, immorality, and lies. I was not going to let him get away with it.

"Unless you pay back the money promptly, the superintendent of education will hear about this. You have until next payday."

I turned on my heels and left that poor excuse of a man standing in the middle of the street. When I asked Mergim about the girl, he said that she was a nice person and that nothing had ever happened between them. Some time later, the brother made one payment on what he owed. Then he disappeared for good. We got back half the money he owed us and decided to drop the matter.

In Dukagjin, I had met two teachers from Shkodra, Ndue Vatë Gjelaj and his wife. She needed a medicated skin cream and Lel Vata had it in his pharmacy. When they and I were transferred to Shkodra, we ran into each other from time to time. By way of background: To save fuel, Shkodra's electricity was cut off at midnight and started up again in the morning. For psychological reasons, to create terror in the minds of the victims, the security people arrested people mostly during the wee hours of the night. On such occasions, the lights stayed on throughout the night. Thus, Mergim and I spent many an evening waiting for the lights to go out before going to bed. One night I stayed up almost until dawn before the lights went out. The next morning I ran into Ndue Vatë Gjelaj.

"What happened to you? You look like death warmed over."

"The lights stayed on last night," I blurted out and immediately regretted my words as I had no reason to trust the man.

"Come stay at my home," he replied. "No one will suspect that I am hiding you."

I took a good look at him. He looked me straight in the eye and his body language supported what he had just said. I had no reason to doubt his words.

True, no one would have suspected that I was hiding in his home, but there was also Mergim. If we spent the nights at Ndue Vata's, our absence from home and our presence at Ndue Vata's would sooner or later be noticed and would make the neighbors, and therefore the police, suspicious even if we were not about to be arrested.

"Thank you, Ndue. I truly appreciate your offer. I may have to take you up in the future. This time, let's see what happens. Thanks again." With these words, we parted company but I made a mental note. In case of need, Ndue Vatë Gjelaj was a man I could count on.

Over the months, Ndue would come and visit us from time to time. Mom liked him very much and called him Gino Cervi, an Italian movie star whom Ndue resembled. We discussed politics frequently and held nothing back. One day, Ndue came to see us again. This time he came with a proposal. He was going to escape with his wife and some friends and asked whether Mergim and I were interested in joining them.

He came from a simple family. During the civil war, he had been with the communists and had risen through the ranks. At war's end, what he saw was not what he had fought for. He resigned his commission and began working as a teacher. The authorities did not suspect how much his political views had changed. On one occasion, he and some of his friends had taken a boat and had rowed across Lake Shkodra to the village of Shiroka on the opposite shore. He intended to do the same on the feast day of the patron saint of Shiroka. He and his crew would have an accordion and some guitars aboard. They would play music and sing as they rowed toward Shiroka. Halfway there, they would change direction, enter Yugoslav waters, and request political asylum. This was an easy way to escape in full daylight. There were few if any difficulties compared to those facing people who tried to cross the border on foot. No one had ever tried to escape in daylight, in full view of guards on both sides of the lake. The plan was so brazen that it was bound to succeed.

Mergim and I looked at each other.

"Can you get us into the boat without arousing suspicion?"

"No problem at all. Get ready and on the feast day, I will pick you up. I'll take care of everything."

Mergim and I were delighted. Here was the answer to our prayers. Ndue Vatë Gjelaj's plan was simple and had one additional advantage. Once the boat reached Yugoslav waters, all of Shkodra would know that the escape had been successful and Mom would not worry about the outcome beyond the morning of the actual escape. Now it was a matter of waiting and keeping our fingers crossed.

Meanwhile, infiltrators from Yugoslavia kept coming into Albania. On such occasions, they also distributed propaganda leaflets that indicated the political climate in Yugoslavia. Such propaganda made me realize that we did not belong there.

I showed the leaflet to Mom and Mergim. The verdict was unanimous. Mergim and I had to back out from the promise we had made to Ndue Vatë Gjelaj. We told him so and he understood.

"I regret that you won't be with us. Please, understand. I cannot cancel now. Too many people are counting on me."

We understood completely. On the feast day of Shiroka's patron saint, we heard with great joy the news of Ndue's successful escape. He and his friends had tweaked the noses of the communists in Shkodra and had gotten away with it. Mergim and I were also disappointed to the extent that we realized that Yugoslavia was no safe haven for us.

Meanwhile, Mergim and I went to work in a quarry near the southern entrance to the city. The crew there was a motley one. One man drilled holes into the mountainside, placed the explosive charges, and blasted large amounts of rock off the face of the mountain. He was the silent type but seemed friendly toward the rest of the workers. We, "enemies of the people," formed the bulk of the work crew. Most were former students who were kicked out of school. One was a graduate of an Italian university who had taught and had taken an active part in Albanian politics, against the communists of course. The rest were women from surrounding villages who had run out of food and needed to work so they could get ration cards for their families. Quite often, these women could not come close to fulfilling their minimum quota and we young men helped them achieve that critical goal. Ration cards were very important. They entitled one to buy bread, eggs, meat, and other foods unavailable without ration cards. Usually, with the exception of bread, most of the food items were not available even with ration cards.

One autumn the rains were late. The water level in Lake Shkodra fell to the point that fishermen caught fish in great abundance. At first the population could buy fish with meat coupons. When people ran out of such coupons, the administration faced a problem. For lack of ice or refrigerated trucks, it could not ship the fish to markets beyond Shkodra. It could permit the local population to buy fish without coupons. That would have been preferential treatment detrimental to the rest of Albania. Thus, for the sake of social justice, the local government certainly with the approval of central authorities—buried the fish en masse deep and far enough from the city to avoid the stench of rotten fish and other possible complications.

The lack of refrigerated trucks had created similar problems in the past. To save on fuel, a regulation stated that no truck could travel unless it was fully loaded. Albania's villages were small and the time before a truck could be fully loaded with eggs or produce took days. Frequently, by the time a truck was fully loaded, the goods had spoiled. This approach caused the loss of scarce goods but prevented trucks from traveling half empty. The logic of a centralized economy!

Even with ration cards, to get an article of clothing or shoes, in addition to availability, a worker needed a special authorization from the employer.

Assuming that the merchandise became available and one had an authorization, one still was not sure it came in the right size. Needless to say, "enemies of the regime" were always at the bottom of the list for such items. In 10 years under communism, I got a pair of sandals and nothing else.

A few months before my escape, a friend of mine named Ismail Troshani came to see me.

"Genc, I have come to ask a favor of you. My girlfriend's cousin has come from Tirana and I need a date for her for tonight."

I was less than enthused. I was tired from working hard all day long. Dates cost money and I didn't have any. Ismail's girlfriend was short and made Olive Oyl look like the Venus de Milo. If her cousin was anything like her... I really was in no mood to spend effort, time, and money to escort somebody's ugly cousin. I stalled.

"What do you have in mind?"

"We can go out, the four of us, and have a bite to eat and a drink at a café, my treat, of course. Then we break up and each couple goes its own way. What do you say? Please say yes, otherwise I am stuck without a chance to be with my girl for another week or two."

Ismail worked at the hospital all week long and slept there when he was on duty. He had few evenings a month when he and his girl could have fun together. He was a good guy despite his poor taste in women. I had to find out whether the cousin was halfway good looking. I pushed him hard.

"I'll come on one condition. If the cousin from Tirana is uglier than your girl, I'll take your girl and you take the cousin."

"It's a deal! Let's meet this evening at eight o'clock sharp outside the Big Café."

That suited me fine. At that hour, it was dark and I planned to suggest that instead of entering the Big Café, we go elsewhere where we would be less conspicuous. We shook hands and Ismail left. I washed up and shaved carefully. I put on a nice silk shirt and a pair of slacks. Both had seen better days but at night they would do.

I was in front of the Big Café at eight o'clock sharp when Ismail showed up with two girls. The newcomer was stunning—tall and slender. I was sure that my eyes were not fooling me, nor had hard labor weakened my taste for pretty girls. Ismail's girl was safe from me. Ismail introduced us briefly. I proposed we move to a less conspicuous but nice café. As we walked, I had a chance to look her over. She wore a nice dress, buttoned in the back, with a light top and a dark bottom. She walked well and seemed unaffected by the effect she must have known she had on men.

At the café the conversation was awkward. It turned out she was a Party member. She had come to Shkodra to inspect the provincial section of commerce and the cooperative producing footwear. There was no sense hiding who I was. She must have already known the essentials from her cousin because she showed no surprise when I told her a little about myself. We had something to eat and drink. Soon what little conversation we had came to a grinding halt. Ismail and his girlfriend were obviously eager to leave for darker places. We got up, the other couple a few steps ahead of us out of earshot and making no attempt to disguise their hurry. The pretty communist from Tirana and I followed somewhat hesitantly. Finally, she took my hand.

"Don't you like me?" she asked bashfully.

"That's not it. You are beautiful but my hands are rough and cracked."

She took my hands and stroked them. "I noticed them at the café."

We walked that evening, sat a while, and walked again. We did not say much, and there was not much to say. She was a member of the communist party. I was the enemy. Yet that night there was no trace of enmity, no anger, no clash. If anything, there was sadness. Two young people, attracted to each other, who felt lost, almost unreal, caught up in a struggle they had no control over.

Time came to say goodbye.

"When are you going back to Tirana?" I asked her.

"Tomorrow afternoon. I'll come to the construction site and say goodbye."

"You will do no such thing. You would only harm yourself. I don't care, there is not much more they can do to me, but you must not endanger yourself." There was no need to explain who "they" were and what they were capable of.

"I will come and see you before I leave. Is there some way I can help you?"

I hesitated a moment.

"Yes, there is. I need sandals. The cooperative refuses to make me a pair without a special authorization saying I had deformed feet. The commerce section says that my feet are not deformed, just big, and refuses to give me an authorization. Can you help?"

"I'll bring you the authorization when I come to see you tomorrow."

The next day I went to work and kept an eye on the road. In the morning, I felt fairly confident she would come. She had sounded so positive. As the day went on it became obvious that the magic of the evening before had worn off before the cold reality. Well, chalk it up to experience, I thought. Besides, I had known all along that she would not come. I had lied to myself. Now I realized that her not coming to say goodbye had apparently rankled me more than I cared to admit.

A few days later, Ismail came to our room and, in my absence, dropped off an authorization for a pair of sandals. She had kept that part of her promise. I needed sandals that had leather tops and heavy rubber soles from old truck tires. I looked at the authorization. Her signature was at the bottom. Her handwriting showed she had little formal schooling. I smiled at the thought that I needed the sandals to escape and that a communist had given me the authorization! She had been good to me that evening and had provided the much-needed authorization. She had made the right choice when she did not come to say goodbye. I wondered how she felt about a party that controlled individual lives to that extent.

At the quarry, our pay depended on fulfilling the daily norm. That sounded reasonable except for the fact that the norm reflected the amount of gravel a mechanized stone crusher could produce in eight hours, if we had one. We were the next best thing. Our productivity, however, still had to match that of the machine that existed only on paper. We got only part of the full pay but got the precious ration cards that covered our daily bread, if nothing else. The bread ration was 400 grams a day, which was a little less than a pound. The bread was not always baked through, but between Mergim and me we managed to also feed Mom who was not working and, therefore, was not entitled to ration cards.

Mom was ingenious. She always managed to prepare sandwiches with a touch of jelly, a little cheese, a pickle, or something to keep us going at noon. In the evening she prepared a soup—some stuffing boiled in water with a touch of oil, most of the time something edible with some flavor. Occasionally we had to skip supper. That was the exception. Going to bed hungry was not.

At work, we got along famously. The rock formation near the Buna River looked inhospitable, and the work strenuous—a just punishment for "the enemies of the people." In reality the work was physically not too demanding for us young men who sat down with hammers and reduced 15- to 20-pound rocks to gravel. There were no spies among us. Quite the contrary, some had been tested by fire, i.e., they had withstood torture in prison and had emerged with flying colors. Hence, the conversation and the humor bouncing back and forth among us gave us respite compared to the bleak atmosphere prevailing elsewhere.

Once a year Catholics celebrated the feast of Our Lady of Shkodra. Legend had it that when a statue of the Blessed Mother had left the sanctuary in Palestine on its way to Italy, it had rested a few days at a church across the river from our quarry. On the eve of the feast day, we were told to report the next morning at the home office. There they issued us rakes and shovels and sent us to the main drag running smack through the center of Shkodra where the faithful would come through on their way to the church. The intent was, of course, to put us on display as "enemies of the people" and humiliate us before the people walking by. After all, one of us was a professor, and I had taught anatomy in high school and was well known among the students. Then there were the young men, such as my brother, who had been schoolmates with throngs of young boys and girls who would see them in rags, handling shovels and rakes. That was the plan. The reality turned out differently. People stopped, talked with us, encouraged us not to give in, and continued on their way to church where they would pray for us., That afternoon they sent us back to the quarry.

October came and I was called before the draft board. Because I have described in detail what happened on that occasion, I won't repeat myself but refer the reader to Chapter 1. The letter ordering Mergim to appear before the board came as a complete surprise to me. It shouldn't have. He was of draft age. Once he was fired from his job as a teacher, I could not expect him to be deferred for reasons of employment as I had been for a number of years. The draft board assigned Mergim to the Labor Battalion headquartered in Tirana. From there he sent word that his feet were killing him because the army had issued him boots that were too small. I rushed to Tirana with a pair of bigger boots and found him at a location west of Tirana, amid a group of friends with similar backgrounds, joking and laughing and making the best of a bad situation. We were able to secure some privacy and hurriedly assessed his "call to arms" and the impact this had on us as a family. Before we parted company, we agreed on one important issue: If one of us had a chance to escape without being able to reach the other, the one with a potential break could escape even if it meant leaving the other behind.

I saw Mergim once more. This time his unit bivouacked south of Tirana near the airport. I had to leave because the Labor Battalion was to march into Tirana; I don't recall for what reason. I left and was walking north on Kavaja Street when I heard the Labor Battalion marching right behind me. I stopped to see them all once more. As they were closing the gap, they started singing an Italian song, "*Noi siamo i cadetti di Gascogna, andiamo a Bologna, andiamo a Bologna...*" (We are the cadets from Gascony, on our way to Bologna, on our way to Bologna...). When they were level with me, they all turned their heads smartly toward me and I, like a fool, stood at attention and saluted them as if I were reviewing a military parade. What can I say? We were all young, full of laughter and mischief. It was too bad. Those young men in tattered uniforms should have been going to college instead of forced labor. It was a testimonial to communist class warfare, irrespective of the cost to the nation. Thirty-nine years would go by before Mergim and I would meet again.

CHAPTER TWENTY-FOUR

OBLIGATORY LABOR – GOODBYE SHKODRA

With Mergim gone, we lost one set of ration cards, which made Mom even more reluctant to eat part of my daily bread ration. Dear Mom! She was a strong, optimistic person, generous to a fault and a staunch anti-communist. If she walked on the street and her foot bumped into a stone, she unhesitatingly cussed the communists. Whenever she needed to vent her anger toward the Red regime, she always invoked the power of the United States on Albania's behalf: "What would it take for the United States to kick the communists out of Albania? No more than two battalions, that's all it would take. So why doesn't America bring in that handful of troops and put an end to our misery?"

I had heard her say similar things so often that one day I decided to stop her in her tracks. "Mom, if we had accepted Uncle Faik's invitation to go to the United States in 1936, today Mergim and I would be American citizens. We would also be of military age. And since the military expedition you are talking about would involve Albania, it would be both logical and fair that we two brothers be drafted to fight for Albania's liberation."

"Nonsense, America is a big country. It would not need you two to free Albania!" Spoken like a true mother, right? Dear Mom!

In Chapter 21, I mentioned how I met Riza Butka, an inspector of the Ministry of Health, who had come to Shkodra to review our campaign against the typhus epidemic. We had a chance to discuss many things, including the political situation in Albania. His visit to Shkodra gave rise to a lasting friendship. I had not seen Dad for years. In 1951, I decided to go to Tirana and seek a way of getting to Burrel where Dad was imprisoned.

337

In Tirana, I stayed at Riza Butka's who, in addition to his hospitality, also offered to provide me with a forged travel pass. When Mom went to Burrel once a month, she had to make the round trip to Burrel in the backs of trucks and had to spend the nights in Burrel under a bridge because the farmers could not take in families of political prisoners. Riza Butka's pass would let me travel by bus and take a room at the hotel in Burrel.

This was great. I went to the bus agency, purchased a round-trip ticket, and got ready to board the bus. I had to walk by a tall, young police lieutenant who, when he saw me, broke out in a grin, thrust out his right hand, and said in a loud voice, "Comrade Assistant, don't you recognize me?"

I shook his hand, trying to remember him. Then it dawned on me. In 1947 or thereabouts he was hospitalized in our aseptic surgical ward. He had a large swelling near the middle of the left buttock that the Italian surgeon, Dr. Augi, and the Albanian surgeon, Dr. Frederic Shiroka, had diagnosed as an aneurysm of the femoral artery. The patient understood that this was most serious and that, once they opened him up, it was touch and go. When Dr. Augi made the incision, instead of an aneurysm, the surgical team found itself looking at a deep, ordinary abscess that was anything but life threatening. Both surgeons had erred in their diagnosis. Everybody was happy, of course, and happiest of all was the patient. He, however, was happy for the wrong reason. He remained convinced that he had had an aneurysm, that the surgical team had saved his life, and that I—since I had administered the ether that put him under—was also a member of that team.

Now he was absolutely delighted to see me. On the bus he sat next to me and for the next four hours he kept quizzing me about everyone he remembered from the hospital. In reply, I had to make up stories to fill the gap; I had left the hospital in April of 1948. I was glad when we reached Burrel and I got off the bus. Gratitude is a virtue, indeed a rare virtue, but in excess it can make one, as the object, very uncomfortable.

I got a room at the hotel, ate dinner at the restaurant, and slept in a bed instead of under the bridge. In the morning I saw Dad. He was behind two sets of iron bars and I was on the outside. Several partisans stood in between. The conversation was reduced to a minimum, and by the time I told him all was well at home and he had told me his needs, our five minutes were up.

That afternoon I was strolling along the highway when the bus appeared, homebound for Tirana. The ticket agent on the bus stuck his head out and asked whether I was ready to go back. I nodded, ran to the hotel to pick up my small travel bundle, and boarded the bus. *With no police lieutenant on the bus like the day before, things ought to go smoothly,* I thought. About half an hour went by when some commotion broke out behind me.

Two other men in civilian clothes had boarded the bus after me. We were barely underway when they started grumbling about something. Soon they started tossing around Dad's name and mine. That got my attention. They were berating the ticket agent.

"How come you put that civilian up front in first class and you put us in the back of the bus? How much of a bribe did he give you?" They spoke with arrogance. Their choice of words marked them as members of the communist party, presumably of a higher party rank than the ticket agent.

"What are you talking about?" the ticket agent asked. "I had one free seat in first class and two in the back. You two were traveling together while he was alone. So, I put you two together and put him up front."

"Don't you know that he is a reactionary?"

"No, I don't. I don't know him at all. Besides, the man is traveling with travel orders. That's all I know."

"Are you traveling on official business?" They asked me.

"No," I replied, "I came to see my father."

They turned their attention back to the ticket agent. "Where did you get the idea he had travel orders? Don't you know that he is a reactionary, son of a reactionary, and that we two are officers of the State Security?"

"How am I to know that you are Sigurimi officers?" the ticket agent replied. "You are in civilian clothes."

"Never mind that. It is obvious that the man has bribed you and that you have no respect for Sigurimi."

Finally, the ticket agent lost his patience. "Look, I don't care who you are. To me you are two tickets and nothing more. The man did not bribe me and you who are so proud of being members of Sigurimi—wasn't Koci Xoxe head of Sigurimi?"

Koci Xoxe was executed as a traitor in 1949. He was Tito's anointed, intended to rule Albania after he had eliminated Enver Hoxha, the first secretary of the communist party, and Mehmet Shehu, the butcher of Albania.

Now the officers began screaming.

"How dare you call us traitors!" They continued, concentrating on the poor ticket agent who had done nothing wrong, except perhaps when he lost his patience. This went on for hours, it seemed. I had shriveled in my seat trying to be invisible and the other passengers kept silent lest they too be struck by lightning just like the poor ticket agent.

Finally, we reached a big bridge that at one time had borne the name of King Zogu. The two officers stopped the bus, got off, and ordered me to follow them. We were standing in the middle of nowhere. I did not know what they had in mind, but did not have to wait long. They ordered me to empty my pockets. I did as I was told. Now I knew what was going to happen and there was nothing I could do to stop what lay ahead. They would find the forged paper and the gates of jail would open wide for me. First I would suffer the worst beatings and tortures in the Sigurimi manual. Then once they broke me, it would be Riza Butka's turn. Riza, who had forged the travel permit for me, was married with small children. He would suffer the same fate as I and perhaps worse, as he might have been a party member. Besides, who knew what other terrible details torture would bring to the surface?

The two Sigurimi officers began going through my papers while I was dying on my feet. One held a flashlight while the other went through the papers one by one. As the pile of papers in his hands got smaller and smaller, I felt the end coming closer and closer. Finally, he was done. He had failed to find the forged travel orders. He returned the papers, got back on the bus and waved me aboard. I felt my knees give way as I approached my seat. I was stunned. I didn't know what had happened. We traveled for a while and finally got off in front of the bus agency in Tirana where, barely 36 hours before, I had run into the police lieutenant who wouldn't stop thanking me.

A few months later, in Shkodra, I was returning home from work, filthy and in rags. A man stopped me.

"Are you Genc Korça?"

"Yes," I replied as I looked at the stranger.

"Did you travel to Burrel some time ago and on the return trip two security officers created quite a disturbance?"

"Yes," I replied. "I remember what you are talking about."

"I was the ticket agent on the bus. When we got to Tirana, I was arrested and tortured for two days and two nights as they pumped me for information about you."

"I am sorry," I replied.

"Yes, I know you are sorry," he said as he walked away.

One Sunday morning, we had to do "voluntary work" at the stadium under construction. We all disliked the place intensely. Besides having to work there half a day on Sundays, we could not help but notice that the various levels of steps consisted of gravestones taken from cemeteries. First the communists had let herds of pigs forage for food in old Muslim cemeteries. The obvious intent was to desecrate the cemeteries and offend the Muslim population. Then they removed the headstones and used them for the stadium. Even though the people of Shkodra followed soccer with a passion, the overall effect of the stadium deeply offended Muslims and Catholics alike.

That Sunday morning, a lifelong laborer challenged me to compete against him in digging a ditch with our picks. It did not take me long to see that I was unable to dig as fast and as deep as he did. In order not to fall behind, I started digging less deeply and was able to keep pace with the man. At this point, the head of the province, Qamil Gavoçi, saw us.

"Good for you, Comrade Genc. This is more suited for you than handling puny syringes."

"Comrade Qamil, as you can see I am able to handle both," I responded.

Qamil Gavoçi kept smiling and walked away. I wondered what was going through his mind at that moment. My answer had lacked prudence but I just could not let him get away with his sarcastic comment.

Soon after Mergim joined the army, I was fired from working at the quarry. I was at the end of my wits. If I could not earn my daily bread breaking stones, what did my future hold? I did not want to plead with the head of the province, for obvious reasons. On the other hand, without work and my daily bread ration, Mom and I could not last long. I decided to see Shyqri Hafizi, Qamil Gavoçi's second in command. He looked to be around 50 years of age. He was a communist of long standing and had held responsible positions. Nonetheless, he was down to earth and approachable. He was laid back, factual, and not discourteous like most Party members. Rumor had it that one day, while in the mountains, the guards gave the alarm that German troops were coming in hot pursuit. Everybody grabbed their weapons and other belongings and started running while Shyqri kept lacing his boots meticulously.

"Come on, let's go. Why are you lacing your boots so slowly, eyelet by eyelet?"

"That's my job."

"But the Germans are coming!"

"That's their job."

Shyqri Hafizi received me without having me wait outside his office. I told him that I had been fired from breaking stones in a quarry. While I was speaking, life's hardships and my responsibility to take care of Mom got the better of me. "If I cannot even work at a stone quarry, then there are only two alternatives. One, that I be arrested, and the other that I escape."

As soon as I said those words, I regretted them, but by now, it was too late.

Shyqri Hafizi looked at me calmly. "If you no longer work at the quarry, you will be sent somewhere else. Is there anything else on your mind?"

"No, thank you. Do you advise me to go to the labor employment office?"

"Yes, that's where you should go."

I could not detect any hidden meaning in his words or body language. I felt relieved that he had not reacted to my emotional outburst and I went down the steps to the labor office feeling better. In due course I was assigned to a new factory under construction north of Shkodra.

Here the work varied. Sometimes I worked with pick and shovel, sometimes I helped carpenters or bricklayers, and sometimes I took care of an injured worker requiring first aid. Overall, the job was easier than at the quarry.

In surgery a few years before, when I scrubbed I had learned to stay one step ahead of the surgeon so I was ready with the proper instruments without the surgeon having to ask or wait for them. That same technique came in handy with the tradesmen. Once I learned the fundamentals, I could be of real help, allowing them to work faster to meet or even exceed the norm.

Pick and shovel, of course, were the toughest. Sometimes we fell behind schedule and had to work 10 to 14 hours each day. Considering the lack of food we all suffered from, on such occasions we paced ourselves to make sure we lasted until the end of the shift.

One morning a Bulgarian engineer came to inspect our work. People thought he was not really an engineer but had been given the title because he was a communist party member and from Bulgaria, i.e., a foreign specialist. He watched me and decided I was not working to full capacity. He grabbed my pick, started swinging it with all his strength, and then gave it back to me.

"That's how you work with the pick," and then he proceeded to insult my mother, the worst insult in the eyes of an Albanian.

Having the pick in my hand, according to our code of honor, I was expected to bash his skull in. Naturally, that was not an option. I looked around questioningly, as if I had not understood his insult. Next to me was Hamid, in his early twenties, built like a bull, and of simple mind. One day earlier, we had all been gathered around a fire inside a shed. Several tree trunks, about 6–10 inches in diameter, were laid out in a circle, pointing at the heart of the fire. As the fire consumed part of the tree trunks, we pushed the trunks forward into the fire. One man there decided to make fun of Hamid.

"Hamid," he asked, "how old are you?"

"Twenty-four, I think," Hamid answered.

"I once had a donkey exactly your age," the man then said and started rolling with laughter.

Hamid realized he was being made fun of. He turned toward the man, hurled an insult at him, and then hit the man with a burning tree trunk on the head, flames, embers, and all. Clearly, once Hamid was provoked, he lost any inhibitions that would restrain a normal individual from hurting someone beyond measure.

So when the Bulgarian insulted my mother, Hamid raised his pick over his head.

"No one, no Bulgarian, is going to insult an Albanian mother and get away with it!"

Another young communist jumped between the two, grabbed Hamid, and yelled, "Get the Bulgarian out of here!"

The Bulgarian realized how close he had come to having his skull bashed in and let some of the workers push him out of danger. Fortunately for me and for all concerned, that was the end of that. I continued to work at that construction site for a few more months and we never saw the Bulgarian again.

Some weeks later, I was done working for the day and had just turned into Quku Street where we lived when I saw a police jeep near our gate. A couple of policemen in uniform were in the car. I had the sinking feeling that my time was up. I had to pass by them and decided to act, as their presence was no concern of mine. I entered the front yard. Nothing happened. I mounted the steps leading to the anteroom, but the police did not come after me. Mom was in our one-room apartment.

"How was work today?"

"Fine."

"Wash up, dinner is almost ready."

That evening I waited until midnight when the lights went out. There was no knock at the gate and no one forced his way into our room. I bid Mom a good night and went to bed.

The next morning the jeep was still near our gate. I exited and started going to work. The jeep came to life, the car drove up behind me—and then stopped. Phew, my knees were shaking. Since no one stopped me, I continued on my way. I kept recovering my composure and strength as I got closer and closer to work. Just as I entered the construction site, I first heard and then saw the jeep, like a fury out of hell, driving toward our construction site followed by a huge cloud of dust.

I did not even bother reporting for work. I walked into the first aid station and collapsed on a chair, with cold sweat streaming down my face. A feeling of helplessness, of panic, had drained me of my strength. I sat there waiting for someone to call my name. If they did not find me at my workstation, sooner or later someone would look for me in first aid.

I sat there for maybe 10 minutes and nothing happened. I ventured out and saw the jeep parked in front of the main office. Then it dawned on me. This jeep belonged to the construction enterprise. It was identical to the police jeep that had spent the night in front of our home. Once I understood, I tried to act normally and reported for work. My wobbly knees, however, stayed with me most of the day. When I returned home that evening, Mom told me they had arrested a neighbor of ours.

Then came the day when all "fat bellies," meaning the rich, would be fired from the construction job for fear of potential sabotage by these "class enemies." I was called into the director's office where I was told that I was among those fired. In truth, I was neither fat nor rich by any stretch of the imagination. In fact, I was skinny and poor. Nor was I a "class enemy"—I had no quarrel with any particular class or social layer. I had to admit, though, that I was an enemy of the communist party for the evil it had brought upon our people.

As I was walking out the gate, one of my coworkers approached me. He was quite young, probably under 20, blond, slim, and very alert. He was also a member of the communist party. He shook hands with me and then pressed a much-worn silver ring into my hand. It was in the shape of two hands clasped in friendship. I was touched. Whatever his message, it clashed with the official decision to fire me from my lowly job. I had no chance to thank him as he had already walked away. Judging by his action, he seemed unwilling to walk through life with his eyes closed. I could not help but wonder what life had in store for him.

My next job was also at a construction site. We were building a two-story children's home. It was rather modest, perhaps 100 feet long and 50 feet wide. In what would eventually be the backyard was the mortar pit. One worker stood in the pit and shoveled mortar onto trays that had handles in front and back. As I arrived at work one morning, the accountant, a distant cousin of mine, was measuring the mound of dirt I had dug up the previous day. He shook his head.

"I can't believe that you dug up 13 cubic yards yesterday."

"Why can't you believe it? You measured it yesterday and it was 13 yards, wasn't it?"

"Because your digging dirt earns you more money than I make as an accountant."

His voice quivered as he spoke more to himself than to me. He had been a rich merchant at one time. Now, somehow, instead of digging dirt with the rest of us, he was able to get a relatively cushy job. Instead of being grateful, he was envious.

"Obviously, my hands and feet are worth more than your brain," I replied in disgust and walked away.

One afternoon a woman was shoveling mortar out of the pit. She had brought with her three little children that were sitting alongside the pit. The older girl, kneeling on the ground, had several pebbles lined up in front of her. She chanted some verses and grabbed first one pebble, then two, then three, and so on. Obviously, success was hers if she could grab all pebbles in one fell swoop. Her little sister, also on her knees, sat nearby admiring the older sister's skill even when she goofed and had to start from the beginning. The youngest was a boy, maybe two years old. He sat motionless near the edge of the pit, looking straight ahead, staring without seeing. That afternoon I was transporting mortar with a wheelbarrow.

"May I give your little boy a ride in the wheelbarrow?" I asked the mother. She nodded.

I put a rag inside the wheelbarrow and put the boy inside. He clamped his little fingers to the sides of the wheelbarrow hanging on for dear life. I ran a couple of times around the pit making sure he could always see his mother. When I stopped, the tiny tot did not crack a smile. I offered him a little piece of bread I always carried with me to still the pain when I had hunger cramps. He took the bread and just looked at me. I felt frustrated.

"Does your son ever smile?" I asked the mother.

"You obviously don't have children. Hungry children don't smile," she replied matter-of-factly.

As winter progressed, it got so cold I could not stand it anymore. One day I reported to the hospital. As I stood in the registration area, Dr. Tahsin Karagjozi, the director of the hospital, came in. He was a distant relative of mine, a relative also of the accountant at the construction site where I worked. Dr. Karagjozi was in his mid-fifties, with silver hair and the manners of a gentleman. He had studied medicine in Berlin before the war. He spotted me.

"What brings you here?"

"It is too cold to work outdoors. I am claiming I am suffering from rheumatism and hope to stay at the hospital until the cold spell is over."

"We can keep you here for a while but you will get a series of salicylate shots. Is that OK with you?"

"Certainly; anything is better then working in freezing temperatures atop a building with the wind blowing like crazy."

He nodded and disappeared.

I got a bed in a room with about 20 other patients. The food, as hospital food goes, was adequate. I got my daily shots and could stay warm. Medical care was free and Mom could use my ration cards.

Two episodes stick out in my mind. One of the patients differed from the rest for two reasons. He was the only one who had a hemorrhoid operation. In such cases, the third post-op day was always bad. That was when they removed a rubber tube wrapped in gauze from the site of the surgical intervention. The gauze had a tendency to stick and when the plug was removed it pulled off the scabs all around, the patient felt pain, started bleeding, and this condition would continue until the area healed completely. The man was also the only illiterate person in our room.

Every day around 2:00 p.m. when we were all asleep, a paperboy would scream at the top of his voice the names of the newspapers and magazines he offered that day. Usually the room bought a daily newspaper and one of the patients would read it aloud so everyone could hear the wonderful progress the country was making under communism. Obviously, we never called on the hemorrhoid patient to read the newspaper to the rest of us.

One day we all woke up as we heard the booming announcements of the newspaper boy. To our amazement, the hemorrhoid patient asked for a newspaper with a firm voice.

"Which one do you want? *Zëri i Popullit, Bashkimi, Hosteni...*"

By this time, we were all wide awake, awaiting the patient's decision.

"The one with the most pages," the patient answered, less assuredly than before. No one dared laugh openly but there was a lot of repressed laughter as we understood what he wanted the newspapers for. At that time we had no toilet paper in Albania.

In the bed next to me lay a young man, the director of the local leather-tanning factory. He was of humble origin, had been invited to join the communist party, and had been sent to Moscow to learn all about leather tanning and related processes. Despite his present position that exceeded by far any hopes he might have had when he worked as a simple laborer at the factory, he was pleasant and remarkably modest. One day, as we were chatting, I said to him, "I wish I had your knowledge of Russian."

"Why are you so interested in Russian?"

"I speak some foreign languages but I lack a Slavic language and Russian would, of course, be most important."

"Do you speak German?"

"Yes, I do."

"I would gladly trade you my Russian for your German," was his unexpected reply.

"Why would you want to do that?"

"Because the best texts we read in school were translated from German."

I had to admire the man for his perceptiveness and sincerity.

When I was discharged from the hospital, the worst of the winter was behind us. Furthermore, the construction project where I had worked no longer needed a large unskilled labor force. I reported to the labor office and was assigned to a work crew that was cleaning up the grounds of what had been the Italian consulate.

Here, work differed greatly from what I had done so far. There was the two-story building with large rooms and high ceilings. The entrance to the building led to a large foyer and several interconnecting rooms. The upper floor was particularly attractive because of the glass-enclosed veranda that in good weather reverberated with light. Large trees around the building attenuated glare and provided welcome shade during summer. The entire building looked solid, comfortable, and of an architectonic style that stressed beauty and comfort. Its windows were not just rectangular openings in walls but caught one's eye with their decorated frames. The entire building conveyed grace and character compared to modern structures shaped like enormous cubes of complex, frozen, geometric forms in steel and concrete. The building before me spoke of a time of leisure and grace compared to the fear, anger, and hatred that convulsed the communist world. The building had large front and back yards surrounded by an 8-foot wall. A large front gate and a small rear entrance led onto the premises.

The man in charge of the project was a builder by trade. In his fifties, he was soft-spoken, of medium height, and a bit slouching. His cap had seen better days. Long hair strands protruded from his cap and covered his ears. He had soft, light eyes, bushy eyebrows, and a walrus mustache. His cheeks were red, laced with thin veins, his nose red and bulbous, and his eyes watery. He looked like he enjoyed imbibing. He wore a baggy jacket and pants with bulging pockets. The average age of the work crew was older than elsewhere. The men had belonged to the middle class and now had to earn a living as laborers. None had been particularly active against the communists. They had lost their comfortable lifestyle, had to do manual labor, were not really hurting compared to what others were enduring, but knew they were being watched and could suffer a worse fate at any moment and without recourse. I suspected they were given their soft work assignment because they had probably done favors to some communist friend or relative during the civil war. Why I had landed among them was a mystery. Since no one questioned my being there, I asked no questions and merged easily with the rest.

We had one young man among us who did not quite fit in with the group. He was in his twenties, tall, strong, and someone who had worked with his hands all his life. He was semi-literate and rough around the edges. One day, when we were removing old, dried-out garbage, someone found an enameled potty that looked brand new. When the young worker heard about it, he asked whether he could take the potty home, as he was the only one with small children. He got it and everyone felt good about it. The next day we found out that he had traded the potty for some booze.

A few days later, the young man came to work wearing a big smile. He greeted us individually, politely inquired how we were doing, took his pick, and moved toward his assigned work station, paying no attention to the surprise that had gripped some of us. Moments later, someone screamed. The young man was on the ground, thrashing about, convulsing, and foaming at the mouth. We grabbed him to keep him from hurting himself. After he recovered, he reverted to being his rough, normal self. Now I knew. He was an epileptic. That was why they had assigned him to this job where there was no danger of his falling off a wall, into a pit, or in front of moving machinery. He was not a bad guy and we got along reasonably well.

I was doing quite well on the job. Removing dried-out garbage was easy and relaxing. We dug up the old piles, loaded the material on wheelbarrows and from there onto trucks that took it away for final disposal. I had learned to dig carefully. Sometimes I got lucky and found intact glass jars, drinking glasses, or other reusable containers. I would lay them aside, wash them at the end of the workday, and take them to a little grocery store where the owner bought them for a few pennies or exchanged them for a handful of plums or other fruit. Added to our meager income, these extra earnings served to perk up our meals or buy a few cigarettes for Mom. Even in times of greatest need, Mom would find money for cigarettes. I had never realized how addicted Mom was to smoking. She had told me that she had started smoking at age 12, unbeknownst to her parents who also smoked but who would have disapproved. Over the years, Mom had never stopped smoking, except when she was not well and cigarettes just did not taste right. In fact, I could always tell when she felt better because she would start smoking again. Until that time, I had never realized that she just could not quit. Here we were, living off my ration cards. She was splitting my meager rations with me, always feeling guilty because my rations were not quite enough for one, let alone for the two of us. Yet she had to buy those smelly cigarettes. I never said anything to her about her smoking out of respect, but also because I had come to realize that this was her only relief. Mom had so few pleasures in life.

At work we were almost done with removing the garbage when our foreman called me from his shed. He asked me whether I could come up with a layout for a small park or something similar for the area in front of the building that now served as the House of Culture for the city of Shkodra. I of course agreed, and prepared some drawings with flower beds around a small reflecting pool and calculated the amount of dirt to be removed. When I presented my drawings to the boss, he seemed pleased.

A few days later, some fellow workers came running to me. "The boss is in great pain. He wants to see you."

I ran to his shed and there he was. Half standing, half sitting, he was flushed, breathing hard as sweat ran down his cheeks.

"Where does it hurt?"

He pointed to his groin.

"Lie down and let me take a look. When I checked his inguinal area, an incarcerated hernia was clearly visible. Carefully, I began reducing the hernia by pushing down on the swelling and pressing the bowel contents upstream. Fortunately the muscles had not tightened completely. Within a few minutes, the hernia disappeared and with it the excruciating pain. The boss breathed a sigh of relief. He felt good and was ready to get up. What I did not know was that he had been wearing a truss for years but was afraid to undergo an operation. I advised him to have the operation and walked away content, as I had done my good deed for the day. Besides, I was sure that out of gratitude, the boss would give me a particularly easy assignment for the rest of that day.

That afternoon the boss called me.

"One of our men just dug up a hand grenade. Get rid of it."

That was not what I had expected. Instead, he singled me out to remove a hand grenade. In other words, he was asking me to risk my life to protect the rest of the work crew. I saw the grenade. It looked old and encrusted with dirt. I was furious. I grabbed the grenade and flung it as hard as I could into the ditch in front of me and the boss. Fortunately, it did not explode. I turned around and walked away without saying a word or looking at him. It occurred to me only later that he might have picked me as being more knowledgeable in general and more familiar with weapons. What was done was done.

After Mergim was drafted, I got into the habit of taking longer walks before going home. I used side streets and, in tattered work clothes, I felt I attracted little attention. After work I was tired and hungry but I still needed to let my mind roam, if not to explore reality, to seek relief in daydreaming. More often than not, I returned to the past. I had one or two vague memories of my years as a toddler in Yugoslavia. I remembered my childhood in Austria quite clearly. In Austria we had moved quite often. We spent a year or two in Vienna and I remembered some episodes at home and at the Montessori kindergarten. In Graz, we had moved four times in about eight years and each time I had to change schools. The fifth time we moved to Italy and I had to change country, schools, and learn a foreign language in a matter of months. In Italy, I learned the importance of assessing events according to perspective. General Radetzky, the conqueror of Milan and northern Italy, was a hero in Austrian schoolbooks but a hated invader in Italy. Memories of events during my years in Italy from the seventh grade on felt as if they had taken place but yesterday.

Each country had offered a different ambiance. The way I learned how to shake hands and bow in Austria provoked hilarity in Italy. Whatever behavioral patterns I adopted in Italy branded me as someone mimicking foreigners in Albania. No matter where I found myself, I was the outsider, the stranger, even if I spoke the language flawlessly and without a foreign accent. Even in Albania, I was the outsider in my land of birth, even before the communist takeover. I had no roots here, no childhood friends, no schoolmates. I was accepted by my peers but I remained different from everyone else. I had left my best friends behind in Italy and had little hope of ever seeing them again. I had no illusions. Even if I escaped and made it somehow to Italy, long years had gone by and no friendships, no relationships would be the same as before.

During these walks, when I daydreamed of escaping into the mountains, I never, ever was able to see myself crossing the border into Yugoslavia. For years after my arrival in the United States, I had a recurrent dream of escaping to Yugoslavia. In my dreams, I saw the same mountains and passes that would eventually carry me to Yugoslavia. Initially these obstacles were formidable, but I would conquer them. Then my flight across the border got increasingly easier. After about 10 years in the United States, all I had to do in my dream was enter a large tunnel that started near where we lived in Shkodra when the Albanian guard was not looking. The tunnel was short and a minute or two later I was in Yugoslavia. I would walk to the Yugoslav border post, identify myself as an American, and ask that the U.S. consulate be notified of my arrival. I had finally arrived; no more nightmares in Detroit, no more having to defend myself from communist troops in pursuit, no awakening bathed in sweat and with my fists skinned from hitting the wall trying to defend myself from my pursuers. About 13 years had to pass—and much water had to flow over the dam—before I did rid my subconscious of the fear the communists had burned into my soul.

There is a saying that the night is darkest just before dawn. Some subtle forces were shifting in my life without my being aware of it. The communists had tried to hurt me in a number of ways. First they had arrested me on the day they conquered Tirana and kept me imprisoned for 13 months to the day. Without the time I spent in jail, I would have never met Albania's past leaders, men I had known by name but now had a chance to see from a close distance—without the artificial glitter of office and power that would have obscured the picture.

The communists transferred me to Dukagjin, one of the poorest and most neglected areas of the Albanian mountain regions. Here I met the simple, brave, and strong people that had fought and defended the good name of Albania during the centuries of Turkish occupation. I broke bread with them when it was available, shared their difficult lives, and sometimes was able to help them in case of injury or illness. Without my stay in Dukagjin, I would have never made contact with our mountain people and would not have had an opportunity to make valuable friends.

Finally, the communist regime had me work as a laborer for a while. This hardened me physically in preparation for my escape. The regime had even provided me with sandals for my escape. How considerate of them!

Now I was prepared and ready for what was to come. The wheels started turning in the direction I had sought for years. October 6th was getting close, only I did not realize what was about to happen.

CHAPTER TWENTY-FIVE

I MEET THE INFILTRATORS

As the reader may recall from Chapters One and Two, Mergim and I had failed in our escape attempt in 1951. Our home had been put under quarantine for a case of typhus among the owner's family and we had lost our liaison with the group of infiltrators that was to pick us up. Mergim had been drafted in 1951 but one year later, thanks to Peter, I had met with the man who would take me to his home in the mountains. I had said goodbye to strong, loving Mom, and then I had left Shkodra with a great sense of relief. We had walked as far as the Cukal Mountain where we slept a few hours. The following day we walked most of the day and made it to Kola Murreci's as darkness was approaching. I had spent the night on some barrels, fighting with cows that were tugging and pulling to get a hold of cornstalks that lay on top of the barrels. From then on I would sleep in more comfortable quarters. At least that's what Kola promised.

OCTOBER 12, 1952

At dusk, Kola Murreci led the cows back into his stable.

"Let me check whether my cousin is gone and everything is under control. It shouldn't take me long. I'll be back and we will have dinner."

I knew that Kola's use of words such as "soon," "promptly," or any such expressions did not relate to a time span. I remembered the incident with the widow. Hence, I stayed on my perch. The cows did not seem to mind nor did they give any sign of resenting me. Perhaps they had seen other escapees in their stable before and had become blasé about such a presence.

Eventually Kola showed up. The coast was clear. We walked from the stable past a baking oven through an anteroom facing the main entrance and into a room with a fireplace against the farthest wall. The room was simply furnished. There were a few three-legged stools, a heavy wood chest with a lid and lock, and a round, low table propped up against a wall. There were two kerosene lamps and little else in the room.

Then there were Kola's wife and his two children, a boy and a girl, both under 10 years old. Kola introduced me to his children. He told everyone that I was a physician who had come from Shkodra to examine their mother who had been ill. First we would eat.

Kola's wife rolled the table toward the middle of the room. The children sat down cross-legged, and Kola and I sat on little stools. His wife put a steaming bowl of bean soup before us and gave us spoons. Then she removed hot embers and ashes from a round metal top that covered an earthen dish in the fireplace. She flipped the dish over a board and a large, round loaf of cornbread, crisp and steaming hot, came off the earthen dish. Before cutting the bread, with her knife she marked three signs of the cross on the loaf and proceeded to give each of us a hefty chunk of bread.

Meanwhile, her husband cut off and placed before us generous slices of boiled pork and lard. An old tin can with a handle attached with solder served as a water pitcher. The water was from a nearby spring, ice cold and delicious. There was little conversation around the table while everyone concentrated on the food. The obvious delight with which the children attacked the meal was a clear sign that this was not their daily fare. While they ate, they also kept their eyes on me. I was wearing clothes such as they had never seen before. I spoke a funny kind of Albanian. Perhaps this was the first time they had ever heard the Tosk dialect. In their young minds, they may have thought that physicians wore such clothes and spoke this way.

We finished our meal and Kola's wife rolled the table away and used a little hand broom made of thin twigs to remove whatever food remnants had fallen on the floor. Her little daughter helped her while the boy sat with his father and me. Men, even little ones, had their privileges.

During the meal the mother had seen to it that everyone was taken care of. She started eating last and finished before the rest of us. Now I had to earn my meal and this was her moment of glory. She finally had a chance to speak about her aches and pains to a man, to a physician. He would pay close attention to what she was saying, would interpret it scientifically, and would give her prescriptions. The latter would wind up in the large chest with other prescriptions that other physicians had given her in years past. From time to time, men and women went to see a doctor. They were poor folk, however, and could not afford to pay for the prescriptions. Kola's wife knew the routine but this did not deter her in the least. She mentioned how her knees and elbows ached, particularly in the morning and when the weather was bad. She mentioned that sometimes she suffered from heartburn and that her back hurt, particularly when she carried heavy loads.

My heart went out to her. What she told me, and what I had heard from other women in our mountains, was simply a tale of women getting up before dusk to prepare breakfast and get everyone going. Then they toiled until late, until after everyone else had settled down for the night. In between, they cooked, worked in the fields, tended the animals, did the laundry, cut and sewed shirts and underwear, and did a hundred other things. When pregnant, they worked in the fields until the very last moment. Then they disappeared behind the bushes and, with the help of other women, gave birth, secured the newborn in clean wrappings, and went back to work in the field. They got married young, moved into the husband's home where they had one year to learn the ways of their new mothers-in-law. After a few years they grew prematurely old with very few privileges granted because of old age. That was the fate of women and they were resigned to it.

Having heard her story, I asked her to remove her jacket and with the rest of her clothes on, I probed her elbows and knees, poked around the abdomen, listened to her heart and respiration, checked her pulse, and went through the motions. After all, even though I was not a physician, I had been the "doctor of Dukagjin" and had to uphold my reputation. Besides, the better the impression I made, the better my chances of getting some respect from the people around me, despite my dependence and helplessness. While this was going on, the children stared at me with big round eyes, with an expression somewhere between curiosity and awe. Kola leaned back on his stool with his back against the wall, smoking a cigarette he had rolled himself, and never showing anything that might have been going through his mind.

Once I wrote the prescriptions, antedating them to a period when I might have seen the patient in some village our health team had visited, the evening was over. The kids left the room and Kola motioned that I follow him. We backtracked to the stable but now things changed. I was no longer to sleep atop the barrels. Instead, Kola removed some medium size rocks from a spot just above the straw on the floor. A hole large enough for me to crawl through appeared. Kola told me to slide in, feet first. He then replaced the rocks and I heard him say, "Good night."

The hole I found myself in was about seven feet long and was high enough for me to turn freely and even to rise on my elbows but not enough for me to sit up. There was fresh straw for me to lie on. The air was relatively fresh, certainly not stale, as I had feared initially. I could not make out where the fresh air came from. It made no sense to investigate my "refuge" any further because of the darkness all around me. Besides, the silence and the darkness were getting the better of me. I said my prayers and fell immediately asleep. When I woke up some hours later, it was morning and Kola was letting the cattle out of the stable.

The next few days ran into one another. Kola removed the rocks early in the morning and I crawled out, washed up a bit, and did whatever else needed doing. After breakfast I crawled back into the "tomb." In the evening, after the kids had gone to sleep, Kola led me to the family room and we shared dinner. After some time spent talking with Kola and his wife, he would lead me back to the stable and I would crawl back into my hiding place. At one point Kola told me that he had built it when he had first built his house. One never knew when such a hiding place would come in handy, considering the many troubles our mountains had suffered from; people would hide from the government, there were blood feuds, sometimes there was a need to hide papers or weapons, and one could always find use for such a hiding place. Now, with a communist government in place and incursions by the security forces, he was very happy to have had the foresight to build the "tomb.. Because of the size of the oven, they could bake bread and even entire lambs indoors. The combination of oven and hiding place was an ideal combination.

One day I noticed an opening about ten inches long and an inch or so high at the distal end of the "tomb" where I could see light. It was coming from near the bottom of the oven. It was through that opening that air entered the tomb. Now I worried that if Kola's wife had to use the oven, the temperature underneath might become unbearable. There was no sense worrying about it now. If the time came, I would find out.

One evening, after I had finished eating, Kola told me that the infiltrators would be here on Friday. Since I had come to Kola's house, the burning question on my mind was the one I could not ask directly, the one he had just answered. I had been out of Shkodra for almost a week. I had told Mom I would be in Yugoslavia in two weeks and nothing had moved yet. When Kola mentioned Friday, I made a quick calculation. The upcoming Friday was October 17. Friday the 17th was considered bad luck. To heck with it; if Friday the 17th would break the impasse of my being stuck in Albania, so be it.

When Kola gave me the news, I tried not to show any emotion. In the Albanian mountains, for a man to show his feelings was unbecoming. Inside, however, I was aglow. That night I crawled into my hole with my mind in high gear. Eventually I got tired. There was no way I could anticipate what the next few days would bring. It was time to go to sleep and that was all for the moment. I said my nightly Our Father and Hail Mary, prayed that God would protect the infiltrators, and fell asleep.

OCTOBER 16, 1952

In the morning, Kola's wife came to the stable, removed the rocks to the entrance of my hiding place, and asked me to give her my laundry. I was happy she thought of it because tomorrow I would meet the infiltrators and once we were on our way, who knows when I would have another chance to have my laundry done. I went through a few contortions, removed my jacket and pants in my hideout, and handed her the laundry. I crawled back into my outer garments and started daydreaming again, trying to imagine my meeting the infiltrators. I had failed so many times in my attempts to contact such groups. Would this time be different?

Slowly, sometime during the day, I began worrying. My shirt and undergarments were those of city dwellers. I hoped and prayed that she would have sense enough not to put my laundry to dry outdoors where someone could see and recognize it for what it was. I had no way of talking to the woman and had no choice but to wait and ask her in the evening when I saw her again. At dusk, when she brought my laundry back, I asked her where she had dried it. As I had feared, she had dried it outdoors. I told her I was worried sick that someone might have seen it and informed the police. She wasn't worried at all. She was sure no one had noticed and there was no need for me to worry about such things. By now, what was done was done. It did not make any sense to worry about things I could not change. The rest of the evening went by and nothing bad happened. We ate our evening meal and Kola and the rest of us called it a day.

When I went out that night to relieve myself everything seemed so peaceful, so removed from everything I was used to, both good and bad. No city crowds to get lost among, but also no nosy neighbors, no informers breathing down my neck. I had no radio, no BBC newscast, no Voice of America, no connection with the world of the living, no voice of hope. But also no anxiety whether the lights would stay on past midnight, a sure sign that arrests were planned for that night in Shkodra.

Here in the mountains the chances of being arrested were slim. It would take someone—either Kola, his wife, or someone who accidentally saw me or my laundry—to betray me to the police. Here there were no omnipresent signs of communism or of communist authorities. While I was far from being safe, this was the safest I had felt in a long time.

As I stepped outside, the cool night was all around me. I was immersed in the smells of the woods, the soothing rustling of the wind among the leaves, and the calm light of distant stars. In Shkodra, even the stars had seemed, if not hostile, at least indifferent to our fate. Here their calm light seemed to say, "Don't worry, we are here. We can see what's happening to you. All of this will pass. Everything will be all right... one day." Could one believe the stars?

My daily routine had also changed drastically from when I had last worked in Shkodra. I was no longer going to work with pick and shovel under the watchful eyes of communist informers. In many respects, living in Kola's dugout under the oven was cozy and peaceful. Of course, I missed home and particularly Mom. For a few years now Dad had no longer been physically in the picture except in our thoughts as a helpless shadow and a source of constant worry. Mergim was in forced labor in the military. Our family nucleus had been reduced to Mom and me.

Life with Mom, however, was also sad. Her garb was no longer that of a sophisticated lady. Her hands were chapped and her face worn. She had to make do with what I brought home. There were days when we had food and others when there was none. All she could do to heat water for me after a hard day's work was to warm it in the sun. She would do the best she could to put before me food that was both nourishing and tasty, which was difficult much of the time. Mom was not entitled to ration cards of her own. Instead, she would buy our daily bread with my coupons and a handful of coins. Even though the ration cards entitled me to a few eggs a month, we never saw any eggs. There was little meat and no fish to speak of.

Here in the mountains, under the starry skies, many thoughts would assail me. The immediate, of course, was always uppermost in my mind. My past lay behind me and my future was uncertain. In fact, I may run out of time that very night, or perhaps before dawn tomorrow. No one could know for sure.

On that particular night, the night of October 16, I was safe. Nothing had happened so far. No one had seen my laundry, or if someone had, he or she had not bothered to report it to the police. Tomorrow would come, and with a little bit of luck I would still be alive. Tomorrow was the day I had waited for, had lived for, planned and schemed for, going back almost ten years. Tomorrow I would meet the infiltrators. Maybe Friday, October 17, 1952 would be my lucky day.

OCTOBER 17, 1952

I don't remember much about that particular day. All day I looked forward to nightfall. I knew when it got dark because I could no longer see the little slit in the wall above my feet. I felt my tension mounting. Would they come tonight? How many men in the group and what would they look like? What would they wear and what weapons would they carry? Would I be able to trust them? How bright, enlightened, or honest would they be in things political? Did they have any contact or cooperation with the West? Above all, would they be loyal servants of the Yugoslavs or of the Albanian cause? Many questions swirled through my head throughout that Friday.

Strangely enough, such questions did not reach as deep or as far into my mind as their importance might have suggested. Meeting the infiltrators was something that still had to happen. Nine past attempts had ended in failure. I could not pin all my hopes on the upcoming meeting before it actually came about. Instead I held back, waiting for darkness, hoping, but without fully committing myself, in anticipation of what that night might bring.

About 10:00 p.m., I heard voices, male voices. Obviously I had not expected to hear a bell or a knock at the door. Were these the voices of "my comrades" as Kola had called them in previous conversations with me?

Then the voices ceased. Time passed and I lay rather passive in my cubbyhole. I lay as in an artificial womb, waiting for others to decide whether I would be allowed to come out and live or whether the visitors had rejected me and I would have to be destroyed because I knew too much.

Finally I heard steps. It was Kola.

"Come out. It is time for you to meet your comrades."

I crawled out, straightened up, and smoothed my clothes, such as they were. Kola walked ahead of me, bobbing up and down with that curious gait of his. Like in a dream, I followed him through the dark kitchen, the hallway, and passed the stairs leading to the attic. When he opened the door to the family room, the light blinded me for a moment, not because it was so bright but because I had been in total darkness for so many hours.

There they were, three of them, wearing the uniforms of the Albanian Sigurimi, from their caps down to their sandals, except they had no red star on their caps. Even their rifles were German Mauser rifles, just like those of Sigurimi. The shortest of the three seemed to be the leader. He was about 5 feet 6 inches tall, thin, sinewy, with piercing, dark eyes. He had an air of authority about him despite his short stature. The other two stood somewhat behind him. One was about 6 feet tall, round faced and with broad shoulders. He seemed cool and detached, not one to trifle with. The other was maybe 5 feet 7 inches, friendly, with smiling eyes. He seemed open, someone you could be friends with.

"So you want to come with us to Yugoslavia," their leader said to me.

I nodded. "Yes, if you will have me." And before I knew it, I blurted out, "It is good to see that Albania still has daring sons."

I said it to no one in particular, and as soon as I said it, I regretted it. I did not want to sound maudlin or ingratiating. I had not rehearsed these words. They rose to my lips because of the turmoil within me. Here were men who took their lives in their hands and crossed into the hell of the People's Republic of Albania. Once they had been in danger like the rest of us but were able to reach safety. Next they had taken up arms and had come back to challenge the communists in their own lair. If they were caught, they could expect the worst. I shuddered.

The leader addressed me once more.

"I am Hila Shllaku and these men with me are Deda Mëhilli and Peter Qafa. We know who you are." We shook hands.

The fact that he introduced himself and his friends was a good sign. Then Hila turned away and spoke to Kola. I did not hear what he was saying. I was too busy looking these men over. So, that's what infiltrators looked like. To me they looked taller than life. They were courage personified. It was exhilarating to see armed anti-communists. In Albania firearms were the symbol of manhood. In communist Albania, only communists carried firearms. Here was tangible proof that it did not have to be that way.

Hila's companions were looking at me, Deda expressionless, Peter with a twinkle in his eyes. I chose to address the latter.

"Peter," I said, "I want to ask a big favor of you. If we are ever surrounded, I want your word of honor that you will shoot me before you kill yourself."

Peter's expression became inquisitive. "Do you have a weapon?" he asked. "No?"

Before I knew what he was doing, he pulled his revolver out of his belt and handed it to me. He reached into his pocket and gave me a hand grenade. It was an Italian aluminum hand grenade intended to make lots of smoke and noise and to allow the user to escape in the confusion. It was of limited use in combat. The revolver was something else. It was a Nagant, originally made in Belgium. It was a beautiful weapon, well designed and balanced. Because of its reliability, it was the favorite gun of political assassins. Under the circumstances, it was also the best guarantee that the communists would not catch me alive. Now it could be mine, all mine, to hold and to use.

"Peter, I cannot accept it. You must not endanger your safety because of me." What I meant was, "You must not risk falling alive into the hands of the communists and without your revolver—that is more likely to happen."

He knew exactly what I meant. His dark eyebrows went up and again that friendly smile.

"Keep it, and don't worry."

I felt warm all over. In my need, I had found a friend. The fear of being caught alive had been with me for many years and had just begun to lift. I tucked the gun under my belt. Now I could behave like a man, as Mom had told me. I could fight and I could take my life to avoid capture. I had lost her knife but now I had a gun! If there ever was a cloud nine, I was riding it.

Years later, in Detroit, I asked Peter why he had given me his handgun.

"I could see the anxious expression in your eyes. It was obvious that you had suffered much. So I decided, instead of me taking your life, I would give you my gun and let you do it yourself."

Because of the late hour, Hila rose and asked us to get ready to leave. There were no farewells. I had packed my knapsack and strapped it to my back. The others picked up their military gear without a word. We fell in line, with Kola heading our column. We exited through the front door as the fresh, invigorating night air gave us a pleasant jolt. We were finally on our way. Then, after a few steps, Kola turned and reentered his home through a side door. Without uttering a sound, he pointed to a staircase. We climbed the steps into the attic, and settled down for the night. I did not quite understand whom we were supposed to fool as Kola's children were standing in a corner of the doorway when we started climbing up the stairs to the attic.

The three infiltrators went to sleep, and began to snore immediately. It did not make much sense. No one was standing guard nor did they take any other precautions, as far as I could tell. I was afraid that if a patrol heard loud snoring coming from the attic, they might get suspicious. Since I couldn't fall asleep, I watched them, and when the snoring got too loud I would shake the culprit until he stopped. As no one objected, it must have been OK.

OCTOBER 18

Eventually I must have fallen asleep, because when I woke up it was daylight. My companions were still there, still sleeping. I felt great. The group had accepted me and I was on my way. Of course, I did not know any details yet, but it would all come in good time. While the three infiltrators were sleeping, I needed to take care of something. I reached into my knapsack and pulled out a roll of gauze bandage. I measured a piece long enough to form a loop from my belt around my neck and back to my belt. Then I ripped it off. I tied both ends of the bandage to the ring at the bottom of the Nagant grip. Then I slipped the loop over my head. Now, in case I fell or were wounded, the revolver could not get beyond my reach. Having done that, I settled back satisfied. Then I must have fallen asleep again.

The next thing I knew, it was light and my companions began to stir. Kola came up the steps and brought us water to wash up and some breakfast. Both morning ablution and breakfast were rather modest. Speaking for myself, I had all I needed.

My companions bid me "Good morning" and then began to chat with each other. They spoke of people and places that were unknown to me. Sometimes they even used words I did not understand, such as "*voz*" and "*granica.*" It did not take me long to find out that "*voz*" meant train and "*granica*" meant border. Any direct questions on my part, however, would have to wait until we were more at ease with each other.

That afternoon, Hila started to ask me questions about various people in Shkodra, people I was likely to know. I answered his questions to the best of my knowledge. I did so until he asked me about a young girl, the niece of a nurse who worked at the maternity clinic.

"Do you know this girl?"

"I know of her, I know her by sight, but I have never spoken to her."

"What can you tell me about her?"

"As far as I know, she is a good person. She works at the post office and is well behaved. I haven't heard anything untoward about her," I replied.

What I said was true, as far as it went. The young girl was in love with an officer of Sigurimi. I did not feel it behooved me to pass on gossip or to blacken her reputation because the poor girl had fallen in love with the wrong person.

Hila looked satisfied and seemed to have run out of questions, at least for the moment. I felt it was now my turn.

"If you don't mind, I would like to ask you some questions," I began. Hila nodded.

"You have been kind enough to accept me as part of your group, even though you know little about me. Can you tell me, how did you decide to take me with you to Yugoslavia?"

The sun was shining into the attic through a skylight. The air was warm and pleasant. The three infiltrators sat in a semicircle facing me, their weapons leaning against the wall. I could feel the reassuring pressure of the Nagant tucked under my belt. I felt in good company and Kola's attic felt like the safest place in all of Albania. Even before Hila answered my question, I felt that I had been accepted.

Hila looked at me with penetrating eyes.

"Actually we know more about you than you may suspect. Obviously, we questioned Peter Kola about you. We also asked others. In fact, I will let you see a written report we received about you just the other day. Any ideas who may have written it?"

He reached in his military satchel and pulled out a letter from among a batch of pieces of paper. I looked at the note in his hand. "May I?"

Hila handed me the note. The brief message read something like this: "The individual you asked about can be trusted to do what's right. I have no qualms recommending him." It was signed "Reja," meaning "the cloud."

The handwriting kept my eyes riveted to the text. I had seen that handwriting before. In fact, I was sure I had seen it more than once. It took me a moment or two, and then it hit me. It was the handwriting of a male nurse who had worked for me in the Albanian public health service in Shkodra. I used to receive monthly reports from about 30 nurses working in the Shkodra province. That's where I had seen the handwriting.

I looked at Hila and blurted out the man's name. Hila just nodded, enjoying the surprised look on my face. I did not know what to think. The man who had written the note was in his late twenties, of narrow build, quite tall and skinny. He had a triangular face with large chewing muscles at both corners of the jaw that seemed in perpetual motion, and almost no chin. He was clean shaven but that was the only clean thing about him. He had a body odor more like a stench. His limbs were long and thin ending in huge hands and feet. Whenever he was near me, I hoped he would keep his arms and legs together. I could not take the odor more than was absolutely necessary. He was also a candidate member of the communist party. He perhaps sensed my personal revulsion whenever he was near me but seemed eager to please me and to win my approval. His was the curlicued handwriting and his signature ending with an upward flourish; like miasma rising from a pile of manure. To think that he had held my fate in his hands, if only for a brief moment! This was perhaps his way of showing me that I should have trusted him instead of loathing him. I shuddered. Fortunately nobody seemed to notice.

I wondered whether I should take this opportunity and ask some more questions that were crowding my mind, but we heard steps coming up the ladder leading to the attic. The trap door opened. Kola stuck his head in and greeted us in his usual unhurried way. While we answered politely, he exchanged a brief glance with Hila. The latter rose to his feet, stretched lazily, and mumbled something about going downstairs. His unhurried movements spoke volumes. He seemed to say that he respected Kola and that the latter had a right to call on him. Hila, however, was the more important of the two, hence his slow response to Kola's unspoken invitation. Furthermore, Hila belonged to those people who mumble when they want to underscore a particularly important point. It was obvious from the way he said it that the three of us were supposed to stay where we were. Then, without looking to see whether anyone was following him, he lowered himself through the trap door and disappeared.

Peter and Deda looked at each other and agreed, without saying a word. They seemed able to converse by just looking at each other, like some married couples after many years of marriage, or partners who have survived many a peril. Then Deda spoke to me.

"You did well to protect the young girl Hila asked you about. She is his daughter."

Deda's voice was even and measured, his words were incisive. He gave the impression of someone stingy with words. Now I had a chance to look at him. He had brown wavy hair, a round face, and a short nose. His skimpy mustache barely covered his upturned upper lip. When he smiled he bared a set of small uneven teeth. He was tall and powerfully built. In addition, he gave the impression of quiet strength. He could be a loyal friend or an unforgiving foe. Either way, you would not expect him to rush you either in friendship or conflict but once his mind was made up... I definitely thought it was better to have him as a friend.

Peter seemed less complicated. He appeared now in daylight just as I had seen him the night before. He too had a mustache. It was black, just like his beard.

"Genc," he said, "you couldn't know that Angje, the nurse at the maternity clinic, is Hila's sister-in-law. You were careful and that's good. You will fit in well with our group. I am not worried about you." He tilted his head and gave me a broad smile. I had noticed before, when Peter spoke heart-to-heart, he would tilt his head.

I thought this was a good opportunity to query the two men while Hila was not with us. "Tell me," I said looking at Peter, "when are we planning to cross the border?"

Peter replied, "First, Hila has some business to take care of with members of our network. Then we will cross the Drini River; actually we will cross it twice. And finally, we will cross the border. So, after all is said and done, we should be able to cross the border in about two weeks."

That was good news. After all, I had told Mom that I would cross the border in about two weeks and she would hear from me soon thereafter.

"Why do we need to cross the Drini twice?" I asked Peter.

"Because the river forms a "Y" here where we are. Hence, we have no choice but to cross it twice."

"Would we have to travel too far to get to where we would have to cross it only once?"

"Yes, that would not be practical."

I felt embarrassed that I knew so little about Albanian geography, about the land and its rivers. I could not help it if I had never attended Albanian schools. I should have learned more about my native country, however, if only in preparation for my escape. I had to admit, if only to myself, that the thought had never crossed my mind. On the other hand, there was no such thing as buying an Albanian map in a store. First, because such maps were not available, and second, even if that had been possible, no one in his right mind would have dared buy one lest he arouse the suspicion of the authorities. Why would anybody want to buy a map unless he wanted to escape?

"Is the network going to feed us for the next two weeks? After all, people have a tough time feeding themselves and their families."

"Don't worry," Peter replied, "we have brought enough money for all of us. We will pay wherever we stay. Ours is a brave and dedicated network. People risk much when meeting with us or offering us shelter. You understand that. On the other hand, they want to contribute to the liberation of our fatherland and everyone is doing their share."

I was impressed. I knew what the communists did to those who opposed them. The present rulers of Albania were exceedingly cruel. Their frenzy and fury knew no bounds when dealing with those who dared oppose them. After all, should the communists lose their foothold, they knew what to expect. That thought was too horrible to contemplate for them. Who could blame them, for what they had sowed, they would reap.

The thoughts that kept crossing my mind replayed moments of insult, callousness, stupidity, and cruelty, all at our expense, all perpetrated by the communists. If they caught us, we knew what to expect. If we made it, who knows what life held for us. One thing was for sure: The communists could never claim they loved Albania, or that they had ruled with mercy or concern for human welfare.

The trap door creaked open. Hila was back. "Get ready. We will eat a bite and then we'll leave."

We started to pack. In my case, there was not much to pack. I folded my blanket and put it in my knapsack. Then I sat down and watched my new friends. Moments later, Kola emerged from the trap door. He had some cornbread, feta cheese, and onions with him, and of course, a bottle of home-brewed whiskey. We sat down and got ready to eat. There were the time-honored rituals. The host raised his glass first.

"Blessed be Christ."

"For ever and ever," we replied.

"You are welcome in the name of the Lord."

Everybody raised his glass and partook of the whiskey. At this point we broke bread and started to eat. It was a simple meal. We were done in a hurry.

"Let's go."

Kola went down the ladder first, followed by Hila, Deda, Peter, and me. We were finally on our way. Silently we filed out of the house. I had strange feelings, as if I were leaving home for the second time. Now there was no turning back. Soon, Kola would leave us and the four of us would strike out toward Yugoslavia.

Well, not quite. Kola did not leave us immediately. As it turned out, that night we visited Kola's cousin. More than a visit, it was a ritualistic expression of trust and confidence intended to show the two men and the rest of the network that the infiltrators had complete trust in Kola and his cousin. It was like slowing down under conditions of imminent danger. It was the Albanian equivalent of partaking of Japanese balloon fish whose flesh is deadly if the gall bladder is punctured inadvertently. It was like toying with death. It was another expression of the chilling rites of manhood. In fact, nothing of consequence happened during the visit. Everyone had some whiskey with some bread and cheese. The conversation was rather lame. Once the visit had lasted long enough to satisfy the rules of the game, Hila gave the signal and we rose promptly. We shook hands all around, mouthed the usual pleasantries, and exited. It was about time!

Now we were finally alone. Deda went to the head of our column followed by Hila and me. Peter was last. The night was dark and I could barely see where I was placing my feet. We seemed to be moving toward the sound of flowing water. Within minutes, we reached a gorge that looked rather threatening. The walls were of stone, black and slippery in the dark of night. In fact, when we reached the bottom of the gorge, I stepped on a wet stone and fell heavily, fortunately without hurting myself too badly. My three companions reacted each in his way. Deda turned around and looked down at me without expression. Hila cussed and hissed at me that I should be more careful. Peter rushed forward and helped me up. Henceforth I knew what to expect.

I wiped myself off and we continued our march. We did not go much further. We had reached Gjoke Vokrri's creek, as planned. Soon we settled down for the night, a very cold night. Besides the chill of the night, the mist rising from the creek seemed to carry off any heat our bodies might generate. There were no ferns or twigs we could gather and lie on. Instead we settled among the stones, covered ourselves as well as we could, and closed our eyes. Again we posted no guards or took other precautions. Recalling Hila's reaction to my fall, I did not think that I should volunteer any advice. It was best not to cross him unless absolutely necessary.

CHAPTER TWENTY-SIX

TOWARD THE BORDER

OCTOBER 19, 1952

We awoke at dawn, cold, stiff, and sore. At least we did not have to go too far for water; a modest ablution, a skimpy breakfast. Then we sat along the creek, seemingly without purpose. Time passed slowly and for me that was hard to take. If I only knew why we were sitting there, taking a chance of being discovered while accomplishing nothing useful. It irked me just to sit there when we could have moved purposefully toward Yugoslavia. What I did not know, and would not be told as a matter of conscious decision, was that we were expecting visitors. What I had first learned during my stay in Dukagjin I had to relearn now. Time in the mountains was always relative: "I'll see you tomorrow at your house," or "Wait for me at Gjoke Vokrri's creek." All four of us carried watches but a watch in the mountains served a different purpose than in town. First, a watch was a sign of affluence and of intellectual importance. Something like reading glasses for a semi-literate among illiterates. Expensive watches accurate to a minute or so per week served no purpose and carried no special distinction. A watch could tell the bearer that there were so many hours to dusk or to dawn, the second being the more important function. After all, the height of the sun above the horizon gave a good indication of the hours until nightfall. Daybreak could also make a big difference as far as starting to move or seeking shelter. Some people could anticipate daybreak by the stars but the skies were often overcast and that's when a watch was important.

I was jerked out of my reveries when I suddenly saw three men half slithering, half stepping down the path toward us. They were Prenk Gjoka and his two nephews. Hila and his companions rose and embraced the visitors. I of course stood up but held back as I did not really belong. After a cryptic introduction, I shook hands with the three men. Hila, obviously, had not yet found a comfortable way of introducing me to members of his network. Personally, I had to admire the self-control mountaineers displayed when they met a stranger like me at a gathering with infiltrators. I had the distinct impression I was witnessing the human species displaying the memory of centuries of persecution, of secret meetings, and of underground resistance.

After the usual pleasantries, the conversation seemed to run out of steam. I wondered. How many more people in the area knew where to find us? Such thoughts made me shiver. Besides, the chill and the moisture of the air did nothing to make me feel better, even in full daylight.

At midmorning, Hila gave the sign for our departure. Prenk and his nephews led the way as we marched—in full view of anyone who happened to be there—toward the village of Kisha. As it was reasonable to assume that none of the men present were raring for an encounter with Sigurimi, I had to conclude that we were marching through safe territory. For the moment at least, that was a comforting thought. We reached the village around noon and, under the friendly gaze of women and children, entered the house of Kola Marashi. All I had ever known about security and self-protection had fallen by the wayside these last few days. I knew it did not behoove me to say or do anything. I had to assume that my guides knew what they were doing. When in Rome, I decided, I would do as the Romans did.

A few days later, we heard that a woman had seen us at the creek and had informed the lieutenant in charge of the local police. He had first told her that those were his men, and after she threatened to inform the captain in the nearest town, had promised to send a patrol to investigate. He then had divulged the contents of this conversation to make sure that we heard about it in time. We had left when the patrol came and no one was hurt. The lieutenant obviously had preferred being a lowly but live lieutenant rather than a dead hero.

That day we ate well. Hila paid for a lamb and we had meat at lunch and supper. We also had the usual feta cheese, onions cut into eighths, pickles, and lots of warm cornbread. Besides, that wonderful water from nearby mountain springs! Who could ask for more?

In the afternoon, another member of the underground, a certain Deda Vuksani, came to meet with Hila and company. Most of the conversation took place in my presence. Whenever issues regarding the network or their political mission came up, Hila and the visitor(s) moved away to discuss the matter by themselves. Most of the time, Deda and Peter stayed with me. Occasionally they took part in the secret conversation.

After nightfall we rose to leave the house. We packed, shook hands all around, fell in line, and marched out the front door. After a few steps, we turned around and re-entered the house through a side entrance. I am sure that such moves made sense as they were intended to hide our continued presence from someone, even if it was not always clear to me as to who was being fooled. We re-entered Kola Marashi's house and climbed into the attic.

As attics go, this was different from Kol Murreci's. The beams, those supporting the roof and those on the floor, were more irregular and only part of the attic had a floor of wooden slats. The rest of the beams were exposed. The rooms underneath had sturdy ceilings and one would not fall through. Nonetheless, if one stepped between the beams one could twist or break a leg, or at least skin a shin. The many years and the smoke had blackened stones and mortar in the walls, particularly over the fireplace. In fact, one could see the smoke seeping through the floor when the fire was lit. Thus, either the chimney leaked or the wind pushed the smoke down through the chimney and into the room, or both. The next morning I also noticed that the attic was dark even during the day because tall trees surrounding the house blocked the small windows at both ends. Obviously, compared to Kola's, this was an older home. Besides, home-building methods may have improved over the years—even in the Albanian mountains. Could cost also have been a factor?

OCTOBER 20, 1952

That day Gjon Zef Bajraktari came to see us. It became immediately obvious that he was an important visitor, more important than anyone we had met so far. When he entered the house, Hila and his cohorts did not just rise, but jumped to their feet as the visitor approached them. There was respect in the way they stood and respect in their smiles as they gazed at the visitor. Perhaps Gjon Zef belonged to an important family. His last name, Bajraktari, meant flag bearer or standard bearer, a function traditionally reserved for the most distinguished family of a region and to its male offspring, generation after generation.

Judging by his looks, the man was in his fifties. He had broad shoulders and strong hands. What I remember most about him was his aura of self-assuredness. Hila stepped toward him and kissed him on both cheeks while shaking his hand with unusual vigor.

"How are you holding up? How are you? How long has it been since we last met?"

The questions tumbled from his lips. They seemed to express genuine pleasure as he fired them off without waiting for a reply. Were his feelings genuine or was he playing politics?

"I am fine. How are you, and how are your companions?" Gjon Zef Bajraktari replied unhurried, looking straight at Hila.

The men chatted a few more minutes, mostly about people I did not know. Deda and Peter listened attentively, without interrupting. The conversation ebbed and flowed without effort as Gjon Zef Bajraktari and Hila showed obvious respect for each other. I don't recall whether they withdrew into a corner to discuss more delicate matters but I do recall one detail that set this visit apart. Toward the end, Hila stopped, collected his thoughts, and said in an official tone of voice:

"Gjon Zef Bajraktari, the Yugoslav authorities fully recognize the importance of your family, of its historic role during Albania's long fight for freedom, and of the contributions you personally have made and are making in the fight against the communist regime. Everyone in Yugoslavia is well aware of your acts of valor, from the men at the very top to the humblest refugee. And these very same Yugoslav authorities have asked me to bring you a sign of their respect and support for your activities and for those your family members are carrying out under your direction."

Hila turned around and dug into his knapsack. When his right hand reappeared it held a shiny Colt revolver which he handed to Gjon Zef Bajraktari with due solemnity. Next he handed him what looked like an ammunition box. Finally, he dipped his hand once more into the knapsack and came out with a bundle of money. He handed Zef Gjon Bajraktari 1,000 lek, and the little ceremony was over.

The gift of money was an interesting twist. Albanians were usually too proud to accept money. The struggle, however, cost money and 1,000 lek was quite a bit of money, particularly in our mountains. On the other hand, there was no need to explain or emphasize the symbolism of the revolver. One had to give credit to the Yugoslavs. They were experts in Albanian psychology, particularly the mores and feelings of our mountain folks. No wonder Albanians and Slavs had lived side by side, in war and in peace, for centuries. They had traded with each other and, sometimes, intermarried.

As I watched the events unfolding between Hila and Zef Gjon Bajraktari, it was hard to tell what emotions or thoughts crossed the latter's mind when he slipped the revolver under his belt and pocketed the money. I was always impressed how well our mountaineers were able to control their feelings and facial expressions. They were most difficult to read. When they spoke, their words were careful and measured. As I recall, Gjon Zef Bajraktari accepted the gifts with no display of emotion and with a few dignified words. He asked Hila to thank the Yugoslav officials for the esteem in which they held him and for their gifts. He thanked Hila for carrying the revolver from far away into the Albanian mountains. He did not make any special commitments nor did he praise the Yugoslavs or their collaborators.

I for one did not know enough about him and his family to understand the undercurrents of what I was witnessing and to this day I don't know whether Hila's gifts to Gjon Zef Bajraktari were a reward or a bribe. Gjon Zef stood up, bid us farewell, and left. For a while we continued to sense his presence among us. There was little question in anyone's mind. Gjon Zef Bajraktari exuded strength of character and personality.

Instead of sitting down to dinner, Hila gave us the signal for departure. Again, I had no way of knowing whether Deda and Peter, or for that matter our host, knew that we would leave at this point. They kept their composure as if everything were going according to plan—which, by the way, was fine with me. The more things went according to plan, the safer I felt.

Outside it was pitch black. The night was cool, pleasant, with only a slight breeze touching, swaying the treetops. One could smell the moist soil and the wisps of smoke from the handful of fireplaces in the village. It felt good to be moving again. We marched in single file for about 15 to 20 minutes. We stopped on a ridge that was at about the same height as the roof of a house to our right. The house was dark and seemed uninhabited. We took a small footpath down toward the house and stopped facing the building. This approach differed from the routine we had followed when visiting various homes in the last few days. We all froze and listened for manmade noises. I heard nothing. I was told to kneel down and stay down no matter what happened.

Peter and Deda fanned out and crept around the building, listening and trying to peer inside. When they had circled the house, they covered the main entrance near the middle of the building. Hila moved toward the side entrance and knocked. The door squeaked open and a man raised a smoky oil lamp toward Hila's face.

"Are guests welcome?"

It was obvious that neither Hila's face nor his uniform gave the host any clues.

"Please come in."

"Is there anyone else in your house beside you?"

"No, I am alone."

Peter and Deda had closed in on Hila and emerged in the small circle of light.

"Come in, make yourselves at home."

Peter turned and waved for me to join them. We entered the house through the side entrance. The house seemed lower than any I had seen so far. Only the part we were in was inhabited. The rest lay in darkness, covered with a layer of dust, as if no one had set foot there in quite some time.

Our host stood there, ill at ease. He must have been in his forties or maybe a little younger. He was taller than Hila, with dark, fairly long hair and a black mustache. His narrow hunched shoulders made him look vulnerable. He looked at us briefly, without betraying any emotion. It was obvious that the uniforms of the three and my presence did not ring a bell with him. He asked us to be seated and shuffled toward the fireplace where he began to stir the ashes.

"Are you hungry? Let me prepare you something to eat."

If Hila accepted the man's food, it was likely that he did not expect a deadly confrontation. On the other hand, if he declined it could be a tacit admission that we had a base nearby. The tension all around us was thick enough to cut with a knife.

"Thank you, my companions and I carry enough food with us. We don't want to be a burden to the people who have a hard time feeding their own families."

Again there was no clue as to where we hailed from, geographically or politically. Hila was the only one who had spoken. His dialect was that of a Catholic from Shkodra, his uniform that of a member of the state security forces.

Hila continued. "Tell me, do people around here have enough to eat?"

"Some do and some don't. Those who don't go into town and find work there. The pay is not much but they do get ration cards for themselves and their families." The man was choosing his words carefully, tipping neither side of the scale. Obviously he had not yet made up his mind as to who we were.

"Lazer Pali," Hila intoned, mentioning the man's name for the first time, "we know you are the village chief. We know you are a good man who cares for the well-being of his villagers. You behave yourself and do not skin those entrusted to you the way other chiefs do. We know that you try to lighten their burden and to act justly. Being honest, however, and trying to shield the people may not be enough. Because of your reputation, my friends and I are here tonight to offer you the opportunity to do more. I am Hila Shllaku and my two companions are Deda Mëhilli and Peter Qafa. The fourth man is a Tosk on his way to Yugoslavia." He paused for effect.

"I have heard of you," Lazer Pali responded.

"Good, then you also know that we have crossed the border from Yugoslavia because we are preparing the forces of the resistance so your region, so Albania at large, may be free again. We need men like you, men willing to lead, who are not afraid of responsibility. What do you say, can we count on you?"

"I am pleased that you have come to see me tonight. We both want to do what's good for our people. You have much political knowledge and insight. I am a poor farmer. You are working toward a better tomorrow.

Our people also need someone who speaks for them today. You and your friends go; work for the Albanian people as you deem best. Let me stay here where the people need me. If I join you, I'll be just one more individual among many. Let me stay here and I will continue to work for my people. You are welcome to stay tonight and break bread with me. Let it never be said that anyone who ever came to my house left hungry. Whenever you choose to leave, may God be with you and your companions."

So, that was it! What would Hila do now? Both speeches had conveyed messages and reassurances at different levels. Hila had introduced himself and his two companions in a sign of trust. Lazer Pali, on the other hand, had refused to join but had wished God's blessing upon them, implying that he would not report this visit to the security forces. Would Hila trust him and spare his life? I certainly hoped so.

"Men, let's go. We have a long road ahead of us." With these words, Hila gave the signal. We rose and moved toward the side door. The host exited first. Outside, we embraced in silence. Hila moved up the path leading to the ridge. I kept a sharp eye on all three of them. I wasn't sure whether it would end with a farewell or whether the man would be killed outside his home. The further we moved away from him, the easier I felt. Soon I lost sight of Lazer Pali in the dark. What a relief! The man had integrity and courage. He also had a sense of mission from which he drew strength. That evening I was glad that Hila spared him despite the risk of betrayal and the loss of face he suffered when the man turned him down. Peter told me later that Lazer Pali lived all by himself, having lost his wife a few years before. That explained the state of the house and the fact that there was no one around during our visit. Lazer Pali continued to be the village chief for a while, until the communists found out about our visit. Then they shot him in the village square for failing to report our visit.

Hila was planning to spend the night of October 20 at Peter Ndoja's home. When we got there, we found the house in ruins. A villager told us that Peter had built a new home in the village of Arra. When we reached that village, we walked up to Peter Ndoja's house. Having reconnoitered the surroundings and the house proper and having found nothing suspicious, we made our presence known and Peter asked us in.

OCTOBER 21, 1952

My notes say that a teacher by the name of Lin Kola came to see Hila and his companions. Otherwise I would not have recalled his name. I never heard what role, if any, Lin played in Hila's efforts and whether he belonged to the network. I recall that Lin was bright and articulate. He did not stay long. Perhaps his was more of a courtesy call, or perhaps there was a degree of urgency to his visit. I never asked and never found out.

As I watched Hila's visitors come and go, I failed to find a common denominator. Most were simple farmers who, in the past, had not taken part in politics but who, for one reason or another, had decided to join the resistance now. Others had already participated in previous attempts to unseat the communist regime. All showed fervor and a willingness to do what was necessary to rid our country of its oppressors. Hila, without actually coming out and saying so, implied that both the Western powers and the Yugoslavs were behind the present attempt to organize a massive uprising against Tirana. I was most interested in this question but had hesitated to broach the subject with Hila. I remembered what Peter and Deda had told me in this regard. To me it was most important to know the truth before we reached Yugoslav soil.

While Hila was secluded in a corner with our host, I asked Peter and Deda once more whether the Yugoslavs worked hand in hand with the Western Allies. Deda did not react. Peter, on the other hand, looked me straight in the eye.

"I wish that what Hila implies were true. When we are in Yugoslavia, we never see anyone except Yugoslav officers of the secret police [UDBA]. Furthermore, the Yugoslavs present themselves as our friends and speak of America and the British as enemies. I am not a politician. I am not even a smart man, but I did want to tell you this before we reach Yugoslavia. You go to college, you understand things. Be careful when we cross the border. I don't want to see you hurt."

He paused for a while but I had the distinct impression that he was not waiting for a response.

"For example," he continued. "Some time ago, the Yugoslavs sent me and some others into Albania loaded with bundles of flyers. I was never one for handing out things blindly. Once we crossed the border, I ripped open one of the bundles. What do you know? The leaflets carried on one side the picture of Koçi Xoxe and a poem addressed to his mother on the other. I don't remember the exact words but the poem said that she should not be sad that Enver Hoxha had killed her son. The day of victory would come and her son would be a shining hero and she and the Albanian people would be proud of him.

"I knew better than that. Koci Xoxe and company were murderers who had slain many and oppressed many more. I was not going to give that stuff to the network. In the mountains, you depend totally on the trust and loyalty of your friends and associates. My friends would throw me out if I asked them to distribute the leaflets. Others may even betray me to the police. I dug a hole and buried some bundles. Others I hid under boulders. As far as I was concerned, Koci was dead and should stay dead. I don't need to tell you more, do I?"

This could be a clever trap and much depended on my answer. Somehow, I felt that Peter meant every word. I looked at Deda. He nodded his head slowly in sign of approval. I decided to take the risk and to place my trust in them.

"Peter," I replied, "I appreciate your warning and your concern for me. I appreciate even more your willingness to share such a secret with me. It is a sign of trust and I assure you that your secret is safe with me. However, since you mentioned that flyer, let me tell you something."

I told him of Ndue Vata Gjelaj's escape across Lake Shkodra and why Mergim and I had pulled out of the group.

Peter and Deda smiled. They were pleased that their confidence in me was justified. I was even more pleased because I needed to forge a bond with these two men as I didn't trust Hila fully.

That night we stayed at Peter Ndoja's. Indoors it was cozy, particularly compared to the night we had spent along the creek.

CHAPTER TWENTY-SEVEN

FIRST DRINI CROSSING

OCTOBER 22, 1952

The next morning we washed up and had a breakfast consisting of warm corn tortillas, feta cheese, and plenty of cold water. The life of Riley! I don't know how much Hila paid for our food but we were getting three full meals a day. Having graduated from obligatory labor, I couldn't ask for more; I was among friends, getting ready to cross the border, one step closer to freedom. While Yugoslavia was not yet freedom, I would at least be reasonably safe from torture and death. I couldn't quite anticipate what awaited me across the border but one thing was for sure: With a little bit of luck, I did not intend to impose on Yugoslav hospitality any longer than I had to!

That day we received two important visitors, the two brothers Shuk and Luka. They were among the few "*vozar*" along this leg of the river Drini. Literally, "*vozar*" meant oarsman. At this point I was unclear about how they were going to get us across the river. I was pretty sure, though, that it would not be by boat. My friends had told me that we would use goat skins as floats. To avoid pestering Peter and Deda with questions, and to hide my ignorance, I chose to hold my peace. When the time came, I would find out. That was all that counted.

Those two brothers differed from our other visitors. They were tall, broad shouldered, dark complected, with very dark eyes and heavy black stubble. They had powerful bodies but moved smoothly, like cats. They would have looked threatening, almost sinister, were it not for their ready

379

smiles. In fact, this last quality was rare in our mountains. While men were generally friendly, someone with a ready smile was the exception. I liked them from the moment we met. I liked the way they looked me in the eye when they spoke. I felt safe with them. I could well imagine that they would attack hazards, such as crossing the treacherous Drini, with flair and courage. Somehow they seemed a cut above most other people I had met. They did not stay long. I didn't dare ask when we would cross the river. All I could do was rein in my impatience and wait, which for someone of my temperament was hard.

At dusk, without warning, Peter and Deda took up their weapons and left. I did not know why or where they were going. I knew better than to ask. This was proof that I was not yet fully trusted. The communists had distrusted me in things political. When they had kept me at arm's length even in matters pertaining to public health, it had hurt initially but I had gotten used to it. Here I figured that I had no need to know and that the less I knew the better. Eventually, but not in Yugoslavia, I would get to where my loyalty and my thinking would no longer be suspect. I would be able to stand up and speak up. I would reveal my innermost thoughts among friends and associates without fear of mistrust. Then, for the first time in many years, I would belong again.

Hila and I had supper with Peter Ndoja and his family. With Peter and Deda away, it was obvious that neither Hila nor I were at ease with each other. Occasionally, usually at dinner, Hila would address me in what he thought passed for German—to impress those around him, I am sure—because I could never make out what he was saying. To humor him, I usually answered in German with the first thing that came to my mind. That evening after dinner, Hila went into a corner with Peter Ndoja to discuss whatever he discussed on such occasions. I went to my layer of straw and my wooden "pillow" and waited for Peter and Deda to return. (Each person had a piece of wood that served as a pillow. Sometimes a chunk in the shape of a half moon was cut out to provide more comfort for the neck.)

Furnishings and tools in such households were very simple. Women did all their cooking in the fireplace—breakfast, lunch and supper. At the crack of dawn, the grandmother, mother, and daughters older than five or six went to work. The younger ones lit a fire. They uncovered the pile of embers in the fireplace, removed the ashes with which they had covered them the night before, and started a fire to preheat the outside of a round earthen dish about two feet in diameter and 4–5 inches deep. Meanwhile, the mother prepared a mixture of corn flour and water, formed "tortillas," and placed them on the preheated back of the baking dish. One of the girls rolled the round, low table on its edge to where the hungry were seated on the floor, while another brought cold water from a nearby spring. Guests and host sometimes sat on low three-legged stools. Within minutes the tortillas were ready, none too soon for the hungry mouths of men and children clustered around the table. Breakfast began once mother gave steaming tortillas to all sitting around the table. Each also got small chunks of feta cheese, or on very special occasions a spoonful of honey. If a cat dared approach the table, she was received with well-aimed kicks by children and grown-ups alike. Our mountain people were no animal lovers. Dogs were not let in as their function was to be outside and protect the house against wild animals and strangers. Cats were tolerated because they caught mice.

The same earthen dish used to bake tortillas came in handy to bake cornbread. The mother mixed corn flour and water and poured the thick mixture, thicker than that used for "tortillas," this time inside the earthen dishes. At this point she took a fork and marked the mixture with one or more crosses representing her personal mark. Then she covered the dish with a metal lid and heaped glowing embers on top and left the dish in the fireplace until the bread was done.

The round table and the low stools were usually the *pièce de résistance* of all the furniture found in such homes, with the exception of a wooden chest holding everything from the married women's dowries to unfilled prescriptions, pieces of soap, and other such items. Iron tongs were near the fireplace. A few dishes and a few whiskey glasses were stored nearby. Empty food cans were omnipresent. Sharp edges along their rims where hammered down and most had simple handles. The entire family drank water from the same can even if one member was seriously ill. Larger cans served as pitchers for milk or water. Each household had at least one wooden tub made of a hollowed-out tree trunk. Such tubs served to do the laundry, bathe the children, thicken milk, and prepare cheese. Cheese and pickle barrels, brooms, and oar-like devices used to put food into or pull out of the oven or fireplace were also of wood. Shovels, picks, axes, kettles, and other such items were bought from the village blacksmith, if there was one, or purchased in the nearest town. In general, the tools and pieces of furniture were much like the century-old furnishings and utensils in display at Greenfield Village in or other historical museums that the reader may have visited.

The nearest town was not always close by. To walk from Theth in Dukagjin to Shkodra in the winter took about 24 hours, as cars and trucks could not cross the snowed-in mountain passes. Even in the summer it took me about 18 hours on foot to get from Kodër Shën Gjergj, where I was stationed in 1948, to our apartment in Shkodra. Now, I understand, there are highways connecting Dukagjin with Shkodra the year round.

In our mountains, lunch was usually a meal adults and children consumed on their own. During the day, most adults were out in the fields while the children tended the flocks and herds. In the evening, the family got together for a simple meal that once in a great while went beyond bread and cheese, or beans, or boiled greens. If there were guests, they were welcomed with whiskey, bread, and cheese, perhaps even hardboiled eggs. Next came helpings of "white" and "red" meat (chunks of lard and pork), boiled beans, raw onions, pickles, and lots of fresh cornbread. For dessert, if there was dessert, there were grits with butter and honey. Eating this dish was an art. It was served in a wooden bowl at the center of the round table. One had to handle the spoon just so to skim the proper amount of butter, honey, and corn meal. I must admit I never acquired this art to the satisfaction of my native friends despite their attempts to teach me proper table manners. It reminds me of a story I heard many years later. A woman from New York was at a supermarket checkout counter in Atlanta. When it was her turn, she asked the cashier whether she had a good recipe for cornbread. A woman from behind spoke up and said, "With your accent, Ma'am, you will never make good cornbread."

OCTOBER 23, 1952

When dawn broke, Peter and Deda had not yet returned. I was ill at ease, since I could not ask any questions as to their whereabouts or their anticipated return. I had no choice but to sit tight and try to hide my discomfort.

Shuk returned and told us that Peter and Deda had been at his home the night before but had left again. Why did they visit him and his brother

Luka when both brothers had met with us that afternoon? Why did they leave without returning to where Hila and I waited for them? How long would they be gone? These questions kept churning in my head. The longer they went unanswered, the worse I felt. What would their absence, a lengthy absence, do to Hila and me?

Outside it got dark early. The wind rose and began howling and whipping furious squalls of rain against the house. The tree branches lashed out at the dark sky as night replaced dusk. The slate roof began to leak in places. The family grew silent as the adults sought ways to keep busy and the little ones clustered around Grandma. You could hear the fire hiss in the fireplace and the animals get restless. Even they were frightened by the fury of the cloudburst, by the darkness of the night broken up by lightning after lightning that seemed to want to rip up the yellow sky. When the whipping rain subsided, one could hear the trees groan. It was a frightful night.

Finally the wind subsided and the rain settled into a steady stream. The adults put the children to sleep and gathered around the fireplace. Outside there were noises of people brushing against the side of the house. Then I heard someone shaking himself off. I heard muffled voices. I peeked above the straw in the attic where I had been resting. Peter and Deda were back! My friends Peter and Deda were back, thank God. Even though most of my questions were still unanswered, I did not care; now things were back to normal. The two men had not disappeared for good. They were not on their way to Yugoslavia without us nor had they decided to stay in Albania and surrender. Their return cleared away the cobwebs of fear and suspicion in my mind.

OCTOBER 24, 1952

I woke up just before dawn to the soothing drumbeat of steady rain. The feeling of well-being lasted but for a few moments. Then reality hit me in the pit of my stomach. What was happening to the River Drini with all this rain? The people in the house began to stir. They were yawning, stretching, and scratching themselves. Then everyone got busy. A new day was upon us. We rose, washed up, and passed the time in the usual manner. We chatted with each other. I cleaned my revolver, and my three friends would move aside and discuss things among themselves or with the host. Meanwhile, the rain kept coming down, flooding the ground and swelling the river.

Toward dusk, the pace inside the house suddenly picked up. I did not see anyone coming or leaving but my friends were in a great hurry. A quick goodbye and we were on our way. As usual, nobody bothered to tell me where we were going. We stepped out into the rain but didn't go far. We traveled in daylight, which meant that we were in a region "safe" from communists and informers. Our path led generally downhill, just as during the last few days. I soon saw the reason for this downward movement. As we exited from behind a cluster of trees, there was the mighty Drini, shiny, rapid, and still rising. Normally, one could see embankments along both sides of a river. That day there were no embankments. Bushes and trees seemed to grow right out of the water as the waves impatiently tugged and pulled, trying to drag half-submerged branches toward the sea. Obviously, the water had risen well above its normal level. It was still raining. Would we be able to cross the river under these conditions?

We continued to walk rapidly. Behind a bend, I saw the outline of a house, obviously our goal for the day. A man was coming toward us. I recognized Shuk, one of the two brothers who were going to get us across the river. Now we were making progress. I liked both brothers when I first saw them. Now that we were at their house it wouldn't be long, nor could we be far from where we would cross the river. Things were falling into place. Well, they had been all along but now our progress from village to village and from house to house made sense. All this time, while Hila was getting together with his contacts, we kept moving steadily toward this house from where we would cross the Drini. After we crossed it a second time, there would be no more natural obstacles between us and the border. There would be, of course, border guards, roving patrols, land mines, machine-gun nests, and whatever else the communists had chosen to keep the border "safe." For the moment though, those hurdles were down the road and seemed less threatening than the river that, according to Shuk and Luka, had yet to crest.

They welcomed us and we settled down. Hila bought a sheep and the women of the house prepared another meal that had me licking my fingers. Until now, I was eating better as an escapee in the mountains than at any other time since the communist takeover.

I don't recall anything special about the house or about the women and children, nor does my diary carry much detail: *"Rain. The river Drini is rising. We go to Shuk's home where we spend one day and one night. Hila pays for a sheep and Shuk serves us a Lucullan meal."*

The brothers told us we had to wait until it was safe to cross the river. Once more the forces of nature carried the day. At least it stopped raining. When was our date with the group that was supposed to pick us up on the other side and help us cross the other leg of the Drini? Were we wasting time? Would this delay have an impact on our schedule or was there plenty of time built into it? I didn't know, nor could I ask those who did.

OCTOBER 25, 1952

No rain since yesterday. Unfortunately, from where I sat I could not see the river. Otherwise, I could pick a point of reference, a tree or a bush, and check whether the river was receding. I could tell by the intermittent shafts of sunlight that penetrated the indoor darkness that probably there was glorious sunshine outside.

The day went by slowly. Peter and Deda spoke with a low tone of voice but loud enough to include me in their conversation. Once we crossed the river, we would have a very steep climb ahead of us, probably the steepest we would face on this trip.

"Worse than the border?" I asked.

"Yes, worse than the border."

I wanted to ask whether they thought that I would manage to climb the embankment. I held back, though, as such a question would have made me look like a weakling seeking reassurance. Once we crossed the river, I would have to muster all my strength and climb as if my life depended on it, as indeed it did.

Today was Valnea's 29th birthday. Would I ever see her again? When we parted in 1943, she gave me a handkerchief on which she had poured some of her perfume, *"Asso di Cuori,"* (Ace of Hearts) that I liked so much. This handkerchief was one of the few things I had carried on me for these many years. The scent was still strong. I was positive it was not my imagination. Whenever I smelled it, the scent brought back powerful memories of less complicated, happier times.

After passing our college exams in the summer of 1943, I had returned to Albania and she had gone to Fiume where she and her family lived at that time. At one point in the fall, Fiume was surrounded by Yugoslav partisans, and two Albanian students on their way home by land were trapped there for several weeks. Valnea recognized one of them, Ismail Troshani, a second-year medical student from Shkodra, and offered them food and financial help. When she wrote me later about this incident, she added that she had prayed that someone would be available to help me if I ever were in trouble. Was this the time she prayed for?

Eventually, it got dark. We ate. After dinner, the conversation went on as the adults stayed up longer than usual.

"Men, the river has crested and is down to a level that my brother and I can handle. No other swimmer along this river would try to cross tonight and the police know this. This makes tonight extra safe. We'll wait another hour or so and then, with God's help, we'll get you across." Shuk looked at each of us while his brother nodded in agreement.

My heart began to pound. This was the day, this the night we had been waiting for. I watched the brothers as they began their preparations. They pulled out some goatskins and lined them up neatly. The skins had been specially prepared and had been sown together like wineskins, including all four legs down to the tip of the fourth. The open tip served as a vent to be tied or untied, as need be. Then the brothers inflated the skins and tied them securely, one at the time. They tested them for leaks by squeezing them tightly under their arms. Finally, they were satisfied that the tools of their trade would not let them down. Next they reached for some pieces of rope that they had stored away since the last time they had used them (had they helped other escapees?) and began to pull hard. The ropes did not break. The brothers rose to their feet.

"Let's go—it's time."

We stood up and grabbed our belongings. I slipped my arms through the straps of my knapsack, checked my revolver and the hand grenade. I put on my cap. I was ready and eager, but I still could not see how they would get us across with those inflated skins and the pieces of rope.

We left the house without saying goodbye as the women and children were out of sight. A few steps down a steep embankment. We stopped near the water. The river glittered in the silver moonlight and the waves seemed to move slowly, deceptively slowly. Obviously, the brothers had picked a point where the river was wider but less rapid. Shuk and Luka disappeared briefly and came up with an armload of pre-cut branches. They wove the branches together to form two resilient platforms and tied about ten inflated goatskins under each platform. That was how they were going to do it! They were going to use pontoons to get us across! Before I knew it, both brothers stripped and were waist-deep in the water. I could see their silhouettes against the shiny surface of the river. I didn't know why, but they reminded me of Ulysses' companions on their long and arduous trip back to Ithaca.

One of the brothers motioned for me to lie flat on a pontoon. As soon as I lay down, I felt the pontoon move. My guide had slipped into the water and was swimming toward the other side, silently, with hardly a ripple to give us away. I stepped ashore. He waved good-bye and was gone before I could whisper my thanks. I looked at the hill facing me. It looked dark and threatening. By the time I turned back toward the river, all three companions were at my side.

"Let's go. We cannot stand here forever."

It was Hila in his usual brusque manner. We started climbing. I threw myself at the task before me. I took in every tuft of grass, every stone, every rock that stuck out as I concentrated on each step, one step at the time. After a while, perhaps not more than 10 or 15 minutes later, I found myself on top of the hill. I didn't dare hope.

"Do we have to climb much further?" I asked.

"No, that's it," was Peter's reassuring reply.

I felt good all over. I took one last look at the river that peeked through in places. We moved toward Hila who hissed his ritual "Let's go." We resumed our usual formation with me toward the tail of the column as we moved away from the river.

"Goodbye Drini, until we meet again." I couldn't help but wonder. "The next time will you be friend or foe?"

Deda took the lead. The night was enchanting. Shafts of moonlight danced between trees and branches, casting intricate patterns on the ground. We slid from islands of shadow to pools of light, on and on, almost without effort. Such a night could not help but make you feel good. Our march took us out of the woods along the steep hills flanking the river. We walked for a couple of hours seeing neither houses nor stables. Finally,

Hila came to a stop. I could clearly make out the face of my watch. It was close to ten o'clock. Would we take a short rest or was this it for tonight?

Hila called Peter and Deda into a huddle. They talked briefly and then reached a decision. We would visit Gjoka Lazri at his house. He was not a member of Hila's network. In years past, he had worked with the resistance against the communists and had been a supporter of Kolë Biba. Hila had met him at that time. Dropping in on him would be a good move. The man was likely to be impressed with Hila's position as head of the Yugoslav network for all of north Albania. One never knew when one might need his help; hence, the reason for the visit.

When Gjoka answered our knock, it was obvious that he and his family had retired for the night. He remembered Hila and greeted him by name. It was less clear, though, whether he considered Hila a friend. Gjoka asked us in and awoke his family. The women got up, uncovered the embers, and started a fire.

"Would you like to eat something?" Gjoka asked in Hila's general direction.

"No, thank you, we have eaten. We are here for a different reason. You are a man of stature and the Yugoslav authorities are well aware of the esteem you enjoy among the people. My two companions, Deda Mehilli and Peter Qafa, and I have come to touch base with you and bring you up to date on recent developments in Yugoslavia and here. We knew that your door would always be open to us."

The struggle on the man's face betrayed his feelings. It was clear that he would have preferred that we had continued on our way without knocking at his door. If the communists ever found out that he had sheltered Hila Shllaku and company, he would be in big trouble. On the other hand, Hila was too dangerous a man to throw out on his ear. To gain time, he turned to the women and murmured some instructions.

As I was only an interested spectator, not a direct participant, I kept my ears alert but I also kept an eye on the women. I saw them grab a frying pan and soon some bacon and eggs were smiling at us. Some warm bread, a few onions, and a bottle of whiskey, and the round table was rolled in front of us.

"Praised be Christ."

"Forever and ever."

While we men munched away, the women moved silently around us, making us comfortable and filling our glasses.

"As I mentioned before," Hila began, "we are here on an important mission and are on our way back to Yugoslavia. We have completed our contacts. The network is primed. Weapons are in place and more weapons are on the way. The allies have decided that it is time to remove the regime in Tirana. I cannot give you exact dates but the end is near. I am sure that you are aware of some of the ongoing things. Let me assure you that there is more going on than even you know. This is probably our last secret trip to Albania. The next time we may come in plain daylight."

Hila leaned forward, eager to see the effect his speech had made.

"Hila, you and I are among the early ones that grabbed a rifle against the communists. You also know, however, how the communists treated us when Kolë Biba and the rest left and we locals had no place to hide. Almost all men were tortured and many were shot. You know my feelings but you also know my responsibilities toward my family. What do you want from me?"

"Nothing more than I have already told you. I wanted to bring you up to date. I think I owe you that much because of your past commitment and devotion to the anti-communist cause. I want to report to the Yugoslav authorities that we can count on you when the struggle for the liberation of Albania begins in earnest. And, as a friend, I wanted to break bread with you and be on my way." Having finished his speech, Hila rose.

Gjoka Lazri looked relieved. He rose to his feet.

"Hila, you know how we await the dawn of freedom. When that day comes, our dead will be able to rest in peace. Until then, we who live under communist oppression can do little but wait."

It was clear that he wanted to get by on as little as possible. He wanted no trouble with either side. He had fought and had paid for it. This time he wanted to survive unscathed. Whatever the outcome of the struggle, he wanted to be with the winner. He showed us to the door, embraced us, and wished us Godspeed.

Once outside the house, we wasted no time and took off in full moonlight. We had marched a couple of hours when Hila took off his backpack and laid it on the ground. Then he started turning around in small circles, the way dogs do before settling down. I don't say this in any negative way,

Hila was smart and knew his business. This was his way of preparing a place to lie down to sleep, doglike.

We were settling down for the night on a small meadow surrounded on two sides by woods but still out in the open. The grass was short and dark green. I felt we were rather exposed and visible from all sides. If it were up to me, I would have chosen a more protected spot. But who was I to tell the experts? I watched my companions very carefully. Would we take turns standing guard? Like Hila, they bedded down for the night. I would have felt more comfortable if we had posted a guard. Besides, our "sawing wood" could be heard loud and clear. I knew, of course, that they were just as interested in surviving as I was and held my peace. All of a sudden, somebody or something swished through the underbrush. Startled, we jumped up and reach for the weapons. Peter chuckled.

"It must have been a boar!"

Everybody grunted something in reply (no pun intended). Peter seemed to be one with nature. He was always the first one to catch on. We settled down and soon we were all asleep again. What if it had been the police instead of a wild boar?

October 26, 1952

We woke up with the first rays of the sun. It was a glorious feeling to wake up rested, surrounded by beautiful trees, with three armed companions, on our way toward the border. Besides, I had a wonderful dream. Peter was our official augur, interpreter of dreams and omens. He predicted the future in many ways. If he drank a cup of Turkish coffee or coffee substitute, he turned the cup over on the saucer and let it rest for a while. Then he looked at the coffee grounds and interpreted what he saw. If we had chicken, he removed the meat from the breastbone and "read" the future from the capillaries in the bone. He did the same thing with the shoulder blade of sheep or goats. I didn't know whether he believed it himself but others listened to him with great interest and respect. Usually, he would start out by asking the host whether the animal was bought or was born on the premises. It made a difference because, for the first six months, the fortune etched in the bones was that of the family where the animal was born.

I remember Dad telling me an amazing story. Michael Grameno's band of insurrectionists, including Dad, were hiding in a house. They had just finished eating a roasted lamb when Michael asked for the shoulder blade. As Dad told the story, Michael took one look and yelled, "Grab your guns, we are surrounded." By the time they took up positions by the doors and the windows, the Turkish troops opened fire. He must have seen something in that shoulder blade…

I proceeded to describe my dream. "Peter, I had an interesting dream last night. I dreamed we were all on top of a hill, bathed in glorious sunshine. We ran through waist-high, luscious grass, down one side of the hill and up the other and I took in the freshness and smell of the meadow."

I was so happy with my dream. I could still savor the sight, the touch, and the smell of the grass. It had to be a good omen! I looked at Peter with anticipation. Instead, Peter shook his head.

"Your dream means much trouble and suffering lie ahead of us. But don't worry, everything will turn out fine at the end."

As usual, he was trying to reassure me. His reply was not what I had expected. I had thought he would tell me that any difficulties lay behind us and that we would move on without further problems. Well, what did Peter know? Chances were he was wrong. Besides, life would go on no matter what my dreams or his interpretation. If perchance he was right and we ran into trouble, well, we would face that too.

When we broke camp, Peter took over as point man. Our goal was the Krrabi Mountain. We walked through tall woods all day with hardly any rest. This was free territory, safe as safe can be. My companions were confident and relaxed. I, too, had never been so lighthearted since the communists had taken over. It was a great feeling. As we walked, I had plenty of time to let my mind roam. I thought happy thoughts but they stopped short of the border. Somehow, I had failed so many times in my escape attempts that I could not bring myself to count my chickens before they hatched. This time things were different, though. As we marched toward our meeting place, the other team of infiltrators was proceeding toward the same spot from the opposite direction. What a good feeling.

Before I knew it, the sun was disappearing behind the mountains. Peter motioned and our little column came to a halt.

"We'll wait here until nightfall. We are near my aunt's home. She expected us the night of October 24 but we couldn't make it because of the rains. I am sure she will be glad to see us tonight."

Before too long, Peter was on his feet leading us downhill. A few more steps and we were out of the woods. In the dark, we could see the outline of a typical farmhouse. We could not see any light but we could see and smell the smoke curling toward the sky. Smoke meant fire and fire meant warmth and food. What a great feeling!

CHAPTER TWENTY-EIGHT

FAILED ENCOUNTER

OCTOBER 26, 1952 (CONTINUED)

We were now on the other side of the Krrabi Mountain. As we approached Mara's house, we went as far as the bushes would give us cover. We strained our eyes and ears but saw or heard nothing suspicious. Peter moved into the open and circled the house. He paused at the door and the windows, listening for any voices or noises that might betray the presence of strangers. After a little while, he knocked in code and the door cracked open. He disappeared inside without a sound. A few moments went by and the door creaked open again. There stood Peter waving us in. Mara and her 10-year-old son stood next to Peter, with big smiles on their faces. She hugged us, one at the time, as she mumbled words of welcome. Her son shook hands with us. He seemed shy and impressed with the visitors. I remember how impressed I was the first time I met Hila and company!

We took off knapsacks and weapons and sat by the fire. Chatting with us, Mara started to prepare a simple dinner. She said she did not know we were coming that night so she had no meat to offer us. She had expected us on the 24th. That night, she continued, the police had searched her home. They had also searched neighboring homes as well as homes in other villages. The farmers thought this was a routine search. She did not think that they had gotten wind of our presence. By the time she was done talking, she had bread and cheese, raw onions, and whiskey on the table.

"Praised be Jesus Christ." She pronounced the ancient words of welcome with obvious pleasure as she looked at her nephew Peter.

"For ever and ever," we responded, raising our glasses and taking a sip of whiskey.

We did not stay long after dinner. It was better for her and her son to have us out of the house quickly. It was also better for us to be in the open where we had freedom of movement. After a brief farewell, we were on our way.

With Peter as a guide, we made our way to a meadow about half an hour from Mara's home. A hedge surrounded the meadow on three sides. The fourth side sloped downward out of sight. We settled down for the night, again without any one of us standing guard. In view of the recent search-and-destroy mission by the police, this seemed strange to me but I had adapted to the ways of my companions. Before long, I was asleep.

October 27, 1952

Toward three o'clock in the morning, it started to rain. It rained hard and sleeping was out of the question. We moved closer to some bushes. Even if they would not protect us from the rain, we were at least less visible. When morning broke, I could see that the meadow ended downhill at a sharp angle because there were treetops sticking out beyond the edge of it. We sat there for hours; hungry, motionless, and soaked to the bone. Fortunately, the day was warm and so was the rain. Peter got up.

"I'll get us some breakfast."

Off he went toward the lower end of the meadow and out of sight. The others did not react. These three men gave the impression they were all acting out a well-rehearsed play and yet, I was sure, there was much individual initiative and improvising going on. Like Peter's sudden departure. Sometimes it gave me the creeps. Peter was gone no more than five minutes when he returned.

"We'll have something to eat in about half an hour," he said as he sat.

Again, no one said a word. Half an hour later, a man in his seventies came climbing up the hill. He had a canvas bag on one shoulder. When he got close, we all stood up. Again, it was that unhurried ritual of greeting one another. Marka Ded Alija shook hands and then embraced all four of us cheek to cheek, on both cheeks. You couldn't tell from the way he greeted us whether he had met Hila and Deda before. We all sat down.

"How are you? Are you cold? Would you like to eat a bite?"

He looked us in the eyes with a steady smile. Soon we had before us cornbread, cheese, and watery yogurt, the latter from a banged-up canteen. He watched us as we dug into the food. When we were done, he rose.

"I'll see you shortly before sunset. I'll carry you across a stream not far from here and then I'll bring you to the bridge on the road to Puka. From there you are on your own. Is there anything else I can do for you?"

Deda spoke up. "A tooth has been giving me trouble. Can you pull it for me?"

Marka Ded Alija looked into Deda's mouth and nodded. "Yes, I can pull it for you." Then he turned on his heels and disappeared beyond the bottom of the meadow.

I could no longer contain my curiosity.

"Peter, how did you get ahold of Marka Ded Alija with such ease?"

"There is a tree at the bottom of this meadow. Marka Ded and I have an agreement that if I am hiding in this meadow and want to see him, I place a stone on a low branch of the tree. Marka Ded saw the stone this morning and knew where to find us."

"Peter, how often does Marka Ded pass by that tree?"

"He walks by daily when he takes his sheep to graze. So it really is no big deal for him to look for that branch."

"When was the last time you reached him this way?" I continued.

"That was about five years ago."

"You mean to tell me that for five years Marka Ded has checked that branch every day?"

"We are friends," Peter answered, surprised at my question. I was dumbfounded.

"Marka Ded Alija is a remarkable man," Peter continued. "He is known throughout these mountains for never telling a lie. Some time ago, a captain of the police and some of his men had stopped at Marka Ded's home. During the conversation, the captain asked him what he done the evening before.

"'We had some infiltrators for dinner.' The captain and his group broke up in laughter and changed the topic. Fortunately for Marka Ded, these men were from the south and did not know of Marka Ded's reputation. Otherwise they would have taken him seriously."

The hours passed slowly. Around three in the afternoon, it stopped raining. The sky cleared and the temperature dropped sharply. Marka Ded came about an hour before dusk. He walked over to Deda.

"Ready?" Deda nodded.

Marka Ded pulled from his pocket a pair of dentist's pliers. I wondered whether they were the right pliers. Before I knew it, Marka Deda had pulled the molar. Next, the "dentist" gave his patient a swig of whiskey and asked him to rinse his mouth and spit out the rinsing. One more swig of whiskey and the deed was done.

By now, the sky was turning red. We shouldered our knapsacks and weapons and were ready to go. Marka Ded pulled from his pocket a knitted brown cap with two straps. He placed the cap over his white skullcap and tied the straps under his chin. He noticed the question in my eyes.

"Years ago when I was a young man, my friends and I used to cross into Yugoslavia to steal cattle. Because our white caps might give us away at night, our wives knitted these brown caps for us. I still keep mine as it comes in handy once in a while."

He turned around and led the way toward the bottom of the meadow. Hila followed right behind him, then Ded and I, and finally Peter. It was getting chilly. We crossed a footpath and reached a stream that was knee deep because of the recent rains. Marka Ded stopped.

"I will carry you across the stream, one at the time. Your feet must stay dry. You have a long way to go tonight."

He sat down and removed his strap sandals and his socks. First he took Hila across and then Peter. He motioned to me. I felt embarrassed because I was less than half his age. This was no time, though, to dilly-dally. I hopped on his back and away we went. Then he went back for Deda. Hila and Peter had left their knapsacks on the other side before climbing on Marka Ded's back. Deda was last. He was also the heaviest. He grabbed his and the other two knapsacks and got on Marka Ded's back. I hated to watch what was going on. The old man never wavered, never lost his footing. Slowly, carefully, he waded through the water and deposited Deda on our side of the stream. Then he put on his footgear and led us up the hill. We were moving fast.

At first, I had no trouble keeping up. Then I began to shiver. I felt chills all over my body and all my muscles ached. I wondered what was happening. I could breathe deeply, without pain, and I wasn't coughing. I didn't think I was coming down with pneumonia. It could not be the flu yet as I had no sore throat or runny nose. It was unlikely that I had caught malaria in the mountains. Whatever I was coming down with, I did not need it. What would happen to me if I became seriously ill? Would my companions leave me behind? Would they wait and give me a chance to recover?

After about half an hour, I began to feel first warm and then hot. Maybe I had a high fever. It did not make sense, though. I was no longer shivering and I felt strong again. I had no trouble keeping up with the rest. Then I understood. I was not coming down with anything. As we started walking, I began to warm up and my clothes started drying because of the body heat. However, they were robbing me of heat faster than I could produce it. That explained why I had shivered so much. What a relief. The others must have also felt the chills but no one said a word. They knew from past experience what was happening.

We were moving through the night steadily, silently. Suddenly we stopped at the edge of a stream about 30 feet wide. Normally, this was probably a gentle little stream. Now the angry waters rushed over rocks and branches, dragging with them everything in their path. A tree trunk lay across the stream. It was round, wet, slippery, and without a handrail. Sometimes the waters washed over it. My friends walked gingerly across the tree trunk and waited for me on the other side. I was quite surefooted during the day. At night, I often stumbled over rocks or stepped into holes despite warnings from my friends. Peter looked at me with concern. I stepped on the end of the tree trunk and promptly froze. I closed my eyes and prayed to the Blessed Mother with all my strength. I do not recall moving my feet. All I know is that when I opened my eyes I was on the other side of the stream and we were on our way again. At first, I did not realize the significance of what had happened. Later it dawned on me where my help had come from—and I was most grateful.

My friends started forging ahead as soon as I joined them on the other side. A few more minutes and we found ourselves facing the big bridge that leads to Puka. A truck was barreling down the highway just as we hit the ditch. Its bright headlights cut a swath through the night and blinded me for a moment. I was no longer used to electric lights.

Marka Ded Alija had intended to leave us here. He changed his mind.

"I will walk across the bridge, past the guardhouse," he whispered. "If there is no guard there I'll turn left. If there is one, I'll turn right. It is up to you what you do next. God be with you."

He crawled over the side of the ditch, stood up, and followed the footpath to the bridge. I kept him in sight as he stepped on the bridge. I followed him until the guardhouse and then lost him. What were we to do now?

"Move," someone hissed in my ear. "He turned left."

I went over the top of the ditch and followed my friends. I told no one that I had lost sight of Marka Ded Alija before he had turned beyond the bridge.

This was the second time that night that something happened and I failed to realize its significance until later. It should have been obvious to me by now that I had impaired night vision. Yet all my life I had excellent eyesight. In fact, my vision was 40/20. I could see at 40 paces what others saw at 20—in daylight. Unfortunately, at night my sight was deficient.

Peter took the lead. We crossed the bridge in bright moonlight. Then we turned left and followed the highway for a few hundred feet. Next, Peter turned right and began climbing uphill along a footpath. We must have walked close to an hour at a brisk pace. Finally, Peter stopped near a vineyard.

"We are now near a farmhouse located atop this hill. I'll lead you away from the house into a field where we can spend the night."

While Peter was speaking, I found a few Concord grapes the harvesters had missed on the vine. The grapes were all wrinkled and sweet. I looked around and found a few more. My friends also found a few. Those grapes were delightful! Thank you, Lord! We climbed a bit further and found ourselves at the edge of the field Peter had mentioned. He had one more idea.

"I am going to get some hay for us to sleep on. Be back in a minute."

We picked a spot to sleep along the edge of the woods. Then we waited for Peter. A few minutes went by, then ten, and finally close to half an hour. We got worried. When he finally showed up, he was white as a ghost—and no hay.

"What happened?"

"You won't believe this. I managed to get to a haystack without awakening the farmer's dog. As I started to pull hay off the stack by the armful, I suddenly found myself looking into the eyes of a large wolf. He bared his fangs, snarled, and leaped. Paralyzed by fear, I fell backwards, unable to lift one finger. The wolf disappeared into the darkness. I sat there for a while, too weak to stand up. I touched my head and face. Not a scratch. Slowly it dawned on me. The wolf must have crawled into the haystack to spend the night there warm and cozy. When I started pulling the hay away, he got scared and jumped not at me but over my head." Peter chuckled. Then he added, true to form, "I hope the wolf feels better than I do right now. I'm still shaky."

It was no laughing matter, but we couldn't help grinning as Peter told us about his misadventure. I am sure, deep down, we three listeners were glad that, if wolf had to meet man, it was best that it happened to Peter rather than to one of us. On that note, we went to sleep. Thank God, the rest of the night turned out to be uneventful.

OCTOBER 28, 1952

We woke up before dawn and marched back into the woods. Soon the sun was out, birds warbled from trees all around us, and a nearby brook was running fresh and clear. We stopped, had a bite to eat, and started to clean up. We shaved, combed our hair, and straightened out our appearance as best we could. That night, the good Lord willing, we would meet the group that would take us across the Drini and on to Yugoslavia.

Here are some things the infiltrators carried in their backpacks: In addition to spare socks and underwear, they carried Gillette shaving cream and brushes, razor blades, DDT powder in small cardboard dispensers, and probably other goodies I never saw. Hila had binoculars and Peter carried clippers that he would use later to trim our hair when it got long.

That morning Hila called me aside and gave me a few words of advice on how to behave. "If spoken to, answer," he said. "The men who are picking us up are among the bravest and most skillful infiltrators. Hold your inquisitiveness to a minimum, particularly with regard to political questions. You are bright and will learn soon enough all you need to know once we get to Yugoslavia. There you may even meet some of the high Yugoslav officers in charge. They are very capable and committed, men like Colonel Četo Mijović. Until then, remember—the people we are meeting tonight are soldiers who are risking their lives to save us. Be thankful."

I wasn't sure why Hila delivered this sermon. In fact, I couldn't quite figure out where I stood with him. Naturally, I would keep my mouth shut and my ears open. I knew more or less what to expect in Yugoslavia. My immediate problem was to get there. Once there, I was confident I would know how to behave and how to proceed. First we had to get ready for tonight's meeting with the other group. Then we would face the second Drini crossing, and finally the border. These were three important hurdles facing us. I would tackle the rest all in good time.

We set out for the Sakat Forest. Our instructions were simple. We were to meet our companions at 10:00 p.m. We would snap two dry branches and they would snap three in return. That day everybody was in a good mood. We continued to walk all day at a leisurely pace, resting frequently. Late that afternoon Deda pointed out that we were just about even with a police station housed in several buildings on the nearest hill west of us. Hila pulled out his binoculars and examined the police station and surroundings. With the naked eye, we could make out some people moving about but not much more. I felt uncomfortable being so close to the enemy.

All of a sudden, Peter spoke from a few feet below us. "I am going over to see what's going on. You go ahead. I'll meet you at the next hill." said he was pointing at the top of the hill.

Before anyone could say a word, Peter hopped, skipped, and jumped toward the bottom of the little valley between us and the police station. Hila followed him with his binoculars for a while. When it got too dark, he put the binoculars back in the carrying case. There was no sense staying where we were. We started toward the next hill. We got there before Peter. I felt quite uncomfortable when Peter first said that he was going to "drop in" on the police. My initial discomfort was now slowly changing to anger. Why did Peter have to do such stupid things? Here we were about to meet with the rescue team and Peter had to play games and take chances! Before too long Peter was back. His eyes were sparkling in the dark. Something must have happened after he left us, something that had pleased him.

"What took you so long?" Hila asked.

"The commissar was just calling the troops together for the evening conference when I first got to the wall outside the police station. I could hear them talk as they all sat on the ground around their beloved commissar. I had not attended a conference in so long that I could not resist. I sat down outside the wall near some large pots the cook had left there to dry. I listened for a while. It was the same tripe the Commies have been pushing from the beginning. I decided not to wait for the end and got up. I hated to leave without saying goodbye or at least leaving something for them to remember me by. Impulsively, I grabbed two of the pots and dragged them behind some bushes. Imagine their faces when the cook first tells them he cannot find his pots. Next, I can just see it. The cook goes to the commissar and asks him to unravel the mystery. I sure wish I could be a little bird perched on a tree and could watch them scratching their heads. And then, when they finally find the pots, they won't be able to explain how they got there!" Peter was in stitches. I had to bite my tongue as I saw nothing funny in the entire episode.

We started moving again and I gave my thoughts free rein. I had dreamed of this day for years. Even though my thoughts kept running hither and yonder, I found it difficult to think beyond the imminent encounter. Actually, there was no need to think beyond. We would take the hurdles as they came, one at the time. We would "hurry slowly" as the Romans used to say. That was exactly what we were doing as we moved steadily toward the Sakat Forest. These thoughts kept going around in my head until it whirled like a spinning top. It got dark. Would they be punctual? Might they be early? We came to a full stop and began our wait. How would we know where to wait for them in the midst of a forest? Would they be able to find us? Would they come close enough to be within earshot? How would we know when to snap those dry branches? How long would we stay here if they did not show up by ten o'clock? It got to be 10:00, and then 11:00, and finally midnight.

Hila decided we would sleep here and stay until they came. That was fine with me. Leaving without meeting the other group could spell disaster. Once a link broke, the chain broke and our plan would go down the drain. I must not entertain negative thoughts. I had to be optimistic. The group would come and everything would turn out fine. I could not listen to that little voice deep down in my mind that said, "You have failed nine times before. This is one more failed attempt—you'll see." I had to believe that this time would be different. I had never come so far nor been in such expert company. If worst came to worst, they would know what to do. After all, Peter had a wife and children in Yugoslavia. Besides, all three, Hila, Ded, and Peter, were in mortal danger as long as they remained in Albania. Hence, what was good enough for them would be good enough for me. Besides, the group might come tomorrow night.

OCTOBER 29, 1952

We woke up at the crack of dawn. For a moment, I felt great. Then it hit me: Our rendezvous had not taken place as agreed upon. Well, perhaps tonight. After all, Hila had said that we would not leave before getting together with the others. There was fog all around us. It magnified noises while it gave a sense of isolation. Birds' voices seemed to float in a milky ocean, disembodied yet so sweet. Some just chirped, others sang full-breasted songs. Morning progressed and the sun came out. The fog started to burn off. As I looked toward the valley, there was a silver ribbon reflecting the rays of the early sun, the mighty Drini. It looked peaceful and conciliatory. Despite its bucolic appearance, I would have gladly traded the enchantment of this scene for an encounter with three or four rough-looking infiltrators from Yugoslavia.

Later that morning, we heard voices. They belonged to shepherds that were taking their flocks to pasture. The tinkling of bells was coming closer. My friends crouched and motioned for me to do the same. We moved rapidly but silently away from the flocks. We did not go far, just far enough to be out of the shepherds' range. I had moved a few steps away when I caught words bouncing back and forth among my companions. Peter and Hila were proposing various ways of crossing the river on our own while Deda kept rejecting every proposal. Peter said that he could help Deda swim across.

"Absolutely not," was Deda's answer.

"We can inflate our pants to help us float and cross the Drini that way." Again, Deda shook his head, unconvinced.

"What if we steal a wooden water barrel and empty it? We can put you in the barrel and we push you across." Stubbornly, Deda shook his head.

"Genc, can you swim?" Peter asked.

"Yes, I can."

"Would you be afraid to swim across the river?"

"No, I would not."

"Deda, three of us can push you in the water barrel. You'll be as safe as when Shuk and Luka helped us across the first time."

"Peter, I am not going near the river without the group from Yugoslavia." The way he spoke made it clear that Deda's mind was made up.

"So that's that," Hila said. "We either cross together, or we wait until we can."

I could only shake my head. It was incredible that someone as strong and agile as Deda would be so afraid of water. Obviously, I was not included in this discussion except for Peter's brief question concerning my swimming ability. It was also obvious that Hila would back Deda. The river had won again. We waited all day and into the night. That night we heard a rifle shot. Nothing else happened.

OCTOBER 30, 1952

The next morning it started to drizzle. Hila told us to get ready to move. I was hoping against hope. Couldn't we wait a little longer? One more night? The reason for moving soon became apparent. My companions had spotted a man who was chopping kindling wood while his dog sniffed hither and yonder. We began slithering diagonally down the face of the mountain we had climbed two days before. My friends knew where the homes were and managed to pass downwind, between the homes and the man, without his dog spotting us. We walked all day. Soon I lost track of the direction as I focused on where I was putting my feet. I did not want to stumble, make noise, or fall behind my companions. I concentrated on walking and left everything else to them.

By midnight, we had circled back to where we had left that morning. That felt good! My friends really knew what they were doing. With a little luck, we would meet our rescuers that third night. Before going to sleep, my three companions dusted themselves with DDT powder. Then they passed one of those little brown cardboard containers to me and I applied DDT meticulously all over my skin, but particularly under the arms and along skin folds. We had problems. At least we didn't have lice.

OCTOBER 31, 1952

That morning, around 5:30, Hila motioned for us to gather around him. The fog was heavy and there was rain in the air. I had a heavy heart.

"We can't stay here any longer. We have taken too many chances already. We shall move to our secondary meeting place. If the group does not find us here, they'll know where to look for us." With those words, Hila rose and began to move downhill. The rest of us followed.

What a development. This was the first time I had heard of a secondary meeting place. Obviously, these men meant business. They were committed to free Albania from the communists, at the cost of their lives if necessary. This was no game for amateurs. We began to move away from the place we had reached with such optimism three days before. The further we got, the worse the weather. First came the fog. Then the rain settled in. By noon, we were shrouded in fog and soaked to the skin. Being wet was one thing, marching in the rain for hours was something else. The wet collar and the sleeves chafed my skin until it was raw. Even worse, my socks turned to mush and my feet were slipping inside my sandals while the latter were slithering in the mud. My feet kept banging into rocks and roots while my toes were getting increasingly sore. I fell a few times without hurting myself too badly. When the rain got bad, Peter gave me a one-man pup tent sheet that was water resistant and could be worn like a poncho with hood. Unfortunately, it lacked drawstrings. I would have loved to fix that but didn't dare ask the others to stop on my account. Water kept running from my wrists to my elbows as I held the sheet wrapped around my shoulders. It did not let me move my arms and body freely but it was keeping me perhaps a little drier.

Things got worse. Hila began to falter. He was suffering from what may have been sharp kidney pains. Twice we got lost in the fog. By the time everything came together, Hila and Peter were exchanging harsh words, not once but twice that day. It was a day to remember. We reached Kuror'e Dardhes in daylight and by nightfall we were at Mara's, Peter's aunt. This time she had not expected us at all.

"How come you are back?"

"We had a change in plans," Hila replied. "Can you put us up for the night?"

"No, I can't. A neighbor's wife is coming over tonight. I promised I would help her with some sewing."

"Can you find an excuse and send her away?" It was obvious that Hila did not cherish the idea of spending the night out in the rain.

"No, I can't do that. I had to renege on my promise once before. This time she might get suspicious."

Hila persisted. "Is there a cave nearby where we could spend the night?"

"No, there are no safe caves nearby. At least, not that I know of."

I had an idea. Normally, I would not have spoken up. Under the circumstances, I decided to risk it. "Could we spend the night in the loft?" Mara looked at me for a long moment.

"Yes, of course, better than being out in the rain!"

I had noticed a tree trunk with notches, like a ladder, leading into the loft. Without wasting any more words, Mara climbed up the ladder and asked us to follow. The loft was very primitive. In other homes, there was a platform, a portion of the loft covered with planks. Here there was none. There were the rough beams that went from wall to wall and the ceiling boards of the room underneath that were fastened to the underside of the beams. We could lie on our side on top of the beams but not for long because they were not wide enough for us to turn without falling between two beams. We decided to lie down between beams because we were tired to the bone and knew we would fall asleep before too long.

While we were taking off our sandals and settling down for the night, Mara appeared with a bucketful of boiled potatoes. Now, I always disliked boiled potatoes. These, however, smelled delicious. I grabbed one hot potato and ate it skin and all. In the dark you couldn't have skinned it anyhow. Besides, the potato tasted good as it was. Then I grabbed a second one. This time something was different. The worst of my hunger had been satisfied. When I sank my teeth into this second potato, I found myself with a mouthful of mud! Mara had not rinsed the potatoes before boiling them and I had been in a hurry to eat. I had not noticed anything unusual when I devoured that first potato. My companions had also slowed down. I noticed that by now they had their pocketknives in their hands and were scraping the mud off their potatoes. Obviously, when Mom had boiled potatoes at home in years past she did not know that leaving the caked dirt on the skin gave potatoes a pleasing flavor, at least to the first one.

NOVEMBER 1, 1952

In the morning, Mara climbed up to the loft with some bread and cheese. Poor woman. As a widow with a young son and very little to her name, I wondered how she managed to keep alive. No one to work the land she might have, and taxes to pay like anyone else. In Albania, taxes were assessed based on the size of the property and were paid in nature. Farmers had to hand over so many measures of grain, corn, etc. per acre. Furthermore, irrespective of whether they had any sheep, goats, or cattle, they had to turn in so many pounds of meat per family. One year, a farmer who had no animals turned in a basketful of turtles as these were the "only animals" growing on his property. He was fined and imprisoned for making fun of the duly constituted authorities. The regime had absolutely no sense of humor. In demanding that farmers bring in meat, the authorities meant to force farmers either to raise animals or to buy meat from others and turn it over to the government. Either way, it was a win-win situation for the government. As to the farmers, well, that was their problem. The communists never worried about details, as long as the solution was in their favor. Government-owned grocery stores in cities, for instance, had clear-cut rules. If you wanted to buy potatoes but the store had rotten tomatoes on its hands, you had to buy a pound of tomatoes with each pound of potatoes. That was only fair. Otherwise, the cooperative would have lost money. According to the communist creed, if the cooperative lost money, the people lost money. Since this was the regime of the people, each individual had to bail out the cooperative by buying the spoiled tomatoes. *Voila*, another problem solved easily, equitably, even elegantly. This situation prevailed for nearly half a century, for as long as the communists stayed in power.

At dusk we left for Mug. The sky was clouded over but the rain had stopped. Hila was feeling better and things went well for a while. Then it started to rain again. Overnight I had inserted a strap into my poncho. Now I put it on so that it covered my head, shoulders, and arms. I had free hands and could walk better. For whatever reason, we left the beaten path and started climbing downhill cross-country. My toes started to hurt because they kept bumping against the tips of my sandals. I had trouble keeping up. When we first reached the original meeting place, I had seen our rescue operation rapier-like: with the rescue team like a thin, sharp blade crossing the border, arching across the Drini, reaching into our hiding place and extracting us with surgical precision. Weeks later, when we found out that our rescue team had arrived hours after we had left, the failed rescue operation had looked more like a dull, rusty knife poking in the dark, searching without seeing, aimlessly, without ever reaching us.

NOVEMBER 2, 1952

Through the fog and rain, we walked until about 2:00 a.m. Then, suddenly, with Peter at the head of our column, we stood before the house of Gjoka Lazri. The only time Peter had been there was when we had visited Gjoka a few days before. How he found the house after a march of about 10 hours, walking under the most unfavorable conditions, was a testimonial to Peter's sense of orientation. They say that pigeons orient themselves by the earth's magnetic field. How did Peter do it?

Hila took over at this point. We would tell Gjoka that our plans had changed based on new instructions from Yugoslavia. We would try to spend the remainder of the night and the next day at Gjoka's. It might take some doing based on the lukewarm reception of a few days ago. Besides, it would not take Gjoka long to realize that the change in plans was not a change for the better. This time we were dealing from a position of weakness. It was up to Hila to make the most of a weak situation and see how much help he could wring out of Gjoka.

CHAPTER TWENTY-NINE

THE CAVE

NOVEMBER 2, 1952 (CONTINUED)

When Gjoka opened the door, he was taken aback. The last people he had expected, the last he wanted to see, were standing right in front of him. He asked us in, even less graciously than the first time. "Come in," he mumbled as he moved aside to make room for us. The rest was almost a replay of our last visit, but with a difference. We sat down. After the usual exchange of inquiries about each other's health, Gjoka spoke again.

"What time is it?" he asked Hila. "How many hours until daybreak?"

"It is about an hour until dawn," Hila replied. "It is too close to daybreak for us to venture out. It would be too dangerous for us as well as for you and your family. If we are seen nearby, the communists will immediately suspect you of harboring us. No sense in taking chances."

Gjoka did not seem convinced. "Is it already that close to dawn?"

Hila and his two companions nodded vigorously.

This time Gjoka didn't ask us whether we wanted to eat. We looked hungry and tired. First he told the women to prepare food for us. Then he turned toward someone lying along the wall in the shadow of the darkened room and nodded.

"I want you to meet Zef Toma," he said.

He gave no details about the man and none were probably needed. Hila, Peter, and Deda stood up and greeted the figure emerging into the circle of light as if he were at least an acquaintance. Zef Toma also shook hands with me. Then he sat down.

407

This was an interesting development. Gjoka may not have wanted Zef Toma to know that he, Gjoka, had dealings with us. On the other hand, Hila may also have preferred not to get involved with Zef Toma. Well, here we were and here he was and neither side had a choice. Obviously, Hila must have known the man or must have known enough about him to trust him, because when he began his prepared speech, he stuck to his original plan.

Looking at Gjoka, he said, "We are back because of a change in plans. We don't know too much at this point, but for now we will stay in Albania to await further developments. We expect a courier with new instructions. Until then, we just have to wait."

Gjoka was not buying it. One could see the struggle on his face. With dawn so close, he did not dare throw us out. On the other hand, if Hila were expecting new directives, why hide at Gjoka's when he had a whole network at his disposal? It was as clear to Gjoka as it was to us that something had gone wrong. He had wanted no part of us when things were going well. Why would he want to have us under his roof now that things had gone awry? While Gjoka was thinking furiously, Hila drew me apart.

"Do you have any money? You are not part of our group. I am going to pay Gjoka for me and my two companions but I cannot pay for you."

"I have no money to speak of."

"Do you have anything of value on you?"

I felt hurt. I knew I had not belonged when I worked in public health under the communists. Now Hila was telling me that I still did not belong. What was I to do? He stayed bent over me like a vulture. Then I remembered. One day while I was digging in a mound of old garbage at the House of Culture, the former Italian consulate in Shkodra, something at the tip of my pick had glistened in the sun. When I looked closer, I saw a gold wedding band nestled around the tip of my pick. I looked carefully at my coworkers but no one seemed to have noticed. I quickly pocketed the ring and went back to work. Now at Gjoka's, Hila was still leaning over me.

"I do have a golden ring. If you want it you can have it."

I pulled it from my coin purse and gave it to Hila. Perhaps he wanted to bribe Gjoka. He put the ring in his pocket without saying a word. I don't know what happened to the ring. All I know is that I saw Hila give Gjoka three gold coins. I am sure he did not hand him the ring.

We had reached an impasse. We had failed to meet with the group from

Yugoslavia meant to get us across the Drini River. What was worse, the Yugoslavs would not know where to look for us if they wanted to send another posse. Gjoka was not a member of Hila's network. A few years before, he had sheltered followers of Kol Biba, an anti-communist from the Puka area. Now Gjoka was trying to avoid trouble and we spelled trouble with a capital "T." I didn't know how long the impasse would last and how much money Hila had with him. The thought struck me that Peter's interpretation of my dream of luscious meadows may have been on target. *Come on*, I told myself, *don't let the first obstacle throw you off balance.* There was no denying that we were in trouble, deep trouble. I reminded myself I had to keep up a stoic front, no matter what. After all, I didn't want my three companions to see how upset I was.

By now, we could see a glimmer of daylight through the windows. Gjoka rose and mumbled a few words in our direction. "I am going to Skura. You can stay here until I return." Before I knew it, he was gone.

Why did Gjoka want to go to Skura? Then again, why not? It was we who needed him, we who must strive to stay in his good graces and not become a burden. He was free to come and go as he pleased. All we could do was be alert and pray—pray that he would not betray us.

Then it was Zef Toma's turn to speak. "Have you heard? A husband and wife who belonged to your network have been arrested."

I don't recall whether he mentioned their names or whether I just forgot them because of the consternation the bad news evoked in me.

Zef continued. "Life is getting more and more difficult in our village. The police don't trust me and are keeping an eye on me. I may have to escape. Perhaps it is best that I join you. Yes, my mind is made up, I will join you."

His tentative way of speaking—as if he were trying to convince himself—did not suit me. He was not a true victim nor was he a true opponent of communism. He would be one more mouth to feed and an individual to keep an eye on. Under the circumstances, though, Hila had no choice but to accept him. If Zef were sincere, he could be of some help. He had friends and relatives; he knew the area and could find food. As far as I was concerned, I did not trust him. I could be wrong, but I did not trust him.

When it got dark, Hila looked at us. Without saying a word, he signaled that we should get ready to leave.

"Zef Toma, we are about to leave. If you want to come with us you're welcome."

That seemed to me like a good move. Gjoka had not returned yet. If he had betrayed us, it was time to get out before we were surrounded. We did not have to go far, just far enough to be out of reach at a location where we could observe any suspect activity or movement by communist forces.

Zef Toma got up and left with us. We walked about half an hour and settled down among some rocks that offered protection against sudden discovery or a surprise attack. Zef Toma spent the night with us.

November 3, 1952

When we awoke, dawn was upon us. I watched my companions to see whether I could anticipate what we would do next. They gave no sign of imminent departure. We ate a bite and settled down again. What were we waiting for? Were we staying here because we had no place to go and one place was as good as another? Or did we want to keep an eye on Gjoka and find out whether he could be trusted? What was going on in Hila's mind? Did Ded and Peter know something I didn't? I had no choice but to hold my peace and seem as unconcerned as the others. If they knew what they were doing, good for all of us, if not, there was nothing I could or should be doing. Nonetheless, sitting here without doing anything, without knowing anything, was very hard on me.

Suddenly we heard steps. It was Gjoka. My friends did not seem concerned that he found us. He settled down. After the usual exchange of greetings and questions about each other's well-being, Gjoka spoke to Hila.

"Your liaison in Skura has not heard from the group. He will get in touch if they contact him. I spoke with Shuk and he will come to see you."

So, that was it. Skura was the secondary meeting place and Hila had spoken with Gjoka in private. Gjoka also knew where we would spend the night. Obviously, Hila had trusted Gjoka more than I thought. Perhaps things were not as bad as they had seemed. Maybe, but I was convinced that the situation had to get much better before we would be out of the woods, so to speak.

That afternoon we had another visitor. This time it was Shuk. He and his brother had ferried us across the Drini. After the usual exchange of amenities, Hila took him aside. Zef Toma, Ded, and Peter stayed with me. The conversation between the two did not last long. They rose and Shuk came toward us. He shook hands and left. I had the distinct impression that he was avoiding making eye contact.

After he left, Hila said to us, "I explained to Shuk that for the time being, and perhaps for some time to come, we would remain in Albania. We have some bases on this side, and most of our network is on his side of the river. Furthermore, there is still work to be done while we await further instructions. Thus, I asked him that he ferry us back to the other side. He refused."

Having said those words, Hila sat down. I didn't quite know how to react. I was disappointed that our friend Shuk had refused a request from Hila. I had seen him as a friend in need but, for whatever reason, he did not want us on the other side of the river. Was it because eventually he would have to get us across once again? Was it that he was afraid of having to feed us? Or was it that, in case we were discovered or if any member of the network were caught, he and his family were at risk? I did not know. On the other hand, I was glad that we were on this side of the Drini. Obviously, we would have to cross the river once more but once was better than three more times.

Then Zef spoke up. "Men," he said, "I will go to Kryezi and speak with my uncle. He is wise and has many contacts. I will ask for his advice. I will also ask him to find us a swimmer we can trust. Once we are across the river we can cross the border on our own. The problem right now is to find someone who can get us safely across. You know, no matter how well a man can swim, unless he is trained to swim across the Drini, he can never make it. Particularly now that the river is so swollen and ice cold."

Those words seemed to support Deda and his refusal to challenge the river without proper help. Zef Toma said goodbye and left just as dusk was descending. The night was warm and comfortable. We ate a bit and settled down for the night. Things were moving again. A bit hesitantly and not as planned, but they were moving. Good night, Hila; good night, Deda; good night, Peter, and may God be with us.

NOVEMBER 4, 1952

We awoke to a friendly sky and a warm morning. While my mood was not exactly bouncy, I had adjusted. I was with comrades-in-arms of whom one, Peter, was also a friend. As long as we stuck together, we had a fair chance of making it. They knew the area and had connections. Of course, I did not cherish the idea of having lost contact with our rescue group but I couldn't argue with reality. Now we, my comrades, had to find an alternate route and other people who could help us across. While things were dark, all was not lost.

As there was little to do, I had time to myself. I wondered what Mom was doing, what she was thinking. I had left home on October 9 and had told her that within two weeks either Valnea or I would confirm that I had successfully crossed the border. Instead, almost a month had gone by and she was still waiting to hear from me. In fact, I was further away from crossing the border than when I spoke with her last, when all was proceeding according to plan. Had she told Dad of my escape? What about Mergim? Did he know that I had left for Yugoslavia? How did he feel about being left behind? We had previously agreed that if either one of us could escape, he should not waste the opportunity. Did he realize that under the circumstances I could not get to him in time to join me on my tenth escape attempt? Furthermore, if I failed to cross the border this time, no explanation would be necessary, ever. Otherwise, if I made it and we got together again, I would explain to him how and why I had to leave without him. For the time being, each of us had enough problems and I need not worry about explaining or justifying my actions, at least not to Mergim. If I got caught trying to escape, I would have to explain a lot to my captors, heaven forbid. To avoid that kind of explaining, I had to make sure I was not caught alive. *Remember Mom's parting words*, I told myself: "return with it or on it." It was what Spartan mothers told their sons when they left for the war. The "it" was their shield. If they won the war, mothers expected them to come bearing the shield, i.e., to come back alive. If they lost the war, they should return on the shield, i.e., dead, carried by their comrades. With that thought in mind, I began a daily routine for as long as I was in the mountains. The Nagant revolver Peter had given me was special, different from any other type of revolver. Cocking the hammer caused the cylinder to slide forward, pressing the uppermost chamber against the breech of the barrel. This was intended to form a seal that enhanced the bullet's muzzle velocity. Or at least that's the way I understood it. One thing I did know: The Nagant had been the favored weapon of political assassins in Europe for a long time.

I started cleaning my revolver daily. I began by turning the cylinder manually as I emptied one chamber at the time until I had removed all seven bullets. Next, I cleaned the barrel, the cylinder, each individual chamber, and wiped and inspected each bullet carefully. As they had different colored rims, it was easy to keep them apart. Two bullets, one with a blue and the other with a red rim, looked reliable, without nicks or scratches. I made sure I inserted the blue one in the sixth and the red in the seventh chamber. Now I was all set. In combat, I would use the first five bullets against others. If unable to escape, the sixth one was for me. If it failed, there was still the seventh, the one with the red rim. This became a daily ritual, and by its very repetitiveness it made me feel good. Overall, I was optimistic. I had to be. If worst came to worst, there was always my trusted Nagant; tied to my neck, always within reach, five bullets for others, the last two for me. The thought of carrying insurance against capture by a cruel, hateful enemy felt reassuring. Having cleaned my revolver, I would tuck it under my belt until the next day. Then I would start all over.

Suddenly we heard steps. Peter motioned for us to lie low. He crouched behind a boulder, ready for action.

"It is Marash Bardheci." He smiled as he stood up.

Marash Bardheci appeared to be in his fifties or sixties. He was tall and wiry and moved well for his age. He had been part of the underground in the mid- and late forties. His nephew had been recently arrested because of his contacts with infiltrators and was presently in a concentration camp in Tepelena, a camp known for its inhumane treatment. Geographically, Tepelena was at the other end of Albania. That's how the communists divided their enemies. Opponents from the north were sent way south and vice versa. Thus, they lost contact with their families and the friends they grew up with.

When I first sighted Marash Bardheci, I didn't know this. All I saw was an agile farmer with a big smile on his face. Peter told me these details later, when we spent weeks in a cave readied for us by Marash.

"Hila Shllaku, must a man hear about your whereabouts from strangers? Am I too old for you to knock at my door? Have we not shared enough bread and have we not drunk more than 40 buckets of water together, more than enough to be called friends?"

"My friend," Hila replied, "you have had enough trouble without my knocking at your door each time I travel through this area. This time, however, sooner or later we would have come to see you."

Marash climbed over the rocks and jumped among us. He embraced Hila more warmly than anyone else since I had joined the group. Then it was Peter's turn and finally he hugged Deda. I couldn't quite make out how well the latter two knew him. Hila introduced me as someone the group was escorting to safety in Yugoslavia. Everybody sat down and Marash offered his silver box full of tobacco so we could roll a cigarette for ourselves. I was always ill at ease when my friends smoked. The odor of burning tobacco carried far and could give us away. Again, this was not a matter for me to offer advice on. I was a novice dealing with pros. Besides, I was a nonsmoker; what did I know?

"I understand you have lost contact with the group that was supposed to get you across the Drini," Marash began.

So much for Hila's cover story, I thought. It had fooled neither Gjoka Lazri nor anyone else.

"The problem right now is to find shelter for you and your comrades until either we contact the group or they find you first. It should not take too long. Actually, a group was in the area just a few days ago. They reached their contact point at the Sakat Forest. They were three days late because the rains had kept them on the other side of the river Drini. When they finally crossed, they found a spot where their comrades had waited for them in the woods. They even found a small box that had contained DDT powder. Someone had discarded it as it was empty."

He stopped and looked searchingly at the three infiltrators. Hila looked at his two companions who nodded silently.

"That was us, Marash, and that was our group. We too were delayed by the rains but not as long as they were. We waited for them on location two days and three nights. Finally, we had to leave.

"We must now get in touch with them. We have checked with our other contact but they have not heard from the group. Are there others in this area that can be trusted and are likely contacts for other groups from Yugoslavia?"

Let me digress for a moment. At that time, different groups infiltrated into Albania from different directions. Those coming from Yugoslavia were armed and handled by the Yugoslavs. Those crossing the Greek border were under American direction. The British brought their people in by boat or submarine, while infiltrators from Italy dropped into Albania by parachute. Each agency cultivated its own support network, which it shared with no one. First and foremost, such networks consisted of relatives and friends of the infiltrators. Second, because the less anyone person knew the less he or she could reveal under torture. I knew this from personal experience. Thus, there could be trustworthy bases in the area that Hila was not aware of.

"Let me talk to some people," Marash answered. "If we make quick contact we can get you out of here before word of your presence spreads."

From his bag, he handed Hila a boiled chicken, some bread, cheese, and a bottle of whiskey. "I'd better be on my way," he said with a sly smile. "God willing, I'll be back tomorrow evening."

We rose, shook hands and embraced. Before we knew it, Marash had climbed over the boulders and was gone.

Things were looking up again. It seemed to me that the four of us stood straighter and embraced Marash more vigorously then when we first greeted him. Obviously, things had changed very little, if one discounted the positive effect of boiled chicken on hungry men. Except now we were more hopeful. Gjoka Lazri had helped us because he had no other alternative. Shuk had taken the easy way out by refusing to take us back to the other side of the river. In the long run, that might be better for us but he did refuse to help. Zef Toma, somehow, did not seem serious about escaping. But Marash, well, he was different. He appeared when things were bleak. He was definitely on our side. He was willing to help and take risks on our behalf. No wonder we felt good!

NOVEMBER 5, 1952

The weather was warm again. It was nice and sunny, somewhat unusual for the season, but no one complained. That day there was not much conversation among the four of us. Obviously, we all thought about making contact with the group, Hila probably more than the rest, as he was responsible for the safety of his two companions. Deda was his favorite. Hila often talked to him with great intensity as if he wanted to impress his thoughts deeply on Deda's mind. Deda listened but said very little in return. He and Hila stuck together. They were geographic neighbors; Hila from Shllak and Deda from Dukagjin. At night, they slept near one another. Hila treated Peter differently, with respect but differently. Peter was from Mirdita. His traditions differed little from those of Shllak and Dukagjin. Nonetheless, he was somewhat of an outsider. I of course was the real outsider. They kept me at arm's length when discussing their political and other activities. I realized I was a burden to them as I lacked their background and experience. Beyond that, Hila didn't seem to care for me as a person. I stayed out of his way as much as I could. If he got me to Yugoslavia, I would be indebted to him. Once there, I did not intend to give up my freedom of thought and action. Anyhow, for the time being such thoughts were premature. First, we had to get across the border. Anything else was secondary at this point.

Zef Toma returned shortly before noon. He was ill at ease. He did not sit down but kept shifting his weight from one foot to the other. Finally he blurted out that he had talked with his uncle and had decided not to escape at this time. He was happy he had met us and might still join us if the police put more pressure on him. As he was delivering his prepared speech, I wondered whether Hila and his companions would try to stop him. I looked at all three but, as usual, I could not read their minds.

Obviously, Zef Toma was anxious to leave. None of the three tried to stop him. The farewell was brief. We had run into each other at Gjoka Lazri's by accident. We were parting company without regret on either side. All concerned seemed glad it was over.

That evening Marash returned. No, he had not been able to make contact with the group. He had some plans, some people he wanted to see. He brought us some food and would get back with us in a few days. Hila and Marash stepped aside and had a few words with each other. By the time

Marash left, it had gotten dark. At a signal from Hila, we rose and gathered our belongings. In silence, we moved to a new location about half an hour up the mountain. We sat down and ate our dinner. Then we picked a spot to sleep, Hila and Deda as usual next to each other. Peter moved close to me. We slept under the thin blanket Mom had given me that faraway ninth day of October. Peter was turning into a real friend.

NOVEMBER 6, 1952

The day was a scorcher. The weather had been very strange that fall of 1952. As luck had it, I had picked that season for my escape.

Over the years in Albania, my plans and daydreams had been strictly seasonal. When the first snow covered mountaintops and passes, my hopes grew cold, not to be rekindled until the following spring. After all, no one in his right mind infiltrated into Albania when you could see footprints in the snow. If no one could enter, anyone escaping had to do it on his own. In the spring, when the snow melted, infiltrators became suddenly active again and hope was reborn.

I couldn't help but think that I had tried to escape before—mostly to Yugoslavia, once to Italy, and once to Greece. Here I was now, on this hot November day, stuck somewhere in the mountains of northern Albania, dripping with sweat, without contact with our rescue group and with no real bases in the area. Winter was upon us, never mind the heat of that day. Four weeks had gone by since I left home, when I thought we would cross the border in one week. To give myself a margin of safety, I had told Mother that I would reach Yugoslavia in two. Instead I was trapped between the White and the Black Drini, unable to advance toward the border or penetrate deeper into Albanian territory where Hila and his friends had support among the population. What a predicament.

Not much happened on November 7th, 8th, and 9th. We had food that Marash had left with us—some chicken and thick yogurt. We also had some cornbread. While prospects were dim for the moment, things were not too bad. We had food, we were in good health, and we had our weapons. Personally, I was better off than in the past. I even felt better. I was more in control of my destiny than I had ever been since I had fallen into the clutches of the communists. If everything else went wrong, I still had my Nagant.

NOVEMBER 10, 1952

Shortly after midnight, the weather changed. The wind began to howl and blow and whip trees and bushes as if to uproot them, followed by a rainstorm. Solid sheets of water were trying to drown any vestige of life that might have survived. We had no choice but to sit there and take it. Finally, by daybreak, things seemed to improve. Peter and Deda moved about to gather wood. Hila and I stayed behind. He was too important to engage in such a menial task. I didn't go as I didn't know what kind of wood to gather. It had to be wood that would not smoke because the smoke would be seen for miles as it rose among the trees.

Our two companions returned with armfuls of branches. The wood was dripping wet. I wondered how they would light it and make a half-way decent fire. I had a healthy respect for people who could light a fire, particularly with wet wood. In fact, ever since that episode with the little girl in Dukagjin who lit a fire so I could boil two eggs), I divided humanity into two groups: those who could light a fire from scratch and those who could not. To make a long story short, Peter and Deda started out with halfway dry tree leaves. Then they went from twigs to small branches, to bigger branches until they had a roaring fire going. I figured out that the system was always the same: from small to large, from large to larger. In theory, I had no problem. Actually lighting a fire, however, was something else.

The four of us stood around the fire and turned from side to side, like oversized kabobs without the skewers. Soon our clothes were dry and our complexion pink. Next, we warmed our cornbread and had some break-fast. After all was said and done, life was not so bad as long as you did not expect too much.

At dusk Marash came to fetch us to his home. As it turned out, his home was not too far. I knew we were getting close when I smelled smoke. The usual low-slung building greeted us in the dark. The windows were shuttered tight. Now we could see whitish smoke rising from a soot-covered chimney. Marash walked in first and turned toward us.

"Welcome in the name of the Lord," he greeted us, pronouncing the traditional greeting with warmth and a friendly smile.

We trudged in, one after the other. I don't know how the others felt but I was greatly relieved. I always felt that way when I had a roof over my head and the prospect of a warm meal. That night I felt particularly grateful that I didn't have to walk far, because my sandals were hurting my feet.

After dinner, Marash announced that he was taking us to a nearby cave. "No one but my family knows about this cave. We sometimes hide corn in the cave when government inspectors go around checking the harvest. In fact," he smiled, "the cornbread and mush we had tonight came from corn we hid in this cave in the fall."

He proceeded to tell us that he had cleaned the cave and had thrown out snakes that had sought shelter there for the winter. I noticed that Deda and Peter exchanged a quick smile. Obviously, the two farm boys had thought of snakes when Marash mentioned the cave. Marash reached behind the fireplace and pulled out a canteen.

"You'd better fill this canteen with water at night because the spring is somewhat removed. I'll give you some tobacco, bread, cheese, and walnuts. I'll see you often, perhaps daily, and bring you supplies and news."

To us, both food and news were very important. As long as we were in the cave, we had no contact with the outside world except through Marash. He promised that he would contact a number of people who could help. He would seek out those with likely underground connections who could get us in touch with rescue groups that may be looking for us. He would also look for a swimmer who could get us across the Drini.

After dinner, I took off my right sandal and sock. My big toe looked angry. It was red, swollen, and throbbing. There was an infection along the inner edge of the toenail. I decided to trim the nail as far back as I could with the help of a razor blade I carried with me. I tried to be inconspicuous. Soon I felt Hila's disapproving look on me. I pointed at the toe to indicate it was in bad shape. Hila continued to glare at me. I felt I had to do what I had to do. After all, the toe could be very troublesome if it festered.

Finally, we all rose and got ready for our nocturnal march to the cave. I left the warmth of the house reluctantly. What kind of cave were we going to? I had been in the Grotto of Postumia before the war. It was incredibly large and deep, full of stalactites and stalagmites, with water dripping all over the place. I remembered hearing hidden streams that seemed to come from nowhere and went nowhere, always noisy, always in a hurry. I did not know what to expect. Would this cave be different? If so, how? Limping,

I fell in line. Off we went toward the unknown that awaited us somewhere in the night.

The sky was limpid, studded with myriads of stars. The air was warm and pleasant. The path toward the cave was mostly downhill, sometimes steeply; sometimes it flattened out. My right toe kept throbbing while I tried to keep it curled up to protect it from bumping against the tip of my sandal. Our night march was dragging on, or so it seemed to me, probably because of my toe. It struck me how dependent I was on a body part as humble as a toe. Somehow, I managed.

Eventually, we made it to the cave. The entrance to the cave was quite small. The cave itself was narrow at the entrance but widened somewhat as you moved farther in. It was just large enough to accommodate the four of us. Hila took a brief look and then decided. He would go in toward the back of the cave. Deda would be next to him, followed by Peter. I, the tallest of the four, would lie near the entrance. As ordered, I entered last. Marash had covered the floor of the cave with fresh ferns. I put my knapsack against the side of the cave as my pillow. Then I lay down. It was quite comfortable, except that I could not stretch my legs. In fact, I would not be able to stretch them for the next three weeks, except at night when we left our hiding place for a breath of fresh air.

CHAPTER THIRTY

THE CAVE...CONTINUED

NOVEMBER 11, 1952

Upon awakening, I felt warm, almost cozy. It dawned on me that our body heat was heating our little cave compared to the temperature outdoors. The air must have been stale but I did not notice it. Outside it was getting light. I was close to the cave entrance and could stick my head out. That's when I noticed the clean and fresh smell of the outside air. A few hundred feet below there was a carpet of dense fog that stretched as far as I could see. Across the gorge, stark cliffs emerged from the gray lake of mist and fog. The sun began to pierce the clouds. Everything gained color and brightness. Now I could see that the cliffs across were topped by meadows. Then came some foothills, and beyond them stark mountains that towered like horsemen in glistening armor, impassive, above the lesser hills. I could see a path leading to a house whose black roof topped walls of dark gray stone. Smoke was escaping from the short stack. I could not smell the smoke but I could imagine what was going on inside. Women around the fire were preparing breakfast. Women be blessed! Wherever they were, there was warmth, food, a kind word, a caring touch. With the eyes of my imagination, I could see the men sitting up and scratching their bearded faces, their hairy chests. They too would get up soon and tend to their chores. Another day had begun.

As the morning fog began dissipating, I could see that our cave was maybe 600 feet above a foaming river. I would have liked to plunge in and drink the cold, frothy water with long, long gulps. Then I would scrape my skin and wash off the scum, sweat, and grime that had accumulated over time. My God, one month and two days had gone by since I had walked out on Mother. I wondered how she was holding up. I had promised that she would hear from me within two weeks. Now twice that length of time had gone by and she still had no word from me. What was worse, it seemed I would never be able to cross the blasted Drini River, let alone the Yugoslav border. Sometimes I felt I should have sent word and waited for Mergim before leaving town. Lately, however, I had thanked the Lord that Mergim was in relative safety in forced labor in the military. Better in forced labor and alive than hiding in a cave at the mercy of circumstances that were playing cat and mouse with us.

My three companions started to stir beside me. I pulled my head back into the cave. Now I could see more than the previous night when we had first entered the cave. Farther in, the cave broadened until ceiling and walls converged, leaving a small opening in the back that seemed to lead to another cave, probably a smaller one. The opening was large enough to let small animals get through. If you looked into our cave from the outside, it must have looked like a human mouth with the back wall forming the soft palate. Like in a human mouth, the walls were wet and kept dripping.

Each of my three companions had his own way of awakening. Peter hardly moved when he woke up. It seemed that he wanted all his senses to be fully alive and reconnoitering the area before he let the world know that he was awake. Deda would sit up and stretch as hard as he could. Then he would look around and smile. He looked funny—he had small brownish teeth with ridges across the middle, and a stunted mustache. Nonetheless, his smile was a friendly acknowledgement of his companions and his way of letting us know that he felt well. Hila, on the other hand, woke up smirking. He would not move. Others were supposed to notice and wish him good morning, thus acknowledging the master's awakening. Morning ablutions were no problem. Since we had no water, we didn't wash. By now, all three of my companions were sitting up, ready for breakfast. Breakfast in bed this morning, as there was no room to get up inside the cave. As usual, Peter was our *maitre d'*. He had black stubble and wore a rumpled gray-green uniform. He had neither a white tie nor white gloves. Under the circumstances his friendly smile would do. He pulled out some cornbread and broke off one half. The rest he saved for dinner. He cut it in four portions. Hila and Deda had first and second pick. I was next. Peter always kept the smallest piece for himself. We each got three or four walnuts and a pinch of salt; not bad. Unfortunately, we had only what little water the canteen could hold. It was stale and not enough for four men. Maybe we could ask Marash for a bottle. When I mentioned it to Hila, he chewed me out. It was bad enough we had to impose on Marash for food and everything else. To ask him for a bottle was inconsiderate on my part. Asking Marash for tobacco almost daily, as Hila did, that was OK. Asking for an empty bottle was an imposition. I knew better, however, than to speak up.

Having eaten, we all settled down, each with his thoughts. As I looked out the cave, the fog was gone. I could see everything in detail, bathed in glorious sunshine. Way down at the bottom of the gorge was the Drini River, cold and wild, mist rising above the rapid waves. The thirst made me grouchy. Of course, the sun was shining and the sky was cloudless, now that we were cooped up in a cave! Yesterday it had to rain cats and dogs to make my feet sore and my life miserable!

Speaking of feet, the night before I had prayed to the Blessed Mother. "Please, Mary, don't let my toe fester. I lack bandages and disinfectant. I have no sulfa powder. I lack a clean blade if my toe festers and I have to cut it open. Then I won't be able to walk for quite a while. That could spell disaster." I took off my right sandal. The toe still looked angry but it throbbed less—or was it just my imagination? I thought I could feel Hila staring at me. I did not turn my head. I decided to leave my sandal off for a while. I should have done so the night before; the less pressure on the toe, the better. I didn't even have hot water to soak my toe in. Perhaps with some rest it might get better.

It was time now for my morning prayer. My thoughts wandered to Dad and Mom, and to Mergim. I began to pray: "*Pater noster qui es in coelis…*" and "*Ave Maria, gratia plena…*" I had said those prayers over a number of years, not daily, but deriving great comfort from the familiar words and phrases. When in trouble, prayers were simple. They spoke of survival, of a bite to eat, of divine protection for our family, until the day we could embrace each other once again.

Here I was in my cave, relatively safe and comfortable. Yet we had lost contact with the rescue group. Hila had no idea what to do next. Deda stuck to Hila, silent and unapproachable. Peter was always optimistic, always of good cheer. He did not have much to say but what he said had meaning. He usually was somewhere near me. From that first night, he had always slept next to me. Even in the cave, he bedded down next to me; good, reliable Peter. The day began to fade into dusk. Peter pulled out some bread and the rest of the walnuts. Then he passed around the canteen he had filled with water from a spring outside the cave. We ate in silence. Before long, darkness was upon us. My companions had one last smoke; even at the risk of someone finding us by the smell of burning tobacco. Before too long, all four of us were deeply asleep; no guard, nothing. I was sure, outside the cave—and for miles all around—you could hear us snoring in concert.

November 12, 1952

Outside the cave, it was a gray day. It rained. Clouds and fog filled the gorge, competing with one another for every peak. The house across was nowhere in sight. We seemed suspended in mid-air, drifting aimlessly in an eerie, soundless world. With the walnuts gone, we ate bread and salt twice, once in the morning and then again at dusk. Then we fell asleep. Another day was gone as we drifted into sleep toward an uncertain future.

We did use some of the water for shaving. Shaving was important. If we ever had to emerge from our cave, we had to look halfway decent, at least by local standards. Thus, we shaved every third or fourth day. I may not be able to explain to you what it felt like to be on the special shaving cycle among the great unwashed. If any male reader wants to know how it felt to shave under the circumstances, I can help. Let him grow a beard for a few days. Then let him wet his face with cold water, rub in some shaving cream (we had Gillette shaving cream); use a brush to soften the beard, and finally, use an old blade and go to it! That's what we did every few days. In addition, Peter had a pair of hair clippers. I must say, he was quite skillful with them. Our haircuts looked no worse than those given by civilian or military barbers. In addition, he did not pull the hair with his clippers. That's more than one could say for many a barber, even in Shkodra.

Back to the morning of November 12. After the usual exchange of pleasantries, we switched to discussing our predicament. There was hope. There had to be. Marash had connections. True, he had not been part of the most recent network headed by Hila, but he had the reputation of being honest, trustworthy, and a solid anti-communist. His nephew was in Tepelena, in a concentration camp for having engaged in subversive activities, wasn't he? Marash would do his best to help us. Besides, it was also in his best interest to get rid of us as quickly as possible. If he could pull it off, it would be another feather in his cap, besides freeing him to go after his own affairs. After all, as long as he had us under his wing, he did not dare go too far for fear that something might happen to us. According to the ancient canon of the mountains, that would put him in a most difficult position. If anything happened to us, even if no one suspected him of betraying us to the police, he would still lose face. Hence, both he and we were most anxious to get going, we to Yugoslavia and he to Tepelena to bring food to his nephew.

As we could do nothing on our own behalf, at least for the time being, Marash would do everything in his power to get us on our way. Thus, hope and wishful thinking gave birth to a modicum of confidence. As far as we were concerned, Marash would not rest until he succeeded. After having reassured each other that our logic was firm and feasible, all of us fell silent. We all had our doubts, but we had to deal with them in private, each in his own way.

When I daydreamed in Shkodra, I always imagined my way from the city to the border. I saw before my eyes infiltrators and secret footpaths, steep mountainsides, brooks, and pastures. When I dreamed, I dreamed in color and in detail. However, my dreams and fantasies always stopped at the border. I never dared imagine myself crossing that fateful line. Somehow, any images, no matter how vivid, vanished as I stepped beyond the pyramids marking the border between Albania and Yugoslavia. In the mountains, my daydreams changed. I started thinking about what would happen on the other side. To whom would I write and what would I say? The two logical people would be Edward, my uncle, and Mustafa Kruja, Dad's friend of many years.

Edward was not really my uncle. My grandparents on Dad's side had, I believe, two sons. I remember vaguely Dad telling me that he and his brother fell very ill at one time. Unfortunately, only one dose of medication was available and Grandma gave it to Dad who was the smaller and weaker one. Dad made it and his brother died. Grandma lost her husband at a young age. When she remarried, she gave birth to two girls, Nigjar and Gjylka. Then Grandma died and her husband remarried. He had two sons, Muamer and Edward, and a daughter, Dashuri, Dashka for short.

Thus, Edward and I had no blood in common but, as Dad, Muamer, and Edward had half-sisters in common, they considered themselves brothers. We saw each other from time to time. In Korça we stayed at our own house but were frequently at Muamer's. When they came to Tirana, they stayed at our house.

Of course, there was also Valnea. A letter to her would have to be quite different. I would announce my arrival, just like with the other two. I would give her news of our family in Albania but would not ask for help. Ten years had gone by since we had said goodbye to each other. For all I knew, she could be married and have a slew of children. I did not blame her. Life in the West had normalized. Only the millions behind the Iron Curtain had been cut off from the rest of the world. They had stopped living as human beings. They were exploited, bruised, humiliated, lashed, mocked, and often killed. Valnea had continued her studies, had probably graduated, and could be married to someone who could offer her a normal life, while I was buried alive in Albania. But then again, maybe she had not married. I always stopped at this point because I could not afford this trend of thought. It weakened me; it lowered my defenses if I ever made it out of Albania and had to face harsh realities. It was bad enough if she were no longer my "Vali." To face her with my defenses down was too much. These and similar thoughts kept going around and around in my head, morning, noon, and night, day after day. What stopped them or displaced them was either the sobering thought of whether we would survive or when I fell asleep.

My right big toe continued to throb. At least in this respect it was good I could stay off my feet. Perhaps the toe would heal without festering and without losing the nail. I remember how long it took toes to heal when we twisted nails off surgically at the Military Hospital. Hila could not stand me as it was. He blamed me for not belonging, for not being part of the group, for stumbling at night, for not knowing the area, for not being able to mingle with the natives without sticking out like a sore thumb. I could imagine how he would react if I could not keep pace with him and the rest of the group. He would go into conniptions. Yes, at times he could be childish, particularly when he was wrong or circumstances were beyond his control. Fortunately, such episodes were the exception. Even so, I never learned to enjoy them.

NOVEMBER 13, 1952

I woke up and found Hila tense and irritated. Deda had wrapped himself in hostile silence. He could express more moods and nuances with his silence than most people can with words. Today he was difficult. He was not just mirroring Hila's black mood. He was in a nasty mood himself. Peter was smiling as always, but even he was tense under his smile. Obviously, the relative safety of the cave was fine, but it was getting us nowhere. The hopelessness of our situation was getting under everyone's skin. Hila felt he had to assert himself as our leader.

"Listen, we have been cooped up here now for four days and without someone to get us across the Drini River; we are as good as finished. Our contacts here have failed us, God only knows why, but we cannot and will not give up. To some extent we are handicapped because we cannot move as swiftly as before, because of Genc."

You can imagine how I felt, particularly because he was right, at least in part.

"There is a way out of here," he continued. "We can reach ..." and here he named a place I was not familiar with. "A steel cable is strung there across the Drini River. We can probably hang from the cable and cross the river hand over hand."

He looked at Deda and Peter to see their reaction. Deda remained expressionless.

Peter cleared his throat. "Hila, I know that village and the cable across the river. I don't know if we can hang on to the cable loaded with gear as we are. After all, the river is wide at that point. Furthermore, I suspect that the waters have risen to a level where there may be little clearance between the cable and the water."

Hila resented being contradicted. His temper rose and so did the pitch of his voice. "There is another solution. Let's get out of this cave where we are buried alive. Let's get into the nearest town and shoot it out with the police. We'll kill a few until we get killed. I say that's better than starving to death. If we die in a shootout, at least we die like men. If we starve to death in a cave, when they find us they'll make fun of us."

Hila began with a bang but ended without conviction. Obviously, it was not yet time for such a desperate move. A few moments went by in silence.

"All right, here is one more solution," Hila continued, more subdued. "We can steal the raft and cross the river at night."

This raft was in a village, tied to a steel cable strung across the river Drini. In fact, there was a story connected with this raft. I had heard it in Shkodra but without the names of the people involved. It was an interesting story worth repeating.

Several years before, three infiltrators were stuck on the wrong side of the River Drini. They wore uniforms but without the red star on their caps and they carried weapons identical to those of the Albanian security forces. They approached the village where the raft was tethered. One of the men took over as they marched into the village in full daylight. Here they found themselves in the midst of a battalion of security forces on maneuvers. Now there was no going back. Their leader, with his head erect and full of self-assurance, marched toward the man in charge of the raft.

"Take us across the river now. We are in a hurry," he said to the man, looking him straight in the eyes and with a tone of voice that left no doubt he meant what he said.

"I cannot do that," the man replied, "unless you show me your travel orders."

The leader had to think on his feet. "We are a special security unit. We have our travel orders but I cannot show them to you. You are a civilian."

The man began to waver. On the one hand, everything about the three men—their uniforms, their weapons, even the leader's self-assurance—seemed to vouch for them. On the other hand, the operator of the raft had strict orders not to ferry anyone across without checking their papers. He was in a bind. If he refused to take them across, he would risk their ire. If he agreed, he would place himself in danger even if they were who they claimed they were. Suddenly he saw a way out. "The captain commanding the battalion is coming this way. If he tells me to take you across, I will."

The three men looked up and saw a captain accompanied by two soldiers coming toward them. The leader saluted the officer, while the other two stood at attention.

"Comrade Captain, we are part of a special security unit. We have our travel orders and must cross the Drini as soon as possible. I have explained all this to this man but he insists he must see our travel orders. This I cannot do. He is a civilian. Please order him to take us across. You are an officer and he will obey you. He'd better!" the infiltrator added in a threatening tone of voice.

The captain felt flattered. "My soldiers and I are about to cross the river. You can come with us but I need to see your orders." The infiltrator smiled broadly.

"Of course, Comrade Captain. As soon as we cross the river I will show you our orders."

The captain was satisfied. He nodded toward the man in charge of the raft. They all climbed aboard the rocking platform and minutes later they were on the other side.

"Now let me see your orders," said the captain.

The infiltrator's hand moved briskly toward his pocket, but instead of coming up with travel orders, he drew his pistol pointing it at the officer. "Comrade Captain, tell your soldiers not to do anything foolish!"

Turning to his two companions, who were pointing their weapons at the soldiers, he said, "Take cover behind that wall." The wall was about a hundred yards from where they stood. "When you are in position, aim straight at the captain. If anyone moves, shoot."

His two companions crossed the field and took up position behind the wall. "Ready!" they yelled. Their leader saluted smartly, turned around, and joined his two friends while the three communists seemed nailed to the ground. The three infiltrators wasted no time. They dove into the forest and moved as fast as their feet and the terrain would allow. As far as they could tell, no one followed in pursuit.

As I started telling the story, Peter smiled broadly.

"Yes," he said, "I have heard that story. In fact, Hila, Deda, and I were the three infiltrators whose story you had heard in Shkodra."

"Was it you who led the group when all this was going on?"

Peter nodded. When Peter repeated the entire story at my request, I listened with fascination. "Did you kill the captain?" I asked.

Peter looked surprised. "Why should I have killed him? The man did us no harm. In fact, he helped us. The man was in deep trouble without my adding to his problems. Besides, the communists would probably shoot him for dereliction of duty."

This line of reasoning was typical of Peter. He was a truly courageous man who would shoot only in self-defense.

This was not one of our better days. We had missed our rescuers. We were hiding in a cave without contact with Hila's network. We were imposing on an old man who had been in prison for subversive activities and whose nephew was presently in a concentration camp in Tepelena for political reasons. The present looked dark, the future even worse. Thank God, Mergim was not with me.

The weather was dismal; fog and rain, rain and fog. Our collective mood matched the weather. There was little conversation in our cave today. Marash came to bring us bread, salt, and a few walnuts. Besides the food, he had news. A family had escaped from Fierza. According to Marash, the head of the family was a swimmer, an individual born along the river Drini and able to swim across that rapid and treacherous river. Marash had heard of no troubles that would force the family to take off and leave everything behind. Could it be that our rescue team needed a swimmer?

The mystery of the vanishing family persisted. Why would they take off without an apparent reason so late in the season? They must have had a guide to see them safely across the border. It was unlikely that our rescue group would come into Albania without bringing their own swimmer. Furthermore, why would they decide to go back to Yugoslavia without trying to track us down? After all, their mission was to find our group and see it back safely.

CHAPTER THIRTY-ONE

WE ARE DISCOVERED

NOVEMBER 15, 1952

It continued to rain. Our cave was wet on the inside even when everything around us, hills and mountains, gorge and river, luxuriated in sunshine. The walls of the cave oozed moisture; in spots they also dripped. Today it was worse, or so it seemed to me. Besides, my spot was near the entrance, at the narrowest point of the cave. I could never stretch my legs nor relieve my cramped knees. Hila, who was the shortest, had claimed the widest spot in the cave. Deda, the second-tallest among us, lay next to Hila. Then came Peter, and finally me, the group's tallest member. Of course, it did not behoove me to complain because I was not really part of the group, Hila kept telling me. Hence, if it dripped worse where I was, it did not really matter. I was ticked off. The accommodations were poor, the food was minimal and lousy, and our chances of survival were bad and getting worse. One could say that my companions had the same troubles as I. True, but my legs were sore. They had been sore since the day we had entered this cave and I had been handed the short straw, the short end of the cave. I also felt discriminated against in other ways. If these were not the only reasons for my resentment, they sufficed. I was in a bad mood and I felt I had good reason to be.

NOVEMBER 16, 1952

The rain kept pelting trees and rocks as far as the eye could see. My companions and I hardly exchanged a word. Sunday was upon us and their thoughts were probably going back to other, happier Sundays. My three companions may have thought of Sundays spent in church, followed by festive family reunions. They may have remembered Sunday meals lovingly put together by mothers and wives, with their children around them as they, the heads of families, had said grace before breaking bread.

My memories were different; not just because of our Sunday meals. Mom had always made an effort to make our Sunday meals festive. When times were good, our Sunday meals were excellent. But even in hard times, even when Mergim and I did manual work, Mom always tried to make the Sunday dinner special. It wasn't easy, but I could tell when she scrounged little morsels here and there during the week—until times got truly bad. On good days, I dug up glass bottles at work, washed them, and sold them for a few pennies. Those few coins went for a handful of plums or a few cigarettes for Mom. On bad days, I came home empty handed. At that point, Mom gave up on Sunday dinners.

My Sundays had also been different from those of my three companions when I lived in Austria and in Italy. My churchgoing days had started in Austria when I was seven years old (See Chapter 3). While in high school in Italy, I used to go to church once in a while, usually not on Sundays. I paid my respects in other ways. There was a crucifix behind the Capuchin church in Fiume. Whenever I walked by the cross, I lifted my cap or my hat in sign of respect when I was alone. I would have been embarrassed to do so in the presence of others who knew I was not a Christian. Sometimes I went to Mass during the week, particularly on afternoons.

In high school, I was not required to attend religious instruction like the rest of my schoolmates. Occasionally, I did attend religious instruction even though the old priest who taught the class demanded so little of the students as to make the class uninteresting. In high school, we had history of philosophy for three years while the priest kept asking the students to rattle off the cardinal virtues and the seven deadly sins. What was even worse, some students caused the poor man such aggravation that he had to stop because his heart gave him serious trouble. Such cruelty on the part of one girl in particular was so offensive to me that I preferred to stay away from religious classes.

A few years had passed since I had attended religious instruction in high school in Fiume. It seemed more like a lifetime. Here I was, stuck in a cave with three companions. Our chances of making it to Yugoslavia were slim, to say the least. Nonetheless, we were not going to give up. We had faith in God and in our just cause. Somehow, we were going to make it. I was sure of it...sometimes.

NOVEMBER 17, 1952

The rain kept coming down. The outside world was gray, our mood even worse. Marash had brought us an extra ration of bread and salt the night before when he announced a trip to Breshat in the province of Puka. Without Marash we were even more lost. He was our faithful supplier, our link with the outside world. He brought us news and kept his ears open. Just in case, if a group of infiltrators ever entered the area.

On the other hand, hope was eternal, even if it was at the bottom of Pandora's box. Who knows, when Marash returned he might have good news for us.

NOVEMBER 18, 1952

My notes for this day are skimpy: "Hila is daydreaming again about how to get out of the impasse." Being the leader, he had the responsibility of getting us out. Or at least of keeping up our morale. Furthermore, he felt that the mantle of leadership required of him, or perhaps even conferred upon him, superior ideas, imagination, and judgment. Hence, he kept his mind, or at least his mouth, going—so it seemed to me. I often found him hard to take.

NOVEMBER 19, 1952

Things had gone from bad to worse. We were left hanging. No contact with the outside world, except through Marash. He was kind and generous. The man was in his fifties or sixties. He had been in prison for political reasons. His nephew was in Tepelena right now, also as an enemy of the regime. Yet Marash kept insisting that he would take care of us as long as we needed it. He came every two days or so and brought us bread, walnuts, and coarse salt. He also brought us tobacco, plenty of it, as my companions smoked like chimneys. I wondered how he managed.

Today Hila and I crossed swords. We had a small canteen for the four of us. We filled it with water, late at night. The contents had to last four grown men 24 hours. I ventured to ask whether we could ask Marash to lend us a bottle. Hila hit the ceiling.

"How can you even think of bothering Marash? Don't you think he has done and is doing enough for us? He feeds us despite being poor. Do you realize he is among the poorest in this region? He risks his life and that of his family daily when he climbs up here to help us. And you, you want to ask him for another bottle. Do you or don't you realize how hard it is for our farmers to give up even one bottle?" Hila was almost foaming at the mouth.

"Hila," I replied, "all I am saying is that we should ask him whether he can spare an empty bottle. That doesn't sound like asking for too much." I kept my voice under control lest I upset him even more.

Hila ranted and raved for a while. It was obvious that the bottle was just the spark he needed. Any pretext would have set him off. Our companions didn't speak up one way or another. They knew Hila.

I certainly did not enjoy being the object of his ire. I could have pointed out that he, Hila, had asked more than once that Marash bring more tobacco. I was sure that parting with an empty bottle was less of a burden to Marash. Anyhow, I decided that this "conversation" had gone far enough. I dropped the water bottle, figuratively speaking, and Hila focused his thoughts on something else, probably on how to get us out of the mess we were in. As it turned out, salvation was not to come from him.

November 20, 1952

I woke up feeling ill. It was not my toe. The toe had healed. No more angry redness, swelling, or throbbing. I had prayed that my toe would heal and my prayers had been answered. No, it was something else. I didn't feel hot, I didn't cough. I felt weak and nauseated. It couldn't be something I ate. We all ate the same meager rations and the others seemed well. It wasn't the water, since we hardly drank. Yet I had this feeling of emptiness in the stomach, different from hunger because I was well acquainted with the latter.

Toward five o'clock in the afternoon, we stepped out for a breath of fresh air. The air was nice and cool. The mountaintops were bathed in sunlight while darkness covered the bottom of the gorge. We could hear but could no longer see the foaming river rushing toward the sea, eager to free itself from the squeeze of the chasm it had dug for itself over the millennia. The darkness was spreading upward effortlessly, up the steep rocks along both sides of the riverbed. I felt the urge to relieve myself. I hadn't had a bowel movement in three days. Maybe that's what made me feel lousy. I moved away from my companions and around a bend that afforded some privacy. I lowered my pants and underwear and crouched down near the edge of the cliff.

I had barely raised my head when my feet slipped. In a fraction of a second, I slid over the edge, twisted around toward the cliff, fell, and grabbed a thin root that stuck out from a crevice. Below me was the chasm. I looked up. I was about three feet below the lip of the ledge. I feared the root would let go! I started to pull myself up. Overhead near the ledge was a bush. If I could only reach the base of that bush! Luckily, the root held. One more pull. I grabbed the bottom of the bush. Slowly I hoisted myself up. I lay motionless for a moment. Then I stood up. I pulled up my underwear and fastened my pants. I no longer felt the urge to go. As I walked toward the cave, Peter looked up.

"What happened? You look as if you've seen a ghost."

I mumbled something in response as I climbed back into the cave. As I lay down, I began to feel the fear I had not felt while I was dangling over the gorge. It did not last long. I said a prayer of thanks. The nausea was gone. My companions climbed back into the cave. I loved them all. I loved the sense of security offered by the cave. I loved the brave underground that daily risked its all. I felt warm and protected. O Lord, I love you.

Darkness had taken over. Another day, one I would remember for sure, had slipped away. I slid down on my back, my feet on the floor of the cave, my knees pointing up toward the low ceiling. I closed my eyes. "Our Father, who art in heaven..." Before I knew it, I was fast asleep.

NOVEMBER 21, 1952

The next morning Hila was on the warpath again. Today it was my fault. I had borrowed a needle to fix my pants that were coming apart. I never was good with my hands. As long as my clumsiness did not affect others, it had been OK. Today, however, I managed to drop the needle among the dried-out ferns that covered the floor of our cave. Deda, who had given me the needle, shuddered with disgust.

Hila erupted. "If you knew you were clumsy, why did you ask for a needle? Do you think we can go to a store and buy another one? We have never had luck with any city people we have taken across the border into Yugoslavia. They cannot walk, they need lots of food, and tire easily. City folks should stay home and leave the mountains to those who can handle them."

I knew how Deda felt. I was about to reply that I was forced to flee. Otherwise, I would have stayed in Shkodra and shared the fate of my parents and Mergim. Instead, Peter spoke up.

"This is the 44th time that I have crossed the Yugoslav border illegally.

You and I have saved many a person from arrest, torture, and even death. Of all the city people who have come our way, Genc is the toughest, the strongest. He has been in prison and in obligatory labor. Unfortunately, this is the most difficult situation we have ever found ourselves in. God will show us a way out. Of this I am sure. Even if we have to split up."

This last comment was probably in response to some of Hila's crazy schemes. Everyone was stunned. Hila and Deda had not expected it. I shuddered at the thought that if Peter left I would be stuck with the two of them. In a sense, Peter had thrown down the gauntlet. Anyone answering would have to think and choose his words carefully. For the moment, no one said a word. The topic would resurface several weeks later as our situation got desperate.

Somehow, the day slipped by. I cleaned my revolver, as usual, keeping the two best-looking bullets for last. In combat, if I could not break contact with the enemy, I would shoot myself rather than surrender. Death was nothing compared to the tortures that I could expect. Thanks to Enver Hoxha, we were more afraid of falling into his hands than of dying. Death was only the end of our hopes, of our lives. At this point, we had few hopes and our lives were not worth a plugged nickel. The thought of suffering torture by the hands of Sigurimi was enough to curdle my blood, because I had seen the results of tortures at the Military Hospital in Tirana.

NOVEMBER 22, 1952

I woke up feeling good—until it sank in where I was. Even in prison in Tirana, those first few moments in the morning I felt great; a young man bursting with health and strength. The true awakening came once I realized that Dad and I were prisoners and that his life was in danger. That's when reality set in. Here in the mountains things were better, for I was beyond the control of the security forces, at least for the moment. My companions and I were in this together. We would make it because as long as there was life there was hope. Or we would fail together. That was still better than being in jail.

Breakfast today was different. We had run out of bread and walnuts. Today we could have water, or we could have salt, or we could have water and salt. What we could not have, however, was peace. Hila was on the warpath again.

"What we need is to get out of this cave. We need to contact our bases. We will find somebody to swim us across the Drini River. We have made it so far, and we will make it again. We are not yet at the end of our wits. They have not yet seen the end of Hila Shllaku. We can always fight to the bitter end and take a few of them with us. We are not there yet. What I need is to do some thinking. I am sure I can come up with something. Just leave it to me... Of course, it would be much easier if we didn't have Genc with us."

He turned to me. "You realize that you have slowed us down. It's been a problem feeding you. The network pays for us. As you are not one of us, we have a problem with the people who give us shelter."

His beady, dark eyes were fixed on me. He didn't sound as malevolent as he had at times. He sounded almost relieved that he could put some blame on me. Without me, he would have probably led his men from triumph to triumph.

"In fact, we have a problem right now. Some of our bases may be reluctant to deal with us if we bring an outsider with us."

The last statement was, of course, pure nonsense because he had lost contact with all his bases. I didn't know whether it was better for me to play dead or respond with a few salvos of my own. I decided for the latter.

"I admit that I have slowed you down at times, particularly at night. It seems to me, however, that we are where we are not because we didn't walk fast enough or far enough. After I joined you, once you had me pay for my food and I did so. Also, I paid 10,000 lek before I left Shkodra—at the request of the network."

That sum was the equivalent of two months' pay. For us that was a lot of money.

"When the group from Yugoslavia failed to pick us up, I was ready to swim across the Drini. The weather was good, the river low."

As soon as I said those words, I knew I had made a mistake. That day, on October 29, Deda had refused to cross the Drini River and had kept us on this side. Today he shot me a dirty look. I had to try to remedy my blunder.

"Perhaps we could not have made it on our own without a swimmer and things would have been worse," I added hastily. Unfortunately, the harm was done.

For whatever reason, Hila chose not to zero in on me beyond what he had already done. He picked up his general theme of "beating the odds" as he had often done in the past. He would start out on a positive note. He would wax optimistic, then defiant. For a moment, he would consider a hero's death. Then he would start from the beginning. As usual, Deda and Peter kept quiet. I of course stayed out of it as I had already done enough harm for one day.

NOVEMBER 23, 1952

When I looked out in the morning, the weather had taken a turn for the better. It was no longer raining. The clouds below us looked like ripped sheets floating in the breeze between the cliffs. In places, I could see the river. The entire landscape was in shades of gray. In mid-morning, from out of nowhere, two visitors moved in front of our cave. They had nice white and brown coats and pointed beards. Their beards had no pretense of wisdom. They also had horns, but their horns were not threatening. They were not interested in us, just in the grass that grew all around our cave. They didn't even bleat. Perhaps they knew that bleating would bring the shepherd and thus end their freedom prematurely. All in all, they were enjoying themselves. We cave dwellers saw it somewhat differently. To us, goats were just the beginning. Shepherds and perhaps sheep dogs were already on their trail. That was not good for us. We had few options. We could push the goats over the cliff and create a ruckus. We could shoo them away, another poor option. We obviously couldn't shoot them. Trying to catch them could bring search parties to our cave. That was no good. While we were going back and forth on the subject, our visitors left. We waited but no one else showed up all day and into the evening. Thank God for little favors.

NOVEMBER 24, 1952

I'll remember November 24 because Hila and Peter exchanged words. It started more or less with one of Hila's rambling monologues. Deda kept silent. I had nothing to offer, so I too held my peace. Peter spoke up this time, gently.

"We have been in this cave for a while thanks to Marash Bardheci's courage and generosity. Marash, however, is in trouble. He would like to stay and take care of us. If he stays, he must neglect his nephew in the concentration camp of Tepelena, one of the worst. Families can bring food to the inmates only once a month. If Marash doesn't go now, he must wait until next month. Can his nephew wait that long? Marash is in a bind. If he leaves for Tepelena and something happens to us, according to the law of our mountains, he is held responsible. His nephew is being persecuted as an anti-communist. He too depends on Marash and Marash is not even a member of our network. He is helping us because that's the kind of man he is. Now we must help Marash. I will go to Sakat. I will get help and will come back for you."

Hila was stunned. "Peter, we cannot break up our group. We left together and we must return together. I am responsible for our group. Don't forget that." It was obvious that Hila could see his leadership slipping away. This he could not afford.

"Hila, you are from Shllaku and out of your territory. I too am out of my area but not too far. It won't take me long to get help. With luck, I may even find a swimmer to get us across the Drini. By that time you will have plotted a plan and we will cross the Yugoslav border together, just as on our way in."

Peter let Hila save face without giving up on his plan. However, I had mixed emotions. Obviously, Peter was not going to die of starvation or inaction in a cave. I had met some of Peter's friends (remember Marka Ded Alija?), and had great confidence in them. However, if Peter left I would be stuck with Hila and Deda, neither of whom were my friends. My thoughts were interrupted by Hila.

"Peter, what if the rescue group came to get us and we were unable to reach you? You know that we have a secondary base as a contact, Marash Ndoja's. He has not asked for us because the group from Yugoslavia hasn't arrived yet. The weather has been bad. It has rained for days at a time. The Drini River is probably too rapid for them to cross. They are due any day. You know that neither the Yugoslavs nor our personal friends will let us down. I don't think this is the time for us to break up as a group. What do you say?"

Hila had a point. One thing I didn't understand, however. If they had another base, why had they not made our presence known to them?

Peter thought for a moment. Then he looked Hila straight in the eye. "You are right. I'll wait a few days. If nothing has moved by then, I'll be on my way."

Everybody felt better. Hila was still in charge. Peter had listened to reason and had grown as a man, at least in my eyes. He was willing to wait but he would not bow to Hila's faltering leadership. Deda seemed pleased, perhaps out of loyalty to Hila or friendship to Peter, or simply because the group had not broken up. This time I agreed with Deda. No matter what the reason, peaceful consensus was better than discord, which could threaten us all.

That evening Marash Bardheci came to see us later than usual. The lateness of the hour was baffling, to say the least. What had happened or was about to happen? Had someone spied on us? Had the police discovered us? Such thoughts flashed through my mind as I kept my eyes fixed on Marash Bardheci. His expression told me nothing. Neither did his opening remarks.

"How are you?" he asked us. "Did you have enough to eat? Are you tired? Has the weather been hard on you?"

Hila gave the conventional answers. We were fine. The lack of food did not bother us, neither did the weather. After all, we were used to such circumstances. It was obvious, however, that Hila could not have continued this charade for very long. After all, he was city bred, never mind his peasant roots.

Marash offered Hila his tobacco box and Hila rolled himself a cigarette. His impatience was showing. "So what is new?" he asked Marash, while keeping his eyes averted.

"Not much. Today I visited Marash Ndoja." Marash Ndoja was our other network base.

"He received me like in olden times when we had both been involved in the struggle against the communists. He offered me tobacco and coffee. He asked no questions but waited for me to explain the purpose of my visit. I did not beat around the bush. I said, 'If someone were to come asking about a lost group, tell him I know where to find his friends.' Marash Ndoja nodded but asked no further questions. 'I'll relay the message, if the time comes,' he had replied. That was good enough for me. I thanked him and left. That happened this afternoon. I thought you may want to know so I came despite the late hour."

There it was. The secondary base had been activated. Now all we had to do was wait until the group came looking for us. Things were not so bad, after all. Just this afternoon it had seemed as if our little world were falling apart. Things had changed in a hurry. Peter need not leave. Hila was vindicated, and I need not worry about being stuck with Hila and Deda without my friend Peter. I looked at my companions. I must admit, Hila didn't gloat. The halo of wise leadership, however, shone brightly atop his head.

Boy, I felt good. That night, when we said good night to each other, we sounded like a team, a real team. With pleasant thoughts swirling through my head, I must have fallen asleep before the rest, because for once I didn't hear them snore.

NOVEMBER 25, 1952

The day was uneventful in view of what Marash Bardheci had told us the day before. Suddenly, at dusk, he stood once more at our cave entrance. He climbed in. His face told me nothing, nor did his opening inquiries about our health. Darn these mountaineers! Why could they not come to the point? The news had to be good, after yesterday's developments. I could hardly wait.

The preliminaries were coming to an end. Our visitor and my three companions had finished rolling themselves a cigarette. They had reassured each other that their health was good, that they had rested well, and that they had plenty to eat. I had been half listening, waiting for the news. Marash Bardheci finally came to the point.

"Marash Ndoja came to see me today." He paused and dragged on his cigarette. "Yesterday he told me that I could count on him for help. Today he had changed his mind. He wanted no part of me. He would never come to my house again. If I went to his, I would find the door shut. If I ever approached him again with the tale of lost infiltrators, he would report me to the police."

His cigarette and those of my three companions glowed in the dark. Darkness filled our cave, darkness in every sense. For a while, no one said a word. Then, Marash Bardheci spoke again.

"We are not going to give up. If Marash Ndoja is unwilling to help, there are others. For now, lie low and wait. Things can change at a moment's notice. Eventually, your friends will come and things will straighten themselves out."

Good old Marash Bardheci. We were stuck in the cave and he was stuck with us, and because of us, his nephew would suffer hunger in the concentration camp at Tepelena. Clearly, this situation could not go on much longer. Hila spoke for all of us, assuring Marash that this was just another hurdle. The Yugoslavs were well aware of the importance of the Albanian network, and sooner rather than later they would mount an operation to get us across the border. The war against Enver and his gang had intensified recently. It would be won and Marash Bardheci would gain the recognition he so richly deserved.

What else was there to say? Marash shook hands all around and climbed out of the cave. For a moment, we could see his silhouette against the dark sky, the silhouette of an agile old man. Then he was gone. I felt dejected. The others must have had similar feelings. We murmured "good night" to each other and withdrew into the loneliness of our thoughts. What was there to think? Another day gone, another hope lost.

NOVEMBER 26, 1952

Morning light reached into our cave with gray fingers. I had been up for a while. When the others awoke, we all went through our usual motions. We greeted each other, ate a bite of stale cornbread, gnawed on some salt, and settled down, each caught up in his own web of thoughts and memories. I looked at my watch from time to time. Sometimes the hours passed slowly, sometimes they seemed to vanish in big chunks, depending on the intensity of my daydreams. Suddenly, Hila erupted like a firecracker.

"My name is not Hila Shllaku if I can't get us out of here, one way or another. By God, if need be, we will fight our way across the border."

For a moment, he seemed to be forgetting that first we had to cross the Drini before we could attack the border.

"We have run into difficulties before and they never stopped us. We have friends and allies in these mountains, people willing, yes, eager to help us. All we have to do is show ourselves."

He looked around. As always, Deda's face was expressionless. Peter looked friendly but no more than that, at a time when Hila was looking for approval and support. He looked at me. I don't know what my face showed. If anything, I was the most interested in crossing the border as I was the most helpless. Then Hila's expression changed from euphoric to one of grave concern. He lowered his voice as he continued.

"I am responsible for you, Deda and Peter. You have both left your families to follow me. I cannot and will not forget it." He looked at me with a semblance of sorrow.

"When we break out of here it may be with blazing guns, on wings of eagles. It is your misfortune that you chose to join us during this trip. We have run into difficulties before and we have overcome them because we were by ourselves. You have slowed us down. We have had to share with you our meager rations. Our bases don't trust you. You have turned out to be a serious burden for the three of us."

He looked at me with his small, shiny eyes, waiting for a reply. I realized that the deck was stacked in his favor but I would be even worse off if I did not respond to his attack.

"Hila, I respect and admire you, the three of you, for the courage you have displayed, risking your lives and those of your families year in and year out. In addition, you have helped many refugees cross the border. That too is well known, wherever people dare hope that some day the communist regime will be overthrown and Albania will be free again. In the meantime, those who have no choice flee Albania to save their lives. I would not have left my family except that I was about to be arrested for the second time. Instead of helping them, I would have become a heavy burden and a source of great anxiety. Never mind what I would have had to face from the hands of Sigurimi. I knew the risks when I asked to join you. I am most grateful that you have accepted me. I assure you that I will do my best not to slow you down nor hinder you in any way." Hila was happy I had picked up the gauntlet.

"You have not slowed us down? How many times have I warned you to watch where you were going? Yet you keep stumbling and falling as if I had not said a word."

He knew and I knew that he was right. What I had not realized yet was that I had impaired night vision. Besides, how could I suspect it when my day vision was 40/20?

He continued, "We pay our bases for food and shelter. In your case, they feed and shelter you for free. Is that fair? They are poor but are willing to sacrifice for us. That does not include you." His eyes told me that he enjoyed sinking the knife into me, at least verbally. I felt my temper rising.

"Now wait a minute. Before I left home I had to scrape together 10,000 lek. I handed the money over to Peter Ndoja, the liaison man. That sum is equivalent to two and one half months' pay. That's a lot of money by any measure. It should pay for a lot of food and shelter." Hila got red in the face.

444 ONE MAN'S JOURNEY TO FREEDOM: ESCAPE FROM BEHIND THE IRON CURTAIN

"We don't do what we are doing for money. There is not enough money in the world to pay for the risks we take." He stopped to fill his lungs with air. I interrupted him.

"Furthermore, you asked for payment at Gjoke Lazri's and I gave you a gold ring. That was the last thing of value I had on me. I have no more."

Hila seemed totally off balance. Was he not supposed to collect payment under the circumstances? Had he kept the ring for himself? Deda and Peter sat quietly, as if the discussion were of no interest to them. Hila exploded.

"What are you talking about? Don't you realize what a precarious position you are in? I want you to know that these two men are my responsibility. If you slow us down or endanger us in any way, I will have to kill you. So now you know where you stand."

"I want you to know," I replied without bothering to hide my fury, "that if it ever gets to the point that I endanger the group, I will know what to do. As for you killing me, the Lord knows I would not keep my hands in my pockets."

The words we had thrust at each other lay like daggers between us. We had both painted ourselves into a corner, into opposing corners, to be precise. He was the leader and probably felt he couldn't back down. I could hardly apologize if I wanted to be considered a man. I had little else left. So, Hila or no Hila, I was not going to cave in.

"It is time for our evening meal." Peter's voice was firm and friendly. He pulled out his knife and carved a slab of cornbread into four pieces. As usual, he got the last and smallest one for himself. A little rock salt, a slug of water, and our meal was over before we knew it. Yet Peter's calm voice and the routine of passing the water jug from one to the other renewed the bond that held us together.

"Good night, men," said Hila's voice in the darkness. He did not say "Good night, Deda and Peter."

"Good night," three voices answered in reply. We had just smoked the Albanian peace pipe. I must admit, I felt good about it. We settled down and no more was said that night.

NOVEMBER 27, 1952

In the morning, as I looked out of the cave, all I could see were shreds of fog halfway up the valley, a dense cloud cover overhead, and angry rain as far as the eye could see. The mood in the cave matched the weather, minus the anger. Sometime during the day, my companions began to talk about the feast of St. Andrew. He was the patron saint of Telumë. He was also Deda's patron saint. For a while, my three companions debated whether we should leave the cave and spend St. Andrew's in Telumë. Why they wanted to take the risk, who they wanted to visit, and why Telumë had not been considered sooner as a possible way out of here were never discussed. I would have liked to know but didn't ask. It was bad enough that I was the outsider. It was best for me to keep quiet. Anyhow, the conversation went back and forth among the three. Soon the idea was dropped, which suited me just fine. Perhaps we could have eaten better in Telumë. But was it worth the risk?

NOVEMBER 28, 1952

Dawn was beautiful. The sky had rained itself out, washing all the clouds down the steep mountainsides and into the river. As I lay near the cave entrance with my knees pulled up, I dreamed with open eyes. I had become quite good at it. Often I relived the past. Sometimes I tried to peek into the future. The most I dared dream of was to compose letters to Mustafa Kruja, Edward Lico, and Valnea. My mind was like a merry-go-round with the same thoughts bobbing up and down. I would write to the first two to inform them of my escape, tell them about their families, and ask for help. I would write to Valnea to tell her that I had made it out of Albania and ask her to send a telegram to Mom telling her that I had finally made it. Whether Valnea still cared for me and whether she would come to see me was up to her. For all I knew, she was happily married and I would stay out of her way.

Today, as my eyes roamed beyond the cave entrance—looking without really seeing—I thought I saw a man in front of our cave. He was so close I could almost touch him. I stared at the man and he stared right back. The next thing I knew, I was pointing my revolver and waving him inside the cave. By now, the rest of the group had also seen him. I moved over to make room as he climbed into the cave. He crouched down and stared perplexed at the four of us, one at the time.

"Who are you?" Let me see your ID." Hila fired both sentences in rapid sequence, without pausing for the man to answer the first.

The man pulled a bundled kerchief out of his coat pocket. He undid the kerchief, opened his wallet, and gave Hila his ID. His name was Ded Nikollë Pjetri.

"Give me your belt and move closer." The man obeyed.

Hila checked the man's belt and waistband for hidden pockets. Communists often kept their party IDs tucked away in or under their belts. There was no evidence here of any such hiding place. What struck me was that the man carried a picture of the Blessed Mother in his wallet. Hila must have noticed the same thing.

"What brings you here?" Hila wanted to know.

"Christmas is near. I was taking a goat into town to sell it and buy provisions and a few gifts for my family."

"Where is your goat?"

"It ran away. I tried to follow the animal but lost it in the woods. Then I smelled cigarette smoke. Thinking that someone else may have caught the goat, I followed the smoke and found myself before your cave."

The man sounded plausible. Particularly his comments about the cigarette smoke. There was a fairly long pause. Hila decided to pursue another line of questioning. "Do you know who we are?"

The man shook his head.

"I am Hila Shllaku. This is Deda Mëhilli and the third man is Peter Qafa from Mirdita."

The man seemed relieved. "I know you by reputation."

"Tell me, are you glad that you met us?"

"I am both glad and sorry that I met you," the man replied.

"How come?" Hila was persistent.

"I am glad that I met you because you are brave men who risk their lives on behalf of the Albanian people. It is always good to meet such men. It gives the rest of us hope and courage. On the other hand, I would have preferred not to run into you. I have a neighbor who killed my brother by betraying him to the communists. If I had known, I would have killed him and would have joined you with my honor vindicated. There is another reason why I would have preferred not to meet you. Under the circumstances, I cannot come with you. If anything were to happen to you after I leave you, how could I convince you or anyone else that I did not betray you?" He looked Hila straight in the eye. He made an impressive witness on his own behalf.

The time had come to fish or cut bait. I tried to anticipate what Hila would do. The man looked sincere if somewhat ill at ease. Hila had not introduced me and that seemed like the right thing to do under the circumstances. Would Hila ask me to step out with the man and keep him covered while Hila consulted with his friends? Would Hila keep him in the cave until dark and then let him go while we left in another direction? Would Hila take him outside, away from the cave, and tie and gag him to give us time to get away? What would Hila do? The three men looked at each other without saying a word. As hard as I tried, I could not read their thoughts.

Hila then said to the man, "Listen, Ded Nikollë Pjetri. You are a good man, someone who cares for his family and for Albanian traditions. It is better that you not kill your neighbor before joining us. The police would try to catch you and us. The day will come when all those who have betrayed our Albanian traditions will be brought to justice. That's what we work for in the mountains, and that's what you pray for in your homes. We are part of the same struggle, wherever we are. We'll let you go now. You are a prudent man. May God protect you. Go and may you find your goat."

The man lost no time. "May God protect you all." He barely finished those words when he jumped out of the cave and disappeared from sight.

"Now we have to get ahold of Marash Bardheci and get out of this cave as quickly as we can."

So that's what was on Hila's mind. Getting ahold of Marash Bardheci was easier said than done, however. Today was his turn to come and bring us bread and whatever else he could spare. Once again, we had to buckle down and wait. We could do little else at this point. Finally, it got dark. Marash was nowhere in sight. Was he not coming tonight? I kept staring into the darkness. Suddenly, a broken twig, a dark shadow in front of the cave entrance. Marash swung himself inside the cave.

"How are you, men?"

"Thank God, we are well. How are you? Could you make it? Are you tired?" we answered in chorus. These were conventional Albanian phrases that sounded natural, rather than stilted, as they do in English.

Marash smelled of alcohol. His voice was shaky, his words slurred.

"I was at a funeral; many guests, lots to eat and drink. We had a good time. We bury the dead then life goes on. It does a man good to be with friends..."

His voice stopped in mid-sentence. What he did not say was, "and forget the present." There was no question that the present was harsh for Marash. He found himself between a rock and a hard place. He had his nephew in Tepelena and us in a cave, and was responsible for both parties. At least liquor had given him a respite for a few hours.

Marash seemed to have run out of words. Hila spoke next. He gave a succinct description of our surprise visitor and his brief stay with us. Hila concluded by saying that time had come for us to leave the cave, preferably that very night. Marash had trouble focusing his thoughts, no matter how hard he tried.

"Listen," he said. "I have to move you from here. Right now I don't know where to. I'll think it over tonight and be back tomorrow."

He wished us a good night and mumbled a few words. Despite his unsteady condition, he was out of the cave and out of sight with dispatch. He was a remarkable old man.

He left us in a quandary. Had our morning visitor betrayed us in the meantime? Would he? Could we spend another night in the cave? Where would we go from here, to another cave? Was there another cave? We could expect snow any day now. How would we handle that, ill equipped as we were, as I was? We said good night to each other and withdrew into our private worlds, as we had done so many nights before. Except that tonight our private worlds were colder than usual.

November 29, 1952

My mind was in turmoil. We probably washed up and ate breakfast, like always. I have no details, however, neither in my notebook nor in my memory. As to washing up, it was rather primitive. Cats in the homes across the gorge did a better job when they licked their paws and wiped their faces! Breakfast also was not much to brag about. Sometimes we had a little bread, a few walnuts, a few chunks of rock salt. More often than not, we had only two out of three. Both washing up and eating breakfast were part of routine events that went by without leaving tracks.

That day Marash didn't show up before dawn when he could come with relative safety. The morning and the afternoon went by and still no

Marash. Would he come in the evening? Did he understand Hila correctly, that we had been discovered by a stranger? Did he realize that we as well as he were at the mercy of this stranger? Last night Marash was drunk to the gills. Would he remember what Hila told him?

At dusk Marash popped up in front of the cave entrance. One quick swinging of legs and he was seated among us. The greetings proceeded as usual, unhurried and dignified. To a city boy like me they were nothing less than exasperating. Finally, Marash got down to business.

"I am sorry to tell you, but I know of no other cave in the area. There is, however, a boulder formation that will hide you from sight and protect you against the weather. When you are ready, we'll be on our way."

I wasted no time. I shoved my thin blanket into my knapsack. I tightened my belt and secured my (Peter's) revolver. I stood up in my sandals and noticed with pleasure that my toe had healed in the meantime. Whatever lay ahead, I was ready. Within minutes, we were on our way, Marash at the head of the column, Peter bringing up the rear. It took us less than half an hour to reach the rock formation. I was somewhat taken aback. If we were within easy walking distance from the cave, were we not within easy reach of a search party headed for the cave? As none of my friends objected, I knew better than to speak up.

The rock formation was like a hand with spread fingers sticking out of the ground. Several large boulders formed a semicircle at one end while one lonely boulder blocked one approach. Hila and Deda laid their blankets in what seemed to be the most protected corner of the enclave. Peter and I claimed the opposite corner.

The weather was not bad. It was cool but not windy. There was no precipitation. Here and there, you could see stars in the sky. Overall, things were not bad. We had no roof over our heads but we also had no dripping cave walls surrounding us. Above all, the air was fresh and clean. That stench in the cave eventually had gotten to me! Who knows, maybe here in the open my friends may not want to smoke for fear of being discovered. Nah! It would take more than that to keep them from smoking. Peter and I snuggled together. We laid our tent sheets on the ground, covered ourselves with my blanket, wished the other side of the house good night, and went to sleep.

November 30, 1952

When we woke up, the sun had gilded the mountaintops on both sides of the gorge, the air was fresh, and we felt full of vim and vigor. We got up and folded our blankets, which were moist with dew. Once we had our usual breakfast behind us, it became clear to us that something was not right.

Mother Nature had surrounded us with an array of colors. The sky was blue, and some trees still displayed their brilliant fall garb while the meadows sparkled like emeralds. The four of us, on the other hand, looked grimy, unshaven, and with hair down to our shirt collars. Something had to be done. First, Peter located a sparkling brook. We undressed to the waist and washed up. We rubbed and scrubbed until our faces, necks, arms, and chests were deep red. Then we shaved. That was the pits. We each picked a blade from a bunch of used blades and sharpened it in the palm of the hand or against the side of a water bottle. Assuming that this procedure helped, I hate to think what these blades were like before we sharpened them! Anyhow, I cried in silence while I shaved the stubble off my face. Finally, Peter cut our hair with hand clippers and scissors. Judging by the job he did on Hila and Deda, my haircut must have been OK.

Now we felt much better and in step with Mother Nature. We felt clean and uplifted. The day went by and our morale stayed way up. A cold night followed. We didn't mind. When it was time to settle down, Hila and Deda went to their corner, and Peter and I lay down in ours. No one stood guard. We may have snored, but no unpleasant surprises befell us.

December 1, 1952

The weather was again beautiful, even warmer than the day before. In fact, at noon it was downright hot, too hot for the season. Even I knew that such hot weather was the precursor of storms to come. Well, we might as well enjoy the good weather while it lasted. Anyhow, the good weather and the improved morale made Hila more loquacious than he had been in the last few days.

Marash had mentioned that rumor had it that the government was about to proclaim a major amnesty. He started to speculate as to who might be included. I must admit that I lent him only half an ear.

As I listened to Hila's speculations, I could not help but remember Osman Gazepi and his "innocent" question in jail early in 1945 (See Chapter

13). According to Hila, the party could just be smart enough to reduce tensions in the country by declaring a broad amnesty and thus gain the cooperation of many. I said nothing but I could clearly hear the echo of Colonel Gazepi's voice and see the broad smile on his face, the face of someone who had played the buffoon because it had suited him best. Mercifully, Hila's soliloquy finally ended. We wished each other "Good night," and sought refuge from reality in dark corners of our dreams.

DECEMBER 2, 1952

My diary quotes Peter discussing the ferry at Dardha. The description went something like this: The River Drini could be crossed at Dardha by means of a raft attached to an overhead steel cable. Peter preferred not to force the operator to get us across. Instead, he thought we might use the steel cable to cross the river hand over hand. I remembered a similar conversation that took place in the cave, except that time it was Hila who had the idea and Peter had opposed it. Now Hila took over like greased lightning.

"Of course, we can cross at Dardha but we can do better than try to hang onto the cable by hand. What we need is a pulley. We hook the pulley up to the steel cable and cross the river one at a time. Since we don't have a pulley we must make one. Here is the plan. We ask Marash to get us an ax and a hand drill. We make a pulley and a frame attached to both sides of the pulley with enough space for the cable to pass through. Crossing the river in this manner should be no problem at all."

I could not visualize this project. Would they make the pulley out of wood? Would the concave rim of the pulley fit the dimensions of the cable? What if the pulley or the frame broke? What if the pulley with one of us hanging on for dear life stopped at the lowest point of the cable, i.e., above the widest point of the river? How would we pull ourselves to the other side? Would the frame be hooked up to a rope so the pulley could be returned for the next trip?

Apparently others were also having second thoughts. I don't recall anyone raising any objections but I do recall vividly that the next proposal dealt with relying on our pup tents to cross the river. We would tie the four corners together, inflate each pup tent, and hang on to it as we swam across. Needless to say, this idea was all wet (forgive the pun, please!) and met with less-than-roaring success. The conversation went back and forth for a while. The initial enthusiasm started dimming. Fewer and fewer ideas were offered for discussion. Finally, the conversation died out like a smoldering fire choked off by its ashes.

After dark, Marash came to see us and told us of his decision. Marash was caught between his nephew who needed food in Tepelena and us who depended on him for survival. In his gentle but firm way, he told us that he had decided not to go to Tepelena.

Hila objected. "Marash, you must go. If you don't, your nephew will be without food for at least a month. No one else will be able to help him there. You have no choice. You must go. One way or another, we will survive."

Marash looked at Hila. His expression was calm. His eyes showed the wisdom of suffering. They spoke of courage, of an inner source of strength. Was it the memory of obstacles overcome? Was it trust in God? Whatever it was, there was no need for words.

Marash started to rise. "It's getting late. I won't see you tomorrow. I'll be back the day after tomorrow with some food. May God protect you."

By the time he finished those words, he was gone.

I was impressed. Hila had no choice but to ask Marash to reconsider his decision. On the other hand, neither Hila nor we could muster any arguments that Marash had not already considered. The way old Marash had handled himself—and us—was most dignified. He did not belabor his dilemma. He either had to sacrifice his nephew or his friends. As a man of the Albanian mountains, he had chosen to sacrifice his relative. His was a spirit that drew strength from traditions and from within. The communist party could not tolerate this. It demanded—and depended on—complete submission of the individual. The Party had to destroy the bonds of family and friendship. It could not allow religion or tradition to be sources of strength outside and beyond the reach of the Party. Everyone had to depend on the Party for food, shelter, employment, safety, and even self-respect. It was obvious how the Party controlled the means of subsistence.

How did they control self-respect? Here is how: The Party was most successful in cities where its control was strict and its tentacles far reaching. For instance, if someone made a decision while on the job and did not hear about it from the boss, he was likely to conclude that he had acted properly. The next time he acted the same way, confident that he was doing the right thing. This time, he got reprimanded and even punished. There seemed to be no rhyme or reason to the way the communists acted. But there was. Such a strategy had a devastating effect on the affected person. It blurred the dividing line between right and wrong and kept him from making independent decisions.

Years later, I read about a study with rats. A rat was put in a cage equipped with two levers. The blue lever delivered food, the red lever an electric shock. It did not take long for the rat to learn to avoid the red lever. Once the rat learned its lesson, conditions were reversed. Now the blue lever delivered an electric poke, the red lever food. It took a while, but the rat adapted and went to the red lever for food. When researchers reversed conditions a second time, the rat crawled into a corner of the cage, refused to come out, and died of starvation.

I cannot help but wonder whether the communists had worked out similar strategies to paralyze entire nations. They had, of course, other tools at their disposal. They chose their pressure points carefully for each person. In one way or another, they would stress the individual beyond endurance. Next, they would exert pressure on the victim, asking him or her to become an informer. Those who caved in paid with their self-respect. Those who refused were in trouble and at the mercy of the Secret Police. Either way, this method was most destructive.

Marash had been part of the underground in years past. He was caught, probably tortured, and spent years in prison. He was not part of Hila's network. Yet he had eagerly come to our aid. And now, having to choose between his nephew and us, he had made the honorable choice, honorable according to the Code of Lek Dukagjini, the code of our mountains. Men like Marash, old and young, gave me hope that Albania had a future.

CHAPTER THIRTY-TWO

OUR GROUP BREAKS UP

DECEMBER 3, 1952

The rain must have started during the night. We were wide awake well before daylight, and by morning we were soaked to the skin. Not surprisingly, the weather and our morale went hand in hand. Had we been a regular military outfit, our commander would have had us sing or march around to boost our spirits. As we could do neither for obvious reasons, Hila tried another approach. He asked us to discuss ways of crossing the Drini River. Whatever discussion followed was lame, worse than previous conversations on this topic. After all, one full month had gone by since we had crossed the Drini at Skvina. Instead of crossing the border in a matter of days, we were stuck, literally stuck on this side of that darned river. It was enough to make a grown man cry. Instead, I devoted my time to tearing up my shirt that, by now, was worn through in places and full of lice and their eggs along the seams. That shirt was good for one more thing. I removed all parts with seams, such as the collar and cuffs.. The rest I cleaned as best I could, ripped it into strips, and stuffed the strips in my pockets. You never knew when they could come in handy.

DECEMBER 4, 1952

The day before, it rained all day. Then the rain grew into a regular rainstorm. Our morale was so low that it was in danger of drowning in the rivulets of water running down our backs, our sleeves, our socks, out again and down the mountainside. Hila described once more for our benefit how we could cross the river on inflated tent sheets. This idea had never been very palatable. Today it had all the charm of regurgitated food. Besides, how did he think Deda would take to such a proposal when his original refusal to

455

cross the Drini River in a barrel had gotten us into all this trouble? A good barrel was like a motorboat, compared to an inflated pup tent!

Toward evening, Marash came to see us. He was soaked to the bone. He brought us some bread but no news. He had trouble hiding his low spirits. Hila asked him not to come to see us every day. What else could he say? Marash shook hands with us and disappeared into the night, a lonely old man caught in a deadly trap.

DECEMBER 5, 1952

It seemed impossible, but the rain was getting steadily worse. Despite what Hila had said to Marash the day before, we hoped all day for the old man to appear. Well, he didn't. He had taken us at our word, and he was right. In daylight, I first worked on my underwear. It needed mending. My long underwear had worn through at the knees and the rear. To some extent, I had contributed to the damage in trying to kill as many lice as I could. I had poked holes into my pant pockets so I could reach under my underwear and catch a louse as I felt it move across my hairy legs. I would hold the "predator" between my index finger and thumb. Then I turned the thumb so that the nail could cut the louse in half. They said that one could not kill a louse with one's fingers. Well, I had just found a way. Mine was a losing battle as my "guests" multiplied faster than I could destroy them. Nonetheless, getting back at them was a minor victory. Please remember, there was little else that would give me that feeling under the circumstances.

With threads from my shirt and blanket I was able to repair some damage to my underwear. Next, I cleaned my trusted revolver. I cleaned the barrel. I emptied the cylinder and cleaned it. The last two bullets were for me. There was one thing I couldn't afford. I couldn't afford to get caught alive. I repeated these thoughts in my mind over and over again. Cheerful as they were, there was little else for me to do. I know that I have previously described these thoughts. But they were part of my mental merry-go-round. That's how it was at that time.

Having run out of things to do, I chewed on a recurring thought. Was there a farmer anywhere in the world who had sown and harvested wheat or corn or anything else intended for me to eat? I write "anywhere in the world" because Albania imported food from the East Bloc. In reality, you never knew where it came from. If the answer to my question was "yes,"

I was meant to survive. Otherwise, this was the end. The same, of course, held true for Yugoslavia. If there was no food intended for me there, I would not make it. I tried not to let my thoughts get away from me. We were not yet in Yugoslavia, and perhaps we would never make it. Today we still had some bread that Marash had left with us. If we kept our hunger in check today, we still had bread for tomorrow. What about the day after? Marash was bound to come with bread and salt, maybe even with something fancier. After all, tomorrow was the feast of St. Nicholas. Who knows, maybe the day after tomorrow we may have our own culinary feast. It was a reassuring thought, a pleasant one to sleep on.

DECEMBER 6, 1952

Because of the rain, Peter and I had gone to sleep huddled together on top of one tent sheet, under my blanket, with the second tent sheet on top of us. It sounds snuggly and warm but our covers were no match for the rain that had pelted us for days. This morning, though, we felt dry, warm, and comfy under our covers. During the night, the rain had changed to snow. When we woke up, there were several inches of snow all around us, as well as on our covers. The air was cold and crisp. Our breath immediately condensed into vapor.

We could have felt good beyond when we first awoke had it not been for our predicament. It weighed heavily on us all day long and sometimes even in our sleep. I remembered the dream when I had run downhill through a luscious meadow and up the other side. Peter had said it meant we would meet with hard times but would eventually make it. In my mind, I had scoffed at his interpretation. The dream had been most pleasant. I had smelled the fragrance of the tall grass and felt the warmth of the sun on my skin. Where did Peter see any sign of sufferings to come? Nonsense! At least, that was how I had reacted to his words at first. Now we were steeped hip deep in hard times.

December 6 was the feast of St. Nicholas. I had memories of my childhood in Austria. Those were childhood memories; reality was very different. That afternoon we heard the sound of airplane engines overhead. We heard the plane twice, to be exact. We had snow in the mountains and could see fog in the gorge below us. Was this good weather to insert parachutists into Albania? I was no expert but I did have my doubts. Something deadly had been going on. Every time infiltrators from the West attempted to enter

Albania, they invariably ran smack into the arms of Albanian security forces. This was true whether they came by land from Greece sent by the CIA, by submarine from Malta (British MI6), or by air from Italy. Some were killed, many were captured, a few made it across the border into Greece. Those who fell into the hands of the communists suffered beyond measure until death freed them from pain and torture. In between, of course, there were the public trials where the prisoners, more often than not, said what their captors wanted them to say. The communists were masters at orchestrating such show trials. They had had plenty of practice since the days of Kamenev, Zinoviev, and all the other victims of Stalin's bloody purges. Only infiltrators from Yugoslavia seemed relatively safe from the clutches of Sigurimi.

What bothered me were not so much the trials, tragic as they were, but the fact that the communists seemed to have detailed information regarding all penetration attempts. Other things also were of concern. Western propaganda aimed at Albania was very poor. Leaflets dropped from airplanes were quite ineffective. The small print was hardly legible under less-than-optimal lighting. Obviously, very few people read such leaflets out in the open in full daylight. The paper was of poor quality and tended to tear if folded and unfolded a few times. The text was simplistic and the cartoons so amateurish that I felt ashamed for the authors. I felt bad about the so-called Radio Free Albania. It was allegedly broadcasting from inside Albania. One day it mentioned that Comrade Rita Marko was dishonoring the good name of Albanian womanhood with her brash and shameful behavior. The trouble with this news item was that Rita Marko was a man and a member of the communist government! Radio Free Albania didn't know that?

Sometime before, lightning had struck and destroyed an ammunition dump near Vlora. About six months later, Radio Free Albania broadcast that Albanian freedom fighters had attacked and successfully destroyed this same ammunition dump. The communists called a meeting and read the text of the broadcast to the assembled population, asking them to compare what they had just heard to the truth. Whoever wrote the piece showed little common sense. To broadcast such misinformation to Albania could only play into the hands of the communists. It further confirmed that it took six months for news to reach Radio Free Albania. What about the claim that the radio station was located inside the country?

Such thoughts truly bothered me. Eventually I would find some of the answers to these and other questions. For the time being, the answers were hundreds of miles away, buried in a world I had yet to get to know. Some were due to the individual naïveté and incompetence of certain Albanian refugees and their Western handlers. The more important answers were buried deep in the mind of Kim Philby, head of British counterintelligence for the Soviet Union and a skilled Soviet agent.

When we said good night, I noticed that Deda was particularly sad. As I understood it, the poor man was within easy walking distance of his home and family.

DECEMBER 7, 1952

I woke up with a question on my mind. Yesterday was the feast of St. Nicholas; would Marash bring us meat today? After all, it was customary to eat meat on feast days. We didn't have to wait long. Marash came in full daylight. He seemed in the dumps. He brought us some roasted lamb, including liver and spleen. He left us soon, seemingly unaware that he could be seen for miles and that his footsteps in the snow would lead directly to our hiding place. We sat down to eat. The meat was cold and almost raw. Poor Marash; he had probably cooked the meat himself and had paid little attention to what he was doing. The problem was that we couldn't light a fire for fear of being seen and we couldn't eat the meat the way it was.

Worse was yet to come that day. For the first time since I had joined the group, Hila and Peter exchanged words. Peter took the initiative. It was clear that we had lost contact with our bases. The groups from Yugoslavia had probably come and gone, unable to contact us. Time had come for him, Peter, to contact friends in Mirdita who may be able to help. I expected Hila to explode. He didn't. His tone was measured, his words carefully weighed.

"Peter, do you realize what you are about to do?" Hila asked. "You are breaking up the group, endangering yourself and us and risking the success of our mission. Your decision is likely to hurt us here and will seem harmful to the Yugoslav authorities. There are better ways to achieve what we all want at a lesser cost. I urge you to rethink your position."

"Hila, I have given it a lot of thought. Our situation is getting worse from day to day. We are a burden and a threat to Marash. He is in no position to continue feeding us. We are a threat because if the security forces find out that he has been hiding us they will make an example of him—and we know what that means. We have lost contact with our primary and secondary bases. If a group were to come looking for us, they would not know where to reach us. At this point, we are stuck. We need to break our chains, and the sooner the better. I am planning to go into Mirdita where I have trusted friends. With their help, I will come back for you and the four of us will make it into Yugoslavia. Trust me; I know what I am doing."

Deda, who had always stayed in Hila's shadow, spoke up. "I will go to Telumë. I have friends there who can hide and feed me for a long time. I don't know whether I can summon help to get us out of here. But in Telumë I have considerable freedom of action. Who knows what may come up."

The three of us, Peter, Deda, and I, looked at Hila. It was his turn.

"I have not yet decided where I will go and what I will do. I still think that breaking up the group is a serious mistake. In fact, the decision to break up is so serious that I will ask both of you to sleep on it tonight. Tomorrow, if you still feel this way, give me your decision in writing. After all, as leader of this group, I need such documents as evidence that your decision was taken of your free will and without undue haste."

Hila was obviously stalling, trying to delay the departure of his companions as long as possible. It was a skillful move on his part. Both accepted. They felt they owed it to Hila. Besides, to ram their decision through at this time would seem disloyal. Hila's move had gained him 24 hours. Would it matter? What about me? So far, no one had said a word as to what I should do. Under the circumstances, with each one deciding and speaking for himself, it was up to me. My first move was to get Peter aside.

"Peter, please let me come with you. You know that I won't be a hindrance to you. Besides, you cannot leave me with these two. You know how they feel about me. Please, let me come."

"My friend, I am sorry but I cannot do so. I will move day and night. I will be on terrain I know well. So I must make the most of the time available. I promise that I will return. I will stay away the minimum necessary. You must trust me. We will separate, but only for a little while. Then we will make it to Yugoslavia as I have promised you."

Now that Peter had turned me down, I had to come to a decision. Deda was even less likely to take me with him. That left only one choice.

"Hila," I said, "I have decided to come with you, if you are willing to take me." Hila was surprised and strangely pleased.

"I am glad that you have such trust in me. Thank you."

I was taken aback. He was my last, my only choice. Was it, perhaps, that my vote of confidence came at a time when even Deda was abandoning him? I did not know what Hila was thinking. Whatever it was, it was not a bad beginning—under the circumstances.

The rest of the day was steeped in gloom. The group had more or less broken up. We were each immersed in our own thoughts. We didn't know what tomorrow would bring. All we knew was that it cast a long, ominous shadow. My diary reads: "Snow and ice in place of rain. I have abdominal cramps. The cold is such that I almost faint." What a day!

DECEMBER 8, 1952

A sad mood prevailed in the morning. Deda was to go to Telumë. Hila could not make up his mind, and I would follow Hila, whatever his decision. The only one who was serene was Peter. He probably struggled until he reached his decision. Now he was ready to go. Peter was a man of action, of thoughtful action. I regretted that he would not take me with him. I could only trust in the Lord and pray. He had brought us thus far, and He would see us through, if that was His will.

We sat down to eat our last lunch together. Hila tried once more to dissuade his companions from taking off, but to no avail. Strangely enough, Hila seemed at peace. Peter, on the other hand, appeared less sure of himself than that morning. I had the impression that Peter did not want to break up with Deda. The latter was his usual inscrutable self. I wondered whether he read Peter the way I did? Where did that leave me? Holding on to Hila's apron strings, in the middle of nowhere. Actually, the worst was over. The die was cast. There was nothing I needed to do but wait. I felt more or less at peace, a peace akin to fatalism.

We sat around the fire, a very modest fire, steeped in individual misery. It was mid-afternoon. Everything that needed saying had been said. The moment of saying goodbye to each other was rapidly approaching. I felt sad as I looked at my friends. After all, we were friends. We had shared the good and the bad. We had laughed and sometimes quarreled, like members of a family. Now at dusk our family would break up.

The skies were pale blue. The mountains glistened in the afternoon sun. I could see for miles. Under different circumstances, I would have rejoiced at the beautiful sights, at the snow-laden trees, the lengthening shadows. Our little fire spread warmth and comfort. The smoke added a homey touch; the flickering flames and the smell of burning wood giving an illusion of peace and serenity. Unfortunately, my mood, our mood, was very different.

Suddenly, we heard the crunch of footsteps in the snow. Marash was climbing toward our refuge, in full daylight. My heart was in my throat. What was happening? Was it the police?

Marash would not have come at this time without a strong reason. Hila jumped in front of him. "Speak up! What's happening?" Thank God; for once Hila was skipping the usual formalities.

"Nothing to worry about," Marash replied. "A group from Yugoslavia has arrived to pick you up. They sent word to Marash Ndou who got in touch with me. Get ready. We'll be leaving soon."

I walked to the farthest rock. I removed my cap, my eyes filling with tears. Thank you Lord for your help at the very last moment!

Hila called us together. "Let's finish the meat and whatever else we have. We will need strength once we get going."

You never saw a bunch of men move faster. There was again laughter in our eyes and bounce in our steps. We roasted the meat, warmed the bread, and sat down, the five of us, including Marash. We ate, packed, and were ready to hit the road in nothing flat. We moved out from among the cluster of rocks with Marash at the head of our little column, Peter at the end. I took one last look at the rocks that had offered us shelter. What had felt like home for a few days looked like a pile of rocks, swallowed up by darkness, without a sign of life.

We were moving at a good clip when Marash took shelter behind a rock and motioned for us to stop. We fell to our knees, arms at the ready. Marash rolled a small stone toward the path where a stranger has materialized out of nowhere. Moments later, Marash stood up, moved out from behind the rock, and embraced the stranger.

Turning toward us he said, "This is Martin Ndou. He will take you to your next station."

Hila came out in the open. He introduced himself and the rest of us. Martin wasted no time. "We will go to my home. There you will eat and rest a bit before continuing on to the next leg of your trip."

Home, food, rest; it all sounded wonderful to me. Then we would be moving again, toward the team that would take us to Yugoslavia. After the bleakness of the last few weeks, there was sudden light. The trap that was closing all around us had sprung open. Hope was replacing gloom. No more Telumë for Deda or Mirdita for Peter. Instead of breaking up, we would stay together until we crossed the border. Thank you Lord, thank you Blessed Mother!

After about three quarters of an hour, we stopped on a little hill overlooking Martin's house and property. The house was built of stone, like all houses in the area, except that it was larger than the ones I had seen so far. Fields surrounded it on both sides and beyond the barn at the back of the house. Martin whispered for us to wait and disappeared inside the house. I could hardly wait for him to come back and ask us in. We had spent weeks in a cave and days among the rocks. It would feel good to be inside a house, surrounded by thick solid walls, to smell the food, and sit near a roaring fire. Our clothes would finally dry and our limbs roast and relax.

When Martin reappeared, he told us that some neighbors had dropped in, making it impossible for us to enter the house. We should not worry, however. There would be a fire for us behind the barn where no one could see us. We would eat and drink to our heart's content. When we were good and ready, we would proceed to the house where the rescue team was awaiting us. There was also a man who wanted to meet us. Who was this man? Was it one of the infiltrators who had come this far to pick us up? Soon we would know.

It all sounded good. Perhaps not as good as I had hoped, but we were still on the right track. Martin disappeared once more. Then we saw the glow of a fire behind the barn. Martin returned and led us down a footpath to a hollow at the end of the property. Around the fire, there was hot cornbread, roast lamb, feta cheese, onions, and whiskey. In the shadow stood a stranger. Martin introduced us to Ndue Deda, who would be our guide for the next leg of the trip.

Ndue was rather short and stocky, with rugged features and a brown mustache. He had piercing but friendly eyes. His clothes were typical of the area. He carried a short Italian rifle, a Carcano, the type of weapon the communists gave to auxiliary police and to local Party members. Who was this Ndue Deda? I had no choice but to trust Martin Ndou—whom, by the way, we had just met. I did not expect to find out much more about Ndue Deda in the next few minutes. They would be devoted to the conventional exchange of pleasantries and then we would eat. What else could a traveler want?

We dug in and no one spoke for a while. When Martin raised his glass to drink to our health, everyone responded in kind, including me. I never liked the taste of the stuff but tonight maybe I needed some of the liquid fire in my belly. I drank a glass and tried not to make a face. I declined a second drink. One glass was enough. We ate and drank aplenty. We had, however, no time to rest. Martin explained that we had a long way to go that night. We shouldered our backpacks, straightened our weapons, and said goodbye to Martin Ndou. Ndue Deda headed the column, Peter was last. We stepped away from the fire and into the night. Soon we lost sight of Martin Ndou's house.

Next came a long climb up a steep mountain face. It started to snow. Whether it was the whiskey or something else, soon I was out of breath. The climb continued and so did the snow. After a while, I felt exhausted. We had to cross a stream. To keep our feet dry, we jumped from boulder to boulder. I was doing fine until I slipped, landing on my chest. It felt as if someone had stuck a dagger between my ribs. There was no time to rest. My friends kept moving forward at a steady pace. By now, it was close to midnight.

December 9, 1952

We reached another stream in the early morning hours. Its waters rushed down the mountainside, gurgling and splashing as they disappeared into the dark of night. The stream must have been treacherous because Ndue had us stop. Then he carried the four of us piggyback to the other side, one at the time, including Deda and Peter, who were no slouches. Even though I could not see anything in the dark, we must have been near a village because a dog started to bark furiously. We stopped briefly. Fortunately, no one came after us. We started up another mountainside.

My feet were killing me. My toe had healed the last time because we had rested in the cave for several weeks. This time the pain was bad and was getting worse. Furthermore, I kept slipping on ice and snow that covered the footpath. I sat down for a moment, took off my sandals, and rubbed my feet. The bottoms of my socks had rotted away. My feet were slipping inside the sandals, and my toes were bumping against the tips of the sandals and hurting a lot! I decided to go barefoot. I fastened my sandals to my belt and stood up. When I looked around, my friends were gone. Panic stricken, I raced up the path. Thank God, there they were, walking single file at their steady pace. I caught up with them and ignored my cold feet.

I felt my strength draining away as we continued our forced march. My feet were hurting but my chest began to hurt much worse. My heart felt as if it were in a vise. Peter, who had taken up position a few yards behind me, came close. "What is it? Are you tired?"

"Peter, go ahead. I am sorry but I cannot walk anymore." I was thinking furiously. What could I tell my trusted friend?

"You are tired, that's all. We all are tired. I'll cut you a walking stick, no, two walking sticks. Give me your backpack. Don't worry, you will walk just fine."

Even with the two sticks, I could not walk more than seven or eight steps without stopping. If we delayed, we were in danger of being overtaken by daylight. The pain was squeezing the air out of my lungs. Peter and I stopped from time to time while the rest of the group kept forging ahead. Finally, the pain got so bad that I collapsed on the path.

"Peter, you go ahead with the group. I am sorry. I can walk no more. Sooner or later, the police will come. Do not worry. They will not take me alive. I'll take with me as many as I can. Go now."

"Nonsense, I'll stay with you. If necessary, I'll carry you to a home where we'll spend the winter. Come spring, we cross into Yugoslavia. OK?"

"Peter, you have a wife and children in Yugoslavia. If there is one among us who must make it safely across the border, it is you. Please go now; don't lose contact with the rest of the group. Go now." I could hardly speak.

"Rest a while. See, Hila and Deda are also sitting down. Ndue left to see whether it is safe to enter his house."

The idea of resting was fine with me. I don't remember what followed. I must have fallen asleep. When a noise woke me up, my chest pain was gone. I heard Peter say, "Ndue is back. It is safe to proceed. Give me your backpack."

He helped me up and we were on our way. I could have burst into song. My heart felt fine, my lungs were rejoicing, breathing the clean, brisk mountain air. My feet were doing what they were supposed to do; I was able to keep up with the group. Thank you Lord, thank you so much!

We entered a little village. In the dark, I could make out a few scattered houses. Judging by their appearance, this was a poor village. We had reached Mertur'i Gurit. Ndue pushed the door open and walked in. I could see a fire in the fireplace and two women scurrying around. Three men gathered around Ndue Deda. Hila, Deda, and Peter walked toward the older man standing next to Ndue Deda. They embraced. It was obvious they were more than acquaintances. I heard my companions address the older man as Mark Zogu. Ndue Deda then introduced the two younger men.

"These here are Peter Toma and Mark Deda, the swimmer." I was also introduced at this time. We shook hands. While the two groups chatted with each other, I had a chance to look around.

I saw a couple of children, half asleep, clinging to their mother's skirt. Plenty of pork, sausages, onions, and peppers hung from a wooden ceiling grate. I could smell freshly baked bread. The mistress of the house spoke to Hila.

"Would you and your companions like some meat?" That was sheer music to my ears.

"No, no. No meat for us. This is not a day for meat."

I didn't understand what was going on. To the best of my knowledge, this was not a Friday. This certainly was not Lent. Was there some other occasion when Catholics didn't eat meat? I didn't know of any. I was tempted to say that I was not Catholic and that I would be happy to have some meat. As a Muslim, however, how could I ask for pork?

Within minutes, the women rolled a low round table into the center of the room. They put a steaming bowl of cabbage in the middle. They put quartered raw onions, chunks of feta cheese, and lots of warm cornbread within easy reach. There was also plenty of cold water. Obviously, the women had been preparing the meal since Ndue Deda first confirmed that we were coming. That must have been while I was recovering from my chest pain. Blessed women! Ndue asked us to sit down and break bread with him. He need not ask us twice. We began to wolf down our food. Everything was delicious. While there was no meat in the cabbage, there was plenty of fat to give the dish taste and substance. Did the women perhaps boil pork with the cabbage? Did they remove the meat after Hila's refusal? It really didn't matter. We finished the first bowl and they brought a refill. We nearly killed that one, too. I ate as much as I could, and that was plenty. Before leaving the table, I stuffed a chunk of warm cornbread into my pocket. Who knows, I might get hungry during the night...

When everyone was full, Ndue rose from the table. He and members of the two groups of infiltrators withdrew into a corner to discuss business.

I remained standing for a minute or two when the older woman took me by the hand.

"Come, sit here on this stool by the fire where I can see you better."

She looked old. Her face was wrinkled, her back bent, her hair stringy. She was in her fifties, sixties, or maybe even in her seventies. Women in our mountains aged beyond their years. Only her eyes were lively. She scoured my face while she began to rub my feet with both hands, but first she removed what was left of my socks, i.e., the tops that barely covered my ankles. The rest of the socks had rotted away.

"Your feet are ice cold. I will find woolen socks for you that will keep your feet warm." While she talked, she kept rubbing my feet. I had a tough time keeping my composure. Here was an old woman risking everything for the sake of a stranger.

"Mother, why are you doing this for me? I am from the south, you are from the north. You are farmers, I am city bred. You are Catholic, I am Muslim. If they find me here, they'll know I don't belong. My looks, my dialect, even my clothing will give me away. Once they are done with me and the group, they'll kill the men in your family. They may even kill you women and the children to make an example of you. They will burn down the house and barn. They'll cut the trees and take all your animals away. Why are you doing this for me?"

She replied slowly but without hesitation. "You are young and you may not have helped others. Your parents, I am sure, have done so and so have your friends. Today it is our turn to help you. You are going to make it out of Albania and one day it will be your turn to help others. Because that's why God has put us on earth."

That was the best sermon I had ever heard. No, not a sermon; she was willing to sacrifice herself and her family for me. Her words burned themselves into my mind and I will never forget them as long as I live.

Meanwhile, Ndue and the other men had finished their business.

"Let me take you to where you will spend the night," Ndue said, speaking to all seven of us. "Take your things with you."

I didn't know what he had in mind. We did as we were told. Ndue stepped out into the dark night and we followed him. Would he take us to a cave or to some ravine? We had taken but a few steps when Ndue opened the door to his stable. Inside it was warm and reassuring. The stable had thick stone walls, heavy beams, and a massive roof on top, just like the house. There was plenty of straw on the floor. One could smell cows and hear their calm, rhythmic breathing. Thank you, Lord, for food and shelter! There was plenty of room for the seven of us. We settled down for the night and said good night to Ndue and to each other.

My companions and I were lying next to one another. Hila, Deda, and Peter began to whisper so they would not awaken the other three. They had found out that Ndue Deda was the village chief, hence his rifle. Ndue Deda had worked with the anti-communist underground for many years. He did not belong to Hila's network but was linked to Marash Ndou's. How lucky for us! When he left us the first time to make sure that it was safe for us to enter his house, he had scratched the window shutters and meowed like a cat. His family's reaction would tell him whether the police or other security forces were inside. The family woke up and stirred the embers in the fireplace. The cat was near the fireplace, so the cat was not outside. They started to talk about a cousin who had escaped to Yugoslavia. If the police were doing the scratching and meowing at the window, they would not know about whom they were talking inside. If it was Ndue, he would understand that there was no police inside. Otherwise, the family would not have spoken about an escapee. Reassured, Ndue entered the house, told the family that we would arrive shortly, and returned to fetch us. Now, safely inside Ndue's stable, my companions and I whispered good night to each other and soon everyone was asleep.

Actually, not everyone; dead tired as I was, I could not go to sleep—perhaps because of my emotions, or perhaps I had eaten too much. No, it could not be the latter, my stomach felt fine. I touched my pocket. Yes, the cornbread was still there, just in case. What a day it had been. I began to relive the last 24 hours. We were about to break up when Marash had brought us the good news. We met Martin Ndou and Ndue Deda. We had an ample meal, and started the long climb up the mountain. Then came my slip and fall, the walk barefoot on snow and ice, and my excruciating chest pain. Was it an angina attack caused by the fall? More likely, it was an angina *a frigore*, caused by walking barefoot on snow and ice. My decision to stay behind and fight to the end seemed unavoidable under the circumstances. Then came Peter's loyal offer of help, my miraculous recovery, a friendly home, the rescue group, hot food, the kindhearted and wise old woman, and now a warm shelter. Was it surprising that I could not fall asleep?

As I was lying on the floor, I could hear my friends snore, the cows breathe, and the restless goats move around. Goats are like babies. They pay no attention who or what they step on. When stepped on, the men would shoo them away. One goat stepped on my feet and got a gentle kick in the rear. Then it happened. Another goat came and plopped itself down on my feet. Can you imagine the goat's warm, soft underbelly on my ice-cold feet? It felt wonderful. I could not believe it. Had the goat come of its own volition? What had made it lie on my cold feet? Anyhow, this was no time for me to fall asleep lest I turn and cause the goat to move away. In fact, I had to make sure the goat wanted to lie on my feet. I had an idea. I began to feed the goat bits of cornbread, a few morsels at the time. The goat ate the bread and was satisfied, and I could feel my toes and feet warming up. Happiness was having warm feet!

It did not take long, and I began to see pale daylight filtering into the stable. The night was over, the men began to stir. The door opened and Ndue Deda entered the stable, bringing with him cold outdoor air.

"Good morning, men. I hope you all slept well. I brought you some bread and cheese for breakfast." He pointed at one corner. "There is water in a pail for you to wash up."

I could not help but muse about our personal hygiene. Under the circumstances, the lack of personal cleanliness could actually be an asset. Take last night, for example. Goats are known for their rotten odor. To tell the truth, I had not noticed. What was more important, the goat did not notice or did not mind my body odor.

We washed up and ate. Now we were ready for whatever the day might bring. Ndue came again and walked us back to the house. Obviously, he was not afraid that someone might spot us. Hila, Mark Zogu and their men withdrew again into a corner. Ndue Deda's family drew me aside where there was some privacy. They had found out that I was a medic and wanted to tell me their woes. First, I checked Lezja, the wife of Marash Mëhilli, who was not home. Then I checked Drana, Ndue Deda's mother, Ndue Deda, and some young man. They all had their aches and pains. In some cases, the cause was obvious. In the case of Ndue Deda's mother, the arthritic fingers and joints told the story. In others, the problems were less obvious, at least to me. Lezja seemed to need more thorough medical attention. I wrote her a prescription and retro-dated it as if I had seen her in

Dukagjin. I told her to go to Mom in Shkodra and show her the prescription. Mom would recognize the handwriting and Lezja could bring her up to date. Mom would then take Lezja to a real physician who could perhaps help her. I thought this stratagem would work well. Mom would get news from me and Lezja would see a physician.

The night before, Ndue Deda's mother had spoken of socks. Now she gave me a brand-new pair. "The tops of these socks are made of sheep wool, the bottoms of goat hair. These bottoms do not absorb water. Thus, your feet will not get wet. Tomorrow I'll make a pair of sandals for you. The bottoms are of cowhide with the fur on the outside so they do not slip on ice. I'll also give you strings so you can tie them around your feet and ankles."

That sounded just great. Obviously, I could no longer wear my old sandals. Now I would get a simpler and less protective type of footwear, but one I could wear. That was a big improvement. The socks were most welcome. I had seen similar socks before. Some were very ornate with gold embroidery. Others were simpler but still very decorative. These were without embroidery. The tops were whitish, the bottoms gray. The very idea that the tops would keep my ankles warm and the bottoms my feet dry was great. The socks were part of the younger woman's dowry.

"Thank you, Mother. I have nothing to give you in return. Would you at least accept my old sandals?" They were all pleased with my offer. Women also wore such sandals except that mine were too big for any of the women. If one of the men could wear them, he could get many miles out of them.

That day we had a good lunch and an even more abundant evening meal. Then it was back to the stable for the night.

DECEMBER 10, 1952

We spent the day in the stable. We had ample food both for lunch and supper. We were offered pork and goat meat, cabbage, and plenty of cornbread, and ate as much as we could. Hila asked Ndue Deda for some Albanian communist publications to take to Yugoslavia. I couldn't care less about the publications; the idea of going to Yugoslavia, however, sounded good! That border had been in my dreams so many times, but never closer than in my dreams. Now we still had to cover long distances, we had to cross the river once more, and then—only then—would we reach the border. Crossing it unharmed was the last major hurdle. Maybe this time we would make it.

Around 8:30 that evening, Ndue Deda escorted us out of his house in the direction of Fjerza. It was a moonlit night. Five to 15 inches of fresh snow lay on top of the old layer and gave everything a fresh, joyful look as if nature were getting ready for Christmas. The air was sparkling clean and invigorating. I inhaled deeply as I walked in the middle of our column. I felt young, strong, and happy. I moved easily. My new moccasins did not slip on ice and didn't hurt my feet. It was good to be with these men, it was great to be here, it was wonderful to be alive. Ndue Deda accompanied us beyond the borders of his village and bid us farewell.

"May the Lord protect you. May your and our efforts be successful so that we may soon see a free and proud Albania." He embraced us one at the time. He waved once more and turned back to Mertur'i Gurit.

At Ndue Deda's home I had felt safe and cared for. My friends had told me that he and his mother had entrusted me to Mark Zogu and his companions with the strongest possible recommendations. I wondered why.

We were on our way. We moved down a steep path when one of the men slipped and fell backward. The column stopped immediately. The man rose to his feet, broke off a branch from a nearby tree, and erased his imprint in the snow. I must have looked baffled because he turned toward me and explained. "I had to erase the imprint in the snow because of the outline of my rifle." So that was it.

We must have walked for quite a while when our leader raised his hand. We stopped. Our leader was listening intently. "Footsteps in the snow...the men are wearing boots...just a few of them...they must be discharged soldiers who are returning home. Let's go!"

I heard nothing, let alone that they were wearing boots. I did not think the man had made it up. This was just one more example that I was moving in a world other than my own—not a very reassuring feeling. Well, at least I had friends I could rely on who knew their way around.

December 11, 1952

We walked all night without resting. The terrain was arduous, the snow hip deep in places. Just before dawn, my companions realized that we could not reach Fierza before daylight. We cut toward the river until we reached the riverbank that was free of snow. We marched on to put distance between our tracks in the snow and our present whereabouts. Our leaders pointed at some bushes that were some 30 feet from the river. That was where we would spend the day.

The bank was steep, the ground muddy and slippery. Fortunately, the bushes were rather thick. They gave us something to hold on to and protected us from being seen from either side of the river. Actually, we were not bad off except we had no water to drink! We each had some food but we had no water, nor could we expose ourselves and go to the river in daylight.

The day went by without a mishap. At dusk, a flock of sheep headed our way. They were probably thirsty. Somehow, my companions didn't hear them. Perhaps they were dozing. I hissed to alert them to the danger. Meantime, the shepherd had rushed to get ahead of the flock, to keep the sheep from being washed away by the river. He had turned his back toward us as he stood no more than 30 feet away from us. We all pointed our weapons at his back. If he turned and saw us, we would have to grab him, if not worse. We certainly would not shoot him, as we could not risk firing our weapons. As fate had it, he was able to turn the sheep away from the river and toward home. The shepherd never realized the danger he had just avoided and we were happy to be off the hook.

Under cover of darkness, we reached Fierza and entered the home of Mark Deda, our swimmer. His mother and father seemed old to be his parents. They were so happy to see him that they did not mind us either. In fact, we enjoyed their friendly hospitality and had another ample meal.

After dinner, Mark, his mother, and Peter Toma went out to find a safe shelter for us. I was hoping they would be successful. After all, a comfortable shelter after an abundant meal was just fine with me. To my chagrin, they were not successful. Around midnight, we took up our marching formation and walked into the ice-cold night. As we began to climb up the mountainside, it got so cold that I had a nosebleed. Fortunately, it did not last long. I had enough trouble keeping up with my companions as it was.

DECEMBER 12, 1952

We had reached the village of Porav and entered the home of Gjokë Deda around 4:30 a.m. Our clothes were soaked from the snow and perspiration. We took off our clothes from the waist up and dried ourselves with rags as best we could. We were unkempt, hairy, and rough. I must say, we looked uninspiring.

Gjokë and his wife fed us and bedded us down for the night. By that I mean, they put fern on the floor and gave each of us a small piece of wood for a pillow. As usual, Peter and I slept near each other. In fact, we had slept like this since we had first met.

We spent the day inside the house, well fed and rather relaxed. Mark Deda stated that he would not attempt crossing the Drini River for the next few days even though Gjokë Deda assured him that the water level was lower than when they had crossed it on the way in. These matters were beyond me. Besides, I didn't mind being indoors, well fed, and fairly safe. Speaking of well fed, it really boggled my mind when I thought that people like Ndue Deda and now Gjokë, who did not have enough food to feed their families the year 'round, fed seven of us for days at a time. Such people truly gave of their want, not of their wealth.

DECEMBER 13, 1952

Around midnight, Mark Zogu woke us up. During the night, it had started to rain hard and the snow was melting. The Drini was bound to rise. We had no choice but to leave right away and try to cross the river, if we were still in time. We said goodbye to Gjokë and his wife and stepped into the darkness. Within minutes, we were soaked to the skin. The creeks were overflowing. The night was pitch black. I fell twice. So did Hila. Mark Zogu fell once but hurt himself rather badly. At one point Mark Zogu slipped and almost fell into the river Drini where the path had been swallowed up by a mudslide.

At dawn, things improved a bit. We had to wade through an ice-cold creek but at least we could see. I crossed it three times as I forgot one of my moccasins on the other side of the creek. We finally reached the point where we would cross the Drini River. It was about 200 feet upstream from the creek. In daylight, we had a better view of the river. It looked swollen and angry with chunks of ice floating downstream. Because of the mild weather, the snow was melting and the river would rise some more. Now was the time to make the most of a situation that would get worse by the hour.

We lit a fire, ate, and dried ourselves. Meanwhile, Mark Deda settled down and began to spread the tools of his trade. He had ten goatskins. When he inflated them, three burst. The rest were not much to brag about either. Mark tied the goat skins together, cut some branches, and tied them atop the goatskins to form a raft. This procedure took about an hour. Then he spoke.

"I will take you across one at the time. I had hoped to get you across in pairs but the raft is weak."

By the time we were ready for the river crossing, heavy fog had filled the valley. The fog might help. Mark Deda undressed. Hila decided that Peter would cross first. He was a good marksman who could cover us while we crossed the river. Peter took our bags, including my knapsack, and climbed on the raft. He waved goodbye with his characteristic winning smile.

"See you on the other side of the river!"

His farewell sure sounded good. The swimmer got into the water, wet his chest, and started to push the raft across with short, powerful leg movements. When the raft reached the middle of the river, we heard a man's voice give the alarm. Other voices answered from other hilltops. I could see Peter raising his rifle halfway. The yelling continued but there were no shots. I estimated that the river was about 100 yards wide at this point. We saw Peter get off the raft and light a fire. Mark Deda crouched near the fire to warm up for the return trip. If I figured right, Mark Deda would have to cross the Drini 11 more times to get us all across. The thought was so ominous that I banned it from my mind.

Meanwhile, my companions were gathering wood to have a fire ready for Mark Deda when he returned. As usual, since I did not know the difference between wood that smoked and wood that did not, I brought whatever wood I could lay my hands on. Then Deda or someone else would pick what wood could be used. Obviously, we could not afford to advertise our presence by creating lots of smoke. When Mark returned, he was cold and scared. After resting for a few minutes near the fire, he entered the water again. Hila climbed on the raft and they took off for the other side. Whoever was giving the alarm started up again. The cries bounced from side to side across the river, like the first time. They were getting to me. I could see that soon we could have unfriendly company on either or both sides of the river while neither half of our group was able to leave its present position. When Hila reached the other bank of the river, we could see a heated discussion taking place between Mark Deda and Hila. Peter seemed to enter the discussion from time to time. Finally, Mark Deda got once more into the water.

When he reached our side, he made it very clear that this trip was his last. He picked up his clothes and asked Deda to climb on the raft.

I approached Mark Deda. "Mark, I have a check for fifty dollars. Take me across and it is yours." Mark agreed while Peter Toma helped me get on the raft. That's when we heard Hila yell from the other side of the river.

"Not Genc, take Deda!" I had no choice but to get off the raft. Mark Deda and Deda Mehilli, my old companion, began to cross the river while the rest of us looked on.

The $50 check I mentioned to Mark had been sent to us by Sadie three or four years before. I did not know that checks expired if not cashed within a reasonable time. I thought they were as good as cash. I had forgotten my wallet one day in a store in Tirana. I realized my loss within minutes, ran back to the store and retrieved my wallet with the precious check. Phew!

In the mountains, I had mentioned the check to Hila. "Give me the check," he had said. "You may need the help of the authorities to have the check cashed." Reluctantly I had given him the check.

At this point, Hila, Peter, Deda, and Mark, the swimmer, were safely on the other side of the river. They waved.

Peter yelled, "Don't worry, we'll send help as soon as possible!"

We waved back in silence. What a mess! I was stuck with strangers on this side of the Drini while my friends were on their way to the border.

Sure, they would send help! The mountains were snowed in. Any footprints across the border were a deadly giveaway. We were stuck here until spring, if we lasted that long. Perhaps I was not meant to make it to Yugoslavia.

Peter Toma and Mark Zogu came off the top of a hill from where they had been surveying the area. "Did your friends desert you?" Mark asked.

"Yes," I replied.

"What shall we do with you?"

"Whatever you wish. You have the rifle. If you want to shoot me, it's up to you."

"By God, then," Mark Zogu replied, "as long as I live you need not worry. Whatever I do for myself, I will do for you. If I am killed, you are on your own." I felt reassured. The man gave the impression of being as good as his word. I should have asked myself why he preceded what he had said to me with an oath.

Years went by before I found out that Peter Toma had made Mark a proposition: "The security forces will be here soon. Most likely, they will engage us in combat. Genc does not know the lay of the land and will fight to the end. Here is a chance for us to take off. You take off in one direction, I in the other. Twenty-four hours later we meet somewhere; what do you think?"

Mark had replied, "As long as I am alive I'll take care of Genc. Once I am dead, he is on his own." Hence, Mark Zogu's oath to me. Peter Toma had gotten the message.

At this point, we drew deeper into the woods. We still had a couple of hours of daylight. Mark opened our last can of meat. We ate in silence. Suddenly we heard voices. Three men, two in military uniform, appeared on the path about a hundred feet from us. They were armed but seemed unconcerned. They spoke aloud and joked with each other, hardly a posse looking for us. Mark Zogu decided that we could not stay here any longer. We moved out and followed the footpath. For whatever reason, I was point man. Suddenly, a civilian came around a bend, a few feet from me. I drew my gun.

"Put your gun down," Mark said forcefully, "he is a friend." Mark pushed by me and embraced the stranger. The stranger spoke first.

"So, you are who the alarm was all about. All men are being called to a meeting. We don't know why. Mark, take your men and wait for me at my home. I have to go now. Later we can bring each other up to date."

"Good, we'll go to your house. We'll tell you what we are doing here and you tell us why they called the meeting." We said goodbye. The stranger went off one way and we the other.

The three of us, Mark Zogu leading, followed the footpath that soon led us to a house. Two women were in the courtyard doing chores. A fierce-looking dog started barking furiously while straining at the chain. Thank God, the chain held. Otherwise, we would have had to shoot the dog and that would have created other problems with the local security forces as well as the owner of the dog. The younger of the two women looked at us, got scared, and ran to release the dog. The older woman recognized Mark Zogu and sharply told the daughter-in-law to stop.

"Mark Zogu, is it you?" she asked.

"Yes," he answered, "with two companions."

The young woman had stopped in her tracks. She looked at us and still seemed unconvinced. When her mother-in-law hugged us, starting with Mark Zogu, she relaxed and stood by, awaiting instructions. The older woman welcomed us and led us into the house.

"Welcome and thanks that the Lord brought you here. My husband is not home, he had to go to a meeting."

I appreciated her words of welcome, so typical of the people in our mountains. Guests were welcome and a gift of God, even in our case when we spelled real trouble. I was also touched by her wisdom. First, she stopped her daughter-in-law from unleashing the dog, thus avoiding a crisis. Having recognized Mark Zogu, she welcomed us but let us know that her husband was not home, another proper and important move. Now it was Mark Zogu's turn.

"We saw your husband as he was going to the meeting. We spoke briefly and he asked us to come here. We will wait for him and take it from there."

The older woman nodded, pleased to hear what Mark Zogu just told her.

"If you don't mind," she said, "I'll put you in the cellar in case other travelers drop in. Our house is on the beaten path and we often have guests, including security patrols that come here frequently for a meal or to spend the night under a roof."

We descended a few steps and found ourselves in a cellar with several wooden barrels in one corner. The lady of the house left us, taking her oil lamp with her. In the dark, we moved toward the corner, sat on the ground, and rested our backs against the barrels. No one spoke. I for one was confused. It was the first time that I had entered a home, had been welcomed, but was offered no food. Could this be because the husband was not home? Was there some other reason? Whatever, I would have loved to eat a bit. My share of the can of meat we ate in the woods when we expected to go into combat had been rather skimpy. The woman of the house had not mentioned food nor had my companions made any move in that direction.

I decided to investigate the barrels behind us. I carefully lifted the lid of the nearest one and dipped my hand inside. As I poked around, I grabbed a pickled cucumber. It was better than nothing. I pulled it out, sank my teeth into it and consumed it with pleasure. Then I thought of my companions.

"Would you like some pickled cucumbers?"

"No, thanks," they both refused.

Well, I decided to get myself another one. I bit into it and I realized how salty these cucumbers were. Here I was, holding a cucumber I did not want. I dropped it back into the barrel and realized too late what I had just done. I could imagine how embarrassing it would be for the host to pull from the barrel a half-eaten cucumber! Now it was too late for me to go after it inside the barrel and in total darkness. I slithered to the ground entrusting my sinfulness to the deep darkness surrounding us.

The hours passed very slowly. It was midnight by the time our host came into the cellar with an oil lamp in his hand. After the usual exchange of pleasantries and having determined that we were fine, and had suffered neither from the cold of the cellar nor from hunger, he and Mark Zogu got down to brass tacks.

"What was your meeting all about?"

"They talked to us about the new rules concerning our income taxes, how much corn, wheat, and other cereals they expected from us, and of course how much meat each of us had to deliver based on the size of our property."

"Did they say anything concerning the crossing of the Drini by our companions? Did they say anything about us who remained on this side of the river?"

"No, not a word."

That was funny. Someone had given the alarm the moment Peter had reached the middle of the river. They must have seen the fires that Peter lit on one shore and we on the other. They must have suspected that some of us had remained on this side, and yet no one had said a word about us? I did not know what to make of it. It also struck me that neither Mark Zogu nor Peter Toma asked any questions. Needless to say, I held my peace.

He asked us to move upstairs where the women had prepared a meal for us, a rather skimpy and simple meal. While we were eating, the host added a few words. "As you know, we often have unexpected guests, including security patrols. They have depleted our food and even tonight they could still drop in—and that would be most unfortunate for all of us. My suggestion is that you leave and aim for the summer hut of our neighbor." He mentioned a name I did not catch.

"He is a communist of some importance here in our area. No one goes to these summer huts in the winter. Furthermore, no one would be looking for you in a hut belonging to a communist. You should be safe there."

We took the hint. We finished what little food there was in front of us, my two companions grabbed their weapons and knapsacks, we said goodbye to our host, and we were on our way. This time, I had nothing to carry as Peter had taken my backpack with him on the raft when he had set out for the other bank of the Drini River. Henceforth, I would have to do without my blanket and the few things I had taken with me when I had left home 65 days ago, when I had left Mom.

CHAPTER THIRTY-THREE

CHRISTMAS—OUR LIBERATORS ARRIVE!

DECEMBER 14, 1952

My companions and I slipped out of the house, crossed the road that ran alongside, and began climbing up the side of a steep hill until we came to another footpath. The going got easier. We followed the path that zigzagged upward until we saw the first lights of dawn. When daylight broke, the footpath seemed to flatten out. There was no one in sight and no smoke rose from the chimneys of huts that dotted the landscape; nor could we hear any noises that domestic animals usually make at this time of the day. Everything seemed frozen in snow and time—and that suited me just fine. Mark Zogu seemed to know where he was going. After a while, he turned from the path and walked toward a small hut. It was less than half the size of a regular home. The walls were of stone, with two windows facing the path. The hut had a thatch roof. The door was securely tied with strands of bark. It looked as if no one had been here in quite a while.

Mark Zogu cut off the primitive rope and opened the door. The floor was uneven. Most of it was under water except for the part that rose up against the wall opposite the door. To our left was a lattice partition that went from floor to ceiling with an opening that led to the other half of the hut. Along the lattice partition and against the wall facing the entrance was a wooden frame about three feet above ground where one could lie down to sleep without getting wet. On top of the frame was a low, three-legged stool.

We entered the hut but did not quite know how to position ourselves. Once our eyes got used to the darkness, we saw that there was not much water on the floor. In one corner there was a primitive broom propped up against the wall. Peter Toma grabbed the broom and pushed most of the water through the door opening out into the open. It was cold inside the hut. We discovered a small heap of charcoal in a far corner that was not under water. Starting a conventional fire was impossible as the smoke could betray us, but a charcoal fire would provide smokeless heat. That charcoal was a godsend!

My friends tried in vain to light the charcoal while I was racking my brain how I could make myself useful. I had been a burden to Hila and company, yet Hila had used me to impress others with his German. On a number of occasions, I had been "the doctor of Dukagjin" and had earned some respect. Now I was with two men who did not know me at all and who owed me no allegiance. I had touched on some political subjects but neither Mark Zogu nor Peter Toma had responded or shown any interest. I prayed and prayed hard. If I could only prove myself useful. I racked my brain. How could I start the charcoal fire? Suddenly, I had an idea. I turned to Peter Toma.

"Do we have the meat can from yesterday?" I knew we did not throw it away to avoid making tracks.

"Yes, but it is empty."

"Never mind, just give me the can." He did as I asked. "Give me a strip of cloth. Rip it off the bottom of your shirt."

"Why?" he asked somewhat defiantly.

"Please do as I tell you." He handed me the empty meat can and a strip of cloth.

I wiped some fat off the inside of the can with the cloth, plugged the cloth into the little heap of charcoal at our feet, lit a match to the greasy cloth and started blowing cautiously so as to provide oxygen without snuffing out the flame. Once Peter Toma saw what I was doing, he also went down on his knees and before we knew it we had a fire. Of course, there was the danger of carbon monoxide giving us a headache, but what was a headache compared to the warmth that would drive the chill out of our bones? We ate a bite and then Mark Zogu spoke up.

"Genc, you heard that this hut belongs to a communist. Peter and I are going to lie down while you stand guard. From the window, you should be able to see anyone approaching from either direction. It is unlikely that anyone will come at this time of the year. If someone should approach, wake us up."

That was fine with me. Finally, someone was standing guard while the others slept. I took up my position near the window, dutifully scanning with my head from side to side while submerging myself into my private world of thoughts. Some time had gone by when I saw a man coming down the path toward the hut. I made a double take. Yes, there he was, coming straight toward our refuge.

"Wake up, Mark, Peter. Someone is coming."

Mark Zogu peeked out. The owner of the hut was coming our way.

"Quickly, Genc and Peter, hide in the stable." So, the part behind the lattice was the stable.

Mark Zogu put the stool in the middle of the room across from the entrance. He sat down, laid his rifle across his knees, ready to face the visitor.

Peter and I could see the man first through a window and then through the lattice. He was tall, relatively well dressed, with a dark, large mustache. He approached the door and stopped, perplexed. He had just noticed that someone had cut off the primitive rope that kept any animals in search of shelter out of the hut. Then he pushed the door open and saw Mark Zogu. The newcomer showed no surprise nor did he miss a beat.

"How are you, Mark Zogu?"

"I am well. How are you and your family?" and here Mark Zogu mentioned some family members by name. Obviously, the two knew each other.

"We are all doing well. I am glad to see you. I had heard that you had been ill some time ago." The man was referring to a recent incident in Yugoslavia. Two Albanian refugees had quarreled and one of them had drawn a gun. Mark Zogu had stepped between the two and had caught the bullet meant for the other man. Fortunately, he had recovered and this was his first trip into Albania since the incident. It was interesting that the communist knew about it. Obviously, the Albanian spy network in Yugoslavia was quite efficient.

"Yes, I am well again."

"Are you alone on this trip?" the man asked.

"No, I have a companion with me." Then Mark Zogu turned toward the stable.

"Peter Toma, come out." Peter stepped out and hugged the stranger.

After a few more banalities, the stranger said to Mark Zogu, "I will go home and get you two some food. I am sure you can use it."

The three of them embraced and the man left. I stepped out of the stable and was surprised that my two companions were getting ready to leave.

"Are we not going to wait for him to bring us some food?" I asked.

Mark Zogu shook his head. "The man is a viper. He cannot be trusted."

That made me feel foolish. Besides, I was somewhat miffed. "How come you did not introduce me to the man?"

Mark Zogu answered very patiently. "If anything bad happens to me or Peter Toma, our families will kill in revenge. Who will avenge your blood?"

Now I had really made a fool of myself. I tightened my moccasins and fell in line as we left the hut. No one bothered to tie the door shut.

As usual, no one told me where we were going. I was used to it and approved of it. Besides, I did not know my way around and would have been unable to find my way wherever we were going. I trudged along, trying not to fall behind. By now it was pitch dark. At one point we stopped. Mark Zogu exchanged a few words with Peter and disappeared in the darkness. At first, I did not notice. When I became aware of his absence, I began worrying. Was he coming back? Had he told Peter Toma where we were going? Did he leave us for good and henceforth we would be on our own? I did not like it. Peter Toma was an unknown quantity as far as I was concerned. Then Peter Toma spoke up.

"We are going down this slippery path to a creek at the bottom. Stay behind me and hold on to my hand to keep me from slipping in the mud."

I did as I was told but instead of keeping Peter Toma from slipping, my moccasins slipped, and I bumped into him; he almost went over the edge.

"You dumb son of an ass. I told you to keep me from sliding, and instead you crashed into me!"

I was furious. To call me the son of an ass was more than I could take. I cocked my revolver and pressed it against his chest.

"Repeat what you just said," I hissed. "Go ahead."

He realized that I was ready to shoot him. Under the circumstances, he was as good as dead. Obviously, I did not care what happened to me.

"Wait a minute, I did not mean it. I almost fell down the ravine and was upset. Let's climb back and rest a bit."

I made room for him. We climbed up the muddy path and he led me into what looked like a former chapel. Dogs began to bark. Then they fell silent. The quiet of the night and the peaceful atmosphere of the chapel calmed me down. But I still had some steam to let off.

"In your opinion, how much sulfa guanidine a day would you give to a patient suffering from typhoid?"

"What are you talking about?" he asked.

"No, go ahead and answer me. Second, what diet would you prescribe for a patient with typhoid? Are you in favor of the French theory regarding feeding the patient by mouth or do you follow the German school?"

Again he replied, "I don't know what you are talking about."

"That's my point. When you were learning how to walk at night, how to walk in the mud or on snow and ice, when you were learning what bells belong to what herd and where their grazing limits were, I too was learning something. Unfortunately for me, today I am in your world and not in mine."

He did not reply, nor did we speak for a few minutes.

"Let's go. We will skip the shortcut. There is another way to get to Gjokë Deda's house."

Now I knew where we were going. Not that I could have made it on my own, but at least I knew our destination. A few minutes later, we knocked at Gjokë Deda's door. Mark Zogu had preceded us and welcomed us with a smile in his eyes. He had no way of knowing how wrong things could have gone at the creek just minutes before.

DECEMBER 15–18, 1952

Three days went by and not much happened. Mark Zogu and Gjokë Deda were personal friends. With Hila, relations with our bases were usually rather formal; I wouldn't say stiff, but more formal. As far as my role was concerned, whether with Hila or now, I stayed in the background. I contributed little or nothing, yet had to be included in their calculations. Nothing of medical significance had happened so far. Thank God, there had been no broken bones or major cuts where I could have been of help. I knew that, under the circumstances, I counted for little. For how little, though, I could not have guessed.

One afternoon, Mark Zogu, Gjokë Deda, and Peter Toma withdrew into a corner to discuss business. I was sitting at a distance near the fireplace when Gjokë Deda's oldest son joined me. He was all of eight years old.

"Roll yourself a cigarette," the boy said, tossing me his silver box.

"Thank you, I don't smoke," I replied as I returned the box to him.

Slowly and deliberately, he opened the silver box and took out a piece of rice paper from under the lid. He grabbed a wad of tobacco from the depth of the box, laid it on the paper, and rolled paper and tobacco into a cylinder. He licked the edge of paper that stuck out, folded it over the rest, and held the finished cigarette between the first two fingers of his right hand. I didn't quite know whether he did it so slowly because the ritual deserved his full attention or because my answer had rattled him and he needed time to compose himself. He turned toward the fireplace and lit his cigarette. Then he squinted and asked the first of four questions whose answers could make or break me.

"Why don't you have a mustache?"

That's an easy one, I thought. "Because I shave it off."

"Are you married?"

"No."

"Are you engaged to be married?"

"No, I am not."

"How old are you?"

"I am 29 years old."

I could see the wheels turning in the young boy's head. I was 29, yet I did not smoke, I had no mustache, I was neither married nor engaged to be married. The eight-year-old turned toward the fireplace and spit into it with great determination. He had established beyond a shadow of a doubt that I counted little among men. Neither he nor I spoke a word. There was no need for words because all that needed to be said had been said. He was grim and I was furious. What a day.

By way of background, I found out that before the boy was born, his father and a friend whose wife was also expecting made an agreement. Gjokë said to his friend, "What do you say, my friend? If our wives give birth one to a son and the other to a daughter, shall we strengthen our friendship with bonds of marriage?"

"Why not, friend?" They shook hands and the agreement was sealed. The two unborns had become engaged. Well, practically.

At that moment I really couldn't have cared less about engagements and the traditions of our mountains. The boy had insulted me and there was nothing I could do about it. I sat there and stewed for a while. The runt owed me one.

DECEMBER 19, 1952

Gjokë Deda was ill at ease with us around the house. He and his wife had five children and probably not enough food for themselves. In these areas, if a family could grow enough food for six months, it was considered rich. Gjokë Deda was not rich. He might be nearly out of food. For four days now he had been feeding three more adults. Who knows how much longer we would stay here? Besides, he told us in confidence that a communist in their village had been accusing him of collaborating with the infiltrators. Those were most serious charges that could cost Gjokë Deda his freedom and more. He grew restless.

"Your situation could be solved easily if we could find a swimmer to get you across the river. He wouldn't even have to escape to Yugoslavia. Once you were on the other side of the river, the swimmer could return home and no one would be the wiser," Gjokë Deda said to us.

His tone was urgent. He wanted us on our way and out of his home, and I could not blame him. Besides, that was fine with me—the sooner, the better. That day Gjokë Deda left to seek help.

Mark Zogu was not much of a talker. Peter Toma also kept to his own devices. The woman of the house and her five children took care of the chores and filled the house with the noise and confusion that I, as a bachelor, didn't exactly cherish. I must admit, though, she was strong and tough. Physically she seemed tireless. Her toughness helped her keep her mental balance. Her oldest son was my "friend," the eight-year-old son. Her youngest was one month old. The rest jumped and played, laughed and cried, and ran to their mother for refuge whenever they felt threatened, i.e., whenever one of their pranks backfired. I kept myself apart and spent the day immersed in my own thoughts.

The woman of the house set the table for the three of us and fed us pork, bread, cornmeal, and cheese. When we finished, what was left was for the children and herself. When eating, we had to curb our appetites and keep in mind that the rest of the family was waiting for our leftovers.

It was already dark when Gjokë Deda returned. He was wet, perspired, and dejected.

"Good evening, men. Are you tired?"

"No, we are fine," Mark Zogu answered for all of us.

Mark kept his answer brief and spoke no more for the time being. Gjokë

Deda's wife put some food in front of her husband while the children were jumping and climbing all over their father. The poor man was always very good to his children. Tonight, however, he did not feel like playing.

"I went to a friend's home today looking for a swimmer. First I sought help as a friend. I got nowhere. Then I offered money, good money, hoping that you could pay him. Even that didn't work. I tried everything I could think of but got nowhere. I don't know where to go from here."

For a moment no one spoke. Then Mark Zogu spoke up.

"At this point it may be safer for us to move away from the river and go someplace where the communists don't expect us. We will aim for Mertur'i Gurit and stay with Ndue Deda, who has kept us before. He is not a suspect and may be able to keep us for a while. I expect a group from Yugoslavia any moment now. Hila and his friends crossed the river on the 13th. Twenty-four hours later, they probably crossed the border. Once in Yugoslavia, it will take them maybe a week to put together another rescue party. Today is the 19th. I would not be surprised if someone will come for us within the next two or three days.

"Gjokë Deda, you have done much for us and are in danger because of us. When our friends arrive, I promise, we will not cross the Drini River without contacting you first. Think it over. You may be running out of time fast. When we come back, it may be best that you and your family join us."

Gjokë Deda looked relieved.

"Woman, prepare food for these men to take with them. Mark, I understand what you are telling me. I have often asked myself whether my family and I may not be better off in Yugoslavia. We have friends and relatives there while here we are helpless and at the mercy of scoundrels who would like nothing better than to see me in jail."

His asking his wife to prepare food for us shortly after we had eaten showed he was in a hurry to get us on our way. Mark Zogu and Peter Toma gathered their belongings while I had nothing besides what I wore or carried on my person. Peter had my knapsack, my blanket and tent sheet, and my pair of spare socks. I had my clothes, Peter's revolver, and a hand grenade. I traveled light, that's for sure.

DECEMBER 20, 1952

We left Gjok Deda's house past midnight. It was cold but the snow on the ground reflected what little light there was, making it easier for us to find our way. Mark Zogu and Peter Toma walked at that steady, unhurried pace that allowed our mountaineers to cover great distances with a minimum of effort. I did not recognize the area even though we had been this way once before when we had gone from Ndue Deda's to Gjokë Deda's. Of course, I could not be sure that we had gone along these same footpaths, but chances were that we did.

Anyhow, after a few hours of walking without rest, Mark Zogu pointed at a small wooden shelter. A farmer had nailed together a few boards no more than five or six feet long and about four feet wide. He had secured one edge to the ground and had fastened the other end to poles about four feet high. Wooden posts kept it from collapsing. Underneath, the farmer had stored hay for his animals.

"It is almost daylight," Mark said. "We'd better stop and spend the day here. At dusk we can go on to Ndue Deda's." We crawled under the hay, and before we knew it we were all fast asleep.

The hay kept us warm and cozy. When we awoke it was daylight. My watch said it was about 8:30 a.m. We sat up and ate the bread that Gjokë Deda's wife had packed for us. I could not help thinking: These people were incredible. They shared with us what little they had, knowing that their own families would run out of food well before the harvest.

The day was cold and cloudy. Looking around, I could see maybe ten homes occupying the bottom of the valley. They were far apart and of very simple appearance. They reminded me of Dukagjin, of the poverty and generosity of that region. One of these homes in the valley must be Ndue Deda's. There was no need for me to ask; by evening I would know. At dusk we were on our way. Mark Zogu led us down along the flank of the hill. I could see the sparks and smell the smoke rising from chimneys. Smoke to me meant warmth, food, and a night or two under a roof—between solid walls and protected from the howling winds of the season. I had hardly walked the stiffness out of my joints when Mark Zogu veered toward a house and stopped at the entrance. He took pains to stand in the shadows and gave some sort of signal that I did not catch. The front door opened and we hurried into the sparsely lit, primitive, warm, hospitable, living space I remembered so well from our first visit. I could see the outlines of several people against the flickering light of the fireplace.

Ndue Deda spoke up. "Welcome. We thank God that He brought you safely to our house. Take off your wet clothes and sit near the fire." He could not have been friendlier or more hospitable. He then turned to the women. "Quickly, set the table. Our guests need food and drink."

Really, there was no need for him to spur on the women who were already in high gear. Mark Zogu and Peter Toma took off their heavy coats and backpacks, and gave their rifles to Ndue Deda. I had nothing to take off. Then the three of us snuggled up to the fireplace while the women scurried around. They put logs in the fire, pushed a kettle toward the middle of the fireplace, and built a wall of embers around it. They prepared flat cornbread tortillas as they loaded the table with goodies. We started to wolf down the food while the family sat around us, helping us, giving us cold water to drink, tending the fire, and doing their best to make us comfortable.

Our chewing must have slowed down somewhat, because Ndue Deda decided to ask us a question that must have been on his mind for a while.

"Where did you spend the day? How were you able to come here so early?"

"We left Gjokë Deda's after midnight and reached the hay shelter before dawn. We spent the day there and left at dusk."

"It's good to have you here. I had heard about the incident at the river crossing. Lucky for all of us; things could have been worse. Now that you are here, you can stay with us as long as you need to. Besides, it won't be long and your friends will come to pick you up."

I wished I could share his optimism. But I must admit, staying with him and his family until we were picked up sounded very comforting. We stayed up a little longer and then followed our well-worn trek to the stable. We had our favorite corner and lay down for the night. We wished each other a good night. As for me, I had a full tummy and was ready to fall asleep. My mind swept back to the first time I had come here. This time I was in good physical shape, no aches and pains, no frozen feet—and no visit by a friendly goat.

Lord, thank you for taking care of us. I prayed, "Our Father who art in heaven..."

DECEMBER 21–23, 1952

Not much happened during those three days. The usual routine: sleep, food twice a day, and a visit with our host and his family each evening. As far as I was concerned, I could take this routine for a long time. Except... except, of course, that we were in danger, all of us, from the oldest member of the family to the baby.

DECEMBER 24, 1952

Christmas Eve. The day was no different from yesterday or the day before. Yet...it was Christmas Eve. Many different images and memories from years past flooded my mind. I thought of Christmas in Austria (See Chapter 3). Twenty years later, and I would be hiding in the Albanian mountains, utterly helpless, were it not for some kind and brave strangers.

That Christmas Eve of '52, my thoughts reached back to the rest of my family. Mom in Shkodra, probably by herself. No visitors, no cheers, no *Glühwein*. She had a roof over her head, however, thanks to the kindness of the Quku family who had taken us in. Mergim was in the army, in forced labor, under the command of sadistic ignoramuses while Dad was in prison at the mercy of jailers without mercy. What a state of affairs.

In 1944, when we could still leave, Dad had decided that he would weather the Red storm in Albania. "I haven't done anything," he would say to the rest of us. "Besides, even if I had reason to leave, where could we go without funds? We suffered 15 years in exile without a regular income. This time I am not leaving Albania, come what may. If you want to continue your studies in Austria, you can have a scholarship, go to Vienna with the rest of the Albanian students." That's what he used to say, because that's what he believed.

Mustafa Kruja had gone even further. "If I didn't have to leave for Vienna to see Besim who is ill, I would stay in Albania with the rest of my family. I have served Albania for over 30 years as an employee of the state. The communists won't give me a job but I will have my pension. You, Genc, worry without reason. You got a scholarship from the ministry of education because of your high marks in school. They won't send you to Italy. So you'll go to Belgrade. It will take you one year to learn Serbo-Croatian. Then you'll go back to medical school and finish your studies." That's how Mustafa Kruja and most of Dad's friends saw the situation. I had a foreboding that the communists had other ideas. So, I refused to go to Vienna because

I knew that Dad, Mom, and Mergim would need me. However, I had not imagined how bad things would get. These were not new thoughts; I had entertained them many a time. They did strike me powerfully that Christmas in the Albanian mountains, when my fate and that of my companions seemed to keep swinging from disaster to success and back to disaster.

One evening at Ndue Deda's, Peter Toma and Mark Zogu left after dinner for Porav. Peter Toma's brother Dedë had been discharged from the military and Peter could not wait to see him. That was understandable. Why Mark Zogu also was going was not clear to me. I did hear, however, Ndue Deda's warning loud and clear:

"Do not bring Dedë Toma with you when you return. Heavy snow is blocking the mountain passes. People will know that Dedë Toma has gone into hiding. The communists will mount a house-to-house search to find him and those responsible for his disappearance. If you bring him with you, I cannot keep you here any longer." That was that.

One could not argue with the premise or the conclusion. I was sure that Mark Zogu, if not Peter Toma, would heed the warning.

Dec. 25–Dec. 26, 1952.

I spent those two days alone, without Mark Zogu and Peter Toma. We were not bosom pals but I still missed them, especially Mark Zogu. I spent the days in the barn and the evenings with our host and his family. One morning the women asked that I take off my suit because they wanted to wash it. I must have been filthy—even by mountain standards. When they returned the suit in the evening, I removed my underwear, what was left of it, and handed it over. The women brought me hot water and a hollow gourd. I rose to the challenge and took a hot and cold bath. I felt hot, burning hot, where the water ran over my body and felt very cold everywhere else. I dried myself with some rags and tried to put on my suit. That was easier said than done. The women had boiled the suit and had dried it over a fire. It was stiff as a board. Once I forced myself into it, I noticed it had shrunk to the point where sleeves and pant legs were at half-mast. I must have been something to look at! Anyhow, the suit smelled of smoke. It felt like armor. It barely covered me, especially now that my shirt and underwear were gone. On the positive side, when I got my underwear back, I felt clean and things were back to normal—minus the lice.

There was another sign that Ndue Deda and his family cared for me. One evening, after the meal, Ndue Deda said to me, "Genc, here in our mountains, in our home, you are as safe as in your own home."

I couldn't help but wonder, as safe as in my own home? Had I been safe there, would I have fled into the mountains? Besides, why was he telling me this? Did I look scared?

"Even if the security forces come looking for you, they will never find you," he continued.

"How come?" I wanted to know.

"Look, we have no trouble hiding one person. We can hide you anywhere, even in the stable. We simply cover you with hay and dry leaves and they will never find you. Besides, no one is looking for you here in my house."

His words did not explain why he had started this conversation. I knew Ndue Deda well enough to know that he did not speak just for the sake of hearing himself speak. Whatever the reason, his words made me feel better.

The women were covering the embers with ashes in the fireplace and busied themselves with their nightly chores. I was sure they heard every word. In fact, it seemed to me that Ndue Deda's words stemmed from a previous conversation between him and his family members. I didn't know how to show my gratefulness with words. So I smiled and they all smiled in return.

DECEMBER 27, 1952

In the evening, Mark Zogu, Peter Toma, and a third man materialized out of the dark. They were soaking wet, part sweat and part precipitation. Who was the third man? Could it be they had found a swimmer who would get us across the Drini? Ndue Deda welcomed them in his usual calm, measured manner. He knew the newcomer and welcomed him by name. I didn't catch the name at first, but after a while I made out that our host was calling him Dedë. Was this Dedë Toma, Peter Toma's brother, the man Ndue Deda did not want under his roof? No, it couldn't be. Mark and Peter would not take the chance of being thrown out. He had to be another Dedë. After all, Dedë was a very common name in our mountains. I felt somewhat reassured. Then Ndue Deda spoke up once more.

"Men, tomorrow I will take you to a cave where you will be safe. I can't take you there tonight because we need to clean the cave first and remove the snakes that winter there. Sleep well tonight. Tomorrow night I'll take you there."

It was Dedë Toma after all. Why the dickens did they do it? Why did they bring him here? Couldn't they wait until we were ready to cross the Drini before picking him up? It made no sense to me. I was upset. I thought I had spent enough time in a cave with Hila and the rest to last me a lifetime. Now I had to do it all over again. No warm food or cozy evenings near the fire, and very little human contact. All of this because Peter couldn't wait to bring his brother to Ndue Deda's house—despite clear and ominous warnings. It was enough to make a grown man cry.

Later that night, when we settled in the barn, I thought I might hear some explanation. Nothing, not a word was said about this act of sheer madness. After a while, resignation replaced my anger. What was done was done. I had no control over it or over myself. I was still at the mercy of mountaineers who chose not to tell me what was going on. So be it. I rolled over on one side ready to sleep.

"Our Father who art in heaven..."

December 28, 1952

Another Sunday; my 12th Sunday in the mountains. How Sundays had changed. In Italy, I sometimes had a chance to go to Mass. More often, I would drop in at church and say a prayer during the week. In Albania I had not gone to church probably because people knew me and it would have been hard to explain. Besides, I had a problem in the family. Dad had told me more than once that I could choose my religion once I was of age. However, when I returned from the audience with the Pope and started wearing a small chain with a religious medal, Dad let me know that he disapproved. Mom, on the other hand, was on my side.

When the communists took over, I didn't even attempt to go to church. My respect and admiration for the Church and the Catholic faith, however, kept growing. I remember so many courageous priests and nuns. Priests were suffering the insufferable with dignity. Nuns had to leave the convent and could no longer wear their religious habit. They had to do menial work to earn a living. Priests were being killed left and right. Yet, with all the indignities and suffering surrounding them, priests died like martyrs. When I met nuns on the street they seemed to float, instead of walking like the rest of us.

In Ndue Deda's barn, it struck me that most calendars abroad marked Sundays and other holidays in red, as a mark of joy or distinction. In Albania, weekdays should be marked in red in honor of the innocent blood that was being spilled relentlessly. Sundays and holidays should be marked in black, in sign of sorrow.

That day I kept imagining a cave, wet walls, dripping ceiling and all. The more I thought about it, the less enthusiasm I could summon for what lay ahead. I remember I was crouched against the stable wall when Ndue Deda walked in. I expected him to tell us to gather our things and get ready to move out. In fact, I had tightened my moccasins, secured my revolver, and was ready to go. I kept my head low, waiting for the inevitable. Then I heard Ndue Deda's voice.

"I did not have a chance to clear the cave today. Tonight you will stay here and tomorrow we'll move you to the cave. Now let's eat."

Thank God, one more night with Ndue Deda and his family—and another couple of hot meals. The execution had not been cancelled, just postponed for 24 hours. Every day gained was a success. O Lord, thank you! After dinner I lay down in the barn and slept like a baby.

DECEMBER 29, 1952

Today was for real. Dedë Toma was still with us. This was Ndue Deda's house and Ndue Deda had told us we would move to a cave because of Dedë Toma's disappearance from circulation. I was still hot under the collar, not because I had something against Dedë Toma, but because I didn't want to trade the comforts of living with a family for the discomforts of a cave. Once again, I checked my meager belongings and was ready to hit the road. As if I had another choice! I checked my watch. It was getting late. We usually ate early in the evening. I did not know what was keeping Ndue Deda. Perhaps he had not yet returned from the cave. Anyhow, better later than sooner. At 7:30 p.m., Ndue Deda entered the stable.

"Men, the rescue team from Yugoslavia has arrived. They are in the house, five men eager to meet you. Let's not keep them waiting!"

I couldn't believe my ears. When the truth sank in, I thanked the Lord. Once more, when the night seemed darkest, a ray of light had broken through. Like in a dream, I crossed the few yards separating the stable from the house. There they were: Shtjefen Zogu, Zef Pjetra, Ndue Gjoni,

Osman Hyseni (the only Muslim in the group), and Çun Jakiçi. I had heard Çun Jakiçi's name before. He was known for his unfailing courage and was perhaps the best Albanian swimmer in Yugoslavia. He made it a point to embrace me and shake hands with me.

"I bring you greetings from Peter Qafa. He told me that you should not worry. This time you will cross the Drini."

A thousand thoughts swirled through my mind. "I am grateful to God that He brought you across the border and the river hale and hearty. I have heard much about you and am honored to make your acquaintance."

I sounded so formal, so stilted. My only hope was that since I meant what I said, our rescuers would take my words at face value. Heaven knew I meant them.

Mark Zogu, Peter Toma, our host, and our rescuers all seemed to know each other. As usual, I was the outsider. It didn't matter. Peter was the link between me and this group. I could see Peter's smiling face telling me to trust his friends. I must say, they were something to behold. They looked tough, reliable, and self-confident. I would have no trouble following them through thick and thin. After all, they were the best; they were Peter's friends.

Together with the newcomers, here we were—nine men, nine "enemies of the people," gathered under the roof of the village chief who had worked with the underground for a number of years. We ate at Ndue Deda's table, partook of his friendship and hospitality, but endangered him and his family by our very presence. The courage, graciousness, and hospitality of Ndue Deda and his family, of these simple mountain people, would put most city folks to shame. Thank God for such people!

The evening went by in a hurry. Finally, it was time to go to the barn. There was room and hay for everyone. Thanks to the type of quarters we had, the arrival of five guests created no problems as to bedding and other facilities. Who cared about comfort? What mattered was that men such as these might one day break the communists' grip and wrestle them to the ground. That's what the communists feared most: the strength of spirit and the dedication of men like these. That's why the communists unleashed their terror at the slightest sign of resistance. They could not admit to others what they feared all along, i.e., that some day, the oppressed would rise in rage and fury and give the communists what they deserved.

The night before, we were about to move to a cave. We did not. Tonight I was sure we would. Look what happened! Our rescuers had reached us. For some reason, I felt exhausted. I closed my eyes and fell asleep, like a stone sinking to the bottom of a deep well.

DECEMBER 30, 1952

When I woke up, my eyes swept the entire stable. I wanted to make sure that the rescue group was still with us. It was. With men such as these, I felt warm and secure. Today Mergim was 20 years old; a member of the Labor Battalion, somewhere in the Tirana area. When we said goodbye as he was leaving for the service, we had given each other a free hand. If he had a chance to escape, he was to make the most of it and not take chances because of me. I, of course, would do the same. Would I want him next to me at this point? There had been so many ups and downs since I had left home. There were times when the border seemed within reach. How I wished that Mergim were with me. Then there were the other times, the times when everything seemed to go wrong and I could do no more than thank God that Mergim was far away in relative safety. What about today? Could I be sure we would cross the border? Would I want Mergim to face the same perils as I, at the risk of Mother and Dad losing both their sons? Lord, you know what's best for us. You put us where we are, you move us to where you want us. Blessed be the name of the Lord!

My companions were stirring. Each had his own morning ritual. I didn't expect to hear much about future plans. I was used to the secrecy with which these men operated. Besides, I was in no particular hurry. When the time came to act, I would be one of them. And that suited me just fine. Nothing particular happened until dinnertime when Ndue Deda led us from the stable to the house. Even though I had covered that ground often, I always wondered. Whenever we entered or left the house, anyone could see us clearly in the door opening, against the light of the fireplace. Did Ndue Deda first reconnoiter the terrain? I never saw him take any special precautions. Like in so many other things, I had no choice but to trust him and the others.

The evening meal was abundant, as always, and the conversation much livelier. Çun Jakiçi could be a lot of fun. He teased anyone within reach and took whatever he or she dished out in return. Some of the others participated, but it was obvious that Çun was their natural leader. Then Ndue Deda rose to his feet.

"Men, I want to ask our friend Genc a favor." He turned toward me. "Would you accept to become my blood brother?"

I was taken by surprise. Everyone was looking at me. I knew I had to reply and that it had to make sense. Why would Ndue Deda want to become my blood brother? What did he have to gain? Why did he make this request at this time? I had no answer to any of these and other questions swirling through my head. The entire room was spinning at an incredible speed all around me. All I could see were the eyes of those present staring at me. I could see nothing else, just so many pairs of eyes fixed on me, awaiting an answer. At last I figured I had nothing to lose. I cleared my throat.

"Of course, I will," I replied. "It is an honor for me."

I was glad my voice did not stick in my throat. The words were out. I heard their sound and so did the rest. I was not sure they made sense. Furthermore, I had no idea what would come next.

"Good."

Ndue Deda reached out and one of the two women handed him a needle. He pricked his finger and then he pricked mine. He squeezed until some blood came out. I did the same. Then he put the tip of his finger over mine and rubbed the tips together, mixing the drops of blood. Next he moistened his lips with the blood on his finger. I figured I had to do the same. I raised my finger to my lips and sucked the blood. Ndue Deda hugged me and the men around us grunted their approval. It was all over before I had a chance to collect my wits.

Next, I heard Çun Jakiçi say, "It is almost ten o'clock; time to hit the road."

The men stood up. There were handshakes all around. Ndue Deda greeted us one by one. When he said goodbye to me, he acted no differently now that we were brothers than before. I was still baffled. We went into the barn one last time. As the men shouldered their loads I strained my ears to hear where we were going. Çun Jakiçi spoke up.

"Secure your loads and weapons. Ndue Deda told me that a police battalion is in the area on maneuvers. We will have to move fast. I'll take the lead. Osman you'll be last. We have to make Porav before dawn. We must avoid the police at any cost."

Çun would get no argument from me. We left the stable moving rapidly and almost without a sound. The night was clear and cold. We fell in line and began climbing the foothills. This was the third time I was following this same path. Would I go on to the Drini River and beyond? Or was this another one of those round trips that ended just about where it had started? God alone knew. I must say, though, that there was a song in my heart and bounce to my step. I didn't know how far we would get this time. I felt, however, that we were much better equipped this time than when we had gone this way last.

We marched and slithered, single file, like shadows in the night. The moon was out, which was both good and bad. I could see where I was stepping but the chances of being seen were also greater. My mind flew back a few years to when I had read Ernie Pyle in jail. He used to mention how American planners had to consider the phases of the moon as well as the time when it rose and set. Tonight I felt very close to Ernie. I felt good. I marched well and sure-footed. I was 28, healthy and strong. I was with friends who had the same friends and enemies as I did. We knew we had to avoid clashing with the police battalion on maneuvers. We were faster, we were motivated, and my friends knew the area better. Unless we had bad luck, we were bound to come out on top.

DECEMBER 31, 1952

We reached Gjokë Deda's house at about 3:00 a.m. We had covered the distance in five hours. Normally, it took six. Çun Jakiçi motioned that we surround the house. He knocked and Gjokë Deda answered immediately. Perhaps he had not yet gone to sleep.

"Listen, Çun. I have an overnight guest. I cannot take you in. Furthermore, I am not yet ready to come with you. Give me one day. Go into the woods to the place where we met the last time. I'll come and see you during the day."

"You got it, but remember, the police are wise to you. Come to our camp. We'll discuss things in the morning."

Gjokë Deda got back into the house and closed the door behind him. Çun turned around and motioned for us to follow him. Within a few minutes we were in the woods, in an area sheltered from the wind, where we settled down for the night. There was no need for words. Çun knew what he was doing. That was good enough for me and my companions. Daybreak found us up. Some were washing their hands and faces, rubbing them with snow until they were red. Others were eating breakfast. Once we were done, everybody settled back into their private world. I wondered what the others were thinking about.

I for one felt good about these last few days. The group inspired confidence, no doubt about that. Its members were team players, cohesive, and loyal to each other. They had the best swimmer, and all of them were handpicked. They viewed Peter Toma as the border expert. He really must know the area. That was good.

CHAPTER THIRTY-FOUR

DRINI CROSSING

DECEMBER 31, 1952 (CONTINUED)

Our camp in the woods was almost cozy. It was pretty high up the mountain, with trees, mostly conifers, gathered around as if to protect us. The men had scattered in a circle with their weapons pointed outward, like a wagon train crew pointing its rifles toward the enemy.

I rose in surprise when Çun approached me. He was smiling as he kept his piercing eyes fixed on mine.

"Let's sit down," he said. We sat down, each trying to find a dry spot.

"Peter Çub Qafa told me all about you in Yugoslavia. He told me that he and you had some tough times in the mountains. He also told me that the Drini River had made life particularly hard for you. The first rescue group was delayed and missed you because of the swollen Drini. The second time, the river separated you from your friend Peter when the goatskins burst and the swimmer had to leave you behind. Well, don't worry. The river is not going to defeat you again. You told Peter that perhaps you were not meant to cross the river a second time; that perhaps you were not meant to reach Yugoslavia. This time we have come prepared. We won't have to depend on goat skins. We have a rubber dinghy. Furthermore, I promise you that you will be among the first to cross the Drini River."

Çun put his hand on my shoulder and smiled warmly. He squeezed my shoulder, rose, and returned to his spot. Mixed emotions welled up within me. As he was walking away, I could barely stammer a few words of thanks. I was afraid that in his eyes I might look like a little child, petulant, a city-born brat afraid of the river. Of course, he could not know that my escape attempts had been thwarted nine previous times and so far the

499

river had proven an implacable enemy so far. My life and my future lay on the line. On the other hand, his friendly tone and his warmth told me he was my friend, someone who would try his best to help me across river and the border despite the difficulties that lay ahead of us. That made me feel good! I would do my best not to be a burden and to help as much as I could—with God's help!

Late that morning, the conversation suddenly stopped. The men had spoken in hushed tones until that moment. Now you could almost hear a snowflake hit the ground. I held my breath. Then, one of the men turned around and waved. It was all right. A person was approaching our camp. It was Gjokë Deda. Soon, the tall, lanky Gjokë appeared, greeting and shaking hands with all the men. What a fraternity they were! To leave their families, to leave the safety of Yugoslavia and cross into Albania while the border and every mountain pass lay buried in snow. It blew my mind. Gjokë made his way to Çun Jakiçi and stopped. They embraced with feeling.

"It's good to see you, Gjokë."

"It's good to be here," Gjokë replied. "I regret that last night I could not ask you in. I had a visitor from a neighboring village, an old man who would not have betrayed you, I am sure, but I could not risk it. I hope you didn't freeze too much."

"No, the woods kept the wind out. We slept well and now you are here. That's good. Here, roll yourself a cigarette," said Çun Jakiçi as he handed the guest his silver box with tobacco and cigarette paper. It took them about a minute to roll and light their cigarettes according to ritual.

"Gjokë, my friend, you have been generous and have helped us and many others on our way to and from Yugoslavia. You have offered us food and shelter. Most of all, you and your family have protected us from communists and spies. We are grateful. However, we are not the only ones who know what you have been up to. Somehow, the police also know. We know this for sure. They know and are about to strike. Go home and get ready. We will come at dusk. By tomorrow morning we can all be safely in Yugoslavia." Çun stopped. He drew on his cigarette and waited for Gjokë to reply.

"Çun, I have felt the danger and I am grateful for your offer. I have to prepare things at home. I have to talk with my wife who finds it hard to leave. Trust me, by the time you get to my house, we will be ready. We'll eat and then we will be on our way, God willing." When he had started to speak, he was troubled. At the end, he sounded relieved. He had voiced his concerns and reached a decision. Everything was in the open now.

Gjokë stood up and hugged Çun. He turned around and waved to the others. When he first came to our camp that morning he shook hands with each of us, like a politician running for office, or rather, like someone reluctant to come to grips with a difficult situation, someone unwilling to make a fateful decision. On his way out, his face was determined and his step bouncy. I wondered what a mountaineer, a family man, would do under the circumstances. Would he say goodbye to his friends? That was unlikely. What would he do with his sheep and his goats? Would he repay any debts or would that look suspicious? Would he make himself visible to show the flag or would he keep a low profile to avoid attracting attention? What would he do or avoid doing? I knew better than to ask questions. I had to be patient for another few hours and I might have the answers to some of my questions.

Slowly, it grew dark. Peter Qafa might have left earlier. Çun waited until it was good and dark. We were ready and packed when he gave the signal to move out. Single file and without a sound, we left what might well be our last camp on Albanian soil. We approached Gjokë's house in such a way that the trees and their shadows offered us protection. We stood before the same door that had kept us out the night before. This time it opened, silently and swallowed us up one by one.

Next to Gjokë stood his oldest son, the one who had spit in the fireplace when he found me wanting. He stood next to his father as if to say that he was next in charge. Gjokë's wife was busy near the fireplace, seemingly unaware of our arrival. I looked around. The large wooden grating hanging from the ceiling was full of meat, many hundreds of pounds of meat. So, Gjokë had slaughtered his animals rather than have the communists drive them off once his escape became known. Good, that meant that he and his family were ready to join us.

Gjokë bent down and talked to his wife. She straightened up and welcomed us, starting with Çun. She mouthed the traditional greetings with little joy on her face or in her words. She set two low round tables and after a while, after a long while, we were all seated and ready to eat. She went to the kettle in which she had boiled the meat and each of us got a steaming, large chunk. I waited for the others to start eating. Once they got going, I grabbed the chunk in front of me, bit off a piece and dropped the rest back on the table. It was burning hot. I started to chew but not for long. Others did the same. Some started chewing again until Çun spoke up.

"The meat is too salty." He turned toward the woman. "Bring water so we can rinse off the salt."

The woman looked sullen but did as she was told. She fetched water and a basin. We all held our meat under a stream of water, hoping this would make it edible. Rinsing helped. The water cooled off the meat and got rid of some of the surface salt. We started to chew again. The meat was still so salty that only hunger and the prospect of a long and arduous march to the border made me finish my meat. I couldn't help but think: Was the woman so absent-minded that she had salted the meat every time she had walked by the kettle or was she so much against leaving her house that she had made the meat inedible on purpose? She was the only person who knew the truth and she was not likely to confide in any of us.

The evening dragged on. It was almost ten o'clock when Çun turned to Gjokë, saying, "Gjokë, time is running out. We got to move if we want to make it to the border."

Gjokë looked at his wife. She said nothing but her body language spoke volumes as she busied herself around the room. If he and his crazy friends wanted to leave for Yugoslavia, that was fine with her. She wasn't going to move and neither would her children. Furthermore, she seemed to say, "If you as head of the family and father of five children don't know that your place is with them, then I am not going to waste my time explaining it to you."

Çun grasped what was going on. He spoke to Gjokë's wife directly, saying, "Listen to me and listen well. My men and I are about to leave. You, your husband, your children, you are all in danger. If the police arrest him, you will be in trouble and in danger. Now get the children ready. If you don't want to come, I'll put a rope around your neck and drag you after me. I am not going to risk any lives because of you. And don't think for a moment that I don't mean what I say."

No one in that room, including Gjokë's wife, had the slightest doubt that Çun meant every word. All evening the woman had been more or less silent. Now she found her voice. If she had to cave in, she wasn't going to do so without bargaining.

"I have about 80 pounds of wool. I am not going to leave the wool behind."

"Fine," Çun answered. "We'll carry it." He turned around and pointed at one of his men. "You carry her wool, OK?" I was surprised that Çun was so flexible and willing to put up with her.

"I also have 60 pounds of tobacco," she continued.

I was even more surprised when Çun laughed and said, "The doctor doesn't smoke. He will carry it and we won't have to worry."

I was in no mood to carry tobacco or anything else on my back. I had back trouble as it was. I looked around to see whether I had any allies; no such luck. Everyone was smiling and looking at me.

"OK, I'll carry the tobacco, but only to the river. I am not going to carry it to the border and get killed with tobacco on my back, like a common thief."

"Fine then, that settles it," said Çun.

Well, it was not quite settled as far as she was concerned. "One more thing. I want someone to carry my wedding gown."

Çun stared at her. "Woman, if you think any of my men are going to carry your gown, you are wrong. We'll carry the wool and the tobacco, and that's it. Now get going."

Well, this time she got busy. She dressed the children in their finest outfits: dark pants or skirts, white shirts, and bright red kerchiefs. I'll be doggone if she did not have them wear their Pioneer uniforms, the uniforms of the communist children's organization! I thought for sure Çun would object to the white shirts that could be seen a mile on that moonlit night. He said nothing, so I held my peace.

We were finally ready. I shouldered my 60 pounds of tobacco and marched out under the amused looks of my companions. I was mad. We gathered in front of the house as for a picnic. Gjokë locked everything. The kids were in a festive mood, and we took off.

It was a splendid night. The moon was high in the sky, the air warm although it was New Year's Eve. We started going down the footpath that Peter, the rest of the crew, and I had taken on December 13. That day seemed so far away, though it was barely over two weeks ago. I don't know why nobody saw us this time. The moon was so bright it seemed almost like daylight. This time there were 16 of us: Gjokë with wife and five children, Çun Jakiçi and his four companions, Mark Zogu, Peter Toma, his brother Ded, and I. We walked one behind the other. One man carried the wool, I carried the tobacco, and Gjokë's wife wore her dark woolen wedding dress and carried on her back a heavy, hand-carved crib with her one-month old son in it.

We reached the Drini shortly before midnight. It looked innocent and beautiful, like a silver ribbon bathed in moonlight between brightly lit shores. The air was warm and pleasant. I dumped my load of tobacco on the ground and watched as the men pulled out an orange rubber dinghy with "U.S. Air Force" stenciled on it. They attached a foot pump and soon the dinghy began to take on an oval shape. Finally, it was fully inflated, a firm oval roll with a firm rubber bottom. Could this be the time when I would finally cross the Drini River? The spiteful river had stopped me several times before, the last time on December 13 when it separated me from Peter, Hila, and Deda. Maybe this was my lucky time.

Suddenly, the rubber stopper popped up and air hissed out of the filler neck. Fortunately, the stopper was attached to a chain. One man caught the stopper and forced it back into place. Then the men reattached the foot pump to the dinghy. This time the foot pump burst.

Is the Drini going to have the last word once more? I asked myself. Darn it! Darn it! Darn it! Çun inspected the damage. The pump was worthless. He stepped into the dinghy. Its rubber bottom was flat. The rubber dinghy was too small, however, to take all of us across in one trip.

"You, and you, and you..." Çun was counting off his men who would row the dinghy. Next, he nodded to Gjokë's wife. Holding her infant son in her arms, she stepped into the dinghy. Çun smiled and turned toward me.

"Doc," he said, "you are next." I stepped into the dinghy followed by Peter Toma.

We began to glide silently and rather placidly away from the shore. Suddenly, the current became swift. We began to shoot downstream. Under load, the rubber bottom of the dinghy was sagging, and the current was dragging us downstream, away from the opposite shore.

"If we continue to move this fast, the communists will never catch us." These were the first cheerful words the woman spoke all night. Unfortunately, she had not grasped the danger we were in as the current carried us inland. Fortunately, farther down the river made a bend and the current slowed a bit. One of the men jumped into the water and dragged us out. Thank God, we made it.

When the men pulled the dinghy out of the water, it was as flabby and wrinkled as the neck of a skinny old chicken. Without a pump, how would we ever inflate the dinghy and get the others from across the river? Çun, Gjokë, four children, and the rest of the men were still on the other shore. I looked at the group around me. Peter Toma and some armed men were on this side. If we had to, we could manage on our own. I felt relieved. Those left on the other side would have to fend for themselves. We had a chance. I looked at my wristwatch. It was exactly midnight. *Happy New Year, happy 1953*, I said to myself. Then, ashamed of my selfishness, I looked around to see what the men were doing.

They had started inflating the dinghy by mouth. I felt guilty and offered my services. We took turns blowing. The second time around, instead of blowing air into the dinghy, I felt air gushing from the raft into my lungs. So much for that! The others kept blowing and soon the dinghy was hard, flat, and fully inflated. One man rowed it back across the river. I saw him dragging the boat upstream. Everyone on that side jumped in and soon we were reunited. I wondered if we would set out for the border, or was it too late?

Moments later, Çun asked everyone to settle down for the night and take cover among the bushes. Not far from us was the main road leading toward the border. We had to be careful, keep the children quiet, and not move from dawn to dusk. We all had some food and water. There really was no need for any of us to move. Çun wished us all a good night.

"By the way, doc, where is the tobacco?" he asked me.

"I left it behind. I told you, I was going to carry it as far as the river and no farther, didn't I?"

"Yes, but you didn't tell us that you would leave it on that side of the river. Well, we are not going to go back for the tobacco. Good night!"

In a few hours, dawn would be upon us, the first day of the new year. Would it be a good year for me? Moments later I was fast asleep.

In the morning, half asleep, I could hear noises. I could hear water gurgling, birds singing, the soft sounds of the wind whispering among the treetops. A new day was here. The thought of where I was finally pushed everything else aside. Last night, my friends and I had defeated the mighty Drini. Today, nothing stood between us and the border except foothills, mountains, border guards, machine-gun nests, land mines, and whatever else the communists had installed to make sure that Albanians stayed within the borders of the glorious People's Republic.

I raised myself on an elbow, half expecting to see a whole new world. Instead, the river was still there, lazily rolling in its bed like a feline stretching out and licking its paws, always ready to slash out at any prey that ventured within reach. The bushes were also still there. They were no longer last night's silhouettes merging with each other and the surrounding darkness. In daylight, they were three-dimensional, tall as men and thick enough to offer shelter to birds and anyone able to crawl under their lower branches. Low fog filled the valley. My face was moist, my clothes wet, and my joints stiff. Good thing I did not suffer from rheumatism.

My companions were up, some cleaning themselves, others eating, others again stowing away their gear. Gjokë and his wife busied themselves with their five children. It struck me how disciplined these children were. They sat around, playing alone or with each other without making a sound. They sensed the danger, and danger was no stranger to them. They had learned early on that to survive they had to know about two worlds: about the world at home and about the outside world. Both were real. Except that what they heard at home was at odds with what the outside world tried to teach them. At home, their parents told them that Enver Hoxha was a crook, a liar, a murderer. In school, the teacher exalted Enver as the country's most beloved son, its fearless leader, its savior, and the man who struggled day and night against the forces of darkness trying to deny Albania its glorious destiny. How could children function in this dual world? They could because they believed their parents, whose love was real, tangible, and ever present. The oldest child knew from experience that "Uncle Enver" lied. The eight-year-old boy had heard Enver Hoxha glorify Tito as Albania's greatest friend, its older brother, its invincible ally. He had heard that same Enver Hoxha rant and rave with impotent fury when he had prophesied that one day Stalin, Enver's latest and everlasting idol, would with his little finger sweep Tito from his palace into the deepest abyss of communist hell. So much for "Uncle Enver's" credibility.

The day passed slowly. The fog lifted, followed by a warm, intermittent drizzle. Pressed under the bushes and behind natural berms, we hardly moved all day. We had filled our water cans during the night and had enough bread, cheese, and meat in our satchels or pockets for the whole day and then some. All day long, I didn't see anyone walking along the road that ran parallel to the river. Even if someone had walked by, he could have missed us very easily.

Dusk crept in on cat's paws. First the shorelines, then the hills, and finally the mountain tops seemed to coalesce into a billowing wall of gray. I tried to make out what time it was. My wristwatch said it was about 5 p.m. When I looked up, Gjokë was coming toward me.

"Doc," he whispered, "soon we'll be on our way. My wife will carry the baby on her back and I will carry our three-year-old. Here, take my rifle and ammunition belt. Also, please stay with my wife. If we are ambushed and you can shoot your way out, take her with you. If not, shoot her first before you kill yourself."

He had risked his life and family for us and now he needed help. I owed it to him.

He handed me a long Italian Carcano infantry rifle and his ammunition belt. This rifle had an excellent reputation. It carried six rounds in its magazine and was particularly effective in piercing wood. The German Mauser was perhaps better balanced and thus seemed to weigh less on one's shoulder. It carried a clip with five rounds and was better in shattering boulders and stones. Both rifles had an effective range of hundreds of meters.

The last time I had held a rifle in my hands was in 1948 in Dukagjin (see Chapter 20). Then I was viewed as an enemy not to be trusted under any circumstances. Four years later, and on the other side of the political divide, Gjokë entrusted me with his wife's life.

I nodded and rose to my feet. I took his rifle and fastened the ammunition belt around my waist. As he turned around, I followed him and took up my place behind his wife. I turned and pointed the rifle toward the road. I could barely make out the rifle sight. We were ready to take to the road toward the border. It seemed like a dream. Would we make it through rough terrain, between machine-gun nests, up the mountain, to and across the border? I did not want to think that far ahead. It had not served me well in the past when events had turned everything upside down. It would not serve me well today. I told myself to take care of the moment and forget the rest.

I looked at myself. Both soles of my moccasins had gaping holes, but I did not care. If we made it, God would provide; if not, I would need no other moccasins. The same applied to my torn pants that exposed my knees and to my jacket whose sleeves had shrunk halfway to my elbows after being washed in scalding water.

It started to drizzle again. Quietly, we started to march single-file behind Peter Toma, our guide. The infiltrators split into two, some at the head and some at the end of the column. The rest of us were in the middle. Gjokë was carrying the three-year-old while the other three children marched behind him. His wife had strapped to her back the heavy hand-hewn wooden crib with her baby son in it. I inserted myself behind her.

At first, the path was level and visible because night had not yet settled in. We proceeded at that measured step so characteristic of our mountaineers; unhurried, almost soundless. Our column started to cross a brook when the men ahead raised their right arm, telling us to stop in our tracks. I could not hear or see anything. Several of us found ourselves in the middle of the brook. We stood there for several minutes. For whatever reason, I felt laughter welling up inside me.

"Men," I said, "my feet are getting wet. It must be because my moccasins have holes."

They looked at each other. I could see them thinking: *Could he be so foolish as not to realize that we were knee-deep in water?* No one answered me. I did not bother to explain nor did my mood change. Somehow, I felt things were finally going my way.

We began to move again. Placing one foot in front of the other, picking each spot carefully for firm support, we began to climb the foothills. We did not want to slip. We could get hurt and the noise could put everyone at risk. By now, it was dark and the drizzle had changed to rain. Another arm signal and the column stopped once more.

Someone whispered, "There is a machine-gun nest ahead of us. All infiltrators move up front. We will split into two and come at it from both sides."

For a minute or two, I neither saw nor heard anything. Then came the word. "The position is empty—let's go."

Suddenly, the baby started to whimper and then to cry. Darn it, the last thing we needed was a crying baby! The woman lowered the crib and started to breast-feed the child. Finally, it shut up. It seemed like an eternity.

We had one more such episode. The warning came down the line that we were close to communist positions, and again the baby began to cry. The woman swung the crib off her back and onto her knees as she fed the baby. By the time the baby stopped crying, the whole garrison could have been on our backs, or so it seemed to me. The system didn't make sense. When the men knew that we were approaching a high-risk zone, why not alert the woman so she could feed her baby before it endangered the lot of us? I could not tell this to the men so, in my frustration, I told it to the mother and added that I had no doubt that her infant son was a communist informer. I am not sure she even heard me. It helped me let off some steam, though.

By now, we had been walking for a couple of hours. At times, we went off the beaten path, particularly in danger zones. We left the foothills behind us and began climbing up some steep slopes. The wind was brisk and the rain changed to snow. I had been walking with my eyes tied to the ground, watching my steps. By the time I noticed these changes, the snow under my feet was one or two inches deep. Things got slippery.

Once more, a warning came down the line. "A communist machine-gun nest ahead of us. We will split as before."

On cue, the baby started to cry. Again, the mother gave him her breast but this time the baby kept crying and crying. The men were getting edgy. To no one in particular, the mother said, "My breasts are dry. I have no more milk."

I remembered that under similar circumstances during another escape, one of the men, the father, had choked the baby to death. I shuddered. Fortunately, the machine-gun nest was empty and our column took off again—and the soothing swaying of the crib put the baby to sleep.

By now, of the five children, only the eight-year-old, the oldest, was still walking. Three men carried the other three. The oldest kept asking, "Dad, can we stop and light a fire? I am freezing."

"See that ridge? As soon as we pass that ridge, we will stop and warm ourselves. Be patient," he kept telling his boy, ridge after ridge, as we continued climbing.

By now, we were in the midst of a raging snowstorm. At least a foot of snow on the ground gave everything a soft, padded, almost friendly appearance. The wind howled through the trees and over the ridges, hitting us from time to time squarely in the chest. Suddenly, Peter Toma stopped and asked the men to gather around him.

"We are seven hours from the border and will never make it before daybreak. Let's drop the children. The police will find and take care of them."

There was something unreal about this whole scene. While he was speaking of getting rid of the children, one of the men, Osman Hyseni, took off his coat and wrapped it around one of the little ones. I was thinking that the family was in danger for helping us and that the police knew that the family was aiding the underground. How could we abandon the children? Peter Toma, on the other hand, was our guide, the one who knew the border best and he wanted to abandon the children in the snow. I wondered, as thoughts seemed to flow as slow as molasses through my mind, who would answer him. Would it be Çun, our official leader? Would the father of the children challenge him? Would anyone want to speak up? Was there a need to speak up? Mark Zogu, the oldest one of the group, took him on.

"Do you know why these people are running away from their home? Because they hid and fed and helped you and me when we knocked at their door. And you want to drop their children? The children will go wherever we go."

No one else said a word. Our column started up again as we began to climb toward the next ridge. The woods seemed particularly dense at this point. Between the trees and the falling snow, I could not see much ahead of me beyond the woman and her baby. We kept trudging higher and higher. We had been walking maybe ten minutes when Mark Zogu's voice rang out in anger.

"Peter Toma, stop running, or by God and on my honor I will shoot you dead."

There was no reply. I didn't know whether Peter Toma heard him. We kept walking without a break and without lighting a fire. Even the eight-year-old had stopped complaining. Numbness had taken over.

By now we were off the beaten path. We were stepping on some rocks and avoiding others. The men began to slip. Every so often, I could hear someone crashing to the ground. I lost my footing several times, but for me this was nothing new. Once I hit the ground with such force that I stopped breathing. Then I started to breathe again, got up, and kept going with the rest. Suddenly I realized that the only one who had not fallen was the woman. I saw her slip once. She fell on her knee and there was a nasty sound, but she never fell on her back like the rest of us. She was protecting her baby in the crib.

On previous occasions, even marching in the snow, I had been quite warm. Tonight my hands were so cold that I could not remove the safety catch on my rifle. For a moment, I panicked. If I could not remove the safety catch, I would not be able to fire the rifle. That could be most ominous. Then the solution hit me. All I had to do was remove the safety catch once. Then I could raise the bolt. All I had to do was lower the bolt, and the rifle was ready to fire. I tried hard and I managed to remove the safety catch. Now things were OK, as long as I did not get hung up on the bolt somewhere. I had to keep that in mind.

The snow kept falling in great tufts. Entire minutes would pass when I could neither see nor hear anyone ahead of me or behind me. The night was so dark and the snow so dense that occasionally I held the woman by her skirt so as not to lose her. At other times the column seemed to shrink and I found myself near one of the men.

"How much longer to the border?" I kept asking.

"Four hours...two hours...we are almost there."

At one point, someone said, "Look straight ahead, see those small pyramids? That's the border."

I did not see anything resembling what the man called "pyramids." A strange sensation came over me. I was about to cross the border, to leave my beloved Albania, my native country, perhaps for good. At my feet, there was a trickle of water seeking its way downhill. I fell to my knees for a last drink on Albanian soil. I got a little water and a mouthful of little stones. Then it struck me. The worst years of my life were those in Albania. Our family was marked for destruction. I was to be arrested for a second time and perhaps much worse. Now I was running for shelter. Yes, the Yugoslavs were our enemies. At least I would not have to dread unprovoked arrest and torture. I spit out the stones, rose to my full height, and stepped toward the border. I must admit that even at this point I did not see the pyramids. I did not care. I had made it. I had dreamed about and had imagined in so many different ways the paths that would lead me to the border. In my imagination I had always stopped at the border, unable to think beyond that line where Enver Hoxha's authority came to an end. Until the summer of 1948, Tito was our big brother, our leader, our demigod. Now, I was seeking asylum in Yugoslavia because under their communist version, my chances of survival were better than in my own country! I glanced at my watch. It was three o'clock in the morning. The date was January 2, 1953 and I, Genc Korça, or even better, Genc Kortsha, had finally crossed the border.

January 2, 1953

There was an eerie quiet all around us. There had been no Albanian guards anywhere along our path. That may have been the merit of a good guide, and ours, whatever his other shortcomings, was one of the best. Likewise, there had been no guards on either side of the border. Our true savior had been the snowstorm that had forced the guards to seek shelter in their barracks. One of our men fired some shots in the air and the sound ricocheted softly from one snow cotton puff to the next as deep, glistening snow covered everything in sight. I surmised that we were fairly deep inside Yugoslav territory if we felt safe enough to fire a rifle to attract the attention of the guards.

A few minutes went by and there came three men, a sergeant with a dog on the leash and two border guards. They seemed to know the infiltrators, judging by the way they exchanged greetings. After some conversation in Serbian, the men built a fire while someone handed out stale cornbread that had appeared out of nowhere. I knelt near the children whom the men had dropped off near the fire. Before shouldering my rifle, I pressed down the bolt and engaged the safety. Thank God, I may have to carry the rifle for a while longer but I would not have to use it.

Next, I concentrated on the cornbread. My hands were so swollen that I could not break the slab of bread. I started to bite off bits of stale bread while my mind was almost blank. I neither thought nor saw beyond the immediate. The wind had started blowing and was pushing the flames toward us, forcing me to pull back a bit. The children were like frozen figurines, unable to move their heads back as the fire singed their eyelashes.

The sergeant said a few words; my friends rose to their feet and fell into the usual single column. The footpath was so narrow that we had no other choice. The path led downhill and whenever we approached a fork in the path, someone would leave the column in the direction of a house that was emerging from the darkness. Eventually it was my turn. The sergeant motioned to me and I followed him toward a rather substantial-looking house with massive stone walls. He knocked and shortly thereafter a man in his bare feet and clad only in a shirt and long underwear opened the door. The sergeant said something, and the man mumbled what sounded like an invitation for me to enter his house.

Once inside, he and I climbed upstairs into what seemed like a large room with a fireplace and not much else in it. Soon another man appeared, shuffling in the dark. He handed me something. I found myself holding a metal bowl filled with watery yogurt, a piece of cold cornbread, and a spoon that had seen better days. One of them pushed a three-legged stool toward me and then they both crouched on the floor in the opposite corner with their knees pulled tightly against their chests. They glared at me from as far away as they could without leaving the room.

I felt myself blush as anger rose within me. "Since when is it Albanian custom not to break bread with a guest?" I made no effort to hide my feelings. The answer startled me.

"You are not our guest. UDBA brought you here."

UDBA was the acronym for the Yugoslav secret police. I could sense the hatred in his voice and the utter disregard for what his words might cost him if indeed I was a Yugoslav collaborator.

"Why did you leave Albania?" he wanted to know.

"To escape from communism," I answered lamely, anticipating what he would say next.

"Here, too, we live under communism."

"Yes, but in Albania they wanted to arrest me and perhaps even kill me."

"It would have been better for you to die in Albania than to live in Yugoslavia." Having spit out those words, he lowered his chin until it rested on his knees. He had said all he intended to say. I decided to go on the offensive.

"When I was here in 1944 with a battalion of Albanian nationalists to fight with you against the Yugoslavs, you did not speak to me like this." They both looked at me with surprise.

"Where were you stationed?"

"In Morine and at the pass of Çakor. In fact, one of our men, Hamit Troplini, died during a partisan mortar attack."

Perhaps they knew what I was telling them. Their first words to me had been words of insulting challenge. Now they both came closer. I could see the deep lines in their faces, the pain of living under foreign oppression, the light flickering in their eyes when they spoke of Albania and things Albanian.

"Do you know how the Yugoslavs treat us?" The word "*shkje*" that the older brother used to designate the Yugoslavs was a term expressing all the pain and hatred Albanians had accumulated over the years toward their traditional enemies.

"They want our land. We are to be moved out of here so Serbs can take over. They want our honor, and if we resist, they want our very lives. We are Muslim. Now they tell us that we are Turks and should go to Turkey where we belong. The weaker among us are leaving just to get out from under the Slavs. If they take our land, they take our honor. What is left for us to live for?"

There was a knock at the door. A soldier was asking for me. In a sense, I was glad to leave at this point. All my words could not change reality, the daily reality he and his brother and hundreds of thousands like them lived under. The brothers saw me to the door. We embraced each other in silence as I stepped into a cold yet exciting dawn. After all, I had left Albania behind me. Of course, I was in enemy hands but I would probably have easier choices and more options than I had in Albania. Life was simple, at least for the time being: Get away from the border and try to get ahold of Peter Qafa. He was the one who had given me a revolver when I was unarmed. He had slept under one blanket with me in rain and snow. When the river had separated us, he had promised he would send people to rescue us and had kept his word. Now we were just a few miles from the town where he lived with his family.

As I looked around, our group had reformed. I could hear my companions joking and walking taller, unconcerned about melting into the background. We began our trek toward the plains of Gjakova.

CHAPTER THIRTY-FIVE

REUNITED WITH PETER

JANUARY 2, 1953 (CONTINUED)

Daybreak was upon us. The deciduous trees seemed to reach for the sky with their thin, leafless branches, like lost souls with skinny arms seeking contact and comfort from heaven. The needle trees looked healthy, snow covered, and self-sufficient. Even the chirping and singing of birds seemed to come from the latter. The members of our group looked different in daylight. Now that the tension had left their faces, all looked haggard and tired. Yet there were significant differences. The men who had penetrated the border to come to our rescue had homes and families here in Yugoslavia. Gjokë, with his wife and five children, was walking into the unknown. The parents were obviously more relaxed and the children seemed to sense it. The four older ones were again walking, chatting and giggling, running, jumping, and picking up stones and branches, only to drop them a few steps later. I wondered. What were they talking about? What did this major break in their lives mean to them? They were away from home, probably for the first time, and in all likelihood would never see their mountains again.

We ran into a man coming from the opposite direction and no one pointed a weapon at him. My companions, in fact, smiled and greeted him. I could not tell whether they knew him but he smiled back and returned their greeting. Who cared? We could walk in plain daylight, without fear of being seen, turned in, or shot at. The situation was not rosy, but it was better than what we had left behind. The Yugoslavs were communists. Well, I knew how to speak and behave with communists if they gave me but half a chance. I had proven that in Albania, under the worst communist dictatorship in the Balkans. Besides, in Albania for years we had lived under the lackeys of Yugoslavia; here, at least I was dealing with the master himself, which was always easier. He who made the rules could also bend them. During the war and for the first four years, Albanian communists, like frightened dogs, had watched their Yugoslav master before barking or biting. All they had done on their own during that period was wag their tails hoping for a bone.

What about me? How did I feel and what was I thinking about my future? Well, I noticed a bounce in my step that I had not had in a while. The ever-present danger of torture and death surrounding me and oppressing me in Albania was gone. But there was still danger. They would question me, they could send me to a refugee camp, or even arrest me, but the likelihood of maltreatment was remote. Given the chance, I would ask to continue medical school. If not, a refugee camp might beckon. Now I could write the letters I had composed in my mind in the Albanian mountains. I remembered them verbatim—I wanted them to be factual and to the point. To Mustafa Kruja, to Edward, and to Sadije, I would write about their families, describe my circumstances in Yugoslavia, and not ask for anything specific but not too proud to accept help. To Valnea, I would describe conditions in Albania, our family situation with Dad in prison, Mergim in forced labor, and Mom all alone in Shkodra. About myself, I would write the same way I had written to her after the communist takeover, as a friend, but prepared for either possibility, for her being married or ready to start anew at the point where we had parted in July of 1943. Either way, I should be able to function with dignity. After all, ten long years had gone by and Valnea had lived under normal or near-normal circumstances while I was buried alive.

A tightness around my thighs brought my reveries to an end. My pants, or what was left of them, had become so snug around my thighs they fitted like leotards. I had no explanation, but who cared? I was no longer an outcast. It did not hurt and if I needed it, medical care should be available. What a good feeling. I looked at myself. I had started out with an almost-new American-made suit, a shirt, long underwear, one pair of wool socks, and heavy sandals with soles from truck tires. When I left home, I also had a knapsack with spare socks and a thin blanket. I lost the knapsack with its contents when Peter Qafa took it across the Drini River that fateful December 13. Now my long underwear was worn through at the knees and across the bottom. The pant legs had shrunk to mid-calf when the women had boiled the pants at Ndue Deda's. They had also boiled my jacket and the sleeves now reached up to the middle of my forearms. Well, maybe I was unfit to be featured in a magazine for the well-dressed man, but I was across the border. I was safe, and one more effort, one more border to cross illegally, and I could be free again!

We had been walking for a while. What would come next? I was told we were aiming for the Baba police station. After a few hours, we could see the plain of Gjakova. A few more minutes and we reached the valley and the Baba station. There was little if any snow; instead, large water puddles covered the ground. As far as the eye could see, there was dead grass, broken corn stalks, and mud, half-frozen, half-mushy mud. It seemed as if the good Lord had a special effect in mind when He limited his palette to a few basic colors ranging from dirty yellow to muddy brown. As we left the woods behind, we saw that our column was heading toward a small, squat, rectangular building that looked just as desolate as the rest of the landscape.

The police station's appearance matched that of the crew it housed. As we came close, some policemen came out to look us over. I grant you, we were a motley crew, but they looked just as bad if you considered that they were leading a normal barracks life. Their uniforms did not fit. The men were unshaven and looked unwashed. I must admit, they blended well into the landscape. They brought us bread and then left us alone.

I had learned in the mountains to be patient and not to ask questions. This was no easy lesson as I was impatient by nature, inclined to lead the target. Well, at this point I was not alone. Whatever happened to the rest would also happen to me.

The men were standing around or sitting on some little knoll, going through their meager belongings. No one was washing up or shaving. I was still standing when Prenda, the woman who had escaped with us, came to me and looked me in the eye.

"Last night everybody was running and looking out only for himself. Not you; you stayed with me through thick and thin. You are my brother."

For her that was a long speech. She reached out, grabbed my right hand, pulled me to herself, and laid her cheek against mine. I had nothing to say in reply, as I was not going to tell her why I had stayed close to her throughout the night. She let go of my hand, her eyes lowered to the ground, and walked away. We parted a few hours later. I would not see her again until we met in New York in December of 1995, almost 43 years later.

518   One Man's Journey to Freedom: Escape From Behind the Iron Curtain

I found a tree trunk to sit on. The view all around us was just as frozen and monotonous as when we first arrived, except for the shadows. They kept pointing away from the sun, doggedly, untiringly, traveling from west to east. I do not know how long I sat there. I remember standing up, perhaps to stretch my legs. As I stood there, lost in my reveries, a small hand reached for mine. It was Gjokë's oldest son, the eight-year-old who was engaged to be married and smoked, the one who had spit into the fire when he heard me say that I was 28 but did not smoke, that I was neither married nor engaged, and that I shaved off my mustache. I had not spoken to him since that incident at his house, intentionally. He was looking at a nearby field where a buffalo was pulling a cart with two big wheels.

"Is that a cart?" he asked, his big eyes looking at me.

It struck me that he had perhaps seen pictures of carts in his schoolbooks but had never seen a cart in real life. His mountains were too steep, the paths too narrow to hold anything on wheels. The youngster who had spit into the fire as he questioned my manhood had shrunk and become a little boy again who found himself in a world he had only read about. I felt ashamed. How could I have held a grudge against a child!

"Yes, my son, that is a cart and the animal pulling it is a buffalo."

He nodded trustingly as he absorbed these first impressions of a new reality and walked away. I wondered why he had come to me in the first place. Whatever the reason, I began to feel better. After all, this was the threshold to my world, the world I had known and could function in. This was my springboard to the free world, the good Lord willing.

Some policemen came out chatting, carrying two slim poles and a net. I could not believe my eyes. They set up a volleyball net, split into two teams, and started to play. They were clumsy, heavy footed, and had no idea of how to handle the ball. They held it too long, twisted it around, broke every rule, and hit the ball whichever way they could. The play field was muddy and their feet slipped. I had played with some of the best teams in Albania. My hands and feet began to tighten up each time the ball flew toward one or the other team. I was reacting instinctively, wanting to take position, to raise my hands and send the ball toward a player on the team or over the net into an empty spot and score.

Before I knew it, I was on my feet. My hands were pointing at myself, my eyes were asking to join them. They nodded. Now I could show them how to play volleyball. The ball came toward me. I spread my fingers before impact to direct the ball with precision toward the player next to me. The ball was heavy and muddy. It twisted and slipped between my hands. I blushed and bent down to pick it up. As I straightened up, I saw the players grinning. The next time the ball came in my direction it was near and above the net. It was not ideal but I should be able to spike it. I bent my knees and pushed hard. My arm went up with my fist clenched, ready to spike. Instead, my feet slipped and I found myself kneeling in the mud, with my feet spread apart. I had to put both hands in the mud before I could get up. I rose and walked off the field without a word. What happened? I did not know, but I had made a fool of myself and had embarrassed my companions. I took my place on the tree trunk and life went on. The policemen went back to their game, more convinced than ever of their talents as players, and my companions returned to whatever each had been doing before.

It was getting dark. Per my acquired behavior, I did not ask "What next?" The Yugoslavs certainly had plans for these 16 individuals stranded somewhere in the plain of Gjakova; particularly for the men they had sent across the border to rescue us. Mark Zogu and Pjeter Toma had crossed into Albania and got stuck when Peter, Deda, and Hila had crossed the river Drini. Six men had come with this latest group. Thus, half our group consisted of infiltrators. There was no doubt that the Yugoslavs would come to where we were, sooner rather than later.

I noticed some movement in our group. Quietly, the men were standing up and gathering their belongings. I began to meander from one to the other, hoping to catch a word here and there. A truck was coming to pick us up. It had left Gjakova and could be here any minute. How did they know? I had seen no one speaking with the police either inside or outside the building. By now, the sun had gone under and the faint glimmer in the sky served as a shimmering background. Some pale pinks and blues lingered on, seemingly reluctant to let go. The translucent darkness had mercifully wiped out the muddy yellows and browns of the landscape. For a moment, the world around me stood motionless, as if to impress an everlasting image in my mind. The men were like black cutouts against the sky, their rifles piercing the cold air, symbols of protection rather than fear.

I don't know how long this image lasted. Next, the sky grew dark and the silhouettes vanished. I heard a heavy engine in the distance while headlights were swaying through the night, up and down because of the ruts, left and right as the truck followed a twisting road. Was it our truck? I could not tell. To me it seemed as if it kept coming closer, as if the head-lights were searching for us. Was it wishful thinking? Heavens no, the po-licemen came out and turned on the lights outside their post. Minutes later the truck came to a full stop in front of the building. A policeman and the driver exchanged a few words. With remarkable self-control, none of our group moved toward the truck. Finally, the driver stepped out, lowered the rear gate, and motioned for us to climb aboard. Silently, without pushing, the men loaded first Gjokë Deda and his family and then took their places on the truck. It struck me that none of them tried to ride inside the cab. The driver raised the gate and locked it in place. Then he slammed the door of the cab. The engine came back to life, the truck moved beyond the lights of the police station, and we were off to the next phase of this trip. As dark-ness swallowed us up, I might have felt that all this was a dream, had it not been for the headlights peering into the dark and the bumps in the road.

We bounced quite energetically until we reached the paved highway. Our truck gathered speed as we moved toward the city lights, like a horse that felt the nearness of the barn. I had not seen electric lights, city lights, in months. We drove between small stone buildings, not unlike those of Shkodra. Then I saw a bakery with large, round loaves in the display win-dow! The store was closed and yet there were these light brown loaves, maybe ten of them, right there where anyone could break the glass and grab them. Clearly, this could not be Shkodra! Our bakeries never had any bread left over, let alone in display windows. After all our hunger and suf-fering, we had arrived in Gjakova.

As the truck got near the center of town, we saw more and more lights and people on the streets. The truck came to a full stop near some govern-ment building. People crowded around us as we got off, pushing and shov-ing, as if they had been waiting for us. I jumped off the truck, and before I had grasped what was going on, Peter stood before me grinning, his big round eyes sparkling, flashing a warm welcome. His arms were around me, his unshaven cheek rubbing against mine, as he whispered, "Didn't I promise I would get you out of there?"

"Yes, Peter, you did and you kept your word."

We moved away from the crowd, holding hands, each of us flooded, overwhelmed with joy bordering on disbelief. After Peter's farewell across the river Drini, I had never tried to visualize us getting together again. He was beyond reach, in an environment I had no feel for while I was in deep trouble on the wrong side of the river, suspended between a harsh reality and a nightmare. Now I was in Gjakova, a small crowd of Albanians still pushing and shoving, reaching for that one special person or persons for whose sake they had braved this winter night.

Peter pulled me by my hand. He walked over to someone whose features I could not make out in the dark. Peter mumbled a few words and the stranger nodded. Then I heard Peter's voice again.

"Come, let's go to my house. My wife and children are anxious to meet you in person."

We did not have far to walk. In the dark, I could not make out much but it seemed to me that Peter lived in a new house. As we entered, I did not have to bend to get through the door. The walls were smooth and white with fresh paint. Peter's wife, Lisa, came to greet me. She was short, sturdy, and looked up at me with piercing, laughing eyes.

"Welcome, and praised be to God that you made it. Come, you must be tired. Wash up and then we'll eat."

Cleanliness and food; both sounded heavenly. By the time she was done speaking, I found myself in a small bathroom. She carried in a tub full of hot water, handed me a hollow gourd with a handle and a bar of soap—real soap.

"Don't be stingy with the hot water. We have lots of it. When you are done, here is a towel. Here are Peter's razor and shaving cream. And here are some pants. They are nice and sturdy; they belong to Peter. Don't worry, he has others. They will fit you but they may be short. Here are socks, underwear, and a shirt. Leave the old clothes on the floor when you are done. I'll burn them."

What a luxury, all that hot water. I had not seen hot water since before Christmas at Ndue Deda's when I had bathed in the cowshed and the women had boiled my clothes to kill the lice. On the other hand, I did not want to be late for dinner. I dropped my rags in one corner. Under the glaring light in the clean bathroom I saw them in the fullness of their grime and wretchedness. There lay the jacket with holes instead of elbows, with its shriveled sleeves. Then came my shirt minus the cuffs. I dropped what was left of the shirt on the jacket. My moccasins came next. The cowhide had lost its hair and had worn through in several places. Not even the twine was worth saving. Then came my pants and long underwear. Both had worn through at the knees and in the back. Fortunately, the holes in the pants and in the underwear did not overlap and I had been spared the ultimate embarrassment. I could not help but marvel. Those rags had helped me survive three brutal fall and winter months, and if necessary, would have lasted me a little longer. How could Bessie's father have ever dreamed when he bought that suit in Detroit that it would last me three months in the Albanian mountains and would get me across the border into Yugoslavia? Farewell, trusted suit. You had faithfully stood between me, snow, and ice. Now the time had come to say goodbye. Crumpled on the floor, it looked like the ghost of the suit it had once been. The nice material, the good cut, and the elegance were gone. Its job was done, and in good conscience, it had given up the spirit.

I went to work pouring water all over me with the gourd and scrubbing myself with the soap, lather flying in all directions. I managed to wash and rinse myself carefully. Then I shaved with a new blade and Palmolive shaving cream. When I slipped into Peter's clothes, I marveled that his pants fit me around the middle and yet I was so much taller than he. The pants and the shirtsleeves were of course too short, but compared to the clothes on the floor, they were sheer luxury. I stepped out of the bath and into the living room. There was Peter, smiling from ear to ear. Was it because he was so happy to see me? Was it because of the way I looked in his clothes, or was it a little bit of both? All I knew was that I felt clean, among friends, and ready to sit down to eat.

Lisa and Dava, her daughter, rolled in a round table, balancing it on its edge. Kujtim, Peter's son, peeked from behind his father to see this stranger who looked and talked funny. I was perhaps the first Toskë he had ever seen or heard. As mother and daughter lowered the table, it stood about 10–15 inches above the floor. Then came the goodies: white cheese, onions, and whiskey; the main course consisted of steaming pork and beans, plenty of fresh, hot cornbread, and plenty of cold water.

Peter raised his glass and, of course, so did I.

"Praised be Jesus Christ," said Peter, the host.

"For ever and ever," I echoed the traditional answer.

Yes, praise and glory and majesty for ever and ever to the Holy Trinity that had protected me and all of us who would sit cross-legged at this round table to partake of God's gifts after months and years of want and hunger, of uncertainty, of fear, threats, danger, and possible death. I could not help but return in thought to those I had left behind, in the clutches of communism. May the Triune God hold them in the palm of His hand and protect the innocent, the helpless, and the suffering.

We exchanged a few more traditional well wishes and then came the moment when I sank my teeth into the warm bread, the rich cheese, and the crisp onions, followed by pork and beans. Every time I drank cold water, the food settled in my stomach and I had room for more. Lisa and Peter saw to it that there was always plenty of food before me. They encouraged me to have some more, and I obliged. Finally—I don't know how long it took—I felt full, bursting at the seams and sleepy.

I did not have far to go. I ate sitting on a mattress on the floor. The women cleared the table, rolled it out, swept the crumbs off the floor, covered the mattress with sheets and blankets, added a pillow or two, and voilà. Everyone wished me a good night. Once I was between the sheets, Lisa returned and tucked me in, turned off the light, and I fell asleep as if I were a heavy stone and someone had dropped me into some deep, dark waters.

JANUARY 3, 1953

When I woke up, morning light flooded the room. The soft mattress, the clean sheets, the ample covers, all felt wonderful. I could have stayed longer in bed but my watch told me it was time to get up. Yes, my watch, the one Mergim had given me to replace the one the guards had stolen in prison. It had followed me through thick and thin. During the months in the mountains, the face had blistered and the steel case had deep scratches, yet it kept telling time faithfully and fairly accurately. And right now it was telling me it was time to get up—and so did my hydrostatic pressure.

Peter and his family were all up and dressed. Kids kept peeking at me with big smiles on their faces. Who knows what Peter had told them about me? Anyhow, I washed up and joined the family at the breakfast table. Pork, fried sausage, scrambled eggs, plenty of fresh bread and cheese, and a circle of friendly faces. What had I done to deserve all this? When we were done eating, Peter and I got up while Lisa and the children cleared and removed the table. I was not without some reminders of my recent past; my feet hurt and my legs and feet were swollen.

A few visitors dropped in. They seemed to have known about my arrival and had timed their visit to coincide with the end of our breakfast. One did not have to live in the jungle to suspect the existence of the jungle telegraph. Furthermore, if I had wondered what Peter had said about me to friends and family, I was about to find out.

The men in Peter's living room were of medium height, gaunt, with sharp features. They stood with knees slightly bent and looked alert, taking in whatever was happening all around them. They spoke and moved slowly, deliberately. They wore the white felt caps of northern Albania and seemed to favor wide jackets and tight pants. Their clothes were rumpled, as if they had slept in them. More likely, the wrinkles in their clothes were due to their habit of stuffing too much into their pockets and of spending most of the day sitting cross-legged, pushing their pants through at the knees and at the seat.

Before the conversation could start in earnest, each visitor in turn put his right hand on his chest and asked about my health. There was nothing hurried at this stage of the conversation. In fact, they all waited for me to answer these questions in full, as if different answers to the same questions were quite possible. With my hand on my chest, I thanked each of them for their interest in me and assured them that I was well. In turn, I inquired about their health and that of their families, without being able to ask about their wives and children by name, as good Albanian custom would have demanded.

At this point, their answers made it clear that, unfortunately, none of them was in the best of health. They did agree, however, that one young boy not far from Peter's house needed medical attention the most and that the rest of them would bide their time, hoping, however, that I would find it in my heart to visit them also. One look at Peter confirmed my suspicion. He was avoiding my eyes, tending to his guests and their needs, and nodding to confirm that he would plan our return visits so that we would see each of them in their homes. That pleased them. After a while, they rose to their feet, embraced me, kissing me on both cheeks, and wandered off with a warm feeling. After all, they had put their names on the list of patients the Albanian Dr. Schweitzer would visit that very day.

I looked at Peter and shook my head.

"How could you tell them that I was a physician? I never claimed to be one. In fact, I distinctly remember telling you that I had finished the first year of medical school and had worked in a couple of hospitals and in public health. Peter, my friend, I worked as a physician's assistant in Dukagjin in the absence of a real physician. We say in Albanian that when you have no chicken you eat crow meat. Peter, here in Gjakova there are plenty of physicians, and besides, the ill can go all the way to Belgrade or Zagreb, to university hospitals if they need specialists or special treatment. How could you tell your friends that I was a physician?" I felt like an impostor.

Now it was Peter's turn. "I understood what you told me but now you listen to me. True, I spoke of you as being a physician but you must also understand that local physicians may know more than you do but they see hundreds of patients each day. They have no time to do their patients justice. On top of that, many of them are Serbians who despise us Albanians. You will look at the patients here caringly because I know you. That's really what my friends are after. Remember that one grave patient they wanted you to see first? He has been seen by physicians and specialists here and in Belgrade. Everyone has told his parents that there is no hope. They really don't expect you to tell them differently. They know that only a miracle can save their son. Nonetheless, they don't want to leave anything undone. You understand."

Of course, I understood. In Dukagjin, people had appreciated that someone from the city, someone other than their kinfolk, actually cared for them and was willing to climb and sweat and bring what modest relief he could. The two lives penicillin had saved while I was there had certainly helped. But what counted most was that they, the mountain farmers, and I, the city dweller, had related to one another as human beings. If I had helped them, they had repaid me a hundredfold with their friendship. Dukagjin was an example of my life under communism. The Reds had aimed to hurt me when they imprisoned me. In jail, I met Albania's past leaders, well-known politicians, military men, and professionals, from the time of Turkish domination to the years of the bloody civil war. Only in jail could I have met them all, devoid of the glory of their official status and the trappings of power. In 1948, when we were expelled from Tirana, I was transferred to Dukagjin, one of the poorest regions of Albania. Again, what better way was there for me to get to know the Albanian mountaineers and their century-old traditions? Where else could I form better friendships with hardy people, strong foes of the regime, whose region also bordered with Yugoslavia? Besides, running up and down those mountains, followed by about two years of heavy manual labor, prepared me physically for what was to follow. I could see Peter's point. I nodded in agreement and a big smile spread across Peter's face. Had he perhaps feared that I would not agree with him?

That afternoon he and I began our visits but not before Peter presented me with a pair of galoshes; mind you, soft galoshes to be worn over regular shoes—except that I had no shoes. Besides, I said a *pair* of galoshes. I should have said two left galoshes. I looked funny wearing Peter's clothes and two left galoshes. Nobody said anything except for some little children who giggled.

Peter began to knock on doors. People's faces blurred in my mind. I recognized some of the men I had seen that morning, but after a while, their wives and children all looked alike; too many people, too many impressions in too short a time. The patients were easier to remember. The most serious was the young boy I had heard about. He was about fourteen, and unable to control his limbs, sit up, or walk. He had the gaunt look, the dark, deep-set eyes, the wasted body with which suffering marks those who do not have far to go on this earth. I asked what they had said in Belgrade and nodded agreement, washed my hands, had a cup of Turkish coffee, and left. I had done what they had expected of me. If nothing else, I had shared their sadness for a little while. We saw some more patients. I vaguely recall seeing children with the usual winter coughs and runny noses, and one with purulent pimples above one elbow.

When Peter said that was all, I thought I was done for the day, but I had another surprise coming. Instead of staying behind, some men kept walking with us. We walked toward an area with taller, more elaborate buildings than the quarters of Albanian immigrants I had seen so far. We stopped and Peter opened a door, motioning for me to enter. Even before entering, my nose told me I was entering a pharmacy. I looked around and there they were, all those milky glass jars with gold lettering, the scales, mortars and pestles of different sizes, the packaged goodies, and bottles full of colored liquids so typical of a pharmacist's empire. And there was the pharmacist himself, wearing a white lab coat, looking me over from head to toe, as if he had trouble pegging me. He was probably Serbian but Peter spoke to him in Albanian.

"Here we have an Albanian physician who has just seen some patients. Would you please give him a prescription pad?"

Absent any chance of my disappearing into the ground, I turned to Peter and murmured, "Peter, I don't know what drugs they have in Yugoslavia. I am pretty sure they are different from those we had in Albania."

While I was mouthing these words, I was hoping that Peter would control the temptation to shine in front of everyone at my expense and would find a way out. Instead, he nodded, as if he were saying, "Go ahead; I know you can do it."

There was only one way out of this predicament. The pharmacist had pushed a pad and pen in my direction. I turned toward the men who had followed us inside the store.

"Let's do this one at the time. What was the name of the patient I saw at your house and what did I say he or she suffered from?"

One by one, they stepped forth and gave me the information. I remember writing prescriptions for cough syrup for those with colds and for sulfa ointment for the little boy with the infected elbow. While writing, I kept wondering: Would the pharmacist actually fill the prescriptions? What if he refused? What would Peter or I do if push came to shove? I held my breath.

The pharmacist looked first at the prescriptions and then at Peter and the rest of us. "It will take me about ten minutes to fill these."

Peter nodded. "We'll wait."

The men followed with their eyes as the man in his white coat began to pour red syrup into smaller bottles, and were fascinated when he put what looked like Vaseline into a mortar, added some white powder which he had weighed, and began to work it with a pestle until thoroughly mixed. He carefully put the cream into a shiny round can and marked the contents on the label with his pen. Phew, thank God it was over. I turned toward the men.

"Let's go; outside I will explain to you how to use the medicine."

I don't remember how we got home. I remember, though, that we had another substantial meal, Peter was clearly pleased with himself and my performance, and once again I could go to bed sated, warm, comfortable, and full of friendship for Peter and of gratitude for the Lord, who had directed my footsteps.

JANUARY 5, 1953

Nothing of significance happened yesterday. This morning, when I got up, Lisa told me that Peter had gone out but would be back soon. I could not help but wonder what he was up to. How many more patients would I have to see, and would one trip to the pharmacy suffice now that my fame was doubtless spreading wherever Albanian was spoken, at least among the refugees?

When Peter returned, he told me that Captain Pero had asked to see him at local UDBA headquarters, seat of the Yugoslav secret police. If I had any sleepiness left in me, that bit of news woke me up. What did Captain Pero want? I had heard my companions speak of him back in the mountains. From their words, it appeared the man spoke good Albanian and was a reliable friend. *Whose friend?* I wondered. He was probably either Serbian or from Montenegro. He could even be a Macedonian. The fact that Peter and Deda considered him a friend meant that the captain knew our customs and traditions and used them to his advantage. Friend of Albania? Considering the work he was doing, that was unlikely.

"What did Captain Pero want? Can you tell me?" The way I asked the question implied that Peter was important enough for Pero to tell him secrets not intended for my ears. Thus, I hoped to encourage Peter to share with me things I was not supposed to know. There was really no need to play games, since Peter came right out with it.

"Hila has asked for you and tomorrow you are leaving for Prishtina. Captain Pero said that some policemen are also going that way so that you will be traveling together."

What a lucky coincidence, I thought. "Did Captain Pero say anything else?"

"No, except that you should be at the police station by 8:00 a.m. tomorrow morning."

So, tomorrow would start a new phase in my life.

"Don't worry, I'll get you to the police on time," Peter added. Captain Pero is a good man and I trust his word. Besides, I will join you in Prishtina in a few days and then the four of us will be together again."

Despite his guileless smile, Peter seemed pensive. I wondered whether there was more depth to Peter than met the eye. Well, whatever tomorrow would bring, my immediate goal was to learn as much about Yugoslavia and policies toward us refugees as I could. After all, the first goal was survival. The second was to reach the West as quickly as possible, because I had not come to Yugoslavia to sink roots. The first goal I could share with Peter but not the second, not even with him. While Peter would never betray me, I strongly believed he did not need to know, at least not at this point.

The day passed more or less like the previous two. About 30 visitors came, and some more made return visits. I remember one home where they had a wooden tub where they let milk thicken by letting some of the water evaporate. Our hostess scooped up the thickened milk with a spoon and presented some to each of the men. It was delicious, probably because of the high fat content. At that time, that was not one of my worries. What struck me about the tenor of the conversations was that the refugees felt insecure, at the mercy of their Yugoslav hosts. Even those who had worked themselves up the ladder seemed concerned. After all, centuries of blood feud between Albanians and Slavs had left their scars.

At dinner at Peter's, the talk around the table made it clear that I was one of the family. Since Peter had returned from Albania, he had spent 29,000 dinars for coffee, cheese, whiskey, and cigarettes. In fact, Peter had reached the point where he would ask Captain Pero to transfer him to some village where he would not have so many visitors. The sum of 29,000 dinars was enormous compared to the monthly stipend of 3,000 dinars that the authorities paid out to refugees. In Peter's case, it may have been somewhat more as he had a family, and perhaps for services rendered; even so, it was a lot.

Having said what was on his mind, Peter laughed. "The house belongs to God and to our friends, so let's not worry. God will take care of everything."

Still, the mood around the table remained subdued. In part, it may have been the sorrow that our paths were parting again. Or was Peter having doubts about my leaving for Prishtina? There was no sense in asking him so I pretended not to notice. We chatted for a while and then decided to go to bed. I may have tossed and turned a little but then I fell into a deep, restful sleep.

JANUARY 6, 1953

The next thing I knew, Peter was standing next to my mattress and shaking me gently. "Time to get up. Wash up and let's have breakfast. We don't want to be late."

I quickly washed my face and shaved. Lisa had prepared breakfast and then handed me a kerchief with some bread and cheese. "For the road," she explained, "because it will take you a few hours to get to Prishtina."

For obvious reasons, I had no packing to do. I grabbed the kerchief and off we went. As it turned out, the police station was not far, and I recognized the building where our truck had dropped us off three days before, except that in daylight, everything seemed smaller, including the police station and the buildings around it.

Captain Pero came out and greeted first Peter and then me. He was trim and tall. He wore a heavy military topcoat and cap and looked good in uniform. As he shook hands, he said in good Albanian, "I apologize I could not come to see you at Peter's but I was very busy. Anyhow, I am sure you had a good time with Peter and his friends. When Peter left you behind at the Drini River, he promised that he would come for you. Well, I did not let him. He was tired out from the hard times in Albania. He was strong enough, though, to come and pester me every day asking that we send a group to rescue you. I knew that if I did not comply, he himself would cross the border into Albania without permission. So he and I traveled to different villages and put together the best team we could and sent them to rescue you and the others who were stranded with you."

It was a long speech and one I could not take exception to. He stressed Peter's friendship for me and implied that he himself had been fully behind the undertaking. Now it was my turn.

"I don't know how to thank you. Frankly, when Peter yelled across the Drini that he would return for me, I did not quite believe it. In fact, I could not see anyone crossing the border amid all the snow to rescue us. It probably meant that we would have to wait until next spring. I was surprised when the group came and so was everyone, including our hosts in Albania. Needless to say, I am happy to be here, and thank you for all you have done for me." I had said all I was going to say.

"Good. Today you are going to Prishtina to rejoin Hila Shllaku. He will treat you right. We thought of leaving you a little longer with Peter, but Hila insisted and it so happened that some of our policemen were also going to Prishtina. So, we thought, this was a good opportunity for you and them to travel together."

There it was again, that cock and bull story.

"Anyhow, I see everyone is ready," he continued. "You will be traveling to Peja by truck and from there you will take the train to Prishtina. Good luck." He smiled and his expression said no more than he intended. Captain Pero was good at his job.

I must have looked funny with two left galoshes, and with pants and sleeves at half-mast. Frankly, I did not care. I looked around. Peter obviously didn't want to leave but neither one of us knew what to say once the captain had spoken his piece. Two army officers who had been meandering around jumped on the back of a nearby truck that stood there idling. A policeman also climbed aboard while a second one came toward Peter and me. He looked straight at me and motioned for me to get on the truck. It was time for us to part. Peter and I embraced.

"Say hello to Hila and Deda for me and tell them I'll be there soon," he said.

I mumbled something in return. At Peter's I had been in a cocoon but time had come to go on to the next stage, even if it was enshrouded in darkness.

When I climbed aboard the truck, the officers had moved up behind the driver's cab from where they looked with some annoyance at the policemen and me who had kept them, at least for a while, from their all-important endeavors. The truck began to move, I waved to Peter, and off we were toward Peja where a train awaited us. We rumbled through the outskirts of Gjakova and were soon on a bumpy two-lane highway. I pretended I was looking at the landscape but was really watching the officers. They wore fitted uniforms, solid boots, and heavy winter coats. They were appropriately dressed for the cold weather. That was not surprising. After all, Tito had created a new army whose backbone consisted of the cadres who had proven their loyalty to him in the mountains. In return, he had rewarded them royally. Those with leadership qualities had formed the higher officer's corps. The others either kept their lower ranks or were discharged from the service and given civilian positions with pay, position, and responsibilities well above anything they may have held before the war even if their present jobs exceeded their abilities.

Yugoslavia, like any dictatorship, valued loyalty higher than ability or qualifications. Anyone with loyalty and either ability and/or qualifications had it made. There was, of course, a fly in the ointment, because no one could rest on yesterday's laurels. Loyalty was tested time and again, demanding of such individuals blind devotion to Tito and the Party, even at the cost of personal integrity. Fortunately for the new ruling class, their acquired privileges and accouterments of power helped deaden any pangs of conscience they might have felt initially, making it ever easier to follow the communist party's clarion call, whatever the cost to others.

It began to snow. The two officers leaning on the cab faced into the wind as if on a submarine conning tower, ignoring the gale and the ice-cold air flailing their faces. The two policemen and I sat crouching down with our backs against the truck railings, our knees pulled tightly against our chests. After all, we did not have to prove anything. After a while, one of the officers turned and started to ask me some questions in Serbian.

When he saw that I spoke no Serbian, he started to speak in broken Albanian, helped by one of the policemen.

"Tell me, how much bread do workers receive in Albania?"

"I received 450 grams a day," I replied. "Others received less, but I worked as a laborer."

"How much sugar and how many eggs a week?" he continued. I replied that we received about a pound of sugar a month and that we had not seen eggs, meat, or milk in ages.

He snorted, "No wonder that you and others like you are seeking a better life in Yugoslavia."

I felt my temper rising. "Actually, people don't risk their lives for better food. What is good enough for our families is good enough for us. It's the political climate, the persecutions, the capriciousness, and the unfairness of the regime that force us to risk our lives, even if it means leaving our families behind."

Had I said too much? Had I given him the impression that the Yugoslav system was better? For the moment, my answers must have sufficed because our conversation stopped as abruptly as it had started. Maybe the wind and the snow flurries had convinced him that silence was better than engaging in an inane conversation.

We made it to Peja. I could not help but look for sights or buildings that I recalled from that summer of 1944 when I had been in Peja with the Besnik Çano Battalion. I remembered the hotel and the surrounding area. I remembered the communist prisoner who was being moved from city to city prior to his execution. I remembered...but I have spoken of these events before.

Anyhow, perhaps because of the snowstorm or because we were in another part of town, I failed to see any familiar landmarks. We did make it to the railroad station, a neglected and sooty building. Here we could wait inside, out of the snowstorm. There was even a stove and benches to sit on. The officers disappeared, never to be seen again, at least not by me. I sat between the two policemen, whose watchfulness and manners toward me could not fail to attract the attention of those sharing the waiting room with us. The latter were so much aware of my presence that they made it a point to ignore me completely as if I were transparent. The way they walked past us or glanced unobtrusively clearly showed their curiosity, but also the care with which they separated themselves from our little group. Who could blame them?

The train huffed and puffed as it entered the station. My guardian angels motioned for me to get up. One got on the train while the other tugged my sleeve to indicate that he and I would wait on the ramp until the first guard had found a safe compartment. Finally, the first guard stuck his head out a window and motioned us aboard. It turned out that he had chosen an otherwise empty compartment. The compartment seemed dirty. What made it look worse was the obvious lack of paint and maintenance. As there was little passenger traffic, it did not take long for the train to be on its way.

There was little for me to do. I could look at my two "travel companions" at the risk of engendering hostility. I could stare at my hands or I could look at the landscape. I remember doing all three, but carefully so as not to run any needless risks. Staring at the guards was obviously not the thing to do. Was I trying to memorize their faces for some obscure, nefarious purpose? If I kept looking down at my hands, was I weighing my chances of attacking both guards? If I fixed my gaze at the window, was I measuring our speed of travel and the lay of the land so I could pick the best moment to jump off the train? Just in case the reader might think I was being paranoid: When I asked to go to the rest room, my guardian angels consulted with each other and one of them took me to the rest room and waited impatiently outside. I wonder whether the other stuck his head out of a nearby window to make sure I was not escaping through the toilet window! I remember having to suppress laughing out loud at the thought of all the trouble it had cost me to get to Yugoslavia and now being under suspicion that I might risk life and limb by jumping out a train window somewhere between Peja and Prishtina!

By mid-afternoon, we made it. The policemen took me to their station where, after a few formalities, I was released to the care and custody of Hila and Deda. I must say I was glad to see them, truly glad. I remember Hila's look when he saw me in Peter's clothes. I could not blame him. I myself felt conspicuous, but then who cared?

It was not far from the police station to the villa where they lived. It actually was a nice villa with several bedrooms, a living room, and a kitchen without utensils. This I noticed because food was uppermost on my mind. Had I been at ease, truly at ease with Hila, I might have asked about food. As it was, I kept my mouth shut, remembering our run-ins in the mountains. There, little of what I had said had met with his approval unless it was in response to his German gibberish to which I was to lend substance by replying in German. Anyhow, I was grateful to him that he had accepted me into his group and had brought me this far. The rest was up to the good Lord and to me, and one thing was for sure: Hila would play no further part in my future if I could help it.

It was barely 6:00 p.m. when Hila and Deda looked at each other and then smiled broadly at me.

"Would you like to go to dinner?" and off we went. The restaurant was nearby. It was large, very warm, and full of people. I could see waitresses scurrying around with their arms loaded with food and beer steins. I forget whether we went to an empty table on our own or were guided by one of these heavenly creatures dispensing food and drinks. In the background, there was also music, perhaps just an accordion. At this point, I found the music distracting. All I wanted was food, good hearty food, lots of bread, and cold water. A waitress finally wound her way to our table. She mumbled something and my friends mumbled in return.

When they looked at me, I just nodded. "The same for me." Heaven knows what they had ordered. It did not take long for the woman with robust arms and white apron to return to our table, her arms loaded with plates filled to the brim with pork and sauerkraut! She also brought a basket full of fresh bread and beer for the three of us.

If I ever was a dainty eater, this was not the time. I dug in and before my two companions had finished half their portions, I was wiping the last of the sauerkraut juice with half a slice of bread. Hila looked amused.

"Would you like another dish like the first one?" he asked. I looked at Deda. He looked friendly as he nodded.

"Yes, if it is all right with you."

Hila motioned to the waitress and before I knew it, she placed before me another steaming plate of pork and sauerkraut. This was heaven! The food was all mine. There was no need for me to hurry as Hila and Deda still had a ways to go to finish their first plate. I must admit, the second plate was just as tasty as the first one, but now I could relax. My stomach was no longer in such a hurry. I tasted each morsel. I took my time and looked around. I finally noticed that the accordionist was very good. I had always liked Slavic music, and at this point it was adding to the pleasure of my meal. I glanced at Hila. Maybe he was not such a bad fellow after all. Maybe I had done him wrong.

All good things must come to an end, but this time it was not a premature end. Hila rose and we followed. Soon we were home. As we were saying good night to each other, I asked where the toilet was.

"Outdoors," Deda replied. "Let me show you." Across from the house was a low brick building like a shed. The restroom was in the shed. Before going to bed, I used the facilities. As it turned out, I would visit it some more during the night, in my underwear and with cold galoshes on my feet. A couple of days passed before I realized that my legs were naturally slim in the morning but heavy and swollen at night. Clearly, I was getting rid of this accumulated water during my nightly excursions into the snow-filled nights of January. After a few weeks, youth and nature provided the solution. My legs were less swollen and I no longer needed to leave my warm bed and march out to the cold shed.

Chapter Thirty-Six

Medical School—Belgrade

Soon after my arrival in Prishtina, Major Kaplar Ljubović of the UDBA sent word for me "to pay him a visit." The subtlety of the invitation was nothing short of touching. Well, this was neither the first nor probably the last interrogation I would face. That morning I rose early, washed, and shaved as well as I could and made sure I was on time at the major's office. I felt ill at ease in Peter's clothes, but that I could not help. Anyhow, I was sure he wanted to see me and take my measurements rather than those of my clothes.

If I was punctual, so was he. At the appointed time, his door opened and a guard asked me in. His office was spacious and bright as the sun's golden rays flooded through two windows. The good major rated a corner office. He nodded and rose to shake hands with me. He was perhaps 30 years old, about 6 feet tall, and a bit on the heavy side. He had wavy light hair, a reddish face, and light eyes. That day he wore a light brown corduroy jacket, a sure sign that he belonged. In Albania, you could get such a jacket only with a special authorization. Furthermore, such authorizations were only for "important people."

"Please come in," he said in very good Italian. "I am pleased to meet you in person as I have heard a lot about you from Hila, Deda, and Peter. You made some real friends in the mountains and I am pleased that we could help you. There is much I would like to discuss with you, since we don't get to meet Albanians of your caliber very often. But first..."

He rang a bell on his desk and a tall, uniformed man entered the office. His face changed abruptly from the friendly smile with which he had greeted me to a frown. He spoke sharply, this time in Serbian. He gestured in my direction, pointing at my clothes and shoes. I caught the word "intellectual" more than once.

He turned toward me and asked, "What size clothes do you wear? What about shoes?" He translated my answers to the man who stood at attention before the major's desk. Having received his instructions, the man left the office.

While this was taking place, I mentally translated the major's greetings to me into their true meaning. I had been a topic of discussion between him and my friends and they may have bragged a bit, as refugees were known to do to give themselves more importance. Is that why he spoke to me in Italian, to test me? He was pleased they (the Yugoslavs) had been able to help me; i.e., I owed them my life.

I could not help but ask myself, had it not been for Peter Toma and Mark Zogu, the two infiltrators in the mountains with me, would he have sent a rescue team just for me? In his words, I was an Albanian of caliber—flattery to butter me up. I remembered well Hila's words in the mountains, when he had handed a beautifully inlaid Nagant revolver to Gjon Zef Bajraktari and had told him that the Yugoslavs were fully aware of his and his family's merits. Next, the major was going to make me feel even more indebted by buying me new clothes. I remember a fellow student in Padua who used to shower his girlfriends with gifts until they felt indebted to where they could no longer resist his advances. To top it off, by calling me an intellectual—practically an equal, almost a comrade in arms—the major raised me from the throngs of faceless refugees to the heights inhabited by superior officers. Wow, I ought to be impressed.

Having dismissed the tall soldier, he turned toward me. His face was still friendly but a cloud seemed to darken his eyes.

"I am disappointed that my colleagues in Gjakova and here in Prishtina let you run around in these rags. How long have you been in Yugoslavia? Ten days, you say? I must apologize. I am truly upset that we failed to offer you the hospitality you deserve, not only for your sake but also for our own."

I mumbled something in return, something like "Such things take time," or "I have always been hard to fit," or something equally bright and original.

"Well," he said, "that will be taken care of. Meanwhile, let's talk a little about conditions in Albania." I wondered whether he would ask about the price of cigarettes.

"I regret that our relations with Albania have gone awry. We fought together and should have continued to stand together shoulder to shoulder. Well, what's done is done. However, I remember with great pleasure my friendship with Stefo Grabocka." He paused but did not seem to expect an answer.

Stefo Grabocka's brother, Llazar, was an NCO with the prison detail when I was imprisoned in Tirana. He was rude and mean. I had met Captain Stefo Grabocka the night I left prison. He was all business when we were brought to his office. According to him, we were released because of the generosity of the people. The eyes of the security forces, however, were upon us. If we ever broke the law again, we would be right back in jail but this time there would be no mercy for us (See Chapter 16). I could not quite fathom why Major Ljubovi mentioned Stefo Grabocka. He could hardly expect that his alleged friendship with a harsh Albanian communist was going to sit well with me. It was equally unlikely that he wanted to test me to see if I would send word back to Albania that Grabocka was a friend of a Yugoslav UDBA officer. His comment mystified me. Major Ljubović continued.

"Enver Hoxha has been in power now for over eight years. How is it that no poet or writer has emerged during this period?"

I was not sure what he was driving at and I told him so. He repeated the question, adding that in Yugoslavia, the years of struggle against the fascist invaders had inspired many poets and writers to hail the revolution and its heroes. I remembered that when a Soviet writer had visited the Albanian League of Writers and had met some members, he had commented, "You call this your League of Writers but so far I have met only translators of foreign works. Shouldn't you rather call it the Translators' League?" So, my Yugoslav host had a point. Did those who joined Albania's communist ranks lack talent? Was the major implying that Albanians were inferior? Was he trying to make me feel inferior? I remember answering something along the lines that perhaps the Albanian political climate was such that it denied writers the proper inspiration, that it kept them from putting their true thoughts and feelings on paper.

I had the impression that my answer failed to satisfy him. Somehow, I had missed the mark as he saw it. Anyhow, one point could not fail to please him. If my answer was inadequate and the lack of writing talent among communist Albanians indicted Enver Hoxha and his sycophants, this further added luster to the Yugoslav communist regime and to the poets and writers that shone like stars in Tito's firmament. My host changed the topic.

"I understand that you had a very hard time in the mountains. Even

Peter Qafa, one of the best and most experienced among our Albanian friends, said that this was his most dangerous and complicated trip across the border. I believe that a lack of reliable and swift communications was at the bottom of it. We had to send several groups to rescue the men. The first missed you by hours. The second did not make contact at all. The third found you by accident but brought only half of you back. We then had to send a fourth one. Now, if we had good communications, like those offered by a clandestine radio, much of this could have been avoided." He finished and looked at me with a pensive and deeply sincere expression.

After all, he had confessed a weakness and bared his soul to a mere refugee—well, to a soul brother as he had already noted. I could sense that he was leading up to something.

He continued. "Let me come to the point. We believe that for us to be able to help you, our Albanian friends, regain your freedom, we must set up a radio transmitter in the Albanian mountains. We need someone who knows the area, who enjoys the respect of the resistance, and who has the intellectual wherewithal to pull it off. From all we have heard, you are that person." He stopped at this point to give me a chance to reply.

"I regret to say that I cannot see myself as that person. I don't know the area at all. We walked mostly at night and even when we walked during the day, I made it a point never to ask any questions. In fact, I never asked where we were, who our contacts were, or anything of that sort, so that if I were captured and tortured, I could not endanger the group. As you know, I am from the south of Albania. I am a Toskë and the inhabitants of the region are Gegës. They are Catholic, I am a Muslim. My dialect and even my appearance would give me away. No, I don't think I am a good choice. Besides, I know nothing about radios."

I should not have made this last argument. It was weak and at the end of my rebuttal. I should have started with it leaving the stronger arguments for the end.

"I disagree with what you just said," the major replied. "We can teach you all you need to know about radio transmitters and we can do much better with you than if we had to deal with a less educated person. Trust me, go back to the Albanian mountains and install the radio transmitter. Once you have it running properly, which should take you no more than a month, we will send someone to replace you. Then, return to Yugoslavia and ask for anything you want. You want to go back to your studies? No problem. But first help your friends by setting up the radio transmitter."

"Since you have someone who will take over the radio transmitter, why do you not send this person in the first place?"

"That we cannot do. He is a good man to take over the radio once it is running. First we need you to install it." His frontal attack left no room for me to maneuver. For better or worse, I had to end this discussion.

"In addition to what I have already told you, there is one more reason why I cannot go back. As you have discussed my stay in the mountains with my friends, they must have told you that I suffered a heart attack that almost cost me my life. I very much appreciate your willingness to send me back to college, and I thank you for it. I must stress, however, that I see no way for me to return to the Albanian mountains." That was that.

He thought for a moment and then replied, "We expected that you would accept our proposal and were ready to send you to the university in Belgrade. In view of your refusal, we have no choice but to send you to a *privatilishte*, to a camp with the rest of the refugees." Clearly, I had fallen from grace, from the apex to the slums in one long step.

"Major, I have come to Yugoslavia as your guest. Whatever you decide is right for me, is fine with me." He rose. The "visit" was over.

Actually, it was not quite over yet. A few days later, they delivered a very nice, dark blue winter coat (12,200 dinars), a black suit (8,000 dinars), an off-white shirt with brown stripes, some underwear, three pairs of socks, and a pair of military boots, size 15. I wore size 12 or 13 at the most. Just for the record, Hila and Deda asked me for some socks and received one pair each.

My diary refers to a joke Italians used to tell under Mussolini. A farmer, hard pressed for cash, decided to write to God. In the farmer's words, God knew that the writer of the letter was an honest and hard worker who needed 1000 lire to bridge him over until the new harvest. He, the farmer, and his entire family would be most grateful to the Lord for His timely help. Having signed the letter, the farmer needed the Lord's address. Since the pope, the king, and Mussolini all lived in Rome, the farmer addressed the letter "To God, Rome." Eventually, the letter reached Mussolini's private secretary.

After presenting that day's mail to Mussolini, the secretary added, "*Duce*, here is a letter that will make you chuckle. As Italy's greatest modern leader, you receive petitions for help practically every day. This man, however, addresses you as God, asking for 1000 lire, which makes him different from the others."

Mussolini ordered that the man receive 500 lire in reply, and with that he forgot all about the farmer. A few days went by and Mussolini's secretary received a second letter from the farmer, also addressed "To God." It thanked the Lord for the 1000 lire he had sent the farmer but added that if there was ever another occasion when he needed money, would the Lord please send it directly to him rather than through Mussolini, because of the 1000 lire sent, the farmer had received only 500.

Under the circumstances, I was grateful to the Yugoslavs but not nearly grateful enough to set up a clandestine radio transmitter for the benefit of the UDBA.

About a year earlier, the Yugoslavs had sent leaflets into Albania proclaiming that Koçi Xoxe had not died but lived in our hearts. The same Koçi had presided over the tribunal that had sentenced Dad and his friends to death and was planning to overthrow Enver Hoxha with the help of Yugoslav troops. Yugoslav propaganda in Albania also claimed that Yugoslavia worked hand in hand with the West and that they were jointly attempting to rid Albania of its communist rulers.

This was, of course, a blatant lie, meant to convince Albanians to collaborate with Yugoslavia. Now I was supposed to set up a radio transmitter to help the Yugoslavs! Well, I would have loved to go to the university in Belgrade, but not at this price. *So privatilishte, here I come,* I thought.

That day we heard that Gjon Jaku, mayor of Shkodra, had contacted some infiltrators asking for their help because he wanted to flee to Yugoslavia. When everything was set, instead of meeting with them, he had sent the security forces. The infiltrators had resisted and had died fighting.

One evening Hila told us that Peter Qafa would join us soon. When Peter arrived, he filled our villa with his friendliness. He was the same he had been in the mountains—calm, smiling, never in a hurry but always on time. I never found out what brought him to Prishtina. It did not matter. I was convinced that whatever his activities inside Albania, Peter would never knowingly betray his country. As Peter saw only a small part of the overall picture, would the Yugoslavs be able to trick him into doing things beyond his understanding? What was Hila's role in all this? I had seen Hila in action. He was intelligent and quick. Was he also reliable?

The day came when Peter left us to return to his family. I truly missed my friend even though his departure was not as critical as it would have been on December 6th deep in the Albanian mountains, when our group was about to break up. We did not know it then, but we were only hours away from finally meeting with a group from Yugoslavia looking for us.

Now I was left with Hila, who was his explosive self, and with "Deda, the Silent." That same day Hila told us the important news: Lt. Colonel Četo Mijović, the highest Yugoslav officer in direct contact with the "heads" of the Albanian refugee colony, was going to meet with Hila that afternoon. Normally, his name was spoken in hushed tones. He was a favorite of namedroppers who usually inserted a pause after mentioning his name to give the rest of the world time to catch up and listen in awe. Hila, instead, spoke with respect but with some degree of self-assurance, because if Colonel Mijović was as high as Albanians could reach, Hila was first among the Albanian infiltrators. The colonel would come around 4:00 p.m. and stay a couple of hours. Deda and I would leave around 3:30 and reappear by dinnertime. If the colonel's car was gone, it was OK for us to enter the house. We, of course, stood in silence. Having given us our marching orders, Hila strutted away satisfied.

That afternoon Deda and I went for a long walk. The sky was gray. It was not cold even though there was snow all around us. The roads were full of slush and I was glad I had my Yugoslav army boots. In fact, I was grateful for my whole outfit, from top to bottom. I remembered with a shiver when Hila found lice in the villa a few days after my arrival. My bathing and the change of clothes at Peter's must not have done the job. Hila insisted that I go to the public baths that very afternoon. I pointed out that I had no clean clothes to change into, as the Yugoslavs had not yet delivered them to me, but Hila was adamant. Out we went, the four of us. I was concerned that after a hot bath, the frigid weather on the way home might give me pneumonia. Neither Deda nor Peter spoke up on my behalf. Who was I to challenge Hila? Besides, deep in my heart, I could not blame him. Anyhow, we got to the public baths and they were closed that day! I was safe once more, maybe with lice but in no danger of catching my death from pneumonia.

When Deda and I went for a walk that afternoon, the road was full of ruts made by cars, trucks, and carts, with hoof imprints and animal droppings here and there. Deda was by nature very reserved. He had barely spoken during the eight weeks we had spent together in the mountains. That after-noon he opened up. He questioned Hila's blind trust in Colonel Mijović. After all, the Yugoslavs had never been our friends and we had no reason to believe that they had changed of late. He added that Hila respected my opin-ion, something Hila had certainly kept well hidden from me. Deda believed that we could not fully trust Hila's judgment. Hila was a good man but his decision to collaborate with the Yugoslavs had put him on thin ice. It was obvious, Deda said, that the Yugoslavs were not part of the Western effort to unseat the communists in Albania. He further suggested that I ask Hila whether he would talk to the Yugoslavs on my behalf to secure a scholarship so I could go to Belgrade. As far as Deda knew, Peter was due back soon and the three of them would go to Kragujevac. By that time, the Yugoslavs would certainly have decided my fate. Hence, time was of the essence.

I listened with great interest. This was the first time that Deda had stepped out of Hila's shadow. He showed good judgment and spoke with prudence. If he trusted anyone, he trusted Peter, with whom he had bonds of friendship. I contributed some thoughts to our conversation but was careful never to cross the line. I needed to play it safe. Thus, I never said anything that could have hurt me with the Yugoslavs. Obviously, an in-former could always make up things. True charges, however, had a differ-ent ring to them and I had lived long enough under communism to know how far I could go.

January 10 was Dad's 60th birthday. Who knew where and how he was spending this day? After so many sacrifices for Albania, after death sen-tences and imprisonment by foreign countries, he had been in Albanian prisons and at hard labor for over eight years. He had been mistreated, worse than when he was in the hands of foreign enemies. He had been tor-tured. When ill, he was denied medical treatment. There was no question that my escape would make things worse for him as well as for Mom and Mergim. I hoped and prayed that they would forgive me. *May the good Lord reunite us one day*, I prayed, *free, healthy, happy, and under one roof.*

Shortly after my arrival, Hila gave me some pocket money, probably from Yugoslav sources. As I was not asked for something in return and did not have to sign for the money, I decided to accept. I needed a haircut; I had not had one since Peter had given all of us one with his hand clippers in the mountains. There was no question about it: Peter was a man of many talents.

In addition to being a pretty good barber, in the mountains he had been a veritable homing pigeon with his incredible sense of orientation. He could move with the stealth of a cat, always blending in with the surroundings, always careful, knowledgeable, and courageous in a humble way. He knew how to steal and slaughter a goat without making noise, and he knew how to cook it in a loosely covered pit with the meat inside the goat's stomach, covered with embers. He also played the *çifteli*, a kind of mandolin with two strings. Often he would sing, accompanying himself on his homemade instrument.

Now I had a chance to go to the nearest barber, but I had to pass a pastry shop and there in the window was a tray with baklava, neatly cut, with plenty of syrup. I glanced at the dessert but kept walking. It would have been unseemly for me to partake of such a luxury while my family in Albania went hungry. I entered the barbershop and when my turn came, I sat in the chair and answered the barber's questions as briefly as possible. Nonetheless, it felt good to be in the hands of someone who handled clippers without pulling the customer's hair, who had a strop for his razor, and who used cologne at the end of his ministrations.

I left the barbershop, and as I started to walk toward our villa, I had to get past the pastry shop once more with its display window and the aroma of freshly baked goods wafting through the open door. I looked at the pastries and tried to think of my loved ones in Albania. Doubtless, they were suffering. If given a chance, however, would they not tell me to enjoy a slice or two of baklava for their sakes as well as mine? Despite my efforts to resist temptation, I reminded myself that yesterday was Dad's birthday and today was Mom's. Mom was 46 years old. She married at 17, became a mother a year later, and spent 15 years in political exile. Since the end of 1944, she was without Dad. Furthermore, my flight had greatly complicated her life. Poor Mom!

I told myself that both Mom and Dad would have wanted me to have the baklava. I entered the store, bought myself two slices, and devoured them before my conscience could convict me of self-indulgence. Outside the store, I became remorseful. The slices of baklava had been microscopic; the taste was OK, but not as good as I had thought it would be. Finally, this concession to my palate had made a major dent into my finances. My first expense was when I bought and mailed a postcard to Valnea announcing my arrival, and asked her to send a telegram to Mom to let her know that "her brother was in good health and had been discharged from the hospital." Then it was the barber's turn, and finally the baklava. What little money was left would barely buy me a cup of coffee.

I still had to write to Mustafa Merlika Kruja, Dad's best friend and Mergim's godfather, to Edward, our relative in Rome, and to Valnea to bring them up to date on matters regarding their families and mine, except for Valnea, of course, who had no family in Albania.

I mentioned to Mustafa that his immediate family had been living in concentration camps for years. Those first few years they were all in the same camp, which was a blessing, all things considered. Their property had been confiscated. His two sons, Petrit and Fatos, and Lena, Petrit's wife, were in forced labor. I listed the names of relatives and friends who had been executed or sentenced to prison terms. I gave some guarded details of my three months in the mountains, and ended by giving him my temporary address, promising that I would write again once I had a permanent domicile.

Edward's family had also suffered greatly. Edward's half-brother and one brother-in-law were executed. Another was sentenced to a long prison term, and his dad to lifelong imprisonment. One half-sister had died and the other was having a hard time healthwise and with her husband in prison. The rest of the family had been dispersed and was doing the best they could to survive. I told him about my life in the mountains and promised to write again.

Valnea, on the other hand, was a chapter onto herself. I had fallen in love with her at age 14 and my love for her had never ceased. We started dating in the 12th grade and said a tearful goodbye to each other in July of 1943, when I returned to Albania after attending the first year of medical school. Until November 1944, when the communists came to power in Albania, we wrote to each other two to three times a week. To paraphrase the words of an author whose name I forgot, these were typical love letters where one sat down to write without knowing what one was going to say, and after completing the letter, one did not quite know what one had written. There was no question, however, about the feelings behind such letters.

Late in 1943, she wrote about seeing two Albanian students, acquaintances of mine from Padua, who were stuck in Fiume while Tito's partisans temporarily surrounded the city. She had crossed the street, had introduced herself, and had invited them to her home for a meal. She had ended her letter by saying that she prayed that if I ever were in need, someone would come to my help. I had often thought about her words during my escape when my very survival depended on others.

During the years under communism, when all incoming and outgoing mail was censored, the tone of our letters changed to the type schoolmates might write to one another. She wrote about her life and common acquaintances, I described my life in Albania, and both of us wrote letters that could have started with "Dear censor." Valnea also sent us some packages for the family and medicine for Dad. She was no longer in Fiume; that was now under Yugoslavian rule and was renamed Rieka. She continued her studies and told me about schoolmates from high school days who had gone on to the university, gotten married, and had done all those things people do under normal circumstances.

Her letters were like a breath of fresh air blowing in from faraway shores, but they also made me feel buried alive. In Albania, the population suffered a great deal but such sufferings were part of normal life. However, when Valnea wrote, I realized that for us in Albania, life had come to a screeching halt: no school, no getting married, no going on vacation, no traveling, and no future. Instead, there was discrimination, persecution, prison, forced labor, and death, and all this in the name of a Marxist class struggle.

A colonel in charge of a military tribunal in Elbasan had told me once that the innocence or guilt of the accused was immaterial. What counted was whether the accused would use his or her talents for or against the communist party. It was on this basis that the court decided on a verdict. He neglected to say that the communist party headquarters handed down the verdict and that he and his tribunal simply made it public.

What made life for "reactionary" individuals and their families in Albania close to unbearable was the feeling of helplessness. Dad and I were arrested the day the communists occupied Tirana. Mom and Mergim were kicked out of our apartment, also among the first. In 1948, we were thrown out of Tirana as soon as the first list of expulsions was published. I was transferred to Dukagjin because of the very primitive living conditions prevailing there. Next, I was appointed as public health inspector for the city of Shkodra because they needed me. As soon as they thought they had a replacement, I was fired from my job and was sent to mandatory labor. You can imagine the mixed emotions within me when I received letters from Valnea describing life in Italy.

Ten years had passed since she and I left Padua at the end of the spring semester in 1943. For all I knew, she was married with children. If she had married in the meantime, in no way must I create a problem for her. If she was still single, there was hope. On the other hand, she could still be single but no longer interested in me. I still carried the handkerchief in my pocket she had sprinkled with her perfume. She used *"Asso di Cuori"*—Ace of Hearts. I could still smell the perfume. Perhaps no one else could have, but I could. I was convinced of this. I remembered her birthday, October 25, and her phone number, 14-76. One day, while still in high school, I had called and when a female voice answered, I greeted her with a cheerful, "Hi, darling." There was a slight hesitation at the other end of the line, and then came the reply, "This is not your darling, I am her aunt. But I'll call her to the phone."

These and many other such memories, of significance only to me, had kept me company for ten long years, particularly in the mountains when I had time to think and to reminisce.

Anyhow, no matter what her state in life, even if she were married with three children, I was sure that she would send Mom the telegram announcing my safe escape.

One day, we were told to leave the villa and move to a hotel across the street. We did not know why but we did not ask for an explanation. After all, we were soldiers, sort of, were we not? We landed at the top floor of the hotel. The room was OK; the beds were comfortable, there was a washbasin with a water jar. Running water was at the end of the hallway and so was the bathroom. We ate lunch and dinner at the same restaurant as before, where pork and sauerkraut reigned supreme. Hila may have lost some of the prestige that came with living in a villa but surely nobody was going to make such a comment to his face.

Our stay at the hotel would have been quite unremarkable except for one incident. One day, I returned to our room while the maid was making our beds. She was pushing 50, cubic in build, with legs like Doric columns. She had high cheekbones, a large mouth, and a rather friendly face. I entered the room and greeted her in Serbian. She answered and followed up with a veritable torrent of words. When she saw that I did not understand her, she smiled slyly. She pointed sequentially at herself, at me, and finally at the bed. I understood what she had in mind but I wanted to let her down gently. I had to come up with an excuse quickly, and do so within my very limited Serbian vocabulary. Furthermore, I had to do so before her smile froze and she reacted like a woman scorned. I pulled myself up to my full height and announced solemnly, "*Ia sam voinik*," translated as, "I am a soldier." Then I turned around and marched out of the room. As a soldier, I was bound by the highest ideals. Anything less would have been incompatible with the dignity of my mission in life, if not of my uniform since I was not wearing one. Surely, she must have seen the strength of my logic. I got safely out of the room and out of her life, and that's what I wanted.

One day, with several Albanians, I paid a visit to an Albanian dentist and his wife. They were nice, hospitable people. During our visit, the wife brought me a light blue shirt that was quite nice except for a rip near the buttons up front that she had mended with white thread. Unfortunately, I had no sweater in my wardrobe and my suit jacket would not have covered the rip. While these thoughts were passing through my mind, she read my hesitation as a refusal and walked away with the shirt. In a stage whisper audible to all, she said something about people who wore rags until the day before and who now wrinkled their noses at a perfectly good shirt. What ingrates! Maybe it was because of the shirt, maybe there were other reasons, but I was never invited back to their house.

The Albanians in Prishtina were a mixed lot. Most refugees were Catholic farmers from the north. They had come to Yugoslavia seeking refuge after Tito's break with Moscow and Albania in the spring of 1948. Many lived in refugee camps, while some lived in Prishtina and seemed to move about freely. Refugees received 3,000 dinars a month. I don't know about those with families and those who "served" the regime. I suspected they got better pay. Most refugees in Prishtina did not serve the authorities and probably did not cuddle up to the UDBA. As a matter of self-protection, I did not trust any of them. If there were innocents among them, it would not hurt to keep them at arm's length. And as to the "friends" of the Yugoslav police, the farther away from them, the better.

Speaking of innocence, one day a Catholic priest and I were strolling along the main drag in Prishtina. He was most pleasant, kind, and trusting.

"Do you know," he said to me, "that some Albanian refugees are actually Yugoslav informers?'

I replied with a noncommittal "Is that so?"

He continued, deeply immersed in thought. "I think I will speak with Apostol Tanefi and tell him about this shameful situation."

I shuddered deep inside. Tanefi was head of the Albanian Refugee Organization. To complain to him about Albanian informants was akin to complaining to Satan about mischievous minor devils. There is an Italian saying: "May God protect me from my friends, I will keep an eye on my enemies." The priest was a good example of a friend who might get me into trouble unintentionally. At that juncture, Apostol Tanefi was hardly a man I would trust. Years later I heard that Apostol Tanefi was not a bad man. Perhaps the stress of working with the Yugoslavs had gotten to him. Eventually, it was said that he became an alcoholic and may have died of cirrhosis of the liver.

One day shortly after my arrival, I was sitting at a café all by my lonely self. Some northern Albanians were sitting at a table nearby and discussing what they would do to the Tosks, the southern Albanians, after Enver Hoxha's overthrow. What they had in mind was harsh and threatening, at least to me as a southerner.

"Gentlemen," I said to them, "you mean that I too will be in danger?"

They looked me over and one of them replied, "I believe you will be safe; you seem like a tame Toskë. We are speaking about the others, the bad ones." With that, they turned away from me and continued their conversation as before.

At about that time I had a chance to attend my first refugee congress. Albanian refugees converged on Prishtina from all directions. The Yugoslav organizers were hoping to get the refugees to commit themselves to a concerted action against Enver Hoxha's brand of communism. The hall never quite filled up. I saw my first tape recorder, a rather large unit with two reels. The organizers probably wanted to give the impression of a high-tech meeting to flatter the attendees. The prevailing sense, instead, was that the UDBA was going to make a permanent record of who said what. The Yugoslav hosts tried to encourage and cajole the attendees to say something worth recording. In all fairness, they put no pressure on anyone beyond what they were willing to say on their own. Thus, for us refugees the congress was a letdown. Our Yugoslav hosts must have felt worse.

It turned out that for me the highlight of the congress took place in the hallway. I ran into Ndue Vata, the man who had offered to take Mergim and me to Yugoslavia by boat in full daylight across Lake Shkodra. Following

Ndue Vata's escape, Mergim was drafted and I joined Hila in the mountains. After his escape, things had changed drastically and in a hurry.

At the Congress, when Ndue Vata saw me in the hallway, he threw his arms around me and nearly choked me to death. He was a very handsome young man, very strong and effusive. Without letting go of me, he pulled his head back, arched an eyebrow like the Italian actor Gino Cervi whom he resembled, and said, "Genc, what happened to you? You look ten years older than when I left you in Shkodra."

With what breath I had left, I mumbled something about having spent three months in the mountains. Mercifully, he let go of me but kept staring at me. Then, he reached in his pocket and pulled out a very wide, very loud necktie. He or someone else had probably received it from the American Red Cross. He gave it to me with a great smile. I thanked him profusely because I suspected it was among his most precious possessions and that he was giving it to me in sign of friendship.

It was good seeing him. He was one of the most trustworthy individuals I had met during my eight years under communism in Albania. This time he had another surprise up his sleeve. He led me into a room and introduced me to a young Franciscan priest who was standing in a corner. The Franciscan was tall, with sharp, intelligent features, and a smile that could melt an iceberg. Ndue Vata introduced me to Fr. Daniel Gjeçaj. We shook hands and I expected we would exchange the usual pleasantries and that would be that. Instead, Fr. Daniel, without changing his friendly smile, popped a question that took me aback.

"Do you intend to stay in Yugoslavia?"

What was I supposed to answer? If I said yes, I would be lying. If I said no, I was running a risk: Fr. Gjeçaj could harm me, if not intentionally, then unintentionally by blabbering to the wrong people. I had already run such a risk when I met the priest who wanted to complain to Apostol Tanefi, head of the Albanian Refugee Organization, about the many UDBA informers among refugees. I looked at Fr. Daniel. He looked most trustworthy. I felt that I had to tell the truth.

"No," I answered, "I do not intend to stay in Yugoslavia."

"Good," he replied, beaming all over his face.

"I have a friend who will escape this summer to Austria. He has already been to the border once and knows his way to the brook that separates

Austria from Yugoslavia. I'll tell him about you. The two of you can escape together to safety."

Well, that was unexpected. How could he trust me to that extent? He did not mention the name of his friend but would doubtless name him to me when the time came.

"How wide is this brook?" I asked.

"Oh, about two meters."

I thought that I could jump two meters with both hands tied behind my back. We said no more that day. We shook hands and I did not hear from him for months to come.

During one of my walks, I had seen the marquee of a movie house announcing an American movie entitled *Neptune's Daughter* with Esther Williams. I had no idea what to expect, but the photos were gorgeous and reflected a life I didn't even dream of. I paid 40 dinars for the ticket, for me an exorbitant sum, and went to my first American movie. I took in all the luxury; the fast pace, the beautiful scenes, and shapely girls. I enjoyed the theme song, "Baby, It's Cold Outside," and assumed that the dialogue was witty based on the facial expressions and body language of the actors. By the time I left, however, I was in the dumps. I had understood little of what was said. The movie might as well have been in Serbo-Croatian for all the good my English had done me. Later I realized that what had failed me was not my knowledge of English or my vocabulary but the fact that I was not used to spoken English.

I have already mentioned Apostol Tanefi, the head of the Albanian Refugee Organization. Hajrullah Ishmi was his second in command. I usually tried to stay away from "big shots," but one day I could not avoid running into Hajrullah without being obvious. After the initial greetings, he complained that he lacked good people to direct some refugee publication that I had never heard of. I got immediately suspicious. Was he trying to recruit me for the job? He proceeded to tell me that a male nurse at a hospital in Tirana had been selling penicillin—had filled the bottles with water and administered the contents to the patients. The money he had pocketed. He was discovered, convicted, and executed. The refugee publication had reported the incident as an example of the communist reign of terror. There was little doubt that the male nurse was guilty and may have deserved the death sentence. The incident, however, should have never been reported as a communist atrocity. I made some sympathetic noises but tried not to get involved. Maybe it was my attitude or maybe Hajrullah had no intention of recruiting me, but that's as far as the story went, thank God!

We heard that General Eisenhower was elected president of the United States and were most impressed with his statement that the hardships in a soldier's life weighed less than the chains of slavery. Could this be an indication of President Eisenhower's views of Eastern Europe under the Soviets and of his determination to do something about it?

On a lighter note, one day I was having a cup of coffee with some Albanians when Bardhyl Shyti, whom I had meet but a few days before, insisted on "reading" the coffee dregs in my cup. I refused but he would not take no for an answer. He turned my demitasse over on its little saucer and let it rest for a minute or two. Then, he looked into the cup.

"You will leave Prishtina and feel much joy. You will get some money. An officer has wanted to get together with you not once but twice but has changed his mind. You will soon receive a letter and a package from abroad. There are three girls who want to meet you. A relative of yours is under strict surveillance and in danger of being arrested." He looked up and smiled at me. His predictions were by the book. They involved money, women, and danger. I returned his smile and let it go at that. Was he trying to convey a message to me or was he just having fun?

I noticed that in Prishtina teenagers and young men were sporting ducktail haircuts. Those who could afford it also wore leather jackets and boots with heavy soles and heels. They swaggered down the street and thought they looked very spiffy. I wondered what the girls thought of them. I for one would have liked to see them in the hands of military barbers. Or was I, a future baldy, simply being jealous?

I went to the movies once more. This time it was a Mexican movie entitled *Day of Life*. It was full of riots, arrests, trials, and executions. I found myself riveted to my chair, helpless, and caught up in the action. I found out that movies dealing with oppression, arrests, and executions were not for me, at least not for a while—probably not for a good while.

Listening to foreign broadcasts was not encouraged but was not as dangerous as in Albania. One day we heard that Italy and Greece had renounced their claims on Albania and its territories. Furthermore, a U.S.

senator had asked for new elections in Albania under international supervision and after disbandment of the communist security apparatus. Both news items sounded important to us. We were particularly delighted with the senator's statement, but did not realize the modest impact or consequences of such statements.

The days followed one another and the end of January was getting closer and closer. Then one day we heard the news that a communist army captain from Albania was captured on Yugoslav soil. His name was Galip Sojli. He was an infiltrator caught in the act. Then came the flip-flop. No, he was not an infiltrator, but a bona fide political refugee sympathetic to the Yugoslav brand of communism. We heard that Galip Soili had made similar statements on the Yugoslav radio and was therefore welcome in Yugoslavia. I had met him once in Tirana when he was in charge of sports equipment for the Albanian army and had issued uniforms and shoes for various volleyball teams. I don't recall how his story ended but I do know that I was going to stay away from him and any potential complications to the best of my ability. For the time being, I was a "guest" of the Yugoslavs. If things went my way, I would not impose on their hospitality for too long but would soon put on my walking shoes and try to reach Austria.

Frankly, I was much more interested in the fact that the membership of the Italian communist party had declined from 2 million to 300,000. Hallelujah!

Another bit of unexpected news came from Edward Kardelji, one of Tito's close collaborators and the chief ideologue of Tito's brand of socialism. In a recent speech, he accused the Soviet Union of falsifying historical facts and of leadership idolatry, akin to that of absolute monarchies. Kardelji pointed out the pay gap in the Soviet Union. It ranged from 400 rubles a month for simple workers to 15,000 rubles a month for heads of enterprises. That was a lot for a classless society. He called Soviet policies neonationalistic and accused them of disregarding the history and culture of other nations. He chastised Soviet Russia for its agreement on spheres of influence with capitalist societies, and concluded by accusing the Soviet Union of choking off the initiatives of the masses. Coming from a communist, this was quite a *tour de force*. Of course, he could have saved himself a lot of trouble had he listened to what we "reactionaries" had been saying since well before 1953.

The day arrived for me to apply for membership in the Albanian Political Refugee Organization. When it all came about, I was underwhelmed as I put my membership card in my wallet next to my card as member of the Albanian Trade Unions. Let me explain. In Albania, anyone working for a living, unless he or she was self-employed, had to be a trade union member. Direct participation in union activities was practically a must. When I worked as a public health inspector for the city of Shkodra, I was one of 21 employees at city hall. In age, we ranged from an 18-year-old mail boy to a janitor who looked very old. He walked with a shuffle, his head bowed down, expressionless, and with his tongue hanging out of the left corner of his mouth. He was an innocuous old soul who somehow managed to come to work. I am not sure he could do any actual work but he did show up every day. In our union, we had a president, a vice-president, a secretary, a treasurer, and umpteen members of the board. All 20 of us, in one function or another, worked with great dedication for the benefit of the old janitor, who was the only one without an official union function. Far be it for me to make fun of the old janitor. He was simply another sad example of how badly people needed an income, however meager, and of the importance of ration cards for themselves and their families. This was also an example of the sham of Trade Unions in Albania.

As far as membership in the political refugee organization was concerned, it was just as important as being a member of the Albanian Trade Unions. You had to be in it but being a member made no difference in either case. Well, almost. Personally, I did benefit as I received a free copy of a German-Serbo-Croatian dictionary.

Hila, Deda, and Peter would be leaving any day now for Kragujevac. Why? I had no idea. There had been passing mention about my going to the university in Belgrade. However, nothing of substance had come about. I had probably blown my chance when I refused to return to Albania at the service of the UDBA.

Actually, I had never counted on going to the university, just as I had never wavered in my resolve not to work for the Yugoslavs. I did not intend to stay in Yugoslavia for very long. I was determined to try to reach freedom with or without the permission of my hosts.

This second point was less foreboding than it might have seemed. Anyone trying to escape got one year in prison. Compared to Albania, where I would have been tortured and executed, jail in Yugoslavia was no serious deterrent. There was too much to gain and too little to lose.

Meanwhile, I received 5,000 dinars as a clothing allowance. I bought myself a shirt, a few handkerchiefs, and some underwear. I also sent Peter 600 dinars so he could buy himself a holster as a memento from me. He had loaned me his revolver when we had just met in the Albanian mountains. More than for use in combat, sidearms were an insurance against being caught alive. I had lost the knife I had stolen from my mother. When I met Peter and the others, I was without weapons of any kind and while I did not fear death, I did fear torture. I was determined never to fall alive into the hands of the Albanian communists. Peter gave me his revolver and I kept it tied around my neck, just in case. Peter's generosity was engraved in my mind and I could never forget it.

News reached us that six infiltrators from the Scanderbeg Battalion in Munich had parachuted into Albania. According to our information, five were killed and the sixth was taken prisoner. There had been other such episodes. Somehow, every time resistance fighters tried to infiltrate into Albania from the West, there was Sigurimi awaiting them. This happened whether they came by air from Italy (mainly members of Blloku Kombëtar, an organization led by politicians active during regimes preceding the communist takeover), by sea from Malta (sent by the Brits), or on foot from Greece (dispatched by the CIA). There were too many such incidents to ascribe them all to coincidence. My experience of spending three months in the Albanian mountains without clashing with the security forces made me wonder how Sigurimi always happened to be at the right place at the right time to meet infiltrators from the West. There was no question in my mind that there was a leak somewhere. The question was where.

Time passed slowly since I had little to do. I had asked Valnea to send Mom a telegram to announce my arrival in Yugoslavia. I had also asked her to send Mom a letter I had written in Valnea's name. Finally, I had asked Valnea to send me my university registration papers from Padua in case I could attend the University of Belgrade. I was confident that Valnea would do as I had asked. Whether Mom would get the telegram and letter was another question as it depended on the Albanian censors. The uncertainty weighed heavily on me, particularly because I knew that I had added to Mom's troubles.

February 16 marked my 29th birthday. I did not tell anyone. Hence, there was no celebrating, no cake, no special food. While I bought myself some baklava for Dad's and Mom's birthdays, I did nothing special for

mine. I had, however, a great source of strength—I had the support of my
faith. In the evening, in bed, I would turn my thoughts to God. I could not
quite fathom how I had deserved such goodness on His part. It could only
be His mercy that surrounded me with such tender care that held me up
when I stumbled, that made my steps firm in darkness, over torrents and
cliffs. Everything spoke to me of Him, the Lord and Creator of every leaf
and every creature. I understood the essential role of chlorophyll in nature,
but why the need for such a variety of leaves, from chestnut trees to conifers, from palm trees to algae under water? How could one deny the divine
essence of moral concepts? Where could such sublime peaks of human
integrity, of love and self-sacrifice, and of sainthood arise from the lowli-
ness and transience of the human condition? Concepts and mores changed
with time. Man might embrace diverse lifestyles influenced by geography
and latitude, but in the depth of his conscience one could always find a
quest for righteousness. This was in flagrant antithesis with man's material
interests. To me it seemed useless to strive to understand God. However,
one could feel God, absolutely, every moment, as He spoke to us through
His creation. If we failed to hear His voice, it was because our senses had
failed us, because our flesh had made us blind and deaf. At the end of the
day, when I lay down to sleep, having had three meals and a roof overhead,
I prayed humbly, with boundless thankfulness as I joined millions of others
in reciting: "Our Father who art in Heaven..."

My life in Yugoslavia was very different from that in Albania. Instead of
hard work, here time weighed heavily on my shoulders. Instead of feeling
helpless, of fearing arrest and torture, I still had a sense of helplessness but
it lacked the sharp edge of impending doom. I was not hungry—in fact, we
ate rather well—but I missed the joy of sharing the food, of living under one
roof with my family. There were the eternal informers. They could hurt you,
but less than in Albania. If you kept your nose clean, you need not panic.

Everything depended on the authorities, but they were less threatening
than back home; they were better educated and seemed less violent. One
more thing: if they said yes, they meant yes, and their no meant no. If one
were to speak in colors, life in Albania was colored red, a burning, flaming
red, the red of danger, the red of emergency and tragedy where the flames
could strike out unprovoked, at any moment, in any direction. In Yugoslavia, my life as a refugee was mostly grayish-brown, the color of slush, of

dirty snow, of mud that surrounded me. The sky, however, was tinged with pink. If Albania was hell and freedom in the West heaven, Yugoslavia had to be purgatory, a place of fear without panic, of hope for the future.

Yugoslavia was not where I wanted to stay any longer than I had to. I wanted to escape, and the sooner the better. Having survived three months in the Albanian mountains, I had gained confidence in myself. At the right opportunity, I would know how to attack and cross the border. After all, I had good teachers in Albania. That's when lighter colors, pastels, entered the picture all around me: the light blues of the sky, the golden rays of a sun that lit and warmed without scorching, the shades of red of the sunset promising a better tomorrow. One thing at a time, I had to tell myself, one thing at a time.

In fact, things were starting to move in the right direction. Valnea wrote that the telegram informing Mom of my successful escape had reached her; also, that soon she was going to send my school documents from the University of Padua. Perhaps I had to wait until spring or summer and then, with my guide, we could start our trek to Austria and freedom. I had learned that his name was Zef Shllaku and that he was from Shkodra. He had studied first in Belgrade but had transferred to the University of Zagreb. With a friend, he had gone once as far as the Austrian border but had turned back for reasons unknown. Father Daniel Gjeçaj was going to speak with him and Zef would contact me in Belgrade.

Now Peter joined us, just in time for Hila's announcement on February 26. On that day, ten days after my birthday, Hila came to us with wings on his feet. "Peter, Deda, get ready, we are about to leave for Kragujevac. You too, Genc, get ready. You are going to Belgrade, to the university."

I should have been dumbfounded. Well, I was not. Helpless and under pressure, I had built up a wall of ice that surrounded and protected me. It rendered me immune to intensive joy or sorrow, a useful defense mechanism that over the years had served me well. I had learned not to be crushed if an anticipated joyful event did not materialize, nor to worry needlessly about a sorrow that may never reach me. This sense of detachment had helped me in times of persecution, particularly during my nine failed escape attempts. I needed it now that there was a possibility of reaching the West, of meeting Valnea. I did not dare hope that she had waited for me. What if she had? What if she came to Yugoslavia to see me? Well, the one thing I was not going to do was daydream.

For the moment, that was not a problem. Short range, I was going to the university in Belgrade. It did not take me long to pack. Deda congratulated me most heartily on my returning to my studies. He and I had grown closer during the long hours together in Prishtina. In the mountains, my lack of experience had made me a burden. My strengths, such as foreign languages and scholastic background were never needed, and therefore had been of no use. Now, I was going to the university and Deda rejoiced and was proud of me. Hila seemed very busy, for whatever reason.

Maybe Hila was being modest. Maybe he had tried to help me behind the scenes or maybe he hadn't. At this point, it mattered little. I had prepared myself to go to a refugee camp, and now I was going to the university. Either way, I was moderately grateful to the Yugoslavs, because in Albania I had been a marked man.

As it turned out, I did not need to say farewell to Hila and friends in Prishtina. That evening, we got on the same train and left for Kragujevac and Belgrade. The train was relatively comfortable, even in third class. There were not too many travelers aboard and we had no problem securing good seats. As the train moved out of the station, the four of us started out on a trip that would take us into uncharted territory.

I had always liked to think ahead and be prepared. During my formative years, during the war and under communism, I practiced short-range planning and it had served me well most of the time. In times of war and danger, long-range planning was seldom called for. I had learned what to say and what not to say without compromising my fundamental values. This was important, because if I abandoned my principles, there was nothing left to sustain me in adversity. In prison, I had learned that words often traveled in unexpected directions. Among prisoners, unless they were true friends, and those were rare, I would say as much as I would say to the warden face-to-face. An Arab proverb said that words were like arrows. As long as they were in the quiver, you were their master. Once an arrow left the bow, you no longer had the power to stop it or change its flight. This policy kept me out of trouble much of the time. Remaining true to my values kept me in prison longer when I refused to repent for having fought in Kosova. Later, it got me into isolation for 42 days, but what an opportunity to get to know Fr. Anton Harapi! That had been well worth the price I paid.

On the train as we left Prishtina, I kept to myself. I had plenty to think about and to prepare for. I had received papers that would permit me to get a room at the *"studentski dom"* (student dorm) Ivo Lola Ribar on the Red Army Boulevard in Belgrade. I also had the necessary documents to register in medical school. That night on the train felt unreal, and I touched my pockets with the papers more than once.

Now that I would have a fixed address, I wanted to write to Mustafa Kruja, to Uncle Edward, and to Valnea. Would she come to see me? I had trouble keeping this last thought from my mind. I usually did it through sheer willpower. This thought kept me from thinking through other problems and alternatives I needed to work out in my mind before facing reality. It also tended to keep alive hopes that must remain under control.

I probably dozed off from time to time but I was wide awake when it was time to say goodbye to Hila, Deda, and Peter. Our farewells were mercifully short because of the train's brief stopover in Kragujevac. Another chapter had closed behind me. I had come to feel true affection and friendship toward Peter. Deda I had come to know and like in Prishtina. Hila remained a mystery that I did not have to unravel at the time. Having placed these memories into imaginary cubbyholes, I was finally master of my own decisions, if not of my destiny. At best, Hila had been like the caricature of a mother-in-law, looking me over disapprovingly and clucking away even when silence would have been preferable.

I could tell the train was nearing Belgrade. Pairs of rails kept getting ever more numerous, converging and diverging, as is typical on approaching major railroad stations. The clangor of the wheel was getting ever faster as we changed tracks, and the railroad cars were swaying perceptibly. Finally, I saw the station signs with "Belgrade" in Cyrillic letters. We had arrived.

It did not take me long to exit from the station, and as I did so, I found myself staring at tall buildings. I broke out in laughter. As a child in Graz, Austria, my parents had often asked me to take sons or daughters of visitors from Albania to the city park and adjacent areas. Many children had stared at nearby tall buildings in awe and that had made me smile, me: their sophisticated host. Well, after ten years in Albania, here I was, staring at tall buildings in Belgrade!

I shouldered my knapsack, asked for directions, and soon I was on my way to the student dorm Ivo Lola Ribar. It was quite a walk but eventually I made it. Once the secretary found out I was Albanian, she called an interpreter. Heaven knows what they talked about, but soon the student took me in tow and I wound up in temporary quarters way up in the attic. The place was OK as far as I was concerned. It had a bed, a washbasin, and some storage space that was more than adequate for my modest wardrobe.

The next morning, my interpreter showed up again and this time we went into the basement where I was to share a room with a Serbian student who suffered from pulmonary TB. Again, these were temporary quarters until more suitable ones became available.

My helplessness in the new environment brought the best out in these "older" Albanian students who were competing with each other as to who would take me to the medical college, etc. It turned out that I had to satisfy some preliminary formalities before I could register in medical school. I had to get the right papers, present so many ID pictures, take a number of steps in the right sequence, and were it not for my "guardian angels," it would have taken me much longer. In truth, I was not worried. Of course, I wanted to take care of these things. I had decided to study Serbo-Croatian seriously and to attend classes. Learning the language was a must—the sooner the better. My knowledge of Italian, German, some English, and Latin were of little help as this was a Slavic language. As I had some talent for languages, I began to progress reasonably well. I could not follow the lectures in medical school, but after a while, I began to read the daily newspaper and understand the gist of news blurbs.

One of my early experiences at the student dorm dealt with an Albanian student who refused to submit to Yugoslav pressure. He had decided to return to Albania and nothing, neither inducements nor threats, could change his mind. He was quiet, polite, and firm. I came to respect him, and on impulse I gave him some of my meager cash that he accepted. Being pro-Tirana of course made him an opponent but one I could respect because of his unbending stance toward the Yugoslav authorities. I never found out what happened to him.

The oldest Albanian student I had met so far was Prenk Gruda, from Gruda in Montenegro. He was in his second year of studying history. He told me he came from a very poor family. He had started grade school in his late teens. He was the oldest of several children, some of whom lived presently in Albania and seemed in good standing with the Albanian regime. He spoke some English and made it a point to speak English with me. One day, he took me to meet Martin Camaj, a student of literature, for whose talent and ability Prenk had much respect. I didn't quite know what to expect. Prenk told me that Martin was from Dukagjin and he had married a Serbian girl, the daughter of a former royalist mayor of Belgrade. As Albanians had a tendency to exaggerate, I took this latter statement with a grain of salt.

We walked maybe 20 minutes and reached a nice home. We entered through the front yard and walked along the house until we came to a lean-to that could have been a hothouse at one time but was converted to an apartment. It looked neat and compact from the outside. As it turned out, the inside was even better. Prenk knocked and Martin Camaj opened the door. He was tall, handsome, and very friendly. He had brown hair that seemed to part naturally in the middle and fell lazily sideways toward his ears. He had bright, intelligent eyes, wide lips, and good, healthy teeth, something rare among Albanians—particularly among highlanders. When we shook hands, I noticed that his were large and soft. In fact, his tall frame appeared rather delicate, the frame of one who had grown up away from sports or from hard physical labor. As it turned out, he had spent most of his life in school, reading and writing, with but little exposure to anything else.

He asked us in with words echoing the beautiful sounds and inflections of Albania's northern highlands. The inside of his home looked inviting. We met his wife Nina, a tall, attractive young woman in her late twenties. She moved gracefully and with ease as she took our coats and bid us welcome.

As I recall, the living room was comfortable, and despite the winter season, full of light entering through wide windows. The furniture was also quite light in color, which added to the airiness of the room. I don't remember what they offered us or what we talked about. I do remember that Prenk introduced me to the young couple, mentioning some of what he viewed as highlights of Martin's and my past and trying to regulate, to direct the conversation. After all, he had brought us together. Martin and I somehow hit it off from the very first moment. The more we talked, the more Prenk faded into the background. In fact, I don't remember a single thing he contributed to our visit until it was all over and he and I returned to the dorm.

"It was most impolite of you to monopolize Martin," he pouted. "After all, it was I who brought you two together." I was genuinely surprised, because Martin and I had not ignored Prenk intentionally. Prenk walked more or less in silence on the way back to our dorm.

One afternoon, some Albanian students decided to gather in the room I shared with the Serbian student. Martin was among them. Prenk pulled out his diary and asked for permission to read some passages that went back to the early 1930s. The subject matter was of interest only to Prenk. The students made no effort to hide their lack of interest. I felt obliged to listen carefully, which was the least I could do as the host of this gathering. Prenk was so pleased and inspired by his prose that he asked for permission to read another few pages. The students grunted. Martin looked at me, beat his chest with his fist, and asked me, "Do you know what this gesture means?"

It was a gesture used by the congregation during the Catholic Mass while uttering the words "*mea culpa, mea culpa, mea maxima culpa,*" meaning "through my fault, through my fault, through my most grievous fault," and I said so to Martin. He smiled broadly, shook his head, and whispered instead a very strong Albanian expression meaning more or less "May he do thus-and-so to my mother [if I agree with his request]."

I found it hard to keep from laughing aloud. The irreverence of the expression and the sense of complicity it created strengthened the bond that was forming between Martin and me. This bond of friendship would last a lifetime. Subsequently, I quoted the incident, the gesture, and its novel interpretation to Zef Shllaku and to other friends for use when appropriate.

While this was going on, Prenk ignored the grunts. He may or may not have seen what Martin was signaling across the room, and continued his reading. Years later, he would publish his memoirs and derive much pleasure from distributing and selling the tome.

Immersed in a new environment, I experienced it with all my senses. The view of a large city such as Belgrade, its hustle and bustle, the way people dressed so much better than in Albania or Kosova, the many cars, some with diplomatic license plates—everything was very different. The will and whim of the authorities still ruled supreme. One sensed their ideological hostility toward us, bolstered by rabid aversion toward anyone and anything Albanian. Nonetheless, the authorities were less heavy handed or insulting than in Albania. The police were still omnipotent but exercised their power less obtrusively. The same held true for their secret service. Their unfettered power was still there, and on occasion one could see the clubfoot and smell the sulfur, but it was not overwhelming if one minded one's manners.

For example, when I registered a student approached me and asked whether I spoke German. He offered help and told me that his father had previously taught at the Belgrade School of Medicine. Subsequently, he had escaped to Switzerland where he again taught at a university. I was surprised that the student told me such politically dangerous details of his private life. I thanked him for his offer of help and made it a point to avoid him thereafter. He could be sincere but I wanted to avoid the risk of guilt by association. Alternatively, he could be a plant, in which case he was dangerous. In either case, it was best for me to avoid him.

The sounds, the speech of the people, the songs, and the very street noises were part of an environment where I was the outsider. The Albanian students all spoke Serbo-Croatian, giving me an inferiority complex. I knew some profanities I had learned in Fiume, and was absolutely taken aback when I heard college girls greeting each other with vulgar sexual expressions that may have lost their literal meaning but were nonetheless repugnant to me.

I registered at the School of Medicine with the help of an interpreter. What a sinking feeling; my inability to follow the lectures made me feel awful. I only derived comfort from the yet-to-be firmed-up plans of escaping to freedom in the summer.

Meanwhile, life went on. The authorities cashed my $50 check for the equivalent of $25. I cannot say that they gave me only half the money. As I learned more about personal checks, I wondered whether the check was any good, it now being three years after it had been issued. Anyhow, with all of $25 in my pocket, my first major purchase was a pair of black wing-tip shoes that went well with my one black suit and dark blue winter coat. I was on cloud nine. I was wearing new shoes, something I had not done for over ten years, since my student days in Italy. In Albania, I had bought only sandals with leather tops and heavy rubber soles from old tires. They had killed my feet. The new shoes fit well. They were quite elegant and moved me one more step away from looking like a refugee.

One day, I had gone to the USIS (U.S. Information Service) library. It was in the center of town and quite impressive, well lit, with beautiful office furniture and staffed with attractive young women. I approached one and asked for help in my best English. She greeted me with a big smile and stood. As her eyes wandered down to my Yugoslav army boots, her smile vanished and she simply turned away. That would not happen again, now that I had black dress shoes!

This was also the first time in years that I had a chance to attend Mass. Belgrade had a large Franciscan church and Prenk Gruda took me there. The feeling of being able to go to church and attend Mass overwhelmed me! The familiar sights of statues of saints, of the Blessed Mother with Baby Jesus and St. Joseph, the large crucifix above the altar, the atmosphere of prayers said in faith and of divine response hoped for in reply. The incense, the beautiful Latin text of the Mass, everything made me feel welcome and at home. "*Introibo ad altare Dei, ad Deum qui laetificat juventutem meam...*" The Mass began and I was back to the years when I was free and could go to church. Except for the sermon in Serbo-Croatian, I could follow and understand the text, the familiar gestures of the priest building up to the consecration, Holy Communion, the final blessing, and the sending of the faithful into the world to take Christ with them and to carry on His holy work.

I did experience one moment of resentment during the Mass. From the opening words, I was on cloud nine until the ushers came with their collection baskets. I did not mind contributing what little I could, not at all. I did resent, however, their bringing me down to earth when I had been soaring in spirit close to God. At night, I could not say my prayers without asking God what I had done that day to deserve food, adequate clothing, a roof over my head, and a warm bed. I felt so unworthy and so grateful at the same time.

With the passing of time, I began to get around and feel less helpless. I needed, of course, to study Serbian, at least to the point of being able to follow my classes in medical school. Prenk Gruda came up with the idea that I could teach German and get Serbo-Croatian lessons in return. He introduced me to a Serbian girl who was taking German in college and felt the need for extra lessons. She was tall, well dressed, and self-assured. Her father had been a royalist general. Prenk was impressed with her social credentials while I hoped to benefit linguistically from such an arrangement. Through Prenk, the young woman and I agreed on a date for our first lesson. The day came, and she showed up accompanied by her sister. She said she had some shopping to do. So the three of us went from store to store, until it was too late for our first lesson. As it turned out, she did not show up at our next get-together and I called it quits. I could not afford to waste time.

One day we students were told that the Red Cross would provide us with clothing articles. I got a very nice light blue summer jacket and a pair of light gray slacks. I felt like a king. I was deeply grateful to the donors of those garments that came just in time for my escape to Austria—if it were to come about.

The day dawned when I would finally meet Zef Shllaku. He came from Zagreb and spent a day with a group of us in Belgrade. He was very reserved. In fact, besides a glimmer of recognition when we first met, he never spoke to me during the entire day. I began to doubt whether in fact there had been this glimmer in his eyes. I decided not to crowd him. If we needed to work out our plans, we would get together one way or another.

Even though I was making a serious effort to learn Serbo-Croatian, I could not stay away from the British Cultural Center and its library. The English language attracted me powerfully, but more importantly, the varied viewpoints about historical events and about World War II in particular proved irresistible. I started to borrow volumes of Churchill's *History of World War II* and fell in love with the contents and the elegance of his prose. It was a different world. Ernie Pyle had taught me English and had carried me beyond the walls of the Tirana prison. Winston Churchill took me back to El Alamein, to the American landing in Africa, to Anzio Beach. I agonized over his attempts to convince Roosevelt and Stalin to land in the Balkans. How much suffering would have been avoided, how many lives saved, if the Allies had landed in the Balkans instead of in Italy! Nonetheless, I could not fault the objections to such a landing where the mountainous terrain would have nullified, at least in part, Allied air and armored superiority. Anyhow, by now that was water under the bridge.

Life in Belgrade began to take on color. One day I served as guide to an Albanian seminarian. I knew my way around downtown Belgrade and the beautiful Kalemegdan, a hill near town with well-kept gardens, coffee houses and restaurants, a zoo, tennis courts, and other amenities. From the top of Kalemegdan, one could see the confluence of the Danube and Sava rivers. The weather was splendid and the landscape before our eyes enchanting. The seminarian looked at me and murmured, "This view reminds me of Shkodra."

"Why?" I asked him.

"Because of the confluence of two rivers and the fortress atop the hill."

While I loved Albania, I was not oblivious to her warts.

"Just because two rivers come together in both instances, you compare Shkodra to Belgrade? How can you look at Kalemegdan and equate it with the Fortress in Shkodra? Do you know that I spent several years in Shkodra and never visited the fortress because it was snake infested?" My guest looked shaken by my reproach. Perhaps I should have kept my mouth shut.

One day Fr. Daniel Gjeçaj came to Belgrade. I had heard that the authorities had tried to isolate him from the Albanian refugees by offering him a scholarship to study in Belgrade. He had answered that their universities taught nothing of interest to him. His sharp answer left no doubt about where he stood.

On a trip to Belgrade, he ran into an Albanian Franciscan who had accepted a scholarship and was studying at the university. It so happened that his Albanian fellow priest was with a pretty college girl. The priest-student was deeply embarrassed at the sight of Fr. Daniel. He introduced the girl adding, "Father, isn't she beautiful?"

"Not as beautiful as the Blessed Mother," Father Daniel had answered tersely.

"But she is also very kind hearted."

"Not as kind hearted as St. Francis."

At that point, Fr. Daniel had nodded to the girl and had walked away.

One evening, a Kosovar student came to my room. He insisted we go together to a dance at the School of Medicine. I had no desire to go, but he insisted so much that I would have hurt his feelings had I refused. So off we went. At this dance, a tall, rather attractive Serbian girl seemed to enjoy dancing with me. At one point, we sat down. I had spoken English with her, and at a certain point, I turned and spoke to my Kosovar friend in Albanian. She asked me what language we were speaking. When I said that we were conversing in Albanian, she said with great surprise, "He is a *shkiptar*," using the word as a derogatory term. "But you are Albanian."

I replied that we Albanians and the Kosovars were brothers. We shared the same language, traditions, and history. She wrinkled her nose and stuck her tongue out at me. I turned to my Kosovar host and said to him, "Tell her exactly what I am about to tell you. I understand enough Serbian to know whether you are translating my words correctly. Here is what I want you to tell her in my name: 'When I was escaping, I carried a revolver with seven bullets. At the border, I surrendered it to the Yugoslav authorities. If I had it with me tonight, I would have fired all seven bullets right into your belly.'"

She rose and sailed away, like a schooner with her blouse and skirt flapping in the wind. She returned a short while later and apologized for her remark, but the harm was done. Of course, I accepted her apology but left shortly thereafter. I did not want to go to the dance in the first place. Now it had ruined my evening.

One evening, upon returning to the dorm, I found my Albanian colleagues in a huddle and all excited. That afternoon, they were asked to go to the Albanian Student Club. They had to remove all rifles and other weapons that adorned the walls as well as the pictures of "martyrs" who had fallen for the "joint cause." Shortly thereafter Dushan Mugosha had appeared.

In 1941, when the three Albanian communist groups of Korça, Tirana, and Shkodra had failed to unite, Yugoslavia had sent two emissaries, Miladin Popovic and Dushan Mugosha, to bring about the unification the Albanians communists had failed to achieve. Both emissaries spent the rest of the war years in Albania. They successfully torpedoed the Mukaj agreement between the communist Front of National Liberation and Balli Kombëtar, the main nationalist organization in Albania. These emissaries orchestrated the Albanian civil war and returned to Yugoslavia at the end of World War II. The Albanian communists obediently surrendered Kosova to their Yugoslav brethren, who proceeded to kill Albanians by the thousands. Eventually, Miladin Popovic was killed by a Kosovar and Dushan Mugosha made general.

Mugosha told the assembled Albanian students that the UN high commissioner for refugees would be visiting that afternoon. Also, that they were to state they spoke only Albanian and Serbo-Croatian and that any conversation with the high commissioner should be made through the interpreter. Eventually, the high commissioner did show up.

"Good afternoon," He greeted them in English. In response, the students smiled and nodded their heads.

"Do you speak English?" They all shook their heads from side to side.

"*Parlez-vous français?*" Again they responded negatively.

"*Sprechen Sie deutsch?*" The students again pleaded ignorance.

"What kind of college students are you who don't speak any foreign languages?"

The interpreter intervened. "They speak Albanian and Serbo-Croatian."

The high commissioner stalked out of the room in disdain and frustration. At that point, one student had smuggled a memorandum written in French into the hands of the commissioner's secretary, a Briton.

Now the students wondered whether the high commissioner's visit would have any consequences. Perhaps the visitors did not know Dushan Mugosha, who had acted as the interpreter. The students hoped the charade had fooled the high commissioner who, of all people, must have been very much aware of such communist shenanigans. The episode would have ended here had it not been for my meeting the high commissioner's secretary in Klagenfurt after my escape, but more about that later.

Meanwhile, my acquaintance with Martin Camaj had bloomed into a full friendship. We got together and talked for hours about things dear to our hearts. We spoke of politics and literature, about our sufferings and hopes. When Martin sold a poem, he would pick me up and take me to a restaurant where we spent his hard-earned money on shish kebab and beer. What a life!

One day, he told me the contents of a short story he had written but not for publication, at least not in Belgrade. It dealt with a Kosovar father and several of his sons who lived in Belgrade. Of his sons, one attended the university. The rest earned a living helping the father cut wood, load or unload trucks, and polish shoes in public squares. One day, when the college student had no classes, he joined his father and brothers in a public square, carrying his box with brushes, rags, and various jars of shoe polish, ready to spend some pleasant hours with the men of his family.

Unexpectedly, he saw a dainty shoe with a high heel pop up on his box. Without looking up, he started to ply his "trade." He wiped the dust off the shoe, brushed it clean, applied shoe polish, and finished the job with care and pride. Then he treated the other shoe in the same manner. Finally, he knocked the brush against the box to indicate that the job was finished. At that point, his customer spoke to him.

"Can you do other things beside polish shoes?"

He looked up and saw a young, attractive woman gazing at him. She obviously wanted to talk to him.

"I can chop wood and do chores," he replied, intent on giving her little or no information about himself.

"I have some cords of wood I need split. Can you do the job?"

He nodded.

She pulled a little notebook from her purse and wrote her address on it. "Can you make it tomorrow afternoon around three o'clock?"

He nodded again.

The next day, he borrowed an ax from his brothers and went to her house. It was an elegant house on the outskirts of Belgrade. A neat, good-looking maid opened the gate. She had been expecting him. She took him to a pile of wood and left. When he was done splitting and stacking the wood, he knocked at the door of the house to collect his money. The maid opened the door and told him that her mistress wanted to see him. Then, she led him into an elegant drawing room and exited quietly.

It soon became apparent that the lady of the house was quite taken by him. Also, that she was not bashful. After they had said and done everything that needed saying and doing under the circumstances, he left the house. He had barely closed the gate behind him when the maid came running.

"Wait, wait," she cried, "You forgot the money we owe you."

Without slowing down or turning his head he replied, "Your mistress has paid me in person." That was the last he saw of that house or its mistress.

I chose to summarize this story because Martin never published it. The story accurately portrayed Kosovar feelings toward their Serb rulers.

One day, Martin came to the dorm and out we went to a restaurant across the street. After lunch, Martin asked me to take a walk into the hills surrounding Belgrade. It was a most pleasant afternoon. The conversation flowed easily, as between good friends who have much in common and who trust each other completely. Late that afternoon, Martin told me he had two tickets to the Belgrade Opera. They were giving *La Traviata* and he insisted that we go together. I objected. We had spent practically all day together. Now it was time that he go home and take his wife to the opera. Martin spoke up, very matter of fact.

"You and I are going together to the opera. If you won't come, I will tear up the tickets." His tone left no doubt that he would carry out his threat.

That evening we went together to the opera. I must admit that I did not expect much of the performance. Growing up in Italy had given me a taste for Italian opera of a high artistic level. While Fiume was not exactly the center of the world, it had a beautiful theater, a carbon copy of the Opera Haus in Graz. Very good operatic companies came to Fiume during the winter season. In the summer, thanks to the government-sponsored Carro di Tespi Lirico program, artists of world renown would come and perform in the open. Thanks to this cultural program, I had the good fortune of hearing Beniamino Gigli as Radames in Verdi's *Aida*, Gino Bechi as Rigoletto,

Tancredi Pasero in *Mefistofele*, and other artists of caliber. I must admit that the Belgrade performance of *La Traviata* was much better than I had anticipated. Martin and I had spent a grand day together. I was concerned, however, about his relationship with his wife who loved him so much.

One day she was at her parents' house when her father and his cronies were playing cards. They got together every so often. They were all VIPs of the past regime and politics was high on their agenda. That day Nina was sitting on the floor knitting. The gentlemen were commiserating with each other about the restlessness of the Kosovars, their lack of appreciation of being citizens of Yugoslavia, and their obstinacy of wanting to be a full Yugoslav republic. Some Kosovars went even further, demanding to be a part of Albania. As the old gentlemen listed all the outrageous demands and the incidents the Kosovars were causing, Nina spoke up.

"If the Kosovars are giving us so much trouble, why not let them join Albania? They would be happy and we would get rid of them."

Her father spoke up with ice in his voice. "I should have killed you myself instead of letting you marry that Albanian."

Nina had told Martin about the incident, and for months he would not permit his in-laws to enter "his" house. Only in his absence would Nina's parents dare visit their daughter.

At this time, Prenk Gruda came to me with another candidate willing to give me lessons in Serbo-Croatian in return for German lessons. She was a freshman, her dad a railroad worker. She was studious and very serious, he hurried to tell me as he sensed that I had had it with the previous girl student he had recommended. Other Albanian students also encouraged me to study with her. Everyone who had tried to seduce her had failed. Maybe she would succumb to my charms and "our national honor would thus be vindicated." I was not looking for girlfriends. I was getting ready to escape and did not want to get involved. On the other hand, the fact that she had rebuffed all advances by our Romeos spoke well of her. She came from a simple family and lacked the airs of my previous "pupil," the general's daughter. What made me accept was the thought I might have to postpone my escape, as had happened so many times in Albania. I agreed to meet her.

She was cute, rather short, but shapely. I could see why the Albanian students had been after her. She was about 18 and quite timid. I liked what I saw. I was even more impressed when I saw how intent she was on improving her German. We started meeting regularly. She worked hard and was pleased with the Serbo-Croatian I had learned so far. One day she asked whether I would come to their apartment for our usual lesson. I traveled quite a distance by streetcar until I reached the apartment building where she lived with her parents. The apartment was modest but well kept. I met her parents and then she and I proceeded to a room where we could study in peace. At the end of our lesson, I left, never to set foot again in that apartment. To this day I don't know why she wanted me there. Did her parents want to look me over? It really did not matter to me. The more I focused on my escape, the less I concentrated on learning Serbo-Croatian. My progress started to slow down and one day she mustered all her courage and told me so. I mumbled some explanation and life went on. On the surface, everything was normal, but underneath I was making, modifying, rejecting, and considering new escape plans that would get me to Zagreb, to Zef, and to the border where Zef would take over.

"*Der Mensch denkt und Gott lenkt,*" say the Germans, meaning that men may do the thinking, but it is God who sets the course. Once again, Prenk Gruda triggered a major development. One day he and Ndue Vate Gjelaj, who had come to Belgrade for a visit, came to my room at the dorm. After mumbling a few conventional greetings, they came straight to the point. Hila Shllaku was in Belgrade spouting oaths of loyalty to Albania while continuing to serve his Yugoslav masters. His frequent oaths went something like this: "I swear on the tombs of my father and my brother who lie buried somewhere in unmarked graves."

Prenk and Ndue viewed me as Hila's friend and wanted me to tell him to stop collaborating with the Yugoslavs. I replied that I was not Hila's friend. I was thankful that he had made my escape possible, but we had never become friends. In fact, we had never discussed politics. Second, I was in no position nor did I intend to discuss such matters with Hila. That, however, was not what they wanted to hear from me.

Shortly after they left, I decided to go to the center of Belgrade to a café frequented by Albanians. Sure enough, there was Hila with his inseparable companion Deda Mehilli. Hila invited me with a grand flourish to join them for a cup of coffee. There were also some other Albanians present and the conversation was both conventional and lame.

This changed with a bang when Prenk Gruda and Ndue Vata showed up and sat down with the rest of us. Prenk turned toward Hila with these words, "Hila, when you want to make a point you swear on your father's and brother's graves adding that you do not know where they lie buried. Yet you continue to be a pawn of the Yugoslavs. Hila, this is treason, pure and simple."

Hila was taken aback. No one had ever dared call him a traitor to his face. He sank his eyes into Prenk's and growled, "Is that what you think of me?"

Prenka squirmed and stuttered, "I am n...not th...th...the only one who thinks so. Genc also thinks that you are c...c...c...committing treason."

Hila turned slowly toward me. "You too think that I am a traitor?"

Prenka had just done me a great favor! I could pay him back by denying what he had just said by telling the truth. In that case, Prenka might have to go to jail. I decided to take another tack.

"No," I said, "I don't think that you are a traitor. Today, we and the Yugoslavs have a common enemy in Enver Hoxha. The Yugoslavs, however, are superior to us in many respects. They are better organized, they have military and economic resources we lack, and they have more talent available than we do. If our interests were to drift apart tomorrow, they may be able to dupe us without us understanding or being able to counter their maneuvers."

Hila pondered my words in silence. He then turned around and told Prenka and Ndue Vata to leave. Both rose and left in a hurry, and so did the others. Hila then looked at me. "What would you advise me to do?"

I decided to risk it all. "Hila, I am about to escape to Austria. Come with me and get out from under the Yugoslavs."

His first comment was vague, clearly meant to gain time. "If you are caught escaping, you will spend one year in jail. If they catch you with me, you'll be in jail twice as long."

"Hila, it's worth the risk."

If I could persuade Hila to escape to Austria, the Yugoslavs would lose their foothold in northern Albania, at least for the time being, since much of their network in that region would collapse. Any weakening of their influence in Albania was obviously in our best interest. After all, the Yugoslavs wanted a Koçi Xoxe-type regime in power, i.e., a communist regime serving at Belgrade's pleasure.

It was Hila's turn. "I have another friend in Belgrade whom I hold in the same esteem as I hold you. I want to discuss the issue with him also."

"Who is this friend?" I asked.

"Martin Camaj."

"Fine, let's go together to Martin's," and off we went—the three of us, Hila, Deda, and I.

On the way, we did not talk much. As fate willed it, Martin was home. Hila summarized my suggestion of escaping together and asked for Martin's opinion. Martin caught fire.

"Excellent thought," he exclaimed, "but we can do better. Let Genc go to Austria and reach the Americans while you and Deda insert yourselves into Albania. Then Genc can fly in on an American helicopter and pick you up. That way we'll take the network away from the Yugoslavs and hand it over to the Americans. That would be a great victory for Albanian nationalism and the liberation of the country from communist oppression."

Hila's wheels were turning feverishly. He could see himself side by side with American generals and diplomats. What a coup! How much better than his present subservient position to Yugoslavs who were enemies, ready to attack and swallow up Albania as part of the Yugoslav Federation.

I objected. "First of all, will the Americans believe me? If yes, do they have helicopters capable of carrying several people? Finally, will they be willing to violate Albanian territorial integrity by landing a helicopter inside Albania and taking such risks? I think we are taking too much for granted. I for one am in favor of my original plan."

Martin and Hila were not. Martin, the poet, was flying high on the wings of his imagination. Hila, the gambler, could only see advantages if he switched sides. Besides, the melodrama suited his character. Then Deda spoke up.

"What do we do with Peter? We cannot take him out with us because of his family in Yugoslavia."

"That's no problem," Hila answered. "We won't tell Peter anything. The three of us will go into Albania. The night of the pickup, we will send him away. He can then return to Yugoslavia, to his family, and tell the authorities the truth that he had no prior knowledge of what had happened." So much for Peter.

"OK. Let's work out the details of the pickup." Martin pressed on and was in a hurry to flesh out his idea. "Where could Genc pick you up?"

"There is an island in the Drini River that would make an ideal landing place for a helicopter," said Hila. He drew a little map on a piece of paper and handed it to me. "When the American helicopter comes, we will light some fires and it can land to pick us up."

Martin and Deda nodded. It was clear that I had been outvoted. Now it was a matter of how best to implement the plan.

"Just a moment," I said. "Before we get to the island, there must be a way to let you know that things are proceeding according to plan and that the Americans are willing to pick you up. Let's set up a timetable. Say I make it to Austria late in May or early in June. I will need time to get to the right people. I will need to convince them that the plan is worth their effort and give them time to organize the means to get you out.

"I propose that we set up a two-stage plan. Can you, Hila and Deda, be somewhere in the mountains surrounding Shkodra, say, from July 10th to the 12th? An American plane will fly over the new tobacco-curing factory in Fushë Shtoj and drop some flares as if taking pictures. Will ten days give you enough time to be near the Drini island by July 22nd through the 24th?"

"Yes, that would be no problem," Hila replied.

"OK, if you see no flares in July, we will have another chance in August. You will be above the Fushë Shtoj from August 10th to the 12th and if you see the flares, you will be ready to light three fires on the island between August 22nd and 24th as soon as you hear the helicopter. Let's agree on three fires. Most people choose four fires when they want to light an area. Let's make it three. If you are caught and forced to go through with the plan, light two fires and the helicopter will know that you are in the hands of the police."

We agreed on how they would receive word that the Americans were ready to pick them up. We had sketched out the rough details on how the pickup would proceed. The rest was in the hands of the Americans. If the mission never came about or failed at some point, Hila and Deda would be on their own. There was little left to discuss.

"Genc, be careful," Hila said. "Much will depend on the success of your mission. Remember, you have our full confidence." He reached into his coin purse and from a hidden compartment drew a gold coin. "Here, take this coin, in case you need money."

The meeting broke up rather suddenly, considering the heady subject and the emotions generated during our short get-together. Hila and Deda left first. Hila was an adventurer with a clear vision of where he wanted to be, namely, on top of whatever structure or organization circumstances made available. Seeing himself aboard an American helicopter flying to Rome to climb a podium, applauded by American representatives and Albanian nationalist leaders, was heady stuff. I imagined such might be Hila's thoughts. I wondered what Deda was thinking. Deda had common sense and was not much of a dreamer.

After Hila and Deda left, I did not linger at Martin's. He, red-cheeked and with shiny eyes, was looking deep into an entrancing, inebriating future while I could only see the difficulties of the undertaking. If anything was left to discuss with him it would be to give substance to the plan he had sculpted with such determination.

The meeting at Martin's had lasted less than an hour but had upset my priorities from top to bottom. Obviously, my interest in learning Serbo-Croatian had slipped from first to near last place. Yet I could not afford to let the girl I was tutoring realize this during our weekly lessons when our roles switched and she became my teacher of Serbo-Croatian. She had already remarked once that I was studying less than in the past. I needed to come up with an excuse. One day when I was obviously falling short of her expectations, I told her that I suffered from a recurring ear infection and that I would seek medical treatment. No, I was not yet ready to go to the student clinic. I thanked her for her concern and promised I would study harder once I was well again. Phew, the first thing that had come to mind was the tactic I had used while I was getting ready to disappear from public view in Albania.

Clearly, the ball was now in my court. Martin, the mastermind, could lean back and let the "field operatives" take over. Hila and Deda would get ready for another trip to Albania, and I had to do my utmost to successfully carry out my part of the plan. Zef still had to be activated, as he would be the guide who would lead me to the stream separating Yugoslavia from Austria. Once in Austria, the rest was up to me.

The days came and went, dreamlike. I got in touch with Zef several times. Traveling near a weekend might be our best choice. There would be more travelers—more confusion on railroads, buses, and highways—and there would be fewer policemen on duty. Hence, we decided that I would take the midnight train in Belgrade on Thursday, June 4. Zef would join me the next morning around 6:00 a.m. at the railroad station in Zagreb and we would leave immediately for Bled. Thus, we would waste no time in Zagreb, raise no eyebrows among the Albanian students or any others who may have noticed my presence, and we would be on our way without fuss or delay.

Now Martin came up with an excellent idea. On his typewriter, he would forge two travel permits, one for Zef and one for me, allowing us to visit Bled and a nearby museum, the former home of a Slovene poet of renown. That the permits were typed rather than printed was no problem as most government offices used manual typewriters. The documents did need some official stamp to look reasonably authentic. I knew that to transfer official ink stamps was relatively easy. Martin procured two university documents with such stamps. We took two hard-boiled eggs, peeled them and rolled each egg first over the stamp on the real document. Now we had the stamp on the egg. Next, we rolled the egg over one of forged travel permits. We repeated the same procedure for the second permit, and *voilà,* we had two official-looking travel documents authorizing Zef and me to be in a border zone. We needed such documents because just beyond the Bled mountains was Austria! The travel documents could not stand a careful scrutiny, but with a little bit of luck we should be able to fool a casual observer.

The closer June 4 got, the more nervous I got. Furthermore, I could not afford to let anyone notice the tension within me. Most Albanian students at the Studentski Dom were good men. However, we knew of at least one informant among us. Besides, there was no need for anyone to know—other than Martin—what I was up to. I continued to attend university lectures I did not understand. I had my Serbo-Croatian lessons with the girl, but now with cotton in my left ear and telling her the same fake earache story I was telling my Albanian colleagues. I kept eating in the cafeteria and sleeping in my room, counting the days until June 4.

Time went by like molasses. By the evening of June 3, I had divided my meager possessions into two piles: things to take with me —and the rest. In addition to what I was going to wear, I was taking with me a pair of shoes, gray slacks, a summer jacket, and some socks and underwear. These I could fit into my knapsack without too much difficulty. The rest could stay in Yugoslavia, my gift to the regime or to whichever student realized first that I was gone for good. The thought of being captured almost never crossed my mind, and then not seriously. Was it a case of youthful optimism or was it awareness of the seriousness of my mission? The fact was, I did not worry about it. Furthermore, even if I were captured, no way would the authorities have suspicion about my plot with Hila. That's what counted.

Finally, it was June 4. We students were notified to present ourselves at the police station to receive the supplemental 9,000 dinars we received every three months. I went with mixed emotions, half ill at ease because of the police office I entered, yet with glee in my heart as they could not read my thoughts. An employee handed me the money with a glance that went straight through me and to the opposite wall, with an expression of a very important functionary throwing food on the ground without paying attention to the dog that would snap it up.

The money gave me an idea and prompted me to take another risk. That afternoon I went to Martin's. We all knew that the dinar was worth next to nothing in the West. Why did I not buy something with it, something of value I could resell in the West if I ever needed to? Martin agreed and off we went to a pawnshop on the Red Army Boulevard. Associating the name "Red Army" with the purpose of my side trip made me feel naughty.

We agreed that Martin would do all the talking. We entered the store and Martin explained to the storekeeper that I wanted to get married and was looking for two gold wedding bands, while I tried to look as innocent as I could. The shopkeeper disappeared. When he returned, he weighed the two gold bands and priced them at 3,000 dinars.

I was taken aback. "Martin, can't we find something more expensive?"

Martin had also failed to anticipate this turn of events. He could not think of a plausible objection, such as looking for heavier, more valuable rings. Instead, he translated my question verbatim.

"Does your friend want to buy wedding bands or gold?" was the shopkeeper's terse reply.

Martin looked at me. It was 4:00 p.m. If the shopkeeper notified the police and they identified me, if indeed they could, I would be on the train leaving Belgrade behind. The point was to make sure that the shopkeeper did not detain us needlessly and for us to cut bait as quickly as possible.

"Tell him gold."

Martin spoke his piece and the shopkeeper disappeared again. He reappeared promptly with a gold chain in his hand. He weighed it and said that the chain was worth 6,500 dinars. I paid and out we went with me clutching in my hand something that felt like a chain wrapped in tissue paper. We moved in a hurry. At a safe distance from the store, I stopped to see what I had bought with the Yugoslav government's money. For a moment, I stared at the chain, almost unable to focus my eyes.

Martin exclaimed, "What a beautiful gold chain with a medal of St. Anthony!"

"Martin, do you know in Padua I used to attend Mass at St. Anthony's Church? I tell you, I feel good all over."

Martin and I parted ways. He went home and I went to the Studentski Dom. I had packed my belongings in a knapsack. As Zef and I were going to pose as tourists, knapsacks would be less conspicuous than, say, briefcases. I checked my travel permit, the railroad ticket I had bought that morning, the gold coin Hila had given me—just in case—and St. Anthony's medal, which I put around my neck. Everything was ready. All I had to do was go to Martin's for dinner and stay there until it was time to catch the train for Zagreb. Nina, Martin's wife, was in on our plot and there was no need for further explanations.

I reached Martin's home and rang the doorbell. Martin opened the door with a smile and skillfully made my knapsack disappear. When he stepped aside, I saw Prenk Gruda and another Albanian sitting in the living room. I got myself a chair in a corner, out of the limelight. After the usual amenities, I clammed up as I was in no mood to make conversation.

Prenka being there was not a problem. He had a tendency to talk a lot, jumping from topic to topic. Today would be no exception. Most of what he said was against the Yugoslavs. They were not so different from the Albanian communists; besides, they had always wanted to take over Albania, all of it if possible—the northern and eastern portion only, if the first option was beyond their reach. The money they paid us students was insufficient; also, that he, Prenka, had delivered several memoranda to the American embassy to keep them fully informed about the Albanian question. Score one for Albania! As I listened to Prenka, I could not help thinking that he was a member of the Albanian Political Refugee Council set up by the Yugoslavs.

I must admit my mind was wandering hither and yonder when I heard Prenka say that he was planning to escape from Yugoslavia. All of a sudden, he had my full attention. Was he trying to tell me that he knew about my plans? There was no way unless Hila or Deda had squealed, and that was unlikely. Perhaps Prenka suspected me personally of wanting to escape. I decided to keep my mouth shut. If he wanted to carry the subject any further, it was up to him. It did not take long and Prenka went on to the next burning topic and lost my interest for good.

Well, time went by, and finally Prenka and his companion decided it was time to go. Nina and Martin saw them to the door. At last, we were alone.

Nina served dinner. Besides having classical features and being highly intelligent, she was also a good cook. We had a good time, and before we knew it, it was time for me to leave for the railroad station. We hugged and wished each other well. I promised to let them know when Zef and I had crossed the border. I would send a postcard to an Albanian student who was the police informant among the Albanian students. I was sure the word would spread like wildfire and Martin would certainly hear about it. One more hug, with the knapsack on my back, and I was out on the poorly lit street.

I turned toward the streetcar stop when I heard someone walking very fast behind me. Instead of running, I hid in the entrance of a tall building. It was Martin, who was trying to catch up with me.

I stepped into the street. "Martin, what's the matter?"

"Here, I want to give you this picture of Nina and me."

Before I could reply, he pressed the photograph into my hands and ran back home. Dear, impulsive Martin. If they found the picture on me, they would immediately suspect him of having been involved with my escape. I stuffed the picture into my knapsack and hurried toward the streetcar. When I got to the railroad station, the train was already at the ramp. I climbed aboard and got myself a corner seat in a tourist compartment. One half-hour to go. I was exactly on schedule. I pretended to be reading while I kept an eye on my fellow passengers and on anyone who might be watching our compartment from the corridor. So far, I saw nobody or nothing suspicious looking.

"All aboard!"

It was midnight. A whistle blew, lots of hissing sounds from the engine, and the train began to roll. Before long, we were out of the railroad station, off the many intersecting railroad tracks, and beyond the reverberating noise reflected by nearby buildings. The train started gaining speed. The wheels were clattering with the rhythmic, relaxing beat of the rails of that time. Po-pom, po-pom...po-pom po-pom...My tiredness finally overcame the excitement of the day, and before I knew it, I was fast asleep. My stay in Belgrade had lasted from the end of February to the beginning of June. Not bad!

CHAPTER THIRTY-SEVEN

FREE AT LAST...

If the train did stop during the night, I never noticed. When I woke up, it was daylight. The passengers, including me, appeared rumpled, like after a night on the train. They all seemed to mind their own business and no one looked particularly suspect. I checked my pockets. Everything was in place: my money, the forged travel permit to Bled, and my knapsack with my spare clothes. The winter coat and other heavier garments I had left behind. I would either make it or I would get caught. In the first case, I would get new ones. Otherwise, I would chalk it up to the failed escape.

As I looked out the window, the weather was splendid. A clear blue sky and trees, meadows, and buildings luxuriated in sunshine. From the knapsack, I pulled out a sandwich that Nina had given me. It wasn't bad; I would have liked it even better if I had also had something warm to drink.

Now it was time to find out how long it would take to reach Zagreb. Judging by the map in the corridor, we should be in Zagreb in about half an hour. Next, how should I handle Zef? How could I assert my leadership without antagonizing him? Once Zef boarded the train, and when the opportunity arose, I would share with him the details of the plan regarding Hila, as Zef was not aware of the latest. Plus, I was the one who spoke German and English, and the leadership role would fall into my lap automatically once we crossed the border.

Finally, the train pulled into Zagreb and there, big as life, was Zef. Through the window, I motioned vigorously that he should come aboard. Zef kept shaking his head, indicating that I should get off the train. I grabbed my knapsack and walked to the door of the railroad car. Zef was smiling but firm.

"Get off the train. I have some business to attend to and we can take the next train."

Because he carried no briefcase or knapsack, I had no choice but to comply. "Now that you got me off the train, what's the big deal that you have to take care of before we leave?"

"I have not yet gotten my 9,000 dinars from the government and I don't intend to leave without the money." He looked determined with his chin thrust out. This was important to him. He was entitled to the money. It was a matter of fairness. I knew that when passion was involved, there was no room for logic.

"OK," I said, resigned. "Where do we go from here?"

"The offices don't open until nine o'clock. We have two or three hours on our hands."

I thought I could use the time to share the new plans with him. "Take me to a church," I said.

Zef had to be surprised. I was Muslim. Why would I want to go to church? I watched him closely but he hid his surprise well. We walked less than half an hour and there we were, in front of a small, very ornate church. We entered and I looked around as if I were interested in the church as such. When we reached the altar, I stopped.

"Zef, I ask you to give me your word of honor as an Albanian and to swear as a Catholic on this altar that you will follow my instructions to the letter. Our escape is but the beginning of a broader mission. I will share with you all I know. If one of us is wounded or killed at the border, the other will abandon him for the sake of the mission. I will not hesitate to leave you if circumstances demand it. I expect you to do the same. Do I have your word and your oath?"

I was not sure how Zef would react. After all, we knew each other very little. Would what I told him sound farfetched, even melodramatic?

Zef looked at me. "You have my word of honor and my oath as a Catholic."

I was relieved. Thank you, Patron Saint of the Church. Zef could not know how close I felt to the Catholic Church, but that could wait. Now I had to tell him about the plan.

"Let's go where we can talk without being overheard."

"I know just the place," Zef answered, "but we need to take a streetcar."

We got on a streetcar and traveled quite a while in silence. I noticed that we were moving away from the densely inhabited area. When we got off, we found ourselves at the entrance to a cemetery. According to Zef, Zagreb's main cemetery was quite famous. There were many crypts and sculptures in honor of famous people who lay buried here.

Zef was right. The cemetery was everything he had said and then some. The large area occupied by the cemetery was such that we were sure to find a safe corner where we could talk freely. We meandered from section to section until we found one where the headstones were the right height and the field of vision wide open in all directions, affording us both safety and privacy.

Just in case someone had followed us and had a parabolic mirror, before we spoke, we turned toward a headstone, bent forward, and spoke our piece.

I explained our plan as best I could. I broke it down into sections. First, Hila and Deda needed to know whether the Americans had accepted our plan. Hence, they would be near Fusha Shtojit on July 10–12. If no American plane flew overhead and dropped flares the first time, they were to return to the same location on August 10–12. If no American plane dropped flares over the factory during either period, the plan was dead. However, if they saw the flares, they had ten days to go to an island in the Drini River and wait. Once they heard a helicopter overhead, they were to light three fires on the island to mark the landing area. If they were in the hands of the police, they would light only two to warn the pilot.

After I was done, I asked Zef to repeat what he had heard from me. Zef had paid attention. He repeated everything accurately and in detail, dates and all. Now he understood why I had insisted that one of us must reach the West even if it meant abandoning the other.

I felt relieved and encouraged by his prompt acceptance of the plan. I shared with him my misgivings about the Americans buying into the plan, but assured him that I intended to do my utmost to carry it to completion.

We decided to drift toward the exit, looking around and stopping to comment about one or the other memorial. To the casual observer, we were sightseers, a role we would play with abandon over the next couple of days.

"Zef, where do we go now?" I was getting sleepy.

"Let's take the streetcar and I will drop you off at the university library. The UDBA offices are not far from there. I should not be long. Then I will take you to my room where you can take a nice, long nap."

That sounded good to me.

We took the streetcar to the university library. Zef helped me pick a book or two, put me at a roomy table, nodded with a smile, and disappeared.

Now I was on my own and quite uncomfortable. What if someone spoke to me? Would I feed him the story about going to Bled? As finals were approaching, that story would raise some eyebrows, probably followed by focused questions that we could ill afford. To make matters worse, anytime I tried to read the book before me, the individual letters and words would start dancing before my eyes and I would nod off. I finally gave in and fell soundly asleep. An inner voice whispered to me that many students fell asleep out of boredom or tiredness when reading their textbooks. So I said to myself, *Don't worry, just don't sleep too long.*

I woke up with a jolt and glanced at my watch. I had slept about a quarter of an hour. Thank God, no one had challenged me and now I should last until Zef's return. Speaking of Zef, what was taking him so long? The minute hand on my watch advanced slowly, too slowly for my taste. Zef was nowhere in sight. He and his 9,000 dinars; he had to know dinars were of no value outside Yugoslavia. Why did he waste our time?

Finally, he showed up with a sheepish grin on his face. I stood up and together we walked out of the library.

"Did you get the money?"

"No, the money has not reached the office yet. The clerk said I should come back in a couple of hours."

"And I bet that's exactly what you intend to do."

"You are darned right. I will not leave my money in Yugoslav hands."

"OK, do what you think is best. By the way, when is the next train to Bled?"

"First let me get my money, then we will look at the train schedule."

Zef had made his point. He would return to the UDBA office shortly before noon and try his luck again. The way things were shaping up, I could not see us leaving in the afternoon and reaching Bled at night and either renting a room, and thus exposing ourselves, or sleeping in the open and running the risk of being discovered. One way or another, we would leave for Bled the next day, probably on the same train that had brought me to Zagreb.

Well, Zef went to get his money around noon and was told to return in the afternoon. By now, I was so sleepy that I asked Zef to take me to his room and to forget lunch, at least as far as I was concerned.

That's what we did. Zef took me to the Studentski Dom and I crawled into his bed. I must have gone out like a light. Sometime later—it turned out to be about four hours later—I began hearing Albanian voices amid dreams that kept racing through my tired mind. Gradually, my survival instinct began to take over. I began listening to the dialogue while pretending I was still asleep.

"Why is this bum here?" someone asked.

"As far as I know," I heard Zef's voice answering, "he wants to transfer here from the University of Belgrade."

"Having made a pigpen of the university in Belgrade, now they want to do the same thing here, these bums."

Who was the one speaking with such authority and self-assurance about "the bums" I seemed to personify? I decided to stretch and give signs of waking up. I opened my eyes and there stood Mustafa Bushati, whom I had known from way back in Shkodra.

"Genc, how are you?" he said, all smiles.

I sat up and rubbed my eyes. "Mustafa, what a pleasure to see you. How have you been?"

We shook hands and everything was peaches and cream. Thanks to Zef, now I knew why I had come to Zagreb. It was a good enough reason and I decided to use it if I had to.

Zef's trip to the UDBA in the afternoon was as successful as his three previous trips, except that by now he was ready to leave for Bled without his 9,000 dinars.

We spent the afternoon with various Albanian students and split off at dinnertime. We ate a simple meal in a little restaurant. I had enough money left from my 9,000 dinars to pay the restaurant, courtesy of the UDBA. We also bought bread, cheese, sausage, and onions for the next day. It was too early in the season for fruit.

That evening, I met Zef's roommate. Zef had never met anyone like him and wanted him to talk about his peculiarities. He was Dutch, tall, skinny, and otherwise nondescript. His claim to fame was that he preferred boys to girls. Also, he was always glad to procure boyfriends for his sister. This was so far removed from Zef's world that he had to try not to break out in loud laughter as he listened to a story he had heard before. I was less impressed and anything but amused.

"Zef, we better go to bed early, because we want to get up early tomorrow morning," I said in fluent Serbian, as I had been rehearsing these words while the Dutch student was dwelling on his lifestyle.

We said goodnight, climbed into bed and turned off the light. I fell immediately asleep and was lost to the world until I heard Zef's alarm in the morning. Zef had already washed up and shaved. I hurried also because I preferred not to have to speak to Zef's roommate. The fewer explanations we had to give, the better for us.

We hurried to the streetcar and were at the railroad station by six o'clock. If Zef had joined me on the train the day before, I had planned to buy the tickets to Bled aboard the train. That morning, we bought them at the ticket counter and approached the ramp from where our train would leave. Both of us had a knapsack with our belongings plus the food we had bought the night before. It was obvious that we were traveling light. That fit our image of students as well as our official intent of wanting to visit some Slovene poet's home/museum and then return to our homes in Zagreb and Belgrade, respectively. I sported a very simple Kodak camera that, in our opinion, added to our image as tourists, while Zef carried a mandolin.

As Zef had traveled this route before, he was the leader. We got off at Bled. The morning was sunny but cool. We walked downhill along a road that led to the center. The morning mist was just lifting off the lake and the scenery was breathtaking. On the other side of the lake, atop a steep hill, was a rugged, well-preserved castle. To our left and far away across the lake was a white church on a small island. Struck by the sun, it was like a glittering diamond in a setting of precious sapphires. Before us the lake, calm and mirrorlike, reflected all the beauty surrounding it. For a brief moment, Zef and I forgot that we were there under false pretense, and let the beauty of God's creation sink deep into our souls.

Along the lakeshore were some buildings that looked like hotels. We avoided those and chose a little bench along the lake where we had breakfast.

We had to whittle away the morning because our plan called for lunch at a village near the poet's museum, an afternoon departure toward the museum, and then a sharp turn north toward the border. We would time ourselves so we would reach the border area in darkness and spend a few hours looking for border patrols. Once we had their schedule down pat, we would cross the brook and enter Austrian territory. At least, that's the way I saw it.

In the beginning, everything went according to plan. In Bled, we took a boat ride that carried us to the church on the little island. Architecturally, it reminded me of Austrian village churches. It was relatively small, stern on the outside, dark on the inside, with impressive paintings and sculptures. The caliber of the artists whose works adorned the church was impressive. The island was small; the ride in the small wooden boat could have been relaxing were it not for our particular state of mind that prompted us to look beyond the immediate to what we had planned for that afternoon and night. Anyhow, the boat trip took up quite some time. Upon our return, we meandered around town and finally boarded the bus that would take us to the village that Zef had picked as our point of departure for the border.

As we reached the village, Zef marched toward a rustic restaurant. There was a menu posted at the entrance. I did not quite understand what it said but the prices were within our means, and that was most important as we wanted no trouble. The dining room was on the second floor. There was a table laid out with food, intended probably for foreign tourists who could order just by pointing without any need to speak with the waiter. When the waiter came, I pointed at something that looked like a wienerschnitzel. Zef ordered the same. Some time went by and I felt that the delay was justified because a wienerschnitzel had to be made fresh to be any good. Finally, the food came. I let it cool off a bit and then bit heartily into my wiener-schnitzel. It turned out to be a piece of gut coated with breadcrumbs. It was a letdown, of course, but I was hungry and wanted absolutely no trouble with the waiter or with anybody else, for that matter.

Zef was less prepared to sacrifice his taste buds. He pushed his plate away and made it very clear that he did not intend to finish his meal. Whatever I said to him was to no avail. Zef was not going to eat, and that was that.

I was still trying to change his mind when a bus pulled up in front of our restaurant and a number of teenagers got off. Zef glanced at them and shouted in my direction, "Those were my students!" and he took off to greet them.

I waited a minute or two and rose to follow him. Two men in the doorway stopped me. They were tall, had dour expressions, and wore dark leather coats down to their ankles. They were obviously UDBA, state security.

"Did you come with this bus?"

"No."

They lost interest in me and moved to a table near a window.

Meanwhile, a bunch of students surrounded Zef. They were yelling excitedly in Albanian, happy to have run unexpectedly into their former teacher. Zef started to play his mandolin and they broke out in song. It was a heartwarming picture, or would have been, were it not for the shadow the two men in the long leather coats were casting on our plans.

Zef, too, was not as calm as he appeared. His students had switched to another song while Zef was still strumming the same one on his mandolin. By the time I reached Zef to tell him to either change the song or stop playing, his students were getting on the bus. Zef pressed his mandolin into the hands of a student.

"Teacher, I cannot accept your mandolin!"

"No, no, just carry it. You like to play it. Play it during the trip to Bled. I too will get on the bus with you and when we get there, you can return the mandolin to me."

While Zef was struggling to get these words out without his voice cracking, we both stood near the rear door of the bus while the students were climbing aboard. We kept stepping aside to make room for the students. Meanwhile, the two security men entered the bus through the front entrance. We helped the last student aboard. The bus closed its doors and left without us. We wasted no time and marched off in the general direction of the museum.

We had walked a few minutes when Zef said, "Time has come to change direction away from the poet's museum." Now things were getting serious.

"Zef, from now on, we have no legitimate excuse for being here. First, we have to destroy the travel permits Martin forged for us."

I pulled mine out of the wallet, ripped it to pieces, and hid it under a stone. Zef did the same.

"Now show me. Where is the border?"

Zef looked toward a tall mountain towering above the foothills.

"I think the border runs along the top of this mountain, the Stol."

"What do you mean 'I think'? Where is the brook that separates Yugoslavia from Austria?"

"No, no, you got it all wrong. See the nearest foothill?"

"Yes."

"Well, the brook runs between that foothill and the next."

"Wait a minute. Father Daniel in Prishtina told me that the brook was the border with Austria and that you had reached the brook during your first trip here."

"Oh no, Father Daniel was wrong. When I tried to escape with Lin Delia, we came as far as this brook. When Lin inquired how far it was to the border and I showed him the top of the mountain, he seemed taken aback. All of a sudden, he cried out. He had twisted his ankle. He began limping and whining that it hurt so much when he put any weight on that foot. His complaints did not stop until I said that we could not proceed like this. I could not see crossing the border all by myself. Instead, we turned around and took the train back to Zagreb. A miracle occurred that day. As soon as we began backtracking, his complaints stopped and so did his limping."

Zef was done speaking. He looked at me with a blank expression. Days later in Austria, he confessed that he had worried at that point that I too would turn back as he and Lin had done the previous time.

I had to do some quick thinking. Going back would put an end to our whole mission and was out of the question. From here on, Zef would no longer be of any help in getting us to the border, but he would be useful in case I did not make it. He was intelligent and cooperative. Clearly, we had to continue our efforts to reach Austria.

"Zef, we will have to take a good look at the mountain before we decide how to attack it."

The mountain towering above us differed from the rest because of its timberline and two humps at the top. From a distance, we could see a path that cut diagonally from left to right as it climbed toward the pass between the two humps. Having surveyed the mountain, I spoke again.

"We will need to reach the timberline before daybreak and spend the day hidden in the bushes. With luck, we will see the Yugoslav patrols and figure out their path as well as the frequency with which they cover the ground between the two humps, that is, between their respective border patrol stations. At that point, we will finalize our plans. Let's go."

It took us less than half an hour to reach the brook between the foothills. It was not even six feet wide as it gurgled its way downhill. We jumped across the brook and started climbing the next foothill. Near the top, Zef spoke up. "I'm hungry."

We had been walking less than an hour and had many more to go. Besides, what little food we carried would provide us with two modest meals. This was no time to splurge.

"OK, let's sit down and you eat something. I'm not hungry."

We sat down amid luscious vegetation, surrounded by tall trees silhouetted against a verdant backdrop. Everything gave off that marvelous smell of healthy green plants. Nothing stirred and one had the impression that, if we stayed here forever, we would be perfectly safe. Of course, we knew better than that.

Zef finished his sandwich with sausage and spoke up again. "Now I am thirsty."

"I am afraid I cannot help you."

"We have some juicy onions," he replied.

"They will make your thirst worse."

"I don't think so." He peeled off the outer layers of an onion and sank his teeth into it. Even though he must have been very thirsty, it took him but a moment to spit out his mouthful of onion. I knew it would be best if I said nothing. There was one detail, however, I had to bring to his attention.

"Zef, pick up the sausage skins and onion peels and bury them under a stone. And please, follow this practice as long as we are on Yugoslav soil."

He did as he was told and no more was said at this point.

We continued to climb, zigzagging up another foothill. I stopped. At some distance, I could see a small shack, maybe four feet high, four feet wide, and six feet long. I could not make out anybody moving outside, however, someone or animals could be inside. I decided to look, carefully of course. The shack was empty. We crawled inside and I decided that we had better sleep there for a couple of hours and then proceed as far as we could.

For whatever reason, we could not fall asleep. Out we went and started climbing once more. We were alert, but strangely enough, without a sense of danger, except for one minor incident. Zef, who was walking behind me, veered off to the left along a small footpath. He followed the path for about 100 feet and saw that the path ended abruptly at the foot of a tall tree. Halfway up the tree, there was a lookout platform, probably for the border guards. When I turned around looking for Zef, I saw him, his mouth agape, with his nose pointed skyward toward the platform. Fortunately, the platform was unoccupied. Phew!

It got dark. The night was cool and very pleasant. We could see well because of the brilliant moon overhead. We kept climbing, following a zigzag path until we reached the timberline at dawn. Now we must rest until dusk. As luck had it, I recognized some bushes that domestic animals would not eat. This was one survival lesson Peter Qafa had taught me in the Albanian mountains. We cut some branches and made a thicket that would hide us from casual observers. For the time being, this was good enough and Zef and I lay down.

As daylight broke, we had a chance to see the surrounding area more clearly. We already knew that we were at the edge of the timberline that meandered up and down to our right and our left. The sky was partly sunny with small good weather clouds. As the sun rose higher in the sky, we could see the deep, healthy green of the vegetation all around us as well as the blue summer sky above. It was a pretty sight and I let it sink in. Somehow, I was filled with a sense of awe. We couldn't be far from the border. We had not seen a human being since we left the valley and that seemed way back in time. I had the sense as if a magic crystal bubble surrounded us that let us look out but rendered us invisible to the rest of the world. It was a wonderful feeling.

That was fine but I could not afford to lose my sense of reality.

"Zef, now let's get some sleep. Chances are we'll be up all night, first observing the border patrols and then cutting to the top and beyond, once we know their routine." I put my knapsack under my head and closed my eyes. What seemed like just a few minutes later, Zef spoke up.

"Genc, let's talk."

"Zef, we have nothing to talk about. We need the rest and I, at least, am going to sleep. So don't talk to me again until dusk."

Little time went by and there was Zef again: "Genc, let's read *Lahuta e Malcise*." This was a work by an Albanian Franciscan beloved by many and an important work in Albanian twentieth-century literature.

I barked in return, "Zef, we had that book in Dad's library and I never touched it. Do you understand? I never touched it, and now you want me to read this book? If you wake me up again I'll give you a punch in the mouth you won't forget for a long time." I lay back to enjoy some well-deserved rest, or so I thought.

"Genc, some sheep are coming our way."

I could hear bells, some bleating, and a man's voice, probably the shepherd's. We could not move at this point. The fact that he was permitted to graze his animals this close to the border marked him as someone trusted by the border guards. That was not a good sign. The animals were coming closer and we could hear them now ripping off grass and pulling leaves off bushes. Zef and I froze. What if the shepherd found us? The minutes dripped away slowly, like molasses. Finally the animals started moving away and Zef and I looked at each other as we began breathing again. That was close. Clearly, Peter's lesson of botany half a year ago had saved us. Bless him. Also crucial was the fact that the shepherd had no dog or else we would have been in trouble. Thank God, our crystal bubble was still intact and working!

At about 5:00 p.m., the weather started changing. All of a sudden, we were surrounded by fog so dense that we could see no more than about 50 feet in any direction. The rest was dense, whitish-gray soup, impenetrable to the eye, both comforting and tempting. Comforting in the sense that shepherds would gather their flocks and rush homeward. Also, that it would protect us from roving eyes. On the other hand, it seemed to beckon to us to move out of our leafy hiding place and climb in daylight the rest of the way to the border.

Zef and I discussed the alternatives. We could stay, wait for nightfall, and then complete our climb. However, if the fog continued, we might have to climb in both fog and darkness. That was an unattractive perspective. It was also essential that we hit the low point between the two peaks, as they were likely to have lookouts covering the border. We decided to move on, hoping and praying that the fog would not lift suddenly and leave us exposed.

We started climbing under the protective fog cover. We kept focusing on where we would step next and listened intently for any threatening noises. We reached the ridge in about an hour. The top was above the fog. From the ridge, we witnessed a spectacular sunset, as we looked north, deep into Austrian territory. We felt so good and full of energy that we could have started our descent immediately, were it not for a glistening layer of ice that covered the northern, Austrian face of the mountain. We were about 7,342 feet above sea level. We realized what had happened. The Yugoslav side of the mountain faced south and the sun had melted the snow and ice, watering the rich vegetation we had encountered. The Austrian side faced north. The sun had warmed the northern slope during the day and had melted the surface snow that had frozen during the night, creating the sheet of ice we saw as darkness fell. We decided to climb down the northern slope as far as we could. We covered some ground, but when we started sliding dangerously on the ice, we realized we had no choice but to spend the night on the Austrian slope but within reach of the Yugoslav border guards.

Between the excitement and the cold, we stayed awake all night. Besides, falling asleep on a slippery, icy slope would have entailed the risk of sliding downhill, and more likely than not, being smashed against a rock or falling off a cliff. Zef and I sat up all night hunched down with our hands under our armpits, trying to keep warm. The lights in Austria were coming on in clusters, forming glittering islands that seemed to mimic the stars in the sky. Some clusters were rather small while others must have been a part of larger communities, perhaps of cities. The latter stayed bright and shiny until late into the night. I tried to pin names on these islands of light and decided that Klagenfurt and Villach were probably the two closer ones. There was one far away. Could it be Graz? Since there was no one to contradict me and I had spent years of my childhood in Graz, I felt that with Graz in sight I was almost home.

Zef and I did not speak all night, each being lost in thought. At daybreak, we did not see any details in the valley because of ground fog. There was, however enough light for us to continue our descent. Zef had shoes with rubber soles that slipped dangerously on the coarse icy surface. I started kicking the surface to make steps Zef could use on our downward trip. Unfortunately, I was kicking so energetically with my left foot that the shoe came off and slipped merrily down before it came to rest on a little plateau about 50 feet below. Now I did something really stupid. I continued to kick the slippery surface with my bare left foot without thinking what I was doing to my toes. I soon gave up, not because of any pain but because I was not making much of a mark on the hard surface.

By now, it was almost daylight and the fog in the valley was dissipating. Way down, we could see a rather massive two-story building that stood all by itself. It was too large to be a farmhouse and without stables, granaries, or tilled soil nearby. Suddenly, we saw two people emerging and walking away at a brisk pace with a German shepherd trotting ahead. Here was our chance. Zef and I began to yell.

"*Hilfe! Hilfe!*"

The two men stopped and began to move in our direction. We were delighted at the prospect of this unexpected help. Then the men slowed down and seemed to hesitate. Finally, they turned back toward the valley. We again started crying for help. They stopped, and this time they seemed to have made up their minds. They started climbing toward us and did not stop until they were about 100 feet below us.

"*Hände hoch!*" (Hands up!), one of them yelled. We complied promptly. The exchange was in German but I will report it in English.

"Do you have any weapons?"

"No."

"Do you carry knives?"

"I have a pocket knife."

"Who are you?"

"Two Albanian college students escaping from Yugoslavia."

That seemed to convince them. They had steel cleats on their shoes that gave them a good foothold on the icy surface. Within minutes, they were at our side. They secured ropes around our chests below the armpits and lowered us gradually down to where my left shoe had been resting. I put it back on, and with the help of our rescuers, we got to the foot of the mountain where we could proceed under our own power. I had to sit down. I was feeling strong chest pains, like in the Albanian mountains when I had walked barefoot on snow and ice. At that time, I saw no way out and had considered committing suicide. Here I was not worried.

I told the men to go ahead with Zef. I would rest a while and then I would join them at the rather large building we had seen when Zef and I were about three quarters up the mountain. They nodded and took Zef with them.

I found myself alone. Under communism, being alone was the exception. Most of the waking hours you were with people or surrounded by them, always watchful, often being watched. I began to relax. I sat down, waiting for the pain to stop. Eventually it ebbed away without my having noticed. For the first time in years, I felt free, as if I had wings. I stood up, there at the foot of the mountain, to my full height. I felt the warm sun flooding me with a sense of well-being that was new to me.

Then a strange, almost bizarre thought struck me. I looked at the mountain and asked myself, "Was communism a reality or just a bad dream, a long nightmare? Could its poisonous tendrils lie in ambush just beyond that mountaintop? What about my years behind the Iron Curtain? Were my memories of discrimination, suffering, and persecution real, memories of a long illness, or were they haunting images contrived by a troubled mind?"

This dreamlike state did not last long as reality took over. Communism lay behind us but its tentacles still held our families in its grip. Personally, I was moving within a new reality, one that would break the chains that had fettered my mind and life for so long. I was free, well almost, but I could not—would not—do anything that would compromise my ideals or jeopardize my family. What if the project of switching the Yugoslav network in Albania to the Americans failed and Tirana found out about it? In my mind, the project was so important that I was willing to risk my life to see it through. If I failed, I was willing to pay the price.

For now, I wanted to enjoy the present. I sat down, luxuriating in the sun. As I looked away from the mountain, I saw two teenage girls coming in my direction. They greeted me with an engaging smile, put their arms around my middle, and began walking me toward the refuge. They giggled and chattered away, unaware that I spoke German. They were cute and I hoped that I would see them again. As it turned out, that was not to be.

At the mountain refuge, I met Zef as well as our two male rescuers. After exchanging a few pleasantries, I asked them why they had first come toward us, then had changed course, and finally had come to our rescue. One of the men started to speak.

"My friend and I belong to a mountain rescue group. Four of us came to our mountain refuge to practice rescuing people stranded in the mountains. Because of the dense fog, we decided to call off the exercise and to return to town. We were to leave early this morning. Our two colleagues left first and we followed a little later. When we heard your call for help, we decided to investigate. Then we had second thoughts. Our two colleagues had left before us and were probably trying to fool us. Hence, we decided to turn homeward. When you began calling again, and there was urgency in your voices, we thought we would investigate, even if our friends were poking fun at us. When we reached you, we approached you with caution because Yugoslav border guards often call for help and then shoot anyone trying to lend a hand to the 'escapees.' Hence, we asked whether you were armed, and so on. As it turned out, we could help you two and for this we are glad."

Zef and I thanked them profusely but had no way of expressing our gratitude in a tangible way. An employee of the refuge took a picture of the four of us. Later, he gave each of us a copy that I still cherish. Then he directed Zef and me to the attic where there were several made-up beds for occupants like us.

When I took my left sock off, the left big toe was swollen, discolored, red and blue, and bloody all around the toenail. I realized my foolish behavior when, after losing my left shoe, I had kicked steps into the snow on the mountainside. Now it was too late.

We lay down to sleep, in freedom after so many years, while our loved ones in Albania would probably suffer because of our escape. I prayed with all my heart. I thanked God for my good fortune and entrusted my parents and my brother to the Lord. Then I fell asleep and rested for a few hours.

Zef was already awake when I opened my eyes. I don't recall whether the refuge staff had awakened us by ringing a bell or by some other signal. The fact is that when we got dressed and descended the steps, they were serving lunch in the dining room. Several persons sat around the table. They made room for Zef and me. Soon we had a steaming bowl of pea soup before us and slices of hearty bread within easy reach. I was delighted and started to eat with gusto. After all, we had not eaten since the preceding evening and had spent much energy trying to overcome the last obstacles between freedom and us.

A gentleman in his sixties sat at my left. He was good looking, dressed in a dark gray jacket made of heavy wool material, with green lapels and green piping along the seams of his jacket and his pockets. His pants were of the same dark gray material, also with green piping along the seams. He was interested in us, particularly when he heard that we were Albanians. He had been in Albania during World War I and was quite upset that the Albanians had not appreciated Austrian help as much as they should have. He had no specific complaints that would have made it easier for me to respond. I responded in generalities, saying that Albania had been occupied by a number of combatant armies, such as the French, the Italians, the Austrians, and irregulars from neighboring countries. These forces had pursued their own interests that often clashed with those of Albania. The gentleman said that Austria had built a narrow-gauge railroad and had not torn it up when the troops had retreated. I replied that the railroad might have served Austria's military needs but that it was neither built nor intended for the benefit of the local population. My answer did not satisfy him and he said so.

In truth, his remarks had a special meaning for me. In 1917, Dad had started his trip as a student to Vienna on the very railroad the gentleman was talking about. Despite the gentleman's personal chill toward me, the atmosphere around the table remained congenial.

While this conversation was going on, I had paid little attention to Zef. His bowl was still full of pea soup and he was munching on some dry bread. I looked at him, smiling, and said in Albanian, "Eat the soup and don't make trouble for us."

"I hate pea soup," he answered.

Having just gone through a lengthy discussion during which I had defended Albanians against charges of ingratitude, I was in no mood to have Zef refuse their soup and thus provide another example of thanklessness. They, the Austrians, had just saved our lives, had offered us a roof over our heads, and were sharing their food with us, and all we had to say was "I hate your pea soup!" Was that ungratefulness or what?

"Zef, eat or I'll dunk your face in that bowl of soup."

"I don't care, I cannot eat this soup."

I could tell that I had pushed him far enough and could go no further, So I changed the topic. I asked when we could contact the gendarmerie. My hosts smiled. Zef and I would stay at the refuge for a couple of days and then they would contact the authorities. There was no hurry and we had nothing to worry about.

"But don't you have to inform the authorities within 24 hours following the arrival of refugees?" I asked.

They replied, "This is Austria. Stop worrying." And with that, I laid my mind to rest.

CHAPTER THIRTY-EIGHT

ST. MARTIN

The next two days went by in a hurry. No more pea soup; instead, we had different kinds of meat, cabbage, potatoes, rice, noodles, fruit preserves, and sweets. We had fresh pork, smoked pork, and pork sausage. Zef was a finicky eater; thank God, he was no Muslim!

Life was good. We had shelter, good food, and friendly people all around us. Because of the frostbite on my left big toe, I walked very little outside the mountain refuge. What a pleasure it was for me to read Austrian and German newspapers and magazines, even if they were two days old or older. The kind of news they reported was different, their point of view far removed from the communist dogma that was forced down our throats for so many years. God bless Austria!

Finally, someone said we would leave that afternoon.

"Will you please inform the police station of our arrival?" I asked.

"Not to worry, we will hand you over to the gendarmes when we reach the first village. Before that, we will stop at a restaurant to transact some business. Then the owner, who has a jeep, will drive both of you to the gendarmerie."

The Austrians put together a light but sturdy stretcher and asked me to lie on it. Three of them, plus Zef, lifted me up and off we went, into the deep green yonder.

Zef started to grumble. "May the devil eat your bones," he hissed into my ear. "Why are you so heavy?"

"Shut up, Zef. The Austrians are doing it out of the kindness of their hearts. You, as an Albanian, owe it to me." I am sure my words made him feel much better.

It was not far to the restaurant. I climbed off my stretcher and both Zef and I got something to drink. Here, a surprise awaited us. The Austrians introduced us to a Slovenian refugee who had just crossed the border. He would join our group and we would ride together to the gendarmerie.

I did not like this development at all. The Slovenian was of average height, in his forties, slim but muscular, and rather tight-lipped. He was dressed like a farmer. He had rough hands and claimed he did not speak German. I could not help but wonder whether the Yugoslav authorities had sent him after us.

Soon the restaurant owner showed up, and to Zef's delight (no more stretcher carrying), we climbed into a jeep. The gendarmerie was just a few kilometers away. When we got there, the sergeant in charge received us. He was in his mid-forties, tall, overweight, with a uniform that was bursting at the seams. He looked at one of his gendarmes.

"Do you speak Slovenian?"

"No."

"Any Serbo-Croatian?"

The answer was again, "No."

"And how are we going to process these two Albanians?"

That's when I spoke up. "Sergeant, don't worry. I speak German and my friend and I can interpret for this Slovenian. But before we go any further, I would like to mention something that worries me. This man says he crossed the border this afternoon. This may be true. I am concerned, however, that the Yugoslavs may have sent him after us. We don't trust the Yugoslavs and would appreciate it if you would keep this in mind when you question him."

The sergeant looked greatly relieved now that communication with the three of us would not be a problem. I also made it a point to speak with an Austrian accent. This was easy for me, as I had spent ten years growing up in Austria. It also had a positive effect on the sergeant and that was in our favor.

"You realize that I must search you for weapons," replied the sergeant.

"Please go ahead, that's fine with us."

With Zef and me, he just went through the motions. He was much more thorough with our Slovenian "comrade," which pleased me as it confirmed that the sergeant had understood my concern.

He asked a few routine questions to establish our identity as well as details of our border crossing. When I told him our story, he shook his head.

"You came early in the season. Most escape attempts from Yugoslavia take place in the summer and fall of the year. At this time of the year, you could have followed the footpath above the timberline and could have walked into Austria without any difficulty, because the Yugoslav border guards have yet to take up their summer positions along the border."

Too bad we did not know that. It all made sense, since the icy descent on the north side of the Hochstuhl was enough to discourage anyone with half a brain. We, of course, did not know.

"Take the Slovene into the village overnight. You too take a room there as I am housing the two Albanians in your room," the sergeant said to his subaltern. "Tomorrow, we send them to Klagenfurt."

That evening Zef and I had a good time with the sergeant. He was interested in life behind the Iron Curtain and particularly in Albania. He offered us a decent meal and some wine. That evening, as we spoke with the sergeant, we had a chance to take a close look at him. He was chubby with a florid red nose and even redder cheeks. He walked in a way that was somewhere between strutting and waddling. Off the bat, he made a friendly impression. We knew from the way he handled our Slovenian co-traveler that he took his job seriously. Separating us from the Slovene gave us an added sense of security. On the other hand, Zef and I could have actually been in cahoots with the Slovene. In that case, the sergeant had a chance to size us up separately while his subordinate could do the same with the Slovene, assuming they found a common language. Zef and I agreed that the sergeant was a good and competent man.

By ten o'clock, we were ready to go to bed. The sergeant showed us to our room, wished us a good night, and so ended our first night in the hands of the Austrian authorities. I fell asleep almost immediately, even though we knew that tomorrow we would go to Klagenfurt. Each day, in fact any change, was a new page for us. Who knew what fate chose to write on it?

The following afternoon, a British military truck pulled up. Several armed British soldiers got off the truck and motioned to Zef and me to climb aboard. The Slovenian was nowhere in sight. We did as ordered and the soldiers sat themselves between the rear gate and us. They carefully lowered the tarp, thus blocking the view from where we sat, and off we went.

Austria in 1953 was divided into four zones occupied by the Americans, the British, the Russians, and the French. The fact that the British

picked us up meant that we were in the British zone. We traveled for almost an hour, bouncing at every pothole, and there were many. To our
great surprise, when the truck stopped, we found ourselves at the steps of a
building with barred windows. Judging by the uniformed police officer at
the entrance, this was probably a prison run by the Austrians.

We were ushered into a large room with a wooden floor. The floor-
boards were rough but spotless. The room had several large windows with
iron bars. The walls were white and much daylight streamed in. There was
a walled-off toilet affording adequate privacy. The beds were clean, with
fresh sheets and pillowcases, and quite adequate. Aside from the barred
windows, the room made a friendly impression. At least that's the way it
struck me, a graduate of Tirana's political prisons No. 1 and No. 2.

Later that afternoon Zef and I were taken to an office for the obligatory interrogation. There were about four police officers present and I did
not notice anyone with rank insignia. The questions were the usual ones:
name, place and date of birth, occupation, reason for escaping, etc. We
had answered such questions the night before and we had no reason to be
anything but truthful.

In my case, they wanted to know where I had learned German. That
was the opening I had been waiting for. I mentioned that, as a youngster,
I had spent ten years in Vienna and in Graz. I told them about the feelings
of traditional friendship Albanians felt toward Austria and Germany, and
added that during World War II, the German authorities and the German
troops in Albania had behaved in exemplary fashion.

Everything I said was true. After Italy's surrender to the Allies on September 8, 1943, Germany invaded Albania. Under Italian rule, Albania
was forced to join Italy in declaring war on the Allies. Now the German
authorities offered Albania a chance to withdraw from the war and declare
its neutrality. Germany needed access to its troops in Greece and would go
to any length to enforce it. If attacked, for each German killed, 40 hostages
from an area within 10 kilometers of the attack would be executed. That
was the standard German law of war. Left alone, the German forces would
treat Albania and the Albanians as friends. Germany was willing to supply goods such as drugs and other industrial products at market prices and
would pay a fair price for food and other goods purchased in Albania. It
turned out that the Germans were as good as their word.

The only exception occurred during the troop withdrawal, at the end of the German occupation. The German rear guard was Battalion 999, made up of convicts originally sentenced for major crimes. In jail, they were given a choice. They could stay in prison and suffer what they had coming to them, or they could join Battalion 999 and take their chances as permanent rearguards during the withdrawal in the Balkans. In Albania, they found a way to make a quick profit. Their technique was simple. They offered military goods to civilians for hard cash. As soon as the sale was transacted, they shot the buyer for possessing German military goods. Then they repossessed the goods and offered them to the next "customer."

The Austrian policemen liked what I had to say about the German occupation of Albania and the traditional friendship between Albanians and the German-speaking countries. Their body language said so and they did a friendly exchange of furtive glances among themselves.

"One of our colleagues here was a member of the führer's *Leibstandarte*," one of the policemen said with obvious pride as he pointed at a tall, dark-haired, muscular man who was standing at the back of the room.

The man came forward, somewhat embarrassed. I wanted to hear more from him. "What impression did you have of the führer? Was he easy to talk to? How did he treat you of the *Leibstandarte*?" I wanted to start with easy questions but could think of many more, depending on the man's answers.

"Actually, I have little to tell you. I was part of his bodyguard. Besides the spit and polish you would expect from such an outfit, we had no contact with Hitler except for seeing him on formal occasions."

That was that. Either the man had no information or was unwilling to talk. I am sure there must have been occasions when Hitler had talked with his bodyguards. There must have been some incidents, funny or otherwise, that must have taken place during this man's service with that top outfit. Obviously, he was not going to elaborate in response to my questions. Too bad; I would have liked to glean a few interesting details from him.

The gendarmes told us why we had to spend some time in jail. It was the penalty for crossing the Austrian border illegally. I don't know who had dreamed up that legal curlicue. Either we were entitled to political asylum and had no reason to be in jail, or we had broken the law and deserved proper punishment. After all, political asylum was the greatest reward they could give refugees. Who was I to quibble?

The real question was what came next. After a simple but tasty meal, Zef and I talked for a while, mostly about our plans and the uncertainty of the future, and then went to bed.

The next afternoon, a British jeep picked me up and took me to see a young lieutenant who probably worked for Her Majesty's military intelligence. He was in his early or mid-twenties, of average height, with light hair and skin. As I entered, he was seated behind a desk in his office and pointed at a chair across from his desk. There was an open file in front of him. He read from this file for a minute or so and then looked at me. He did this several times. I had the impression that every move of his was meant to put me off balance. Eventually, he spoke to me.

"Please, give me your name and your last address in Albania and in Yugoslavia." When I did so, he seemed to enter everything in the file in front of him.

"Thank you. Now tell me why you escaped from Albania and recently from Yugoslavia." I complied and again he took everything down.

"According to your narrative, all industry in Albania is in the hands of the state. What do you think should happen with such industries once the communist regime is overthrown?" I had given no thought to the problem he was raising. I gave him the first answer that came to mind.

"Pre-existing industries should of course be returned to their legitimate owners. Any industries established by the communists should be kept to provide competition for new industries that will be built after the liberation." He scribbled in his file: "Has vaguely socialist tendencies."

"Where did you learn English?"

"In prison, in Tirana," I replied, giving him whatever detail he asked for.

The interrogation continued for another ten minutes. Then he asked again, "Where did you learn English?" I repeated what I had told him previously.

He proceeded to ask me about some of my activities in Albania, and lo and behold, popped the same question one more time.

"Sorry, I missed some of the detail. Please tell me, where did you learn English?" It was time to stop this nonsense.

"In Tirana there is an institute for foreign languages. Colonel so-and-so is in charge. There are two sections. The English section has about eight students, the American section 14. Students are assigned to one or the other depending on their next assignment. I was part of the American section."

The lieutenant was scribbling furiously. He raised his head and encouraged me to go on.

"Lieutenant, twice I told you the truth—that I had learned English in jail by myself. The truth did not seem to satisfy you. I hope you are happy now that I made up an intriguing story that, however, falls short of the truth." He was obviously displeased.

"Tell me something about the health institutes that came under the jurisdiction of the city health department of Shkodra."

I started rattling them off but when I came to the Center for Hygiene, instead of pronouncing it correctly, I pronounced it "heegeen." After all, in Italian and Greek the first syllable of the word hygiene was pronounced like the "i" liver. In German it was pronounced like a "ü" as in "über." The lieutenant covered both his ears with his hands.

"Where did you learn that awful pronunciation? It is 'hygiene' of course."

"Fine, this is the end of our conversation in English. Find someone who speaks Albanian and English and then we will continue." I had had it.

Now the ball was in the lieutenant's court. He had to get things back on track. He pressed a button on his desk and a sergeant appeared.

"Please bring us some tea."

A few minutes later, the sergeant reappeared holding a tray with two cups, milk, and sugar. The sergeant turned the tray in a way that put one cup directly in front of me. I hesitated, wondering whether there was some drug in that cup. The lieutenant read my mind, took the cup nearer to me and offered me the other one.

"To me this seems like a double reverse. Thank you, Lieutenant, I don't drink tea."

The conversation came to a screeching halt. He called for the jeep and I returned to the Austrian jail where Zef and dinner awaited me. The lieutenant and I were both losers. He had fallen short of his intended goal and I had failed to make a good impression on the young officer.

Before we knew it, a brand-new day, full of hope and promise, was shining through our windows. We got up, washed, shaved, and were ready for whatever the day would bring. After all, we were free; well, almost free.

We had breakfast but practically no conversation with the guards. Somehow, the intimacy of the previous evening had receded under the glare of the new day. All they told us was that we would move to the Jesu-itenkaserne, to the Jesuit barracks, whatever that was.

We waited, but not for long. A vehicle pulled up. We said goodbye to our friendly guards, grabbed our modest belongings, and climbed aboard. After a ride through town, during which we craned our necks to see as much as we could, we stopped before an imposing building, several sto-ries high, that dated back to the Austro-Hungarian monarchy. The façade was gray with age and dust. It had style, the style of an aristocrat living in poverty. At the large entrance, a policeman awaited us. Some official papers changed hands. The policeman motioned with his head and Zef and I crossed the threshold into the Jesuitenkaserne. *Well, it is going to be "home" for a while,* I thought, and that was not all bad considering that my left foot was hurting quite a bit.

Zef and I climbed up the steps to the second floor and were assigned two beds. What belongings we had we could store under our beds, unfor-tunately within reach of everyone sleeping in the same room. Some might be interested in perusing what we had and perhaps in sharing or abscond-ing with "the goods," depending on the individual's personal preferences. Well, I had lived under worse conditions in jail in Albania and had sur-vived. Hence, I was not worried. Zef, I hoped, would learn to roll with the punches. The more I saw of him, the more I liked him. He turned out to be a gentleman, which was not surprising considering that Fr. Gjeçaj had put me in touch with him.

Soon after checking in, we met the police captain in charge of the Je-suitenkaserne. He was about 40 years old, tall, and bulging around the middle. He was shaped like a pear and walked leaning back a little. His kindness and simplicity shone through. Toward us, he was always consid-erate, even caring.

Again I stressed my Austrian accent that had served me so well once we crossed the Yugoslav border. He was glad that I spoke German and enough Serbo-Croatian to converse with other refugees and act as an inter-preter for them. He did not say so expressly, but it was obvious that Zef and I were on his favorite list. If there was food left after everyone had received their ration, the cooks would motion to Zef and me to come for seconds, ahead of the rest. I got preferential treatment because of my severe frost-bite and Zef, of course, was my helper.

The rest of the refugees consisted mostly of young Yugoslavs in search of a better life. Among them were a few college students awaiting transfer to a student refugee camp in St. Martin near Villach. According to what they told us, we too would go there before long.

The captain insisted that I be seen by an Austrian physician. I, of course, was all in favor of it, and soon a lady physician gave me a physical exam and looked at my left foot. She was in her early forties, of medium height, and quite attractive. There was, however, an undercurrent of resentment in her one could not miss. She found my blood pressure high for my age (140/90) and was not pleased with the way my left big toe looked. There may be a need to amputate it, she told me. As I would see her every day, she thought it was safe to wait a few days while keeping the foot under observation. Her wait-and-see approach paid off as the toe began to heal.

As we got to know each other better, our conversation began to cover ever more interesting subjects. One day I asked her why she seemed to be so resentful and against whom.

She replied quite frankly, "After a few years at the hospital, I was promoted to head the gynecology and obstetrics section. After the war, the Allies demoted me and assigned me to the Jesuitenkaserne. Do you find it hard to understand my resentment and anger? And what do I have to show for all those years of hard work? Now I take care of healthy young refugees."

"Permit me to ask you a question, Doctor, if you don't mind. Were you ever a member of the Nazi party?"

"Yes, I was but I never hurt anyone," she replied heatedly.

"Doctor, if you had been just a few miles to the south, if you had been in Yugoslavia, chances are you would not be alive." I decided that, for the moment, I should press no further.

Soon after I met the lady physician, I also met a cute woman in her twenties, an employee of the Austrian Red Cross. She was bubbly and easy to talk to. She also seemed to have the gift of keeping young men at arm's length without being unfriendly. My speaking German made for easy conversation.

"Is there something I can do for you?' she asked me. I couldn't think of anything and I said so.

"Would you not be more comfortable if you wore slippers instead of walking in your socks?" She had a point.

"I'll bring you some slippers this afternoon," she said. "We probably have some in our warehouse."

Well, I waited all afternoon and all morning the next day but she failed to show up. Now that she had planted slippers in my brain, all I could think of was slippers, even a pair of simple slippers with the top made of cotton and with leather soles. I was not asking for much, was I? But, no matter how hard I looked for her, she was nowhere in sight.

She came the following afternoon holding a cane and a pair of slippers in her hand. "I turned our warehouse upside down until I found a pair of fur-lined slippers your size. Please try them on."

I put them on. They fit like a pair of gloves. The poor girl! She truly must have looked high and low to find these elegant leather slippers.

"I don't know how to thank you. These slippers will keep my feet warm, and I am sure they will help my toe get well again."

She smiled a pretty, innocent smile. "Well, then this is goodbye. If you have any other needs I can help you with, please let me know." She pressed the cane into my hand and was gone before I could add anything. I never saw her again.

A few weeks later, something happened that brought her back into the picture, even if not in person. Uncle Edward had written from Rome while I was still in Yugoslavia and had included a personal check for ten dollars. The check was drawn on the Bank of the Vatican. I had not cashed it in Yugoslavia, as I was getting ready to escape and wanted no dinars. Now in Austria, I was able to wear shoes and walk with the help of a cane. I knew exactly what I was going to do with that money. I needed some underwear and a briefcase. I needed the latter as I was about to work on the Hila project and would have to carry papers with me.

So one beautiful, warm June afternoon, I put on my light blue summer jacket and light gray pants I had brought from Yugoslavia, put on my shoes that fit me again, grabbed my cane, and set out to find a bank. As the Jesuit-enkaserne was not far from the center of town, finding a bank should be no problem. Indeed, I was looking forward to taking a little walk, in freedom, in a nice clean town, and without need for a permit. I was moving with all deliberate speed, using my cane with flair, and taking in the street life pulsating all around me. The streets were clean, the traffic disciplined, and the pedestrians courteous toward me, as they may have thought I was a war veteran.

I spotted a bank in one of those imposing, massive buildings that seem to attract banks. I entered, limping with dignity, and walked to one of the many windows. A young man smiled and asked how he could help me.

"I would like to cash a check," I replied with self-assurance. Were checks not as good as cash, and particularly one from the Bank of the Vatican? He looked at the check and then, politely but firmly, asked me to come back in a week. I was thunderstruck.

"Why?" I asked, as my first impression of the nice young man began to change for the worse.

"This is a personal check and our bank must be sure that the check is covered."

"What do you mean 'covered'?" My voice was brimming with suspicion.

"You see," he said, "a person may have a number of checks. If he or she runs out of money, the individual could still write checks that would not be covered. This is why we have to write the Vatican Bank to confirm that the check is valid."

I was furious, mostly because he had exposed my ignorance *vis-à-vis* checks, but also because I would not be able to make my purchases as planned.

"Why would my uncle send me a bogus check?" I countered, and then added, "Could you resolve the question by cabling the Bank of the Vatican?"

"Yes, we could," he replied, "but it would cost about ten dollars."

I was hurt. I took the check back and started to leave.

"Wait a minute. Please give me the check and I will cash it for you," the teller said.

"If the check is valid, you should have cashed it when I first gave it to you. If it is questionable, then you should not cash it now." I said grimly and started to walk out again.

"Look. I am sure the check is good. I'll keep the check and pay you with my money. A week from now, when we have confirmation from the Vatican Bank, I'll cash it and pocket the money. After all, I can afford to lose the ten dollars better than you can."

I was deeply touched. "You know, you are the second person since I reached Austria that has been so kind to me."

"Who was the first one?"

I mentioned her name. "She works for the Austrian Red Cross at the Jesuitenkaserne. She is young, pretty, and very kind."

"I know her," he replied. "In fact, I know her well. She is my fiancée and we are planning to marry within the year."

His words touched me deeply.

"May the good Lord bless you both." I accepted the money he offered me and walked out of the bank trying to hold back my tears.

Now that I had all of $10 in Austrian currency in my pocket—and that was a lot of money for me—I could proceed with my purchases. First, I saw an elegant men's store. I entered and asked for underwear. They directed me to the right counter but the only underwear in my size was in a ribbed silver material. It was not too expensive but was not what I had in mind. Not wanting to waste time, I bought two pairs and walked out. I was luckier with buying a briefcase. The leather goods store had just what I wanted at a price I could afford. I got myself a nice leather briefcase in tan with inside dividers and a lock. Now I was ready for what I was planning.

Meanwhile, I kept seeing the lady physician. She had come to realize that I had friendly feelings toward Austrians and so she began to open up. One day she told me the following story in answer to my question about whether she had known about the concentration camps:

"During the war, I befriended the wife of a German police lieutenant. Once a week, she and I would meet at my place for tea and cookies. Her husband used to drop her off and pick her up again in the evening. She was a most beautiful woman, always elegantly dressed, always exquisitely bejeweled. One day I said so to the lieutenant, adding that I had never seen such beautiful custom jewelry as the one worn by his wife.

"He replied coldly, 'Her jewelry is not custom jewelry. It is real and if you knew how I got my hands on such jewels you would refuse to have tea with my wife.'

"Believe me, I was too scared to ask any questions. More importantly, I preferred not to know the answers."

One day, two German ex-soldiers in their late twenties joined the rest of us at the Jesuitenkaserne. They were quite dissimilar. One was short, slim, muscular, and intelligent. The other was tall, rather plump, sporting a perennial empty smile. It was obvious that the short one was the leader of this odd couple. With time, I got to know him rather well. He spoke well, in careful terms, and made a fairly good impression. I became suspicious when he told me that, after the war, he and his friend had signed up with the French Foreign Legion. I knew that many legionnaires were runaways from the law. From what were these two characters running away?

Like many Europeans, I belonged to those who did not hear about the Holocaust and the death camps until after the war. At this point, I was most interested in finding out as much information on the subject as I could and these two looked like a potential source.

"Tell me," I asked the shorter of the two one day, "is what we hear about these camps true? Is it true that people were gassed and others were worked to death?"

"You cannot believe all you hear and read," he replied. "They don't tell you, for instance, that such camps also had artistic groups and orchestras that performed on stage. The prisoners were well fed and treated with respect. In fact, male prisoners had access to women and were well provided for in this regard." He was calm and relaxed as he spoke.

"How do you know these things?" I asked him.

"I was there, in fact we both were there," he replied without hesitation.

"Tell me then, how were these women recruited? Did they volunteer for the job?"

He lost his composure. I sensed that he was reliving in his mind the scenes of how these unfortunate women were "recruited." He stood there for what seemed like a long time and failed to come up with an answer.

I had heard all I needed to hear. I turned away and left him standing there. A few days later, he and his friend disappeared from the Jesuitenkaserne. I never heard whether they were transported elsewhere or had disappeared on their own. I had lost interest in them.

One day, Zef and I heard the faint sounds of children singing festive church songs. We couldn't tell where the voices were coming from. Then we realized that they were getting stronger and seemed to come from the street in front of the Jesuitenkaserne. We rushed to the nearest window. We could see adults carrying religious statues on platforms. There was a throng of little girls in white bridal attire, and boys in white shirts, dark ties, and dark pants singing and marching behind the statues. It was the feast of Corpus Christi. Memories swept through my mind. My early youth in Austria, similar processions in Italy, and then the bleak years of communism where religion was depicted as evil, as the opiate of the people, to be purged at any cost and re-placed by communist dogma. Tears began to stream down my cheeks. Later, Zef would tell me that until then he had thought that my words of respect for and strong attraction to Catholicism were simply strategies to ingratiate myself with him. He believed me when he saw my reaction to the parade in honor of Corpus Christi in Klagenfurt that summer of 1953.

At another time, I was called to meet a visitor who had come to see me. I was happy to see Fejzi Domni, a friend from Tirana whom I had not seen since the summer of 1944. He was part of our group, a gentle, pleas-ant young man, and a graduate of Tirana High School. He was the first friend I met in the Free World. He told me that he had worked in America for some years to earn money for college. Now he was studying in Vienna, hoping to earn a medical degree. In Austria, medical school took five years to complete. What struck me was that all exams, covering every subject from the first to the fifth year, were given at the end of the last year. What an effort that had to be! We spent a few pleasant hours together and then Fejzi left for Vienna.

Let me add another episode that took place the day that we said good-bye to Fejzi in Tirana back in 1944. Germany had offered some college scholarships for students wanting to continue their education in Vienna. This was an excellent opportunity for young people to get away from the fratricidal war and live in relative normalcy by attending school, even though the war was coming closer and closer to Germany's borders. A bunch of us went to the Hotel Dajti where the students were getting on buses that would transport them to Vienna. There was Fejzi, smiling and hugging each of us one by one. To our surprise, there was another student whom I knew from Padua. He had started medical school with me.

Before finals, he had come to see me. As I have related in an earlier chapter, he asked me to take some exams on his behalf, but I refused.

That day in 1944, I spotted him among the departing students at the Hotel Dajti. He had dissuaded a cousin of his from applying for a scholar-ship "because of everyone's patriotic duty to fight for Albania," and now he was getting ready to climb aboard one of the buses. When his cousin, the one whom he had persuaded to remain in Albania, asked him why he was leaving, he lamely replied that his uncles were forcing him to go to school. Many years later, at Mustafa Kruja's funeral in Buffalo, he was preaching to the crowd of attendees about the evils of communism and how he had fought against them. I called him aside.

"If you keep lying through your teeth about your anti-communist stance during the civil war in my presence, I will challenge you and tell people the truth about you. I have not forgotten how you approached me in Padua and I remember vividly how you persuaded your cousin not to apply for a scholarship. In fact, at this point I suspect that you duped your cousin so you could get the last scholarship for Vienna." He blushed and his eyelids fluttered rapidly.

"I have no idea what you are talking about when you speak of Padua or of my cousin in Albania. I don't recall either incident."

"That may be so. Your memory is obviously no better than your ethics. All I am telling you is to stop portraying yourself as an anti-communist in my presence unless you want me to come after you with a vengeance." That shut him up.

Back to the Jesuitenkaserne. The day came when Zef, my dear friend and companion, left for St. Martin. I missed him—his sense of humor, his relaxed attitude, his uncomplicated instinctive understanding of human nature. I knew that eventually I too would transfer to St. Martin and we would be together again.

One day the mail delivered a letter from Fejzi Domni as well as a shoe-box full of cookies. In the letter he told me that his landlady had baked the cookies and that they were intended for Zef and me. This was a welcome gift. I liked cookies and there were plenty in the box. I promptly began to feast on my share. As the box had no divider, some of Zef's cookies would slip into my half and it became difficult to tell his from mine. Well, as long as they slipped into my half, it was not my fault. It was like a branch from a neighbor's apple tree hanging over my backyard. I could certainly pick apples from that branch without committing theft. Well, Zef's cookies kept straying and I kept eating them until, one day, there were so few left on his side that I was sure he would scold me for not finishing them off.

I told Zef what had happened when he came to visit me. I had not anticipated that he would get so mad. After all, I told myself, they were just cookies and Fejzi was my friend who had just met Zef. Well, any reasonable person could make a good case in my defense. I had to conclude that Zef got mad because of his misplaced sense of justice. Fortunately, the crisis did not last and I forgave him his strong reaction. My generosity toward him made me feel good!

One day I was taking my afternoon nap when someone tapped me on my shoulder. I opened my eyes and, to my surprise, I saw the police captain, who in hushed tones told me that a gentleman was here to see me. Half asleep, I got up and followed the captain to his office.

There stood a man, tall and neatly dressed, wearing half a smile. He spoke broken German with a strong British accent, as he asked the captain whether there was someone at the Jesuitenkaserne who spoke Albanian and either German or English. The captain looked nonplussed. Hadn't he and I conversed in German since I first arrived at the Jesuitenkaserne? He kept looking at me and at the Englishman, back and forth, and the longer the impasse lasted the more confused he was getting. The Englishman spoke again.

"A few weeks ago, the UN high commissioner for refugees and I visited a group of Albanian college students in Belgrade. To our surprise none of them spoke any other language except Albanian and Serbo-Croatian."

So, this was the secretary of the commissioner my friends had spoken about in Belgrade. I addressed him in English.

"Would you prefer that we converse in English or in German?"

"Why did you lie to us in Belgrade when you claimed you spoke no foreign language other than Serbo-Croatian?"

Here was that ugly word. According to him we had lied.

"By the way," I asked him, "who was the man who accompanied you during the visit?"

"Some chap from the Yugoslav Foreign Office, I believe."

"Well, sir, that was General Dushan Mugosha of the Ministry of Interior, a cofounder of the Albanian communist party, not some chap from the Yugoslav Foreign Office. The Albanian students had strict orders to avoid speaking directly with the foreign visitors. All of the Albanian students spoke at least one foreign language, such as Italian, French, English, or German. But they were told not to and were in no position to challenge General Mugosha's edict." The Englishman wanted to waste no more time.

"Captain, is there an office nearby where this gentleman and I can chat in peace?"

"Of course, please follow me."

The Englishman and I sat down in a simple office and the captain left.

He began, "What can you tell me about the way the Yugoslavs treat Albanian students and refugees who escape into Yugoslavia?"

I began to explain how the system worked. Albanian civilians were usually assigned to refugee camps and received a monthly financial subsidy from the government. Some worked as teachers, if they had the necessary qualifications. Generally, the Yugoslavs tried to isolate refugees with leadership qualities from the rest of refugees by recruiting the former to serve as infiltrators into Albania, by sending them to universities to continue their studies, or by some other means. College students were paid 3,000 dinars a month plus 9,000 dinars every three months since they had to pay for books, tuition, and room and board.

The Englishman seemed to be under time pressure. He looked at his watch repeatedly, and finally interrupted me.

"I see that you can provide us with much-needed information. Would you be willing to come to Vienna and meet with me at my office? Of course, we would pay your expenses."

He reached out and handed me his calling card. What stood out very clearly was that the office was located at *Stalinplatz No.3*.

"Excuse me, is your office in the Soviet zone?"

"Why, yes," he replied. "Rest assured, though, that the Soviets would not bother you at all."

"Sir, if you want to talk to me, you'd better come to see me in Klagenfurt in the British zone. I will not enter the Soviet zone under any circumstances."

He seemed surprised. We got up and shook hands. That was the last I saw of him.

A few days passed and the captain informed me that I would be transferred to the student refugee camp in St. Martin. My stay in Klagenfurt had been pleasant and useful because it gave my toe time to heal. Now I was ready for bigger and better things. My goodbyes were sweet and short. The captain was not in his office and I had formed no real friendships with refugees. I shook a few hands, exchanged a few good wishes, grabbed my knapsack, and walked out the front door of the Jesuitenkaserne. This chapter of my life was behind me. It was good while it lasted but it was over. Time had come to look forward again, and that was a good feeling. In Albania, I had been deprived of a future for too long. Here, in a foreign land, my future was returned to me. *Gloria in excelsis Deo.*

I walked to the railroad station with wings on my feet, or so it seemed to me. I needed my cane but I had no problem carrying my knapsack and my briefcase. I very much enjoyed the freedom to move around without need of a permit. The railroad station was not far and trains to Villach ran often. I bought a ticket, sat on a bench, and watched the world go by. The familiar Austrian accents, the popular costumes of *dirndl* and *lederhosen*, the respectful behavior coupled with a lack of fear the people displayed toward the authorities—everything contributed to my joyful sense of well-being.

Of course, even in Austria not everything was perfect. I remember the newspaper headline: *"Sprechen Sie Deutsch, Herr Doktor?"* (Doctor, Do You Speak German?) I remembered it because it dealt with an Albanian physician whose parents had moved to Austria when he was a toddler. He grew up and graduated from medical school in Austria. He had probably served in the German army and after the war had returned to Klagenfurt. Now he was being promoted. For some people, suddenly, he did not belong because he was not born in Austria! As I recall, the pettiness did not go any further. It was, a fly in the ointment, but only a little fly when one considers the heart-wrenching injustices routinely committed behind the Iron Curtain.

My train pulled into the station and I climbed aboard. We left on time and a short while later arrived in Villach. The walk from the railroad station to St. Martin was less than half an hour. To my right there was a large refugee camp. I could see men and women in groups, and children scampering around. The camp for college students was to my left. It was much smaller and consisted of a few wooden huts. At the center were the kitchen and the mess hall. To the right was the administration building, and to the left two student dorms.

I presented myself at the administration building. The two secretaries knew of my arrival. The atmosphere grew quite friendly when I replied to their questions in German. One of them rose to tell Mr. Foster, the Englishman in charge, that I had arrived.

When I entered his office, he was standing behind his desk. He was in his fifties, short and thin. His jacket hung from his skinny shoulders like from a coat hanger, and his pants seemed two sizes too large. He smiled a friendly smile and we shook hands. He motioned toward a chair and began explaining the camp rules to me. Breakfast was at 8:00 a.m. All students had to do manual labor to prepare them for what they might run into once they left for their overseas destinations. He knew about my frostbitten toe and told me that I was exempted from manual labor. He further said that the food was good and that the students could ask for seconds. Furthermore, if they got hungry during working hours, they could always drop in and the cook would prepare something for them. Curfew, even though not strictly enforced, was at 10:00 p.m.

It all sounded very good. I offered to work in the kitchen, as I did not want to shirk work. The fact that I spoke reasonably good English pleased him. As I had no more questions or comments, we both rose, shook hands, and I left. Now I could look for Zef.

I had wondered whether he held a grudge because of the cookies. Well, I need not have worried. Word of my arrival had spread and Zef was waiting outside the administration building. We hugged like brothers who had not seen each other in many a moon. It had not been that long but we had missed each other. Not much had happened since we had met last. Yet, like good friends, we had much to talk about. Zef introduced me to some Albanian and Yugoslav students. The conversation was simpler with the Yugoslavs because some had escaped in search of adventures while others were seeking a better future. The Albanians had all suffered political persecution and were strongly loyal to their political parties. One had to be careful lest one step on political land mines. We shared, of course, the strong political bond of anti-communism and nationalism that made it easy to put up a united front if we ever had a problem with the Yugoslav students. In fact, such a confrontation never came about.

While the camp rules said that the students would engage in manual labor, no one was doing any such work at this point. There were some administrative formalities that had to be done first and only then could the work force march, shovels and picks in hand, into the sunrise for a better and ever-so-glorious future. I didn't know about the Yugoslavs, but all Albanian refugees, Zef excepted, had been in forced labor in Albania. I was sure that the work expected of them in St. Martin would be a picnic, comparatively speaking.

A few weeks after my arrival, Prenk Gruda arrived with two companions. They told us details of their escape. Fortunately, everything had gone smoothly. Prenk also told me about the postcard I had sent to an Albanian student at the Studentski Dom in Belgrade announcing my safe arrival in Austria. The student had asked with indignation why I had sent the card to him and not someone else. The truth was that he was an informer for the Yugoslav secret service and my card would not put him at risk with his employer.

I was afraid that Prenk would chide me that when we met at Martin's the day of my escape I had kept mum about what I was about to do. Apparently, he had not realized that I left Belgrade that very night. He also told me that he and the young Serbian girl I was teaching German had gone to a number of ear, nose, and throat clinics trying to find me. Obviously, my ruse had worked.

In St. Martin, my work in the kitchen was not going too well. The cook was reasonable and accommodating. He let me do whatever I wanted, no more and no less. I cut vegetables, peeled potatoes, and I even cooked steaks for hungry (bored?) camp inmates as they drifted in around ten o'clock after an ample breakfast consumed just two hours earlier. There was only one thing wrong with being the cook's helper. The smell of food all day long ruined my appetite. As I would rather enjoy my food than cook it, I decided to let the cook know how I felt. As I said, he was a fine fellow. He let me resign without protest or regret, and I joined the others at their "*dolce far niente*" (sweet doing nothing) as we milled around within or outside our camp.

Zef and I went for walks and chatted about many things, most of them related to Albania. Zef was a fine young man. In Shkodra, he had gone to some anti-communist student meetings and had distributed anti-communist leaflets. When the authorities began arresting students, Zef hid first in a neighbor's home and then left for Yugoslavia with the help of infiltrators. In Yugoslavia, he had finished high school and then had worked as a teacher. He was a fervent Catholic, an Albanian nationalist, and an excellent young man. His dream was to return to Albania and to continue teaching.

In addition to expecting us to work, at the St. Martin camp they also provided us with food coupons. In view of the excellent meals we got three times a day, Zef and I decided to use the food coupons to buy some exquisite chocolate at a local grocery store. It was a fine store, well kept, with a number of teenage boys and girls serving as sales personnel. When we left the store, Zef turned to me.

"Did you see those boys and girls?"

"Yes, what about them?"

"They were all work. They did not flirt or fool around with each other. What beautiful young people!" When it came to girls, he was straightlaced and of high moral character.

He also had a sense of humor. He and I were walking outside the camp one day. At a certain point, Zef looked backwards.

"Albania needs such friends."

When I turned around, I saw that a beautiful German shepherd was following us. I broke out laughing and Zef chimed in with great cheer.

One day, word came that the next morning the students would go to work with picks and shovels. I, of course, was exempted. Prenk Gruda complained of an injury he had sustained some 20 years before and he too could stay home. The next morning, after a breakfast of hearty bread, bacon, and eggs, the students, including our Zef, marched off to work like the seven dwarfs. They crossed the road toward the large refugee camp and disappeared from sight since the other camp was below street level. Some retuned early. The Albanians, to a man, had refused to work under the supervision of an individual selected by Mr. Foster while the Yugoslavs had stood aside. It turned out that the supervisor was Russian and the Albanians flatly refused to work under him. Mr. Foster tried to pacify them by pointing out the man in question was a White Russian, not a Red Russian. As far as the Albanians were concerned, a Russian was a Russian. They had suffered abominably under the Russians and the very tone of his voice, his very accent, offended them deeply. One of the Albanians, Ndue Zef Ndoci, went so far as to threaten the Russian with a pick if the Albanians were forced to work for him.

Ndue Zef Ndoci had spent time in jail in Albania where he had been suspended from his wrists, without food or drink, for days and days. One day he made some gurgling sound that attracted the attention of the guard. The guard tried to pour water down the prisoner's throat but to no avail. The guard then removed the ramrod from his gun and pushed it down the prisoner's gullet. Having forced it open, the prisoner was able to swallow some of the water the guard was giving him. At this time, the Albanian government, and the security services in particular, were under Soviet supervision and direction. No wonder that Ndue Zef Ndoci would not work under a Russian—white, red, or any other color.

Meanwhile, I had some thinking to do. The time was coming for me to set in motion the Hila project. My first loyalty was, of course, to Albania and to Balli Kombëtar, the National Front, in whose ranks I had been active and had fought in Kosova. There was also a problem with Mr. Foster and the British, as we were in their zone. We did not quite trust them because we suspected that, as monarchists, they would favor King Zogu and his followers. I decided to tackle the two problems one at the time.

First, I would write a letter to a Balli Kombëtar leader to inform him that I had important information that I needed to discuss with someone in authority. Midhat Frasheri, the descendant of a most distinguished patriotic family, was the undisputed head and one of the founders of Balli Kombëtar. He also was of advanced age. Those around him were in their forties and fifties, and were distinguished professionals and fervent nationalists who had sacrificed their earthly goods, and were ready to give their lives for Albania. Some had carried arms against the Turks and against King Zogu. The younger ones had fought the Italians and the Germans. Some had fought the enemy with their ideas, others with their arms. Some had done both.

Compared to the founders of Balli Kombëtar, Abaz Ermenji belonged to the younger generation. He was in his late thirties or early forties. He had taught Albanian history in high school. The Italian authorities arrested him and sent him with other Albanian professors to a concentration camp on the island of Ventotene. Recall that, before accepting the office of secretary of education, Dad had demanded that all Albanian professors be released from that camp. At that point, Abaz Ermenji and many others had regained their freedom and had returned to Albania.

I decided to write to Abaz Ermenji because, besides being an impressive teacher, he was also a courageous fighter who had led Albanian nationalist units against the communists. It took a while before he answered. The gist of his reply was that I should write to him again describing my information in cryptic terms that would convey the essence without allowing an outsider to make out the true meaning of the message. I could see that, were I to depend on the mail, I would fail to make the deadlines agreed upon with Hila. I was disappointed but decided to proceed without delay.

Since Zef and I were in the British zone, I decided to speak with Mr. Foster. I mentioned that I had information that may be of interest to the British authorities. He promised he would contact the right people promptly. I went back to my bed, keeping an eye peeled on the highway, wondering whether a British jeep would show up. A day or two went by and no one came. I mentioned before that we suspected the British as being close to the Albanian royalists. Now I felt free to act on my own. After discussing the events with Zef, or rather the nonevents both with Abaz Ermenji and the British, we decided that my next step was to go to Salzburg, capital of the American zone.

Chapter Thirty-Nine

CIC Salzburg

Zef saw me to the railroad station in Villach. I climbed aboard the train that would take me to Salzburg. A quick wave of the hand and off we were, he back to St. Martin and I bound for Salzburg. Until now I had worked within the relatively narrow confines of political refugees set by the Austrians and the British. Henceforth, I would be on my own—within the law but on my own. I checked the content of my pockets. I had everything I needed, including some money I had saved along the way.

I chose a compartment that was half-empty. A couple of middle-aged Austrians occupied the window seats and a woman in her mid-twenties sat with her back to the direction in which our train was traveling. I took an empty seat near the door.

The compartment was relatively dark. As my eyes adjusted to the muted light, I noticed that she wore a large gown and a floppy blouse called for by her florid body build. She seemed relatively tall and was grossly overweight. She had a small knapsack in the overhead rack and a typical European shopping net next to her. In the net, she had a book by Ernie Pyle, the distinguished American war correspondent. I guessed she was an Austrian maid or cook who found solace and self-esteem in reading such books in the original.

We had been traveling in silence when the conductor came to check our tickets. The elderly Austrians and I complied promptly. She was having some kind of trouble.

She looked around the compartment and asked, "Does anyone here speak English?"

"I do," I replied.

"Could you please tell the conductor that I need to buy a ticket to Salzburg? I was in a great hurry when I got on the train."

I translated what she told me, the conductor sold her the ticket, and everything was under control. I, for one, felt sheepish for having misjudged her and so I began by introducing myself to her. It turned out that she was from New York, on vacation, and that Pyle was one of her favorite authors. At this point, I told her how indebted I was to Ernie Pyle. In 1944–1945, in jail in Albania, I had started to study English. I was indebted to Pyle not only for the English I had learned from his books but also for giving me a glimpse of U.S. army life and for taking me beyond my prison walls to North Africa and other remote places. To me, his was a new world. I could not conceive of GIs complaining to the *Stars and Stripes* that enlisted men in the South Pacific received warm beer while their officers had access to ice-cold beer. Even more important to me was Ernie's definition of courage. I was taught that a brave man was unafraid, always and everywhere. I knew I felt fear every time I was in trouble or in danger, and did my utmost to hide my feelings from others. As I was a born coward, I wanted no one else to know my deep, dark secret, and therefore, I picked fights at the drop of a hat. Ernie, on the other hand, described a brave man as one who did his duty despite his fears. What a revelation; what a relief that was for me. I ended by saying that I wanted to write to Ernie Pyle, and asked her whether, by any chance, she could tell me how to find his address.

The American girl listened to me patiently and when I was done she asked, "Don't you know that Pyle was killed during the last days of the war in the Pacific?"

I was stunned. Pyle was a noncombatant; how could he get killed? I felt a sense of personal loss at the news of his death. Despite my euphoria since having escaped from the dark world of communism, there was no escaping the fact that the realities of life struck just as hard in the West as behind the Iron Curtain. What a pity!

"No, I didn't. I feel truly sad as I wanted to thank him for what he had done for me while I was in a communist prison."

I don't recall what we talked about the rest of the trip. The news of Ernie Pyle's death had cast a long shadow on anything that followed. When we reached Salzburg, we got off the train and shook hands. I was in a hurry to get going.

"Do you think we can get together perhaps this evening?" she asked.

"Where are you staying?"

In reply, she showed me an address printed on some type of itinerary she pulled out of her pocket. It was printed on American Express stationery.

"What is American Express?"

"It's a commercial organization that assists travelers in putting together individual or group trips. When I travel, family and friends know where I am supposed to be on any given day. They mail letters for me to the right American Express office and I retrieve them promptly. American Express will cash traveler checks; the office can assist also in case of financial or medical emergencies. They can be of much help all around."

I was impressed. Obviously, I had much to learn about the West and about America in particular. Perhaps I should meet her in the evening and continue my learning process.

"Is it perhaps easier if we meet in front of the American Express office this evening, say around 7:00 p.m.?" I asked.

"Fine. See you this evening."

With that we parted, my mind already in high gear, eager to implement the plan I had worked out for my first trip to the American zone.

I had no trouble finding the American consulate. The building was not particularly impressive. There were some American soldiers at the entrance and the flag fluttered above. My eyes truly feasted on what I saw. How I had longed to see that flag, to see American soldiers in Albania! How our hopes had refused to die for a long time, and how we eventually had to resign ourselves to the oppressive communist reality. Now was my chance to strike back.

Once inside, I moved toward an information desk and moseyed around until I was fairly sure that the employee was an American.

"Could you please tell me where I could find someone connected with American intelligence?" I asked in my best English.

"Get out!"

"Excuse me?"

"Get out. We want no part of people like you."

Well, so much for that. Being thrown out of the American consulate was not part of my plan. I stepped outside and realized I needed to improvise. I started walking. At the street corner, I had to stop for a red light. To my right an American military jeep had also come to a stop. I stooped and spoke to the driver.

"Excuse me, do you know of an American intelligence unit here in Salzburg?"

The driver took a quick look at me.

"Hop in, I'll drive you there."

A few minutes later, he stopped maybe 100 feet short of a three-story building. "Here we are," he said. "Do me a favor, don't mention I brought you here." With that, he stepped on the gas and disappeared.

Above the entrance, there was a five-foot oval, curved shield with the inscription:

U.S. ARMY COUNTERINTELLIGENCE CORP
CIC
Sub-Detachment 430 - A

No one could miss it. I climbed a few steps, entered the building and found myself before a reception desk. An Austrian secretary asked me what or who I was looking for. I told her I needed to speak with someone in American intelligence and that it was important. She asked for my name and nationality and showed me to a room where someone would see me shortly.

As I recall, the room contained office furniture, somewhat more elegant than what I had seen in Yugoslavia and in the British zone. I did not have to wait long.

"I am Captain so-and-so." He mumbled his name that I did not catch. He stuck out his hand in my direction. "And you are?"

"I am Genc Korça," I replied as we shook hands.

"I understand you have important information you want to share with us?"

"Yes, sir, I believe it is very important and rather lengthy. I want to add that the information is intended for the CIA and I hope that you will put me in contact with them." He looked at his watch.

"It is lunchtime. Perhaps it is better we meet after lunch when we are not under time pressure."

As we shook hands, he looked me straight in the eye and said "*Mir'u pafshim,*" and walked out before I could recover from the surprise.

I left the building with different thoughts tumbling through my mind. Where did they find a CIC officer who spoke Albanian or was of Albanian origin? Did they have such experts for different European countries at all CIC stations or did Salzburg just happen to have one? Was Salzburg a center for Albanian counterintelligence? Anyhow, for the time being, my problem was one of finding a restaurant where I could afford to eat and be back by two o'clock as we had agreed.

I took a good look at the building housing the CIC. It was more or less free standing, with no other buildings immediately next to or behind it. Across the street was a fruit stand, and there were streetcar rails and overhead wires.

Having completed my visual reconnaissance, I crossed the street, looking for a simple restaurant. I saw one; in fact, I saw two. One was elegant, definitely out of my class, the other looked OK from the outside. I read the menu and prices posted at the entrance. Yes, this was definitely in my league. I entered, had a simple meal, and was ready for my meeting. I also had a chance to think and put my first impressions into some semblance of order:

1) If they had experts on Albania, as seemed to be the case, it would make my job easier.

2) I intended to give them enough detail of the Hila plan to pique their interest without giving them the full details of the plan. I did not expect the CIC to take over the plan. That would fall under the purview and responsibility of the CIA, I assumed.

With these points in mind, I was ready for the afternoon interview. I entered the CIC building a few minutes before 2:00 p.m. The secretary recognized me and directed me to a different room than the one in the morning. The room was about the same size, but it contained several chairs beside the desk and other pieces of office furniture.

This time the wait seemed longer. Well, I was not going to reproach them for being late. After all, one should not forget one's manners. Or was it that they held all the aces? Either way, I was going to be a good boy. Furthermore, if they were trying to upset me by keeping me waiting, I was not going to fall for it.

Finally, they arrived. I am saying "they" because there were two of them, but the officer who had greeted me in the morning was not among them. What happened to the "Albanian expert"?

This time they skipped the introductions. "Mr. Korça, you said this morning that your story was both lengthy and complicated. Let's sit down and please start from the beginning."

We sat down with the two of them facing me. This was easier for me as I could see them at a glance without having to turn my head one way or the other. I began by giving them a short version of my biography, as I needed to present proper credentials. I spoke in some detail of Hila Shllaku and about his role in Yugoslav anti-Tirana activities as well as about his network in northern Albania. I mentioned the fact that the Yugoslavs had been able to create this network, claiming that they were striving to overthrow Enver Hoxha's regime working hand in hand with the West. I concluded by saying that my friends and I believed we had a way of taking this network away from the Yugoslavs and placing it at the disposal of the United States.

They listened attentively, without interrupting me.

"You have given us a thumbnail sketch of what you want to share with us. It is indeed an interesting and complicated story. We will want to meet with you again. At that point we may need further details of your plan."

"Gentlemen, I live in a refugee camp in St. Martin in the British zone. I will gladly return to Salzburg when you wish to speak with me."

"What we have in mind is something else. Can you stay in Salzburg a few days?"

"Yes, I can."

"We will give you 10 schillings every other day. That should suffice to cover room and board. We will see you tomorrow morning, say around ten o'clock?"

I nodded. They pressed the promised 10 schillings into my hand, smiled, and disappeared. Now I had a little money. I had to look for a youth hostel and see what food I could afford for a few schillings a day. I found a hostel that charged three schillings a night. Tomorrow I would go to a grocery store and see what I could buy with the money available to me.

Now that I had found sleeping accommodations, I had one more thing to do. I had to grab a quick bite, certainly not at a restaurant as I had done at noon, and meet my American "date" at 7:00 p.m. I had no time to waste.

By seven o'clock, I was in front of the American Express office. It was located in an older building and the façade gave away nothing of the customer services the American girl had talked about. She was pretty much on time and when I saw her, I could not believe my eyes. In the morning, to say something kind, I had mentioned to her that the good Lord had fashioned women in a way that some of them should not wear blue jeans. Well, my "date" waddled up to me in the tightest blue jeans Levi's had ever produced.

We greeted each other with polite smiles and decided to make use of the daylight to do some sightseeing. As neither of us had brought a city map, we drifted hither and yonder. We decided not to visit the fortress because of the late hour. Soon we ran out of topics to talk about. The evening was beginning to drag. Had I had money and some interest in my "date," I could have invited her for a snack or a drink. Under the circumstances, we both agreed it was getting late. She said that the next day or so she would be leaving Salzburg and I, of course, had a tight schedule of commitments.

We shook hands and wished each other well. I hurried off in the direction of my youth hostel as quickly as I could. I had expected some interesting conversation with the girl from New York. Absent that, I saw no reason to prolong the evening beyond what courtesy demanded. As I directed my footsteps toward the hostel, I could focus again on next day's meeting with the CIC. So far, I had no indication what was on their minds, except that they had asked for another meeting.

I slept well, probably because the day had been full of new impressions, from being kicked out of the U.S. consulate to concluding the day with a boring date. The hostel offered breakfast at a moderate price. One could buy milk, coffee, tea, or hot chocolate and fresh breakfast rolls. I ate with gusto and got ready for my meeting.

At ten o'clock sharp, I was at the reception desk of Counter-Intelligence Corps Sub-Detachment 430-A. On this day it was "manned" by a gorgeous young woman dressed and made up in typical American fashion. She could have been a beauty queen just out of a fashion magazine. Her dress was fresh and without wrinkles, as if she had just stepped out of the dry cleaner's. Her blonde hair was styled to perfection, and her fingernails were long and polished. It made one wonder whether she could type or do any office work the way she was dressed and made up. Indeed, one could ask oneself whether she really needed to do any work the way she looked. My less-than-reverent thoughts stemmed probably from the fact that she looked at me with a look somewhere between haughtiness and disdain. When the gorgeous creature spoke, she did so in German with an unmistakable Austrian pronunciation.

"What do you want?" she asked.

"I have a ten o'clock appointment," I replied, trying to hide my thoughts that shifted from pure admiration to resentment and back again.

"You can wait here," she said, pointing at a spot a few feet away from her desk.

I moved in the indicated direction and made it a point not to look at her. If I hadn't, my admiration would have shone through unabashedly.

One of yesterday's officers came out, shook hands with me, and asked me to follow him into one of their offices.

"Mr. Korça, would you mind going over yesterday's narrative once more to make sure that I have understood you right?"

I assumed that his request aimed at discovering any discrepancies that might show up during my repeat performance. I did not mind. Anything that confirmed the validity of what I was telling the CIC was in my favor. I needed to convince them that I was telling the truth so they could then proceed and get me in touch with the CIA.

Today he was taking notes. He began asking questions aimed at clarifying certain details of what I was telling him. I had no trouble repeating the story over and over again, because I was telling the truth. On the other hand, I had no evidence that he was familiar with either the geography or the people I was talking about.

"What you are telling me is interesting. I don't know, however, whether the CIA will want to take over. Particularly since you are providing us with little hard data." Clearly, the CIC wanted to know more without committing themselves in any way.

"Sir, I am afraid that my instructions are to provide the specifics only to the CIA. Please, do not misunderstand. We Albanians have been through a most difficult period with regard to Allied efforts to free Albania. Any time Albanian infiltrators have attempted to land in Albania by submarine, by air, or by land, they have found the Albanian security forces awaiting them. This is well beyond coincidence. Obviously, we cannot point fingers at anyone or anything in particular. There is little doubt, however, that buried in Allied intelligence there is a leak that has proven very dangerous to the Albanian resistance. Please, don't misunderstand what I am saying. For all we know, the leak may be within the CIA. Our group had to make a decision, and the instructions I was given leave me no choice."

"I see."

He was obviously displeased. On the other hand, I was wracking my brain as to how I could provide the CIC with more information without violating my instructions. "Sir, ask me questions on points of interest to you and I will try my best to answer them. Please remember that I have instructions I cannot violate."

"Rather than go that way, let's call it a day. You go and rethink your position. We will meet again on Monday and you will tell me all you can at that point. You may need some money to cover your expenses. Here are ten schillings. See you then on Monday at 10 a.m."

We stood up, shook hands, and left the room, he for his office and I for the exit where a splendid sunny day enveloped me, without giving me much pleasure.

I went toward the youth hostel where I was staying. My mission was a failure. Abaz Ermenji had shown little or no interest in what I had to say. The CIC wanted information without commitment on their part. On ten schillings every two days, I was subsisting on bread and sardines for my main meals. It was Friday. I had about two days to kill and then one more meeting with the CIC. Obviously, I could not call it quits. Hila and Deda counted on me. Somehow, I had to break the impasse.

At the youth hostel, some Yugoslav students had told me that there was a Franciscan church nearby that served free meals. People stood in line. Before lunch everyone said grace and after the meal people would clear the tables and wash dishes. The Yugoslav students had eaten there more than once. I, too, should try it. Maybe today was the right day for a free meal. Somehow, I needed a morale booster.

I had no trouble finding the church as well as the place where the people were lining up for a free meal. My heart sank. Those in line were mostly men, unshaven, sickly, and in rags. And there I was, young and healthy, in a nice, clean summer outfit with light blue jacket and gray pants, carrying a new leather briefcase. I was wearing my best, my only outfit, but compared to the others I looked as if I had strayed by mistake into a poor section of town. While I was trying to make up my mind whether to stay or walk away, the line started moving. Before I knew it, I was in a dark, cool corridor and then in a mess hall. Here people picked up soup dishes and approached two Franciscans who were ladling out a thick stew. People could help themselves to hefty slices of dark bread and spoons were available at a nearby table.

Then people sat down and started eating, one bite of bread and one spoonful of stew, grimly, in silence, without looking at anyone, immersed in what they were doing. No one said grace. By the time I sat down, some people were lining up for seconds. I started to eat with my head lowered, afraid that someone would tell me that I did not belong. When I was done, I looked up. There were still a few people eating, fully concentrating on the bowls in front of them. When I was done, I picked up my bowl and followed others to a kitchen table where we put down our bowls and spoons. Those in front of me were walking toward the exit without anyone asking them to wash dishes. I approached the exit and walked out into the sunshine, relieved and determined never to return to this place for a free meal, no matter what.

At the hostel, I went directly to my bed and lay down. The meal at the Franciscans had depressed me even more. It had made me feel like an impostor, like someone milking the system by eating the food of the poorest of the poor. Mercifully, I fell asleep.

When I woke up I had made up my mind. For the next 24 hours, I was not going to think at all about Hila and my mission. Instead, I was going to take in Salzburg, visit the castle, and allow myself to be a tourist for a change, albeit one with little change in his pockets, removed from clandestine operations and all that went with them.

The castle was impressive and so was the view from the castle. However, the more I tried the less I succeeded in sloughing off the burden that had gotten heavier as I had failed in whatever I had tried so far.

I returned to the hostel in a foul mood. In the mess hall, I saw two Swedish students with a girl. She was a new arrival, a young British nurse. The two Swedes were vying for her attention, each trying to outdo the other, each seeking to take the lead. When they saw me they sensed that time had come to declare a truce.

"Why, here is Genc. He is our resident Albanian. He is a medical student, so the two of you will have plenty to talk about. Genc, come here. We want to introduce you to this nice British nurse."

I would have preferred to go to my room and avoid the noisy duo were it not for the nurse who had hardly uttered a word since I had entered the room. I decided that if I wanted to mope I did not have to be by myself to do so.

"Pleased to meet you," we said to each other as we shook hands. She was no beauty but she had all the attractiveness of a healthy, young female. She seemed rather bashful compared to the girl from New York, which was a relief.

"Let's go out to dinner," the Swedes hollered.

"There is a little restaurant at the foot of the castle. The food is good and the prices just right for traveling students," one of them volunteered. "Of course, you, my dear, will be our guest," he said bending awkwardly toward the nurse, without specifying whether I would be included among the hosts.

At this point, I could not care less. I had some money in my pocket and by splitting the bill among the three of us, I would avoid an awkward situation with the stentorian Swedes.

The restaurant was as the Swedes had described it. The food was tasty, the portions abundant, and the bill moderate. When the bill came, we three men threw in our share and the four of us started on the way home. I noticed that I was always next to the nurse without any effort of mine. During the entire evening, I had spoken to her only once when, in an aside to her, I had said that the two Swedes were blocking my Eustachian tubes. She had nodded her head and chuckled. Having imbibed more than they could handle, both had trouble walking in a straight line. I put my arm around the nurse and the two of us were the steady half of the group as we wound our way toward the youth hostel. We said good night and the Swedes disappeared.

I turned toward the nurse.

"How about going on a picnic tomorrow, just you and me? There is a castle outside Salzburg, not the one on top of the hill above the city. It is beautiful, known for its waterworks, and less touristy than some other sights. I can buy bread, sausage, cheese, some soft drinks or beer—whatever you prefer. The weather is going to be sunny and mild, just like today, and we can have a good time." Even though my heart was not in it, I thought the change of pace would do me good.

She nodded. "That would be very nice indeed."

I wished her a good night and gave her a peck on the cheek. "Who knows," I said to myself, "maybe tomorrow will be better than today." And with that thought in mind, I lay me down to sleep.

I woke up to a splendid, sunny day. By the time I got to the breakfast room, the Swedes and the British nurse were eating their breakfast. I grabbed my usual fare and felt a little like the cat that had swallowed the canary. I knew what was coming.

"Well, shall we make plans for today?" one of the Swedes thundered in his normal tone of voice as he looked around encompassing the three of us. I spoke up first.

"Count me out as I have other plans for today."

That obviously sounded like good news to him. "Well, then you are coming with us, right?" he said to the nurse.

She shook her head. "I, too, have plans for today."

The Swedes looked at each other, nonplussed. They looked at me, they looked at her, and then it dawned on them that the nurse's and my plan probably coincided. I must say they recovered with style.

"Have a good day and hope to see you in the evening," they said to both of us, and left without looking back.

The nurse had prepared a little knapsack and told me it contained her more valuable personal belongings including cosmetics and face cream. Somehow, her practicality impressed me favorably. Perhaps we would spend a pleasant day together.

We left the hostel in the direction of a nearby grocery store. Bread, sausage, cheese, fresh fruit, some beer, and a water bottle disappeared in my knapsack without making too much of a dent in my financial reserves. We marched to the streetcar, and before long, we got off in front of the ritzy castle I had mentioned to her.

The sun bathed the castle's white façade in glorious light and made the building seem lighthearted and airy. The portion of the garden in front of the castle displayed well-kept bushes and beds of luscious flowers. A reflecting pool and water fountains created intricate patterns of water jets and droplets that sparkled with all the colors of the rainbow. My companion seemed delighted. We moved along the paved road toward the building. As I had read in the literature, there was a pool and fountain that came to life every half-hour or so. The trick was to maneuver one's date into such a position that she would get soaked by the water fountain. The area around the pool was marked discreetly to keep those in the know safe and dry.

At first, I thought it would be fun to play such a trick on her.

"Did you bath [sic] this morning?" I asked her, trying to hide the malice in my voice.

"You mean 'bathe'," she corrected me.

The lover of languages took over in me. "Why do you say 'bathe'? Isn't the word pronounced 'bath'?"

She explained in her straightforward manner. "You 'bathe' or you can draw or take a bath. The two words are spelled and pronounced differently." She did not call one a verb and the other a noun, but her explanation was clear and to the point.

My original intention was to get her wet at that tricky pool and then offer to take her into the woods where she could take off her clothes to let them dry. That would have been mean. I was so pleased with having learned a little more about the English language that I decided not to get her soaking wet and to let events take their natural course, whatever that was.

We walked around for a while and I explained to her the secret of the dormant fountain and confessed my original plan. She laughed at my naughtiness but did not seem upset. We stood by at a safe distance until the fountain did its trick soaking the unsuspecting.

Lunchtime was approaching and there were no tables or benches on the lawn outside the castle. I suspect this was intentional, as munching tourists would have clashed with the elegant lay of the land. Furthermore, we were getting to the point where we would have liked to get out of the sun and into the shade. The answer to our problem was obvious. We turned toward the nearby woods and started walking briskly just to get out of the sun.

As I looked around out of habit, perhaps because of my suspicious nature, I broke out in laughter. Entering the woods, less than 150 feet from us was the gorgeous, haughty Austrian secretary who worked at the CIC. She was with a very young American officer. She saw me and saw me laughing. Her haughtiness toward me crumbled before my very eyes.

That evening my guest and I went to the same restaurant the Swedes had introduced us to. I mentioned to my date that it was her turn to pay for my dinner. After all, I had paid for part of her dinner the evening before and had also purchased our picnic food. She was truly shaken up. Heaven knows, she must have been hard pressed for money, at least in view of her travel plans that, as far as I knew, would take her to Italy next. I did not want to spoil her evening. After roasting her for a little while, I said that in view of Albanian hospitality, I could never let her pay. The furrows on her forehead disappeared and her pretty smile came right back. We enjoyed a good meal and each other's company. Pleasantly tired, we returned to the youth hostel. We hugged and wished each other a good night's rest. Early the next morning, she would be on her way to Italy.

I spent Sunday reminiscing and feeling better than I had felt in a while. The English nurse was a pleasant person, a trusting soul. She had come so far without seeing the grim side of life. I sincerely hoped and prayed that no one would hurt her down the road. And there was also the "haughty" Austrian secretary. Well, she deserved to get off her pedestal and learn to treat the "lame," the downtrodden, with respect as human beings.

That Sunday, I had time to think. There was not much more detail I could give the CIC regarding my assignment. Their role in this case was to serve as a bridge between me and the CIA group in charge of Albanian affairs. As the CIC claimed to have contacted the CIA, all we had to do was wait for their answer. In the meantime, I might as well return to St. Martin, as there was no need for me in Salzburg. Unless the CIC officers had ideas of their own, that was what I would tell them come Monday morning.

The next morning, the beautiful secretary was not at the desk when I arrived at ten o'clock sharp. Another young lady, having found my name on the appointment calendar, directed me to one of the offices. Before long, there came my contact. He was polite as usual.

"Good morning, I hope you had a nice weekend," he said while motioning for me to sit down.

"Yes, thank you, I did." I stopped at this point. I did not know whether it was proper for me to ask an older man who was also an officer about his weekend. He came straight to the point.

"Where do we go from here?" he asked me.

"Sir, I have given the matter much thought. I don't think I can go into the details of my mission. We believe we have the means either to destroy the Yugoslav underground network in north Albania or to turn it over to the United States. I believe we can do this with a minimum of risk and expense to the United States. I do not believe that you, the CIC, intend to take over this operation. Please tell me if I am wrong."

He did not react one way or another. I continued.

"From what I understand, such an operation would come under the jurisdiction of the CIA, assuming they are interested. Thus, it seems to me that since you have contacted the CIA, it is up to them to respond. As there is no need for me to be in Salzburg, I propose I return to St. Martin and return here if and when you call me."

I still could not tell from his expression how my reasoning sounded to him.

"What you have said is correct; we are awaiting a response from our colleagues at the CIA. We do think, however, that it would be best if you stayed in Salzburg a little longer to keep in regular touch with us. Naturally, we would continue to pay your expenses."

I had decided not to mention money to them lest they felt that I was doing it for material gain. "What do you mean by 'keeping in regular touch,' sir?"

"Well, you could drop in every day to inquire whether we had news for you. If yes, we would take it from there. If not, you would be on your way again."

To me, this was most disturbing. "Sir, I have family in Albania. Coming to see you every day could expose them to serious harm."

"What do you mean?"

'Sir, your building here is rather isolated. Yet there is a fruit stand across the street from you. I for one find it hard to believe that the owner can make a living with the fruit and vegetables he sells your employees. I suspect his main business is to film anyone coming in and out of your building. He is either on retainer or sells the film to the highest bidder." My host kept silent for what seemed like a long time.

Finally, he said, "What do you propose?"

"I will come by every day, on foot, by bike, by streetcar, or even by cab. If you have potted flowers, say, in the corner window on the second floor, someone from your office and I will meet at the entrance to the castle overlooking Salzburg at three o'clock that afternoon. No potted flowers, no need to meet and I come back the next day."

Suspicion seemed to creep across his face. "Tell me and be honest. Who has trained you in such matters?"

"Fine, I'll tell you. Peter Qafa with whom I spent several weeks in the mountains as I was fleeing from Albania taught me this trick." Then

I proceeded to describe to him the encounter with Mark Dedë Alia. "The day we were hiding in the area, Mark came to see us at a certain location because Peter had put a stone on the branch of a tree along the way that his friend Mark took every day with his sheep."

I don't know whether the CIC officer was satisfied with my explanation. He may have been happier had I confessed that the Albanian Sigurimi or the Yugoslav UDBA had trained me. In either case, I would have received my training from fellow professionals, and not from some poor Albanian farmer. However, what I told him was the plain truth. To believe or not to believe me, that was up to him.

"OK," he said, "I am satisfied with the explanation. By the way," he added, "here are 20 schillings. This will carry you until Friday. On Friday at 10 a.m. we'll meet again here at the office."

I had one more suggestion.

"If we are not to meet until Friday, why don't I return to St. Martin? I will leave the address with you and you can reach me by phone. I'll use the money you just gave me to buy train tickets to and from St. Martin." I could not see myself lollygagging around Salzburg for four days. At this point I had come full circle, as this was what I had proposed that morning.

"OK, go back to your refugee camp and be here Friday morning. If we need you sooner, we'll let you know."

We stood up, shook hands, and I was out the door. I zipped back to the youth hostel, packed my few belongings, and caught a train for Villach. I needed to go back to reality, such as it was. Salzburg had lost its fascination as far as I was concerned.

CHAPTER FORTY

CIA ROME

My return to St. Martin was uneventful. I spent time with Zef and brought him up to date on what had transpired in Salzburg. When I walked into the office, the secretaries were all smiles and spoke to me in hushed, conspiratorial tones.

"We know where you have been. You are a sly one and can get away with it," and they kept giggling. "But the next time you go, please bring us back some souvenirs. Of course, we will pay you."

"The next time I go where?" I asked, failing to understand what this was all about.

"Do not think we don't know where you go when you disappear like you did this time."

"Will you kindly tell me what you are talking about?"

Mr. Foster's personal secretary spoke up. "OK, we know you go illegally to Italy. We won't tell anyone but the next time you go, please let us know so we can give you money and you can bring us some nice things from there."

I was at a loss. There was a real chance that I might go Italy to meet with the CIA. I was convinced that the secretaries knew nothing about it. Why did they mention Italy? I started to leave the office, assuring them that I had not been to Italy during my absence from the camp.

"OK, then tell us where did you go?"

I decided that the aura of mystery could be in my favor. "Ladies, I did not go to Italy. However, I cannot tell you where I did go."

This answer failed to persuade them and when I left the office, they were still smiling from ear to ear, like people in on a secret.

Friday morning I went back to the railroad station and returned to Salzburg. At ten o'clock sharp I was at the CIC building. The gorgeous Austrian secretary was at her desk.

"Good morning, Herr Korça," she said, and she directed me to the room where I would meet with the CIC officer. As I had expected, the trip to the woods behind the castle—I with the British nurse, and she with an American officer—had improved our relationship markedly and I was promoted to "Herr Korça."

A few minutes later, my CIC officer entered the room and we went through our usual routine of shaking hands and sitting down for our "*palaver*" of the day. The CIA had failed to respond so far but he, on behalf of the CIC, wanted to add a comment or two. Why did I want to go to Italy? No matter what my reasons, the CIC would be no part of it.

"It is not true that I insist on going to Italy. Rome is in the picture because CIA offices in charge of Albanian affairs are in Rome. That's why I have asked to be sent or, if you prefer, escorted to Italy. Let me ask you: Why are you so suspicious of my asking to go to Italy?"

"We suspect that you have motives other than the ones you have mentioned. For all we know, you may want to carry precious stones across the border."

I spoke almost with contempt. "Do you mean to tell me that you have no laxatives in the West? If you still wonder why I seek to go to Italy, let me set things straight. I will be perfectly satisfied to stay in Austria if a representative of the CIA Albanian section will meet me here. This takes my going to Italy out of the picture and should clarify things." I really could not imagine where the CIC was coming from.

He rose to his feet. "I suppose you will want to return to St. Martin for the weekend?"

"Yes, sir. When do you want me back?"

"See you on Monday, same time, same place."

As instructed, on Monday morning I was back. This time, I had taken an earlier train to avoid running into the secretaries at the camp. In Salzburg, I had seen a neat restaurant not far from the CIC building. It served an American-style breakfast, like ham and eggs and other such delights, for a reasonable price. I had been tempted to go there for quite some time. Well, here was my chance.

Two American ladies were seated at a table next to mine. I was always eager to hear spoken English and so I tried to hear what they were talking about. Their conversation went something like this:

"My husband and I are so looking forward to coming to your house for bridge with you and the colonel tonight." The one lady spoke with such flattery that she almost made the milk curdle in my cup.

"I am glad you reminded me of our bridge party," responded the other lady with a haughty tone of voice. "The Ruskies are giving us trouble again. General Clark is calling my husband and other high-ranking officers to Vienna to discuss these points..." and here she rattled off the problem and the four points on the general's agenda. It seems that the Russians were using private boats on the Danube to promote certain as-yet-unidentified activities. The general wanted to discuss these specific questions:

1. Would it suffice to instruct private owners of such boats to refuse to rent them to the Russians and to alert Western authorities?

2. Did the French, British, and American military have the right to confiscate these boats if the Russians persisted in using them?

3. Should they confiscate the boats or buy them outright from the owners if other means failed?

4. What should the Western powers do to prevent suspected boats from Hungary and other satellites from entering Austria via the Danube?

I could not believe my ears. Such loose talk in a public place. World War II was over but the Iron Curtain had split Europe in two and war clouds were never far off the horizon. I made a mental note of the ladies' conversation and left the restaurant.

The meeting with the CIC officer started on time but was getting nowhere, as usual. Today, I decided to spice it up a bit.

"Do you think I could see the commanding officer in charge of your CIC sub-detachment?" And then, as if catching myself, I added, "I am sorry, that was stupid of me. Of course, he will be with the other superior officers in Vienna to attend General Clark's meeting. The Ruskies are giving us trouble again. Time has come to take a good look at what they are doing on the Danube." Then I quoted the four points the older lady had mentioned to impress her companion at the breakfast table. The CIC officer had grown very serious while listening to me.

"Tell me, what secret service are you with?" he finally asked.

"Do you really think that if I belonged to a foreign secret service I would tell you what I just did? I had breakfast this morning at a breakfast shop frequented by Americans. Two American ladies were sitting at the next table and what I told you was what the older one told her friend."

"The trouble is," said the embarrassed CIC officer, "that we have not been able to teach our wives to keep their mouths shut."

I had a sinking feeling. Should these officers' wives learn to keep their mouths shut, or should the husbands keep *their* mouths shut—even with their wives?

We met again the next day but we had obviously reached the end of the path.

"Mr. Korça, I regret to inform you that the CIA is not interested in your proposal. If I may ask, what do you intend to do now?"

Well, that was that.

"I cannot drop the project at this point. My orders are to contact the CIA in Rome and I tried to do this through your office. As I have fallen short of my objective, I will go to Rome, present the project to the Albanian section of the CIA. At that point I will have completed my mission."

We were done talking officially. Now we were talking as two men who trusted each other, at least to some extent.

"Be careful. When you crossed the border illegally into Austria, you did so to seek political asylum. If you are caught crossing the Italian border illegally, you will have broken the law. The violation will be entered in your file and you will forfeit the right to immigrate to America."

"I did not come to emigrate. I have a mission to carry out and am willing to take certain risks to complete it successfully. But I do thank you for your advice."

We stood up and shook hands, this time more warmly than in the past.

I exited the building and left behind some illusions about the West I had carried with me across the border. The lack of interest shown toward the Albanian students in Belgrade by the high United Nations commissioner for refugees matched the disinterest his secretary had shown when he never called me to continue the conversation we had started in Klagenfurt. Mr. Foster's contacts had made no effort to speak with me when I claimed I had a matter of importance I wanted to bring to their attention. The complete disinterest of the CIC regarding the Yugoslav network in north Albania, however, did take the cake. This of course bode poorly for Albania but it also made me fear that the overall Cold War playing field might be tilted in favor of the Russians who took intelligence matters very seriously.

I was rather dejected when I took the train back to Villach. I had left full of hope the first time I went to Salzburg. I was finally going to make contact with Americans, the hope of Albania and of the people languishing behind the Iron Curtain. The consulate threw me out without asking any questions. It could be, of course, that they were so besieged by refugees trying to make a fast buck that they had decided to kick out any and all such "customers." The CIC in Salzburg seemed to feel they had enough business to justify their existence. Besides, they were well paid, had PX and other privileges, were well received by the local population that would rather be under the Americans than under any of the other three occupying powers, and had the ability to attract beautiful young girls to work for them. That was not all bad, was it now? I wondered, if I were in their shoes, would I worry about the Yugoslav network in north Albania? Well, I was not an American and I did worry about this network. In fact, I had given my word that I would do my utmost to take it away from the Yugoslavs at whatever cost.

At the camp, I spoke with Zef, informed him of the failure of my mission in Salzburg, and laid plans for my upcoming trip to Italy. First, I had to find out whether the CIC or anyone else was shadowing me. I failed to detect anything untoward. It seemed that the CIC truly had no interest in what I was doing. Zef and I went to Villach a couple of times. We entered buildings with more than one exit, went into larger stores, stopped in front of glass plate windows, all with the intent of seeing whether anyone was following us. I must admit this was all very amateurish but we had to do the best we could. As far as we could tell, no one was following us.

One beautiful, sunny afternoon, Zef and I went again to Villach. Zef had shouldered my knapsack with my meager earthly goods. I was wearing shorts, a sport shirt, and leather shoes with heavy crepe soles I had bought in Austria. We meandered in the general direction of the railroad station, keeping an eye out for anyone who might be showing an undue interest in us. We failed to spot anything unusual. I bought a one-way ticket to a village near the Italian border, said goodbye to Zef, and hopped on the train at the last moment.

The trip was so short that I didn't even bother to look for a seat. I got off the train and started walking southward, in the general direction of the border. Soon, I heard the sound of horseshoes on the pavement. Behind me were a horse-drawn cart and a farmer sitting high atop the cart. He stopped and asked whether I wanted a ride. I accepted with mixed emotions. I did not want to make him suspicious by refusing but preferred not to engage in any kind of probing conversation. I had prepared a cover story, just in case. According to my story, I was a college student on vacation. I planned to wander from village to village and look at the many little churches to list names of architects, artists, and organ makers in preparation for my thesis. I thought the subject sounded innocent and plausible. At the same time, I did not expect the farmer to know enough about art to spot my ignorance. I could always switch the conversation to Italy where I had some knowledge of art as we had had three years of art history in high school.

As it turned out, the farmer was no talker. We traveled in silence until the road turned west, running along the mountain chain that formed the border with Italy. I got off and thanked him for the lift. He kept going west while I disappeared first into the tall grass and then among the bushes, southbound.

The weather was just great. The sun shone, giving warmth and light, making things grow, and bringing God's blessing to all from the smallest blade of grass to fruit trees, to animals, domestic and wild, as well as to men, women, and children in God's creation. I kept climbing and the vegetation began to change from grass to bushes to tall deciduous trees. The terrain was as spotty as a leopard with blotches of shade and sunlight forming irregular patterns pleasing to the eye. The climb was not steep, the air breezy and refreshing. I was moving at a swift pace.

I was enjoying myself so much that I completely forgot I was in a border zone between two countries. I stopped to listen. I could neither hear nor smell human beings. By that I mean I heard neither footsteps nor conversation, as one would expect from guards along a peaceful border. As to smelling them, as a nonsmoker I could smell burning tobacco at a great distance. What reminded me of being in a border zone was the lonely, decrepit bunker I ran into, a leftover from World War II.

Beyond the bunker, the mountainside began sloping downward. I was probably on Italian soil. I continued to walk at a fast pace until I saw a paved highway. Still in the woods, I changed into long pants and a dry shirt, ready to hitchhike my way further into Italy. If the occupants of the car were Austrian, I would be Italian, if they were Italian, I would be Austrian. I would speak some English, though, in case we had to communicate to a minor degree. The intent was to keep the conversation to a minimum. I did want to hitchhike to get far enough from the border so that I would not run the risk of passport controls near the border, on the highway, or on the train.

The first few cars did not stop. Finally, a car with Austrian license plates picked me up. The two men in the car were in their thirties and spoke to me in German. Naturally, I was Italian. I spoke some English and so did they. When we got to a little town whose railroad station I could see from the highway, I asked them to drop me off. I thanked them and we wished each other good luck.

My next step was to find a bank and exchange some schillings for Italian currency. Unfortunately, the bank had closed about half an hour before I got there. I had enough lire to pay for dinner and probably enough to buy a one-way ticket to Rome—tourist class, of course. I decided against sleeping in a hotel because of the need for a valid passport or an ID.

As I walked through the little town, I soaked in the Italian ambience. The difference between this little town and one such as Villach was obvious. The people wore dressier clothes than their Austrian counterparts. Their speech was louder, more animated, and underscored by expressive movements of their hands. Boys and girls paid more attention to each other, the boys teasing and complimenting the girls on their appearance and the girls rebuffing the boys, precluding further advances. Social relations were a true art form in Italy and many had mastered it to perfection.

I happened to be walking behind three high school girls when one of two boys passing them within a few feet said in a stage whisper to his friend, "They are on a propaganda tour," while nodding toward the girls. The girls giggled in response, neither accepting nor denying the statement, ready for the next encounter on the return trip.

The stores were different and so was the merchandise they carried. My interest was only passing, since I had to cling to what little money I had. I walked downhill toward the railroad station and disappeared in the wooded area behind the station. I was looking for sleeping accommodations while it was still daylight. There were quite a few pine trees and the needles on the ground formed a passable mattress. A brook gurgled nearby.

I could not ask for anything better, now could I? I made a mental note so I could find the place after dark, and returned into town in the direction of a restaurant that looked promising. I waited until it was almost dark before entering the premises. Italians eat relatively late and if I had arrived earlier I might have attracted attention. I ordered pasta with meat sauce, a green salad, and some wine, not that I liked wine but had I not ordered it they might have remembered me at the restaurant. Though it was all I could afford, the servings were actually quite abundant.

I had no trouble finding my "bedroom" in the woods. I took off my outer garments to keep them from wrinkling, put on my short pants and sweaty shirt, lay down, and made myself comfortable. The next morning I wanted to get up early and catch the first train to Rome. It was going to be a 14-hour trip and I did not want to miss it.

At dawn, I awoke as the full-breasted joyful songs of many birds welcomed the new day. The air was cool and refreshing. I washed up and shaved carefully so as not to be conspicuous in the eyes of ticket controllers or of policemen who might be patrolling the train. With a one-way ticket to Rome in my pocket, I hopped aboard the train and found a window seat facing in the direction of travel. Several mothers with small children crowded into my compartment. To discourage any needless conversation, I decided to play the Austrian for a while. The train whistled and the accelerating beat of the wheels on the tracks was like music to my ears. After all the time wasted in Salzburg, I was finally on my way to Rome.

The train was moving downhill, away from the border that was also the high point between Austria and Italy. When I had climbed up the Austrian side, I felt I was climbing some rolling hills rather than a mountain. It was very different from when Zef and I had approached the border that ran across the top of the Hochstuhl. Here there was no timberline. The grass was luscious and the tree leaves trembled in the wind. These leaves came in all shades of green, ranging from the silver green leaves of ash trees to the dark green leaves of oaks, maples, and other deciduous trees.

From the train I could see signs, posters, and placards, all in Italian. The uniforms, be they military, police, or those of railroad employees, were similar to those before World War II. The people here dressed differently. No more *lederhosen* or *dirndl* dresses—flared skirts with a tight bodice worn over white blouses—and no more loden suits with green piping. Again, I noticed that the attire here was more colorful. People seemed to move faster, speak louder, move their hands, and change their facial expressions for emphasis, all at the same time. Their normal conversation was several notches louder than that in Austria. To me it was a homecoming of sorts. After all, I had spent seven years in Italy from the seventh grade through my freshman year in medical school.

I settled in my corner, making myself as unobtrusive as possible. The cadence and dialect of the other travelers, mostly women with several children each, were cascading over me giving me much pleasure. The topics of conversation were rather narrow, the children always wanting something to eat and drink and the mothers trying to accommodate them promptly and with lots of hugs and kisses. I must admit that, despite my quasi-Olympic detachment, the little ones were getting to me. They started out with whining rising to screaming at the top of their voices if their demands were not immediately satisfied. There was also a more personal reason for my resentment. I had had a skimpy breakfast and nothing to drink. The train stopped ever so often at various stations where one could buy something from vendors with carts along the various ramps. Immediately, the mothers in our compartment would throw themselves toward the window, pull it down, and stick their heads out with their derrieres keeping anyone from getting near the window from the time the train came to a stop to the moment the train started to leave the station. They yelled, gesticulated, and fought each other with such fury that I, not wanting to attract attention, gave up on the idea of beating them to the window.

The farther we got from the border, the less threatened I felt, and the better my Italian got when my travel companions asked me a question or wanted me to do something for them or their offspring. My improving Italian could have aroused suspicions were it not for the fact that my fellow travelers changed continuously. Those who were on the train early on had gotten off. They were replaced by others, mostly mothers, who brought with them droves of ever-demanding brats, all of them indistinguishable as to their manners from their predecessors.

The day dragged on. I pressed some money into the hands of the perennial victor of the battle for the window in our compartment and asked her to buy me a sandwich. By the time I thought also of buying something to drink, the train took off and we were again on our way. The hours went by very slowly. It was getting hotter and hotter in our compartment. Furthermore, I had trouble shutting out the noise, mostly emanating from the mouths of creatures under three feet tall. In addition, I could not afford to let my guard down. To the best of my recollection, I did not sleep or even nap during the entire trip.

On the positive side, we were moving farther and farther away from the border and from the likelihood of any document controls. The occasional conductor, asking for our tickets, was no problem, of course. I had started out that morning from the northeast corner of Italy. As we approached the main north-south travel corridor, I was recognizing names I knew from the past. By the time we hit cities such as Bologna and Florence, I knew it was just a matter of hours until we reached Rome. The scenery outside the window was flat with fields and villages or small cities alternating with regularity. The train was on time; the frantic movements, the loud trivial conversations, and the occasional insults had become routine. I could always tell when the train was approaching a station by the cries of parents trying to keep their flock together and to make sure nobody left their assigned pieces of luggage behind.

When the clock struck 9:00 p.m., our train entered the railroad station in Rome. Mussolini's efforts to make Italian railroads examples of punctuality had survived him and I for one was grateful. I had been in Rome previously and knew the city up to a point. I had the address of an Albanian member of Balli Kombëtar. He was from a very good family from Shkodra, and although I did not know him well personally, I felt I could ask him for shelter, at least initially. He was also the right person to put me in touch with the Balli leadership in Rome. I would tackle the rest one step at the time.

Once outside the railroad station, my immediate problem was to find a bus or streetcar that would take me near the address I was looking for. I approached a policeman and felt very daring.

"Excuse me, could you tell me what bus or streetcar I should take to get to this address?"

"Take streetcar so-and-so and it will take you there."

"Thank you," I replied. I could not help comparing his immaculate white uniform and tropical helmet with the appearance of Albanian police in their slept-in, rumpled uniforms and their uncouth manners. As I walked away, I felt both gratitude for being in a civilized society and pleased with my courage of approaching a policeman for help and getting away with it.

I climbed aboard the designated streetcar, and after a wide-eyed ride amid the clatter and clamor of a major European capital, I got off at my destination.

Mr. Hasan Kazazi lived in a high-rise apartment building typical of large cities throughout Europe. The massive entrance door was locked. You had to have a key or you rang the bell, identified yourself, and were let in by the person whose bell you had rung. I lacked the former and did not want to chance the latter. There was a bar next door, however, and since I had nothing to drink during the day, here was my chance. Years ago, in prison, I had seen Coca-Cola advertisements in American magazines. Austria was jam-packed with such advertisements from newspapers to magazines and billboards. Yet, I had never tried a Coke. Here was my chance. I walked up to the bar and asked for a Coke. I tried a sip. It was cold, bubbly, and for what-ever reason, I could not detect any particular taste. What a disappointment!

I sat down at a table and kept my eyes peeled for someone with a key to open the door of the apartment building. I would approach the individual and enter the building claiming that I had forgotten my key. It did not take too long; a man approached the door with a key in hand. I jumped up, mumbled my excuse, and started climbing the stairs. Once I was sure I had the right apartment, I rang the bell. An older lady opened the door.

"I am so-and-so, a nephew of Mr. Kazazi. Is my uncle home?"

"No, he is out," the lady replied with suspicion in her voice.

"May I come in and wait for him? I am coming from Milan and am rather tired," I said ingratiatingly.

She moved aside and let me in. She looked me over, once more from head to toe, and asked me to follow her into the living room. There was another lady there, also elderly, and also quite suspicious.

The first lady introduced me as Mr. Kazazi's nephew and then added, "I am surprised that he did not tell us you were coming. Usually, he is very good in such matters."

Obviously, they felt safe enough to let me in but their suspicions were alive and well. The living room was cluttered with old furniture. The ladies had their chairs around a medium large table. The one seated was doing some embroidering. The one who had opened the door to me must have been reading, judging by the newspaper and the glasses on the table. The room was well lit and appeared a bit shabby to me. That was perhaps the reason they rented out rooms.

I tried to fight the chill by telling them that I was a medical student in Milan. That did not seem to help. They had a photograph of Pope Pius XII on the wall. So I told them about meeting the Pope in the summer of 1941 when our city choir was in Rome for a contest. I thought that story would awaken their interest for sure. Well, it didn't. I was running out of subjects and they were not volunteering any. Finally, somebody unlocked the apartment door.

"That's him," one of the ladies said.

I was on my feet before either of them could even think of moving, walked to the door, and threw my arms around Mr. Kazazi in a bear hug so he would have to listen to me. He froze when he saw me. I hurriedly introduced myself and whispered, "I told the ladies I was your nephew from Milan."

He replied promptly and with equal resoluteness, "You must return to Austria immediately."

"Not until I meet with Vasil Andoni and Zef Pali," I replied. The two men were professors and members of the Balli Kombëtar Central Committee. Clearly, my friend was not amused.

"Did you have something to eat?" he finally asked me, as Albanian hospitality gained the upper hand.

"No," I replied truthfully. I was ticked off.

He confirmed my assumed identity with the two ladies, informed them he was taking me to a restaurant, and whisked me out of the apartment.

We walked but a short distance and entered what looked like a simple restaurant. Frankly, I was surprised. It was almost midnight and the restaurant was still open. I should have remembered from previous years that Italian nightlife extended into the wee hours of the night.

My host was restless. Clearly, my presence was not welcome. I felt resentful. I was taking all the risks. I had chanced being caught at the border and winding up in prison. I was risking my future for our country and here I was definitely not welcome. At that point, however, I did not recognize that harboring an illegal immigrant could mean trouble for him, as I would learn a few days later.

He pushed a menu in my direction, adding that he had already eaten. I decided that I would bother him as little as possible. The cheapest food on the menu was a stew of dried, salted codfish. I hated the taste but it was the cheapest meal and that's what I ordered. I regretted, though, that my host couldn't possibly know how much I hated this dish.

We returned to his apartment where we shared his bedroom for the night. I slept on some sort of couch and the next morning we left to meet with Vasil Andoni and Zef Pali. We traveled by streetcar and on foot and made it to an apartment somewhere in Rome. My host was not asking any questions about the reason for my trip and I was keeping my mouth shut as the silence between us suited me just fine.

We met with the two men I had asked to see. In fact, there was a third man present, another member of Balli's Central Committee whose name I don't remember.

"Welcome to Rome." Vasil Andoni extended his hand as he rose to greet me. Turning to Mr. Kazazi, he said, "Thank you, Hasan, for hosting Genc overnight and for bringing him here today. He will stay with us and you and I will see each other later."

Finally someone who seemed glad to see me; the fact that he did not include Hasan Kazazi in what was to follow pleased me, I must admit.

"What brings you to Rome?" he asked in his friendly, unhurried, typical way.

I proceeded to give him the highlights of my escape before introducing Hila into the picture. Then I mentioned our get-together in Belgrade, Martin's involvement, and the plan intended to bring Hila and his network in Albania over to the West. I kept it brief but was ready to elaborate if they needed more detail. I also stayed away from giving the details of the planned incursion into Albania for security reasons. As I talked, I had the sense that I was talking about another world, a world they had little knowledge of and few links with. That was not surprising, considering Albania's pathologic isolation.

Vasil Andoni asked most of the questions. Once I was done, my three listeners decided that it was indeed necessary that I meet with the head of the CIA section for Albania. I was delighted. *Now we are cooking*, I thought. Now I would find out whether the CIC had truly presented my case to the CIA. There was still time to carry out the plan to rescue Hila and Deda. Once

I met with the Americans, it would be up to them as to what they did with the information. It was likely that my job was done at that point.

That afternoon, Vasil Andoni and Zef Pali took me to meet Athanas Gegaj. He was a former Roman Catholic priest who had fallen in love with an Italian woman and had married her. They lived in a small house halfway up a hill. Her brother also lived with them. I was introduced under an assumed name. Again, I was a medical student from Milan who, for reasons not included in the cover story, was spending a few days in Rome. I had the impression that Athanas Gegaj was never told the true story. He may have suspected that there was something fishy about my being there but had agreed to take me in. That was fine with me. In fact, Vasil Andoni and Zef Pali picked me up from time to time and Athanas Gegaj never asked a question or displayed any curiosity about my comings and goings.

I had a long session with Zef Pali. He was from Shkodra and we had many common acquaintances. He had known Hila when the latter was an NCO in the police before the communist victory. Zef did not think much of Hila and had trouble accepting the fact that in the intervening years, Hila had achieved prominence as a refugee in Yugoslavia. He inquired about others in Shkodra but knew very few of the local communist leadership. He showed much interest in stories and anecdotes of events that had occurred during the years of his absence from Albania. That, of course, was understandable. As editor of the Balli newspaper *Flamuri,* he was eager to gather fresh material for his paper. When I saw the insistence with which he was looking for details to flesh out my stories, I recognized that here was a contribution I could make to Balli and to the paper. Instead of giving him all the material he was asking for, I thought I would tell him enough to stimulate his appetite but kept the most interesting material for later, when I could contribute it myself, circumstances permitting. For the time being, I also had to hold back on any material that would identify me as the source, because I could not afford to make life more difficult for my loved ones who were still in the hands of the communist regime.

At one point, he asked me whether I wanted to accompany him as he was going to Radio Vatican to see an Albanian priest who worked there. I asked him whether the station was near St. Peter's and when he confirmed it, I asked to visit the basilica while he was at the radio station.

What a powerful emotional experience that was for me. I had been to St. Peter's before and those memories engulfed me in a way I would have had to suppress had I been with others. As it was, I entered the basilica, knelt down in prayer, and let past and present engulf me with unfettered power. Thank you, Lord, bless you Lord...

That evening, Vasil Andoni brought word that the next evening we would meet with the CIA officer in charge of the Albanian section in Rome. He and Zef would pick me up at 6:00 p.m. They left and I spent the rest of the evening with Mr. and Mrs. Gegaj. They were friendly, hospitable, and respected my privacy. Under the circumstances, they were ideal hosts.

The next day, I needed no special projects or preparations for the evening get-together. The plans and deadlines were sculpted in my mind. I was ready to go. That afternoon around 5:30, the two professors rang the doorbell at the Gegaj residence.

I opened the door for them; I had been near the door for about half an hour, awaiting them.

"Are you ready?"

"Yes, just let me say goodbye to Mr. and Mrs. Gegaj," and off we were for the evening.

We took a streetcar and got off at a certain point. "We wait now," Vasil said. "They are usually quite punctual."

That evening would not be an exception. We did not have to wait long. A station wagon pulled up and the driver lowered the window and waved.

"Good evening," Vasil said as he bent down to enter the vehicle. Zef and I followed. The three of us squeezed into the back seat.

The head of the CIA's Albanian section was probably the driver. *Who was the man sitting next to him*? I asked myself. The driver had mumbled an introduction for himself and the other man up front. Then Vasil introduced me to our two hosts.

I could not tell which way we were going but it was plain that we were leaving Rome as we drove first through suburbs and later through open country. Finally, after almost an hour's drive, we pulled up a hill and stopped at the entrance to an elegant restaurant. A waiter escorted us to a table on a terrace with a beautiful view of the countryside below and around us. Even though I had more pressing thoughts on my mind, I could not help but notice the pattern formed by beautiful, bountiful farmland, by farmers' homes, and by barns and granaries, all separated—or rather stitched together—by narrow paths, country roads, and highways.

The sun was still fairly high above the horizon when we ordered our drinks. Once the waiter was gone, our driver took over.

"Mr. Korça, I am glad we have a chance to get together. Your friends have told us much about you. My colleague, who is my counterpart with British intelligence, and I are most interested in what you have to tell us. Mr. Andoni, will you please act as our interpreter?"

Now I knew who the other gentleman was. The American was not aware that I spoke English. Obviously, the CIC had failed to mention it in their reports. I knew that Vasil Andoni was a graduate of Robert College, and therefore spoke English. Zef Pali may have spoken English but he was probably less proficient.

For two months, I had hoped and planned for the day when I would sit with a CIA officer and tell him about our plans regarding Hila and the role we hoped the CIA would play. That day was finally here. The four men around the table now turned toward me since the ball was in my court.

"I apologize for my English. It is self-taught but I will do the best I can. I know I can count on Professor Andoni's help if I get stuck." I wanted to speak without an interpreter and thus keep my part of the conversation under control. If they were surprised that I spoke to them in English, none of them showed it.

I began from the beginning, telling the story I had mentioned to Zef in Zagreb, to the CIC in Austria, and to the two Albanian professors in Rome. It was a story I knew well and the words and terms came easily. When I was done, the American spoke up.

"Why have you waited so long to come to us with this most interesting information?"

"Over a month ago I went to the CIC in Salzburg informing them of our plans and asking to be put in touch with you. I did not provide them with all the details, such as dates and locations for making contact with the Albanian underground. Other than that, they had everything they needed to inform you about our plans. After meeting with them in Salzburg for weeks and weeks, they finally told me that you were not interested in what I had to offer."

He was obviously embarrassed. "Well, yes, they did contact me but what they told me bore little resemblance to what we just heard from you." He reached for his wallet, extracted 50 dollars, and extended his hand in my direction.

"I realize your information is worth more than $50 but that's all I have with me tonight. When I see our head accountant I'll get more."

I blushed, turned toward my two compatriots, and said in Albanian, "Does he take me for someone who is selling information?" The American seemed at a loss while his British colleague kept silent as he had done throughout the evening.

Professor Andoni intervened. "I'll take the money. Our friend needs some Italian clothes to be inconspicuous. We'll take care of it."

The sun had set and the evening was very pleasant with a cool breeze wafting across the terrace. We had finished our dinner and the wine that went with it. The waiter came and presented a bill for $25. I was aghast. In Albania, a family of five could have easily lived a whole month on $25 dollars. Here, our host was paying this for a dinner for five? I tried not to show my dismay.

The evening was over. We climbed into the car and drove back to Rome. Little was said during our return trip. When we reached the point where we had gotten into the car, the CIA officer said that we would hear from him. We wished each other a good night and the car took off while we three Albanians moved toward the streetcar that would take me home.

The next day, Vasil Andoni let me know that within 48 hours I was to leave with the CIA officer for an unknown destination. I had learned my lesson in Albania that hypothesizing or trying to guess what lay ahead was futile under the circumstances for lack of information. Furthermore, the forces controlling my future were beyond my control. I pushed aside all thoughts that were attempting to pierce the clouds of uncertainty. I concentrated on the present, on the "dos and don'ts" facing me. I might stroll in the neighborhood, take in the sights, enjoy reading Italian newspapers, and listen to the radio. It was probably prudent to keep away from Uncle Edward Liço because of his business associates. I would certainly avoid places frequented by Albanians, such as the cafés along the Via Veneto. All I had to do at this point was bide my time and wait for the anticipated trip. After all, two days would pass in a hurry. Things were moving in the right direction and that was what counted.

The evening of my departure, Professor Andoni came around 7:30. I said goodbye to my hosts, who had been prudent and kind and had made my stay pleasant. It was not an emotional goodbye. Our relationship, however, had been such that if we met sometime in the future, I would see them with pleasure.

After a short trip by streetcar, there we were on a street corner awaiting the CIA officer who would pick me up. A few minutes later, I saw the station wagon amid Rome's heavy traffic. The driver pulled to the curb. I shook hands with Professor Andoni and climbed into the car next to the CIA officer who had been our host a few nights before. Smoothly, he eased the car into the hectic, aggressive Roman traffic where only the fittest could survive.

I did not know my travel destination nor how I was supposed to get there. Again, the driver was heading out of Rome. We cleared the suburbs without having said much to one another.

"Would you mind repeating right from the beginning what you told us the other night?" he said for an opener.

I went over familiar ground, repeating the full story with all the particulars. Now he began asking questions. I had the sense that more than wanting to clarify this or that detail, he was trying to punch holes into my story. He had me go over my story again and again, which pleased me because it was my chance to convince him of my truthfulness.

We had been traveling for hours. By now it was obvious that we were going north, because I could see from the road signs that we were bypassing Florence and later Bologna. Outside, it was getting lighter. Now I also had a chance to watch my travel companion from a close distance. He was about six feet tall, with a large head, a ruddy complexion, and sparse reddish-blond hair. He was lean, heavy boned, with large hands and feet. He looked to be in his early forties. Professor Andoni had told me that he, the CIA officer, was a former Air Force colonel.

We kept pushing north. By now, we were more or less talked out. According to the road signs, we were getting close to Padua.

"Soon we'll stop somewhere to eat a bite and freshen up. This may also be a good chance for you to buy some clothes. Do you have any suggestions?"

I immediately thought of Padua. I knew the city center and the facilities it offered. Yes, Padua would do nicely. However, I could not help thinking of the Yugoslav secret service major who, just about six months ago, had also insisted on buying me some new clothes. Coincidence or secret service blueprint? It really did not matter. I still had my "refugee" clothes on and needed to be able to mingle, sartorially speaking, with an Italian crowd without being conspicuous.

"Padua is just ahead of us. I went to medical school in Padua and know my way around. At the center there are several restaurants that serve breakfast. There is also what the Italians call an '*albergo diurno.*' It is an underground facility, with restrooms, showers, barber shops, manicure facilities, and where one can have his clothes pressed."

"OK, Padua it is."

The colonel was a skillful driver. Soon we were at the center of town and parking was not a problem in that faraway year of 1953. I led him to the *albergo diurno,* and here we split up. Furtively, he gave me 100,000 lire.

"See you here in a couple of hours."

That suited me fine. I had enjoyed our "overnight togetherness." It had given me the chance to convince him, if not of the truthfulness of my story, at least of my consistency in telling it. I was ready for a breather.

The *albergo diurno* had been upgraded since my times as a student. I showered, shaved, and left for a quick breakfast. I felt clean, bouncy, and full of purpose. Across the street from the entrance to the main university offices, there had been a good men's clothing store. It was still there. I bought myself a striped tan summer suit, two short-sleeved shirts, socks to go with my new outfit, and some underwear. I did not buy shoes, as the brown shoes I got in Austria were new and very nice. The total expenses at the clothing store came to about 64,000 lire. By now, it was time to go back to the car.

Punctual as always, there was the colonel. He looked me over, from head to toe, and seemed pleased with what he saw.

"I see you made good use of time," he said with a smile.

"Thank you, yes. By the way, here is the receipt from the clothing store and here is your change." I gave him the receipt and 36,000 lire in Italian currency. I wanted to let him know that I had no problem spending money to further our plans. After all, we were both soldiers fighting for the same cause. I also wanted him to know that I was not for sale. I may have imagined it, but I thought he looked slightly surprised. Who knows what was going through his mind.

"Let me tell you what lies ahead," he said after pocketing both the receipt and the cash. "We will drive now to Venice and you will disappear for 48 hours to give us time to prepare some travel documents for you. We want to take you to Trieste for a few days. Trieste is international at this point. Hence, you will need some sort of documents. I'll take you to a designated place and that's where you'll meet with some colleagues of mine who will take you to Trieste two days hence."

I was nonplussed. What did he mean by saying that I had to disappear for 48 hours? Wasn't the CIA as powerful as the Soviet secret service? Could they not do just about anything that pleased them?

"I don't understand why I have to disappear for 48 hours. Can you not hide me somewhere for that length of time?"

"No, we couldn't. If the Italians find you in our company, we would have an international incident on our hands. I am afraid you will have to handle this on your own." The way Hasan Kazazi had received me in Rome a few days before came to mind.

"Well, where do you want me to hide for two days?"

"Why don't you go to a brothel and spend the time there?"

I was furious. In Albania, we had survived our battle with the communists against all odds. They were better organized and had superior means; they controlled the police and the army. They had the power of the state and the party behind them. They were ruthless in conceiving and executing their plans. We had right and justice on our side. We were honest and uncompromising. We cherished and respected the best Albanian traditions. We would never dishonor *"besa"* (our word of honor), just as we would defend to the very last our personal and family honor and that of our friends. And here, the colonel wanted me to spend two days in a brothel?

"I have another idea. In Castello di Godego, not far from Padua, lives a former classmate of mine. She may be married by now but I am sure she will not betray me to the police. Can you drive me there?"

The colonel pulled out a map. Castello di Godego was about an hour's drive from Padua.

"OK, let's go," he replied and off we went.

I spent the time preparing myself to see Valnea. I had been in love with here since I was 14 years old. In high school, we got together for weekly dances and started dating seriously in the 12th grade and through our first year in college. Mine was a pure, exhilarating love where her well-being was all-important and her happiness my utmost concern. When I graduated from high school, Dad gave me as a graduation present two weeks' vacation anywhere in Italy. I, of course, chose Abbazia, a beautiful resort town about 7 kilometers from Fiume where Valnea lived. Mom, who would spend the vacation with me, wanted to go somewhere we had not been before. With the finality and selfishness of youth, I replied that it was *I* who had graduated from high school and that this was *my* graduation present. Therefore, we would go to Abbazia. Mom grumbled, and as it turned out, she had every right to grumble.

I remember we arrived in Abbazia on a Sunday. I took Mom and Mergim to the Hotel delle Palme, rented a bike and took off for Fiume. Thereafter, Valnea came to Abbazia every morning, Monday through Saturday. On Sunday I would again rent a bike and see her in Fiume. Mom and Mergim were left to their devices. For me those two weeks were like heaven. The two of them probably felt differently.

Under communism, I had conditioned myself to accept whatever situation I might face. In self-protection, I had surrounded myself with a sort of impenetrable barrier. I had not allowed myself to grieve when someone died or to rejoice if something good happened. I dated a few girls but never got attached to any and gained a few friends but was not surprised if they failed me. Psychologically, I could afford neither peaks nor valleys, neither enthusiasm nor discouragement.

After my escape, I continued the same way. During those ten years of separation, Valnea could have fallen out of love with me. By now, she could be engaged or even married with children. True, in her letters after my escape, she had not mentioned anything like that. Well, I was about to find out.

Once we reached Castello di Godego, someone gave us directions how to get to the pharmacy where Valnea worked. I entered the pharmacy and had trouble adjusting my eyes to the darkness inside the store. I took a quick look around but failed to see Valnea. I saw a man standing behind one of the counters.

"Could you please tell me whether Miss Valnea Curatolo is here?"

"No," he replied, "she is in San Remo on vacation."

"Thank you," I turned around and walked out of the store. As I had her address in San Remo, I needed no further information.

I got into the car and explained to the colonel what I had learned.

"So, where do we go from here?" he asked.

"Can you drive me to Venice? There I can take an overnight train to San Remo, spend the day there, and return overnight to Venice, in time to meet your people in the afternoon."

"That's fine with me, except that, instead of Venice, I'll drive you to Mestre where you can board the train. For me it is easier to get in and out of Mestre. Is that OK with you?"

"Yes, thank you very much."

About 45 minutes later, we were at the railroad station in Mestre. I shook hands with the colonel, never to see him again.

CHAPTER FORTY-ONE

SAN REMO—TRIEST—GREECE

Inside the railroad station in Mestre it was pleasantly cool. The distance between Mestre and Venice was just a few minutes by train. Mestre itself was an industrial and maritime center.

I went to a ticket counter and bought a ticket: Mestre–San Remo–Venice. The next train to San Remo was leaving shortly and was due to arrive in San Remo the next morning at 7:00 a.m. That fit my plans perfectly. I got myself something to eat and went to the platform just as the train from Venice was pulling in. The train was half-empty. I found myself a window seat and settled down for a trip that would last about 16 hours and would bridge ten long years since the time I had said goodbye to Valnea at the railroad station in Padua.

I made myself comfortable. The rhythmic clatter of the train wheels and the occasional engine whistle gave me a cozy feeling. I pulled out a magazine I had bought in Mestre and promptly fell asleep. I must have slept a few hours because, after all, I had not slept a wink the night before, that long night between Rome and Padua. It was a night to remember. The frequent questions, the coherent answers, and the strange relationship between a CIA officer trained not to trust and a refugee trying to sell a plan that in his mind was good for Albania as well as for the United States.

On the train, I got myself something to eat and drink, relieved that there were no hefty mothers with umpteen whining children in the compartment. I slept some more during the night but woke up at daybreak. The scenery outside the window was breathtaking at times. There were hills and mountains covered with luxuriant vegetation. Wild, colorful bushes and flowers grew close enough to sway as the train rushed by. Sometimes factories and warehouses alternated with farms and barns. At other times, I could see the deep blue color of the Ligurian Sea and rows of white villas glistening like pearls along the seashore.

The closer the train got to San Remo, the more my mind began to wander. Would Valnea be home? How would she look? How would I look to her after so many years? How would she receive me? Should I be cool and controlled or act with self-assurance as if I had returned to my girlfriend after being absent for a while? This last question had an easy answer. Of course, I would act cool, calm, and collected and let Valnea take the lead. It was the proper, safe way. Whatever her reaction, I would not hurt too much if things went wrong.

The train tracks were multiplying rapidly, as is the case near railroad stations. The train began slowing down. I could see signs and shields that made sense to railroaders but to no one else. Finally, there was the large shield with "San Remo" in large letters. The engine came to a full stop. The time was 7:00 a.m. precisely. I grabbed my modest belongings, jumped off the train and moved toward the exit. As I left the railroad station behind, I glanced at my watch, hoping that enough time had passed for me to go to directly to Valnea's apartment. Well, it was about 7:02 a.m., still too early for a visit. I decided to go to a restaurant and have breakfast. Italian breakfasts are not very elaborate. Fruit juice, a croissant, and a cup of coffee was the normal breakfast. The service was prompt and though I dawdled through breakfast, I was done by 7:25. I felt I had waited long enough.

I asked the waiter for directions and stood at the front door of Valnea's apartment building by 7:30. I had waited ten long years for this moment. So what if she lost some sleep on my account. I rang the bell, and moments later the front door release activated. I climbed the stairs and found myself facing a half-open door and Valnea's mother peering at me.

"Excuse me, Mrs. Curatolo, is Valnea home?"

She shuffled away and I heard her say in a muffled voice, "Valnea, I think Genc is here." Then she returned to the door, asked me to come in and pointed at a room off the hallway. I entered, waited a few minutes, and finally sat down, intentionally facing away from the door. A few more minutes passed when I heard footsteps behind me. I jumped to my feet, turned around and there was Valnea. We half embraced.

One long look told me that she had not changed at all. She was exactly as I had seen her in my dreams, awake and otherwise.

"Valnea, how are you?"

"I am fine, how are you, Genc?"

"I, too, am fine." We were both groping for things to say.

She asked, "Did you get the letter I sent you to St. Martin?"

"No, I got no letter from you." I wondered what was in that letter.

Suddenly, the doorbell rang, breaking up the awkward silence that was engulfing us. Valnea excused herself and went to open the door. I could hear voices, hers and a man's, but could not make out what they were saying. I waited for quite a while. Finally, she came back, mentioned that Guido Federighi, her boss, had recognized me in Castello di Godego, and was presently in the other room. She excused herself, as she had to talk to him.

I had my answer. He had seen me, had realized that I was coming to San Remo, and had hurried after me to make sure I did not steal his woman. We must have traveled on the same train to San Remo. I leaned out the window in Valnea's apartment. There was little traffic below and few pedestrians passing by the house. As I looked to my right, I saw Guido looking out the window, tears streaming down his face. I felt contempt for him. How could a man cry, not just under these, but under any circumstances? Besides, he had won and I was the loser.

As on many other occasions over the years, I felt out of place. I considered how I could get myself and everyone else out of this embarrassing situation. I looked down and saw that I was on the third floor of the building. There was no way I could safely climb down. By jumping down, I could break a leg or worse. No, I would face the situation. I could take no chances for the sake of my assignment and of those who depended on me.

Valnea finally returned. "I would like you to meet Guido."

Guido and I shook hands. He was somewhat shorter than I, slim and quite handsome now that he had composed himself. Valnea took over once again. By now, it was about nine o'clock.

"Genc, you remember Nucci. Why don't we pay her a visit?"

That was fine with me. I remembered Nucci well. Her full name was Clementina Niccoli. We called her "the countess," because she had style and was the prettiest girl in our class. She and I had been classmates since the eighth grade; we had been members of our city choir and of the "Saturday

Night Dance Club" at the Bolchis'. We had never been close. Nonetheless, I was glad to see her again. Being with her would bring back memories of our years in Fiume and Padua. Besides, we—Valnea, Guido, and I—would be on neutral ground. And that was good.

As we crossed the street, I instinctively took Valnea's arm. Compared to ten years ago, it had gone soft. When we got to Nucci's apartment, Valnea rang the bell. Nucci opened the door and her eyes popped at the sight of the three of us.

"Genc?"

"Hi, Nucci."

"Please come in," she said ushering us into her apartment.

Compared to Valnea's, it was airy and full of sunshine. Our conversation kept limping along. Everyone was looking for safe topics but could not come up with something that would fill the conversational chasm for more than a few minutes. If we talked about our common school years, Guido was left out. If I told them about communism and some of my adventures, it would sound like bragging or asking for pity. I wanted neither. I could have told them why and how I had come to Italy, but for obvious reasons I was not going to bring that up. Fortunately, Valnea asked no questions. So, I sat back and let the two women do the best they could.

Eventually, Valnea proposed that we return home. Her father liked to go out for an *aperitif* before lunch, preferably with friends. We picked up her father. Nucci's sister and her husband also joined us. Valnea's mother stayed home to prepare some dishes Guido liked. Again, I would have felt hurt had it not been for my body armor. OK, so Guido was Valnea's boss and probably her fiancée, but darn it, didn't my long years of absence and suffering count for something?

On the way to the bar, I pulled Guido aside. "Guido, do you mind if I buy Valnea a present?"

"No, go ahead."

By the time we were seated at a sidewalk table at a nearby bar, there were seven of us. The conversation began to flow smoothly in an atmosphere of easy friendship. Nucci's sister was a darling. She was pretty, bubbly, youthful, and unencumbered. Her husband owned a printing firm in Milan. He was very friendly, sharp, and seemed financially well off. Both he and his wife wore their expensive, understated clothes with style.

Valnea's father was in charge, there was no doubt about that. He picked the topics of conversation and shifted smoothly from one to the next when there was little left to say or if the topic seemed to be going in the wrong direction. I contributed little but took in the friendly, peaceful atmosphere, the feeling of being part of a group of friends without threats on the horizon. It was a feeling I had missed for too many years.

At one point, the conversation touched on smoking. As they were all smokers, they mentioned their preferred brands of cigarettes but agreed that American cigarettes were the best. The day before, the CIA officer had given me a pack of American cigarettes. I had put it absentmindedly in my pocket. Now it was my turn to speak up.

"Since you like American cigarettes, may I offer you some?"

They all reacted with much cheer and my pack began to make the rounds. When it reached Valnea's father, he turned to me. "Where did you get this pack of cigarettes?" he asked, fixating his eyes on me.

"Why?"

"It has no Italian tax stamp."

He was right. Importers of American cigarettes in Italy had to pay an import tax. American military personnel, CIA employees, and some others got them at the PX stores free of tax. I did not want to reveal the source and so I mumbled something in return. The others switched topic, thank God. I wondered, however, what Mr. Curatolo made of my answer.

Nucci's sister and husband left for home while the rest of us got up to partake of the lunch Mrs. Curatolo had prepared. Guido, the guest of honor, was seated at the head of the table. I sat with the rest of the mortals. After lunch, Mrs. Curatolo informed us that it was time for Guido's nap. Valnea and I withdrew into one of the rooms, speaking softly to make sure we were not disturbing Guido.

Around three o'clock that afternoon, Nucci's sister and husband came to pick us up for a brief tour of San Remo. Valnea and I climbed into the back seat. Guido was still sleeping. To me the four-passenger car seemed uncomfortably small compared to the American station wagon that had brought me from Rome to Mestre.

The young couple took us to see the long and elegant sidewalk along the seashore. I saw the statue representing a young woman, symbol of youth, life, and love. Valnea had sent me a postcard with the picture of the

statue while I was still in Albania. I had looked at it many a time, sometimes by itself and sometimes side by side with pictures of Valnea, asking
myself why life had torn us apart, why I could not go back to school, why
the Allies had abandoned us to communism, why...why...why...

I looked at the statue and reminded Valnea of the postcard she had sent
me, while blocking out any thoughts that might weaken me. Eventually,
we wound up in a narrow one-way street and stopped at a store selling
"*Sale e Tabacchi*," salt and tobacco products that were monopolies of the
Italian state. Our driver stopped the car, temporarily blocking the street,
and we all entered the store. As I was looking around the store, we heard
an angry car horn honking, demanding the right of passage.

Valnea turned to me. "Genc, you know how to drive. Would you move
the car?"

I started to leave the store and then I remembered. I could not afford
an angry exchange of words, an altercation, or an accident, anything that
might attract the attention of the police.

"Sorry, Valnea, it is better that the owner move his car." Valnea looked
surprised but I could not explain, not under the circumstances.

During the afternoon Valnea told me that Guido had run after me as I
left the pharmacy in Castello di Godego. He did see that the license plate
of the car started out with the two letters "EE," "*Escursioni Estere*." Such
license plates were issued to foreigners staying in Italy. He had called a gas
station at the entrance to Castello di Godego and had asked the owner to
stop our car so Guido could speak with me. We must have taken a different
route because the owner never saw our car. That's when Guido decided to
come to San Remo to make sure I was not alone with Valnea. It so happened that Guido and I had traveled on the same train. He would have had
plenty of time to talk to me on the train.

Nucci's sister and her husband must have discussed me after we met
that morning. Before dropping us off, he said to me, "Genc, as you know
by now, I have a printing establishment in Milan. I need a supervisor I can
trust. Would you be interested?"

This offer caught me by surprise. I was touched by his desire to help
me and yet I had to turn him down. I needed a moment or two to think how
to formulate my answer.

"Thank you so much but I know nothing about the printing business."

"That's something you can easily learn. What I need is a man who is honest and reliable. That's why I am making you this offer."

I countered, "Well, it is not yet certain where I will settle down—in Italy or somewhere else." I figured that he would accept this, as I had obviously lost Valnea, and without her I had no reason to live in Italy.

"You know best what's good for you," he replied. "Anyhow, should you change your mind, the offer stands." He pulled out his wallet and gave me his card. "You can reach me either by phone or by mail, OK?" Both husband and wife waved goodbye and off they went.

Valnea and I climbed the steps to the apartment and got there just in time for a snack, as Guido's train was leaving around 7:00 p.m., arriving in Venice in the morning. Mr. Curatolo, Valnea, and I accompanied him to the railroad station. I turned toward some posted train schedules on the wall and studied them with utmost attention so he and Valnea could say goodbye to each other in whatever fashion they chose. When the train began moving away from the platform, I turned around and waved goodbye to Guido. He just left, and I would be leaving San Remo at 9:30 that evening. That was how this chapter of my life would end.

As we left the railroad station, her father spoke to Valnea.

"Come, let's go home now."

"Dad, you go ahead. I'll be home before too long." Then she turned toward me. "Come, let's go to a café that's not far from here."

We walked to a café by the name of something like *Trajectory Southeast.*

"Valnea, there are some things I would like to tell you. The name of the café points southeast, toward Albania. I may be going back to Albania on a mission," and I proceeded to give her in broad strokes a description of our plans to transfer to the Americans the Yugoslav network in northern Albania. I told her that good men, personal friends of mine in Albania, depended on me. I told her that I intended to buy her a present in San Remo but that I did not have a chance to do so.

A friend had given me a gold coin in Yugoslavia in case I needed money for my mission. As it turned out, I did not need to cash it. I pulled the coin out of my coin purse and gave it to her, asking her to accept it, as I could not think of anyone I would rather give it to. I concluded by saying that I might be gone for a while but that I would let her know my whereabouts as soon as possible.

The more I spoke, the closer Valnea and I were drawn to each other. By the time I was done, it felt as if someone had spliced the film of our lives, joining our farewell in 1943 to this magic summer of 1953, thus removing the intervening gap of ten years.

Time had come for us to leave. We did not say much as we walked to the railroad station. I climbed aboard my train and Valnea followed. As I looked at her, I could sense Guido's presence between us. Instead of kissing her goodbye, I stiff-armed her and shook hands while everything within me screamed that I take her in my arms. She got off the train and waved, as once again life separated us.

Many things had happened in the 48 hours since I left Rome. Now, I was again on a train, traveling east to meet my "friends" the next day at 1400 hours in Venice. From Professor Andoni I had learned that "friends" was what people called the CIA when they did not want to use its initials in public. I liked that. Besides, the United States and the CIA were indeed our friends.

At this point, my mind was in turmoil. Memories and new hopes all centered around Valnea, pressed to the fore while thoughts linked to the next day's meeting demanded prime attention. The entire day in San Remo had been tiring. I had tried to stay on top of things until evening, and then long repressed emotions had burst forth and taken over. Eventually, the rhythmic pattern of the train wheels lulled me to sleep and I slept for hours and hours.

I woke up refreshed and at peace with myself. Considering how things stood now between Valnea and me, I felt I could tackle anything that would come my way. Obviously, I still had much to do with our "friends," whatever course they chose to take. Once that was taken care of, I would come back to Valnea and the future would be ours.

The train got to Venice on time. I grabbed a bite at the railroad station where the food was neither the best nor the cheapest, but it did the job. Next, I went to the barbershop for a shave. I remember this vividly because of what the barber said to me.

"Did you travel all night?"

"Why?" I asked him.

"Because the skin under your chin is bleeding and yet I did not cut you. That happens when men are tired."

I gave him a noncommittal answer but I knew he was right as it had happened to me before.

Because my meeting was later that afternoon, I had plenty of time to get to the café. At the designated time, an American car stopped and the driver stuck his head out the window.

"Jack, let's go."

As that was the name the colonel and I had agreed on, I joined him in the car. He took off at a brisk clip and drove even faster once we cleared the suburbs. I knew we were going east but I was unfamiliar with the general area. Suddenly, in the middle of nowhere, he came to a screeching halt.

"Get out and climb into the car that's following us."

The whole thing looked like a B gangster movie to me but who was I to object? I did as I was told, jumped into the car that had stopped behind us and off I was, with a different car and a different driver.

This one seemed more relaxed. I decided to ask him a question that had bothered me for a while.

"I see the speed limit has been set at 56.3 kilometers per hour. Can you tell me why not at 56 km/hr or even better, 55 km/hr?"

He chuckled. "Our American limit in this area is 35 mph, which is equivalent to 56.3 km/hr. If the European limit were set at anything other than 56.3 km/hr, we would have two limits, one for Americans and the other for Europeans. Now we could not have such a thing, could we?"

The name "Trieste" began to appear on road signs, so we could not be very far from the border.

"Do you have any documents for me?" I asked.

He shook his head. "No, but we really don't need any. Here is what we will do. I will give you some chewing gum. When we get to the border, start chewing while reading an American newspaper you will find in the glove compartment. I will place my passport between you and me on the front seat. No matter what happens at the border, you do not speak Italian. If anyone addresses you, look at me and I will take care of the situation."

Well, that was clear enough. Except, why did they ask me to disappear for 48 hours when they could get me across the border without documents? Fortunately, they did not and I had a chance to spend time with Valnea.

At the border, we stopped. The driver called the border guard by name. In poor Italian, he told the guard that he had not forgotten his promise and pulled out a can of American shaving cream. The guard took the can and waved us on with a big grin. We had just entered the international territory of Trieste. We drove into the city and the driver stopped in front of a gray, rundown house.

"Here we are. Grab your suitcase and follow me."

He rang a bell; we walked in and climbed several flights of stairs. A woman who was standing in front of an apartment asked us in and showed us to my room. The room was dark, with creaky furniture that matched the outside appearance of the building. I had expected something less shabby, but as far as I was concerned, it would do.

When the woman left us, my driver said to me, "Talk to her as little as possible. She will serve you breakfast and lunch. In the evening, we will pick you up and treat you to a good meal and some fresh air. For this evening, this will have to do." He gave me a rather large package that smelled of sausage, bid me good night, said he would pick me up the next evening, and was gone without waiting for an answer.

Spending the day in a dark room was no big problem. I had learned in the Albanian mountains, whether in a shelter or in the open, to occupy my mind for hours at a time. Besides, staying inside the room was both more comfortable and safer than where I had first learned the art of focusing my eyes inward. First, my mind would stay away from speculating about the future. Next, it would focus on recent information and weigh its accuracy and value. Whatever survived this scrutiny, I would put up against past and present events. If everything fit together, I would weigh its potential impact on the future.

This method had limitations but also a few benefits. Sometimes, "facts" of the past came to assume new meaning in view of fresh evidence. In extreme cases, these "facts" turned out to be the very opposite of how they had appeared at first blush. I had this experience also with people whom I had categorized as friend, foe, or of little import at first. Based on new evidence—and after due consideration—I had sometimes had to move them to another category.

In the evening, my "friend" (case officer?) picked me up around 7:30. Of course, I had an appetite but I longed even more for sunshine and some fresh air. The hustle and bustle of Trieste was most welcome. By the sights and sounds of it, Trieste was just like many other Italian cities on the seashore. This was no surprise to me. What surprised me was that Tito demanded Trieste for Yugoslavia and that the Allies were treating him with kid gloves, reluctant to say no to his absurd demand. There was little doubt that Trieste was Italian. The answer was less clear in the case of Trieste's hinterland. Fortunately, I did not have to make those decisions.

We drove to a nice restaurant and picked a table out in the open. I remember the waiter asking me what kind of dressing I wanted on my salad. The only dressing I was familiar with was oil and vinegar, and that was what I asked for. Except that, since I knew how to spell but did not know how to pronounce vinegar, I pronounced it "winegar." I felt embarrassed when my host pronounced the word correctly as he ordered his salad dressing. Well, live and learn.

The next morning, my case officer unexpectedly showed up at the apartment and asked me to get ready to leave. That did not take me long, nor did I feel sorry for getting out of the apartment.

In the car he told me that the landlady was getting suspicious of me because I spent all day cooped up in the room and did not leave except in the evening and then accompanied by an American. I was going to move in with another American where I would spend the rest of my stay in Trieste.

That was indeed welcome news. I longed to hear spoken English, preferably with an American accent. Meeting another CIA agent was just what I wanted, as I was interested in anything American, and particularly in anything or anybody related to the CIA.

We drove into a plush section of town with broad streets, nice stores, and fine buildings. I do not want to give the impression that I felt I was too good for the shabby building I was assigned to when we arrived in Trieste, but given a choice, I would have opted for one in the nicer parts of town. Well, we climbed a few flights of stairs and my escort rang the bell. A young man, about my age, opened the door. He was about 5 foot 7 inches, of slight build, with dark hair and a friendly smile. We shook hands, my driver excused himself, and here I was with my new "handler."

He showed me to my room, a very nice, large bedroom with a large desk and a comfortable chair. He showed me the bathroom, and after unpacking, we got together.

It was obvious from the beginning that we would get along just fine. He seemed as interested in meeting people from behind the Iron Curtain as I was in meeting Americans. He asked many questions regarding life in Albania as well as Yugoslavia. Obviously, it could all be a show, but his interest seemed too genuine to be just a façade. Furthermore, the conversation was not just a one-way street. I, too, asked questions, mostly about life in America. I obviously stayed away from asking anything related to his job but I did ask questions regarding my immediate future. He replied that a lie detector expert was flying in from Germany to test the truthfulness of my story. I was most pleased. Anything that boosted my credibility was welcome. Furthermore, the fact that they were flying in someone from Germany meant that they were interested in what I had to say.

A couple of days went by. One afternoon I was in my room when I heard male voices in the apartment. Someone else had joined us, and as it turned out, it was the polygraph expert from Germany. Now my curiosity was aroused. Shortly after his arrival, they called me into the dining room.

Next to my host was this man of medium height, rather sturdy, with a light complexion and light hair. My host introduced us. We shook hands and the man started setting up his equipment without wasting much time.

He explained that the equipment measured basically three things: heartbeat, respiration, and electric conductivity of the skin. At least, that's what I understood. Next, he went over a list of questions he was going to ask me. He read the questions one by one, explained their meaning if I asked for it, and even changed the wording of a particular question until I was satisfied that the meaning was perfectly clear to me. I was most surprised at the fairness of the test. The questions dealt with my personal data and with some details of the plan I had brought to the CIA. He further explained that if I had trouble understanding the question, my vital signs would be affected. Hence, it was to his benefit and mine that I be relaxed as I answered the questions. He zeroed the instrument and began asking questions from the prepared list. He went through them once and then once again. I felt confident that everything was proceeding very well. Then he sprang a trap.

"I am going to ask you now a few questions not on our list."

That felt like a low blow. I did not know what my reactions would do to his machine but I knew that I had just been kicked off Mount Olympus. Gone was my serenity and gone was my trust in fair play as far as this procedure was concerned. He asked the first question:

"Why did you not offer your information to our British allies as you escaped into the British zone in Austria?" That was easy.

"I believe that the British favor the royalists, the Legaliteti Movement, and are therefore not on Balli's side. As a member of Balli Kombëtar, my friends and I decided that I would make the information available to the CIA and let the Agency decide how to proceed from there."

He looked at his tracings and went on. "What did you know about the CIC and how did you contact them?"

I told him how I had contacted the American consulate in Salzburg and how an American soldier had brought me to the CIC.

"One last question. Is what you told me the truth?"

"Absolutely. In fact, I wish you would use any methods at your disposal to check out my truthfulness..."

He interrupted me. "Thank you, that's all."

A couple of days went by uneventfully. I would sometimes go for a walk, but most of the time I stayed home and read or listened to broadcasts, preferably in English but also in Italian. In the evening, my host and I would go out for dinner and enjoy excellent Italian food.

One evening he told me very matter of factly, "Tomorrow you are scheduled to leave Trieste."

"Do you know what time I will be leaving?"

"I assume, some time in midmorning."

"Then, we should say goodbye tonight."

He had been a gracious host. He was easy to get along with, and since the wheels had been moving forward, lie detector test and all, I was curious as to what would happen next. We shook hands, wished each other well, and retired for the night. He knew much more about me than I knew about him. I could not even say that the name he used was his real name but that was the way the game was played. I was very much aware of my helplessness. The "friends" had me under their control. They decided where I would go, where I would stay, and when I would leave. Actually, under the circumstances, I would not have wanted it any other way.

The next day, I got up early, prepared breakfast, and was ready to leave at a moment's notice. In fact, I did not have to wait long. The doorbell rang.

"Good morning, ready to go?" It was the same man who had brought me to Trieste.

"Yes," I replied. I grabbed my little suitcase, closed the door, and followed my guide. He had parked the car in front of the house. We climbed in and began driving uphill toward the border. Just like on the way in, the border crossing was no problem. Now I was back in Italy. We had traveled for a while in silence when my driver turned his head halfway back, pointing toward a package on the back seat.

"In there we have an American military uniform for you. Grab the package and unwrap it. I'll tell you step by step how to proceed."

I had noticed the package when I got into the car, but from its shape I could not guess its content. I removed the heavy wrapping paper. I could see socks and a pair of shoes, a military cap, a shirt, and a pair of trousers. Except for the brown shoes, everything else was khaki. Well, not quite. There was a blue braid around the left shirtsleeve at the shoulder.

"Take off your civilian shoes and your socks."

I complied, and kept doing exactly as I was told. Not that I could not have handled the situation myself but my driver was deriving obvious pleasure from changing me from a civilian into an American GI.

"Next, take off your pants and shirt. Put on first the shirt and then your pants. Put on your belt. Now, put on your socks and shoes. Finally, transfer the content of your pockets from your civilian slacks to your military pants. "

I could not say it was easy to change clothes in the front seat of a moving car but it was not too bad. As I looked at myself, my attire was so different from what I was used to that I felt like a different person. I settled down and had to admire whoever had picked the clothes and particularly the shoes for me. That the uniform fit was one thing. I can also imagine that at one point or another they had taken a look at my shoes and the shoe size marked inside. But these shoes fit perfectly without my having to break them in. I must say, I felt good in an American uniform.

We traveled quite a ways before road signs indicated that we were approaching Udine. As we got into the city, my driver stopped the car.

"Is there something you would like to buy?"

"Yes, thank you." I wanted to buy a book for myself and I wanted to write a card to Valnea. I bought *Piccolo Mondo Antico*, a funny book about an anti-communist Catholic priest and his opponent, the communist mayor of a small town. I also wrote a postcard for Valnea, and my companion promised he would mail it. He never did.

Our next stop was the Udine airport. We drove into the airport and near a military DC-3 that was waiting for us. I clutched the envelope with my military papers and climbed aboard. I saluted the two officers in the cockpit and sat down on one of two long benches that ran along both sides of the airplane. Next to me was a civilian who was my new escort. He was of medium height, light-complected, friendly, and built like an athlete.

"So, you are Albanian," he said smiling as we shook hands.

"Yes, I am."

"I don't speak Albanian, but in high school we had several Albanians on our basketball team. To confuse our opponents, we used to call out our plays in Albanian, '*një, dy*' [one, two], etc. Over the years it served us well."

There was little I could say in reply. I made some comments responding to his friendliness. Most of all, I was interested in the cockpit and in the landscape below.

"Can I get up and move about the airplane?"

"I see no reason why you shouldn't," he replied.

After a while, as I looked out the left side of the plane, I thought I recognized the Albanian coastline. If this was indeed Albania, I could not understand why we were flying so close to the Iron Curtain. I could just see something going wrong with the plane and us having to land in Albania. What a triumphant return this would be for me! I had escaped a few months ago and now I was returning in an American uniform. The very thought sent shivers down my spine. I decided to ask the pilot.

"Excuse me, sir, is that Albania's coastline?"

"Yes, it is."

"Then, why are we flying so close to it?"

"If you look out the other side of the plane you will see an electric storm hovering over central Italy."

I looked out and it was something I had never seen before. Amid a blue sky, a bunch of dark clouds were firing lightning after lightning at the ground below.

"Sir, if it is all the same to you, I would rather fly through that storm than risk landing in Albania." He neither responded nor reacted to my comments, and since he was in charge, we continued on the course he had chosen.

It was not long afterward that I noticed we were losing altitude. We were flying over a very large city, a veritable metropolis. The pilot lowered the landing gear. My travel companion looked at me.

"Welcome to Athens."

At that very moment, as I looked out the window, I recognized the Acropolis. We made a very smooth landing and rolled on the ground for a considerable distance as the plane taxied to an out-of-the-way hangar. When we came to a stop, I saluted the officers and followed my companion out of the plane and aboard a jeep that was idling nearby. We left the airport without stopping for passport control or customs. This had to be the American military section of the Athens airport.

The driver got us out of there and onto a highway that followed the seashore. It was a very hot day and the air whistling by as we drove with the top down did not help. From the position of the sun, I could tell we were traveling south. To our left were arid hills, minimally covered with low bushes and sparse vegetation. After a while, we turned inland up a winding road. The driver stopped our jeep in front of a nice-looking villa. My companion jumped out of the vehicle.

"Today is Saturday," he said. "This villa is where you will stay. The smaller building to the right houses the cook's quarters and the kitchen. There you will find a refrigerator with all kinds of food, from steaks to potatoes. Today and tomorrow, you will have to fend for yourself. On Monday, the cook will come. He will cook for you anything you want. On Monday, someone from our office will also come to ask you questions about Albania. Is this OK with you?"

"Of course, that's fine with me." As if I had a choice!

"Let's go inside, I'll show you around."

The villa was quite large, well furnished, and comfortable. On that particular day, it was hotter than blazes! At this point, the CIA officer handed me the keys, shook hands with me, and left. It felt good to be alone. I was tired and sleepy. I went into the bedroom, pulled the drapes, lay down in the buff, spread-eagled, with sweat running freely off my body. Before falling asleep, I turned on the radio, found a station broadcasting classical music, and threw myself into the arms of Somnus, the Roman god of sleep.

All of a sudden, the room reverberated with a harsh Albanian voice. Alarmed, I jumped up, aware of my helplessness. To my surprise, the room was exactly as before. There was no one there besides me. The harsh-sounding voice was that of Mrs. Sopoti, a speaker at Radio Tirana. Her voice blared from the radio, at the end of a program of classical music broadcast from Radio Tirana. Phew, what a shock and what a relief!

I could not go back to sleep. First, I decided to remove all military insignia from my uniform. Then I put on my khaki shirt and pants and sauntered across the front yard and into the kitchen. It did not take me long to find some bread, cold cuts, and cheese. There was also a pitcher full of cold water in the fridge. I sat down, made myself a good sandwich, and did not bother to return to the villa, as it was no cooler than the kitchen.

The next morning a surprise awaited me. As I walked outside, a small but sturdy shorthaired mutt with reddish fur and a light tan belly stood up from his resting place on the steps leading to the kitchen. He had a curly tail with long hair. His eyes were smiling at me as he wagged his tail with great vigor. He strongly resembled the stray dog that had been my steady companion in Dukagjin. I called him and he joyfully hopped toward me. I petted him. Did he belong to the safe house I was temporarily occupying? Was he some kind of a guard dog? It actually did not matter as long as he was willing to give me his friendship in exchange for scraps of food. We both needed what the other had to offer. I liked dogs and he was entering my life at the right time. I needed someone who understood without asking too many questions, someone trustworthy, someone who would not blabber behind my back. I decided to call him "Red."

"Red, let's go into the kitchen and have breakfast together." Without hesitation, he followed me up the steps and into the kitchen. I scrambled some eggs for myself and Red feasted on the eggshells. I gave him sausage skin and some bread with which I had wiped the frying pan, and he polished off with enthusiasm whatever I put in front of him. He liked my cooking and I liked his company. It was obvious that we were meant for each other.

It was a bright and sunny day. I decided to climb up the hills behind the villa before it got too hot. Red bounced right behind me and together we explored the area for about an hour. I was confident that I would not have visitors that Sunday. I felt on vacation and was glad to share my day off with Red. In a sense, we were both strays and we knew it.

Later, I let Red into the house and was pleased that he was housebroken. The next day, when the cook showed up for work, we might have a problem but I was determined to stand up for Red—I was sure that he would have done the same for me.

On Monday morning, by the time I walked into the kitchen, there was the cook. He was in his fifties, with a potbelly and gray hair. He stood up, half smiling, with a cold look in his eyes as he looked me over.

"I am Jack," I said as I extended my right hand toward him. We shook hands.

"My name is Christophoros, Chris for short." He spoke English with a heavy accent but without hesitation.

"I am an American and will spend some time here with you." I had decided to draw clear boundaries early on. If I had said that I was a European, he might have pestered me with all kinds of personal questions. By claiming to be an American, I intended to keep him at arm's length. He seemed unconvinced but that was fine with me.

"What would you like for breakfast?"

"How about a couple of scrambled eggs, bacon, toast, and some coffee?"

"Would you like Turkish coffee?"

"No, thanks. I'll have an American coffee. I think there is some in that cupboard." I pointed at the shelf where the coffee was.

"Do you take cream and sugar?"

"Yes, thank you."

I turned away from the cook and started to play with Red. I expected Chris to say something about the dog. Albanians, particularly farmers, disliked dogs. I suspected Greeks felt the same way. Well, Chris didn't say a word one way or another. When I finished eating, I made it a point to wipe my plate clean with bread, put the bread on a cracked plate I had found the day before, and offer it to Red, who ate the bread with his usual enthusiasm and licked the plate clean. Then we both left the kitchen and entered the villa. I wished I could have turned around to see how Chris had reacted to my feeding the dog. It did not matter. His silence had assured us that victory was ours, Red's and mine.

Around midmorning, a pickup pulled into our front yard. The driver got out and shook hands with me.

"I brought you food for a week. If you have something special in mind, tell me and I will bring it next Monday. Here are ten packs of cigarettes, and two bottles of whiskey. They should last you for a week."

"Could you bring me some razor blades? And, by the way, I don't smoke and I don't drink."

"OK, I'll take the stuff back next Monday." And off he went.

That afternoon, two CIA men came to see me. One of them said his name was Philip Adams and that he was of Albanian descent. The other mumbled a name and let it go at that. We sat down in the living room and they began to ask me questions about Albania. The questions were so vague and so ill defined that I did not know how to answer them. After about half an hour, I finally spoke up.

"Gentlemen, I know quite a bit about northern Albania that might interest you. I don't quite know how to fit this information into specific categories so as to give you this information efficiently. Do you have any ideas how we could do this?"

They looked at each other. They spoke to each other quickly and softly. Then Phil Adams said to me, "Maybe here is what we need to do. We will bring you a couple of books that cover the broad field of questions of interest to us. We will bring you pen and paper and whatever else you may need. Then, at your convenience, you can sit down, read the questions, collect your thoughts, and write down your answers. In the long run, this will probably be the best way to handle the problem. What do you think?"

"I think that's an excellent idea. In addition to pen and paper, I will need a typewriter and a good dictionary. If there is no good Albanian-English dictionary then I would appreciate a German-English or Italian-English dictionary."

"That should be no problem. We'll be back tomorrow." They rose, we shook hands, and that was all for that first day.

I was delighted. Instead of trying to find our way in the dark, I would have a chance to answer clearly defined questions. I would have a dictionary to work with, and I could use a typewriter, since I found it hard to write by hand.

The next afternoon both men returned. I helped them carry the goodies into the living room.

"Don't worry, later I will put everything where I want it. Please, sit down and show me how to proceed."

The man whose name I did not catch showed me the two books they had brought with them. They contained categories of questions to ask of refugees. He gave me a German-English/English-German dictionary, lots of paper, and a few pens, pencils, and erasers.

Then Philip added, "Should you also know something not covered by these questions that you think we should know about, by all means, feel free to add it. From time to time, someone will pick up whatever you have written up to that point. Also, we will drop in to see you and perhaps ask you to explain or expand on something mentioned in your report. OK?"

That was fine with me. They left and I was on my own. I really liked the setup. I could work at my own pace, cover as many pages in one day as I could reasonably handle, and ponder my answers until I was satisfied with the way I had phrased them. I put the typewriter on the desk, put the paper and the rest where it was most convenient, and sat down with the larger of the two books. In the introduction, the author explained that the content was meant to help interrogators elicit information from refugees. If the refugee had detailed information on any one question, specific follow-up questions were listed. If not, the interrogator should proceed to the next category of questions. Again, not doing this orally face to face gave me all the time I needed to answer questions to the best of my knowledge. It also gave me a good feeling as I was putting my knowledge fully at the disposal of the CIA and their struggle against communism. I knew I would enjoy hurting the Tirana regime as much as I could.

CHAPTER FORTY-TWO

RADIO FREE ALBANIA

My days took on a certain routine. After breakfast, I would work for a few hours; next, lunch and a short nap. In the afternoon, coffee and a slice of bread with jelly, cold cuts, or cheese followed by a few hours behind the typewriter. Then dinner and a walk with Red up and down the nearby hills. I felt well. My work was progressing and I was satisfied with my ability to express my thoughts in English. Each day represented a step forward, and I had a sense that the information I was bringing to the CIA was worth my effort and their money.

The pickup appeared on the following Monday. The driver jumped out, handed me the razor blades I had asked for, retrieved the packs of cigarettes and the two bottles of whiskey, and handed me another 10 packs of American cigarettes and two bottles of whiskey.

"Remember? I told you that I don't smoke or drink. So take away the cigarettes and the whiskey and don't bring any for the rest of my stay here," I said to the driver.

"That's OK. I'll pick them up next week. Today I'm in a hurry."

I was so disappointed. To me, God came first, then the United States, the bulwark of freedom, the hope of the oppressed peoples throughout the world. Now this! I could not see Americans stealing from their own government. In my opinion, it was akin to blasphemy. I decided to report the incident to one of the CIA officers who visited from time to time. Then I began to have second thoughts. If the driver stole, chances were he split the loot with a superior for safety's sake. Who knows how far up the free cigarettes and free booze—or their equivalent in money—would reach?

679

I decided to say nothing, but my image of the CIA and of Americans had suffered a blow. This was one more instance where idealistic expectations had to make room for reality. Pity.

As time went by, Chris opened up a bit. He had worked for some years in Chicago. I replied that I had never been there. I told him practically nothing about myself, drawing mostly from what I had read about life in the United States. We got along fine and I saw no need to shorten the distance between us.

Occasionally, a CIA officer would pick up what I had written since his last visit. On one such occasion, he left saying, "See you later." I expected him to show up later that day but he did not. Nor did he come the next day or the day after. Because I did not want to be traipsing over the nearby hills when he came, I stayed home for three days. On the fourth day, he finally showed up.

"Three days ago, you told me that you would see me later. How much later did you have in mind?" I was fuming.

"How do you mean, 'how much later?'"

"To me, 'later' means within an hour or two, not three days later," I said. He could see that I was angry.

"No, no, when we use that expression, we don't mean it that way."

I was not about to be put off. "If you don't mean it, then you should not say it." The absurdity of my telling an American, and perhaps the English-speaking world, how to use that expression never entered my mind; what self-righteousness!

One day I received a phone call from my case officer. The CIA was asking that I provide them with a list of people in Albania who were 100 percent trustworthy in case infiltrators or persons working for the United States contacted them. This was a most delicate and dangerous request. I was to put on paper the names of people such as my brother and others I trusted fully, with no assurance that the list would never fall into the wrong hands. I considered the pros and cons for quite a while. Finally, I agreed to accede to the request. Was I not ready to return to Albania by American helicopter to pick up Hila and Deda? My brother and my friends were just as patriotic as I was and would do their utmost to overthrow the communist regime. Did I have the right to deny them such an opportunity? It was a matter of trusting the CIA's judgment. Had I hesitated one moment when

I approached them with our plan to get Hila out of Albania? Was not my very presence in the villa a testimonial to my trusting the CIA?

I sat down and compiled the list starting with my brother and including the friend who had confessed to me in Shkodra that he had been forced to become a Sigurimi informer and that he was ready to erase that dishonor with his very life. When I was done, I called the CIA. They told me that someone would pick up that list within an hour.

After less than an hour, a cab pulled into our front yard. A Greek cabbie got out and said to me in English, "You got an envelope for me?"

'What envelope?" I replied.

"You have something for me."

I was tempted to send him away empty handed. At last, I handed him the envelope and he took off. My conscience, however, bothered me very much and kept bothering me until the day my case officer came for the usual routine visit. I was all steamed up.

"How could you send a Greek cabbie to pick up the list of absolutely trustworthy individuals I know in Albania?"

"We have worked with him before and we trust him. That should be good enough for you."

"Are we going to play games with the lives of dedicated people? Can you be sure that the cabbie doesn't routinely make copies of the material intended for you in exchange for good money?" This matter was too important for me to let go.

"Look, we are professionals. We know what we do and we screen the people we work with."

"Then tell me, how come my phone calls to you go through Greek telephone operators?"

"Those girls work for us. They have all been cleared."

"They have been cleared by whom?"

"By the Greek police, of course."

"And you trust the Greek police? Until recently, Greece was ravaged by a bloody civil war. And you are sure that communist agents have not infiltrated the Greek police?"

"What would you have us do?" he asked, stressing the word "you." It was hard to miss the irony.

"To begin with, you should have American telephone operators."

"Do you realize that we would have to pay them three times as much as we pay the Greek girls? Furthermore, the American operators would be entitled to home leave once a year. In case of pregnancy, they would go home before delivery and stay there umpteen months, all at the taxpayers' expense. We simply could not afford to replace the Greek telephone operators with our own."

The meaning of his reply was quite clear. According to the American way of thinking, national security was subordinate to cost. I had deeply resented the fact that the CIA pickup truck driver stole cigarettes and booze. Now I caught a glimpse of the American bureaucratic mind. I had seen the Soviets err so much on the side of excessive security as to reduce it to a counterproductive absurdity. The Americans seemed to err in the opposite direction.

Eventually, I finished working my way through the two books the CIA had provided and informed the CIA officer who happened to be the one who had come to see me on the very first visit with Philip Adams.

"Good," he said. "Now we get you a Greek residence permit and arrange for you to stay in Greece. It will take no more than a couple of days. Meanwhile, you can stay here until we take care of the paperwork."

"When I was in Rome, the CIA officer in charge of the Albanian section told me that once I was done here, I would return to Italy. Now that my interrogation has been completed, I ask to go back to Italy."

"That's not true. Nobody has promised you that you could go back to Italy."

I felt my anger rising. "You are calling me a liar. I demand that you contact the head of the CIA section for Albania in Rome. If he denies making that promise, I will plead guilty of having lied to you."

The same CIA officer returned a couple of days later.

"Did you ask the CIA officer in Rome whether he had made the promise that I would be free to return to Italy?"

"No," he said, "we didn't. Even if he did promise, he was not authorized to do so."

At that moment, the CIA sank another couple of notches in my esteem. I had seen this mentality in Albania where the authorities could play games with individuals, misrepresent the facts, and get away with it. It saddened me to see this same approach in dealing with the CIA.

I had packed my humble belongings by the time the CIA car came to pick me up. I said goodbye to Chris, in what was less than a tearful parting of the ways. I patted Red on his head. He put his head down and looked up at me as if he knew that we would never see each other again. He had been a faithful companion and a good friend.

I had entered the villa that first day wearing an American uniform. Now I was leaving as a civilian, one step closer to the truth. My driver took me first to a hotel in the center of Athens. It was not elegant but it was clean and the room was OK.

"By the time you unpack, some friends of yours will drop in to see you," he said. That was enough to arouse my curiosity. It did not take me long to unpack, and shortly thereafter Luan Gashi arrived with an older man in tow.

"Genc, this is Ejup Binaku, a member of Balli's Central Committee, and a colleague of mine at work." I shook hands with Ejup. With the formalities out of the way, Luan and I hugged each other like the old friends we were.

"Tell me," Luan asked, "how did you survive these six weeks?"

I answered with another question. "How long have you known that I am in Greece?"

"We were told soon after your arrival. I congratulate you. You did well. You did give us some trouble but you also did us a big favor."

"What do you mean?"

"It's lunchtime. Let's get out and have a bite to eat."

I wondered whether he suspected that the room might be bugged. I had thought of it but now I decided I would let Luan take the lead, as he knew the situation better than I. It was a pleasure to walk freely, with friends, amid the traffic of a metropolis. The sights and sounds were very different from those in Belgrade, in Austria, or in Italy. Well, this was Greece. The inscriptions above stores, the street signs, everything was in the Greek alphabet. I had studied classical Greek for five years in middle and high school in Italy. At least I could read the signs.

We entered a restaurant and Luan had to read the menu for me. It sounded like good Balkan food with lemon egg soup, shish kebab, and baklava. Soon we were eating and talking with gusto. Now I also had a chance to observe Luan and Ejup. Luan had aged some. His brown wavy hair was thinner, a few wrinkles here and there, but he was as gentle and kind as I remembered him. Thin and tall, unhurried; yes, that was my friend Luan who had recruited me into Balli Kombëtar early in 1943, and with whom I had faced some risks during the civil war in Albania. While I surrendered to the communists and was arrested, Luan fled into the mountains, hoping for a quick Allied landing in Albania. When the landing failed to take place, after a few months he and his companions decided to leave for Greece.

Ejup was in his mid-forties and resembled Omar Sharif. He was dark-complected, with penetrating eyes that seemed to envelop the listener when he leaned closer to make a point. He was slightly stooped and walked with a slight limp. He had been a teacher in Kosova before he had taken charge of a Balli military unit. I liked him at first sight.

I spoke up. "Luan, you told me that I had given you some trouble and had also done you a favor. Tell me, what did you mean?"

"Let me give you an example. You had reported that the leaflets American planes dropped over Albania were ineffective."

"Yes, a number of things were wrong with them. First, the print was very small. Those who picked them up were not going to read them out in the open but hidden somewhere in a dark corner. Under those conditions, they were hardly legible. The quality of the paper was poor. After folding the leaflets a few times, they tended to rip along the folds. You can imagine how those leaflets passed from hand to hand, how often they were folded and unfolded. Within a short time, the leaflets became useless. And another thing: the caricatures were clumsy and lacked humor."

While I was speaking, I could see Luan and Ejup looking at each other from time to time, carrying on a silent conversation, remembering things they had previously discussed with regard to what I was saying.

Luan then replied, "When I said that you had done us some harm, it dealt with the caricatures. Gaqi Gogo is the author of those drawings."

Gaqi Gogo was a well-known follower of King Zogu. The Americans had attributed my negative comments to my being a Balli member and, therefore, against the king. This, of course, was not true. Up to that moment, I did not know that the drawings were Gaqi Gogo's work.

Luan continued. "On the other hand, you helped Balli by making sure that the information you were bringing went to the CIA. In the past, Balli was accused of being anti-American. Again, this is not true. But Balli, as a member of the Rome Committee, has objected from time to time to American proposals or initiatives while the other members have remained passive."

"What's the Rome Committee?" I asked.

"Its full name is 'The Free Albania National Committee.' It consists of Balli Kombëtar, Levizja e Legalitetit [the royalist movement], and some nationalists not affiliated with either group. Recently, the Americans have been trying to make Blloku Kombëtar Independent [the Independent National Bloc] part of the Rome Committee. Its members are politicians accused of having collaborated with the Italians, such as Shefqet Verlaci, Ernest Koliqi, Mustafa Kruja, Kolë Bibë Miraka, and some others. Neither the royalists nor the unaffiliated have objected, while Balli has opposed this move. When we have more time, I will go into more detail as to Balli's position."

Over the next few days, I spent much time with Ejup and Luan. They shared an apartment not far from the city center, quite comfortable for two men who got along with each other. In fact, they did not just get along well; Luan and Ejup were good friends. Once we talked about what I knew of Luan's family and about common friends in Albania, we touched on problems of the present.

"Let's talk a bit about what Ejup and I do for a living," Luan said one day. "We both work for Radio Free Albania. Have you ever heard of this radio? It supposedly broadcasts from somewhere inside Albania."

"Yes, I have heard of it, and I must say, what I know about it has been most discouraging. You too will be discouraged once I tell you what I know."

Luan was looking at me with an embarrassed smile. "How bad can it be?"

"You be the judge. I heard about Radio Free Albania on two occasions. The first one was when lightning struck an ammunition dump near Vlora. About six months later, Radio Free Albania broadcast that forces of the Albanian anti-communist resistance had blown up the ammunition dump. The communists held a meeting with the local people, read a transcript of the RFA broadcast, and asked the people whether they thought that the broadcast was telling the truth. You can imagine how the people responded. It was bad enough that the broadcast was lying. Even worse was the fact that it had taken six months for the news to travel from Albania to RFA headquarters, wherever that might be. Obviously, no one believed that the radio was located on Albanian soil."

"We thought that the news of the destruction of the ammunition dump was dramatic and deserved to be broadcast, and that's what we did."

"Luan, my friend, you could broadcast the news to the rest of the world but not to Albania where people knew the truth. There is worse, if that is possible. In one of your broadcasts, the RFA attacked Rita Marko, the communist woman who with her unconscionable behavior was dishonoring the good name of Albanian womanhood. It just so happens that Rita Marko is a man. Those who heard the broadcast were in stitches."

"How were we to know that Rita Marko was a man?" Luan replied.

"That's what I mean. You don't write on a subject that you know little or nothing about. By knocking about in the dark, the radio has created a bad name for itself."

Now Ejup spoke up. "Your comments are right on target. We need someone who can bring fresh knowledge and insights to the job. Would you be willing to work for the RFA? Obviously, we cannot offer you a job but we can do the groundwork at the office, if you are interested."

I had to do some thinking. The fact that the CIA had flatly refused to let me go back to Italy may have been an indication that they wanted me to work at the radio station. If that was the case, I was better off working in Athens than living in a refugee camp somewhere in Greece.

"Yes, I might be interested. Tell me, what do you two do at the RFA and what would I do if this goes through?"

"Luan works as a writer while I monitor Tirana news broadcasts. We have another Balli member, Gani Hamiti, who works at the station. There are also some other employees who are members of Legaliteti, and one independent. Hence, it is important that you declare yourself an independent so as not to upset the existing political balance at the RFA."

That would not present a problem if the CIA agreed. I had declared myself a member of Balli from the very beginning. Anyhow, we would cross this bridge once we got there.

Soon after this conversation, the CIA asked me whether I was interested in working for RFA. Indeed I was, and so they hired me on a temporary basis until I received my security clearance from Washington. My salary was $100 a month, equivalent to that of a major or lieutenant colonel in the Greek army. I found a very nice apartment in Kolonaki, one of the best quarters of Athens, where I paid $30 a month in rent. A seven-course meal at an elegant restaurant cost $1. Most of the time, I ate simple meals at much lower prices. Thus, the pay was quite adequate for my needs.

When I found the apartment, I had to do some bargaining with the owner. I insisted that I wanted to take more than the one shower a week she was willing to include in the rent. We agreed on my taking two showers a week. That would take care of my having to go to the public baths. The first time I went to a public bath, I tried to explain to the person at the ticket counter that I did not want to take a tub bath, that I preferred taking a shower. I thought that a shower was more likely to be clean than a bathtub. Well, I didn't know the word "shower" but I knew that in German it was called "Dusche." So I said to the girl at the ticket counter that I wanted to take a *douche*. She did not say anything, gave me a ticket, and I was directed to a room with a tub, which I could occupy for half an hour. There was no shower but I did not want to waste time. The tub looked reasonably clean and would have to do for that day.

When I saw Luan, I told him what had happened. He was too polite to laugh. He just smiled, told me what douche meant in English, and that the next time I should ask for a "shower."

The one condition my landlady raised was that if the Greek Internal Revenue Service asked me about my rent, I should state that I paid $10 a month. Her husband was in his eighties; she was so much younger as she put it, probably pushing 70, and they lived on his pension. I could understand why she wanted me to say that about the rent and that was fine with me.

Luan and Ejup arranged for me to meet Gani Hamiti, the other Balli member working at RFA. He was short, in his forties, olive-complected, with wavy dark hair streaked with gray. He was from Vlora and had escaped when he found out that he was about to be arrested. Of necessity, he had left his wife and children behind. Presently, he worked as a writer and speaker at the radio but was paid by British intelligence rather than the CIA. He lived with Mrs. Nina Matathia and her daughter Toula. Nina was born in Greece and was of the Jewish faith. She had gotten married and had joined her husband in Albania. During the war, he had sent her and their daughter to Greece where the war had kept them virtual prisoners. Her husband had sent word to them at the end of the war that they not return to Albania, and so they had remained in Athens.

One day, one of my CIA contacts asked me whether I was willing to meet with a British gentleman who was interested in Albanian affairs. I agreed, and one evening the CIA officer took me into a very dark side street in downtown Athens. I could barely make out the silhouette of a short, slim man who, as we shook hands, mumbled his name to me. Then he asked me in English whether I preferred we converse in English or in Albanian.

"In Albanian, of course," I replied, wanting to make things easier for me, and perhaps less easy for him. I enjoyed having the home-court advantage. We climbed into a jeep and off we went in the general direction of the safe house where I had spent my six weeks with Red, my faithful companion. We did turn off sooner, though, and turned into the front yard of a villa that was very nice but somewhat less opulent than my previous abode.

Now I had a chance to see my host in a well-lit room. He was of medium height, slender, with blondish hair and a reddish complexion. He was about 60 years old, give or take a few years.

I spent just under three days with my British host. From the very beginning, his excellent Albanian surprised me. During our conversation, I further discovered that he knew much more about Albania than I did. He knew many past and present Albanian leaders. Among others, he had known Enver Hoxha and Mehmet Shehu during the civil war as well as after the communist takeover of Albania.

One of the questions he asked dealt with the carrying capacity of bridges between Shkodra and Tirana.

"I am sorry, I don't know; such information is not posted at or near bridges."

"I understand. Can you tell me whether these bridges were widened or strengthened recently?"

Again, I did not know.

He shifted to another subject. "What do you think about the possibility of air-dropping weapons to the Albanian resistance?"

"How many weapons are you thinking of?"

"Say, five thousand rifles and adequate ammunition to go with the rifles."

"I would say that such an undertaking has no chance of success, absolutely none."

"Why do you say that?"

I did some calculating. "Five thousand rifles, at five kilograms a rifle, weigh 25,000 kg. One hundred rounds of ammunition per rifle weigh about 5 kg, so there we have another 25,000 kg. That brings the total to 50,000 kg without considering the weight of the crates. At a load of 250 kg per mule, those receiving the weapons would need 200 mules to get the weapons to the intended recipients. The communists have left only two mules per village and have removed the rest. The resistance would have to mobilize 100 villages without the communists getting wind of what is going on. In addition, they would want to transport the weapons without being detected. That, sir, is impossible."

He seemed displeased. "That's exactly what we did in Albania in World War II," he replied. "Could your reasoning be influenced by the fact that this is a royalist initiative and you are with Balli?"

I did not let him throw me off balance. "Sir, I spoke of the weight of the material to be air-dropped, of the need to mobilize 100 villages, and of moving the weapons without being detected by the communists. None of the preceding deals with political beliefs or the parties involved." Obviously, his World War II experience was a handicap in this regard.

He did share some thoughts and a personal experience with me that I found of great interest. At one point, he spoke of India and of India's efforts to get rid of the British.

"We gave them schools, hospitals, roads, and an efficient administration. We taught them everything they know and now they want to get rid of us. That's gratitude for you."

I could not help thinking that even parents who do as much and more for their children have to let them go once the children grow up. What about India's wealth, abundance of talent, pride, and urge to be independent? Didn't that count for something? My British friend took obvious pride in what England had done for India, while an independent observer might have taken a different view of certain aspects of the British-Indian relationship over the years. Now that India had grown up, would it not be better for Great Britain to stand aside and be India's lasting friend?

The other item of interest dealt with a personal experience. My host had spent part of World War II in the Albanian mountains as part of the British mission. He happened to be with the Kryeziu family when German troops searched the house where he was hiding. He was dressed as an Albanian farmer and the Germans failed to recognize him. After the raid, he agreed with his hosts that time had come for him to leave Albania and, if possible, return to England. The war had started in Europe in

1939. This was 1941 and the United States had not yet entered the war. The Germans had occupied Yugoslavia in the spring of that year. He made his way to Belgrade and managed to enter the American embassy without being stopped. There he revealed his true identity and his hope that they could help him return to England. Instead, to avoid a potential diplomatic incident, the Americans notified the Germans, who arrested him promptly. He wound up in a prison camp for British officers where he stayed for a while. Coached by British physicians, he was able to feign a debilitating back condition. Eventually, the Germans consented to send him back to England after he signed a document in which he gave his word of honor as an officer that he would take no active part in any military actions against the Germans for the duration of World War II.

When it became obvious that I had told him whatever I knew in response to his questions, he ended the meeting. "I will leave you at this point and the driver will take you back to Athens."

I stood up and we shook hands. He moved toward the door of the room, turned around, and stuck his right hand halfway inside the jacket in the direction of an inner pocket.

"Is there a way that I could leave you with something to remind you of the time you spent here as our guest?"

"Thank you, sir. The memory of these three days will suffice to make me remember, with pleasure the time we spent together."

He nodded, pulled his hand out of the jacket, and walked out of the room. I had to think of the dinner with his CIA counterpart in Rome, who gave me $50 and made me feel like a paid informant. Obviously, the Brit knew his Albanians. He was willing to pay if I had asked for something. He simply went through the motions of offering some money, pulled back his hand when I declined, and got all the information I could provide at no extra cost. There is no substitute for experience.

At the first opportunity, I asked my CIA contact who the British gentleman was.

"Don't you know? That's Colonel Oakley-Hill. He has spent many years in Albania."

Now I understood. Colonel Hill had spent years during King Zogu's regime as an organizer of the Albanian gendarmerie. He had infiltrated into Albania during the war and had returned after the war in charge of the

British program at Radio Tirana. When the British and the Americans left Albania, Hill had left with the rest.

Subsequently, I met him a few times at Gani's. On one of these occasions, he told us that his great dream was to return to Albania, buy a few sheep, and wander through Dukagjin, letting his sheep graze while he visited his friends in village after village. I, of course, was not inclined to believe what Hill was saying. To me, this was another ploy politicians and secret service personnel use to win the friendship of their targets.

Another time, he told me that my friend Zef Shllaku, who was still in Austria, had accepted the Expanded Rome Committee. I questioned his statement and he consulted his notebook.

"Well, I have it right here," he said while nodding.

A few days later Zef came to Athens and I had a chance to ask him in person.

"Zef, did you ever tell Colonel Hill that you accepted the Expanded Rome Committee?"

"Absolutely not," Zef replied.

Well, that was enough to get me going. The next time I saw Colonel Hill, I confronted him with the truth, perhaps less diplomatically than I should have. He mumbled a bit, checked his notebook, and said, "I must have confused him with another Zef."

For me it was a great pleasure to have Zef in Athens. By now, we were like brothers. We understood each other, sometimes without exchanging a word. I was quite busy writing for the radio at my apartment. But whatever time I could spare, we spent together.

Zef had brought me mail from St. Martin, including two letters from Valnea. I could recognize her handwriting from a mile away. When Zef gave me the two letters, I could tell from the postmark which letter she had written before San Remo and which after our encounter. I read the older letter first. In it she wrote that a long time had gone by since we had said goodbye to each other in Padua. That even wives would not wait ten long years for their husbands, and that the reasonable thing to do was to sever our relationship and remain friends. The content and tone of her letter hit me like a ton of bricks.

The second, written after our get-together, asked that I forget the first letter and that we go back to loving each other as we had done for so many years. I remembered that one of her first questions in San Remo was whether I had received the letter she had sent to me in Austria. At that time, I had not. Now I knew. I felt deeply hurt by the chill of her prose and the determination with which she had disposed of me in the first letter. I was so hurt that I wanted my pound of flesh.

I wrote her a letter telling her that I had received both letters and that, between the two, I had to agree with her first letter. My intent was, of course, to have her protest and stress again that what she had written after we met in San Remo reflected her true feelings for me. I fired off my reply and waited anxiously for what she would say in return. Days turned into weeks, and she finally wrote back mentioning neither letter, writing in the same detached noncommittal style she had used in her letters since my escape. I had loved her since I was 14 years old. She had been for me a beacon of light during the darkness of communism, a source of strength, a refuge in my loneliness. Now, my first love, my only love, was dead—a thing of the past. All I could do was clench my teeth and go on with my life. This I did. For three days, I could not talk. Zef stood by me, in silence, but always available. After three days, I pulled myself together and life went on.

Soon after completing my six weeks at the safe house, I went to the USIS library. There were so many things I wanted to read up on, so many books that had been published during my ten years of being buried alive in Albania, that at the library I truly felt like a kid in a candy store. I ran into a young lady who worked there and when I thanked her for the information she had given me, she replied, "You are welcome." As I mentioned before, I was not used to spoken English and the expression struck me as being just wonderful. People, particularly employees and salespeople in Albania, considered any customer an intruder, someone interrupting their personal comfort and well-being. In the American environment of the USIS library, my inquiries were actually welcome. Wow!

I meandered a bit through the library until I decided to go upstairs. On the staircase was a picture of Teddy Roosevelt and a saying of his. "There is nothing more frightening than ignorance in action." I stood transfixed. It fit the Albanian communists like a glove! Where loyalty was the main and sometimes the only prerequisite, ignorance ruled supreme.

I decided to ask the reference librarian about information on Soviet MiGs. Behind the desk, she seemed petite. She had honey-blonde, wavy hair, slanted green eyes, pearly teeth, and a beautiful smile. Her nameplate on the desk identified her as Miss Daisy Pastou.

"Excuse me, Miss Pastou, I would like some information about Soviet fighter planes. Could you help me?"

She looked up with a beautiful smile. "Are you a pilot?"

"No," I said, "I am just interested in Soviet MiGs."

"Are you Swedish?"

I had to smile. She was as personal and inquisitive as if she were Albanian. "No, I am not but I'll give you another two guesses and if you guess wrong, I'll tell you my nationality."

"Are you German?"

"No."

"Are you Austrian?"

"No."

"Then what are you?"

"I'm Albanian."

"You don't look Albanian."

"Why, what do Albanians look like?"

"They are short and dark."

"Well, I am sorry to disappoint you but I am 100 percent Albanian."

She checked her index catalogs and could find nothing on Soviet fighter planes. During our conversation, I happened to ask her whether the library had Ernest Hemingway's *For Whom the Bell Tolls*. The movie was showing in theaters around town and I wanted to read the book first.

"Yes," she replied, "we have a few copies but the waiting list is very long. If you wish, I can bring you my personal copy."

"That would be very kind of you."

"Fine, I'll make a note to myself. Are you going to be in town tomorrow?"

"Yes, what time can I pick up the book? Maybe I can pick it up in the evening and we can have dinner together."

"No, I am sorry. I cannot make it tomorrow."

"What about the day after tomorrow?"

"I am sorry."

"What about any evening this week?"

"I am sorry, I would not be able to make it. But do come tomorrow and I will bring the book."

The next day, I picked up the book and promised to return it to her as soon as I had read it. This time I didn't ask for a dinner date. It took me about a week to finish the book. When I returned to the library, I thanked her for the favor she had done me by lending me the book, and as a second personal favor, I asked whether we could have dinner together. She again told me that her evenings were very busy and I withdrew as gracefully as I could.

I continued to go to the USIS library quite often because it offered much that interested me, but I made it a point to stay on the first floor. Well, one day she came bouncing down the steps, saw me, and rushed over.

"How come you visit the library and don't drop in to say hello?"

"I didn't want to bother you. After all, you had made it quite clear that you were too busy to see me after work. So, I decided not to impose on you even at work."

"I am sorry I gave you that impression, I certainly did not mean to."

Had she broken off with her boyfriend in the meantime, or what? Well, that did not matter. "Fine, then tell me what evening we can go out to dinner. I know a nice restaurant that, I am sure, you will enjoy."

"How about tomorrow evening?"

"Fine. When and where shall we meet?"

"Say at 8 p.m., on the street corner across from the USIS library?"

"Thank you, I'll be there. I'll have a rose clenched between my teeth so you will recognize me."

She laughed and that was that.

The next evening I was at the designated corner about ten minutes early. By the time she came at 8:15 p.m., I had been waiting for 25 minutes.

"Why did you come at all if you didn't want to come in the first place?" was how I welcomed her.

"I am sorry I'm late. To get here I take two buses and you know how it is when you depend on public transportation."

I was mollified. "OK, let's go, I am getting hungry."

The restaurant was about ten minutes away. It was a small but elegant restaurant where I had eaten before. The headwaiter was Albanian. He was maybe in his late sixties, somewhat bent and shriveled, but with keen, shrewd eyes. When he saw me with Daisy, he greeted us, and as he was leading us to our table, he winked at me with a smile. I did not like what he was implying and wished he had not done it.

We had an excellent meal. I found out that she had been engaged to a Greek Army lieutenant who was killed during the civil war against the communists. We got along fine. As it turned out, this was the first of many dates to follow.

One day, Luan Gashi asked me to sign an application for membership in Balli Kombëtar.

"Luan, what do you mean? You were the one who recruited me in Padua in early 1943. Now you want me to sign another application?"

"We have all signed such applications. After the war, many people have been hopping from one party to the other; sometimes holding simultaneous membership in more than one party. It is just a formality but a necessary one."

"OK fine, show me the application." The text of the application was straightforward but there was part of one sentence that caught my eye.

"Luan, it says here, 'I will not question any orders issued by my superiors and will carry them out to the best of my ability.' Luan, that's how the communists operate. No way am I going to sign such a blanket statement."

"What changes would you want to make in order to sign?"

"I would insert the words, 'as long as such orders are in Albania's best interest.'"

"Then insert them in your handwriting. Will you sign the application now?"

I changed the wording as indicated and signed the application.

At the apartment, I was getting along very well with my landlady. She taught me Greek and I taught her English. She repeatedly told me she was quite a few years younger than her octogenarian husband. That cast an air of mystery, almost of romance, when she and I sat *tête-à-tête* poring over the books in front of us. I am kidding, of course.

She was a kind lady. She was preparing a New Year's party for a few friends and asked me to join them. When all her guests had arrived, I heard mention that she had invited me to join them. I was apparently "Albanian and a fine gentlemen."

An unknown male voice challenged her. "How can he be both Albanian and a gentleman?"

That was enough to get me going. I entered the room. My landlady, still shell-shocked from that man's comment, mentioned my name without introducing me individually to a room full of people. They looked at me, then turned away and continued their conversation. I stood by my lonely self in the middle of the room with no one paying any attention to me.

Finally, a lady took pity on me. She came to me, greeted me, and proceeded to ask me, "Do you speak English?" As she said that, the room fell silent as everyone turned toward us.

"Yes, I do." After a brief conversation, it was obvious that her knowledge of English was limited. So, she tried again.

"I am sorry, my English is not so good. My best foreign language is German. Do you speak German?"

"Yes, madam, I do." Her German may have been good at one time, but by now it was very rusty. Despite her good intentions, our conversation ground to a halt. It was my turn to take the offensive.

"Do you speak Italian?"

"No, I'm sorry."

"Do you speak Latin?" I was taking a chance. My Latin was fair but I would have found it difficult to carry on a conversation. She shook her head.

"Do you speak French?" Now I was stepping on very thin ice. I could read and understand French to some extent but could not speak it. She again shook her head. I shrugged my shoulders as if to say that I didn't know what else I could do. I stayed a few more minutes, helped myself to an appetizer or two, thanked the hostess, and sailed out of the room. I should have felt remorse for having embarrassed the one person who had tried to be kind to me. However, I was so offended by the boorish words of the unknown man that I could not separate him from the lady who had tried to make me feel at ease. Eventually, I came to regret my behavior. As so often in life, by that time it was too late to do me, or her, or anyone else any good.

One day, my CIA contact told me that a documents expert would come to look at my Albanian documents. That afternoon I answered the doorbell. Before me stood a lady dressed in an ample, flowery dress, wearing a straw hat. She was Hollywood's idea of a retired American schoolteacher on vacation. I stood there staring at her.

"You were expecting me, weren't you?"

"Yes, of course, please come in." I had laid out my documents on a table and she began looking at them, mumbling as she went along.

"I know this, and this, and this."

She stopped and started paying attention to a piece of paper. At one point, she looked at it against the light.

"This is obviously a forgery," she said.

I got up and recognized that she was looking at the travel order Riza Butka had given me.

"How do you know it is forged?" I asked.

"First of all, this is an original travel order that someone modified to meet your needs. To do so, he used a razor blade to insert your name in place of his. His last name must have the same number of letters as yours."

I counted B-u-t-k-a, that was five letters, and so was K-o-r-ç-a (That's the way I spelled my name at that time).

"He made another change in the travel order. He scratched out the name of some other place and replaced it with 'Burrel.' The original name must have been longer than Burrel. So, he inserted 'Burrel' twice, once at the end of one line and again at the beginning of the next. The casual reader would not notice the change; skillfully done."

I looked at the paper. She was right. Having finished what she had come for, she said goodbye and left me feeling guilty for having judged her by her appearance. She was obviously a skilled professional who, for whatever reason, dressed the way she did. Something else was struggling to emerge from my subconscious mind. Then it hit me. Where were my forged travel orders that night in 1951 at the bridge on my return trip from Burrel? (See Chapter 24.) Why did the two officers who harassed me not find the forged document when I emptied my pockets?

I was suddenly overflowing with deep gratitude. The fact that the travel orders had escaped those two communist officers had avoided a catastrophe in the making. To me this was a miracle that had saved at least two lives—mine and Riza Butka's. I prayed from the bottom of my heart: *Thank you Lord, thank you guardian angels*! One more thought occurred to me belatedly. Why had I not destroyed the forged document after I needed it no longer but had carried it around since 1951, from Tirana to Yugoslavia, to Austria and Italy, to that very day in Athens?

Chapter Forty-Three

Lavrion Refugee Camp

Fall was upon us. Both deadlines for Hila's rescue had passed and I had not heard a word about the whole affair. One day I asked my CIA contact what had happened with Hila. After some inquiries at the office, he told me that an Air Force plane had dropped the flares over the tobacco fermentation plant in Fusha Shtojit according to plan. Ten days later, they had flown over the designated island but had seen no fires. The pilot decided to drop a message indicating that they would be back in four weeks and that on that occasion Hila was supposed to light four fires.

I exploded. "That was one stupid move!"

"Why, what would you have done?" he said with resentment and sarcasm in his voice.

"You tell me: What will the pilot do if in four weeks he sees four fires burning on the island? How can he be reasonably sure that the fires have not been lit by the security forces?"

"Let me ask you again, what would you have done?"

"Our original plan called for three fires. Let's assume that the message dropped to Hila had said, 'The next time light one more fire than agreed upon,' and that the second time there were indeed four fires. There was at least a reasonable chance that it was Hila who had lit the fires."

That was the last time the CIA said anything to me about Hila. At one point, they asked me whether I was willing to enter Albania with a group of trustworthy men.

"We have picked the best, the most trusted among our volunteers, to go with you. What do you say?"

I had had my troubles, indeed plenty of troubles, when I escaped from Albania and had to trust infiltrators I did not know. I replied, "I have no intention of entering Albania with a group that I have not picked personally."

"There is no need for you to trust them as long as we do."

"Then be my guest. You enter Albania with those people since you trust them."

"It seems to me," he replied, "your love for Albania has limits."

"I am speaking from experience. Having spent several months in the Albanian mountains, I know success depends on the cohesion of the team. Albania does not lack martyrs. In fact, too many infiltrators run into the arms of Albanian security 'welcoming committees' as soon as they tread on Albanian soil. We know there is a problem somewhere along the line. Too many infiltrators have been captured or have died under torture to attribute it to coincidence. Going with people I do not know would be asking for trouble."

I had become quite skittish when it came to certain plans concocted by the CIA. At one point, a CIA officer asked me to re-enter Yugoslavia to retrieve documents supplied by Albanian students in Zagreb. I knew from Martin that the driver of the American consulate in Zagreb was from Kosova and was a most reliable individual. Martin had also suggested that Albanian students put together documents with information of interest to the United States that the driver could pick up without difficulty or risk. It sounded like a good idea. My CIA contact was suggesting a different approach.

"Why don't you enter Yugoslavia and pick up the material?"

"I just escaped from there. The Yugoslavs would be delighted to get their hands on me." I could not believe my ears.

"You could grow a mustache or a beard and we would provide you with proper documents."

"Why would you want me to take such risks when the driver of the consulate could pick up the material without any risk to himself or to anyone else?"

"That's out of the question. We cannot endanger our personnel."

Obviously, we were expendable in the eyes of the CIA, and so Martin's idea died on the vine.

Meanwhile, the initiative to broaden the National Committee for a Free Albania had grown into a crisis. The United States firmly believed in the attractive but unrealistic idea of total mobilization against the communists. Hasan Dosti, who had taken over as head of Balli Kombëtar after the death of Mit'hat Frasheri, was willing to accept the American initiative. At one point, he had said that one could not say no to the Americans. Abaz Ermenji and most Balli members were just as convinced that accepting to work with "Albanian fascists" was a grave error, something they would never do. Eventually, the CIA gave an ultimatum. The broadened Rome Committee was to become reality with or without Abaz Ermenji and his followers. Those who accepted the American initiative would stay; the others would no longer be a part of the committee.

Push had come to shove and the aftershock reached Athens and Radio Free Albania. We were all asked whether we accepted the expanded committee. Since I worked out of my apartment, my CIA contact came to see me.

"Congratulations, your security clearance has arrived from Washington. Henceforth, you will come to the offices of the radio station and work there. And here is the declaration with which you signify that you are ready to work with the broadened Rome Committee. You will also qualify for an ID card identifying you as an Albanian in good standing."

I had given the matter quite some thought. In my opinion, Abaz Ermenji's labeling as fascists all members of the National Bloc was a broad-brush approach that tarred the innocent with the guilty. On the other hand, through fierce and unceasing propaganda, the communists had branded all members of Blloku Kombëtar traitors and criminals. In my opinion, bringing them into the Rome Committee weakened the nationalist cause and our Anglo-American allies, and played into the hands of the communists. I believe deep down in his heart Hasan Dosti also viewed the members of Blloku Kombëtar as collaborationists but could not reject the American initiative. I decided to side with Abaz Ermenji, albeit for different reasons.

"You told me some time ago that the CIA would issue ID cards to Albanians, and that only those accepting the broadened committee would qualify. I told you then and I am repeating it now that there are two conditions to qualifying an individual as an Albanian. First, anyone born in Albania of Albanian parents is automatically an Albanian. This is something that no one, including the United States, can deny. As to who is a good Albanian, that is a matter for Albanians to judge, not for foreigners.

"You are also telling me that my security clearance has arrived from Washington. I find it quite coincidental that my security clearance should arrive at this time when some of your employees are quitting. Permit me to ask you a question: Do you have a security clearance?"

"Of course I do," he replied.

"I assume you got it because you never did anything illegal or joined any subversive organizations, such as the American Workers Party. That's fine as far as it goes. Were you ever in enemy hands—say in the clutches of communists, under severe pressure, perhaps under torture, in danger of being killed—and yet you remained faithful to democratic ideals?"

He could see which way I was going. I could see him tensing up. "I have asked you to sign this acceptance of the broadened Rome Committee. Tell me now without wasting any more time. Are you or are you not going to sign?"

"I am convinced that broadening the committee is wrong and will weaken it. I am equally convinced that this move is neither in your nor in Albania's best interest. I see no alternative but to refuse to sign."

"Do you realize that you will no longer work for RFA? You are free, of course, to seek other employment in Athens."

"I understand."

He got up and left, visibly disappointed. I wondered how many more individuals he would talk to that same day. I would hear from Luan how things had gone with the rest of them.

The CIA fired all its employees working for RFA who did not recognize the broadened Rome Committee. The British took a different approach. Gani Hamiti, the one employee paid by the British who worked for the RFA, also refused to recognize the broadened Rome Committee but was not dismissed. When the CIA raised this point, Colonel Hill replied that, while he would have preferred that Gani recognize the committee, the British did not consider his refusal reason for dismissal.

I had saved some money but once I lost my monthly salary, I could no longer afford to pay a monthly rent of $30. So, I moved to a basement not far from where I had lived before. It had a bed, a chest of drawers, a small table, and a chair. I put my underwear and my papers in the chest of drawers. I drove some nails in the wall so I could hang up my suits and raincoat. In addition, I bought a little electric hot plate where I could prepare tea or coffee, and cook beans, rice, and other simple meals.

Next, I had to find a job. I mentioned my problem to Daisy, who promised she would talk with a friend who was the secretary of the director of a major American construction company. In fact, the next day she told me that I could start work in a week. I must admit, I felt good about her concern as well as the job.

One day, when my CIA liaison came to see me in my basement, he was shocked.

"How could you quit your job with us? Look at this rat hole!"

"Believe me, it's not so bad. Besides, I have found a job and I may be able to afford better quarters."

He came back a day or two later. "Where is this job of yours? We cannot find it."

I provided the address of the construction company, wondering why they needed the information. I would soon find out.

That evening I met with Daisy, who looked upset.

"If I had any brains, I would not be here with you," she told me. "Today, the director of the construction company called my friend and asked her whether they had an application from a Mr. Korça. To avoid suspicion, the secretary did not want to say yes immediately, so she said she would check. A few minutes later, she returned with my application. The director then told her to pitch it, as the applicant was a communist."

Now I knew what game the CIA was playing.

It got worse. I received a letter from Uncle Edward in Rome who told me that the United Nations had granted me a scholarship to attend medical school in Strasbourg. The CIA, in turn, had annulled it. Edward's comment was that I had said the wrong thing in the wrong place.

That afternoon my CIA contact came to see me. This time I was furious.

"It may have given you some pleasure to know that I was fired from my construction job as a communist even before I started. Furthermore, I heard that you have annulled my scholarship to study medicine in Strasbourg for the same reason. Let me tell you something. Four years ago, Tonin Jakova, the first secretary of the communist party in Shkodra, called me to his office. This was the first and last time I ever saw that office. He congratulated me for controlling and suppressing the typhus epidemic that had been raging in Shkodra. Someone present in his office suggested that I receive a scholarship to continue my medical studies abroad and thus become even more valuable to the people. The secretary broke out in an ugly grin and replied, 'When we build a university in Trush, it will be his turn to go to school.'

"Trush is a God-forsaken village that gets practically buried in mud during the rainy season. That day I attributed the communist secretary's attitude to the red star. Today I realize it is not a matter of color but of shape.

Obviously, there is no difference between the red and the white star as long as it has five points."

My visitor blushed. "How dare you say such a thing."

"I just did. Now it's up to you to do as you wish, right?"

Enraged, he stormed out of my room.

A few weeks went by. It was a warm sunny day in early March, a day with hardly a cloud in the sky. It was perfect spring weather and I would have enjoyed it very much were it not also the day when I accompanied Zef to the Greek police headquarters. As he too had refused to accept the broadened Rome Committee, he had to leave Athens for the refugee camp in Lavrion. A Greek police major, looking past Zef with disdain, handed him to a police officer who would take Zef to Lavrion. Then the major turned to me with an unctuous smile on his flabby face, half bent forward in a servile gesture, and asked me in broken English whether he could be of service to me. He obviously mistook me for an American. I shook my head, thanked him, and asked myself how he would treat me when it was my turn to go to Lavrion.

My turn came about four weeks later. I did not see the major at police headquarters but I cannot say I missed him because I knew from experience that he was not the only hypocrite in the ranks of the local authorities. I traveled by bus to Lavrion, accompanied by a policeman who held my papers. I had visited the camp a few months before, on November 28, the Albanian Flag Day. This time I would not be a visitor but an inmate.

The bus stopped in the main square of town, across from the refugee camp. I was told to wait outside the office building and soon a policeman came out, motioned that I follow him, and took me to the camp depot. There I got two sheets, a blanket, and a mess kit with spoon, fork, and knife. Now I was an official member of the camp contingent, one of about 1,000 refugees from Yugoslavia, Bulgaria, and Albania. Men without families were quartered in low permanent buildings with several dorms housing from 50 to 100 men each. Families lived across the street in small homes built for single families. Now these homes were subdivided with hanging blankets to accommodate two and sometimes three families. Greek families from Romania lived in similar little houses, one family in each house as far as I could tell.

As I entered the refugee camp, it did not take long before Albanians, mostly Balli members, surrounded me who knew me from my previous visit to Lavrion. They spoke with the Greek policeman who was supposed to assign me to one of the dormitories and prevailed upon him to assign me to one of the nicer rooms. Within minutes, Zef was at my side and things were not as depressing as they had first appeared.

The camp was shaped like a figure 8. There were two sets of one-story buildings housing the dorms, with the kitchen and a large recreation room located at the intersection of the two loops. The recreation room was large and almost bare. There were a few chairs and tables along the walls and a ping-pong table at the center. Some people played cards or dominoes while the younger crowd played ping-pong. The room was unremarkable except for a poem mounted on the wall facing the entrance. It was the first American poem I ever memorized and would never forget: "O beautiful for spacious skies, for amber waves of grain..."

There were, of course, things in the refugee camp I had to get used to. There was a shed inside the camp along the outer wall near the main entrance. It housed a row of urinals and stalls without doors, a reminder of my prison days in Tirana.

As in prison, a siren told us what to do and when to do it. Here, it greeted us in the morning, told us to get up, to go to breakfast, and to spend the day within or outside the compound. Before it got dark, the siren got us back into camp until the next morning.

Breakfast consisted of tea and bread. Lunch consisted of soup and some bread, boiled meat, and vegetables. The evening meal was also passable, except on Thursdays when we got a handful of olives full of worms. On Thursdays, my friends and I made it a habit to eat dinner at a local restaurant.

Zef and I developed somewhat of a routine. We would eat breakfast together and then we split up. He liked to play with and teach the refugee children this and that. I went for walks with young Balli members, with Balli Council members, and rather infrequently with the leaders of the other political parties. At noon, Zef and I met for lunch. In the afternoon, we went for long walks up the hills. It was a way of removing ourselves from the camp and its depressing environment.

Lavrion was a small town built around a central square. It nestled in a small depression surrounded by hills partially covered with vegetation, mostly tall grass, bushes, and some trees. These plants gave the town a pleasing, colorful green and tan frame. Weatherworn buildings girded the center; rows of fresh laundry flapped in the breeze behind private homes. The one road from the north came from Athens and led southward toward Sunion. Lavrion had a few thousand inhabitants, a handful of stores, a couple of cafés and restaurants, a movie house, a soccer field, a couple of schools, and not much more. There were no buildings more than two stories high. The town was clean and peaceful. I don't remember a single clash between refugees and the townspeople. If there were some discordant notes, those were more often than not due to political tensions within groups of the same nationality, under the watchful eyes of the ever-present Greek police. A VW minibus wound its way to Lavrion, usually on Fridays, when World Council of Churches employees processed refugees for resettlement.

Sunion was an even smaller place but renowned for the impressive ruins of Neptune's Temple. Lord Byron had spent some time there and had written a poem in honor of Sunion. All told, I was to spend about one year in Lavrion, which gave me a chance to learn the finer points of camp life.

Politics was the main pastime in our camp. That was not surprising, as all inmates were or claimed to be political refugees. Most Albanians were members either of Balli (republicans) or of Legaliteti (royalists). These two groups hardly spoke to each other. There were also a few members of Blloku Kombëtar Indipendent (National Independent Bloc), followers of the prince of Mirdita, of Shefqet Verlaci, of the political leaders accused as Italian or German collaborationists.

Albanian royalists saw themselves as allies of the Greek monarchy. They were the favorites of the camp authorities and provided members for the kitchen staff. They had no problem getting permission to spend a day or two in Athens. Some of them also distinguished themselves by informing on their fellow refugees; the smarter ones to the Americans, the less gifted ones to the Greeks.

Both the authorities and the Albanian royalists saw Balli members as enemies because of their republican beliefs. I noticed early on that when we stood in line to get our food, royalists got chunks of meat while Balli members got what was left on the bone after the cook had shaken off much of the meat. The Greek police stood by and watched. They generally favored the royalists, even more so the informers.

Once a week I went to the public baths to shower. I had to pay but the charges were modest. During the summer of 1955, the United States Escapee

Program (USEP) funded the construction of showers at the refugee camp. The day the showers were ready, American and Greek authorities came from Athens to witness the historic inauguration ceremonies. Selected individuals, all honored members of the BOI (the Brotherhood of Informants), paraded with soap in hand and towels wrapped around their shoulders in and out of the baths in full view of the guests. Once the guests left, the baths closed, not to open again, at least for as long as I lived at the camp.

Greek women from Romania did laundry for pay with customers providing the detergent. I liked Tide best for how my laundry looked and smelled when I got it back.

There were quite a few young intelligent men in the camp. There were some college students among the Yugoslavs. We got along quite well and found it easy to communicate with each other. Some of them went snorkeling and at times returned with fish of unusual colors and shapes. One of the Yugoslav students was an excellent swimmer and diver. He had the quality I so much admired of cutting through the water with the utmost ease and elegance. One day he left our camp for good. We found out that he had been a member of the Yugoslav national swimming team and that the Greek sport authorities had hired him as a trainer.

The majority of camp inmates had little or no schooling, irrespective of nationality. Most were farmers who lived along the border and were able to escape with relative ease. Among the Albanians, a few had to flee once the police discovered that they had helped infiltrators from Greece. Others had left because of their inability to pay taxes or to avoid the draft. Most were good people.

In the early evening, they gathered near the loudspeakers to listen to the BBC news service in Albanian. Even though this was our only daily source of political news, listening with the group was no pleasure. Invariably, one or more of the listeners would approach Zef or me at the end of the broadcast, saying, "There was quite a bit of static on the radio and I could not make out what was said. Could you repeat some of the more important items?"

In truth, the noise did not keep them from understanding the newscast. It was the fact that they had trouble focusing on what emerged from the loudspeakers. They could follow a live conversation where thoughts were repeated, where not every word counted, as opposed to a formal, succinct broadcast script where the listener could not ask for an explanation. Thus, listening to the BBC was a mixed pleasure. Many times I chose to be else-where at the time of the broadcast.

Daisy, bless her heart, kept coming to see me every two weeks or so. Besides the obvious pleasure of spending a few hours with a pretty, well-dressed, educated young woman, there was also satisfaction—perhaps even pride on my part—that she would come to see me during those difficult days. Daisy was taking a certain risk when she came because of her employment with the USIS. After all, I was not sent to Lavrion as a friend of the United States or of Greece. I saw myself as a true friend of the United States, even though they viewed my personal beliefs differently. The Greek authorities blacklisted me for two reasons: First, because they followed blindly any in-structions they got from the CIA. In addition, because I openly opposed Greek claims depicting southern Albania as rightfully belonging to Greece and objected to the ultra-nationalist stance of the Greek Orthodox Church that used extreme nationalism to maintain its grip on the population.

My friends of the Balli youth were proud that I had such a pretty visi-tor who worked for the Americans. They kept a respectful distance but made sure that no royalist would pull a dirty trick on me or embarrass me under the circumstances. One of the royalist leaders from our camp did in fact inform the CIA that an American woman from the U.S. embassy in Athens had come to see me. The CIA became very concerned. They asked all female embassy employees whether they had spent part of their week-end in Lavrion. This got them nowhere. They must also have discussed their predicament with their British colleague, Mr. Hill. My friend Gani of-fered help when he saw the concern my mysterious visitor was causing. He jumped on his motorbike and came to see me in Lavrion. Here he asked me directly who my visitor was and I answered candidly, as I had no reason to hide the truth. Gani, having resolved this important matter, remounted his steed and went back to Athens to inform the powers that be that my friend Daisy did not work at the embassy but at the USIS library.

As far as I was concerned, this chapter was closed. Well, not quite. A few days later, we had pea soup for lunch. The soup was practically boiling. I placed the soup container lid on my hand and the container on top so as not to burn my hand. Just as I was moving toward my dorm, the man who had in-formed the CIA about Daisy's visit popped up right in front of me. I stopped.

"I understand you told the CIA in Athens about the young woman who came to see me this weekend?" and as I was saying these words, I looked at him and then at the container full of boiling pea soup in my hand. He must have read my mind.

"Wait a minute. Albanians at the café asked me how you were. I answered that you were doing well, in fact that a young, attractive lady had come to see you in Lavrion. That's the truth and that's all I said."

"That is not all. You gave your report to the CIA, not at the café. You said that she was an American employed at the U.S. embassy in Athens. And that was a lie because you knew better." I looked him straight in the eye and then I looked at the container full of hot soup.

After letting the moment linger, I continued. "Don't worry; I will not waste the pea soup on you. Just remember, if you ever again stick your nose into my affairs, you will find out what I'll do about it." What held me back from splashing the pea soup in his face was not the loss of the soup but the fact that I could have burned him seriously and that the resulting burns would have exceeded by far his petty act of spying.

The monotonous life in Lavrion continued. Some periods in one's life are like a string of precious pearls embedded in one's mind. My days in Lavrion did not quite qualify. As with pearls, there was pain. My pain was frequent, the pearls were rare. As in Albania, I felt shunted aside, away from the mainstream of life and there was nothing I could do to improve my chances for a better future. I was 30 years old, still sitting in a camp, still the eternal medical student with all of one year's credit to my name. Around me, political passions had gained the upper hand and party loyalties seemed more important than the best interests of Albania. The republican Balli Kombëtar had split into two groups when the CIA had broadened the Albanian National Committee. Those who accepted the broadened committee, including Hasan Dosti, head of Balli Kombëtar (BK), remained members of the old organization. Most members rejected the new committee and joined the newly formed BKA (Agrarian National Front) under the leadership of Abaz Ermenji. Members of both groups in Lavrion were mostly farmers from southern Albania, victims of communist policies of expropriation and repression. The split created much pain masked only by party loyalties.

Camp life had become a true burden to both Zef and me, and so we started looking for ways to get back to Athens. We heard about the Jewish

ORT school in the periphery of Athens. The initials stood for *"Organisation Réhabilitation et Travail"* (Organization for Rehabilitation and Work) where Jewish boys in their preteens could learn crafts and trades, probably in preparation for resettlement in Israel. The school also accepted refugees against payment. The United States Escapee Program promoted two six-month courses, one for welders and the other for electricians, to provide refugees with skills that would allow them to make a living once they emigrated. Zef and I both applied for admission to the welders' course and were both accepted.

The following weekend, we joined the rest of the trainees, some 35 in all, in a villa outside Athens. Several bedrooms were equipped with bunk beds. There was a kitchen with an adjacent eating area. We were under the control of two policemen who seemed to mind their own business—well, at least one of them. The other was less friendly, as I was about to find out.

That very first weekend, two American children, a girl about five years old and her three-year-old brother, meandered into our yard from the villa next door. They were blond, blue eyed, friendly, and cute, straight out of a Norman Rockwell drawing. "Mr. Niko," one of the policemen, walked toward the little boy, squeezed his head hard, and lifted him off the ground. I guess it did not hurt too much because the boy made a face but never cried. Then, Mr. Niko put him down and both children bolted away toward their villa. Mr. Niko grinned.

"Their father is an American colonel," he added by way of explanation. Having satisfied his sense of power and vindicated the glory of Greece, he strutted away toward the sanctity of his bedroom. We never again saw the two children in our yard.

That weekend the food came by truck and we ate quite well. On Monday, we got up early, got ready for school, and traveled about one hour by truck to the ORT school. The school was located in a one-story building. It consisted of the director's office, a locker room, several classrooms, and work areas. The director and his pretty secretary took care of the administration. The director was rather rotund, pushing 40, and quite friendly toward us refugees. His secretary was obviously fond of one of our Bulgarian companions, a tall and handsome college student who flattered her with his attention and enjoyed his status as top dog among us. Amazing what a pretty woman's favor can do for a man's status among his peers.

That first day we also met our welding instructor. He seemed like a no-nonsense man who knew his business. He was friendly but firm, and willing to share his knowledge with those trying to learn. He gave us an overview of what he was going to cover during the six months we would be with him. He explained that we would learn acetylene and electric resistance welding. We would start out welding straight lines on 5 x 8 pieces of metal, making sure the bead was straight and we burned no holes into the base. Eventually, we would know what welding equipment to use to cut and weld together pieces of metal according to a blueprint. As part of the course, we would learn how to make a pair of calipers with shop tools. As far as I could judge, these six months could be a good learning experience. Compared to Lavrion, it would be just great.

Soon, attending school became routine. Monday through Friday, we spent most of our day in school, either working in the shop or attending lectures. We ate breakfast at the villa, lunch at a restaurant within walking distance of our school, and supper again at the villa. On Mondays, we had fish for lunch. The restaurant diet was varied and generally good. Saturdays and Sundays we were off, i.e., we stayed in our villa and the area around it. We had few, if any, problems among refugees. We knew we were lucky not to be in Lavrion and acted accordingly.

Now I had the opportunity to attend Sunday Mass in Athens. On Saturday evenings, I would ask Mr. Niko whether I could go to Athens on Sunday to attend Mass at the large Catholic church near Omonia Square. The answer was always the same: "See me tomorrow morning."

On Sunday mornings, time was of the essence. I had to walk about half an hour to get to the bus. The bus ride would take another half hour or so to get to the church in time for the nine o'clock Mass. Around seven o'clock each Sunday morning, Mr. Niko would twist and turn in bed, pretending to be asleep. Then he would open one eye, glance in my direction, and growl, "What do you want?" I would repeat my request of the night before.

"I want you back here right after Mass." Then he would turn on his side and dismiss me, offering me a view of his royal back.

Ever so often, I would ask for an extension, making sure that I was not incurring his displeasure. Then Daisy and I would attend a concert by the Athens Symphony Orchestra, have a picnic, or go to the seashore for a swim. I kept my demands modest, acutely aware of the need for his good will.

School also had its ups and downs. One day, I was arc welding behind a metal partition when I noticed that the classroom behind me was unusually quiet. I enjoyed the silence for a few moments and then became suspicious. I stuck my head out from behind the partition. All the trainees were gone. I happened to look at a pair of oxygen-acetylene cylinders and saw flames dancing around the connectors fastening the rubber hoses to one of the cylinders. I jumped to my feet. I was just swishing through the exit when I bumped into our instructor who was rushing in. He ran to the leaky cylinder, turned off the gas, and took care of the problem. We trainees were glad that the instructor was present when this happened.

We had not seen the last of it, however. Our little, roly-poly director was in hysterics.

"Here we have all these political refugees, these self-proclaimed heroes of who knows how many battles, gathered like sheep in our yard when all they had to do was turn off the gas, hee, hee, hee..."

The last thing we needed was for him to make fun of us but there was nothing we could say or do under the circumstances.

A few days later, Joseph, an Albanian trainee, returned to our villa very upset and, according to him, with a high fever. He told us that he was dating a Greek girl and was ready to ask her brothers for her hand. That afternoon, before he got to her house, she had swallowed a fistful of pills and was rushed to the nearby hospital. There she told him that when she told her brothers that he, Joseph, would come to ask for permission to marry her, her brothers flew into a rage and locked her in her room. In a moment of desperation, she had swallowed the pills.

The gendarmes told me to examine Joseph. His heartbeat was regular, his skin felt normal. I put a thermometer under his arm and turned away, always keeping an eye on him. After a minute or so, Joseph removed the thermometer and started rubbing it with the woolen blanket on his bed.

I grabbed the thermometer from his hands.

"Joseph, I don't know what is going on and I don't care what you tell the gendarmes. But you are not going to make a fool of me." I had never liked Joseph. He had escaped from Albania to avoid arrest for stealing goods from the cooperative where he worked as an accountant.

The next morning we all went to school except Joseph, who was "ill." At noon we were all rushing toward the restaurant, because it was Monday and we all liked fish, when my friend Zef came storming in my direction.

"Stop. We've got to do something about Joseph."

"Zef, I don't care about Joseph or his love life. I am more interested in the fish that awaits us at the restaurant."

"Wait a minute. Joseph stole the big service revolver from one of the gendarmes at the villa. He is now in school and says that he is gong to kill one or more of his girlfriend's brothers."

This was serious. "Where is he now?"

"In school, waiting."

"Waiting for what or for whom?"

"I don't know."

"OK Zef, let's go back. Here is what we are going to do. We will ask him to tell us what he has in mind. I will get him involved in conversation. I'll be on one side of Joseph and you on the other. At a certain point, I will say 'This is the darnedest story I have ever heard.' At that point, I will throw him down and pin him to the sidewalk. You grab the gun and run to our gendarme on duty, OK?"

"OK."

We returned to school and there stood Joseph. He was hunched together and looked even punier than usual. I put my arm around him and started walking away from the school. I asked him to tell us what was going on.

"As I was telling Zef yesterday, the brothers offended me deeply and nearly caused their sister's death. Today I am going to avenge my honor by killing one or more of the brothers."

While going through the motions of listening to Joseph, I steered us away from the restaurant to get some distance between the other trainees and us. Time had come to act.

"Joseph, this is the darnedest story I have ever heard," then I tripped him and pinned him to the ground. His jacket opened up and the grip of the large revolver stuck out of his belt. I waited for Zef to act but nothing happened. When I looked up, there was Zef staring at us with bulging eyes and his mouth wide open in a silent scream.

"Zef, grab the gun and run!" I yelled.

This time, Zef did as he was told. When I saw him last, he was running toward the school as fast as his legs would carry him.

I picked Joseph off the ground and mumbling something, I dusted his clothes off while he appeared dazed. To my horror, I noticed that this whole episode had taken place across the street from a police station. Luckily, no one had noticed, no one challenged us, and no shots were fired.

Zef entered the schoolyard and rushed into the director's office. There stood the director who looked at Zef, stared at his gun, started to shake, and raised his arms as high as he could. The secretary was also in the office. She just froze. It took Zef a moment or two to understand that the director and his secretary had totally misread what was going on.

He turned to the secretary. "Please put the gun in the office safe until we can return it to our policeman."

The secretary recovered before her boss and did as Zef told her. Once Zef was rid of the gun, he stepped out on the street just as Joseph and I got there. By now, Joseph had recovered sufficiently to understand what had happened.

"Zef, I will never forget or forgive you for what you did to me today. Genc is just a big oaf who did what you told him. I'll get back with you and you won't like it one bit." Having spoken those words, Joseph walked away without looking back. Never before had I been called a big oaf, and I enjoyed it.

"Zef, do you think he will hurt you?" I whispered to him, affecting a raucous, slurred speech of a dimwit. Zef was at a loss.

"Zef, can we eat now?"

"OK, let's go and eat."

At the restaurant, no one paid much attention to us. Having eaten, we returned to school and nothing happened until the end of the class. By that time, the director had returned the gun to our policeman and people were asking Zef and me what had happened. Invariably, I directed them to Zef, stressing he was the one who had taken charge that day. Suddenly, Joseph appeared. He looked distraught. He had met with his girlfriend's brothers but what they told him was very different from what he had heard from her the day before. According to them, they had asked her when she and Joseph were getting engaged. She had replied that she had lost interest in him and that she had made up her mind not to marry him. Her brothers had reminded her that she had pulled a stunt like this once before and that this time she was not going to get away with it. They liked Joseph and she was going to marry him, or else. She then locked herself in her room, swallowed a few pills, and asked to be rushed to the hospital. Having told us the latest version of the "drama," Joseph just stood there until one of our gendarmes took him by the arm and disappeared with him. It was not clear which version was true. The fact was that Joseph had stolen a service revolver and had uttered threats against his girlfriend's brothers. Presently, he was in the hands of the Greek authorities. None of us had any idea what would happen next. This event took place during the summer of 1954. I left Greece near the end of December 1955 but never saw or heard of Joseph again.

We had other minor adventures in school. At one point, the United States Escapee Program (USEP) gave each trainee a five-pound can of ground beef, for a total of about 175 pounds. The owner of the restaurant where we ate lunch offered to add the beef to the various dishes like spaghetti or lasagna since, otherwise, probably much of it would have gone to waste. We all agreed that the suggestion made sense. Well, he got the canned beef and we licked our chops in anticipation. As it turned out, we got the meat supplement just once. This was either a case where each one of us had consumed five pounds of ground beef at one meal or the restaurateur had used one can for that one meal and had found other uses for the remaining 34.

I raised the subject with the owner of the restaurant and had to listen to a torrent of abusive, offensive words describing our lack of gratitude. According to him, we were insulting the very bread that the Greeks so generously shared with us, that had he known how ungrateful we were, he would have never offered to take the beef off our hands, etc. Neither the sound nor the fury of his reaction could hide the theft. Unfortunately, under the circumstances no protest of ours would lead to an official inquiry. We decided to cut our losses, be of peaceful hearts and minds, and forget the remaining 170 pounds of ground beef that had been ours but for a brief moment.

Meanwhile, life was good. At school, we learned some fundamentals of welding and the use of simple hand tools. Daily life and weekends were peaceful, at least without too many rough edges, had it not been for Mr. Niko. One day, one of our Albanian trainees went to Athens and complained about Mr. Niko's highhandedness. Mr. Niko heard about it, had us all line up, and slapped the complainant hard in the face. Then he sent us all to our rooms. No one dared come to the victim's aid or complain to the authorities. We knew that no one would back us up. Compared to what the communist police did to the people, this was nothing. It was a lot, though, for us who had escaped in search of human rights and dignity.

There was one more incident. This one affected me personally. Having finished the welding course, Zef and I applied and were accepted to attend the course for electricians. I was looking forward to another six months in school, with relatively easy access to Athens, and away from Lavrion. Well, one day I was called to the office of Captain Pantazopoulos. I cooled my heels in his antechamber but that did not bother me as I sensed that worse was to follow. Finally, I was called into the inner sanctum. The captain was at his desk and somewhat further in the back was his secretary, a nice lady who had always been polite and friendly with us refugees.

The captain looked up and began his diatribe. "You, Kortsas, see yourself as one above the rules. You walk around Athens as if you were a tourist. You go to the best café in Athens, a camera hanging from your chest and a young lady at your side. What have you got to say?"

"Sir, I don't have a camera. As for going to cafés in Athens, I always behaved correctly, wore proper attire, and paid the check. Had I been told not to go to such places, I wouldn't have."

"Well, we have other plans for you. You will return to Lavrion. The Albanians there need you. You can write letters and applications for them and find other ways of making yourself useful."

"Sir, I would like to know what is prompting this decision."

"Very well, I'll tell you. You are being transferred for..." and here he used a Greek expression I did not understand.

"I am sorry, sir, I do not understand what you just said."

His secretary spoke up. "It means 'for administrative reasons,'" she said in English.

So that was that. I was going back to Lavrion, where I had come from. In truth, I never saw myself as a tourist in Greece. The way the Greek authorities treated us refugees would have quickly dispelled any such notion. My opinion of the Greek authorities had become such that I had never voiced it to any stranger, not even to Daisy—not because I did not trust her but because I might have hurt her national pride. I was well aware of the fact that my status would have gotten much worse had the government officials known the contempt I felt for them.

In fact, I had more respect for the Yugoslav authorities than for their

Greek counterparts. The communist Yugoslavs were our enemies for national and ideological reasons and made no bones about it. Greece, on
the other hand, was part of the "Free World." It was the cradle of classical culture and democracy and had cast beacons of light that had seduced
Alexander the Great to embrace Hellenism. It had inspired writers and
poets throughout the centuries. At this stage in history, however, Greek
ultra-nationalists, the Greek Orthodox Church, and the Greek authorities
still wrapped themselves in yesteryear's glory. They saw themselves as
worthy descendants of the best minds of Athens and the military valor
of Sparta, while presently groveling in the dust of the *Pax Americana.*
These same leaders eagerly kissed the hand that fed them while snapping
for crumbs that might fall from the master's table. They hated the Turks,
their powerful rivals at and beyond the Bosporus. They despised all their
neighbors, and particularly us Albanians who were economically and militarily weaker. They gave free rein to their *"megali idea,"* their dream of a
"Greater Greece," which included southern Albania, Macedonia, and parts
of Bulgaria and of Turkey. To make matters worse, such notions of inflated
nationalism reached deep into the psyche of the people. I mentioned earlier
how my landlady had invited me to join her and her friends on New Year's
Eve and how one of her friends had said that the expression "Albanian
gentleman" was an oxymoron. Daisy's friends, who were well-educated
and held responsible jobs, had asked her how come that in all of Athens
she had found no one better than an Albanian to go out with. Our "friend"
Mr. Niko had asked me one day to walk with him.

"Tell me," he said, "why do the United States and the rest of the Western powers withhold all territories that rightfully belong to Greece?"

"I don't know," I replied.

"Don't say 'I don't know.' You are a college student, you certainly
must know."

"No, I don't. I am a medical student, not a student of law or political
sciences."

Mr. Niko insisted and I kept giving him the same answer. Finally, he
himself provided the "correct" answer.

"The Western powers won't allow Greeks to take what is rightfully
theirs because the Greek population would rise to 17 million and our country would become so powerful that no one, not even the United States,

could stand up to Greece." There was the truth—the pure, unadulterated, dazzling truth, and I had been too blind to see it!

"Blindness," however, was not an Albanian monopoly. When thinking of expanding its territory to the north, Greece had never bothered to mention the deportations *en masse* of Albanians from historical Albanian territories following the collapse of the Turkish Empire toward the end of the 19th century as well as after both World Wars. Such populations had to leave behind goods and properties and move to centrally located Greek areas. Illyrians and their descendants, the Albanians, had populated much of the Balkans since ancient times. Albanians have lived in villages, such as Menidhi near Athens, since time immemorial and spoke Albanian to this day. The Greek fleet in the 19th century had mostly Albanian sailors, all things conveniently forgotten by Athens. Furthermore, present-day Greece claims southern Albania on the pretext that many of its inhabitants are Orthodox, and therefore Greeks. There is an Italian saying that nothing better than human stupidity can render the idea of infinity. Greece's perennial "*megali idea*" is a close second.

These are some reasons why I never considered myself a tourist in Greece. I realized, of course, that Greece was not the only country that lived in the past. There are a few other countries whose present ranking among nations falls short of their past glory. Mussolini had dreamed of recasting Italy in the image of Imperial Rome. The Italians, however, never used the imperial yardstick to measure their present greatness. France, when looking at herself in the mirror, still clings to the apex of Napoleonic glory despite ample evidence to the contrary. It has been Albania's misfortune to have been mutilated, deprived of regions populated by millions of Albanians all around its borders from north to south by the stroke of the diplomats' pen at the London Conference and thereafter. To this day, the European powers are dead-set against correcting the grave sins perpetrated against the Albanian nation. If Albania is to be reborn, the strength and vision will have to come from within.

CHAPTER FORTY-FOUR

DEPARTURE FOR THE UNITED STATES

Thus, for "administrative reasons" I returned to the refugee camp in Lavrion. In my absence, little had changed. While the Balli Kombëtar Agrar (The Agrarian National Front) leadership and we members found ourselves at odds with American/CIA policies and paid a price, the royalists were in lock step with both the United States and their Greek counterparts. Some royalist leaders filled our jobs at Radio Free Albania and enjoyed the pay and prestige that went with the job. Whenever they and their followers had a chance, they would lecture us and rub it in and we would respond without mincing words. Unfortunately, this continuous friction did poison the atmosphere between the two parties.

Whatever small favors or privileges were available in Lavrion, the authorities saw to it that they invariably went to the royalists. A royalist operated a mini tobacco and dime store inside the camp at some profit. Royalists had easy access to travel permits to Athens compared to what I had to go through to get a day pass. My requests, for example, had to be several weeks apart and every time I returned from Athens, I was expected to bring American cigarettes to the police sergeant who had issued the pass. On February 16, 1955, I got a pass to visit my friends in Athens. As it was my birthday, they had prepared a little celebration and dinner for that evening to accommodate those who were working. When I asked for permission to spend the night in Athens, Captain Pantazopoulos at police headquarters flatly refused. Informants, including a confessed emissary of the Albanian communists, were permitted to spend days and days in Athens without any difficulty. I, however, who had objected to American policies that turned out to be wrong in the long run, could not spend my birthday in Athens.

I have already mentioned that on Thursdays, dinner in our camp consisted of a handful of olives. This would have been OK had the olives not

725 ONE MAN'S JOURNEY TO FREEDOM: ESCAPE FROM BEHIND THE IRON CURTAIN

been full of worms. Because I had worked with the medical director of the Greek Red Cross for our camp, I decided to take a sample of the olives to his office in Athens. As luck had it, he was in and was willing to see me.

"Doctor, these are the olives they serve us every Thursday night in Lavrion, They are full of worms and who knows what. Would you please let the camp authorities know that the olives are unfit for human consumption?"

"I cannot do that," he replied. "How can I be sure that these are the olives they actually serve in camp? Perhaps someone picked them from a garbage pile and lied to you."

"Doctor, these are the olives I got yesterday from our kitchen as my evening meal. I am not in the habit of lying. I can understand your reluctance to accept this sample at face value. Please, come to Lavrion some Thursday evening, unannounced of course, and see for yourself." I thought I had scored a point.

"Again, I cannot initiate such a visit unless asked officially. And your invitation hardly qualifies."

Clearly, he refused to look into the problem. I decided to see Mr. Cox, head of the United States Escapee Program (USEP) for Greece. I had met him before and he was kind enough to see me that day. I told him the same story I had told the Greek physician.

"Mr. Korça, the food supply is in the hands of a Greek who is a British subject, a Mr. Bayet. There may be some ramifications if one were to pursue this matter. My advice to you is to skip the camp food on Thursday evenings. Believe me, it is the most prudent course under the circumstances."

So much for that. I did not quite know how Mr. Cox fit into this scheme. I considered him an honorable man who did not want to get his hands dirty. Of course, his response to me could also mean that he was involved in this or other shady deals. In the absence of evidence to the contrary, I preferred to consider him innocent. Either way, I had no higher avenue available to me.

The monotony of camp life was numbing. Life all around us went on but we, the camp inmates, bounced from breakfast to lunch, from lunch to dinner, and from dinner to sleep in a dull, desensitizing, gray atmosphere. Once in a great while, something would happen that would upset our routine. One day, in mid-afternoon, the siren starting wailing, ordering us to rush to the foot of our beds where we would stand at attention to receive the words of wisdom that would soon be pouring from the lips of our "masters." It did not take long before a sergeant and two gendarmes stormed into our dorm.

"You call yourselves political refugees! You are nobodies; you are the scum of the earth. You never saw women before you came to Greece. Now, one of you has raped a goat, an innocent farm animal. All of you have covered yourselves with shame. I don't know how you will go out tomorrow morning and be able to look the honest, God-fearing population of Lavrion in the eye. As for today, you are all consigned to quarters." Having spit out those words of righteous indignation, he and his acolytes stormed out in majesty to carry their message of the goat's violated honor from dorm to dorm.

As it turned out, some young Bulgarian was the perpetrator. We did not waste much time discussing the incident until the next day when Zef gave it a new twist. A small-format newspaper in English reached us once or twice a week. On page three of the issue that arrived the next morning was the picture of a goat as part of an article on farming. The royalist in charge of the miniscule dime store was a man in his mid-fifties, dignified, and slow to speak. In addition, he was illiterate, but few people knew that. Not so our Zef. Zef tucked an issue of the paper under his arm, entered the dime store, and showed the picture of the goat to the old gentleman.

"By now, the shameful news has reached the whole world. Here is the story, and here is the picture of the goat that was assaulted yesterday." Having said those words, Zef left with deep pain in his face and, dragging his footsteps, he left the storeowner steeped in gloom. Once out of sight, Zef came bouncing into our dorm to tell us what he had just done. The whole thing was so outrageous and so out of character for Zef that we could not help but burst out in uproarious laughter.

Life in our camp was not all fun and laughter, even for Zef who was always friendly, even-tempered, and adaptable. Zef was a born teacher who loved little children. He played with them for hours, improvising games and keeping them happy. He could hug and kiss any child, never mind that the child's nose and upper lip shone with semi-congealed, yellowish-green snot if the kid forgot to wipe it off with the back of his hand. One day, someone in the royalist camp came up with the story that Zef was so good with the children because he was trying to convert them to Catholicism. The story deeply hurt Zef's feelings. When he told me about it, he added, "To think that I never ever mentioned the Christian faith to the children."

One day I got a phone call. The caller was with the U.S. military and wanted to know whether I could work as an interpreter for the U.S. Army for a day or two. I would stay in Athens and would be paid for my work. Obviously, that was fine with me; too bad that the assignment was only for a couple of days.

I presented myself at the Tameion Building in Athens, curious as to what I was supposed to do. I got to the designated room and was introduced to a bird colonel. He handed me a document of one and one-half pages and asked me to translate the text. The text covered instructions for foreigners wanting to join the U.S. military. It did not take me long to translate the instructions, which I returned to the colonel who was in the next room. He took one look at the text and made a strange comment.

"I thought Albanian was a short language."

I had never heard of "long" or "short" languages. "I don't understand, sir. What do you mean by saying 'short language'?"

"Our first interpreter translated the same text in only three-quarters of a page."

"Could I see his translation, sir?"

He handed me a sheet of paper with the original translation. It was obvious that the interpreter's knowledge of Albanian was woefully inadequate. His vocabulary was limited and whenever he did not know the Albanian equivalent to an English word or passage, he simply skipped it. Furthermore, many of the words he had used were Turkish words once used in Albanian but that had fallen into disuse over the years.

"Sir, I believe this man learned Albanian from his grandparents or parents who left Albania around the turn of the century, before Albania gained its independence from Turkey in 1912. Whoever taught him Albanian had little schooling. Furthermore, the person who translated this document has never attended an Albanian school. The Albanian version of the document is short because the individual simply skipped parts of the original he could not translate."

"OK, now that explains it. All Albanian applicants for service in the U.S. Army flunked the lie detector test. At first, we thought that the individual applicants were giving us a false name and/or false personal data and were probably communist spies. When we ran into the same problem with all applicants, we began to suspect that something else was wrong. Obviously, if the applicants could not understand the questions the interpreter asked, they would get upset and flunk the test. Would you be willing to ask Albanian applicants questions related to the recruiting interview?"

"Of course, sir." I did not have to do a lot of thinking before coming up with a positive answer. "One more thing, sir: Could I meet your interpreter in person?"

"I don't see why not."

That ended my contact with the colonel. Shortly thereafter, someone brought the Albanian interpreter into the room. He was short and thin, of simple appearance. We shook hands and sat down. He told me, in English, that he was stationed in Germany. His file indicated that he spoke Albanian. The index cards, when queried, located him and he was flown to Greece on temporary assignment.

His parents were farmers from southern Albania. They had immigrated from their village to America where they owned a grocery store. When he grew up, he worked as a meter reader for an electric company. He added that he learned Albanian from his parents. He was a pleasant young man who had been asked to give more than he could deliver. We shook hands and that was the last we saw of each other.

That afternoon, I worked with some Albanian applicants and everything went smoothly. The next day, I translated the questionnaire for Albanian applicants, was paid, and returned to Lavrion.

After I had been in Lavrion a while, a representative of the World Council of Churches (WCC) asked if I would teach English to prospective immigrants. I would teach one hour a day, five days a week, and would be paid $20 a month. Considering that I paid no room and board at the camp, $20 a month was good money. I was most pleased to accept.

A number of young men signed up for the course. They were eager to learn and I was eager to teach. The WCC provided notebooks, pencils, and erasers that, under prevailing camp conditions, lent stature and dignity to the course.

These supplies, in fact, cast a longer shadow than I had anticipated. One day, a sergeant of our camp police came to my classroom and informed me that the captain in charge of the refugee camp wanted to see me. After class, I walked to his office with a queasy stomach. I preferred to stay away from mules, cannons, and officers, as they said in the Italian army. I knocked at the captain's door.

"Come in, Mr. Kortsas. Please be seated."

My queasiness evaporated when he called me "Mister." Normally, I was simply "Kortsas." The Greek camp authorities called me "Mr. Kortsas" only when they needed a favor from me.

"I understand you are teaching an English course for refugees?"

"Yes sir, that's correct."

"And the World Council of Churches provides you with notebooks, pencils and erasers?"

"Yes sir, they do."

"I have three children in school. Do you think you could spare a few school supplies?"

"I will bring you some, sir. That's no problem."

"Thank you, thank you very much."

As I left his office, the captain was rubbing his hands with a smile on his face. His stratagem had saved him a handful of *drachmae*. What a clever devil he was!

On Saturdays, the camp's library got the latest issues of American magazines, such as *Life* and *Time*. On Saturday afternoons, I made it a point to be early at the library to get ahold of the latest issues before they got lost. One day I also found out that the WCC had brought a reel-type tape recorder to our library, an instrument that no one used. I had seen my first tape recorder in Prishtina at a conference that the Yugoslav authorities, i.e., the UDBA, had held with Albanian refugees. Now it was my turn to use the tape recorder.

I hauled the instrument into class, where my students were duly impressed with the magic of the recorder that permitted them to hear their voices as they read their English lesson of the day. None, of course, recognized his own voice, while the rest of the class assured him that's the way he sounded to the class. The tape recorder served us well even after the novelty wore off.

One day, a newcomer to our class decided to hold private conversations with his classmates while I was teaching. He was a young Albanian who had made it across the border with his whole family. When I asked him to keep quiet in class, he challenged me. I asked him once more to save his conversation with his neighbors until after class and he responded that even in Albania, where they had real teachers, he talked in class when he felt like it. Now the ball was in my court. I threw him out, stressing that he could return when he was willing to behave. He promised that he would return with his brothers who would teach me a lesson I would long remember. Well, the brothers never showed up and he never returned to class. I must confess that nobody missed him.

The WCC gave me another chance to make some money. Somebody had compiled a pocket dictionary of about 2,000 words. I was to translate it into Albanian and put together a pocket dictionary. The job was easy and gave me great pleasure as I could see how it could be put to good use. Additionally, it was another bit of money that joined the rest of my savings. I think I did a passable job but I do remember one mistake I made: I translated "homely" as "homey." What do you want, perfection?

The topics of conversation with other camp inmates varied depending on the participants. Each person had a different escape story, and some were more interesting than others. Almost everyone had escaped because of the communist tyranny. One day a member of a well-known nationalist family from Vlora made it safely into Greece. The communists had executed his uncle, and some relatives of his had spent time in jail and in labor camps. He was well received and held in high regard by the Balli Kombëtar Agrar party. In fact, the party immediately offered him a seat on the Central Committee. He refused, as he did not consider himself prepared for such a high position and first wanted to learn more about life and political conditions in the West. Personally, I thought his modesty was becoming. He was intelligent, had good judgment, and did not jump to conclusions. Overall, he was far above most refugees in our camp.

One day, he disappeared from Lavrion. Rumor had it that he was in Athens being interrogated by the CIA and the Greek police. Next, we heard that he had slashed his wrists in prison. Was he being tortured? We did not know what to make of such news. Finally, we heard from reliable sources that the man had confessed that he was a communist agent and that Mehmet Shehu, the butcher of Albania, had personally escorted him to the Greek border. After a while, he, the confessed communist agent, returned to Lavrion. He acted and behaved with bravado to compensate for the ground he had lost among Albanians. In addition, he traveled freely to Athens, spent days and days there, giving the appearance that he had gained the favor of the CIA and their Greek counterparts. At what cost, of course, was anybody's guess.

A few months later, his younger brother arrived from Albania, worried about the older brother's well-being. The question immediately arose whether the communists had sent him too, but no one had any real information one way or another.

One day I was swimming by myself in the Aegean Sea near Lavrion. As I waded ashore, I saw an individual on his haunches staring up at me.

"Are you Genc Korça?" he asked.

"Yes," I replied, "and who are you?"

"You don't know me."

"Were you ever at the Military Hospital in Tirana?"

"No."

"Were you in Dukagjin?"

"No."

"Then, where did we meet?" I asked the stranger.

"I told you, we never met."

"Then how do you know who I am?"

"I served with the Albanian border guards. When you escaped they sent us your photograph and that's how I recognized you."

My concern grew. To my knowledge, I had been photographed only once, in jail, and then I had grimaced, hoping to render the picture useless. Obviously, they must have photographed me without my knowledge. I decided to provoke the man to see how he would react.

"It does not really matter how you recognized me. What's important is that you changed your mind about communism and decided to escape." As I was saying these words, I took a good look at him. If necessary, I knew I could take him. I was bigger, stronger, and had the advantage of standing while he was precariously balanced, hunched on his heels. Not a muscle moved in his face.

"I have not changed my mind about communism." I tensed up, ready to jump him if he made a wrong move.

"Then why did you escape since you still believe in communism?"

"One night, while on patrol along the border, one of my companions asked me whether I had ever asked myself why I was pulling night duty so often. I never had and told him so. My companion said, 'When you are on night patrol, the captain visits your wife at home.'

"I was stunned. The next time I was on night duty, I told the rest of the squad that I had forgotten something and would join them at a designated place. I sneaked home and there was the captain's horse tied to a tree in front of my house. I went in and shot him to death. I left for the border, avoided the guards, and sought refuge in Greece."

His story was unconvincing. He did not mention shooting his wife. More important, the Greek authorities would not grant asylum to someone who had committed premeditated murder. Since he stayed on his haunches, I did not feel physically threatened. I broke off our conversation and walked toward where I had left my clothes, always keeping the man well in sight.

Days and months passed and the man never created a ripple. He did become, however, inseparable with the two brothers, one of whom was the confessed communist spy.

At about this time, the latter came to me and asked that I translate a letter he wanted to send to the American embassy in Athens. In it, he admitted his former role as a communist plant but stressed that his brother was unaware of it, that his brother was innocent and should not pay for the older brother's mistakes. To my knowledge, none of the three immigrated here to the United States but the older brother did come here as a visitor. It was hard to pass judgment in this case for lack of hard information. The communists in Albania may have coerced the man to become a spy. I for one know of no evil he did on behalf of communism. However, I never was in a position where such information would come to my attention. Let God the All-Knowing, the Almighty, be the judge.

Occasionally, I had a chance to meet Albanians who lived outside the camp, mostly in Athens. Among them were individuals who crossed the Greek border into Albania on behalf of the CIA. The reader knows from early chapters that infiltrators from Yugoslavia came mostly by land; a few via Lake Shkodra. Infiltrators from Italy parachuted into Albania, while those working for British intelligence came by submarine. Those working with the West practically always met with an Albanian "reception committee" that did its best to capture them alive. The Albanian captors wanted the most recent news the infiltrators were carrying with them but also wanted to bring them to trial before a people's court. On such occasions, the communist government loved to hold public trials that had little to do with justice and everything to do with spectacles like those held in the Coliseum pitting the defenseless against hungry lions. (At that time, Kim Philby, Soviet agent and head of MI-6 counterintelligence for the USSR, and his companions had not yet been uncovered).

During my stay in Greece, I had noticed that CIA infiltrators into Albania wore Timex watches while on a mission. Now, there was nothing wrong with that except that such watches were not available in Albania and would immediately identify the infiltrator if he tried to mingle with the civilian population. One day, I brought this fact to the attention of a CIA officer. I suggested that infiltrators should wear watches available in Albania and that hundreds of Albanian refugees in our camp had such watches. I for one would be glad to make my watch available in exchange for a Western watch while the infiltrator was in Albania. Upon his return to Greece, I would return the borrowed watch in exchange for mine. The answer I got from the CIA officer baffled me.

"So, you are interested in getting an American watch for free. Is that why you are proposing this scheme?"

"Not at all; I want to prevent infiltrators from Greece from being betrayed by their watches. Let me add that if the infiltrator is captured or killed in Albania, I will return the borrowed watch to you without asking for one in return."

"We are not interested in your suggestion." And with these words my CIA contact sailed out of Lavrion.

I should have known better. For a time, Ditar Kurtesi, whom I met in Lavrion, had worked as an infiltrator for the CIA. He told me that on one occasion, he and his group were near the Albanian border. It was late autumn and both sides of the border were snow covered. The infiltrators-to-be received boots with U.S. Army heel markings. Ditar approached the American lieutenant in charge of the detail and complained that imprints made by the boots would give them away. The lieutenant replied that if the boots were good enough for U.S. soldiers, they were good enough for Albanian infiltrators. Ditar moved away, pulled out his knife, and got ready to cut off the rubber heels. An Army sergeant who had served in Korea approached Ditar.

"Aren't you carrying German weapons, just like the Albanian border guards?"

Ditar nodded.

"If you were to run into an Albanian patrol immediately after crossing the border, could we on this side tell the difference between shots fired by you and those by border guards?"

"No, of course not."

"There is snow on both sides of the border, and your footprints will clearly show that you entered Albania from Greece. What if you ran into an Albanian patrol, exchanged fire, and decided to return to Greek territory?"

The message was quite clear. Crossing the snow-covered border into Albania was ill advised, with or without U.S. Army boot markings. The Albanians got the message. They crossed the border and ran into a patrol. They fired a few shots and had no choice but to scrub their mission. At least that's what Ditar told the CIA liaison officer.

I am not accusing today's CIA of incompetence. But at that time some U.S. personnel in Greece had limited experience. In general, the newly formed CIA may have been overextended, because following the end of World War II, it had to cover countries and territories the world over.

Among other things, during my conversation with the CIA officer about watches, he had implied that I need not entertain hopes of ever seeing the United States. This was a heavy blow for me. The principles upon which the United States was founded were dear to my heart. They had given me strength and hope under communist oppression, when the ideological tyranny and its application had threatened the very survival of Albania, when the country had reeled under the heavy blows inflicted first by the Yugoslavs and later by Stalin and Mao-Tse Tung.

To find myself branded an enemy of the United States was indeed a heavy blow. While it did not affect my ideals, it did clash with the truth. It made me feel betrayed by my best friend. It rendered my present hopeless and destroyed my future. As I remember those days, I still feel the weight on my shoulders, the bleak outlook and heavy clouds that darkened my mind. What was worse, I dared not share them with any of my friends, not even with Zef. This was one case where sharing my sorrow would not lighten my burden but only sadden my friends.

Meanwhile, my fame as an English teacher had spread. The family of a young man who was getting ready to go to college in the United States hired me as a tutor. My young pupil's knowledge of English was most limited. I did my best during the summer months. He left in early fall and I never heard from him again.

That summer, I had two paying students, both female employees at our refugee camp. One worked as a secretary at the office and the other as a teacher in charge of refugee children of school age. The secretary was a jolly, well-rounded woman in her twenties. She was no workaholic, nor was she trying very hard to learn English. The teacher was rather tall, slim, reserved, and pensive by nature. She was quite pretty despite her modest wardrobe. While the secretary was always ready to break out in laughter, the teacher would rather smile than laugh. Rumor had it the teacher had a crush on me.

One day, the two girls asked me whether I would go with them and some of their friends to nearby Sunion for a picnic. I agreed and one early afternoon we took off by bus. The beach at Sunion was full of people, mostly tourists. I found myself at the periphery of the group. The boys ignored me, as could be expected. The one that stayed close by me was the teacher. When most of our group left on a boat tour of the bay, I decided to swim to a small, nearby island. Days before, I had read in the local press that sharks had attacked swimmers in the Sunion Bay not far from the beach. An encounter with sharks that afternoon seemed like a natural way of solving all my problems. Halfway to the island, I noticed that the teacher had followed me at a distance. I felt guilty. If I had decided to throw my life away, I had no right to endanger hers. As luck had it, we reached the island without a problem. We had been there but a few minutes when the boat with the rest of our group turned toward the island. Some of the boys were rowing forcefully while the secretary and others were gesticulating and yelling in our direction.

"What are they saying?" I asked the teacher.

"To stay out of the water because there may be sharks. They will pick us up and take us back ashore." I had no choice but to claim ignorance, but I remember feeling lower than a snake's belly, as they say.

Meanwhile, the World Council of Churches was churning out papers and preparing political refugees for resettlement in the United States, Canada, and Australia. To qualify, candidates had to be bona fide refugees, in good health, and pass an interview with a representative of the embassy of the country of interest. None of the three would accept known or alleged communists. This made it possible for informants, many with a shady past, to do real harm by leveling false charges against innocent people. Refugees in poor health also faced a serious problem. Some found a haven in Sweden, others in Belgium. One chose to face Golgotha.

One day I heard that a Bulgarian, a former infiltrator at the service of the CIA, had decided to return home and surrender to the Bulgarian communist authorities. I could not believe my ears. I decided to talk to him in person. What he told me was sad indeed. He had entered Bulgaria with orders to assassinate a communist leader. He had carried out his orders but had lost contact with his group. Consequently, he had spent an entire winter in the Bulgarian mountains until spring when he crossed back into Greece. He was getting ready for immigration into the United States when the medical examination revealed that he suffered from pulmonary TB. He was declared unfit for immigration into the United States.

"You know, of course, what awaits you in Bulgaria," I said to him.

"I know, but what do you want me to do? The communists have jailed 24 members of my family; men, women, and children. If I stay in Europe, they will suspect that I may try to enter the country illegally as in the past and will keep my people in jail. The United States does not want me. If I surrender in Bulgaria, they will kill me but will free my family. I have no choice but to surrender." What could I say to change his mind? Shortly thereafter, I lost track of him.

Once an Albanian asked me to be his interpreter at the Australian embassy in Athens. We appeared before an Australian team of interviewers consisting of a man and a woman, with the man in command.

"Why did you escape from Albania?" was the first question. It was a reasonable question, one for which each refugee had prepared an answer.

I translated his response, saying, "I had to escape because of my anti-communist activities before and after the Red takeover."

"What would they have done to you if they had arrested you?"

"I would have been tortured and probably killed."

"Your activities were such as to deserve such harsh punishment?"

"Yes, I would say so."

"Why did you not take your wife and children with you?"

"Because they could not handle the very difficult escape route the other men and I were going to take."

At this point, the interviewer's voice became harsh.

"From what you have told me, it is likely that your family will suffer because of your escape. We do not want men in Australia who care more about their personal safety than their families. Your application is denied." With those words he snapped shut the file in front of him and both he and the lady left the room.

The entire interview had lasted less than five minutes. We got up and left the Australian embassy quite dejected. I did not know how the refugee could have handled the situation differently. Furthermore, any one of us who had left a family behind could forget about leaving for Australia, if the same yardstick were applied to all. Some months later, the same refugee was accepted for immigration into the United States.

Meanwhile, many refugees were leaving Greece for their new countries while Zef and I were in Lavrion, stuck in the quagmire that had been ours now for almost two years. I had expected to emigrate, to rebuild my life, to continue my medical training, to get married, and to build a future for my family in the free, glorious United States of America. Instead, the United States considered me an enemy, a communist.

I still had great admiration for the country and what it stood for. Behind the Iron Curtain, I had an overly rosy image of Americans across the board. I could understand up to a certain point the lack of interest of the CIC in the Hila rescue project. They should have contacted the CIA in Rome, however, and let them be the judge. I was greatly disappointed when the driver who was bringing supplies to the CIA safe house near Athens was stealing booze and cigarettes from his employer. The Tameion Building in Athens housed the American embassy, the CIA, and several major army and navy commands. The use of Greek telephone exchange operators in the Tameion Building was a serious security breach, as was the use of Greek cabbies to transport sensitive documents. The insistence of the CIA to bring the Blloku Kombëtar Indipendent (BKI) group into the Committee for a Free Albania was an error that eventually caused the demise of the Rome Committee. It is true that not all members of BKI were Italian puppets but the Albanian communists had seen to it that they were all painted with the same brush as traitors and fascists. Making them members of the Committee for a Free Albania at this stage was ill timed and detrimental to the best interests of the anti-communist struggle. That is why I quit my job with Radio Free Albania. At that point, the CIA branded me a communist, forced me out of my job with an American construction enterprise in Athens, and cancelled my scholarship to study medicine in Strasburg.

Now I had to find a way out. On one of my trips to Athens, I visited the Italian consulate and completed an application seeking resettlement in Italy. Italy was a less attractive choice. My relationship with Valnea was dead. I had no idea how I was going to make a living or where to live. Italy was a true battlefield contested by a number of major and minor Albanian political parties, none of which I could endorse 100 percent. I was a member of Balli Kombëtar Agrar but did not share their indiscriminate, unbending condemnation of all members of the BKI. Sooner or later, I anticipated I might get in trouble with any or all of the Albanian parties. In many regards, there was no comparison between Italy and Greece. Italy offered much better living and employment conditions. But Italy was a poor second choice compared to the United States. At that juncture, however, I felt I had no choice. I filed my application to go to Italy and now all I had to do was await the outcome.

Meanwhile, things were beginning to move on another front. One Friday, as was their wont, employees of World Council of Churches came to Lavrion to process immigration papers. Unexpectedly, they told me to get ready since I could expect a call to undergo my physical and an interview at the American consulate in Athens. Something had changed, perhaps for the better. I had heard that the head of Radio Free Albania had complained to a friend that it was too bad that the men he had respect for had quit working at Radio Free Albania, while he had no respect for those Albanians presently working at the radio station. Apparently, someone in a position of authority had recognized our integrity and understood that we had quit rather than accept a political move that in our opinion was wrong.

Unfortunately, the CIA would repeat the same mistake of "total mobilization" a few years later before the Bay of Pigs invasion. In an attempt to mobilize all anti-communist forces against Castro, the CIA had asked former Batista officials to join, and thus lost some of the best Cuban nationalists who had opposed Batista's dictatorship and who now refused to fight side by side with Batista's people. After all, the Castro movement came to power because of the injustices perpetrated by the Batista regime.

In view of the World Council of Churches' notice, I hurried to a large hospital in Athens where I underwent a thorough physical at my expense. The results confirmed that I was in excellent health. One week later, the U.S. consulate asked me to appear for my medical checkup and an interview.

After a long hiatus, things were moving fast. The U.S. immigration official at the consulate in Athens had the reputation of being very hard-nosed. Having had the experience at the Australian consulate, I said my prayers and felt psychologically ready. Come what may, I was going to tell the truth. It was up to him to accept or reject me.

When the day came, I had prepared myself for a long interview. At least, that's what people had told me to expect. I was called into the interviewer's office. It was large, nicely furnished, with a man in his forties seated behind a massive desk. He looked at me through his gold-rimmed glasses.

"Have you ever been in prison in Albania?"

"Yes, sir."

"Why?"

"Because I was born on the wrong side of the tracks."

"What do you mean, you were born on the wrong side of the tracks?"

"My family was anti-communist. I fought against the communists and we lost. That's why they jailed me."

He looked at me, smiled, stamped a paper in front of him, and said, "Congratulations. Would you please ask the next applicant to come in?"

I felt on wings as I left his office. The medics were next. Their offices were also in the Tameion Building. I finished my physical rather quickly and was given a date to return to Athens and complete the rest of the immigration procedures.

On that long-awaited day, I was to see a Miss Wiesender, whom I had previously met. She had always been very friendly and I expected more of the same. When I entered her office, I had the distinct impression that something was wrong. She was again very friendly but there was an undercurrent of disappointment in her voice and behavior. After we exchanged the usual pleasantries, she came to the point.

"I regret to inform you that you suffer from amebiasis, an infection by intestinal parasites. Under these conditions, we will have to delay your departure for the United States until you are cured."

"I underwent a thorough physical at a Greek hospital here in Athens one week ago. The checkup included a test for amebiasis. I received a clean bill of health. Finding amebiasis a week later is unlikely. There may be another obstacle to my departure, a less obvious one. Two years ago, I worked with an American agency whose name I am not at liberty to mention. You should have no problem identifying my previous employer. If there is an objection to my leaving for the United States, I suspect it comes from that office."

"I understand what you are telling me. Please, take these pills regularly. They should take care of the amebiasis. Come back a month from today and we will talk again."

I thanked her and left her office. Now, the ball was in her court. I did not feel crushed by how things had gone. It was in line with the treatment I had received during most of my stay in Greece. Yes, I would take the pills by the book. I wondered what "the friends" would do next. Whatever their decision, I would find out one month hence.

While life in Lavrion was as "exciting" as always, I had a target date to shoot for. The fateful day finally came. Before seeing Miss Wiesender, I was to provide a specimen to the medical laboratory. A little while later, I was again in Miss Wiesender's office.

"I spoke with your former employers. They told me they were not sure they had treated you fairly. That, by the way, is their way of apologizing. An individual cannot expect more from an agency of the government.

"Now let's come to your health. Congratulations, your intestinal infection is thoroughly cured. Knowing how conscientious you are, I would have sent you to the United States even if you needed further treatment. Doubtless, you would have done so until you had taken care of the problem."

I was relieved.

"You will be leaving soon for the United States. We would like you, however, to stop in Munich for an interview with Radio Free Europe." So, that was what the CIA had in mind.

"Miss Wiesender, I don't think that my stopover in Munich is linked to my being interviewed by Radio Free Europe. I certainly refuse such an interview. My Dad is in prison for life. I have no idea where Mom and my younger brother are. When I left, Mom was with some friends and my brother was serving in the forced labor battalion of the Albanian army. Can you imagine my being interviewed at RFE and adding to their troubles?

"There may be another reason for my stopover, however. The secretary of the Battalion Skanderbeg in Munich passed away recently. The Battalion is looking for someone who speaks Albanian and English. In addition, I speak German. I would be a likely candidate for the job, don't you think?"

She looked pensive. "All right, then we will fly you directly to the U.S. without a stopover in Munich. You will be leaving in a few weeks. Does this give you enough time to get ready?"

"Yes, it does." We both stood up and shook hands. Dear Miss Wiesender!

Things began to change even in Lavrion. I was no longer "O Kortsas" but "O kirios Kortsas" (Mr. Kortsas). It did not take me long to settle my affairs in Lavrion and in Athens. I told Daisy that I would be leaving in weeks.

"Genc, I am willing to wait for you up to three years. My age does not permit me to wait longer than that."

I felt guilty. Daisy was a lady. While I had enjoyed her company, I had never allowed myself to fall in love with her because I had been burned with Valnea.

"Daisy, I don't know what awaits me in the States. I have no job and I still have to complete my education. I cannot predict whether three years will be enough for me to reach the point where I can support a family. I am sorry, but I cannot promise that I will send for you within three years."

"Genc, there is a young engineer who is in love with me. He presently serves as a lieutenant in the Greek navy. I do not love him but I know that I can learn to love him. What do you say?"

"Daisy, I am so grateful for your care and kindness toward me. I do not see my way clear to make any commitments at this point. You are a wonderful young woman and I am sure your friend is a fine person. I wish you, both of you, the very best." We hugged for the last time and I was on my way.

My friends had told me that tailor-made suits were prohibitively expensive in America and I had not heard of ready-made suits. So, with the money I had saved, I bought material for two suits and went to a good tailor. After the initial work, he asked for a second fitting. That meant I had to get another permit to come to Athens. When I asked for it, the captain of our camp asked to see me.

"Kirie Kortsas, why do you think you need a permit to go to Athens? Can't your American friends take care of it?" I was stunned. Since I got my visa for the United States, the captain had been very friendly.

"No, sir. This is Greece. My American friends have nothing to do with giving me permits to go to Athens." I was paying homage to Greek sovereignty to soothe his feelings, while we both knew that at that juncture Americans were the supreme rulers of the country. In addition, I wanted to gain time to identify what lay behind his ill humor. Then I remembered. One day, while having lunch in a restaurant in Athens, an Albanian refugee whom I knew only by sight had asked me what had brought me to Athens.

"The U.S. consulate called to issue me a visa for the U.S." That was all I said. Obviously, he had twisted my words in his report to the Greek police.

"Sir, I never said I did not need permission from the Greek authorities to travel to Athens. Whoever has said something to the contrary has twisted my words."

"You have four hours to go to Athens and come back." Obviously, my words had failed to pacify him. In truth, at this point, it did not matter much.

On another occasion, my friends Luan Gashi and Ejup Binaku urged me to see Captain Pantazopoulos, who had returned me to Lavrion "for administrative reasons."

"Why should I say goodbye to him? He was never friendly to me."

"Do it for our sake; we are left behind."

I saw their point. With Jupi I went to the police station. Jupi stayed outside and I was ushered into the captain's office. Pantazopoulos rose from his chair, something he had never done before, shook my hand, and said a few pleasantries. Then he came to the point.

"Kirie Kortsas, your stay in Greece could have been much more pleasant if you had so chosen. You felt like a caged bird, isn't that so?"

I did not understand some of what he said that day but his secretary, who had always been very friendly toward me, acted as an interpreter.

"Yes," I replied, "I did feel like a bird in a cage."

"But there was no need to feel that way," said the captain. "The door to the cage was open."

I blushed. Now I understood what he meant. If I had wanted better treatment by the Greeks, all I had to do was to turn informer. I rose from the chair.

"Good day, Captain," I said and stalked out of his office.

Outside, Jupi was waiting for me. "How did it go?" he asked.

"The s.o.b. had the gall to ask me why I had not become an informer."

"There is no reason for you to get mad," Ejup said to me. "As a police captain it was his job to try to recruit you. It was your job to refuse. You both did your duty. So, relax and forget Captain Pantazopoulos."

That was one bit of advice I had no trouble taking.

Soon the day arrived when a number of refugees destined for the United States took the bus to Athens and then to Ellenikon International Airport. We arrived there in the early evening. Our flight was scheduled for midnight. I passed the time looking at several Super Constellations parked on the tarmac. They were sleek and elegant. Would ours be such a plane?

While I had been fairly detached during the ups and downs of the last two years, I could not help feeling antsy. If either the Americans or the Greeks wanted to, they could still stop me from leaving. Now that the time of departure was only hours away, I was increasingly aware of my helplessness. I was trying to chase away any negative thoughts. If either side had wanted to keep me here, they could have done so a long time ago, I kept telling myself. Were they playing a cruel trick on me? First, fill me with hope, and then pull the rug from under me? They had never spared my feelings in the past. Could they be playing games with me now that everything seemed to be in my favor?

As I was sitting on a bench trying to chase the demons out of my mind, I heard the loudspeaker, first in Greek and then in English: "*O kirios Kortsas s'tin telefono, parakalo*, Mr. Kortsas to the telephone, please." I got scared. So, they were pulling the plug at the last minute. My limbs felt heavy. I pulled myself together. They had given me a rough time before. I should be able to handle whatever they sent my way.

"Hello?"

"Genc? This is Daisy. My fiancée and I want to wish you the best of luck. Have a good trip. Keep well, and write when you have time."

I mumbled something in return. I could have slapped her until her cheeks got blood red. How could she do this to me? Did she not know that she had almost given me a heart attack?

We finally started boarding a four-engine aircraft. It was not a Super Constellation. That was for regular passengers. We refugees were flying a Flying Tigers Airline plane. All I cared about was that we were finally leaving Greece, the cradle of Western culture, the country that had shown me one of the lesser facets of its complex soul. The engines revved up and got increasingly louder. We were rolling faster and faster, and finally the wheels got off the ground. Athens was under us, brightly lit. The Acropolis and the city got rapidly smaller and finally disappeared into the night.

We had left Greece behind us, headed toward the United States. I shook off the dark clouds that had sapped my strength for so long, leaned back, and fell asleep. Finally, finally, when we touched down in New York I would regain my freedom, my full freedom, thank God! Maybe someday I will return to Greece as a tourist. But I won't hold my breath in the meantime, that's for sure.

EPILOGUE

I want to add a few words about my first years in the United States and my subsequent dealings with the CIA. I arrived in the United States just before Christmas 1955. Within two weeks, I had a job as a first-aid attendant at Great Lakes Steel. I bought a car and in September 1956, I registered in pre-med at Wayne State University. Margaret and I met in January 1957 in an English class and on December 30 of that year I proposed marriage. Margaret accepted and we were married on Easter Monday at St. Joseph's in Detroit. The date was April 7, 1958.

When I informed Mom, she asked why I had chosen April 7. Italy had occupied Albania on Friday, April 7, 1939 and that day was called Black Friday in Albania. We had our reasons. Unfortunately, I could not explain them to Mom. Margaret and I used to attend a German Mass at St. Joseph's. Father Halter, a German priest, had been a prisoner of war in Russia for four years and he and I could converse together without needing to explain elementary details, as when conversing with people unfamiliar with life under communism. Since Margaret and I both attended classes at WSU, we had to get married during vacation. We had no strong reason to receive permission to get married during Lent. Father Halter was leaving for Germany on Tuesday after Easter to see his mother. If we did not get married on Easter Monday, we would have to wait until summer vacation. So, we picked Easter Monday—and in 1958, Easter Monday fell on April 7. With Margaret, God has brought love and happiness into my life. Blessed be the Lord.

Dennis was born on May 8, 1959, and I was baptized at St. Dominic's three days later. I graduated with a B.A. in chemistry in June 1960, and in July General Motors hired me as a junior industrial hygienist. They had wanted a radiation specialist but he asked for more than GM was willing to pay. So, they decided to hire a novice and train him the GM way. That's how I got my break. Later, I learned that my experience in the health field and my age were in my favor. On the negative side, they wondered whether, having qualified for Phi Beta Kappa, I might find little challenge in industrial hygiene. I accepted the job eagerly. By that time, Margaret was expecting Duane, our future industrial hygienist. I really needed the job.

1)

ONE MAN'S JOURNEY TO FREEDOM: ESCAPE FROM BEHIND THE IRON CURTAIN

Before I was hired, the Director of GM Industrial Hygiene, Mr. Castrop, had asked if I intended to become a U.S. citizen, as that was required for the job, and I had answered that I would apply as soon as I had five years in this country. A year later, he told me that I should apply for security clearance. My ears perked up. Nobody had told me that I needed secret clearance to hold this job. He insisted that he had told me and I replied that I would have refused the job under those conditions. Because of my past experience (with the CIA, but I did not mention the Agency), there was the possibility that I would be denied the clearance. What was worse, if I was subsequently asked whether I had ever been denied security clearance, I would have to say yes, at the risk of jeopardizing future employment.

Now I felt I had little choice. Resigning was not an option. I decided to go through with it. Two men from Army intelligence interviewed me and a month or two later I was given "secret clearance." Obviously, I could not have gotten my clearance without CIA approval. I was most grateful. The CIA now had a better understanding of me as an individual. Perhaps they had come to realize that my objections to the expanded Rome Committee were also in the best interest of the United States. Above all, I was elated that the CIA was big enough to admit its error. Except for people who have been in my shoes, others may find it hard to understand not just my relief, but the feeling of finally being vindicated, of actually being told that my life history qualified me as a good American, a good security risk for my new country. In Albania, I was the enemy, a dangerous individual who could not be trusted. Here, I was not only granted U.S. citizenship but also permitted to enter GM factories where we produced armaments and did secret research. Finally, after so many years, I belonged!

God gave me a wife I could love with all my heart. Duane was born on October 22, 1960 and Ann joined our family on May 2, 1963. I was an American by adoption and baptized into the Roman Catholic Church, 28 years after I had heard the Lord's call at age seven at the Sacred Heart of Jesus Church in Graz.

Over the years, I have had the opportunity to serve my new country as a loyal citizen and professionally to the best of my ability. None of this could have come about until I reached these shores and my new country accepted me whole-heartedly. These last next 55 years (as I write these lines) have been living proof, and I am deeply grateful. Thank you, Lord, for all your blessings. God bless America!